Bardic Nationalism

IRISH BARD.

Joseph Cooper Walker, *Historical Memoirs of the Irish Bards*. 1818 ed.
Courtesy of Regenstein Library, University of Chicago.

Bardic Nationalism

THE ROMANTIC NOVEL AND THE BRITISH EMPIRE

Katie Trumpener

PRINCETON UNIVERSITY PRESS

PRINCETON, NEW JERSEY

Library of Congress Cataloging-in-Publication Data

Trumpener, Katie, 1961–
Bardic nationalism : the romantic novel and the British Empire /
Katie Trumpener.
p.   cm. — (Literature in history)
Includes bibliographical references and index.

ISBN 0-691-04481-3 (alk. paper). — ISBN 0-691-04480-5 (pbk. : alk. paper)

1. English fiction—19th century—History and criticism.
2. Nationalism and literature—Great Britain—Colonies—History.
3. English fiction—18th century—History and criticism.
4. Nationalism and literature—Great Britain—History.   5. Bards and
bardism in literature.   6. Imperialism in literature.   7. Colonies
in literature.   8. Romanticism.   I. Title.   II. Series: Literature
in history (Princeton, N.J.)
PR868.N356T78   1997   96-39166
823'.709358—dc21   CIP

This book has been composed in Times Roman

LITERATURE IN HISTORY

SERIES EDITORS

David Bromwich, James Chandler, and Lionel Gossman

The books in this series study literary works in the context of the intellectual conditions, social movements, and patterns of action in which they took shape.

Other books in the series:

Lawrence Rothfield, *Vital Signs: Medical Realism in Nineteenth-Century Fiction*

David Quint, *Epic and Empire: Politics and Generic Form from Virgil to Milton*

Alexander Welsh, *The Hero of the Waverly Novels*

Susan Dunn, *The Deaths of Louis XVI: Regicide and the French Political Imagination*

Sharon Achinstein, *Milton and the Revolutionary Reader*

Esther Schor, *Bearing the Dead: The British Culture of Mourning from the Enlightenment to Victoria*

Elizabeth K. Helsinger, *Rural Scenes and National Representation: Britain, 1815–1850*

CONTENTS

ILLUSTRATIONS

PREFACE

THIS BOOK links the literary and intellectual history of England, Scotland, Ireland, and Britain's overseas colonies during the late eighteenth and early nineteenth centuries to redraw our picture of the origins of cultural nationalism, the lineages of the novel, and the early literary history of the English-speaking world. In the process, it argues implicitly for the disciplinary transformation of English literature, so called, and for a new way of conceiving the disciplinary mandate of comparative literature.

The romantic period sees the consolidation of a new British overseas empire and a new degree of English political and cultural influence in Scotland and in Ireland; Britain's own uneven economic development, at the same time, means that Scots and Irish are disproportionately represented in the British Army that occupied new overseas colonies, as in the early colonial settlements. In Britain Anglo-Scottish and Anglo-Irish cultural revivals partly offset a process of cultural centralization, and a new literary nationalism became visible in novelistic genres and literary scandals, amid discussion of national character, cultural transmission, and modernization. Most existing studies of this period have treated these Anglo-Celtic literary cultures as imitative footnotes to a broadly English culture or, although significant in their own right, as isolated from England and from each other. This book establishes their centrality, interconnection, and international influence.

English literature, so-called, constitutes itself in the late eighteenth and early nineteenth centuries through the systematic imitation, appropriation, and political neutralization of antiquarian and nationalist literary developments in Scotland, Ireland, and Wales. The period's major new genres (ballad collection, sentimental and Gothic fiction, national tale, and historical novel), its central models of historical scholarship and literary production, and even its notions of collective and individual memory have their origins in the cultural nationalism of the peripheries. The book argues therefore for a major revision in the way we think about this particular moment in literary history, as in the way we understand the genesis and function, the centralization and circulation, of literature within an empire.

The first half of the book argues that in Scotland and Ireland, a nationalist and traditionalist worldview takes shape from antiquarian reactions to Enlightenment programs for economic improvement, read as a form of political and cultural imperialism. The case is made in part through a detailed examination of several landmark English Enlightenment investigations of the Celtic peripheries and the critical reception of these works in Ireland

and Scotland. Their famous indifference to cultural tradition catalyzes literary counterrepresentations and the articulation of an oppositional nationalist aesthetics. Responding in particular to Enlightenment dismissals of Gaelic oral traditions, Irish and Scottish antiquaries reconceive national history and literary history under the sign of the bard. According to their theories, bardic performance binds the nation together across time and across social divides; it reanimates a national landscape made desolate first by conquest and then by modernization, infusing it with historical memory. A figure both of the traditional aristocratic culture that preceded English occupation and of continued national resistance to that occupation, the bard symbolizes the central role of literature in defining national identity.

A quintessential product of the late eighteenth century, bardic nationalism continues to have enormous influence on the formal development of the early-nineteenth-century novel, as the second half of the book details. As nationalists argue for the specificity and the separate historical development of particular regions (and as enlightened imperialists, arguing along opposite lines, see this distinct character as a symptom of backwardness), the period's fiction begins to codify the different British peripheries and colonies into distinctive "chronotopes." Mikhail Bakhtin's notion of the literary chronotope theorizes the spatial-temporal parameters that determine the worldview of a fictional genre and the rules of operation that establish the direction, the pace, and the meaning of the stories unfolding within it.[1] If Bakhtin's idea makes sense of the ideological distinction and contest between the different novelistic genres emerging during this period, it is equally useful to describe how the novel (in an era of intense discussion about the developmental pattern of national characters and histories) grasps nations as distinct life worlds yet begins, at the same time, to experiment with the relations of setting and time, plot and character. Thus in the late eighteenth century, the writers of picaresque novels become interested at once in the plot situations generated by travel, in the differences between the places passed through, and in the filtering of their reality through narrative perspective. Whereas some novelists transpose romance plots into a succession of new national or colonial settings or into the bardic, Gothic, or antiquarian past, to see how they are affected by such variables, others carefully localize their characters' movements to explore the microinfluence of locale or historical circumstances on attitudes and actions.

The new early-nineteenth-century genres reiterate and redirect such chronotopic experiments, to analyze both Britain's constituent cultures and her overseas colonies. The early national tale evokes an organic national society, its history rooted in place; the historical novel describes the way historical forces break into and break up this idyll—and yet, through the very upheaval they cause, shape a new national community in place of the old. Nationalist Gothic and annalistic novels, however, refuse this happy ending to stress instead the traumatic consequences of historical transformation and the long-term uneven development, even schizophrenia, it creates in "national characters." Although such novels now seem prescient in their critique of colonialism and modernization, it is Walter Scott's historical novel, with its stress on historical progress, that won out as the paradigmatic novel of empire, appealing to nationalist, imperialist, and colonial readers alike. For Scott insists simultaneously on the self-enclosed character of indigenous societies (living idyllically, if anachronistically, outside of historical time), on the inevitability with which such societies are forcibly brought into history, and on the survival of cultural distinctiveness even after a loss of political autonomy. As he enacts and explains the composition of Britain as an internal empire, Scott underlines the ideological capaciousness of empire, emphasizes the analogies between nation formation and empire building, and argues for the continued centrality of national identity as a component of imperial identity.

Throughout the nineteenth century, indeed, in the new context of the British overseas colonies, the Anglo-Celtic model of literary nationalism that arose in response to British internal colonialism (and that used a conservative model of memory to buttress a movement of radical self-assertion) continues to manifest its characteristic political strengths and weaknesses. A lasting source of anti-imperialist inspiration, it also helps ensure that cultural nationalism (as long as it separates cultural expression from political sovereignty) can be contained within an imperial framework. Some Irish and Scottish writers see in the empire a restaging of the structural injustices of Britain; their sense of systematic parallels becomes the basis of an international solidarity at once militantly anti-imperialist and militantly nationalist. Although equally resentful of the subordination of Britain to England, others see in the empire (as a place where individual Scottish or Irish settlers can rise to prosperity and influence) the sole compensation for these injustices—and allow their nationalist pride and their ambivalence toward English culture to be subsumed into a support for the imperial project.

Where both positions meet is in their awareness of the transcolonial consciousness and transperipheral circuits of influence to which empire gives rise, as disparate cultures find themselves connected not only by their parallel modes of subordination within the empire but also by a constant flow of people—administrators, soldiers, merchants, colonists, and travelers—back and forth between different imperial holdings. Thus even in their deliberate, systematic underdevelopment or monodevelopment by the imperial powers, the most far-flung provinces of the empire (beginning with Scotland and Ireland) simultaneously develop a strange cosmopolitanism, which parallels (if on a much reduced scale) that of the imperial center itself. Such self-awareness marks much early colonial writing. Yet most accounts of Britain's literary empire, seeing as their object of study a literature forged by the influence of English models on English colonists, have either emphasized the cultural subordination of periphery to center or traced the discrete national development of separate colonial literatures. The international address and transcolonial character of today's postcolonial fiction makes clear the need for a synchronous history of empire instead.

The aim of this book, then, is to map the national and transnational lineages of nationalist fiction in the early nineteenth century and to draw a new kind of map of romantic fiction in the process. Read as a sequence, the chapters that follow describe an unfolding series of linked novelistic concerns, generic types, and literary tropes; taken individually, each chapter attempts to describe the way important extranovelistic developments of the period—-Enlightenment land reform and eighteenth-century ballad collecting, the reorganization of British domestic life and the circuits of emigration and influence within the British Empire—not only give the romantic novel much of its content but leave lasting traces in the generic structure, recurring tropes, and formal vocabulary of the novel.

Julian Moynahan attributes the instability of the romantic novel to the political upheavals of its period.

> Romanticism had temporarily unhinged—derailed—the novel by overwhelming it with new expressive possibilities, a new politics of crisis and change, and a new expectation that any substantial story about private persons would reflect the experience of a whole society. Development in the genre, rapid in the eighteenth century, appeared to slow during the first third of the nineteenth.[2]

This book reads the romantic novel very differently. Between 1760 and 1830, British literature is obsessed with the problem of culture: with historical and cultural alterity, with historical and cultural change, with comparative cultural analysis, and with the way traditional customs and values shape everyday life. At the same time, British novelists are rethinking the political and epistemological bases of the novel, taking apart, reassembling its chronotopic framework, and reformulating the relationship between its characters, its plot, and its argument. Many of the novels discussed in the following pages have long been forgotten or overlooked; read against mid-eighteenth- or mid-nineteenth-century realism, they may appear scrappy or odd. Yet they have an aesthetic of their own; although some of these novels develop new and innovative ways of working with the novel as a long and cumulative form, many are structured episodically, with local strengths of scene and characterization. When they are reread in relation to the intellectual life of their period, their true degree of conceptual ambition and formal experimentation becomes clear, for even their hoariest literary clichés or set pieces prove to be saturated with cultural and historical meaning.

Over the course of the romantic period, the history of the British novel is a history of dislocations, bifurcations, and disengagements as much as it is of continuity or accretion. Only an account that describes this history both locally and relationally can hope to capture the complex dynamic of its development. The incremental structure of this book attempts to capture the movement of the literature it is describing, to analyze its leaps ahead and its doubling back, and at the same time to fill in, layer by layer, the novel's intellectual and literary context. As the first half of the book will work to show, controversies around the figure of the bard—and the problem of bardic memory—recapitulate at once the recurring epistemological dilemmas of antiquarian work and a specific history of debate about the politics of cultural memory and the future role of national cultures in the new multinational Britain. Such debates point to a bifurcation of British romanticism by national identifications (whereas many Irish, Scottish, and Welsh writers remain fundamentally suspicious of an English-dominated Britain, most of their English contemporaries take it for granted). This divide is particularly visible in what interests each group about the bard: nationalist antiquaries take up the bard as a figure of cultural situatedness and argue for a reading of aesthetic works as the expression of cultural practices and historical conditions, whereas English men of letters adopt the bard as a figure of cultural fragmentation and aesthetic autonomy.

For much of the twentieth century—and perhaps particularly during the 1980s, when Marxist literary history did battle with a rhetorically oriented deconstruction—literary and historical studies have tended to separate these domains from one another, a divison that replicates and extends the bifurcation in the late-eighteenth-century reception of the bard. This book represents an attempt to develop a kind of literary history that historicizes, explicates, and thereby circumvents this divide, to develop a mode of literary-historical analysis in which literary form itself becomes legible as a particularly rich and significant kind of historical evidence, as a palimpsest of the patterns, transformations, and reversals of literary, intellectual, and political history. To explore the ways in which the romantic novel takes up and reworks the nationalist debates of the late eighteenth century is to watch a process through which ideology takes on generic flesh, and old formats of literary argument reappear to structure the novel in many ways, from the development of character to the unfolding of plot.

ACKNOWLEDGMENTS

As a child immigrant to Canada from the United States in the late 1960s, I experienced "English" Canada as deeply colonial in mentality and mysterious in its cultural practices. Why was everyone so hostile about American influences and so proud of British ones? Why *were* we still celebrating Victoria Day? Why were so many of my schoolmates, those Janets and Heathers, learning Highland dancing? Why was every parade so full of kilted bagpipers? And who watched the interminable televised curling matches?

My relationship to Anglo-Canadian nationalism (as later to Quebecois nationalism) remained fundamentally ambivalent. In that it identified me, and other resident Americans, as the personal targets of its nationalist anger, it left me alienated, defensive, and critical. But I was also caught up in the literary and cultural renaissance that this nationalism made possible. I, too, felt the excitement of reading, for the first time, a newly discovered and newly written Canadian literature, which instead of presupposing detailed knowledge of London (or New Jersey) was about landscapes, weather, histories, and ways of life that Canadian readers knew at first hand. In expressing a shared apprehension of the world, this literature seemed to promise, even inaugurate, a new mode of communal life. Yet as my immigrant friends from India and Pakistan felt even more acutely than I, the lived reality of Canadian life was often considerably less utopian. The final chapter of this book explores the historical reasons for this gap.

As an undergraduate at the University of Alberta, my meditations on the transcolonial logic of the British Empire were sparked by a haunting fragment of Indian statuary on display in Cameron Library: the head of a bodhisattva, presented to the university, a plaque announced, by a British Army major, who had "traded it for rifles in the Kyber Pass." I first began thinking about the multinational character of British culture in David Jackel's wonderful survey course on the British novel, which used Edgeworth, Smollett, and Scott to raise questions of nationalism and regionalism, both in Britain and in Canada. In graduate school, Russell Berman showed me new ways of thinking about cultural history, and Terry Castle and David Wellbery taught me to love the late eighteenth century; together, they guided the comparative literature dissertation on traditionalism from which this book evolved.

My research was supported by graduate fellowships at the Stanford Humanities Center and at the Free University of Berlin, by a Mellon Postdoctoral Fellowship at the University of Pittsburgh, by several short- and

xviii ACKNOWLEDGMENTS

long-term fellowships at the Chicago Humanities Center, and by a National
Endowment for the Humanities Travel to Collections Grant. A number of
libraries granted me access to their holdings: the British Library; the Scottish National Library; the Library of Congress; the Newberry Library, Chicago; Special Collections, Regenstein Library, University of Chicago; the
Beinecke Rare Book Library, Yale University; Widener and Houghton Libraries, Harvard University; McGregor Library, University of Virginia; the
Carnegie Library, Pittsburgh; the University of Pittsburgh Library; the
Osborne Collection of Early Children's Literature, Toronto Public Libraries; the Thomas Fischer Rare Book Library, University of Toronto; and the
Bruce Peel Special Collections, University of Alberta. Many other libraries
generously lent me rare books on interlibrary loan. At a moment in which
most sources of funding for humanities research (and even free scholarly
access to many libraries) are under threat, it is imperative that we remember
how much material support is necessary for all work of historical revision.

A slightly shortened version of chapter 3 appeared in *ELH*; a condensed
version of chapter 6 appeared in Deidre Lynch and William Warner, eds.,
Cultural Institutions of the Novel (Durham, N.C.: Duke University Press,
1996).

Jonathan Arac, David Bromwich, James Chandler, Ian Duncan, and
Richard Maxwell read my manuscript in its entirety; I am deeply grateful
for their searching and detailed criticisms. Many thanks to Marilyn Butler,
Jerome Christensen, Ina Ferris, Jon Klancher, Alok Yadav, Stewart Sherman, Margery Fee, and W. H. New, who read and commented on parts of
the manuscripts, as to Mary Murrell, Dalia Geffen, and Jason Dawsey for
their editorial assistance. The interest, input, and faith of many col-
leagues and friends—especially Elizabeth Heckendorn Cook, Norma
Field, Michael Geyer, Miriam Hansen, Elizabeth Helsinger, Carol Kay,
Loren Kruger, Janel Mueller, Wendy Olmsted, Rita Pappas-Signorelli,
Laura Rigal, Mark Sandberg, Molly Sandock, and Martha Ward—helped
the project enormously; Robert von Hallberg, Philip Gossett, and Arjun
Appadurai created the administrative free spaces in which this book could
take shape.

My work has been sustained, over many years, by the intellectual stimulus, detailed criticism, and unconditional friendship of Nancy Glazener,
Deidre Lynch, and Shamoon Zamir, as well as by the calm support of Nico-
las Maxwell, Betsy Trumpener, and John Trumpener. My greatest debt is
to Richard Maxwell, whose learning, wit, and care strengthened every page
of this book.

I dedicate this book to my parents: Mary Dorris Trumpener, who taught
me to think about cultural differences, and Ulrich Trumpener, who taught
me to think about historical experience.

Bardic Nationalism

A PARAPHRASE OF THE 137TH PSALM, ALLUDING TO THE CAPTIVITY AND TREATMENT OF THE WELSH BARDS BY KING EDWARD I

Sad near the willowy Thames we stood,
And curs'd the inhospitable flood;
Tears such as patients weep, 'gan flow,
The silent eloquence of wood,
When Cambria rushed into our mind,

And pity with just vengeance joined;
Vengeance to injured Cambria due,
And pity, O ye Bards, to you.
Silent, neglected, and unstrung,
Our harps upon the willow hung,
That, softly sweet in Cambrian measures,
Used to sooth our soul to pleasures,
When, lo, the insulting foe appears,
And bid us dry our useless tears.
"Resume your harps," the Saxons cry,
"And change your grief to songs of joy;
Such strains as old Taliesin sang,
What time your native mountains rang
With his wild notes, and all around
Seas, rivers, woods return'd the sound."

What!—shall the Saxons hear us sing,
Or their dull vales with Cambrian music ring?
Thou God of vengeance, dost thou sleep,
When thy insulted Druids weep,
The victor's jest the Saxon's scorn,
Unheard, unpitied, and forlorn?
Bare thy right arm, thou God of ire,
And set their vaunted towers on fire.
Remember our inhuman foes,
When the first Edward furious rose,
And, like a whirlwind's rapid sway,
Swept armies, cities, Bards away.

"High on a rock o'er Conway's flood'
The last surviving poet stood,
And curs'd the tyrant, as he pass'd
With cruel pomp and murderous haste.
What now avail our tuneful strains,

Midst savage taunts and galling chains?
Say, will the lark imprison'd sing
So sweet, as when, on towering wing,
He wakes the songsters of the sky,
And tunes his notes to liberty?
Ah no, the Cambrian lyre no more
Shall sweetly sound on Avron's shore,
No more the silver harp be won,
No—let old Conway cease to flow,
Back to her source Sabrina go:
Let huge Plinlimmon hide his head,
Or let the tyrant strike me dead,
If I attempt to raise a song
Unmindful of my country's wrong.
What!—shall a haughty king command
Cambrians' free strain on Saxon land?
May this right arm first wither'd be,
Ere I may touch one string to thee,
Proud monarch; nay, may instant death
Arrest my tongue and stop my breath,
If I attempt to weave a song,
Regardless of my country's wrong!

Ye Muses, by your favorite son;
Or I, even I, by glory fir'd
Had to the honour'd prize aspir'd.
No more shall Mona's oaks be spar'd
Or Druid circle be rever'd.
On Conway's banks, and Menai's streams
The solitary bittern screams;
And, where was erst Llewelyn's court,
Ill-omened birds and wolves resort.
There oft at midnight's silent hour,
Near yon ivy-mantled tower,
By the glow-worm's twinkling fire,
Tuning his romantic lyre,
Gray's pale spectre seems to sing,
"Ruin seize thee, ruthless King."
                    —Evan Evans (1731–1789)

HARPS HUNG UPON THE WILLOW

The old harper who used to be the delight of travellers at this inn [in
Conway, Wales] is now sitting in an arm chair in the little parlor within
the kitchen in a state of dotage. His harp stood in the room in which I
slept carefully buckled up in its green cover. At Bangor there was no
harper. The waiter told us they were "no profit to master and was
always in the way in the passage so master never let none come now."
—Maria Edgeworth, letter to Mary Sneyd, March 31, 1819

Neil Gow was dead, the last of our bards—no one again will ever
play Scotch musick as he did. . . . Nor can any one hope to revive
a style passing away. A few true fingers linger amongst us, but
this generation will see the last of them. Our children will not be
as national as their parents.
—Elizabeth Grant of Rothiemurchus, *Memoirs of a
Highland Lady* (composed in 1845–54, published in 1898)

[In] pennillion, or unconnected stanzas, [performers at King Arthur's
Bardic Congress presented] in succession moral precepts, pictures of
natural scenery, images of war or of festival, the lamentations of
absence or captivity, and the complaints or triumphs of love. This
pennillion-singing long survived among the Welsh peasantry almost
every other vestige of bardic customs, and may still be heard among
them on the few occasions on which rack-renting, tax-collecting,
common-enclosing, methodist-preaching, and similar developments
of the light of the age, have left them either the means or the
inclination of making merry.
—Thomas Love Peacock, *The Misfortunes of Elphin*

THE BARDIC INSTITUTION

Evan Evans's "Paraphrase of the 137th Psalm" envisions England as the
site of Babylonian captivity. The Thames, here, is not the subject of idyllic
landscape description but a river of Babylon; on its willowy banks, the
Welsh bards (transported from their country by Edward I in 1282) hang up
their harps and vow poetic silence. To play for their Saxon captors, as they
have been ordered, would be to surrender their nation's last cultural treasures along with its political sovereignty, and to allow a eulogistic poetry

rooted in the landscape and culture of Wales to adorn the "dull vales" of England.[1] Evans's "Paraphrase" describes the development of a bardic nationalism, in resistance not only to the military conquest of Wales but also to the arrogant assumption of the English that other cultures are there to be absorbed into their own. Evans's adaptation of David's psalm becomes a manifesto for a new nationalist literature, as it links a latter-day cultural nationalism to a sanctified biblical precedent, to invest the Welsh with the Israelites' self-confidence as a chosen people and to raise cultural self-preservation to the status of a religious duty.[2]

In eighteenth-century Ireland, Scotland, and Wales nationalist antiquaries edited, explicated, and promoted their respective bardic traditions; emphasizing the cultural rootedness of bardic poetry and its status as historical testimony, their work represents a groundbreaking attempt to describe literature as the product of specific cultural institutions and to understand literary form as a product of a particular national history. Its more immediate purpose, however, was to vindicate the bards, to uphold the honor of their respective national literary traditions from a long line of critics and—as Evan Evans argues of the patriotic defense of Wales in *The Love of Our Country* (1772)—from contemporary "slanders."[3]

In 1729 Scottish antiquary Thomas Innes had argued that the uncertain, fabulous accounts "of the origins of nations, and founders of empire," which were "brought down" by "the bards or poets of the ancients," were no more reliable as historical sources than Virgil's *Aeneid*.[4] Because Britain's early inhabitants had "no use of letters," they had "no means of preserving the memory of past transactions, and less yet of calculation of dates or epochs" (1:iv). This left an open field for later generations of "bards, senachies, or antiquaries, poets and genealogists" (all "different names for the same thing") to fabricate whatever version of the past seemed nationally expedient. A "kind of parasites," the bards were "ignorant and venal" illiterates, "famous for flattering their patrons with ancient pedigrees, and whole nations with ancient successions of kings."[5] In the sixth century, King Aidus almost banished "all the race of bards or antiquaries" from Ireland, and over the following centuries, the Irish bards were repeatedly threatened with exile, "their impostures, flatteries, and insolence having frequently grown to that height, that even pagans had a horror of, and could not bear with them."[6] For Innes, latter-day Irish antiquaries who continue to draw on bardic works as historical sources fatally continue a patriotic tradition of deceit and self-glorification. Only a new breed of antiquarian scholar like himself, schooled in the sciences of chronology and historical probability, can counteract the deleterious influence of bardic inventions on the historiography of early Britain.[7]

Fifty years later, Welsh antiquary and harpist Edward Jones not only champions the Welsh bards but defends even their historical forgeries, by reading them as a patriotic resistance to English occupation. As Jones insists in *Musical and Poetical Relicks of the Welsh Bards, Preserved by Tradition, and Authentic Manuscripts, From Remote Antiquity* (1784), bardic poetry is the product of a highly developed and specialized system of literary education, under the direct patronage of the Welsh court and the Druid priesthood; it therefore represents a learned record of civil and religious life in preconquest Wales.[8] Bardic literary activity contributed to the maintenance of national memory, and Edward's legendary 1282 massacre of the Welsh bards was therefore a deliberate and largely successful attempt to destroy an autonomous Welsh cultural tradition: "And had not the fatal accident which overwhelmed, in the hour of its prosperity, the hereditary princedom of Wales, involved in the same ruin its Poetry and Music, our country might have retained to this day its ancient government, and its national arts." Edward I "gave the final blow to Welsh liberty in the massacre of the bards." Those who survived could not give voice to their indignation: "Yet they were not silent or inactive. That their poetry might breathe with impunity the spirit of their patriotism, they became dark, prophetic, and oracular."

Following the example of the "Monks of the Welsh church," who "in their controversy with Rome" had written religious poems, which they "feigned to be the work of *Taliesin*" in order to "countenance their doctrines," the bards ascribed many of their own political writings to Taliesin, or disguised them as "prophecies of the elder *Merlin*."

> Hence much uncertainty prevails concerning the genuine remains of the sixth century, great part of which has descended to us mutilated and depraved: and hence that mysterious air which pervades all the Poetry of the later periods I am describing. The forgery of those poems, which are entirely spurious, may, I think, be presently detected. They were written to serve a popular and temporary purpose, and were not contrived with such sagacity and care as to hide from the eye of a judicious and enlightened scholar their historical mistakes, their novelty of language, and their other marks of imposture.[9]

Innes had mourned the repeated military occupations of Scotland because they deliberately destroyed many of the "ancient monuments" of Scottish culture, damaged the national historical record, and left modern-day historians without the full documentation needed to refute bardic inventions. Jones mourns Edward I's occupation of Wales as a historical and cultural rupture: the extirpation of the bardic caste wipes out a flourishing literary culture and destroys national institutions. In the wake of English conquest, bardic composition not only bears witness to but resists English cultural violence; the bards' insistent retrojection of recent history into a Welsh prophetic tradition insists that the invaders will not be able to destroy literary tradition, after all, for this attack is already anticipated and shored up against by the tradition itself.[10] Jones emphasizes the antiquity, plenitude, and sufficiency of the Welsh record, despite every attempt to destroy it: "There is no living nation that can produce works of so remote antiquity, and at the same time such unimpeached authority as the Welsh."[11] Unlike Innes, Jones makes no concealment of his own nationalist sympathies. In light of the history of national suppression he sketches out in his account, a defensive nationalism appears as a patriotic duty, and Jones can see himself unproblematically at once as latter-day bard and latter-day antiquary.

In Ireland, writes Charles O'Conor in 1753,

> The English were far from being mistaken, when they allotted the severest Penalties for these incendiary Bards; a Race of Men who were perpetually stirring up the Natives to Rebellion; and as constantly giving Rebellion another Name, Nothing less than the Rights of the Nation, and the Spirit of Liberty. Poetry preserved the Spirit of our Language, the Force of Elocution, and in some Degree, the antient Genius of the Nation, even in Ages of Anarchy . . . in the worst, it preserved the People from degenerating into Savages.[12]

Over the following decade, the publication of Thomas Gray's poem "The Bard" (1757) and James Macpherson's *Poems of Ossian* (1760–65) would stir up English enthusiasm for bardic poetry and for the picturesque landscapes of Wales, Scotland, and Ireland. Yet its newfound popularity in England endangered the bardic tradition in a new way, as English poets tried to impersonate the bardic voice and to imitate bardic materials, without grasping their historical and cultural significance. For nationalist antiquaries, the bard is the mouthpiece for a whole society, articulating its values, chronicling its history, and mourning the inconsolable tragedy of its collapse. English poets, in contrast, imagine the bard (and the minstrel after him) as an inspired, isolated, and peripatetic figure. Nationalist antiquaries read bardic poetry for its content and its historical information; their analyses help to crystallize a new nationalist model of literary history.[13] The English poets are primarily interested in the bard himself, for he represents poetry as a dislocated art, standing apart from and transcending its particular time and place.[14] The late-eighteenth-century bardic revival gives new emphasis to the social rootedness and political function of literature, as to the inseparability of literary performance from specific institutions and audiences. English writers insist, in contrast, on literature's social and political autonomy.

These differences of emphasis reflect the very different circumstances under which Irish, Scottish, and Welsh nationalist antiquaries (usually gentleman scholars, clergymen, professors, or other professionals) investigate the cultural history of their countries, and those under which London's new professional men of letters attempt to earn their living in the literary market, in the absence of the aristocratic patrons who had supported and pensioned their forebears. Financially secure yet (as they see it) culturally disfranchised, the nationalist antiquaries see literature as a vehicle of collective expression and historical justice; financially insecure and preoccupied with their own exposed situation, the London literati increasingly understand literature as a vehicle of individual conscience and individual expression, newly independent of aristocratic mandates, but therefore fully aware of its own social marginality. Each group uses the bard to express its very different yearnings for independence and for a lost feudal unity—and each locates the bard at a different moment of cultural and literary crisis. Where English authors celebrate the unity of function manifested by Ossian (as a warrior and adviser, chronicler and bard), in order to mourn the organic character of literary life under feudal patronage, and point out the later specialization of bardic duties as an anticipation of the modern division of labor, nationalist antiquaries see such specialization as devoid of economic significance.[15] And whereas nationalist antiquaries emphasize the collapse of Celtic clan culture under the pressures of Christianity and English conquest, the English poets tend to be more preoccupied with the decline of troubadour culture in the fourteenth century, a development that coincided with an earlier rise of the bourgeoisie and the growth of a mercantile, guild-based town culture; in obvious parallel to the eighteenth-century crisis of literary commodification, courtly poets and musicians lost status and came to be seen as craftsmen instead.[16]

Yet nationalist antiquaries read the English appropriation of bardic poetry not so much as an expression of cultural crisis as a repetition of the cultural subjugation of Wales, Ireland, and Scotland, a restaging of the scene of Babylonian captivity, in which the exiled and imprisoned bards were ordered to sing for their new masters. The conquest of Ireland, argues Sylvester O'Halloran in 1771, fundamentally reshaped the English relationship to Irish history and to their own culture. As long as England had no aspirations to rule Ireland, English writers had only praise for Ireland's artistic and learned traditions. Yet "the moment a *fatal* connection arose between the two people we find the tables turned, and every crime that human malice can invent, or human frailty imagine, imputed to them."[17] Down to the present day, English detachment and disdain toward Ireland conceals a will to domination, motivated both by envy at the cultural vitality of the conquered and by a deep fear of England's own innate inferiority.

The pervasive self-figuration of eighteenth-century England as Augustan Rome, then, is inadvertently revealing, because both societies remained culturally and economically dependent on the labor of their subject peoples; just as Rome's cultural life depended on the wholesale appropriation of Greek literary traditions and the learnedness of Greek slaves, so too the English expect to harness captive traditions of Celtic learning and poetry, harps and bards, for the cause of an imperial state. The poetry of Gray, Macpherson, and Evans dramatizes the refusal of a nation to give up its culture in support of the empire. Yet their bards can meet the threat of cultural absorption only with their own self-destruction; like the Buddhist monks who immolated themselves during the Vietnam War, Gray's bard leaps to his death to commemorate his people's losses, to refuse the surrender of their culture, and to mark forever the injustice of the English. Latter-day nationalists see themselves as carrying on this bardic protest, albeit in a less dramatic register; if the bards of old hung up their harps, refusing to play for their captors, present-day nationalist antiquaries are determined to deliver over no piece of their cultural legacy without fully cataloging where it came from and making clear what it meant for it to be wrenched from its original circumstances.

From a nationalist perspective, Gray's popularization of the legend of Edward as "bardicide" and his portrayal of the bard as a vengeful national hero seems more satisfactory than Macpherson's Ossian, a figure whom blindness and age have rendered at once venerable and feeble. *Ossian*'s success, indeed, might be attributed in part to the reassurance it provides of the obsolescence of Highland clan culture, so recently a military threat to London and now forcibly dismantled under British military occupation. Evans's own bardic poem links Ossianic sensibility, and a desire for the echoing of song in the landscape, to the insensitive Saxon captors, and the Welsh bards themselves articulate a vow of vengeance straight out of Gray and the Hebrew Bible. The "Paraphrase of the 137th Psalm" thus closes with a virtual paraphrase of Gray and with the symbolic suicide of the "last surviving poet," who swears vengeance with his death. Yet the rest of the poem, paradoxically, has been narrated by a group of Welsh bards who have not only outlived Edward's "whirlwind" but outlasted "the last surviving poet" as well, to go on singing. Instead of their traditional songs of praise, they chant new poems of execration against the conquerors; the poem thus describes the simultaneous death and rebirth of national song.

Gray glosses this central, paradoxical topos of Welsh literary historiography as a mythic celebration of the nation and of poetry, both forces strong enough to overcome their own historical eradication: Edward "is said to have hanged up all their Bards, because they encouraged the Nation to rebellion, but their works (we see) still remain, the Language (tho' decaying) still lives, & the art of their versification is known, and practised to this day among them."[18] This myth of survival in destruction is foundational not only for the poetics and vernacular revivals of the late-eighteenth century but also for a long series of novelistic genres, from the sentimental and the Gothic novel to the historical novel. The dying bard in Charles Maturin's *Milesian Chief* (1812), for example, figures the death of Irish court culture under English occupation, anchoring undying feudal loyalties and memories of a former national glory. One of a staff of "domestic bards" retained by the O'Morven family in their castles across Ireland, he was forced to leave their service during the civil wars and returns now, after "years of wandering, to die under the shelter of our walls. He was blind, but his memory was faithful to the path that led us home." Resting "among some ruins," he learns that they are all that remains of

> the roof under which he had lived and under which he had hoped to die. But even this hope failed him, and he felt his age more helpless, and his blindness darker than when he sat down among the ruins. . . . Before he expired on the spot, he poured out his grief to his harp in a strain addressed to the solitary tenant of the ruins—the doves, whose notes the music seems to imitate. The words are beautiful, but I will not be guilty of doing them into English: their untranslatable beauty is like what we are told of the paintings of Herculaneum, which preserve their rich colours in darkness and concealment, but when exposed to the light and modern eyes, fade and perish.[19]

Maturin reenacts this paradox of memory and obliteration. His bard dies with no one to hear his final song, yet the song, somehow, is preserved anyway, so that at the end of the eighteenth century it is still known to the Milesian chief. The chief (and Maturin after him) declines to translate the fragile strains, lest in the exposure to modern, English eyes they "fade and perish."

Maturin's early-nineteenth-century evocation of bardic nationalism is informed explicitly by the events of the 1790s. His novel ends with the United Irishmen rebellion and with the execution of the Milesian chief; revolutionary unrest is both the logical extension and the death sentence of cultural nationalism. Evans's late-eighteenth-century poem works to avoid this outcome. With its emphasis on regeneration in death, its version of bardic nationalism also preaches conciliation in resistance: the end of the poem veers from the literary and historical prototype offered by David and the exiled Israelites to that offered by Gray and his bard, and the result, paradoxically, is both the radicalization and the depoliticization of the poem. On the face of it, Evans's decision to end his poem with Gray's vision of a defiant bardic self-destruction rather than Macpherson's vision of bardic decrepitude suggests a stance that is militant rather than melancholy, aggrieved rather than recuperative. Yet in departing from its original mode of paraphrase (the updating and recontextualizing of the 137th Psalm) for another (the redeployment of tropes proposed by another contemporary poet), Evans blunts the full political force of his original. For although it, too, began lyrically, at the riverside, David's psalm ended by predicting the Israelites' vengeful joy as they witness the murder of their enemies' children. In keeping with its overall emphasis on rhetorical gestures and on literary utterances as the real sites of political power, Evans's poem ends, by contrast, with the suicidal leap and dying curse of the last bard. The violence of cultural annihilation is here internalized, to destroy the poet himself.

Evans's poem is a generalized (and deeply felt) attack on English hegemony, which remains extremely careful to circumscribe the effects of its rage. By "paraphrasing" the Israelites as bards, Evans synecdochically replaces the collective subjects of the biblical Psalm (their sense of group identity shaped by a shared experience of diaspora) with a much smaller cultural elite of distinctly aristocratic sensibilities and loyalties, trained to serve as the living repository of cultural traditions. In lieu of a popular resistance movement, Evans advocates a literary nationalism guided by poets and scholars. Evans's poem represents simultaneously the conjunction of a cultural nationalism with a nationalism of more clearly articulated political, perhaps even revolutionary, goals and a substitution of one set of goals for the other. The consequences of that substitution would be particularly evident from the retrospect of the 1800s, when the failure of the United Irishmen rebellion appeared to divide antiquarian nationalists from revolutionary nationalists forever.

It Is New Strung and Shall Be Heard

The high point of Ireland's "first Celtic revival," as commentators have often argued, was the 1792 Belfast harpists' festival, held around Bastille Day; intended, according to its 1791 circular, "to revive and perpetuate the ancient Music and Poetry of Ireland," the festival gathered twelve elderly harpers from across Ireland, "descendants of our Ancient Bards, who are at present almost exclusively possessed of all that remains of the Music Poetry and oral traditions of Ireland," to perform for a large, appreciative audience, while antiquarian Edward Bunting and a team of transcribers noted each song.[20] Bunting's three volumes of melodies from the festival, published over the next forty years, had a major influence on young nationalist poets; William Drennan and Thomas Moore, for instance, set some of their most influential "Irish melodies" to its music.[21] The Belfast festival thus marks the conjuncture of new and old bards, of traditional music and romantic poetry.

It also marks a much briefer political conjuncture between bardic and revolutionary brands of nationalism. The Belfast festival coincided with a major convention of some six thousand Irish volunteers and United Irishmen; the harpers' performances were framed by processions and parades, debates on Catholic emancipation, and banquets with toasts to the fall of the Bastille and the rights of man. "What a strange contrast is afforded here," writes Charlotte Milligan Fox in *Annals of the Irish Harpers* (1911), "between the politicians of the new era, fired with the principles of the

French Revolution, and the musicians mostly aged and blind assembled in the Exchange Rooms, who waited for the sound of the drums and the cheering to pass into the distance, ere they wakened the clear sweet music of their harps."[22] In retrospect, the separation between a political nationalism, oriented toward the future, and a conservative nationalism, attempting to preserve the national past, might seem absolute—except that here they stage their celebrations together. Busy with the organization of the political convention, Theobald Wolfe Tone records his boredom at the harpers' festival.

> July 11th. All go to the Harpers . . . poor enough; ten performers; seven execrable. . . . No new musical discovery; believe all the good Irish airs are already written. . . .
> July 13th. The Harpers again. Strum. Strum and be hanged.[23]

In the wake of the festival and convention, however, the United Irishmen collectively adopted the Irish harp as their badge, even if the motto to stand beneath it—It Is New Strung and Shall Be Heard—suggests important differences of emphasis between their conception of nationalism and that of the nationalist song collectors.

Beginning with its initiator, Dr. James MacDonnell, many of those associated with the harpers' festival were also strongly committed to the cause of Catholic emancipation. Festival organizer Henry Joy McCracken had also helped found the first United Irishmen society in Belfast the previous year. During the 1798 United Irishmen rebellion, he commanded the rebels of County Antrim; imprisoned and executed for his role in the uprising, he became one of the martyrs of the rebellion.[24] Another founder of the United Irishmen, William Drennan, was tried for seditious libel in 1794, and thereafter turned to poetry as his principal mode of political expression, moving from a revolutionary nationalism back to a bardic one. In the wake of the 1790s, as Drennan's case suggests, a radical cultural nationalism continued to sustain itself in the way that (and partly because) a radical political nationalism could not. Drennan's strong dissatisfaction with the 1802 Act of Union thus finds expression not in a resumption of revolutionary plotting but rather in the composition of poetic strains of almost Ossianic melancholy.[25]

The displacement of political anger into cultural expression had been a central tenet of bardic nationalism from its beginnings. With such displacement as its starting point, this book explores several other kinds of displacements, across periods, genres, and finally national borders. When late-eighteenth-century discussions of bardic poetry and national antiquities are remembered and revived, in the first years of the nineteenth century, this has an immediate effect on the early-nineteenth-century novel, shaping first a new kind of nationalist novel and then a new kind of historical novel.

In turn, these genres are transported out of British peripheries into the colonies of the new British Empire, where they form the primary models for early colonial fiction. And the revival of the national antiquarianism of the 1770s in the novel of the 1800s is possible in part because in the interim the novel has continued to work with many of the conceptual problems raised by antiquarian activity. The transportation of Scottish and Irish novelistic genres to Canada, Australia, and British India is facilitated by the novel's own long-standing obsession with cultural transfer and imperial consciousness.

Although after 1800 the novel appears to take up exactly where the antiquarian theorists and Enlightenment ethnographers of the 1770s left off (and to redeploy literary tropes thirty or forty years old with scarcely any consciousness of the passage of time), the events of the 1790s have transformed the meaning of cultural nationalism. Proto-Jacobin in many respects during the last decades of the eighteenth century, cultural nationalism often appears in the 1810s and 1820s as reactive or reactionary, even if the possibility of a more radical deployment remains. The advent of a class-based cultural analysis and revolutionary politics fundamentally alters the ground of subsequent political life in Britain, so that the revival of cultural nationalism in the early nineteenth century has a very different meaning from what it had the first time around, despite an apparent continuity of rhetoric.

John Galt's historical fiction, both a product of and a critical meditation on this second wave of cultural nationalism, shows us how to interpret these shifts. In *Ringhan Gilhaize, or The Covenanters* (1823), Galt's novelistic annal of three generations of covenanting activity, in *The Entail, or The Lairds of Grippy* (1821), his novelistic annal of a hundred years of Scottish history from the Union to the end of the eighteenth century, and in *Bogle Corbet, or The Emigrants* (1831), a novel that traces the development of imperial ideologies from the Industrial Revolution through the 1790s into the political reaction and empire building of the early-nineteenth century, we repeatedly watch a particular ideological position or political tenet—the yearning for religious freedom, the desire for a classless society or for the restoration of Scotland's ancient glories, the anxiety about the moral price of empire—assume a very different significance as the political ground shifts under it, undergoing radical internal transformations even while its surface propositions appear unchanged. In *Ringhan Gilhaize*, the Covenanter movement (as chronicled by a grandson of an original Covenant signatory) begins as a movement of earnest purpose, ceremonial and festive in its processions, righteous in spirit. Then, as the Covenanters endure persecution, prohibition, and finally, at one horrible moment, the massacre of their families, the tone of Galt's novel and of the movement changes gradually but irrevocably. The movement still continues a generation later, but its vision has darkened and narrowed, until in the novel's final sentences (as our narrator proves to be the assassin of Claverhouse and the self-styled vindicator of three generations of national suffering), we see that we are facing fanaticism.[26]

Cultural nationalism follows a similar pattern as it spans the 1790s—or better, as cultural nationalists dissolve their demands in the face of the 1790s and reconstitute them after 1800. Like the movement for the abolition of the slave trade, nationalist campaigns for cultural recognition are eclipsed by the threat of French invasion and of class warfare. At the same time, however, the rhetorics of both nationalism and abolition reappear, radicalized almost beyond recognition, in the separatist, republican programs of the United Irishmen, of Scotland's Friends of the People, and of the United Scotsmen.[27] In the early nineteenth century, the rethinking of the nature of Britain, in the wake of the United Irishmen rebellion and of Ireland's 1802 Union with England, catalyzes a resurgence of nationalist literature, first in Ireland and then in Scotland. Yet within this literature, paradoxically, nationalist and unionist sentiments often appear side by side more amicably than ever before, and the permanence of national differences is recognized only to be overridden. As John Gibson Lockhart puts it in *Peter's Letters to His Kinsfolk* (1819),

> [A]fter two nations have been long separate in their interests, and have respectively nourished their own turn of thinking—they may at last come to be united in their interests, but their associations cannot be so pliable, nor can they be so easily amalgamated. An union of national interests *quoad* external power relates chiefly to the future—whereas, associations respect the past. . . . The essence of all nationality, however, is a peculiar way of thinking, and conceiving.[28]

Now, for the first time, the novel becomes a prime genre for the dissemination of nationalist ideas. Yet when Irish and Scottish novelists set out to bring the claims of nationalism into the novel, they usually turn to an antiquarian and bardic version of nationalism that is already thirty or forty years old.[29] There are several possible explanations for this fact.

1. This revival is internally coherent. Because the literature of nationalism is concerned, again and again, with the renewal of past glories and traditions, it is only appropriate that it commemorate and celebrate its own history. The nationalist novels of the early nineteenth century need to be understood, therefore, as a kind of explicit homage to an earlier literary nationalism. Sydney Owenson's *O'Donnel: A National Tale* (1814) features a heroine named Charlotte O'Halloran (in tribute to late-eighteenth-century antiquaries Sylvester O'Halloran and Charlotte Brooke), and Alicia LeFanu's *Tales of a Tourist* (1823) an antiquary named O'Carolan (honoring both O'Halloran and the eighteenth-century

harper, composer, and poet Carolan). Indeed, we are able to recognize the late eighteenth century as the formative moment for modern cultural nationalism in part because the subsequent novelistic tradition continually enshrines it as such. Novels such as James M'Henry's *O'Halloran, or The Insurgent Chief: An Irish Historical Tale of 1798* (1824) track the movement from an antiquarian and bardic nationalism to revolutionary nationalism with great explicitness; if M'Henry's title character at first seems only to echo the political rhetoric of his eighteenth-century namesake, he will eventually lead the 1798 rebellion.[30]

2. The early-nineteenth-century revival of eighteenth-century nationalism is reactionary. What the events and the political discussions of the 1790s made visible was the parallel between nationalist and class struggles. Rather than building on this insight, however, early-nineteenth-century cultural nationalists return self-consciously to a prerevolutionary antiquarian rhetoric, signaling their refusal to conjoin the two political causes. Under the sign of the bard (a figure for a national poetry consecrated to the cause of feudal loyalties), they mourn the loss not only of past national glory but also of the hierarchical stability of a feudal past.[31] The new nationalism, argues Thomas Love Peacock in *The Misfortunes of Elphin* (1829) and in *Crochet Castle* (1831), is conservative in every sense.

3. The early-nineteenth-century novel *does* mesh nationalist analysis with the vestiges of a Jacobin critique. In the late eighteenth century, nationalist antiquaries argued the importance of cultural forms both for the maintenance of imperial domination and for any nationalist resistance movement. As E. P. Thompson argues in *The Making of the English Working Class*, the 1790s saw the emergence of a new workers' culture—and this made evident the full power of nationalist arguments. The ubiquitous presence of eighteenth-century cultural paradigms in early-nineteenth-century novels is therefore profoundly unsurprising. Although early-nineteenth-century nationalists may reach back across the revolutionary decades to retrieve the rhetoric of the immediately prerevolutionary period, their reception of late-eighteenth-century ideas remains influenced by the cultural developments and rhetoric of the revolutionary period.

These three possibilities are not mutually exclusive. Genres are subject to uneven political and formal development; an old nationalism, a deliberately conservative nationalism, and a radicalized nationalism can exist side by side within them. Throughout the 1790s, novelists remain obsessed with the formal problem of how to represent the differences between European and non-European cultures (the mental, geographical, and political distances that separate them, their incommensurability and simultaneity) and the political problem of how to use the vantage point and perspective of the colonies to reassess and criticize British society. When novelists return, after 1800, to regional topics and to the problem of British nationalities, the change of direction represents both an attempt to examine Britain, along Jacobin lines, as an imperial state, and an attempt to retreat completely from such radical analysis back into the smaller, ostensibly intact world of Britain itself.

TRANSPORTING THE HARP

Since the eighteenth century, as Tom Nairn argues in *The Enchanted Glass*, the British Isles (themselves a "piece of phony geography") have functioned as a transnational political and cultural empire, a "Ukania" much like "Kukania," the Hapsburg Dual Monarchy (*K[önig] u[nd] K[aiserreich]*) satirized by Robert Musil, Karl Kraus, and other Austro-Hungarian modernists.[32] As formed in 1707 by the legislative union between the kingdom of Scotland and an England that had already subsumed Wales and held Ireland in colonial thrall, the Anglo-Scottish state had the fortune or misfortune to be combined before the general formation of modern national consciousness. As Nairn argued in *The Break-up of Britain* (1977), Scotland subsequently developed a kind of protonationalist consciousness in the course of the Enlightenment, and Ireland developed a classically anti-colonial nationalism. In the meantime, the larger entity of Great Britain was held together by

> the historical apparatus of "Greater"—a combination of formal Statehood, informal authority-structure and ideology soldered together into the formidably powerful identity of Britishness. This is an entity which has no business to exist in the contemporary world, but it does. It "makes no sense" according to the standard concepts of today's nation-state politics . . . because it dates from before the formation of these concepts: it is not . . . "above that sort of thing," but *before* that sort of thing—an anteriority carried forward into modernity by the peculiar survival-conditions of an a-national economy.[33]

If Scottish and Welsh nationalists are driven by a resentment of a hegemonic Englishness, this is, in fact, a nationalist formulation they have invented in their own image and that does not exist in England.[34] Even London functions not so much as the source and center of Englishness but as the nerve center—-and blind spot—of a patched-together empire. As the place from which the empire is ruled, it gathers a cross section of intellectuals, aristocrats, and merchants from every domain. A place from which the all of the isles *seem* visible, it can really give only the most misleading sense of the empire's cultural coherence, its actual economic or political conditions.

British centralization implies not only the spread and enforced imposition but also the systematic underdevelopment of Englishness. To the degree that England becomes the center of the empire, its own internal sense of culture accordingly fails to develop. And to the degree that the English language, coercively imposed on the British peripheries, comes to serve as the means of imperial absorption, it becomes an increasingly minimal basis for identifying Englishness. The peripheries, in comparison, struggle with the contradictions of underdevelopment, yet they each retain their distinct, national, and non-English character. Their very ways of speaking and using the English language remain highly distinctive, marked by a particular cultural and political history.[35] In contrast, the language and cultural landscape of England come to seem ever paler, even to the English themselves.

The canonical British literary tradition of the late eighteenth and early nineteenth century reflects this narrowing sense of Englishness; it remains obsessed with refining, then redefining, English literary style, with analyzing the nuances of English sensibility, and with an increasingly pastoral redescription of the English landscape.[36] Over the same period, however, a formally experimental, and now less studied parallel literature—a new travel literature, a nationally inflected picaresque, a new antiquarian literature, a new Gothic and historical fiction, a new novel of foreign and domestic national manners—begins to explore a much larger repertoire of experiences and places, often taking as its starting point the textures and local sublimities of peripheral culture, landscape, and speech.

The romantic period is one not only of literary centralization but also of literary devolution. In the late eighteenth century, many well-known writers (Sheridan, Goldsmith, Boswell, Smollett, and Thomson) still moved from the peripheries to settle in London (or saw themselves as enjoying their real success through publication there). Yet the same period also saw the development of distinctive new literary cultures in Ireland and Scotland, and by 1800, both Edinburgh and Dublin had become lively centers for novelistic publication. In Edinburgh, argues John Gibson Lockhart, the advent of the *Edinburgh Review* and of *Blackwood's Edinburgh Magazine* helped to stimulate the growth of a new national and nationalist literary culture. And Scott's publisher, Constable, helps to change

> the whole aspect of Edinburgh, as a seat of literary merchandize—and, in truth, making it, instead of no literary mart at all, a greater one than almost any other city in Europe. . . . Instead of Scotch authors sending their works to be published by London booksellers, there is nothing more common now-a-days, than to hear of English authors sending down their books to Edinburgh, to be published in a city, than which Memphis or Palmyra could scarcely have appeared a more absurd place of publication to any English author thirty years ago.

A very large percentage of "the classical works of English literature, published in our age, have made their first appearance on the counters of the Edinburgh booksellers," and the Edinburgh title page consequently carries "greater authority" than "almost any London one."[37] In the mid-eighteenth century, James Thomson and other Anglo-Scottish writers "had no relation to their own country in particular, or its modes of feeling."[38] By 1819, a new literature of distinctly Scottish (and Irish) nationalist feeling was available all over Britain, British novel writing and reading were dominated by a long-standing vogue for Irish and Scottish subject matter, and a number of popular and influential Irish and Scottish novelists (Edgeworth, Scott, Maturin, and Hogg) not only wrote consistently about local subject matter but remained firmly ensconced in regional centers, rather than moving to London. In the first decade of the nineteenth century, even the most nationalist novels still appeared to address themselves primarily to an English audience, and only secondarily to Anglo-Scottish and Anglo-Irish readers. By the 1820s and 1830s, however, the density both of dialect and of cultural references in the works of key novelists (such as Galt and Owenson) suggested that the implicit audience had changed dramatically.[39]

In the early nineteenth century, Scottish and Irish novelists of this period often find their primary inspiration in each other's work, and the constant copying and cross-pollination between the Irish and Scottish novel amount almost to a transperipheral literary life, just as the characters in Regina Maria Roche's *Children of the Abbey* (1796) spend the whole novel crossing back and forth from one periphery to another, from Ireland to Wales to Scotland to Ireland to Scotland to Ireland. London is no longer the center of novelistic consciousness. In the eighteenth century the explosive questions of the early settlement of Britain, of which country had the most complete historical records or the most highly developed bardic poetry, had continually divided Scottish, Irish, and Welsh antiquaries. Yet even in attacking one another's findings, they drew heavily on each other's work; their accounts of the way bardic poetry, oral transmission, and the traditions of Gaelic learning functioned in their respective countries are thus surprisingly uniform.[40] So, too, for all their boundless vituperativeness, the controversies about who had colonized whose country gradually establish many deep-rooted commonalties of language, literature, and social structure in all three nations.[41]

In the early decades of the nineteenth century, the growing nationalization and national bifurcation of the novel, and the enormous popular success of the Scottish novel in particular, led to an increasing dilemma of identification for English novel readers and novelists. In Sarah Green's *Scotch Novel Reading, or Modern Quackery, By a Cockney* (1824), a hapless young English novel reader is swept up in the "Caledonian mania" of the day. Besotted with the heroes and heroines of the Waverley novels, Alice Fennel affects Highland dress and an unconvincing (and utterly literary) Scottish accent: her conversation, "a patchwork of quotations, phrases, and ill-pronounced specimens of Scotch dialect," is pronounced so queerly that one observer wonders "she had not been born dumb, for there was surely some great defect in her organs of speaking." As Green's characters and narrator agree, Scots has an "unpleasant coarseness" even when properly pronounced, "not only a barbarous, but a contracted sound," corresponding to the confluence, in Scottish culture, of "extreme nationality and narrowness of mind."[42]

Writing in the satirical tradition of Charlotte Lennox's *Female Quixote* (1752), William Beckford's *Modern Novel Writing, or The Elegant Enthusiast* (1796), Eaton Stannard Barrett's *Heiress, or Adventures of a Fair Romance Reader* (1813), and Jane Austen's *Northanger Abbey* (1787–88, published in 1818), Green mocks the excesses of female novel addiction. What is at stake in the Scottish novel, however, is not simply a mode of reading but the future of British literary culture and cross-cultural understanding, for the romanticized vision of Scotland purveyed by Scott and his contemporaries actually retards the process of intellectual union it claims to make possible. And the fad for nationalist fiction threatens to trap the English novel in an inauthentic regionalism, just as the hapless Alice is trapped in an inauthentic costume and an inauthentic (and incomprehensible) accent. "[N]othing now goes down" in contemporary literature, her father laments, "but Scotch stories; and Scotch dialect, by the way a very unpleasant one, is thrust upon us, as if there was not another country under the sun worth hearing of than poor, miserable little Scotland."[43] In the long run, Alice is cured of her folly by meeting actual Scots and visiting Scotland, arriving at a more balanced view of Scottish culture and learning to distinguish fact from fiction. So too, Green argues, the English novel must regain its balance by abandoning its attempts to mimic the Scottish novel, returning instead to the English subjects that have traditionally been its strength.

Jane Austen, in contrast, insists on the possibility of a more balanced relationship between the ostensibly native concerns of the English novel and the material of cultural nationalism. In an early scene in *Mansfield Park* (1814), she invokes a nationalist rhetoric of cultural difference and authenticity in order to establish her own localist agenda. Austen works to avoid any exoticizing of national difference, the borrowing of bard, brogue, or national costume. Instead, she draws on the nationalist analysis of cultural condescension to set up the terms of her own critique and to suggest that Mary Crawford's London attitudes are a kind of imperialism. When Mary reveals that her harp is being sent on to her, an already infatuated Edmund Bertram greets the announcement with "pleasure and surprise." Recent Irish and Scottish novels from Sydney Owenson's *Wild Irish Girl* (1806) to Charles Maturin's *Milesian Chief* (1812) and Walter Scott's

Waverley (1814) have imbued the image of the harp-playing heroines with a great deal of picturesque and romantic charm, signifying a poetic soul and a reverence for national traditions.

Yet Mary's complaints about her trouble in finding a farmer to transport her harp reveal the superficiality of her engagement with everything the instrument represents.

> "You would find it difficult, I dare say, just now, in the middle of a very late hay harvest, to hire a horse and cart?"
>
> "I was astonished to find what a piece of work was made of it! . . . Guess my surprise, when I found that I had been asking the most unreasonable, most impossible thing in the world, had offended all the farmers, all the labourers, all the hay in the parish. . . . I shall understand all your ways in time; but coming down with the true London maxim, that every thing is to be got with money, I was a little embarrassed at first by the sturdy independence of your country customs. However, I am to have my harp fetched tomorrow."[44]

As a bardic instrument, the cherished vehicle of Irish, Welsh, and Scottish nationalism, and then as the emblem of a nationalist republicanism, the harp stands for an art that honors the organic relationship between a people, their land, and their culture.[45] In Mary Crawford's hands, it is deployed for purely picturesque effect. Uninterested in the outcome of the harvest, the needs of the farmers, or the state of the countryside, eager to buy convenience at others' cost, Mary plays the harp solely in self-advertisement; her selfish individualism bars her from serving as the genius loci of any place. The episode at once illustrates the transportability of nationalist tropes into the English novel and problematizes the act of transport itself.

The Origins of Nationalism

In the second half of the eighteenth century, local developments such as enclosures, the changing uses of crops and livestock, the building of new roads, and the reorganization of poor relief generated new agricultural abundance and new agricultural fortunes. They also led to increasing political tension and class stratification: a new kind of rural penury, the criminalization of the poor, the escalation of rural depopulation, the beginnings of large-scale overseas emigration, and, in those who migrated instead to Britain's cities, the origins of what would become a new industrial working class.[46] In the Scottish, Irish, and Welsh peripheries of the new Britain, the effects of such modernization were particularly visible and politicized, for they were seen to escalate, exacerbate, or recapitulate processes of political incorporation and disfranchisement already under way, in Wales and Ireland since the sixteenth century and in Scotland since the beginning of the eighteenth century. In Ireland, as in Wales, the English conquest and subsequent disfranchising laws had meant the disinheritance of an indigenous feudal class and its replacement by a new class of English landowners. The eighteenth-century "improvement" and capitalization of rural estates newly called into question the legitimacy of Anglo-Irish ownership and government and the legacy of the penal laws.[47] In Scotland the dramatic political, economic, and social reorganization of the Highlands in the wake of the failed 1745 Jacobite uprising—British military occupation and forced anglicization, the introduction of land-intensive sheep grazing, and the subsequent forced "clearances" of large numbers of peasants whose labors were no longer marketable—was matched by far-reaching changes in landholding and local government in the Lowlands.

Despite their clear significance for the shape of British society, these large-scale economic and social transformations are registered only intermittently (although often with considerable force) in late-eighteenth-century literature.[48] Only under the influence of the Jacobin writing of the 1790s, with its insistence on the social function of literature, does British literature begin to address itself more frequently and consistently to contemporary political and economic life. Thus it is only in the early nineteenth century that a new Scottish historical fiction and an Irish national fiction attempt, for the first time, a panoramic picture of the social changes of the past seventy-five years. In their juxtaposition of plots, as in their story lines, Scottish novels argue for an understanding of the late eighteenth century simultaneously as a period of unprecedented intellectual brilliance for Scotland (in the theoretical work of the Scottish Enlightenment) and as a period of unprecedented economic ruthlessness and political disfranchisement. In rural Scotland, as Scott and Christian Isobel Johnstone argue in *Guy Mannering* and *Clan-Albin*, their respective novels of 1815, Highland and Lowland peasants alike were displaced from traditional lands to make room for sheep, for model farms, and for manufactories. In Glasgow, as Galt argues in *Bogle Corbet* (1832), new imperial and industrial fortunes were made from the sweated labor of a new urban proletariat, as from the slave labor of Britain's overseas colonies. In Edinburgh the building of the New Town by urban "improvers" increased the social distance between the well-to-do and the impoverished. Even in Scotland's smaller towns, as Galt argues in *The Provost* (1822), a parallel reorganization of urban life and structures of local government worked to support the economic interests of a new middle class and to silence a disfranchised poor.

The capitalization of Britain, funded by the booty of imperial conquest and the slave labor of the colonies, accentuates the gap between rich and poor. In the initial, optimistic period of capitalist expansion, landowners depict themselves as public benefactors, "improving" their own property as part of a campaign for greater national prosperity. But once those without property start to feel the ruthlessness of a new capitalist social contract, property owners depict themselves as drained of all personal agency or responsibility, forced into rent increases or clearances only because they, in turn, are acted upon by larger, impersonal market forces.

The rise of a capitalist economy exacerbates not only the inequities of class within all sectors of British society but also the inequities of regional development. Many Scottish and Anglo-Irish landowners find themselves caught between the two developments. Those able to make new capital investments in the improvement of their properties often succeed in consolidating their local economic and political standing. Those without such investment capital, however, often suffer an acute loss of prestige and local importance. In preunion Ireland, for instance, many landowners begin to feel their marginal place within English and British economic, political, and cultural life with new acuteness; when Maria Edgeworth and other Irish national novelists look back on the late eighteenth century, in the wake of the Union, they focus on the figure of the absentee landlord and use the return of the absentee as a catalyst of plot.[49] Such landlords, Edgeworth argues, are driven by contradictory imperatives and loyalties; while they desert their local responsibilities and make continual, unreasonable financial demands on their impoverished Irish tenants, in a vain bid to win status and recognition in London, English society mocks and despises them as backward representatives of a backward people. And indeed, their refusal to invest in or to supervise local development dooms their tenants to dependent poverty. The only solution to these social and economic disorders, the novelists suggest, is a renewed, nationalist identification with Ireland, as a state whose marginality can and must be reversed. By ignoring the judgments of London and taking pride, instead, in local improvement and accomplishment, the landlords could alleviate the sufferings of those beneath them and resume the duties of their station. The emergence of the modern nation-state and the concealment of landed and moneyed power in and as market forces are thus matched by the rise of a new cultural nationalism.

But as Marxists have long argued, nationalists' complaints of past oppression and external misrecognition also work to occlude the actual local restructuring of the country. Benedict Anderson has influentially argued that modern nationalist movements, in spite of their traditionalist and communitarian rhetoric, are actually predicated on the rise of individualism, fueled by political energies generated by the modernization process and shaped by "impersonal" apolitical institutional forces.[50] Anderson points particularly to the parallels between the way the modern census "produces" integral autonomous subjects and the way modern print capitalism creates in its readers a sense of seriality and therefore of historical agency. When the census designates new ethnic (in addition to more traditional racial or religious) categories in which to group inhabitants, and then records identity in integral terms within those categories, Anderson argues, this creates new forms of identification with the state. The newspapers, in their turn, use a standardized vocabulary ("a minister," "the emperor," "a nationalist leader," "the revolution," "the civil war," "the nationalist partisans") to describe political actors and political events emanating from very different situations in various parts of world; the effect is to lead newspaper readers to see developments around them in terms of "everyday universals." Together, census and newspaper create subjects whose self-understanding is at once newly individualized and newly communal, newly generic and newly, ethnically specific—and nationalism creates itself in their image. Grounded in new notions of the universal, byproducts of new systems of categorization, nationalist movements tend to couch their very claims to historical, ethnic, and cultural specificity in a recognizably standard rhetoric. Even as they labor to re-create the lost community of the nation, nationalists work within a thoroughly modern conception of political life. Although they seem not to realize it, their sense of community is imaginary as much as it is imagined.

From its very origins, then, nationalism appears as a species of fiction. Yet if nationalism is a creation of the imperial state, why is the nationalist political stance so oppositional? If the nationalist is a descendant of the statistician, if nationalism is a modernism, a product of rationalization and enumeration, then why does the nationalist sense of temporality appear so resolutely antimodern, so that nationalist revivals often are accompanied by antiquarianism and other forms of traditionalism? Despite their cogency, Anderson's theories cannot account for central features of nationalist rhetoric. Whereas Anderson emphasizes the discursive construction of nationalism, its origins in an official act of naming, nationalists insist that it is the imperialists who are trapped in a discursively bounded and therefore severely limited view of the world. For Anderson, nationalist analysis is derivative, produced by, in, and with imperial categories: the nationalists' sense of group identity derives from their collective interpellation, into the modern state apparatus, and into state classifications. The nationalists frame the causalities rather differently, reacting with particular vehemence to the imperial census; for them, its catalogs and inventories function as claims to ownership and as tools for social control, yet its categories remain deeply inadequate, reflecting grave misprisions about the culture under survey: imperialism does not makes nationalism possible so much as necessary. For Anderson, nationalism is an attempt to wrest or extend the state's attention to a newly individuated, newly visible, recognized, and therefore self-confident body of subjects. Nationalists, instead, see their movement as a collective one, fueled by anger at the authorities' persistent inability to tell the natives apart; they combat the abstractions of the state by insisting on the human fates behind the official statistics.[51]

In examining the prototypical nationalisms of late-eighteenth-century Britain, this book shows Western Europe's first modern nationalist movements emerging from a rather different set of circumstances and displaying a far more complicated consciousness than the one Anderson postulates.[52] Its relationship to modernization is dialectical rather than simply derivative or reactive.[53] New losses invoke the old: the modernization process triggers cultural memory both because modernizers and improvers appear determined to suppress and replace it and because new forms of economic oppression are being joined to old forms of political oppression. The communalist rhetoric of nationalism responds at once to the division of labor, to the large-scale alienation of land and of culture, and to the threat of a new capitalist oligarchy.

In its emphasis on solidarity, as in its communitarian longings, early nationalism anticipates socialism and other utopian movements, just as the nationalist account of the collective roots of culture and the importance of cultural institutions in the struggle against political oppression anticipates central discussions of Marxist aesthetics. Yet from the nineteenth century onward, Marxists have tended to view nationalist politics with great suspicion, as enshrining the wrong kind of collectivity—and Anderson, his protests to the contrary, is finally no exception.[54] Reading nationalism as a relatively unreflexive reflection of modernity, he tends to miss its moment of radical critique, from its prophetic analysis of modern alienation to its recognition of the way in which Enlightenment progressivism overlaps with imperialist demands for social control and cultural pacification.

In eighteenth-century Britain new forms of cultural nationalism emerged in response at once to Enlightenment programs for economic transformation and to Enlightenment theories of historical periodization and historical progress. Anderson identifies the imperial classification of the people as the founding moment of nationalist identity formation; nationalism is constructed by the imperial census and with the categories of the imperial state. In Britain, however, it is not the census but the survey that provides nationalism with its symbols of imperial control: the terrain of nationalist struggle is the land itself.[55] The intellectual roots of nationalism are in an antiquarian practice concerned with conjoining the material and the discursive realms. And nationalist analysis tries to steer a course between what it condemns as the excessive nominalism of imperial discourse and the excessive materialism of Enlightenment practice.[56]

Well into the eighteenth century, as Michael Herzfeld has argued in *Ours Once More*, the Greek-speaking inhabitants of the Ottoman-occupied territory now known as Greece thought of and referred to themselves as Romans. By the early nineteenth century, however, they had come to see themselves as Greeks, and as such they fought together for the liberation of what would become Greece from its Ottoman occupiers. Herzfeld ascribes this radical shift in consciousness to the influence of a new breed of Hellenizing antiquaries, whose researches (and forgeries) assembled convincing evidence that a modern Greek culture and language were descended from those of the ancient city-states. As a result of their arguments, the Greeks came to understand themselves both as members of a shared national culture and as the bearers of an illustrious national history. This new sense of history and of collective identity, in turn, gave them a new belief in their political agency.

In Ireland, Scotland, and Wales, antiquarian scholarship played an equally influential role in awakening a new historical consciousness.[57] In their reconstruction of indigenous cultural forms and institutions suppressed after the English conquest, as in their arguments about the continuities of language and culture from ancient times to the present, the antiquaries demonstrated both the enormous cultural damage wrought by imperial occupation and the continuing strength of culture to oppose its homogenizing force.[58] But although they played a crucial role in explaining the historical basis and the historical fate of ethnic identities, what they did not do, and did not need to do, was to establish identity itself.

The cultural divisions between occupying and occupied populations, between Milesians and Anglo-Irish, between the disfranchised and the politically ascendant, between Highlanders and Lowlanders, were clearly marked by language and by accent, by religious affiliation and by the legal status it afforded or denied.[59] In Wales, Ireland, and the Highlands, the day-to-day operations of an occupying government, its legal codes, and the structural discriminations that barred indigenous inhabitants from full access to education, property, or government office repeatedly made clear the precise differentials of status and power.[60] Given the long history both of legal disfranchisement and of cultural denigrations by the English (from the rhetorical denunciations of the Irish during the Elizabethan occupation to the vehemently anti-Scottish campaigns during the Bute ministry), any anti-English or anti-imperialist movement had a vast repertoire of historical resentments on which to build. According to Charles Hamilton Teeling, writing in 1828 to explain the long-standing anger that led up to the United Irishmen rebellion,

> It has been the policy of Britain from the first hour her footstep was imprinted on our shore to render her name hateful to Ireland by the most flagrant acts of injustice; to irritate—to weaken—to divide; to insult every monument of national respect—to deride every feeling of national pride. The sneer of imag-

ined superiority meets the native proprietor in every walk and station of life,
and the most insidious means are employed to debase him in the world's estimation and his own.[61]

A new nationalism may be called into being in several parts of Britain, but
only where a firm sense of national identification, pride and anger, has long
preceded it.

In an imperial situation that functions by categorical exclusions, in a
climate of long-standing political and religious antagonisms, it does not
take the advent of a census taker to make visible the lines of demarcation
between various groups. It is all the more remarkable, then, that late-
eighteenth-and-early-nineteenth-century cultural nationalisms found important supporters and advocates not only among those directly oppressed
or disfranchised but also among intellectuals who, by virtue of ethnic, religious, regional, or occupational background, might have been expected to
oppose them. In Ireland, especially, some of the most impassioned denunciations of English imperialism and some of the most dedicated attempts at
literary restitution come from Anglo-Irish antiquaries and novelists; convinced of the intertwined destinies of Catholics, Anglicans, and Presbyterians, Milesian peasants and Ascendancy gentry, they work to explicate a
past full of ethnic shame.[62] Nationalist movements may have found their
emotional center in the memory of ethnic suffering, but they also move and
mobilize sympathizers beyond the ethnic groups most directly affected.
Identification is at least as complicated as identity itself.[63]

The question, then, is less how a consciousness of national aggrievement
first comes into being than when and why it takes on a more systematic and
militant form, and under what circumstances it can mobilize broad support.
In Britain and Ireland the measurement and mapping of land, the remaking
of rural topography, in the name of agricultural improvement, reawakens
and renews questions of ownership, tradition, and occupation. Often a prelude to enclosure (as to other improvements that fundamentally altered access to and the use of common lands), the surveying of land functioned
symbolically as an announcement of the new terms of ownership. At the
same time, the eighteenth-century development of government ordnance
surveying is clearly linked to the consolidation of British military control
in Scotland and Ireland, North America and India. In domestic as in overseas territories under occupation, such surveys functioned quite explicitly
as acts of incorporation; the first major ordnance survey was begun in the
Highlands in 1746, to facilitate pacification and military occupation.

In the seventeenth century, official "plantation" maps were produced
in Ireland as a basis for the redistribution of forfeited Irish property and for
the systematic "plantation" of English soldiers and adventurers on these
lands.[64] In the early nineteenth century, the systematic remapping of

Ireland, in the famous 1824 General Ordnance, was accompanied by its renaming, as the surveyors devised a new anglicizing nomenclature with which they systematically replaced each Gaelic place-name on the map.[65] The survey's determination to inscribe English and Anglo-Irish cultural and religious values on the Irish landscape was clear—and galling—to nineteenth-century Irish commentators.[66] But although Anglo-Irish land-owners served as the main local informants, and then the main beneficiar-ies, of the survey, the attempt to verify place-names and land boundaries involved the surveyors themselves in philological and cultural reconstruc-tion and brought them into contact with nationalist antiquarian circles.[67]

In 1833, indeed, it was proposed that the ordnance maps be accompanied by extensive "memoirs" of each area in question, detailing monuments, geological formations, and sites of local history. The subsequent official decision (after two pilot studies had proved more costly and compendious than expected) to curtail the program and devote the survey strictly to the surface features of the country provoked prolonged nationalist anger. "In proposing to suppress the study of place-names, antiquities and local his-tory," writes one modern commentator, "it was widely felt that [the] Peel [government] was making a deliberate assault on Irish national feeling."[68]

In the mid-eighteenth century, an occupying British Army that surveyed and built military roads through the Highlands to facilitate troop movement encountered even more direct protest. Traveling in the 1770s along these same military roads, Samuel Johnson notes that their milestones have been systematically removed by local inhabitants. Far from sympathetic to any form of Scottish cultural nationalism, Johnson nevertheless recognizes this vandalism as political protest: "[W]e proceeded southward over Glencroe, a black and dreary region, now made easily passable by a military road. . . . Stones were placed to mark the distances, which the inhabitants have taken away, resolved, they said, 'to have no new miles.'"[69]

Where the milestones of the British Army appear in the Highland land-scape, the mile becomes an imperial term, marking distance in the abstract and on a larger and more systematic scale than anyone local needs.[70] The survey, likewise, identifies local specificities but only to subsume them into a new, alien, and ungraspable totality. Far from experiencing such standardization as the precondition for a new self-understanding, eigh-teenth-century nationalists experience it as a form of occupation and cul-tural alienation. "Improvement makes strait roads," concurs William Blake in "The Marriage of Heaven and Hell" (1790–93), "but the crooked roads without Improvement are roads of Genius."[71]

Nationalist consciousness began with the recognition of imperial occu-pation and with the attempt to grasp its economic, political, and cultural consequences, from the appropriation of land and the loss of self-government to the alienation of cultural inheritances. The material difficulties involved in recovering and reconstructing the national cultural legacy of an oppressed people brought home, as little else could, the full effect of imperial occupation. While free nations could collect, protect, and publish all available historical and literary records, the colonized were forced to look on as "their" governments hastened the dispersal of private and national libraries, discouraged the propagation of national literary traditions that might have stirred up "separatist" sentiments, and attempted to suppress or supplant the national language. If the immediate political consequences of conquest were a loss of sovereignty and a loss of national pride, the long-term cultural consequences were even more damaging: threats to the historical record and to the national sense of history, the determined undermining of cultural traditions, the erosion of language, and the gradual loss of national identity.[72] In an age of localized and national uprisings, mass executions and deportations, in a political context that produced real national martyrs, the nationalists' new attitude toward the past must be understood as historical mourning and as national self-defense.

On one level, the effect of antiquarian work—and the problems of conservation and of heritage it brought to light—was to guide the nationalist analysis of imperialism beyond the realm of purely material relations, toward more abstract questions of history, memory, and collective identity. In this historicizing turn, and in its ultimate belief in the primacy of cultural questions over economic ones, nationalist analysis most decisively parts company with Enlightenment discourses of national improvement. Yet the activities of nationalist antiquaries represent a continual attempt to join the realm of materiality to the discursive realm. At the most elementary level, antiquarian work is driven by the belief that the shape of the past—its belief world, its cultural practices, its historical transformation—can be reconstructed through the analysis of the artifactual traces it has left behind. When eighteenth- and early-nineteenth-century intellectuals tried to mock or discredit antiquarian theories, they attacked with particular vehemence the antiquaries' founding premise: the belief in the reconcilability of material and linguistic sources and the elevation of the physical fragment, the worn or broken artifact of everyday life, to the same status as written records.

Antiquarian work is attacked both for the ostensible baseness of its objects of study and for the literal-mindedness of its belief that it can deduce civilizational forms from physical remnants; antiquarians proverbially mistake the discarded chamber pot or the cooking pot found in the bog for an antique urn, postholes dug thirty years ago for the traces of ancient buildings, and on this basis misdeduce the local course of Roman conquest. To conduct researches in the material world rather than in the world of the library is to risk contamination by its debris; antiquarians are depicted as lacking in decorum, ridiculously reliant on the (misleading or

misunderstood) testimony of the local peasants, prey to suspicious parox-
ysms of enthusiasm over individual finds, and given to erecting huge and
wobbly theoretical edifices on the basis of modest or dubious evidence. In
attempting to interpret the evidences of the world, antiquarians enter un-
knowingly into an epistemological quagmire, in which they successively
loses all sense of direction and all sense of perspective.

But if the satirist represents antiquarians as debased and bested by their
materials, the nationalist antiquarians see themselves as ennobled and enlightened by their contact with material evidence. The artifact is of value
not so much in its own right but because of its ability to represent synecdochically the culture and the historical moment that produced it. And because its materiality renders it fragile, the artifact represents not only the
traces of a larger cultural world but also the tragic trials and the triumphant
survivals of its history. Made of transient stuff, it survives only brokenly,
to serve as a reminder of all that has been effaced or swept away. Yet the
fact that it has survived at all is little short of miraculous and suggests the
power of culture to endure its vicissitudes with something of itself still
intact. Far from evoking disgust, then, the brokenness of the object evokes
both tenderness and veneration in the antiquary.

From the mid-eighteenth century onward, antiquarian editors routinely
use the term *reliques* to describe pieces of ancient poetry that constitute the
surviving records of a distant national past. The Christian overtones of this
language are not accidental, but they are not at odds, either, with the materialism of antiquarian analysis. The political and temporal pressures that
would efface the meaning of a culture are legible on the scarred surface of
the artifact; the crucified object serves as a synecdoche for the martyrdom
of the culture as a whole.[73] The attributes of Christ's tortured body are here
transposed onto the fragments of the past; they will reappear in the early
nineteenth century, in the national tale, on the tormented bodies of its allegorical characters. In both incarnations, the metaphor of sacrifice and redemption are deployed with great intensity—but at the same time without
the mystical or racializing overtones with which later nationalists invoke
similar images. If eighteenth-century nationalists devote considerable attention to the way national history is rooted in a particular national landscape, their analysis is grounded in a critique of existing property relations
and the formulation of a new historical reflection theory.

Early cultural nationalists derive much of their historical and anthropological sense of culture from the innovative historical theories of the Scottish Enlightenment, particularly its four-stage theory of human social development, and its careful enumeration of the way material determinants
and institutional forms of culture define each civilizational epoch.[74] Nationalist accounts, however, place their emphasis very differently, insisting
on a notion of cultural tradition left out of the natural and national histories

of the mainstream Enlightenment. For the Enlightenment model is evolutionary, emphasizing the inevitability with which each developmental stage, each historical culture, is replaced by the next, more advanced one. What shapes, destroys, and replaces cultural formations is an apparently impersonal, endlessly recurring historical process.

The nationalist reworking of this Enlightenment model involves a sustained attempt to challenge its assumptions about inevitability, agency, and progress. When cultures change, nationalists argue, it is often due to the violence of outside forces, rather than any inevitable, internal dynamic. The English conquest of Ireland and Wales and the British occupation and pacification of the Highlands involved deliberate attempts to eradicate traditional forms of culture in order to root out remaining sources of indigenous identity and national pride.[75] Such suppressions lead to the lasting psychic and intellectual dislocation of the colonized. Unable, under English occupation, to rebuild their shattered cultural institutions, they are unwilling, at the same time, to adapt themselves to the conquerors' way of life. Their refusal to relinquish the memory of a preconquest society dooms them, personally and collectively, to a shadowy half-life, caught between past and present. Yet this refusal also keeps alive the hope of future autonomy and decisively blocks the conquerors' narratives of triumph and progress.

For late-eighteenth-century nationalists, the insistence on the contemporary cultural forms of educated Western Europeans as the natural telos of all societies amounts to a justification for imperialism. O'Halloran, it will remembered, traced this tactic back to the Elizabethan conquest of Ireland; to justify their military activities, he argued, the English ideologues launched an official campaign to vilify Ireland, portraying it as primitive and uncivilized. Believing in the inevitability of historical progress, Enlightenment historical narratives assign coexisting cultural forms to exemplify different moments in a "historical" hierarchy: "advanced" forms of culture serve as models for the present, and more "primitive" forms will necessarily be doomed to extinction. Nationalist historical narratives, in contrast, posit the noninevitability and undesirability of radical cultural transformation, stressing instead the organic accretion of cultural practices, institutions, and forms over many epochs. Even where external forces succeed in disrupting the coherence of a national culture, and where an imperial culture is imposed in its place, the lasting force of national memory will ensure that its victory does not endure. Thus where Enlightenment histories stress the necessary discontinuities of culture, nationalist histories stress the survival of cultural memory from one epoch to the next.

The historicizing move of cultural nationalists, in the late eighteenth century, represents at once a decisive challenge to Enlightenment cultural assumptions and the attempt to apply and extend the Enlightenment's new

sociological analysis. Antiquarian research derives much of its investigative method, descriptive techniques, and discursive style from Enlightenment encyclopedias and treatises. But if the Enlightenment impulse is
scientific—an attempt to expand, by experiment and by catalog, the scope
of the knowable world—the nationalist project is recuperative. What separates nationalist antiquaries from their Enlightenment counterparts is their
motivation and their partisanship, their identification with their subject
matter and their sense of temporality.[76]

In an era dominated by a rhetoric of progress, nationalists insisted on
looking backward; new visions of futurity gave rise to new visions of the
past. Yet many nationalists also participated in projects for economic renewal: a suppressed history of national suffering and a lost national heritage were to be recovered precisely to speed the economic, cultural, and
political recovery of a newly conscious nation. If some Enlightenment improvers dreamed of a future severed from the past, nationalist improvers
wanted a future in which a relationship to the past, damaged or severed
under colonial rule, could be repaired, a future in which a history of cultural
achievements was at once honored, preserved, and rejoined.

Late-eighteenth-century nationalism is constituted, in many ways, as a
critique of modernization and of the uneven regional development it perpetuates. The ultimate goal of many nationalist sympathizers, however, is
to become beneficiaries of the new wealth that such modernization generates. Thus although it derives its rhetoric of colonization from the experience of the overseas empire and its rhetoric of dispossession partly from the
plight of the British poor, eighteenth-century cultural nationalism is paradoxically enmeshed both in the project of empire (which generates the
money for domestic reconstruction) and in the process of class stratification (as the apparently inescapable result of economic modernization). In
its analysis of the way in which penal laws and other repressive property
laws facilitated the English appropriation of aristocratic estates in Ireland
or Wales, and in its laments for those dispossessed or exiled as a result,
eighteenth-century cultural nationalism may appear to foreshadow a
Jacobin critique of property relations and political absolutism. Yet such
laments often reflect not so much concern for tenant farmers as nostalgia
for feudal privilege and a lost indigenous aristocratic culture.

The cultural nationalisms of late-eighteenth-century Scotland, Ireland,
and Wales served as an important prototype for nineteenth-century nationalist movements throughout Europe, not least in their populist attempts to
invoke a united people without giving unsettling attention to differences of
status and privilege within the nation. Problematic already from the origins
of nationalism, this paradox became painfully acute in the 1790s, in the
light of attempts by the United Irishmen and Scotsmen to forge a revolutionary, anti-imperialist, and Jacobin nationalism, determined simultane-

ously to level class barriers and to eradicate ethnic identifications based on religion or cultural tradition. Prior to the 1790s, the rhetoric of cultural nationalism often resembled the parallel rhetoric of improvement, in the way it masked the powerful interest, and self-interest, of class. Directed against the conquest of the nation by outside forces, the subjugation of the nation to outside rulers, the draining of the nation's wealth by absentee landlords, nationalist polemics sometimes masked the extent to which an imbalance of power and the economic exploitation of the rich by the poor are features of domestic political life as well.

If the British influence in the Celtic peripheries manifests itself overtly, in military or juridical form, the process of cultural homogenization and economic modernization is often more subtle and more localized. The bog drainages that English political economist Arthur Young records so pains-takingly and approvingly in hundreds of locales across Ireland are carried out by Anglo-Irish landowners on dozens of isolated estates, coordinated only indirectly by the force of the agricultural market and by the Dublin Society's information on agricultural improvement and competitions. Anglo-Irish society, indeed, is closely knit precisely because of the geo-graphical, linguistic, and cultural isolation of English settlements, the in-tensity of tenant discontent and unrest, and the relative lack of wealth and pedigree, the provincial manners and pronunciation that separate Anglo-Irish landowners from their English counterparts.[77] At the same time, as Young points out, they are confronted at home by the spectacle of their dispossessed Catholic counterparts, even in some cases by Milesian aristo-crats reduced to working as cottars on their former family estates. What all of these factors make possible, however intermittently, is critical reflec-tion on the price of conquest, modernization, and dispossession. So too, in late-eighteenth-century Scotland, the linguistic and cultural divisions, the increasingly uneven economic and political development between the Lowlands and the Highlands, and the growing gap, during the Bute era, between Lowland consciousness of its own cultural refinement and the cru-dity of English anti-Scottish sentiment, all help to create an Enlightenment culture at once actively involved in the project of modernization, visibly anxious about its consequences for traditional culture, and, thanks to the self-scrutiny of sentimentalism, intensely sensitive to its own ambivalent feelings.

The particular situation of these places, indeed, makes possible in them new kinds of consciousness, far earlier and far more acutely than within England itself. In watching the effects of imperialism and moderniza-tion on the traditional societies within their purview, segments of both Anglo-Irish and Lowland society become convinced of the need to pre-serve indigenous antiquities and traditionary customs, and even to deceler-ate the course of modernization altogether, by reseparating the national governments of the peripheries from the central government in London and from a British economy.[78] The new, middle-class cultural nationalism and antiquarianism that these concerns engender are thus based at once—and this cannot be stressed enough—on a new degree of imaginative sympathy and community with countrymen more directly oppressed and affected, and at the same time on a rhetorical appropriation of their situation and customs as if they in fact constituted a shared tradition. This paradox remains crucial to all subsequent European nationalist movements.

Reinhart Koselleck has argued a dialectical relationship between absolutism and the emergence of the European Enlightenment: "It was from Absolutism that the Enlightenment evolved—initially as its inner consequence, later as its dialectical counterpart and antagonist, destined to lead the Absolutist State to its demise."[79] The cultural nationalism that becomes visible in the political and literary life of late-eighteenth-century Ireland and Scotland develops in similarly dialectical relationship to Enlightenment reform, as to new forms of economic oligarchy and political repression, privatization and modern state formation which accompany the first phases of modernization and industrialization. The late-eighteenth-century development of nationalist thought is internally dialectical as well, as it moves from materialist analysis into new theories of history and new plans for cultural reconstruction.

In the movement of their own argument, the chapters that follow will attempt to recapitulate the logic of this development. The first two chapters analyze Arthur Young's and Samuel Johnson's landmark Enlightenment investigations of the Irish and the Highland peripheries in the 1770s and the groundbreaking works of political economy and cultural sociology each journey produces. Concerned with current national prosperity, both accounts are famously indifferent to nationalist claims for cultural tradition, and both, therefore, catalyze strong nationalist reactions. Taken together, the two cases illuminate both the internal logic of an Enlightenment materialism in which economic prosperity takes priority over all cultural questions and the insistence with which nationalist rereadings of the same economic and political landscape stress cultural factors instead. Wherever improvers aim to replace the blighted ruins of the past—and a paralyzing emotional investment in them—with the promise of a better future, nationalists find themselves defensively guarding the memory of dispossession as the only birthright they have left. At the same time, nationalist responses to specific Enlightenment arguments for improvements vary greatly in their degree of defensiveness. Irish nationalists respect Young's materialist *Tour in Ireland* (1780) even where they dissent from it, impressed with both Young's condemnation of Catholic disfranchisement and his selfless work for a future Irish prosperity; later commentators continue to see Young's journey as a positive watershed in Irish self-understanding. Yet in the case of Johnson's *Journey to the Western Islands of Scotland* (1775), Scottish nationalists react to Johnson's mode of Enlightenment analysis with utmost vehemence, criticizing Johnson as an economic, cultural, and linguistic imperialist; fifty years later Scottish commentators still see Johnson's journey as a moment of national trauma, which made visible the depths of English ignorance and insolence about Scotland, and with it the long-term impossibility of full Scottish integration into Britain.

Angered by Johnson's treatment of Scotland as an experimental physical and historical force field, by his attack on Macpherson's *Ossian*, and by his dismissal of the very notion of oral tradition, nationalists insist on apprehending the Scottish landscape with a sense of its historical depth, as well as its political immediacies, and on opposing Johnson's literacy-based notion of culture with their own voice-centered model. Invoking Aberdeen classicist Thomas Blackwell's theories of Homer as traveling rhapsode as well as Macpherson's blind bard (for whom the landscape echoes with the voices of the past), Scottish, Welsh, and Irish nationalists conceive a new national literary history under the sign of the bard, a figure who represents the resistance of vernacular oral traditions to the historical pressures of English imperialism and whose performance brings the voices of the past into the sites of the present. If the bard himself becomes a ubiquitous figure in late-eighteenth-century fiction and poetry, the new vision of literary history that takes shape around him continues to inform key aspects of romantic literary life in Britain, from its notions of genial authorship and of the social function of poetry to the shape of romantic fiction. As the middle chapters of the book will detail, the two major new novelistic genres that emerge during the first decades of the early nineteenth century, the national tale in Ireland and the historical novel in Scotland, continue to be centrally concerned with the claims of a bardic nationalism, and with the new sense of time and place it engenders, even while their plots of national survey continually invoke, revise, and revile the Enlightenment tours of inspection undertaken by figures such as Young and Johnson.

For nationalist antiquaries, the English refunctioning of the bard merely displays the nominalism of imperialism in a new, aesthetic register. Cultural nationalists systematically distance themselves from the activities of the imperial survey, on the grounds that imperial acts of enumeration, renaming, categorization, and classification intentionally ignored indigenous names, understandings, and investments and treated nations and cultural traditions as chattel, as a means of humiliation. As Johnson admits at the beginning of his *Journey*, "[W]hoever surveys the world, must see many things that give him pain."[80] Here it is merely someone else's national literary tradition, instead of somebody else's national terrain, that is being treated as movable, transferable property. And here again what marks imperial "ownership" of such property is the shallowness of its hold on what it claims to possess. Bardic nationalism insists on the rich fullness of national knowledge, on the anchoring of discursive traditions in landscape, in a way of life, in custom. The English, in comparison, have only borrowed words.

PART ONE

Enlightenment and Nationalist Surveys

William Chaigneau, *The History of Jack Connor*. 1766 ed. Courtesy of
Regenstein Library, University of Chicago.

Chapter 1

THE BOG ITSELF: ENLIGHTENMENT PROSPECTS
AND NATIONAL ELEGIES

[August 1776: T]ook the road to Ballymoat; crossed an immense
mountainy bog . . . found that it was ten miles long, and three and a
half over, containing thirty-five square miles . . . 35 miles are
22,400 acres. What an immense field of improvement! nothing
would be easier than to drain it, vast tracts have such a fall, that
not a drop of water could remain.
—Arthur Young, *A Tour in Ireland, with General Observations
on the Present State of That Kingdom: Made in the
Years 1776, 1777, and 1778*

Everywhere in the mentality of the Irish people are flux and
uncertainty. Our national consciousness may be described, in a
native phrase, as a quaking sod. It gives no footing.
—Daniel Corkery, *Synge and Anglo-Irish Literature*

PS. I am apt to think that those who are of op
that bogs do rise tow: & the middle ha
not distinguished betw^n: an island in al
& the Bog itself—
—Anonymous, "Letter to the Publick Concerning Bogs"
(Dublin, 1757), handwritten addendum to the copy held by
Yale University's Beinecke Rare Book Library

An Immense Field of Improvement

The comprehensiveness of Arthur Young's *Tour in Ireland* has made it at
once one of the most frequently consulted records of eighteenth-century
Britain and a work virtually unread, indeed almost unreadable, in its nine-
hundred-page entirety. In the book's final third, the English agricultural
reformer and "political arithmetician" (2:10) sketches a pioneering political economy of Ireland, illustrating the effects of absenteeism and analyzing the causes of political unrest, advocating large-scale bog reclamation
and economic union with Britain, and calculating the advantages of both
for Anglo-Irish landowners.[1] The book's first five hundred pages, in

contrast, consist of virtually raw data, reproducing in minute detail Young's notes from three years of fact-finding travel, farm for farm and field by field.

> Fallow. 2. Wheat, sow 1 barrel, produce 5 1/2. 3. Peas, sow 3/4 barrel, and get 5 to 10.
> Fallow. 2. Wheat. 3. Oats, sow 2 barrels, get 8 to 15. (2:67)

Young's entries for his visit to Shaen Castle, in July 1776 (to give one of several hundred possible cases), move from the course of crops to record the price of land, the rate of tithes, the yield of particular drained bogs, and the expense of building cabins, interspersed with the opinions of the land-holder on the Union of Ireland with Britain (he opposes it) and on the best procedures for bog drainage. Then Young goes on to the next estate, to repeat his surveying.

In an age schooled by *Sir Charles Grandison* and "much too idle to buy books that will not banish *l'ennuye* from a single hour," such thorough documentation, Young recognizes in his preface, "must necessarily be exceedingly dull to those who read for pleasure: so disagreeable, that they will certainly throw down the volume with as much disgust as they would tables of arithmetic" (2:11). Yet those few readers "who wish to receive real information, should readily give up the pleasure of being amused for the use of being instructed."

> The details of common management are dry and unentertaining; nor is it easy to render them interesting by ornaments of style. The tillage with which the peasant prepares the ground; the manure with which he fertilizes it . . . and the products that repay his industry, necessarily in the recital run into chains of repetition, which tire the ear, and fatigue the imagination. Great however is the structure raised on this foundation: it may be dry, but it is important, for these are the circumstances upon which depend the wealth, prosperity, and all power of nations. The minutiae of the farmer's management, low, and seemingly inconsiderable as he is, are so many links of a chain which connect him with the State. (1:2)

"These little movements" are so crucial to "the great machine of State" that they must be an object of study for all "willing to sacrifice their amusement to their information." The king himself must remember the contributions of "the poorest, the most oppressed, the most unhappy peasant, in the remotest corner of Ireland" (1:2). .

Young's preface argues for agricultural reclamation, scientific investigation, and the reading of his own *Tour* as parallel forms of improving labor. Over three years, Young watches individual gentleman "improvers" reclaiming Ireland's "manures, wastelands and bogs," to increase its yield of produce and profits. Young then takes up the farmers' statistical detritus, sifting its minutiae to assemble a political economy in front of the reader's eyes. The reader, finally, moves through the cycle of production all over again. He internalizes a myriad of tiny facts as a form of self-improvement. Young's book works to call into being not only a new vision of Ireland but a new mode of seeing, microscopic yet all-encompassing.[2]

The Ireland that Young apprehends is in the midst of improvements of all kinds yet riddled with local difficulties; in describing individual estates, Young records not only landowners' reclamation and improvement techniques but also their complaints about tenants who participate in Whiteboy activities (and other, localized forms of agricultural unrest) or emigrate to America. In Armagh the "Oak-boys began at Blewstone upon the county cess; but in a moment rose to rents, tythes, bogs, and every thing else: idle rascals that all went to America" (1:124); in Lesly Hill the "emigrations were considerable in 1772 and 1773, and carried off a good deal of money, but it was chiefly of dissolute and idle people: they were not missed at all" (1:161).

Usually, Young reports these opinions without critical commentary. But he is critical of cases in which landowners take advantage of the poor's dependence. And he identifies Ireland's "cruel laws against the Roman Catholics" as "the marks of an illiberal barbarism" (1:59): by disfranchising and disinheriting most of the population, these measures perpetuate a huge social, economic, and legal chasm between property holders and those without property, prevent the country's full modernization, and condemn the Irish peasantry to a poverty far more dire than that of their English counterparts. Young's own account, the preface announces, will make "the ease or oppression" of the poor the basis for "a multitude of conclusions . . . relative to government, wealth, and national prosperity" (1:4). At the same time, the "value of a country" can be "held in a just estimation" only when its rental value is ascertained; precisely because it is so preoccupied with working out, in microscopic detail, the material conditions of each estate, and the general economic state of Ireland, Young's account tends to obscure social considerations, and it finally fails to calculate the relative prosperity of peasantry and landowners.

From Dublin to Dunkettle, Young assesses the life of the landholding classes by quantification and enumeration, recording incomes and measuring the floor space of castles and manors. The unquestioned basis of all these calculations is the landowners' ownership of their property, so the real issue in Young's political economy is the industry and yield of the peasants on that property, to generate its wealth. Young's tendency, in fact, is to conflate the landowners' "experiments" in irrigation or bog reclamation with the tenant labor through which these ambitious and ultimately profitable improvements are accomplished. On occasion, he does detail the promises of free land or lower rents by which tenants are persuaded to undertake the enormous additional labor of improvement. And he laments one Catholic tenant, an improver of his own initiative who "merited for his life the returns of his industry" (1:58) but whose sole reward (since only Protestants could be granted long-term leases) was a more than tripling of his rents.

Overall, however, it is not the laborers but the landlords who create value through their foresight and investment. Twenty years before, Bally-moat was "a wild uncultivated region, without industry or civility; and the people all Roman Catholicks, without an atom of a manufacture, not even spinning" (1:223). Determined to establish a manufactory, Lord Shelburne imported Protestant weavers from the North. The estate manager estab-lished a bleach mill, built houses for the weavers (designed without space for personal gardens, for "he would not wish to have them farmers, which he thinks does not at all agree with their business of weaving"), and planned a model town to be built around the manufactory, with "a man-sion-house for himself in the stile of a castle, and suitable to the ancient ruins, situation, and grounds. . . . Too much praise cannot be given to a man, who . . . should turn his attention and expence to objects of such national utility and importance, which have for their aim the well-being, happiness, and support of a whole neighbourhood" (1:226). The project, in the meantime, involved the reconfiguration and repopulation of the neigh-borhood, and it generated sufficient profit to build a castle for the benevo-lent manager, with a triumphantly picturesque prospect of the ancient ruins.

Following a visit to the battlefield of the Boyne (where he meditates on the Williamite victory as the triumph of liberty), Young visits the estates of the Lord Chief Baron Forster of Cullen, who "has made the greatest im-provements I have any where met with" (1:110). "This great improver, a title more deserving estimation than that of a great general or a great minis-ter, lives now to overlook a country flourishing only from his exertions. He has made a barren wilderness smile with cultivation, planted it with people, and made those people happy. Such are the men to whom monarchs should decree their honours, and nations erect their statues" (1:113). Yet this "prince of improvers" (1:115) also prescribes the raising of rents as "one of the greatest cause of the improvement of Ireland; he has found that upon his own estates it has universally quickened [the tenants'] industry, set them to searching for manures, and made them in every respect better farmers" (1:114).

Improvement, in Young's account, is "more profitable and easy in Ire-land than . . . in England. There are no common rights to encounter, which are the curse of our moors" (2:98–99).[3] Nor is there apparently much of a shared national culture. Young's only mention of Ireland's traditional feudal structure is a brief account of the homage the common people in Connaught still pay to the impoverished descendants of Milesian aristocratic families. Young's tone, in this passage, is at once distantly sympathetic—"they consider [O'Connor] as the Prince of a people involved in one common ruin"—and frankly incredulous, given the penury of the "aristocrats" involved: "Macdermot, who calls himself Prince of Coolavin . . . though he has not above £100 a year, will not admit his children to sit down in his presence" (1:219). Young's sole mention of the cultural and linguistic differences between Irish peasantry and Anglo-Irish landlords is just as offhand. Lord Shannon, he reports, extends bounties to his laborers "by way of encouragement; but only to such as can speak English and do something more than fill a cart" (1:324). And his sole account of a distinctively Irish custom, a brief note on the keening that accompanies Irish funerals—"both men and women, particularly the latter, are hired to cry, that is, to howl the corps to the grave, which they do in a most horrid manner" (1:249)—suggests both the animal rawness of the howling and the fundamental insincerity of the ritual, which depends on paid mourners for its expression of collective grief.[4]

Here the fact of economic transaction raises doubt about the expressiveness of local custom. But Young himself habitually reduces questions of cultural tradition and alliances to economic terms. As he argues in the preface, the problem of the British, in their attitudes toward Ireland, is that they conceive its management, like their other colonial economies, primarily as "a trader's project . . . governed by the narrow spirit of the counting house" (1:5).[5] Yet despite his awareness of the systemic problems that mercantilism causes, and despite his attention to the local manifestations of peasant "oppression" and, as corresponding "barbarities" (1:82–83), of agricultural unrest, Young apparently cannot see that there are any insurmountable structural problems in the Anglo-Irish system of landholding, or that Ireland's problems are specifically colonial in any way. He has no sense at all of the landholders as a foreign presence, still resented as conquerors by large segments of the population, and correspondingly little sense of the Irish peasantry as a distinct cultural group.[6]

The legacy of political and religious strife in Ireland, for Young, manifests itself most powerfully in property relations. In the period between Elizabeth and Cromwell, he writes, 95 percent of Ireland's landed properties

changed hands from Catholic to Protestant. The lineal descendants of great families, once possessed of vast property, are now to be found all over the kingdom in the lowest situation, working as cottars for the great-great-grandsons of men, many of whom were of no greater account in England than these

poor labourers are at present, on that property which was once their own. So
entire an overthrow, and change of landed possession, is, within the period, to
be found in scarce any country in the world. . . . From hence it results that the
question of religion has always in Ireland been intimately connected with the
right to and possession of the landed property of the kingdom. (2:59–60)

The future alleviation of Ireland's long-standing religious and economic
tensions lies in the transformation of these relations, through the improvement of property. Let Ireland but "transfer her anxiety from the faith to the
industry of her subjects; let her embrace, cherish, and protect the Catholicks as good subjects, and they will become such; let her, despising and
detesting every species of religious persecution, consider all religions as
brethren, employed in one great aim, the wealth, power, and happiness of
the general community" (2:72). As historical grievances give way to historical progress, as economic and political differences are subsumed into the
process of improvement—more bog reclamation, better cultivation techniques, more trade, more economic liberty—greater wealth will be generated for all, eventually alleviating the distresses, and thus the discontents,
of even the most lowly. In Waterford Sir William Osborne has succeeded,
through the course of his improvements, in transforming his tenants into
model farmers; although "nine-tenths of them were White-boys, [they] are
now of principles and practice exceedingly different from the miscreants
that bear that name. . . . It shows that villainy of the greatest miscreants is
all situation and circumstance: EMPLOY, don't *hang* them" (2:398–99). Sir
William Osborne formed model farmers "from the refuse of the White-
boys" (1:399). So too Ireland will be able to generate a new economy from
the reclamation of "Manure—Waste-lands—Bogs" (2:93) even if at first
"the drains will for some time fill up almost as fast as made" (1:269).

Bog drainage synecdochically represents the project of Enlightenment
land reform: the creation of arable, profitable soil out of its former useless-
ness, by bringing it into the light of day, out of the primeval ooze that now
covers it. In the politically charged climate of late-eighteenth-century Ireland, in which riots over agricultural rents often express indigenous resistance to the country's hated conquerors and occupiers, the virtue of bog
reclamation is that (unlike other improvement projects) it need not displace
the local tenants, even if their labor must be harnessed to effect the drainage, and even if, by destroying crucial parts of a peasant subsistence economy, draining functions as an Irish equivalent of the English enclosure of
village commons during the same period. Drainage is an act, furthermore,
that creates new lands ex nihilo; the scale of the reclamation promises to
transform the face of many parts of Ireland. Demonstrating the fruitfulness
of English stewardship, the Anglo-Irish landowners secure their right to the

land they occupy by molding the surface of the country in their own image, bringing new Irelands into being out of the void. Here colonialism and expansionism appear as progress and as the incontrovertible economic salvation of the whole country, Irish peasantry and all. For as Sir William Osborne's Whiteboys make clear, the intense labor of clearance and reclamation reclaims and reshapes resistant rural communities into contented, hierarchical production units.

Arthur Young's account replicates much of this imperial and capitalist logic. Its announced interest is in demonstrating the social and economic connections between rulers and peasants, and at least intermittently, the *Tour* does express intense indignation about the economic and political situation of the Irish poor, insisting that national prosperity depends on peasant liberty. For all this, the *Tour* is finally unable to give a systematic account of the interplay, in Ireland, of political, economic, and cultural forces. For if, in its incredible detail, the *Tour* presents a landscape chock-full of things (fences, drains, sheep, cabins, bogs, and crops), its scale of analysis occludes the history of human presence in the landscape, clearing it of cultural tradition and local attachments and transforming it instead into an open field of agricultural experiment.[7] Young's intention is to lead the reader out of the morass of facts and statistics into a new state of political and economic clarity. But numbers have no history and no temporality. Where they are the main means of marking and grasping the character of the landscape, a sense of historical tradition, attachment, or agency is almost necessarily absent.

There Was an Old Prophecy Found in a Bog

Despite these limitations, Young's *Tour* continues to serve, long after its statistical information is out-of-date, as a central point of reference in the debate over Ireland. For Anglo-Irish improvers, the *Tour* inaugurates new ways of surveying national progress, new ways of thinking about the interdependence of the nation's economic and political development. For cultural nationalists, the example of Young's materialism (at once his greatest strength and his greatest shortcoming) helps them to develop their own, differently inflected account of the Irish cultural landscape.[8] Resolutely presentist and progressivist in its reading of Ireland, utilitarian and utopian in its belief in the country's infinite improvability, Young's *Tour* coincides historically with a very different kind of response to the agricultural improvement and political transformation under way throughout the British peripheries. The 1750s, 1760s, and 1770s see the rise not only of a new nationalist scholarship but also of a new mode of historical, national, and pastoral elegy, which exerts a powerful influence both on the tone of contemporary poetry, from Oliver Goldsmith's "Deserted Village" to Macpherson's *Fragments of Ancient Poetry*, and on the development of the British novel. Preoccupied with the damaging effects of improvement and empire on national cultural life, the new literature of elegy intends its own recording and memorializing activity to effect a compensatory retrieval of national history (if not a sentimental return to an earlier mode of communal life): it will counter the physical destruction of a national sense of place by the literary recovery of a national sense of history and a sense of national destiny.

From an Andersonian perspective, such efforts appear deeply paradoxical, in ways that point to nationalism's founding contradictions: they react to a change in material circumstances with the formation of new discourses, then mistake their own rhetoric for reality. Yet eighteenth-century antiquarianism is founded on the belief in the reconcilability of the material world and the textual record. What the national elegy tries to formulate is a way of linking the concrete circumstances of a culture with its intellectual achievements. The physical space a nation inhabits, the artifacts its people create together, and the physical traces their joint life leaves behind are by nature material and tangible, whereas their beliefs and practices, the time they live through together, the events and conditions that shape their self-perception, are intangible and transient. The space a culture inhabits remains visible, whereas the time a culture inhabits does not; yet any full account of what the culture stands for must attempt to explain both. Unprecedented in the precision with which it analyzes the cultivated terrain and national space of Ireland, Young's *Tour* is nonetheless deeply inadequate, by such antiquarian standards, as a diagnostic account because of its inability to record the intangibles of Irish life—language, history, and custom.

For Maria Edgeworth, nonetheless, the *Tour* still remains a principal inspiration for contemporary Irish fiction; in *Castle Rackrent, An Hibernian Tale taken from facts and from the manners of the Irish squires before the year 1782* (1800), she argues that "Mr. Young's picture of Ireland was the first faithful portrait of its inhabitants" and declares her own intention to follow his analysis of Irish national life by attending to the situation of the humble, right down to "the most minute facts relative to [their] domestic lives."[9] Like other early-nineteenth-century Irish novelists, Edgeworth draws on the format of Young's journey of discovery to organize many of her plots, emulating his detailed descriptions of the rural economy and continuing his focus on the country estate as the principal site to think about the nature of Irish society.[10] To some extent, these writers also subscribe to Young's model of a literature of utility; as Tom Dunne and David Lloyd have recently argued, they imagine the novel as a literary equivalent of model estate or moral school.[11] But they are also preoccupied with the political questions left out of Young's account: the tenuous coexistence of English and Gaelic cultures; the way the experience of expropriation, disfranchisement, and religious oppression continues to shape Milesian consciousness; and perhaps most important, the dubious claims of Anglo-Irish improvers to the land they govern and transform in their own image.

An important series of early-nineteenth-century novels structure their stories around the contrast—and conflict—between Anglo-Irish landowners (whose interest in their usurped property is governed by profit motives) and the dispossessed Milesian aristocracy, still bound to their ancestral lands by bonds of history, memory, and longing.[12] In *The Irish Chieftain and His Family* (1809) Theodore Melville secures the reader's sympathy for the dispossessed Milesian aristocrats by repeatedly describing their mixture of delight and anguish as they view their lost homelands. In the opening scene, Cormac O'Donaghue (the Ossianically named chieftain's son) contemplates a deserted Gothic building and succeeds, at least temporarily, in reanimating it through reverie. In his mind's eye, Cormac superimposes the invisible landscape of the past onto the ruins of the present, while the echoes of a lost, Ossianic oral tradition—the strains of minstrelsy and bardic recitation, the acclaiming shouts of the assembled feudal vassals—resound in his ears. The moment is one of happiness and triumph only because "the illusions of his warm imagination" have subordinated the present-day view to a phantasmagoria of the past.[13] But when, in a later scene, he reverses the emphasis of his seeing, contemplating the present-day landscape through the veil of the past, the effect is correspondingly painful, despite the natural beauty of the prospect before him. The "distant rocks, the Sugar-loaf mountains, the stately Tomics, or the majestic Glenau" are all "objects on which his ancestors had gazed with delight." Now, however, when Cormac wanders in the "domain of his forefathers," and in a landscape "truly emblematic of their heroic deeds," he does so as "an obscure, unnoticed and insulted stranger; yes, a very stranger upon the land which gave him his birth, but of which he could not now call the spot he stood upon his own" (2:19). The more Cormac feels the conjoined presence of his ancestors imprinted on the landscape, the more he is overwhelmed by his own sense of loss and by the loneliness of the present: in his contemplation of the past, he stands quite alone.

On the terrain of the early-nineteenth-century novel, however, Cormac is by no means an isolated figure. In the novels of Sydney Owenson and Charles Maturin, especially, the sense of the national landscape as a site simultaneously of historical plenitude and historical loss becomes a crucial commonplace, the primary touchstone of character, the ground of narrative perspective, and the central philosophical insight around which plot,

themes, and descriptive passages are built. In other forms of literature as
well the nationalist sense of the country's historical layering and historical
plenitude informs virtually all forms of landscape description, whether the
scene described is a sublime prospect or a lowly bog. In the wake of the
nationalist revolution in seeing, even the bog undergoes a complete rehabilitation. Once anathematized as loathsome, it (and every other distinctive
feature of the Irish landscape) gradually becomes an object of national attachment and a source of national inspiration. "Irish poetry," writes Owenson in her 1806 national tale *The Wild Irish Girl*, "is generally the effusion
of some blind itinerant bard, or some rustic minstrel, into whose breast the
genius of the country has breathed inspiration, as he patiently drove the
plough, or laboriously worked in the bog."[14]

But if this reinvestment in the bog reflects a general shift in national
attitudes and the advent of new, self-consciously sympathetic ways of reading both cultural and agricultural landscapes, the bog also receives special
nationalist protection as the long-standing target of Anglo-Irish polemics,
and as a local land form now under threat of extinction by the forces of
improvement. For nationalist commentators, the bog is important as both a
material site and a discursive one, as the locus of a long-running struggle
between improvers and nationalists, beginning already with the Elizabethan colonization and settlement of Ireland.[15] So, too, for Anglo-Irish novelists writing after Grattan's Parliament, the United Irishmen rebellion, and
the Union, the defense of the bog and the rewriting of the Irish landscape
have particular significance, for they mark the novelists' own distance from
an older Anglo-Irish literary, cultural, and political tradition they have
come to condemn as imperialist, and their attempt to found in its place a
new, progressive, and broadly nationalist Irish literature in English.[16]

"There was an old prophecy found in a bog, / Lilli burlero bullen a la, /
That Ireland should be rul'd by an ass and a dog / Lilli burlero bullen a la":
so ran the most famous lines of "Lilli burlero" (1687), the ubiquitous anti-
Jacobite song of the Williamite wars. The "ass and dog," the final verse
explains, are Richard Talbot, earl of Tyrconnell, and his brother Peter,
Catholic archbishop of Dublin, who had fought, during the 1680s, for the
restoration of offices, rights, and lands to Ireland's disfranchised Catholic
majority. Sung throughout the eighteenth century, to mark the defeat of
their cause, the verse mocked both the nonsensical sounds of Gaelic and
Irish English and the chimerical political hopes of Irish Catholics; in *Tristram Shandy*, indeed, Uncle Toby whistles "Lillabullero" "when any thing
shocked or surprised him;—but especially when any thing, which he
deemed very absurd, was offer'd."[17]

In presenting the bog as the ludicrous source of Catholic inspiration,
"Lilli burlero" recapitulates a long line of Anglo-Irish commentaries that

use the bog as an emblem for Ireland's intractable national character. Edmund Spenser's *View of the Present State of Ireland* (1596) presents Ireland as a "wasteland" in order to propose "a programme of displacement, depopulation and geographic transformation . . . whose unspoken fantasy is of a land . . . flat, empty and inscribable."[18] For seventeenth-century commentators, however, the bog represents a lasting physical barrier both to the agricultural development and the political subjugation of Ireland. Irish military tactics, Fynes Moryson argues in the *Itinerary* (circa 1620), have evolved in relation to the local landscape; the Irish rebels are "trayned" preeminently "to skirmish vppon Boggs, and difficult . . . passages of woods." To prevent future rebellions, the authorities level, clear, and transform this familiar terrain, thus crippling rebel forces and improving government surveillance; by cutting passages through bogs and woods, landowners will "not only keepe the Irish in awe, but be to the State as it were spyes to advertise all mutinous and seditious inclinations."[19] Gerard Boate's *Irelands Naturall History. Being a true and ample Description of its Situation, Greatness, Shape and Nature* (1652) invokes the need for bog drainage as a metaphorical justification for the English colonization of Ireland and castigates the Irish for political uprisings that slow their own agricultural salvation.

> [A]s the Irish have been extreme careless in this, so the English, introducers of all good things, in Ireland (for which that brutish nation from time to time hath rewarded them with unthankfulness, hatred, and envy, and lately with a horrible bloody conspiracie, tending to their utter destruction) have set their industrie at work to remedy it . . . with very good success. . . . [I]n case that this detestable rebellion had not come between, in a few yeares there would scarce have been left one acre of Bog, of what was in the lands and possession of the English.[20]

William King's "Discourse Concerning the Bogs and Loughs of Ireland" (1685) concurs, urging the drainage of bogs so that "they may be remedyed and made usefull. . . . We live in an Island almost infamous for *Bogs*. . . . [I]f want of industry has in our remembrance made one *Bog*; no wonder if a Country, famous for laziness, as *Ireland* is, abound with them. . . . [W]ant of industry causes *Bogs*."[21] Yet he also situates the bog at the center of a complex historical and cultural economy. Because of its ambivalent role in recent Irish history, the bog has become a defining feature of the mental and physical landscape of Ireland.

> The *Bogs* are a great destruction to Cattle. . . . They are a shelter to *Torys*, and *Thieves*, who can hardly live without them. . . . The Natives heretofore had nevertheless some advantages by the woods, and *Bogs*; by them they were

preserved from the conquest of the *English*, and I believe it is a little remembrance of this, makes them still build near *Bogs*: it was an advantage then to have them to have their country unpassable, and the fewer strangers same near them, they lived the easyer; for they had no inns, every house where you came, was your inn: and you said no more, but put off your broges & sate down by the fire: & since the natural *Irish* hate to mend highways, and will frequently shut them up, and change them (being unwilling strangers should come and burthen them). (Pp. 952–53)

Once an actual barrier to the English conquest of Ireland, the bog remains an emblem of Irish resistance to the "burthen" of Anglo-Irish rule. King insists, however, that the antisocial behavior that results from this resistance—the refusal to maintain communications to the outside world, the wish to be left alone—ends up punishing as much as protecting Ireland, driving it into a position of isolated eccentricity. Yet this critique of Irish isolationism remains in tension with King's evocation of the warmth, comforts, and unself-consciousness of Irish traditional hospitality.

Jonathan Swift evokes the waste landscape of Ireland to different ends. If Swift's obsession with waste—and with the excremental—has usually been read as a personal neurosis, a new term in the cloacal vocabulary of the early eighteenth century hints at the possibility of a different reading: "boghouse" designates an English latrine rather than an Irish cabin, and yet the Irish referent—and a deliberate political denigration—remains implicit within it. In *Swift's Landscapes*, Carole Fabricant has argued a similar metaphoric link between Swift's cloacal imaginary and his polemical writings about Ireland, suggesting that his aesthetic challenges the decorum of Augustan literature. Whereas his English contemporaries use the well-regulated estate as an emblem of England's political order and economic prosperity, he meditates on mud and excrement. The "ill management of the bogs," for Swift, demonstrates the political and economic misrule of Ireland.[22] If an established tradition of English wit mocked the Irish as "bog-trotters," here Irish swamp water and mud become the mark of political suffering.[23]

Swift's interventions have a lasting influence on the perspective and horizons of Anglo-Irish literature. Although a work like William Chaigneau's novel *The History of Jack Connor* (1751) continues to champion Anglo-Irish paternalism, it also reflects critically on mass poverty and religious repression, on the social responsibilities of Anglo-Irish landlords, and on the enormous handicapping of the Irish economy by its balance of trade with England (documented in later editions with an appended statistical treatise). Part picaresque novel, part didactic prescription, *Jack Connor* suggests the increasing dividedness of Anglo-Irish sympathies. Lord Truegood, Chaigneau's most exemplary character, is the Anglo-Irish proprietor of Bounty Hall, County Meath. Returning from a long absence in England, Truegood quickly transforms his neglected estates into a model settlement. To "reclaim" his tenants from Catholicism, for the British Crown, he establishes a charity school that removes Catholic children from their parents and teaches them the Anglican creed along with the alphabet. To improve his lands, at the same time, he employs "the poor, which is the best sort of charity, in draining and making good land of some bogs."[24] The parallel between the religious reclamation of Catholic tenants and the agricultural reclamation of waterlogged land is not, as we have seen over the last few pages, coincidental. Yet when Mr. Leatherhead complains of the "plague of Irish" descending on England, suggests that "we transport 'em back to their bogs and potatoes," and wishes Ireland "at the bottom of the sea" (2:169), Chaigneau immediately counters this complaint with a long report of Irish political, economic, and religious discontents, stressing English and Anglo-Irish responsibility.[25] Although Chaigneau's view of the Irish landscape is still largely congruent with that of Anglo-Irish administrators and surveyors, his economic critique anticipates Young's reform arguments.

Edgeworth's Irish novels follow Chaigneau and Young in advocating local economic reform and an improved paternalism as the solution to Ireland's problems; the "new" Anglo-Irish novel that Edgeworth inaugurates on the eve of the Act of Union builds self-consciously on indigenous literary traditions as well as Enlightenment treatises. Like *Jack Connor*, Edgeworth's *Ennui* (1803–5, published in 1809), *The Absentee* (1812), and *Ormond* (1817) describe the transformations that can follow the return of absentee landlords to their abandoned Irish estates; encouraging local industry and developing economic infrastructure, their reinvestment of money and energy in their own estates not only ends the vicious cycle of local poverty but causes political discontent to disappear of its own accord, as the people rejoice in their new prosperity.[26] In turn, as the Irish gentry recover from their "Londonomania," Ireland slowly regains respectability in the eyes of English neighbors and tourists. *The Absentee*'s comic English servant, who accompanies her absentee masters back to Ireland, admits:

> "I was greatly frighted at first, having heard all we've heard . . . of there being no living in Ireland, and expecting to see no trees nor accommodation, nor any thing but bogs all along; yet I declare, I was very agreeably surprised; for as far as I've seen at Dublin and in the vicinity, the accommodations, and every thing of that nature now, is vastly put-up-able with!"[27]

The novel locates Edgeworth's corrective account of Irish prospects in relation to the long tradition of "representations and misrepresentations of Ireland, from Spenser to [Sir John] Davies to Young and [Daniel Augustus]

Beaufort" (p. 81), a line that runs from seventeenth-century Anglo-Irish treatises famous for their incomprehension, ambivalence, or hostility toward Milesian life to more dispassionate eighteenth-century statistical and cartographic surveys.[28] Edgeworth's Irish novels reevaluate, synthesize, and reappropriate this tradition by reading it in reverse: they assume a Youngian detachment in order to reopen the fractious questions of cultural difference and political domination which preoccupied Elizabethan commentators. Edgeworth measures Anglo-Irish ideology against the more "impartial" criteria of political economy to diagnose Ireland's problems with a new, clearheaded rigor and to neutralize the historical force of Anglo-Irish prejudices.

For some contemporaries, however, Edgeworth's handling of the Anglo-Irish tradition is not radical enough. Where she emulates the cool utilitarianism of the Youngian survey, they look instead to the outspokenness of Swiftian satire, with its uncompromising political critique, its call for new political solidarities across ethnic and religious divides, and its advocacy of systemic political transformation. Following Swift, Sydney Owenson's 1827 novel *The O'Briens and the O'Flahertys* thus points to Ireland's vast wastes to indict a long history of Anglo-Irish mismanagement and the physical, cultural, and psychic erosion it caused: "[T]he natural resources of the soil were abandoned to neglect and waste, the bogs were overspreading rich vallies, and fertile trackes, the intellectual and moral resources of the nation were alike doomed to sterility and uncultured wildness."[29]

So too in her earlier novel, *Florence Macarthy* (1818), Owenson compares the verdant, abundant Ireland that Spenser described with the Swiftian scene of urban poverty and decay that greets the present-day traveler. The contrast underlines both the progressive material deterioration of the country under Anglo-Irish stewardship and the political transformation of Anglo-Irish literature, from the self-confident (and self-centered) optimism of seventeenth-century commentators to Swift's dystopian, compassionate vision of a ruined, desperate Ireland. In Spenser's day, the colonization of Ireland was still in its early stages, the country still in its "*natural state*"; by the early nineteenth century, two centuries of economic exploitation and political oppression had exacted a terrible toll on countryside and inhabitants: approaching Dublin through "one of the most wretched suburbs that ever deformed or disgraced the metropolis of any country," present-day travelers had to make their way through "collected heaps of mud and filth," breathe air "infected by noxious vapours," and see the "foul," ruined hovels that housed the city's "hordes of wretched and filthy creatures."[30] In comparison with such scenes, the scenarios envisioned by Chaigneau, Young, and Edgeworth, in which Ireland's absentees return to reform their country, bog by bog, appear unduly optimistic. For they ignore the possibility that resident landowners might continue to drain profits as well as stagnant waters from their lands, that agricultural reforms might increase estate incomes and raise tenant rents without effecting general prosperity at all.[31]

When bogs are cleared in an imperial context, as Thomas Chandler Haliburton argues in 1835 from the British colony of Nova Scotia, the activity openly augurs exploitation, not regional economic salvation.

> "This Province is like that 'ere tree: it is tapped till it begins to die at the top, and if they don't drive in a spile and stop the everlastin' flow of the sap, it will perish altogether. All the money that's made here, all the interest that's paid in it, and a pretty considerable portion of rent too, all goes abroad for investment, and the rest is sent to us to buy bread. It's drained like a bog; it has opened and covered trenches all through it, and then there's others to the foot of the upland to cut off the springs. Now you may make even a bog too dry; you may take the moisture out to that degree that the very silt becomes dust, and blows away. The English funds, and [American] banks, railroads, and canals, are all absorbing your [Nova Scotian] capital like a sponge, and will lick it up as fast as you can make it."[32]

From Ireland to Canada, the empire can be profitable only because it siphons off profits from the peripheries and redirects them into the home economy. Yet well into the nineteenth century, the advocates of modernization argue for the far-reaching social transformations caused by the drainage procedure itself, as it joins disparate agricultural sectors into a new regional economy and forms Britain into a new political and economic unit. In his *Code of Agriculture, Including Observations of Gardens, Orchards, Woods, and Plantations* (1817), Scottish agricultural reformer John Sinclair pleads for a "great scale of drainage" across Britain.

> So sensible have landed proprietors become, of the deep interest they have, in executing this most important species of improvement, on a liberal and extended scale, that it is a practise with many, to have a *general plan* for the drainage and regular division of the different farms, when their estates are newly let; and the work is thus likely to be completed in a methodical, substantial, and permanent manner, under professed drainers and labourers solely employed in this essential work. On this great scale of drainage, the connexion of one farm, or part of an estate, with another, renders the effect more complete, and the ultimate charges much less.[33]

Like Young before him, Sinclair sees the drain as a foundation on which to erect a new moral, economic, and political order. Drainage systems link individual estates and landowner interests in new ways, and the process of draining speeds the division of agricultural labor, spawning a specialized class of agricultural workers and improving the quality of agricultural work.[34] The benefit of the estate owners thereby becomes a public good; the tax laws should be reorganized to give improvers even greater financial incentives.

Sinclair describes drainage as the process of "discovering," vanquishing, and eliminating "the main spring or source of the evil." The economic and political justifications for land reclamation are grounded not only on the statistical evidence of the profits such improvements will yield but also on a quasi-theological sense of the bog as a source of sin and sloth, a site of social and moral darkness: drainage takes on the status of an exorcism.[35] In some ways, improvers take over and refashion the Swiftian reading of mud as a figure for the country's long-standing political, economic, and moral quagmires. Yet because they stress the possibility of agricultural and moral renewal, they also transform the bog into an arena of moral choice. If the country appears as a singular instance of neglect and blight, it is also an exemplary site for experimentation and transformation; Ireland's irregularities elicit their most careful planning and their most extreme prescriptions for rationalization, for the long-term reform of the rural economy can be effected only by strategic acts of effacement, replacement, and superimposition. Covered over with firmer soil and new growth, the bogs of Ireland will disappear completely.

A Vegetable Herculaneum

Cultural nationalists are heirs both to Swift's righteous anger and to Enlightenment reclamation programs. Yet the new nationalist mode of describing Irish topography differs significantly from the readings that preceded it, informed by different cultural, political, and epistemological considerations. Where Swift expresses disgust at the state of Ireland, and modernizers seek a new beginning in a radically transformed national landscape, nationalists wish to maintain the terrain of Ireland largely as it stands. For Young, Ireland is a place where a new future can become visible. For the nationalists, it is a place where the outlines of the past can still be glimpsed, where a hidden landscape of historical tradition and emotional attachment can be sensed just beneath the surfaces visible to the modern eye. Such surfaces serve as an accretive national annal, bearing the visible marks of many centuries of continuous human presence, the scars of military battles, and the traces of occupation. For nationalist antiquaries, one devastating long-term effect of English occupation was the suppression of antiquarian learning as of bardic poetry. Where both oral and written traditions have been forcibly suppressed, the national landscape becomes crucial as an alternative, less easily destroyed historical record. Agricultural reforms that would erase the surface of the country, to create an economic and political tabula rasa, thus threaten the vestiges of cultural memory.

In many parts of Ireland, as Young's *Tour* records, improvers' attempts to reshape and reorganize the countryside met with Whiteboy unrest and other physical forms of resistance. Over the long run, rhetorical resistance also slowed the whole-scale transformation of the countryside. For although the nationalists' polemical explications of its historical and cultural significance had little influence on most agricultural reformers, they had a profound effect both on the literature and the practice of a new domestic tourism. The advent, in turn, of tourist itineraries organized around "picturesque" landscapes and ancient ruins gave landowners and municipalities economic motivation to conserve as well as to improve.

The long-term effect of antiquarian tourism was the stylization as much as the preservation of the national landscape. But its secondary effect was to transform the status (and thus the carrying power) of nationalist arguments about cultural tradition. Once, such arguments had been dismissed as extremist, regressive, or crackpot. Then the new tourist literature took them up, softened their militant tone, and refashioned them into picturesque commonplaces aimed at a broad British audience of tourists and readers.

Under the influence of these new touristic surveys, in turn, the political economy survey was itself transformed. John Sinclair's comprehensive *Statistical Account of Scotland*, a parish-by-parish description of Scottish economic, political, and social life, published in twenty-one volumes over the 1790s, includes not only the traditional topics of Youngian political economy—statistics on human and livestock populations; wages, prices, and poor relief; and the effect of the Union—but also recurring discussions of "Antiquities and National Curiosities" and of distinctive features of local landscape and natural history, from hills and caves to indigenous wildlife. Only a decade after the publication of Young's *Tour*, and in part under the pressure of a new, nationalist sense of place, the survey expanded as a genre to include many more cultural materials and curiosities than before, and it began to resemble the touristic guidebook in format and content.[36] And from the 1790s onward, several new literary genres, from a new breed of national miscellany magazine to a new imperial travel writing, developed antiquarian variants of the survey, in which cataloging activities began and ended with the description of antiquities and traditional practices.[37] By the 1830s, even the Ordnance Survey of Ireland experimented with, then controversially rejected, the idea of providing a comprehensive cultural and geographical description of the entire terrain it mapped.[38] The survey's new mandate (as publication officer Lieutenant Thomas Askwin Lancom's 1832 reorientation booklet makes clear) would have engaged surveyors not only in a comprehensive chronicling of Irish cultural forms (customs, festivals, legends, social practices, and conditions) but also in compiling an equally exhaustive historical annal of the Irish landscape. In mapping bogs, for instance, surveyors were to ask themselves many new questions, from the bogs' probable origin to the age and stratification of any timber found within them. The bog, then, was to be interrogated as a stratified historical record in its own right, with its own accretive, localized forms of information.[39]

If the official survey considers the move from enumeration to description, British domestic travel writing shifts with even greater finality from an Enlightenment view of national landscape to one strongly marked by nationalist preoccupations.[40] John Carr's breezy *The Stranger in Ireland, or A Tour of the Southern and Western Parts of That Country, in the Year 1805* (1806) thus insists on the picturesque interest of every conceivable aspect of the Irish landscape. "The bogs of Ireland," in particular, "at first seemed to be a subject of little interest, but as I enquired and reflected, I found them a source of uncommon surprise, curiosity and amusement."[41] The book devotes a whole section to their properties, genesis, and contents. Having "fallen into the usual false notion of Englishmen who have never visited Ireland, that a bog was a collection of thick mud" (p. 303), Carr discovers instead that bogs are repositories of Irish civilization, "a sort of vegetable Herculaneum" (p. 305).[42] Under their surface are not only whole forests of ancient organic artifacts—the horns of long-extinct moose deer and petrified trees (from the period before the Brehon laws)—but also the vestiges of Irish cultural antiquity, musical instruments, "ponderous and beautiful ornaments" (p. 310), and implements of everyday life.

The bog has legendary preservative qualities. One informant claims that the locals preserve their butter and eggs there, another to have found an ancient shoe that the bog had preserved perfectly over several centuries, and a third to have found the skeleton of a modern-day cobbler, "unexpectedly overwhelmed by a floating bog" (p. 304), and recovered, in the course of bog reclamation, in an enbalmed state, with a shoe and some leather fully preserved at his side.[43] Throughout the late eighteenth and early nineteenth centuries, the shoemaker appears in traditionalist writing as a transitional figure symbolizing first the resistance to modern divisions of labor, then lost artisanal traditions and the political independence they represent. Here the cobbler at once disappears into the oblivion of the bog and is restored, in embalmed form, as an emblem of an earlier era and as evidence of the bog's ability to halt the ravages of time.

To Carr, the bogs of Ireland appear as an endangered species; their reclamation is so profitable "that I should not be surprised if, in no very distant period, a bog were a greater rarity in Ireland than in England" (p. 313). Sharing Young's optimism about the course of economic and political progress in Ireland, Carr ends his section titled "Curious Bog Anecdotes— Bog Remarks—Bog Antiquities" by an approving invocation of bog reclamation, for the land, turf, and building wood it yields are the basis of Ireland's future prosperity. Yet unlike Young, he also eulogizes the bog as accreting numerous layers of cultural history, as an antiquity and national landmark in its own right. For Young, the work of improvement and clearance forces the bog to yield up its swallowed lands and breaks the paralyzing grip of the past on the country's sources of wealth. For Carr, as for other romantic writers, the bog contains Ireland within itself, bearing, preserving, and yielding up the artifacts of national culture. The bog, indeed, is "so antiseptic" that the trees within it "are constantly dug up in so perfect, or rather in so improved a condition, that they are preferred to the wood" (p. 305) of live trees: the bog's process of petrifaction represents an improvement over the state of life itself.

In Carr's bog, two faces of Irish history are visible simultaneously. In its muddy depths and unpredictable, sliding extensions, the bog suggests the intractability of Ireland's political situation. But it also evokes an organic, conservationist, and antiprogressive vision of national history.

> As we approached the vast waste called the Bog of Allen, the conversation became influenced by the surrounding scenery, and we talked of these wonderful powers of nature, by which she sometimes revolutionizes her own works. . . . My intelligent fellow-traveller said it reminded him of a part of one of the eloquent sermons preached by the celebrated Dean Kirwan, the Massillon of Ireland, which had taken strong possession of his memory: "Every thing is liable to change," said that great devotional orator, "empires, kingdoms, states and provinces; God, from the summit of his immutability, sports with all human things, and wishing to show how little dependence we should place upon them, has decreed that nothing here shall be permanent, but the inconstancy which whirls and agitates us." (Pp. 302–3)

Carr insists both on the imbricated relationship of past and present and on the intrinsic circularity of history.[44]

In crucial ways, Carr's characterization of the bog, as of Ireland, involves a popularization of nationalist sentiments. His book, however, met with a mixed reception in Ireland. In their highly critical review of the book in the *Edinburgh Review*, Richard and Maria Edgeworth compare it unfavorably with Young's *Tour*, complaining of its haste, superficiality, and irritatingly miscellaneous character: "[T]o save himself the trouble of

thought or arrangement, he has emptied and overwhelmed us with his com-
mon-place book."[45] Building on this critique, Edward Dubois's *My Pocket-
book, or Hints for "A Right Merrie and Conceitede" Tour in Quarto*
(1807) glosses and refutes Carr's text, chapter for chapter, beginning with
Carr's own pseudo-encyclopedic chapter headings.

> *Heads of Chapters to occupy full Half a Page-*
> *It does not matter if they should resemble a*
> *Bill of Fare, which often contain every thing*
> *but what one might reasonably axpect to find.*[46]

Carr's book is a dictionary of received ideas, recycling hoary clichés while
claiming original investigation; *The Stranger in Ireland* depends so heavily on quotation that it comes close to plagiarism. Dubois's critical gloss,
in contrast, involves a sustained reflection on the hypertextualism of travel
writing as on the emerging clichés of romantic tourism. Carr, Dubois suggests, might as well have written the travelogue in England, in his own
library, without ever setting foot in Ireland. If earlier English reports on
Ireland continually recycled the same clichés, projections, and fantasies,
the romantic version of the Irish travelogue, with its equally clichéd defenses, prospects, and mythologies, offers little if any improvement. What
Dubois attacks is not so much the content of romantic fantasies as their
strategies of description, their predictability, their lack of saving irony or
self-consciousness. And when he glosses Carr's bog fantasias, he is especially critical of the way Carr's habitual overidentification with Ireland
leads him to animate and personify the bog, with strange effects on the
logic of his prose.[47]

Owenson devotes much of *Florence Macarthy* to a critical gloss of
Carr's nonlinear theory of history and to the political problems involved in
its application to Ireland. This national tale centers on the contrast and
contest between Milesian and Anglo-Irish claims to Ireland, describing the
return to Ireland of two linked characters, a Milesian nationalist and an
Anglo-Irish absentee, who embody different philosophies of history and
thus different political outlooks on Ireland. The absentee, like Carr, believes history is circular; he therefore views Ireland with fatalism. The nationalist, in contrast, believes in the contingency and therefore also the
mutability of history; although he too acknowledges the determining force
of historical patterns, he believes that concerted collective action can bring
about progress. The first position concedes circularity as the only possible
modality of history and thus remains trapped in the cycles it describes; the
other identifies the cycle in order to break it forever.

Owenson's critique of Carr raises the question of how the traveler's
worldview and philosophy of history determine what he sees. Alicia Le-
Fanu's *Tales of a Tourist* (1823) invokes Carr to raise the related problem

of how touristic modes of seeing limit the traveler's comprehension of the places visited. LeFanu's grotesque Mr. Pendennis comes to travel writing after a stint as a lecturer on mnemonics. Bringing to his new occupation both the discipline and the mindlessness of that other memory work, he becomes "one of that valuable class of men . . . who heroically devote their lives to the united miseries of an author and a special messenger, that no part of his majesty's domains may remain unvisited and undescribed."[48] The comprehensive list of cultural, historical, and economic topics that Pendennis plans to cover in his account of his Irish travels closely parodies Carr's table of contents, both in its specific items and in its overall haphazardness. In some respects, LeFanu builds directly on Dubois's earlier satire: as Pendennis's attention to Irish culinary delicacies reminds us, the most important literary model for the Carrian tourist itinerary is the menu.

> Irish settlers . . . Brehon laws- Bonmots- Charter Schools -Kilkenny theatricals. . . . Beautiful women- Beef and butter- Rotunda- Irish jig- Irish wolfdogs-Saltworks- Fisheries . . . Druidical circles- Round towers . . . Castle balls- Salmon leaps- Masquerades- Mendicity- Linen and woolen trade- Marino-Irish patriots-Trouts in the Shannon- Bog of Allen . . . Sheep's heads- Poems of Ossian. (1:49–51)[49]

Tourist literature presents the same paradox as the survey: its very quest for comprehensiveness leads to incomprehensibility and superficiality. Rather than sorting out and making sense of the different aspects of Irish life, Pendennis's account, like Carr's, presents Ireland as an incomprehensible bog of customs, sights, and fragments. Past and present, cultural relic and economic statistic, remain jumbled together, all apparently of equal interest. Like the Edgeworths before her, LeFanu criticizes such travelogues for their incomprehension about what connects a culture, what gives meaning to individual sites or artifacts. Carr's mode of travel writing lacks either a Youngian sense of the nation's political and economic coherence or a nationalist sense of its cultural coherence. Instead, Pendennis's list reveals a scurrilous imperialist unconscious, a logic that associates Irish learning with theatricality, Irish patriotism with the behavior of fish, and Ossian with indigestible local delicacies.

Throughout the seventeenth and eighteenth centuries, ethnic joke books such as *Bogg-Witticisms* (1700) relentlessly evoked "Irish bulls" and "Macronian blunders," the grammatical illogicalities or inadvert puns purportedly uttered by Milesians in speaking and writing English, as a means of denigrating Irish intelligence. Richard and Maria Edgeworth challenged this savage tradition of ethnic joking in their 1802 *Essay on Irish Bulls*, explaining the "Irish bull" less damagingly as the result of Irish bilingualism, the attempt to translate from one idiom and cultural context into another. In many cases, their analysis uncovered a deep logic and a high degree of abstract thinking in the "bull": the "mistake" came from overloading rather than from failing to comprehend the grammatical structures of English. As Siobhán Kilfeather has argued, the bulls cited by the Edgeworths often contain subversive political content as well and can be read as acts of linguistic protest against English as an occupying language.[50] In *Tales of a Tourist*, Pendennis's Carr-like catalog of Irish sights suggests an obverse, if equally covert, strategy of linguistic attack and denigration by those who describe Ireland and the Irish people. Not only do English travel writers fail to understand the internal connectives of Irish life, but even their most neutral and apparently haphazard attempts to catalog Ireland work, on the deepest levels of organization and association, to reduce Irish culture to agriculture, Irish achievements to natural history.

MY BOG: FROM ALLYBALLYCARRICKO'SHAUGLIN TO THE BLACK ISLANDS

The principal problem with travel writers who set out to describe Ireland, as Maria Edgeworth's novels argue so influentially, is that their mode of cultural explication and commentary replicates the wrong features of the survey. Like imperial surveyors of land, they import an ostensibly universal standard of measurement into a landscape of great historical and cultural complexity. Their accounts mimic the sweep and scope of Young's descriptions of Ireland, but the resemblance is superficial, for they have invested neither the time nor the labor to ascertain the texture of the country. Travel writing, for Edgeworth, represents literary work of the highest political consequence. Yet it is too often undertaken by the arrogant or ignorant, with lasting damage to cross-cultural understanding.

An episode in her *Ennui* points up the investigative shortcomings of Lord Craiglethorpe, a shallowly elegant "English traveller, full of English prejudices against Ireland and everything Irish."[51] Craiglethorpe offends his Anglo-Irish hosts with his "ill-bred show of contempt for the Irish" and his "inordinate arrogance" toward his own cousins; he passes through even the most elegant estates with a "note-book in his hand, setting down our faults and conning them by rote" (pp. 209–10). As his hosts realize with horror, he intends "to publish a Tour through Ireland, or a View of Ireland, or something of that nature." Yet they know he has merely been "posting from one great man's house to another" and can have acquired no information about Irish life, save that of the gentry (who live much as they would in England).

> As to the lower classes, I don't think he ever speaks to them; or, if he does, what good can it do him? for he can't understand their modes of expression, nor they his: if he inquire about a matter of fact, I defy him to get the truth out of them, if they don't wish to tell it; and, for some reason or other, they will,

nine times in ten, not wish to tell it to an Englishman. There is not a man, woman, or child, in any cabin in Ireland, who would not have wit and *cuteness* enough to make *my lord* believe just what they please. So, after posting from Dublin to Cork, and from the Giants' Causeway to Killarney; after travelling east, west, north, and south, my wise cousin Craiglethorpe will know just as much of the lower Irish as the cockney who has never been out London, and who has never, *in all his born days*, seen an Irishman but on the English stage; where the representations are usually as like the originals, as the Chinese pictures of lions, drawn from descriptions, are to the real animal.
(P. 211)

Offended by this preemptory method of surveying Ireland as by Craiglethorpe's desire to believe the worst of her country, his cousin, Lady Geraldine, undertakes appropriate revenge: feeding him endless misinformation. Craiglethorpe will assemble a book so completely untrue that it will be unpublishable, even within the exaggerating and denigrating genre of English guides to Ireland. What he must learn is that it takes real patience and effort to understand an unfamiliar national culture. As Young argues, an investigator can arrive at true knowledge only through the transformative process of labor.

Craiglethorpe's arrogance toward his Anglo-Irish peers requires more subtle punishment. For the sake of a practical joke—intended primarily to embarrass snobbish Miss Tracey—Craiglethorpe consents to be introduced to her as his own land surveyor, Mr. Gabbitt, who in turn assumes Lord Craiglethorpe's identity. The trick goes off very well; the "admiration of Miss Tracey for *the false Craiglethorpe* . . . the awkwardness of Mr. Gabbitt with his title, and the awkwardness of Lord Craiglethorpe without it, were fine subjects of her ladyship's satirical humour" (p. 209). But the joke is on Craiglethorpe as much as it is on Miss Tracey. The self-styled travel writer is exposed for what he really is, a mere surveyor of unfamiliar lands—except that Gabbitt performs his surveying labors more honestly and arrives at a more accurate reading of Ireland.

At the same time, in a novel centrally concerned with the transposition, interchangeability, and hence constructedness of both class and ethnic identities, the joke functions as a parable of uneven chances and the way they are reinforced by social norms and expectations. In the novel's main plot, Lord Glenthorn and Christy O'Donoghoe, Anglo-Irish landowner and Milesian blacksmith, prove to have been switched at birth but cannot successfully be switched back, because a lifetime of education and acculturation has made each unsuited to the other's social position. So too, in the Craiglethorpe episode, English and Irish nobility, aristocratic traveler and humble surveyor, honored guest and "low man" (p. 208) who cannot be fittingly brought into company, are separated solely—but nonetheless decisively—by circumstance.[52]

For Edgeworth, the travelogue (or fictions based on travelogue forms) can potentially explain, to a distant and differently situated audience, just how national circumstances have been shaped by internal and external forces, and thus why national character is formed as it is. Such explanations are at once demystifying and denaturalizing. They ought to instill, in their distant audience, an understanding of things as they are and of the historical contingencies that have shaped them: readers are to finish Edgeworth's novels sympathetic to the dilemmas they describe and determined to see new distributive and retributive justice for Ireland.

Edgeworth is the novelist who most fully shares Young's reading of Ireland, his work ethic, and his antitraditionalism. Her own literary career, famously, begins under the tutelage of her father, a landlord, dedicated agricultural improver, and author of a Young-influenced *Statistical Survey of Longford*.[53] Yet her Irish novels demonstrate the power of immaterial as well as material forces: class and ethnic relations in Ireland not only have economic determinants but are structured at the deepest levels of language, thought patterns, and cognition by the long-standing coexistence and friction between two very different cultural traditions.

The tension, in Edgeworth's writing, between Youngian political economy and an ethnographic analysis sensitive to cultural and linguistic traditions is particularly clear in *Castle Rackrent*. A family annal narrated by an apparently loyal and doting family retainer and ornamented by "antiquarian" footnotes, the novel works to explode both the notion of feudal loyalty (showing a retainer sentimentality driven, generation after generation, by the hope of direct or indirect material advantage) and antiquarian claims to Ireland's former greatness (showing a historical sentimentality driven by deliberate misinterpretation and wild extrapolation). Like Young, Edgeworth advocates the economic and political reconstitution of Ireland, and she is critical of antiquarian traditionalism as an impediment to this process. The regressive character of such traditionalism seems visible in the very conventions of antiquarian scholarship, as *Castle Rackrent*'s pseudo-antiquarian footnotes make clear. There the "editorial" addition of layer after layer of glossing antiquarian footnotes weighs down the narrative action and slows the progress of the reading eye across the page.[54] The reconstruction of Ireland is similarly slowed by the antiquarian mode of reading the present-day landscape as overlaid with invisible layers of tradition, and by the glossing of every discussion of current problems with references to a glorious national past. Antiquarian traditionalism weighs down Irish consciousness with a spurious ancestor worship and an impossibly idealized sense of the old Ireland.

Yet if *Castle Rackrent*'s footnotes indicate Edgeworth's critical distance from cultural nationalists, the glossary notes suggest greater sympathy for their position. Written together with her father, and added to the novel when the novel was already in press, to render the text's "idiomatic phrases" of Irish English "intelligible to the English reader" (p. 123), the glossary promises to give access to the meaning of the natives' utterances, to render transparent Irish thought processes. And yet, beginning with the extended gloss of the novel's captioning first phrase, such transparency proves elusive; both the glossary and the narrative logic of the text continually evince the profound strangeness and thus relative illegibility of Irish life for the English reader. From the famous Irish funeral howl to the most ordinary expressions, Irish vocalization and Irish speech patterns compress and express many layers of historical memory. The idiom of Edgeworth's characters remains incapable of translation, because standard English can have no analogs for the historical undertones and historical unconscious of the original words. If *Castle Rackrent* expresses Edgeworth's suspicion of a political ideology grounded on the principle of cultural preservation, it also demonstrates continually how capaciously, how complicatedly cultural history and cultural practices are preserved—and rendered visible—within language itself.[55]

Edgeworth's attitude toward the Irish landscape is similarly paradoxical. For the most part, her Irish novels avoid both picturesque and sentimental modes of landscape description and insist instead on the mutability of the Irish terrain. Like subsequent national novelists, Edgeworth often uses the journey of an initially uncomprehending stranger in Ireland to orchestrate stories of national discovery. Yet she also invokes the perspective of the stranger in Ireland to question local attachments. In *Castle Rackrent* the inability of Sir Kit's new wife to comprehend the beauties of the local bog suggests the limitations of local perspective as much as of her own.

> Then, by-and-bye, she takes out her glass, and begins spying over the country. "And what's all that black swamp out yonder, Sir Kit?" says she. "My bog, my dear," says he, and went on whistling. "It's a very ugly prospect, my dear," says she. "You don't see it, my dear," says he, "for we've planted it out, when the trees grow up in summer time," says he. "Where are the trees," said she, "my dear?" still looking through her glass. "You are blind, my dear," says he; "what are those under your eyes?" "These shrubs," said she. "Trees," said he. "May be they are what you call trees in Ireland, my dear," said she; "but they are not a yard high, are they?" "They were planted out but last year, my lady," says I. . . "they are very well grown for their age, and you'll not see the bog of Allyballycarricko'shaughlin at-all-at-all through the screen, when once the leaves come out. But, my lady, you must not quarrel with any part or parcel of Allyballycarricko'shauglin, for you don't know how many hundred years that same bit of bog has been in the family; we would not part with the bog of Allyballycarricko'shauglin upon no account at all. . . ." Now one would have thought this would have been hint enough for my lady, but she fell to laughing

like one out of their right mind, and made me say the name of the bog over for her to get it by heart a dozen time—then she must ask me how to spell it, and what was the meaning of it in English. (Pp. 77–78)

Edgeworth's own family had a long-standing preoccupation with bogs and drainage. In the 1780s, her father had "improved, with success and profit, considerable tracts . . . of bog" on his property.[56] And in 1809, when the government embarked on a major survey of Ireland's principal peat bogs (in order to prepare their reclamation), he volunteered to direct the district survey. For almost a year, he and his son William spent long days with the surveying team, traversing the "wastes and deserts" (2:294) of every bog in the region.[57] As Maria noted sardonically during this epoch in the Edgeworth household, "It is bog, bog, bog, night and day."[58]

Castle Rackrent describes an opposite yet equivalent scenario, in which the enthusiasms of the bog aficionado meet with the incomprehension of an uninitiated family member. What could "Allyballycarricko'shaughlin" possibly mean in English, or the bog signify to the English stranger in Ireland, unaccustomed to anyone singing the praises of mud? Not yet inculcated with local pride or inured to the local habit of justifying the area's visible poverty, the outsider sees Sir Kit's ragged "prospect" as simply pathetic, and the bog's extensive, accreted name as ludicrous. Yet Edgeworth depicts the vocabulary and comportment of the critic herself with irony; "my lady" mistakenly and arrogantly expects the landscape of Ireland to meet the standards of the English prospect or the capital-intensive English estate, with its very different geological, historical, and economic formation. For Edgeworth, then, no less than for other Irish novelists of the period, the condescension of the foreign visitor elicits a defensive (and implicitly nationalist) response.

If *Castle Rackrent* inspired novelists such as Owenson and Maturin to develop more militantly national tales, Edgeworth's own subsequent Irish novels shift subtly in their attitude toward nationalism. The last of these novels, *Ormond*, includes a sympathetic meditation on the traditional culture preserved in the boggy isolation of the Black Islands. *Ormond* is organized as a panoramic, geopolitical bildungsroman, in which the stages in the hero's moral growth are marked by his movement from the estate of the opportunistic Sir Ulick to the feudal Black Island court of King Corny to the temptations of London and Paris and finally home to Ireland. Character and action evolve as a function of surroundings, and each of Ormond's places has a distinct logic and a social economy of its own. In some ways, this organization merely reflects the ideas of Montesquieu and Herder, of Thomas Blackwell and Robert Wood, about the causal connection between place and national character, climate and tradition. What is new here is the novel's emphasis on the coexistence of cultures, economies, and ways of life *within* Ireland. And what is new for Edgeworth, in particular, is the presentation of King Corny's rural court, and the world of Milesian feudal tradition, in terms that are consistently more positive than those used to depict the forces of anglicization, as represented by the insincere, corrupt Sir Ulick.[59]

In *Ennui*, eight years earlier, Edgeworth bestowed her greatest approval on Mr. M'Leod. Lord Glenthorn's compassionate and utilitarian Scottish estate agent doubles as the agent of economic modernization and improvement as propounded by the Scottish Enlightenment. "M'Leod perplexed me," reports Lord Glenthorn of his own pre-Enlightened days as the benevolent despot of Glenthorn Castle, with "his doubt whether it would not be better for a man to buy shoes, if he could buy them, cheaper than he could make them. He added something about the division of labour, and Smith's *Wealth of Nations*; to which I could only answer—'Smith's a Scotchman.'"[60]

Yet by the time she writes *Ormond*, Edgeworth's own utilitarianism is softened by a new, sympathetic interest in how traditional societies function as closed cultural economies, staunchly resisting improvement. The outstanding, endearing characteristic of King Corny's domain is the fact that everything in it, beginning with the shoes, are homemade.

> King Corny had with his own hands made a violin and a rat-trap; and had made the best coat, and the best pair of shoes, and the best pair of boots, and the best hat; and had knit the best pair of stockings, and had made the best dunghill in his dominions; and had made a quarter of a yard of fine lace, and had painted a panorama. . . .
>
> But now . . . in consequence of his slight commerce with the world . . . it had occurred to Harry to question the utility and real grandeur of some of those things, which had struck his childish imagination. For example, he began to doubt whether it were worthy of a king or a gentleman to be his own shoemaker, hatter, and tailor; whether it were not better managed in society, where these things are performed by different tradesmen: still the things were wonderful, considering who made them, and under what disadvantages they were made: but Harry having now seen and compared Corny's violin with other violins, and having discovered that so much better could be had for money, with much less trouble, his admiration had a little decreased.[61]

There is a growing separation here not only between the perspectives of Ormond and his affectionate foster father (a potentially tragic "developmental" and civilizational gap that looks forward to the self-conscious sophistication separating Pip from Joe in Dickens's *Great Expectations*), but also between the perspective of Ormond and that of Edgeworth. If Ormond regretfully comes to see Corny's economic self-reliance as superseded and somewhat ridiculous, Edgeworth views it as naive and utterly impractical, yet touching and laudable as well.

Enlightenment sociology understood early societies to precede the division of labor, and this view was reinforced by Macpherson's depiction, in his *Poems of Ossian*, of the many functions of the third-century bard. "I remember Mr. Macpherson told me," writes David Hume in 1760, "that the heroes of this Highland epic were not only, like Homer's heroes, their own butchers, bakers, and cooks, but also their own shoemakers, carpenters, and smiths."[62]

"In rude ages," adds Adam Ferguson in 1767,"men are not separated by distinctions of rank or profession. They live in one manner, and speak one dialect. The bard is not to chuse his expression among the singular accents of different conditions. He has not to guard his language from the peculiar errors of the mechanic, the peasant, the scholar, or the courtier."[63]

The absence of the modern separation between hand and head, then, is the salient feature of the ancient world; the period's equally idealized picture of the medieval world involved the conflation of the whole feudal caste system in the figure of the self-sufficient nobleman. By the early nineteenth century, however, King Corny's mode of life is historically doomed and already deeply anachronistic—and in her account of the near-fatal consequences of an archaic code of honor, Edgeworth suggests that many aspects of feudal culture deserve their imminent death.

Yet when the actual death of King Corny brings the end of an epoch for the Black Islands, and the end of Ormond's idyll there, Edgeworth moves into the mode of national elegy, to mourn what is lost with Corny's passing. As Edgeworth's letters make clear, the writing of *Ormond*, and especially the death of King Corny, is bound up, on many levels, with the final illness of her own father. As the novel took shape, she read it aloud to him on his sickbed, and "he corrected the whole by having it read to him many many times; often working at it in his bed for hours together, once at the end, for six hours between the intervals of sickness and exquisite pain." Writing "in agony of anxiety, with trembling hands and tearful eyes," Edgeworth hurried to finish *Ormond* so that her father could receive an advance copy on his birthday and was deeply moved at the eloquence with which he recounted its story to a birthday visitor. He died two weeks later, and she continued to associate the novel with the memory of his death, particularly because he himself had written King Corny's death scene, up "to the end of that chapter where Ormond 'loses the best friend he had in the world.' "[64] *Ormond*, then, is in several senses a testimonial to a dying patriarch.

Within the novel itself, the mourning for King Corny transfigures the very landscape of the Black Islands, transforming boggy terrain into a site of national memory. Crossing the island for the last time, on his way to the ship that will carry him away, and absorbed in mental leave-taking, Ormond chooses

an unusual path across this part of the Island to the water-side, that [he and his companion Moriarty] might avoid that which they had followed the last time they were out, on the day of Corny's death. They went, therefore, across a lone track of heath bog, where, for a considerable time, they saw no living being.

On this bog, of which Cornelius O'Shane had given Moriarty a share, the grateful poor fellow had, the year before, amused himself with cutting in large letters of about a yard long, the words—

"LONG LIVE KING CORNY."

He had sowed the letters with broom seed in the spring, and had since forgotten ever to look at them,—but they were now green, and struck the eye.

"Think then of this being all the trace that's left of him on the face of the earth!" said Moriarty. "I'm glad I did even that same."

After crossing this lone bog, when they came to the waterside, they found a great crowd of people, seemingly all the inhabitants of the Islands assembled there, waiting to take leave of Master Harry, and each got a word and a look from him before they would let him step into the boat.

"Ay, go to the continent," said Shellah, "ay, go to fifty continents, and in all Ireland you'll not find hearts warmer to you than those of the Black Islands, that knows you best from a child, Master Harry, dear." (P. 175)

To close the Black Islands section of her novel, Edgeworth mounts a brief, yet familiar, scene of feudal leave-taking: King Corny's spiritual heir is seen off by the entire island community, in a ceremony that affirms feudal loyalties, solidarity, and love. By 1817, the assembly of the clan is a well-established novelistic set piece, recurring in feudal fictions from Ann Radcliffe's *Castles of Athlin and Dunbayne* (1789) to Maturin's *Wild Irish Boy* (1808) and Scott's *Waverley* (1814). Yet Edgeworth's framing of the scene is striking and unusual. For the encounter with the feudal community merely reiterates an even more moving encounter with a feudal landscape. Trying to avoid the memory of Corny's death, Ormond and his companion walk toward the shore on an unfamiliar and bleak route that leads through the bog—only to find, in the heart of the bog, a forcible reminder of their love for Corny. It is the bog, blooming in green memorial, that provides him with his final tribute and his last, lingering earthly trace.

At a later point in the novel, impoverished peasants in another part of Ireland will hide stolen silver in their local bog, trusting to its proverbial preservative powers—"the bog-water never rusting" (p. 258)—to safeguard their loot.[65] The moment is one of political unrest in Ireland and one in which Ormond begins to make himself over into a true "improver" of

Irish political and economic life. The modernization project is under siege, and the bog therefore resumes its usual role in Enlightenment writing, as a space of complicity, depravity, and superstition. At the end of the Black Islands episode, in contrast, the bog is suddenly a site of positive memory, as its preservative powers work to enshrine feudal loyalties. And here, however briefly, Edgeworth's treatment of the Irish landscape reflects the memorializing ethos of cultural nationalists rather than the progressive spirit of Enlightenment improvers. No less than all the rest of the Irish landscape, the bog memorializes what is dead and lost, by fostering a living memory. Addressed to someone about to leave the Black Islands and the era of King Corny behind him, to cross back irrevocably into the modern world, the bog's triumphant parting message—LONG LIVE KING CORNY— serves as a reminder that feudal relationships could be experienced as spontaneous love, capable of outliving the epoch that gave them birth, outliving even the state of physical extinction. To Ormond, as to the reader, the bog appears initially as a landscape of desolation and death. Yet what it sustains is memory and hope. The bog, finally, teaches the bereaved how to mourn and how to remember, how to shore up their losses, and how to carry the loyalties of the past into an unknown future.

Chapter 2

THE END OF AN AULD SANG:
ORAL TRADITION AND LITERARY HISTORY

Such were the words of the bards in the days of song; when the king
heard the music of harps, and the tales of other times. The chiefs
gathered from all their hills, and heard the lovely sound. They praised
the voice of Cona! the first among a thousand bards . . . I hear,
sometimes, the ghosts of bards, and learn their pleasant song. But
memory fails in my mind. I hear the call of years! They say, as they
pass along, why does Ossian sing? Soon shall he lie in the narrow
house, and no bard shall raise his fame! . . . The sons of song are gone
to rest. My voice remains, like a blast, that roars, lonely, on a
sea-surrounded rock, after the winds are laid.
—James Macpherson, "Songs of Selma"

Wednesday, 22nd September [Isle of Skye] . . . "I look upon
M'Pherson's *Fingal* to be as gross an imposition as ever the world was
troubled with. Had it been really an ancient work, a true specimen how
men thought at that time, it would have been a curiosity of the first rate.
As a modern production, it is nothing." [Samuel Johnson] said, he
could never get the meaning of an Erse song explained to him. They
told him, the chorus was generally unmeaning. "I take it," said he,
"Erse songs are like a song which I remember: it was composed in
Queen Elizabeth's time, on the Earl of Essex; and the burthen was
'Radaratoo, radarate, radar tadara tandore. . . .'" When Mr M'Queen
began again to expiate on the beauty of Ossian's poetry, Dr. Johnson
entered into no further controversy, but, with a pleasant smile,
only cried, "Ay, ay; Radaratoo, radarate."
—James Boswell, *Journal of a Tour to the Hebrides*

No Echo to Be Heard

In 1773 Samuel Johnson, accompanied by his Scottish biographer James
Boswell, undertook a three-month tour that would form the basis for his
Journey to the Western Islands of Scotland (1775), as well as for Boswell's
Journal of a Tour to the Hebrides with Samuel Johnson, LL.D., 1773
(1786).[1] At the end of the trip, Boswell insisted on visiting Hawthornden,
for the pleasure "of seeing *Sam Johnson* at the very spot where *Ben Jonson*

visited the learned and poetical [Edinburgh writer William] Drummond";
for Boswell, indeed, the whole journey re-created Jonson's 1619 journey to
Scotland (commemorated in a memoir by Drummond, as by Jonson's "My
Picture Left in Scotland").[2] In several crucial respects, however, Johnson's
trip failed to conform to literary-historical precedent. Jonson was so eager
to visit Scotland that he walked from London on foot; warmly received by
Scottish authors and publishers, he left the country with real regret. Johnson, as John Knox argues in 1786, set out for Scotland "under incurable
impressions of a national prejudice, a religious prejudice and a literary prejudice," and although warmly received by Scottish intellectuals, he was depressed and exasperated by much of his journey.[3] In turn, the perceived
"odium which Dr. Johnson bears to any thing Scotch" chilled or infuriated
many interlocutors.[4] The *Journey* was read with bitter indignation by several generations of Scottish readers, for whom it marked the lowest point in
Anglo-Scottish relations and served as a lightning rod for nationalist
anger.[5]

For Johnson's critics, the *Journey* is an imperial ethnography. As
Donald M'Nicol argues in his *Remarks on Dr. Samuel Johnson's Journey
to the Hebrides* (1779), the *Journey* systematically discredits

> the Poems of Ossian,—the whole Gallic language,—our seminaries of
> learning,—the Reformation,—and the veracity of all Scotch, and particularly
> Highland narration. The utter extinction of the two former seems to have been
> the principal motive of [Johnson's] journey to the North. To pave the way for
> this favourite purpose, and being well aware that the influence of tradition, to
> which all ages and nations have ever paid some regard in matters of remote
> antiquity, must be removed, he resolves *point blank* to deny the validity of all
> Scotch, and particularly Highland narration. This he employs all his art to
> persuade the Public is always vague and fabulous, and deserve no manner of
> credit, except when it proves unfavourable to the country; then, indeed, it is
> deemed altogether infallible, and is adduced by himself, upon all occasions, in
> proof of what he asserts.[6]

The *Journey* virtually ignores the intellectual, cultural, and economic renaissance taking place in Edinburgh, Glasgow, and other Lowland cities,
using the bleaker prospects of the Highlands and Islands, areas in political
and economic transition, to characterize Scotland as a whole. As Boswell's
Journal records, Johnson met Adam Ferguson, Lord Monboddo, and a host
of other important Scottish Enlightenment literati during his time in Scotland; Johnson's own account of the journey fails to discuss the work of the
Scottish Enlightenment at all.

Yet the *Journey* does appropriate Scottish Enlightenment paradigms
and investigative procedures to criticize the culture from which they

sprung. Drawing on the Scottish Enlightenment four-stage theory, John-son depicts Scotland as a country that subsumes several distinct stages of cultural development. Each presents the traveler with different conceptual problems, and in each, therefore, the observer must develop a distinct mode of analysis: different kinds of places make possible not only differ-ent cultural forms but different questions and observations. In the Low-lands, Johnson meditates on ruins, progress, and historical change, draw-ing on and questioning the premises of Enlightenment historiography. In the Highlands, observing a society paralyzed by the breakup of the clan system and still resistant to anglicization, he meditates on community loyalties and the physical determinants of culture, interrogating Mon-tesquieu's geographical sociology and Adam Ferguson's historical ethno-sociology. On the Hebrides, finally, Johnson reconsiders human knowl-edge and cultural transmission in terms that question Blackwell's theories of cultural history and extend the epistemological experiments of Diderot or Hume.[7]

Scotland's tripartite geological formation and Johnson's geographical movement are thus synchronized with the movement across several kinds of Enlightenment conceptual terrain, as the *Journey* moves from historiog-raphy to ethnography, and sociology to epistemology, from the progress and decline of civilization to the traditional organization of political and economic life to the nature of human communication and memory. Forty years later, Scott's *Waverley* and Edgeworth's *Ormond* take up this same tripartite investigative model, to give readers a vivid sense of the autono-mous logic and temporality (and ultimate interconnection) of each sector of Scottish, Irish, or British society. Johnson's *Journey* is more successful as a discourse on method than as an integrated ethnographic or sociological survey; it remains a disjunctive work in part because it sees Scotland as fundamentally and fatally disconnected.[8]

The Scottish Enlightenment traced the historical formation of national character to understand the internal logic of other cultures in their own right. Johnson's account continually measures and misjudges the situation of Scotland against the standards of London, as if it provided the only model of intellectual and political life.[9] Its preemptive attitude begins with the physical landscape (and putative treelessness) of Scotland and extends to the country's cultural institutions, using Enlightenment categories to condemn the state of Scotland, and the state of Scotland to criticize the Enlightenment.[10]

So far, my discussion of eighteenth-century nationalism has focused on its embattled, if indebted, relationship to Enlightenment models of de-velopment. Yet Johnson faults the Scottish Enlightenment for its fatal complicity with the work of nationalist revivalists and mythmakers: in

Scotland, all nostalgic clinging to ruins, to dubious past glories, impedes the productive potential of the present. The *Journey* attempts to establish the primacy of a cosmopolitan and imperial vision of Enlightenment activity over what it sees as Scotland's nationalist Enlightenment, of the forces of linguistic normalization over those of vernacular revival, and of a London-centered, print-based model of literary history over a nationalist, bardic model based on oral tradition. Johnson's critics, in turn, refuse to grant him victory in any of these contests, reading the *Journey* as testimony to his powers of projection, displacement, and misrepresentation. As England's leading lexicographer and man of letters, Johnson spends his time in Scotland meditating on alienation, cultural decline, and the relationship between language and thought, yet he never recognizes the contemporary Scots and Gaelic literary revivals going on around him; he even fails to register the complexity of Lowland attitudes toward the English language. He cavils at the sites of past Scottish rebellions, defending the need for military occupations and cultural assimilation, yet fails to notice the complicated power dynamics that frame his own interaction with informants. On Skye, Johnson and Boswell visit a vaunted local attraction,

> [A] cavern by the sea-side, remarkable for the powerful reverberation of sounds. . . . The boatmen . . . inquired who the strangers were, and being told we came one from Scotland and the other from England, asked if the Englishman could recount a long genealogy. What answer was given them, the conversation being in Erse, I was not much inclined to examine.
>
> They expected no good event of the voyage; for one of them declared that he heard the cry of an English ghost. This omen I was not told till after our return, and therefore cannot claim the dignity of despising it. . . .
>
> We . . . came without any disaster to the cavern. . . . But, as a new testimony to the veracity of common fame, here was no echo to be heard. (P. 74)

Unlike the visit to the Marabar Caves in E. M. Forster's *Passage to India*, this expedition ends without any "disaster" or overt violence. Yet Johnson seems surprisingly deaf to the episode's many reverberations; the exchanges with the boatmen, the challenge to produce a competing genealogy, the cry of the English ghost, all echo with a hostility Johnson cannot acknowledge. Instead, he remains preoccupied with the cave's lack of echo, as evidence both of the fundamental unreliability of Highland traditions and of the fundamentally unresonant character of the Scottish landscape, if viewed without nationalist sentimentality.

Macpherson's *Ossian* had turned the Highlands into one enormous echo chamber, evoking an emphatically oral world, from the "echoing halls of Selma" (Fingal's court, where every action is accompanied by voices lifted in recitation, harps lifted in song) to the landscape itself, which echoed with the remembered voices of the past: "By the mossy fountain I will sit; on the top of the hill of winds. When mid-day is silent around, converse, O my love, with me! O talk with me, Vinvela! come on the wings of the gale! on the blast of the mountain, come! Let me hear thy voice, as thou passest, when mid-day is silent around."[11] The rustling, sighing, burbling, and echoing of wind, grass, and water punctuate or accompany many Ossianic poems, serving the blind bard as a natural mnemonic to remember the voices of the dead.[12] Johnson, in contrast, insists on the desolation of the Highlands and describes his decision, during the journey, to write an account of Scotland as motivated by the silence of its landscape, empty of history and of cultural referents: "I had indeed no trees to whisper over my head, but a clear rivulet streamed at my feet. The day was calm, the air soft, and all was rudeness, silence, and solitude. Before me, and on either side, were high hills, which by hindering the eye from ranging, forced the mind to find entertainment for itself. . . . [H]ere I first conceived the thought of this narration" (p. 40).

If the *Journey* is framed as a response to Scotland's barrenness, isolation, and silence, the journey itself seems conceived as a repetition and refutation of Macpherson's prior collecting journey through the Highlands to gather the scattered poems of Ossian from oral and manuscript tradition; Johnson's evocation of river, trees, and wind paradoxically echoes *Ossian*'s anthropomorphized voices of tradition. Like *Ossian*, indeed, Johnson reiterates, ventriloquizes, and perpetuates a long history of nationalist and antinationalist rhetoric about Scotland, from Daniel Defoe and John Wilkes to the Scottish Enlightenment. The *Journey* is a literary-historical echo chamber.[13]

THE DEATH OF SCOTS MUSIC

Johnson visits the Highlands at a moment of transition. The Jacobite defeat in "the '45" was followed by brutal British military reprisals, the occupation and disarming of the Highlands, and a wave of repressive legal sanctions against clan culture.[14] The result was the large-scale collapse of the social and economic infrastructure.

> The state of life, which has hitherto been purely pastoral, begins now to be a little variegated with commerce; but novelties enter by degrees, and till one mode has fully prevailed over the other, no settled notion can be formed. . . .
> The inhabitants were for a long time perhaps not unhappy; but their content was a muddy mixture of pride and ignorance, an indifference for pleasures which they did not know, a blind veneration for their chiefs, and a strong conviction of their own importance.

Their pride has been crushed by the heavy hand of a vindictive conqueror, whose severities have been followed by laws, which, though they cannot be called cruel, have produced much discontent, because they operate upon the surface of life, and make every eye bear witness to subjection. . . . They are now in the period of education, and feel the uneasiness of discipline, without yet perceiving the benefit of instruction. (Pp. 89–90)

Many, however, did not wait to learn the "benefit" of this reeducation: Johnson's visit coincided with the beginning of a large-scale emigration from the Highlands to North America.[15]

During the same period, the Scottish Lowlands began to experience unprecedented material prosperity (reflected in Adam Smith's influential capitalist theory) and an intellectual, literary, and architectural renaissance; Edinburgh, as Tobias Smollett apostrophized it, was a "hotbed of genius."[16] "Is it not strange," writes David Hume in 1757,

that, at a time when we have lost our Princes, our Parliaments, our independent Government, even the Presence of our chief Nobility, are unhappy, in our Accent & Pronunciation, speak a very corrupt Dialect of the Tongue which we make use of; is it not strange, I say, that, in these Circumstances, we shou'd really be the People most distinguished for Literature in Europe?"[17]

The Enlightenment formulation of a new four-stage model of sociological development was one response to Scotland's widening social and economic disparities, transforming the Highlands and the Lowlands into nonsynchronous and separate stages of an impersonal, apparently inevitable evolutionary process. Far from linking the prosperity of the Lowlands or of London to the depletion of the Highlands, and seeing these places as parts of a single economic system, the model detached them one from the other.[18] Transforming spatial distance into developmental time, it both recognized the separate social reality of each place and suggested its fragility and malleability. The model lent itself equally, therefore, to the progressive and expansionist rhetoric of imperialism (backward societies can reach prosperity only by being absorbed by those at a more advanced state) and to the defensively nationalist and conservationist rhetoric of cultural separatism (cultures can maintain their historically rooted character only by maintaining political autonomy, even at the price of refusing progress altogether).

Working within a society at once particularly vulnerable to the first shocks of European economic modernization and possessed by a new kind of intellectual confidence, Scottish literati developed complex notions of the status of literature as historical trace and historical record. Thomas Blackwell's *Inquiry into the Life and Writings of Homer* (1735) read every aspect of Homer's epics as historically contingent and culturally saturated, reflecting the worldview, political organization, and religious beliefs of his society. Blackwell's groundbreaking theories produced new modes of historical thinking and literary history, and new models of the social function and political address of literature, which helped authors to imagine themselves in a new relationship to their works, their public, and their posterity.[19]

Scotland's long-standing linguistic complexity also made Scottish intellectuals particularly sensitive to the intricate relationship between oral and written literatures; effectively monolingual (standard English) in its intellectual and official writings, eighteenth-century Scotland remained bilingual in its speech (with large repertoires of poetry and song in Erse/Scots Gaelic and in Scots English) and trilingual (Erse, Scots, and standard English) in its literary life. Mirroring the country's history of geographical, political, and religious divides, Scotland's complicated linguistic identity confounds any attempt to reduce "the paradox of Scottish culture" (David Daiches) to a simple linguistic or cultural opposition between Highlands and Lowlands. Throughout the Highlands, Johnson found settlements in which no one seemed to understand a single word of English, but also well-educated lairds and ministers whose English usage was exemplary, even elegant.[20] Lowland literature offered similar contrasts. Whereas neoclassically trained poets such as Robert Fergusson and Robert Burns self-consciously turned back to the Scottish vernacular, many Enlightenment intellectuals, wishing to reach English as well as Scottish audiences, or to create a larger British public sphere, labored to anglicize their own pronunciation and to develop a stately prose style in a language not fully their own. "[W]e who live in Scotland," writes Hugh Beattie, "are obliged to study English for books like a dead language which we can understand but cannot speak. Our style smells of the lamp and we are slaves of the language, and are continually afraid of committing gross blunders."[21]

The linguistic particularity of a nation, the historicity of literature: the conjunction of these questions formed the conceptual foundation of a modern Scots literature, laid already, perhaps, when Chancellor Seafield, addressing the last meeting of the last Scottish Parliament, on the eve of the 1707 Union of Scotland with England, uttered a famous eulogy of the long tradition of Scottish political and cultural independence: "[N]ow there's ane end of ane auld sang." The terse phrase announced the end of an autonomous Scotland as the end of an oral, vernacular world, yet it did so with pithy, "couthy" confidence in the survival of the Scots language as a necessary medium for articulating Scottish experience (a confidence amply repaid by the survival, down to the present day, not only of Scots but also of

Seafield's pronouncement as the encapsulation of all that was lost in the Union).[22]

Robert Fergusson's "Elegy, On the Death of Scots Music" (1772) formulates the same paradox of cultural suppression and survival.

> On Scotia's plains, in days of yore,
> When lads and lasses tartan wore,
> Saft Music rang on ilka shore,
>   In hamely weid;
> But harmony is no more,
>   And Music dead.
>
> .   .   .   .
>
> Scotland! that could aince afford
> To bang the pith of Roman sword,
> Winna your sons, wi' joint accord,
>   To battle speed?
> And fight till Music be restor'd
>   Which now lies dead.[23]

The poem's linguistic and rhetorical design, its strategic, harmonizing use of Scots, undoes the elegy initially announced. From the opening stanza onward, standard literary English gives way to the "hamely weid" of tartan, the "Saft Music" and rugged texture of Scots. By the final stanza, both harmony and music are fully restored, mute mourning transformed into a battle cry.

Chancellor Seafield's metaphor of the "auld sang" invoked the breaking off of a poetic tradition as old as the country itself. Yet however threatened in the wake of Union, Scotland's Scottishness remains protected in Scots: a culture lives on in language.[24] The late-eighteenth-century Scottish vernacular revival reveals a reassuring side to Enlightenment theories of social evolution: although cultural forms originate in one specific historical epoch, they can survive into the next.[25] Literature, then, has several compensatory or repository functions. Its timeliness, its link to its own time and place, would give it a tragic frailty, were it not that it can survive, in fragmentary or transmuted form, into the next stage of national evolution, to serve both as historical record of the past and as a foundation for the nation's future writing.

THE DIGNITY OF WRITING

Macpherson's controversial Ossianic publications—first of bardic fragments, in *Fragments of Ancient Poetry, Collected in the Highlands of Scotland and Translated from the Galic or Erse Language* (1759), then of an extended cycle of longer poems—made clear the stake of these theories of tradition and transmission. Macpherson claimed to have translated third-century Gaelic compositions, passed down, as Edinburgh rhetorician Hugh Blair explained, by oral tradition, transmitted "from race to race" by a bardic succession.[26] Scottish Enlightenment literati hailed the first translations as a great, lost patrimony, and their financial support for Macpherson's tours through the Highlands to gather further materials amounted, as Richard Scher has brilliantly argued, to a virtual commissioning of the *Poems of Ossian*.[27]

Invoking and mourning an epic past, *Ossian*'s auld sangs seemed designed to reanimate a Scottish nationalism and an oral tradition on the wane since the "spirit-breaking '45."[28] Enthusiastically received in Scotland and retranslated, with enormous resonance, into many European languages, the poems met with a more suspicious reception in Ireland and in England, for they supplied genealogical evidence for new, nationally gratifying theories about the original settlement of the British Isles, demonstrating the Highland origin of the kings of Ireland. Irish literature was thus of Scottish origin as well. After the English conquest of Ireland, "the Irish bards began to appropriate the Scottish Ossian and his heroes to their own country."[29] Thereafter, as Lowland Scots lost "the language of their ancestors," they lost not only "their national traditions" but the very "story of their country," so that "Irish refugees" found it easy "to impose their own fictions" of origin. But although "ignorant chronicle writers, strangers to the ancient language of their country," and later English, Irish, and Lowland historians perpetuated these mistaken accounts, the songs of Ossian were luckily still preserved in Highland popular memory: "The ancient traditional accounts . . . have been handed down without interruption . . . it was impossible to eradicate from among the bulk of the people their own national traditions."[30]

In Ireland outraged nationalists challenged these historical theories to reclaim Ossian as an Irish bard; in England Johnson and other literati challenged Macpherson's claims for the poems' ancient provenance and oral transmission. The controversy over Ossian, as over questions of bardic and editorial prerogative, oral tradition and cultural memory, historical authenticity and anachronism, would rage for the rest of the eighteenth century.[31] *The Poems of Ossian* itself anticipates such debates to a remarkable degree. Its true subject is not epic heroism but the vicissitudes of oral tradition: acts of heroism are overshadowed by the act of narration, anticipated, recounted, celebrated, commemorated, and mourned, at Fingal's court, through rituals of bardic song. A poem such as "The Songs of Selma" is thus framed as a bardic recital in which a long succession of singers recount narratives of death and mourning, reducing the audience to tears. And at the poem's end, Ossian (as frame narrator) mourns the memory of the recital as well as of the deaths recounted there. The bards who sang to Fingal are no more; the bardic tradition has no more listeners.[32]

Describing the actions of three generations of bards and warriors, Ossian's poems let the time of action and of memory overflow into one another, creating a complex temporality of bardic repertoire and performance that both constitutes history and stands outside historical time. Rhapsodic medium between past and present, repository and vehicle of tradition, Ossian sits alone in a barren, post-Fingalian landscape long after the heroic events of his poems. Yet the desolation and hopelessness of his historical situation animate Ossian's complaint and memories. Left in a present that is empty, he revives the past to fill it; unable to see the landscape in front of his blind eyes, he re-creates a mental landscape of memory and voice, a past composed of earlier bardic songs.

All Ossian's heirs have died before him, he has not managed to pass the poems on, and so the tradition entrusted to him will die too—yet it does live on unexpectedly past the end of the last poem, in Macpherson's "retrieval" of Ossian's repertoire fifteen centuries after it was ostensibly composed. The elegiac pathos of these poems is magnified not only by the subsequent erosion of clan culture but even (paradoxically) by the fact that they are remembered and recovered so long afterward, surviving after all, against all hope, in Macpherson's late-eighteenth-century translation. In the absence of written records, Johnson will argue, an oral culture is incapable of holding on to its past. Yet as Macpherson demonstrates, oral performance functions precisely to keep the past alive, resonating continually in and with the present. And although *Ossian* reaches its readers as a printed text, it evokes a sense of oral performance, of the third century living on in the eighteenth.

When Fingal's culture dies out in the course of the *Poems*, killed by its own fighting spirit, its heroic ethos is transformed into a memory problem; to put it in terms of the eighteenth-century struggle between an aristocratic and a bourgeois ethos, *Ossian* announces the end of a heroic age and the beginning of a sentimental one.[33] Appearing during a moment of virulent English anti-Scottish sentiment, in which the hated earl of Bute, Britain's first Scottish prime minister, was popularly believed to give clannish preferment to his own countrymen, and in which Scots were depicted by the English press as ravenous Highland beggars or as greedy careerists, flooding and devouring England, Macpherson's Ossianic poetry offered English readers new possibilities for sympathetic identification with a defeated people and a dying culture.[34] Precisely because it mixes tradition and forgery, recasting indigenous epic poetry for eighteenth-century sensibilities, *Ossian* drew English readers into an unfamiliar, threatening, and alien cultural world, making it appear to them, for the first time, as sublime, heroic, and tragically doomed.

The lingering resistance to *Ossian*, argues Glasgow novelist Robert Couper in 1803, is both political and aesthetic, a refusal by a neoclassically oriented English intelligentsia to accord a place in the English (and Western) literary pantheon to "an illiterate and half naked barbarian, and a Scots Highlander into the bargain," no matter how "sublime and elegant" his poetry. Unable to "resist the strength, fertility, and tenderness of the Celtic bard," they consigned him into

> the strong hands of the inquisition, armed with Homer and Virgil, with a thousand commentators, and ten thousand prejudices. Still the harp of the old barbarian sounded upon his chord, and with increasing strength. This was not to be forgiven; so it was judged best to lay the ghost, by proving, declaring, and saying in the most incontestable manner, that neither the ghost nor the bard had ever had an existence, except in the visionary heads of some scabber'd highlanders. What a triumph to the learning and the little minded!

A hundred years hence, Couper concludes, Ossian's poetry will be enjoyed for its own sake, without anyone's caring "whether James Macpherson, Esq. or Ossian, the son of Fingal, was the bard."[35] At the moment of *Ossian*'s appearance, however, the struggle between pro- and anti-Scottish factions dominated English public life; Macpherson dedicated an early Ossianic collection to the earl of Bute. The first quarrels over *Ossian* were fought out between Smollett's *Briton*, a Bute-sponsored journal that defended Scotland and Scottish loyalty, and John Wilkes's anti-Bute *North Briton*, dedicated to satirical attacks on Scottish nepotism, penury, and "*national spirit*."[36]

Johnson's skepticism toward *Ossian*, as toward Scottish nationalism, echoes their exchanges.

> The Scots have something to plead for their easy reception of an improbable fiction: they are seduced by their fondness for their supposed ancestors. A Scotchman must be a very sturdy moralist, who does not love Scotland better than truth: he will always love it better than inquiry; and if falsehood flatters his vanity, will not be very diligent to detect it. Neither ought the English to be much influenced by Scottish authority. (P. 119)

Johnson was justified in doubting Macpherson's "improbable fiction" and in questioning Scottish credulity and self-interest in the *Ossian* controversy; Macpherson *was* a nationalist mythmaker as well as an editor and translator, and *Ossian* a modern fantasia on fragments and themes from a much older oral tradition. Yet Johnson's well-publicized skepticism (and in the wake of the *Journey*'s publication, his exchange of insults with Macpherson, ending in physical threats) is also motivated by deeply entrenched prejudices against Scottish culture. For Johnson, *Ossian* is the product of a "Scotch conspiracy in national falsehood," designed to provide a backward, unpopular country with badly needed cultural and literary credentials, and instead providing further evidence of Scottish national dishonesty, the willingness of Scottish intellectuals to perjure themselves for a spurious national cause.[37] The repudiation of Macpherson thus becomes a repudiation of Scottish nationalism itself.

Johnson's *Journey* also investigates and repudiates key aspects of Blackwellian literary history: its postulation of an oral tradition and transmission; its belief in literature as a product of its time and place, of social institutions and geographical conditions; and its belief, therefore, that the "genius" displayed in a great work of national literature is the expression of a collective tradition as much as of an individual mind. Blackwell had taught Macpherson's tutor (perhaps even Macpherson himself) at the University of Aberdeen, and *Ossian* lent support to Blackwell's Homeric theories both in its framing and in its content.[38] So did several other influential literary treatises, from Edward Young's *Conjectures on Original Composition* (1759), with its emphasis on the social preconditions for great art, to Robert Wood's *Essay on the Original Genius and Writings of Homer* (1769), with its emphasis on the geographical situatedness of literature, on the shaping influence of place on literature, and therefore on the continuing touristic interest of literary sites and on their importance for literary-historical reconstruction. As the *Essay* describes, Wood traveled through Greece and Asia Minor to "read the *Iliad* and the *Odyssey* in the country where Ulysses travelled, and where Homer sung," and to understand Homer's epics in living relationship to the country of their birth, by approaching "as near as possible, to the time and place, when and where, he wrote."[39] So too Johnson traveled to Scotland to examine at first hand the culture that had produced *Ossian* (either organically or fraudulently) and to revisit the sites where Macpherson claimed to have collected Ossianic poetry—but in order to refute the postulation of a "bardic institution."[40]

From the mid-eighteenth century onward, nationalist antiquarians in Ireland, Scotland, and Wales had developed a historical model of national literary life which stressed the primacy of national institutions rather than the imagination of individual writers. The Scottish Enlightenment saw itself as living evidence of the shaping influence of favorable institutional conditions on national intellectual life: Scotland's brilliant literati "were not angry or alienated intellectuals, eking out a living as hack writers or translators, satirizing the elite of their society, or dodging the censors and authorities," but professors and other professionals working within the Scottish legal system, the universities, and the Church of Scotland.[41] In London, however, as Johnson anxiously chronicles in *Lives of the Poets* (1779–81), the decline of aristocratic patronage meant that the new, professional men of letters now labored to live by producing salable copy and suffered from the fluctuations of the market.[42]

One "of the first full-dress professional men of letters," Johnson "is both grandly generalizing sage and 'proletarianized' hack."[43] With its enforced, continual productivity in a multiplicity of genres, his career typifies the tenuous livelihood of professional literati in a commercial society. Yet Johnson's philosophical prose style and his elaboration, in *Lives of the Poets*, of a new, biographically based account of authorship (which insists on the links between an author's life experience and his poetic production, and on the power of art to transcend even tragic material circumstances) work to counter the effects of the market. Despite his criticisms of London literary life, Johnson remains uninterested in the alternatives represented by Edinburgh, Glasgow, or Aberdeen or in antiquarian theories of an institutionally produced bardic poetry. Instead, he superimposes his own conditions of work onto Scotland, to criticize the cult of the bard as a deluded, retrojecting fantasy. His attempts to reconstruct the nature of bardic literature emphasize the bard's multiple literary roles as historian, panegyrist, and poet, as evidence not of a literary life before alienation but of undeniable continuities between a literary system ruled by patronage and one ruled by the market; in both cases, the poet works under conditions and in genres not of his choosing, composing under the dictates and pressures of the occasion.

Even when faced with the remnants of a clan society, Johnson searches for signs of a preexisting division of labor. "As the mind must govern the hands," he notes in a passage on the feudal tenanting system of the "tacksmen," or middlemen, that could equally well describe his conception of the intellectual as the mediator of culture, "so in every society the man of intelligence must direct the man of labour" (p. 88).[44] Visiting the Lowlands during its period of greatest cultural vitality, Johnson's melancholy, dismissive accounts of intellectual life there are most telling, perhaps, as an oblique reflection on conditions in London.

Early in the *Journey*, Johnson pauses over a comparison of Scottish and English customs of house ventilation to justify his attention to the details and the texture of daily routine, by arguing for the experience of ordinary people as an index of the country's prosperity. "These diminutive observations seem to take away something from the dignity of writing, and therefore are never communicated but with hesitation, and a little fear of abasement and contempt." Yet much of life is passed "in compliance with necessities, in the performance of daily duties, in the removal of small inconveniencies, in the procurement of petty pleasures"; the "measure of general prosperity" and the "true state of every nation is the state of common life." Throughout the *Journey*, as Johnson describes

the diet, dwellings, footwear, work rhythms, and religious practices of ordinary Scottish people, "in the streets, and the villages, in the shops and
farms" (p. 22), these details are indexical rather than picturesque; what
they measure is the economic viability and cultural coherence of a life
world.

Yet this emphasis on material conditions and on material progress is also
strategic; as the Highland Society argues, Johnson clothes "ordinary sentiments in imperial language."[45] John Wilkes had polemicized against Scottish nationalism (and its rhetorical insistence on the attachment of Scots to
their native land) by pointing to the wave of Scottish opportunists flocking
to London. In a similar spirit, Johnson uses economic emigration from the
Highlands as evidence that Highlanders have no strong adherence to their
native soil. Identity inheres so completely in cultural practices and artifacts, he argues, that a group of compatriots can transport it fully into a new
location; the attachment to a native landscape is incidental. In the meantime, Johnson's analysis of the emigration wave emphasizes not immediate
political and economic pressures but the inherent difficulties of agricultural
subsistence in the Highlands, given its climate, geography, and feudal
landholding traditions. By emphasizing the material determinants of culture, Johnson is able to make a categorical distinction between kinds of
societies, the temporality they inhabit, and the intellectual life they make
possible.

> [W]e were willing to listen to such accounts of past times as would be given us.
> But we soon found what memorials were to be expected from an illiterate
> people, whose whole time is a series of distress; where every morning is
> labouring with expedients for the evening; and where all mental pains or plea-
> sure arose from the dread of winter, the expectation of spring, the caprices of
> their chiefs, and the motions of the neighbouring clans. . . .
>
> The chiefs indeed were exempt from urgent penury, and daily difficulties;
> and in their houses were preserved what accounts remained of past ages. But
> the chiefs were sometimes ignorant and careless, and sometimes kept busy by
> turbulence and contention; and one generation of ignorance effaces the whole
> series of unwritten history. Books are faithful repositories, which may be a
> while neglected or forgotten; but when they are opened again, will again im-
> part their instruction: memory, once interrupted, is not to be recalled. Written
> learning is a fixed luminary, which, after the cloud that had hidden it has past
> away, is again bright in its proper station. Tradition is but a meteor, which, if
> once it falls, cannot be rekindled. (Pp. 110–11)

For centuries the Highland peasantry have lived from day to day, their lives
defined by the practical exigencies of survival. Such a society is incapable
of creating or even conceiving of lasting values. Cultures of the book, in

contrast, are able not only to create records for posterity but also, day to day, to use the act of mental transport involved in reading to transcend its material conditions and inherited intellectual horizons.

Johnson's distinction between literate and illiterate societies depends heavily on Scottish Enlightenment discussions, yet he takes them up so that the Enlightenment vision of society and political implications is utterly transformed. For these theorists, each stage of society, including the pastoral, had its own kinds of poetry; each stage built on the last, inheriting the bases of its own cultural forms from all preceding stages. Johnson's adaptation creates a model of cultural evolution whose stages seem absolute in their dissociation: before writing, and the material conditions that can support literacy, there is no possibility of significant cultural life. Like Young, then, Johnson preempts any sustained account of cultural forms precisely by his attention to the material conditions of daily lives. But whereas Young seems genuinely oblivious to the claims of cultural tradition, Johnson sets aside such claims with great deliberateness and, given his own interest in preserving English religious, literary, and linguistic traditions, what can only be seen as considerable bad faith.

The materialist method could have been used to ground an accretive model of literary and civilizational history. As Jacobin antiquary Joseph Ritson argues in *Pieces of Ancient Popular Poetry* (1791), "enlightened civilisation" is built on humble customs, and the "cultivation or refinement" of modern literature on the compositions of "venerable though nameless bards." Early poetry should therefore be collected and protected with the respect due to "a superannuated domestic, whose past services entitle his old age to comfortable provision and retreat."[46] The classical world created heroic myths and deathless literature. If neoclassicism detached these works from their context, extrapolating and abstracting aesthetic principles from their particularities, a materialist criticism should read classical works into and out of their moments. The result would be at once a liberation from the myth of a golden age and a heightened appreciation for the intellectual and aesthetic breakthroughs these works represent. Just as the great battles of antiquity were fought under circumstances that are not, in themselves, heroic, so too antiquity's great epics are formed and shaped from quite ordinary materials. A truly historical engagement with classical literature might well center on the editorial history—and the original piecemeal nature—of its great epics, thus making visible for the first time how transcendent these works of art actually are, greater than their materials and circumstances seem to make possible.

By these standards, Johnson's critique of *Ossian* does not go far enough. Although he insists on the "edited" quality of Macpherson's poems, he refuses any further recuperative move. Despite his lip service to the dignity of ordinary life, Johnson perceives the material world as debasing, and his denigration of *Ossian* depends on his account of the poverty (and therefore the intellectual impoverishment) of the Highlands. In *Lives of the Poets*, Johnson shows contemporary English poets struggling heroically to transcend the difficulties of their working lives. He uses the case of Scotland, in contrast, to argue that certain material circumstances render aesthetic achievement inconceivable. Yet this thesis is strongly contradicted by the evidence of the ancient epics.

RUINS AND MONUMENTS

"Edifices, either standing or ruined, are the chief records of an illiterate nation" (p. 73). Throughout his *Journey*, Johnson pays particular attention to the ruined buildings of Scotland—monasteries destroyed during the Reformation, ancient buildings that have fallen into decay, fortifications pulled down in the wake of Cromwell's occupation of Scotland—as monuments that stimulate meditation on the course of Scottish history. At the convent cemetery on Iona, he even finds himself relishing the way "reliques of veneration always produce some mournful pleasure. I could have forgiven a great injury more easily than the violation of this imaginary sanctity" (p. 150). Here, the past is particularly poignant, in light of the Islands' present backwardness: "[O]nce the metropolis of learning and piety," Iona now has "no school for education, nor temple for worship, only two inhabitants that can speak English, and not one that can write or read" (p. 152).

When he approaches another Iona cemetery, however, Johnson is noticeably less pious.

> A large space of ground . . . is covered with grave-stones, few of which have any inscription. . . .
>
> Iona has long enjoyed, without any very credible attestation, the honour of being reputed the cemetery of the Scottish Kings. . . . But by whom the subterraneous vaults are peopled is now utterly unknown. . . . [S]ome of them undoubtedly contain the remains of men, who did not expect to be so soon forgotten. (P. 151)

The savage kings who ruled Scotland now lie forgotten in unmarked graves while their country is finally being subdued and anglicized; the tone here is not one of sorrowful awe but of sardonic satisfaction. And the relics of the Scottish Reformation are approached with downright disrespect. In St. Andrews, when Boswell "happened to ask where John Knox was buried Dr. Johnson burst out, 'I hope in the high-way. I have been looking at his reformations'" (B, p. 42). If others see Scotland's current intellectual brilliance as built on Presbyterian foundations, Johnson sees Knox's legacy as literally ruinous.

At Inverness, in contrast, the sight of a ruined Cromwellian fort leads Johnson to extol the Puritan occupation and to condemn Scotland's ingratitude toward its conquerors, past and present. Although no "faction of Scotland" loved or revered the memory of Cromwell,

> [W]hat the Romans did to other nations, was in a great degree done by Cromwell to the Scots; he civilized them by conquests and introduced by useful violence the arts of peace. . . . Till the Union made them acquainted with English manners, the culture of their lands was unskilfull, and their domestick life unformed; their tables were coarse as the feasts of Eskimeaux, and their houses filthy as the cottages of Hottentots. (Pp. 27–28)

The very rudiments of culture were brought to Scotland only in the forced Union with England and by the Cromwellian occupation. "I see a number of people barefooted here," Johnson says to Boswell. "I suppose you all went so before the Union" (B, p. 35).

To its patriots, Scotland's civilizational achievements were impressive not only in themselves but as the transcendence of the handicaps of poverty and isolation innate in Scottish geography. Scottish military bravery had safeguarded the country from a long succession of would-be invaders and preserved a distinct way of life. From this point of view, every military occupation appears as a tragic violation of national sovereignty. Describing the post-'45 military occupation of the Highlands, Smollett's "Tears of Scotland" (1746) rages against the occupiers who reduced once-hospitable houses to "smoaky ruins," transforming them into "monuments of cruelty."[47]

Johnson's account mocks the pieties of this nationalist historiography: only the occasional breaching of national military defenses brought civilization to Scotland in the first place, and even so, its hold on a wild countryside remains partial and tenuous.[48] The Highlands and Islands are locked into barbarism not only by the illiteracy of the population but also by the innately savage character of the Erse language, "the rude speech of a barbarous people," who had few thoughts to express. Because it "never was a written language," anyone who now writes in Erse

> spells according to his own perception of the sound, and his own idea of the power of the letters. The Welsh and the Irish are cultivated tongues . . . while the Earse merely floated in the breath of the people, and could therefore receive little improvement.
>
> When a language begins to teem with books, it is tending to refinement . . . speech becomes embodied and permanent. . . . By degrees one age improves upon another. Exactness is first obtained, and afterwards elegance. But diction,

merely vocal, is always in its childhood. As no man leaves his eloquence behind him, the new generations have all to learn. There may possibly be books
without a polished language, but there can be no polished language without
books. (Pp. 114–15)

Already in the 1755 "Preface" to his *Dictionary of the English Language*," Johnson affirmed the primacy of written, literary language over
the spoken vernacular, announcing his desire to consolidate the proper usage of "a speech copious without order and energetick without rules."[49]
The lexicographer's duty is "to correct or proscribe" the "improprieties
and absurdities" of a language, to impose uniformity on what, in oral
form, "unfixed by any visible signs, is spoken with great diversity."[50]
Only written language can serve as a bulwark of order against "the
boundless chaos of a living speech" and "the corruptions of oral utterance
. . . that which every variation of time or place makes different from
itself."[51]

As Johnson himself admits, the lexicographer's dream that "his dictionary shall embalm his language, and secure it from corruption and decay" is
a delusion. Just as the *Journey* mocks Scottish patriots who take pride in a
history of defensive isolation behind Hadrian's Wall, so the "Preface"
mocks Continental academies of letters

> instituted, to guard the avenues of their languages, to retain fugitives, and
> repulse intruders. . . . [T]heir vigilance and activity have hitherto been vain;
> sounds are too volatile and subtle for legal restraints; to enchain syllables, and
> to lash the wind, are equally the undertakings of pride, unwilling to measure its
> desire by its strengths.[52]

Johnson himself, nonetheless, toys with the idea of a linguistic customs
barrier able to shield the English language from the contaminating
influences of translations, which invidiously introduce foreign idioms and
leave "the fabrick of the tongue" only seemingly intact.[53]

"The chief glory of every people arises from its authours": Johnson's
Dictionary is designed simultaneously to establish a finite body of words,
a standard pronunciation and spelling, as the linguistic identity of the English people and, in using English literature as a source for many defini-
tions, to establish a particular canon of literary works as the literary heritage of the English language.[54] The *Dictionary* deliberately ignores the
work of "illiterate writers," and the "casual and mutable diction" used by
"the laborious and mercantile part of the people," a "fugitive cant" that is
"formed for some temporary or local convenience," is not part of "the dura-
ble materials of a language, and therefore must be suffered to perish with
other things unworthy of preservation."[55]

Yet the necessity for a canon, for the *Dictionary* itself, originates in the way English society divides classes and labor, which results in a linguistic and semiotic flux.

> The language most likely to continue long without alteration, would be that of a nation raised a little, and but a little above barbarity, secluded from strangers, and totally employed in procuring the conveniencies of life; either without books, or . . . with very few: men thus busied and unlearned, having only such words as common use requires, would perhaps long continue to express the same notions by the same signs. But no such constancy can be expected in a people polished by arts, and classed by subordination, where one part of the community is sustained and accommodated by the labour of the other.[56]

When Johnson visits the Highlands and Islands, twenty years later, he ought, at last, to find those circumstances most likely to produce linguistic stability. Instead, he finds the opposite tendency at work, as post-'45 historical, economic, and political pressures destroy linguistic as well as cultural traditions.

> There was perhaps never any change of national manners so quick, so great, and so general, as that which has operated in the Highlands, by the last conquest, and the subsequent laws. We came thither too late to see what we expected, a people of peculiar appearance, and a system of antiquated life. The clans retain little now of their original character, their ferocity of temper is softened, their military ardour is extinguished, their dignity of independence is depressed, their contempt of government subdued, and their reverence for their chiefs abated. Of what they had before the late conquest of their country, there remain only their language and their poverty. Their language is attacked on every side. Schools are erected, in which English only is taught, and there were lately some who thought to refuse them a version of the holy scriptures, that they might have no monument of their mother-tongue.
>
> That their poverty is gradually abated, cannot be mentioned among the unpleasing consequences of subjection. They are now acquainted with money, and the possibility of gain will by degrees make them industrious. Such is the effect of the late regulations, that a longer journey than to the Highlands must be taken by him whose curiosity pants for savage virtues and barbarous grandeur. (Pp. 57–58)

The only way out is to move forward; the improvement of the region depends not only on the disappearance of regressive cultural practices but on the improvement and standardization of Erse itself, to make possible a literate Highlands. "After all that has been done for the instruction of the Highlanders, the antipathy between their language and literature still continues; and no man that has learned only Earse is, at this time, able to read" (p. 116).

Given Johnson's own antipathy toward Erse, as a language "merely floating in the breath of the people," why does he oppose the plans of the Society for the Propagation of Christian Knowledge to anglicize (and Anglicanize) the Highlands by providing educational and religious materials solely in English?[57] Because English cannot serve the region's urgent religious and political needs with necessary speed, and because in the absence of a standard translation of the Bible, Erse is unable to serve even as a standard written administrative language. In several parts of the Hebrides, Johnson meets ministers who attempted to render the Gospel into the local idiom, only to find their translations incomprehensible to the inhabitants of neighboring islands. This confirms the necessity of scriptural "monuments" such as biblical translations and national dictionaries, to establish a new unifying national written vernacular.

Similar thinking informed the Scots revival under way in the Lowlands at the time of Johnson's visit. Yet as its key figures insist, *their* philosophy of language reflects a populist nationalism; Johnson's is statist and elitist, for he fails to grasp that a language is collectively produced and collectively used, the most important shared property of the national community. His profound insensitivity to the cultural performance of language leads him to disparage the verbal vernacular (language at its most spontaneous and expressive) in favor of a static linguistic and literary canon.

Already in the 1750s, Johnson's *Dictionary* had come under sharp criticism in Scotland for its definition of oats—"A grain which in England is generally given to horses, but in Scotland supports the people." Lord Elibank's much-cited rebuttal—"But what men, and what horses!"—attacked Johnson's heartless attempt to reduce Scotland to its poverty, its people to brutes.[58] Johnson's flippant comparison between the English and the Scottish diet betrayed a complete lack of cultural (and agricultural) relativism; national diet has an organic relationship to national climate, yet Johnson treated Scotland's most abundant grain as an inherently debased food.

When Johnson visited St. Andrews in 1773 and the university's professors hosted a banquet in his honor, Robert Fergusson wrote two occasional poems to commemorate the occasion in all its ironies. In both poems—one written in a ponderous, Latinate, mock-Johnsonian English, the other in an emphatically profane Scots vernacular—Johnson's old definition of *oats* is turned against him (as he is shown greedily shoveling in the banquet of Scottish delicacies) and used to indict his lexicography as an imperial philosophy of language. "To Dr. Samuel Johnson: Food for a New Edition of His Dictionary" apostrophizes Johnson as a "verbal potentate and prince" whose inflated language separates words completely from the objects and situations they were originally coined to describe, and whose arrival in

Scotland, appropriately enough, catalyzes a flurry of written record keeping and memorialization.[59]

> Great Pedagogue! whose literarian lore,
> With syllable on syllable conjoined.
> To transmutate and varify, hast learned
> The whole revolving scientific names
> That in the alphabetic columns lie,
> Far from the knowledge of mortalic shapes;
> As we, who never can peroculate
> The miracles by thee miraculized,
> The Muse, silential long, with mouth apert
> Would give vibration to stagnatic tongue,
> And loud encomiate thy puissant name. . .
>
> . . . .
>
> Welcome, thou verbal potentate and prince!
> To hills and valleys, where emerging oats
> From earth assuage our pauperty to bay,
> And bless thy name, thy dictionarian skill. . . .[60]

Fergusson's diction mocks Johnson's linguistic circumlocutions as a neurotic avoidance of the physicality of language and of everyday life. Self-immured in literary language, Johnson is incapable of comprehending the material bases of Scottish culture. Because he is unwilling to immerse himself in the material conditions of Scottish life—to ingest oatmeal and swill whiskey, to trade his London breeches for "the kilt aërian" and sleep outdoors on the chilly heath—he will return to London as he came, unable to understand the forces that created clan loyalties or Highland rebellion, how "naked hinds, / On lentiles fed, could make your kingdom quake, / And tremulate Old England libertized."[61]

Fergusson frames his own fantasies of Johnson's cultural immersion and conversion as communion scenes, in which the glass of whiskey, or the "lignarian chalice, swelled with oats," is held up to Johnson's "orifice."[62] At the beginning of the poem, Fergusson invoked a long-silenced Muse, whose "stagnatic tongue" is awakened to "give vibration . . . and loud encomiate" the mighty name of Johnson. By the poem's end, Fergusson has imagined (and discarded) the possibility of Pentecost, an occupation, liberation, and transformation of the mouth to inaugurate a new mode of orality; Johnson's own mouth would cease to function as a tomb of living language, as a cavern without echo, and the *Dictionary*, in a new, revised edition, would cease its pallid jokes about the Scottish diet and give readers more substantial mental nourishment.

"Lines, to the Principal and Professors of the University of St. Andrews, on their Superb Treat to Dr. Johnson" uses the earthy vernacular of Scots to proclaim the comparative health of Scottish life—and thus to mock the professors of St. Andrews for their cultural cringing and overabundant hospitality.

> But hear, my lads! gin I'd been there,
> How I'd hae trimm'd the bill o' fare!
> For ne'er sic surly wight as he
> Had met wi' sic respect frae me.
> Mind ye what Sam, the lying loun!
> Has in his Dictionar set down?
> That aits, in England, are a feast
> To cow and horse, and sicken beast;
> While, in Scots ground, this growth was common
> To gust the gab o' man and woman.[63]

When Fergusson describes the true Scottish bill of fare, his enumeration of Scottish gastronomic pleasures becomes a celebration of the feast offered by Scots, with its biting vowels and throat-filling locutions. If Johnson's gibes about the paucity of the Scottish diet, as an index of Scotland's material and intellectual paucity, are belied by the heartiness of the feast in his honor, so too his gibes about the intellectual paucity and ungainliness of Scots are belied by this poem in his honor, by the robustness of Scots vocabulary and pronunciation.

Floating in the Breath of the People

One way of defending Johnson against such "vernacular" critique would be to argue that Fergusson holds him to an inappropriate historical standard. Johnson's *Dictionary* was published in the 1750s; by 1773, new theories of language had begun to change the emphasis of linguistic investigation. Rousseau's still unpublished and Herder's recently published work on the origin of language, for example, call attention to many new issues: to speech as the central mode of linguistic expression, to the central importance of language in differentiating human from animal existence, to the epistemological questions raised by individual language acquisition, to the historiographical questions raised by the continual evolution of languages, and to the political importance of a shared language in defining national identity.[64] In light of such discussions, Johnson's continuing adherence to a script-based model of language appears increasingly anachronistic. But it also represents a deliberate refusal of the new mode of investigation. Continental linguistic theory and British literary practice increasingly derive their political, intellectual, and aesthetic mandates from a new vision of a communal national language as the living breath of the people; Johnson insistently upholds the hierarchical separation between a written language that facilitates the retention and accretion of human thought and a spoken language that merely "floats in the breath of the people," at once transient and shallow, volatile and stagnant.[65]

For Johnson, the absence of writing fundamentally limits the mental capacity and historical consciousness of traditional societies, for oral tradition is unable to transmit either complex ideas or great verbal art. "In an unwritten speech, nothing that is not very short is transmitted from one generation to another. Few have opportunities of hearing a long composition often enough to learn it; and what is once forgotten is lost for ever" (p. 116). During the final, Hebridean phase of the Scottish journey, Johnson's prolonged examination of the claims for and against Macpherson's *Ossian* not only defines the limits of oral transmission but relocates the problems of historical progress, historical change, and uneven development within language use. Suspicious of the retentive capacities of even educated minds, Johnson experiments with the limits of his own visual memory and scoffs at the notion of oral memory. At the same time, in a characteristic turnaround, he is willing to entertain the notion that second sight may actually exist in the Highlands as a local "faculty of seeing things out of sight" (p. 109), the product not of traditional belief systems so much as an anomalous physical force field. But if Highland peasants are able to glimpse the future, they can have little notion of the past; any society that lacks written records is doomed to an extremely short collective memory— "what is once out of sight is lost for ever" (p. 65)—and to a cultural identity defined by ceremonies and pageants, by the sites and edifices of everyday life. The "present race" remember "their primitive customs and ancient manner of life" only "very faintly and uncertainly" (p. 112).

Robert Wood argues that Homer was illiterate and relied "on the fidelity of oral tradition and the power of memory."

> In like manner the historians of Ireland have collected their materials from the lays of their Bards, and Fileas; whose accounts have been merely traditional. But the oral traditions of a learned and enlightened age will greatly mislead us if from them we form our judgement on those of a period, when history had no other resource . . . nor can we, in this age of Dictionaries, and other technical aids to memory, judge, what her use and powers were, at a time, when all a man could know, was all he could remember. To which we may add, that, in a rude and unlettered state of society the memory is loaded with nothing that is either useless or unintelligible.[66]

Johnson, in contrast, sees memory as a human constant rather than a historical and cultural variable, and literacy as an absolute epistemological divide. In the Highlands the "nation was wholly illiterate. Neither bards nor *senachies* could write or read. . . . [T]he bard was a barbarian among barbarians, who, knowing nothing himself, lived with others that knew no more" (pp. 112–16). Although Johnson and Boswell hear tales of "manuscripts that were, or that had been in the hands of somebody's father or grandfather," they find no evidence that such manuscripts are indigenous, "other than Irish" (p. 118). As for the poems of Ossian,

> I believe they never existed in any other form than that which we have seen. The editor, or author, never could shew the original. . . . He has doubtless inserted names that circulate in popular stories, and may have translated some wandering ballads, if any can be found; and the names, and some of the images being recollected, make an inaccurate auditor imagine, by the help of Caledonian bigotry, that he has formerly heard the whole. . . .
>
> It is said, that some men of integrity profess to have heard parts of it, but they all heard them when they were boys; and it was never said that any of them could recite six lines. They remember names, and perhaps some proverbial sentiments; and having no distinct ideas, coin a resemblance without an original. . . . If we know little of the ancient Highlanders, let us not fill the vacuity with Ossian. (Pp. 118–19)

Scotland's much-vaunted oral heritage, then, is an unwitting hoax, perpetuated by well-meaning patriot antiquarians.[67] And the very notion of oral tradition is so speculative that Macpherson's biggest tactical error, according to Johnson, was to claim a manuscript at all: "If he had not talked unskilfully of *manuscripts*, he might have fought with oral tradition much longer."[68]

For all his skepticism about oral performance, Johnson is unwittingly impressed when some of Macpherson's supporters sing Erse songs during a stormy boat ride off the coast of Skye. Once back on dry land, however, Johnson puts several local guarantors of *Ossian*'s authenticity under relentless cross-examination, attempting to show them as partisan and unreliable, their notions of oral transmission as vague and unconvincing. When Mr. McQueen *does* prove able to repeat passages of *Fingal* in the original Erse, Johnson simply dismisses this evidence in Macpherson's favor, arguing that Macpherson has merely taken Highland "names, and stories, and . . . passages in old songs" and "compounded" them with his own compositions (B, p. 206). He overrides Mr. McQueen's protest that Homer, too, "was made up of detached fragments" (B, p. 129), by insisting on the organic composition of the Greek epics.[69]

To many Scottish critics of the *Journey*, Johnson's style of cross-examination appears designed to block, rather than to elicit, new information or ideas. Johnson, however, complains to Boswell that "he could get no distinct information about anything, from any of the people" (B, p. 117).

According to some informants, Highland history was traditionally handed down by a succession of oral chroniclers; there was a lineage of native historians, just as there was a "race" of bards. Others, however, draw no distinction between the offices of poet and chronicler. Such contradictory responses merely confirm Johnson's suspicions about the unreliability of oral tradition. Yet his parallel inquiries about the division of labor in clan society meets with similarly contradictory responses: some say that each man makes his own brogues, others that a single shoemaker makes brogues for all.

Unused to strangers, the Highlanders are "not much accustomed to be interrogated by others and seem never to have thought of interrogating themselves; so that if they do not know what they tell to be true, they likewise do not distinctly perceive it to be false" (p. 117). The problem, then, is due at once to the difficulties of translation and cross-cultural communication, to the moral inadequacies of illiterate intellects, and to the narrative inadequacies of oral culture.

> The Highlander gives to every question an answer so prompt and peremptory, that skepticism itself is dared into silence ... but, if a second question be ventured, it breaks the enchantment; for it is immediately discovered, that what was told so confidently was told at hazard, and that such fearlessness of assertation was either the sport of negligence, or the refuge of ignorance.
>
> If individuals are thus at variance with themselves, it can be no wonder that the accounts of different men are contradictory. The traditions of an ignorant and savage people have been for ages negligently heard, and unskilfully related. Distant events must have been mingled together, and the actions of one man given to another. . . . [S]uch is the laxity of Highland conversation, that the inquirer is kept in continual suspense, and by a kind of intellectual retrogradation, knows less as he hears more. (P. 51)

Johnson's own wish to reach a "settled notion," a single prognosis about the Highlands, and thus to reach a position of moral certainty, is undermined repeatedly by the complicated tensions that characterize his encounters with his informants, from Enlightenment luminaries and gentleman improvers to Highland peasants. Although Johnson seems oblivious to it, the dynamic of his informants' responses constitutes an object of study in its own right. Sometimes it seems that his informants are trying to end his "interrogations" by telling him whatever he wants to hear, or that—like Edgeworth's Lady Geraldine, forty years later, feeding Lord Craiglethorpe false information about Ireland to punish the presumption of his survey, or like James Joyce's Buck Mulligan, a hundred years later still, baiting Haines, the English folklorist—they take a patriotic delight in confusing him. Johnson seems oblivious to such possibilities.[70] His brooding on

incompatible and contradictory pieces of information, his repeated attempts to sift the data collected, allow him to ignore the problems of cross-
cultural communication and the limits of his investigative method.

In *The Tourifications of Malachi Meldrum* (1803), Robert Couper satirizes Johnson and Young by sending out his naive narrator to re-create both
of their journeys at once. After spending "many a weary winter night" pe-
rusing Young and "the elaborate pages of the renowned Dr. Adam Smith,"
Malachi Meldrum resolves (as chapter 5 announces in pompous, pseudo-
Johnsonian diction) to "ENTER UPON DUTY AS A TOURIFICATOR AND SCIEN-
TIFICALLY PERAMBULATE THE VILLAGES." The first site of "tourification"
is the town where he has spent "almost every week of my life, and had been
again and again in almost every hold and bore on it; yet in a scientific point
of view I found I knew nothing about it."[71] Now he sallies forth,

> [A]nd wherever the sound of the hammer, or the treddles, or even the whistling
> of a taylor was to be heard, thither I bent my steps. The blacksmith . . . first
> attracted my attention; and I entered the smithy with a countenance formed, as
> well as I could, both to conciliate respect, and to inspire confidence. The black-
> smith . . . satisfied me as to the angle a hobnail ought to be pointed to; and he
> was loud and long on the general abuse and cruelty of fitting the horse's foot
> to the shoe. . . . In recompense for this and a great deal more, I gave him a
> chemical dissertation upon iron, and the easiest and cheapest modes of excit-
> ing heat; and I shewed him how his forge . . . might be Rumfordized to the
> greatest possible advantage. (1:108–10)

Next, he attempts conversation with a weaver, who is "thumping away at
his loom," reading Paine's *Age of Reason*, and "silently unsaying all that
his pious father and mother had taught him" (1:110). When Meldrum addresses him on "the beautiful and immense labours" of his craft, and of the
technological improvement promised by the power loom, he receives in
return only blasting political disquisitions on the current oppressions of
"Aristocratical statutes and edicts" and on the struggle for "civil liberty,"
along with dire predictions that if power weaving ever takes hold, "the
whole race of weavers would be starved, nay extirpated" (1:110–12). Upset
by the weaver's prophetic anger and "profane swearing," Meldrum takes
his departure. His final, reassuring encounter is with a tailor, sitting in the
sun on his shopboard, "chanting an old Scots song, his work seemingly
going on all the better for it" (1:113), at peace with the world.

What we witness here, in the interrogation first of the smith and then of
the weaver, is the passage from a Youngian utilitarianism to a Johnsonian
philosophizing, and an implicit dissection of both modes of investigation.[72]
As we learn from Meldrum's autodidactic preparations for his tourifications, the very attempt to set aside a habitual set of responses to place, to
become a truly scientific investigator, involves acute self-alienation from

the rhythms and relations of everyday life. Meldrum's labored reading of Smith, theorist of the division of labor, has an unwitting appropriateness: the weariness his oeuvre induces in its reader indicts self-improvement as alienated labor. The long-term result of this self-education is that the scientific interrogator becomes a more inept observer than before; his hard-won distance from ordinary life makes it impossible for him to assess it accurately.

Despite Meldrum's self-conscious efforts to establish just the right tone of respectful curiosity, his conversations with both smith and weaver fail completely as exchanges of information. In each case, the investigator's efforts to "bestow knowledge and information where it seemed to be lacking" (1:108) fall utterly flat, because he lacks any inside knowledge of what he advises on and because he is incapable of listening in return. He overwhelms the smith with a disquisition so technical that it bestows no benefit whatsoever. Yet where he achieves a more dynamic reaction, as his platitudinous vision of industrial progress is rejected and dissected by the radical weaver, Meldrum is so unnerved that he is unwilling to converse further. Materialist analysis founders because of its failure to assimilate unsettling information; if the enlightened traveler takes to the road to learn from local informants and assess local conditions for himself, in practice the instruction is all in one direction; the traveler is happiest when his interlocutors give him no information at all.

My Arithmetick Left in Scotland

Sometimes translation fails Johnson visibly in its work of mediating Scottish life. When he watches field workers singing at their work, the apparent untranslatability of what they sing leads him to a reading of the song as pure rhythm and to a cross-cultural and transhistorical free association between their labors and those of Roman galley slaves (unintentionally telling, since many Highlanders perceive themselves under a hated English imperial yoke). During a society evening in Raasay, in contrast, when the ladies sing songs in Erse, the genteel company elevates native music out of its workaday environs. In the field Johnson hears only utilitarian rhythms; here he hears pure voice, emotions that seem to transcend class barriers and almost transcend linguistic barriers as well.

> I listened as an English audience to an Italian opera, delighted with the sound of words which I did not understand.
>
> I inquired of the subject of the songs, and was told of one, that it was a love song, and of another, that it was a farewell composed by one of the Islanders that was going, in this epidemical fury of emigration, to seek his fortune in America. What sentiments would rise, on such an occasion, in the heart of one

who had not been taught to lament by precedent, I should gladly have known;
but the lady, by whom I sat, thought herself not equal to the work of translating. (P. 39)

Able suddenly to appreciate the Erse language as music, Johnson is also—
because this is a moment when linguistic translation fails—able to appreciate the emotional alienation of the Highland peasants, taught to read "only
English, so that the natives read a language which they may never use or
understand" (p. 103).[73] Yet such empathy leads him not to affirm nationalist claims but to anticipate a moment, evoked in the *Journey*'s closing passages, when there will be no difference left: translation will no longer be
needed, because the Scots will be (or be as) Englishmen; they will speak
with the "propriety of English pronunciation" (pp. 36–37); and the most
disadvantaged will interact as free men, the last impediments to cultural
understanding and ideal speech acts removed forever.

> The conversation of the Scots grows every day less unpleasing to the En-
> glish; their peculiarities wear fast away; their dialect is likely to become in half
> a century provincial and rustick, even to themselves. The great, the learned, the
> ambitious, and the vain, all cultivate the English phrase, and the English pro-
> nunciation, and in splendid companies Scotch is not much heard, except now
> and then from an old lady.
>
> There is one subject of philosophical curiosity to be found in Edinburgh,
> which no other city has to shew . . . a college of the deaf and dumb, who are
> taught to speak, to write, and to practice arithmetick . . . the improvement of
> Mr. Braidwood's pupils is wonderful. . . .
>
> It will readily be supposed by those that consider this subject, that Mr.
> Braidwood's scholars spell accurately. Orthography is vitiated among such as
> learn first to speak, and then to write, by imperfect notions of the relation
> between letters and vocal utterance; but to those students every character is of
> equal importance; for letters are to them not symbols of names, but of things;
> when they write they do not represent a sound, but delineate a form.
>
> One of the young ladies had her slate before her, on which I wrote a question
> consisting of three figures, to be multiplied by two figures. She looked upon it,
> and quivering her fingers in a manner which I thought very pretty . . . multi-
> plied the sum . . . observing the decimal place. . . .
>
> It was pleasing to see one of the most desperate of human calamities capable
> of so much help: whatever enlarges hope, will exalt courage; after having seen
> the deaf taught arithmetick, who would be afraid to cultivate the Hebrides?
>
> Such are the things which this journey has given me an opportunity of see-
> ing, and such are the reflections which that sight has raised. (Pp. 162–64)

Johnson envisions Scotland as a deaf-and-dumb school whose scholars,
"delighted with the hope of new ideas" (p. 162), move from the backward-

ness of Erse to the cosmopolitanism of English, their seemingly insurmountable handicaps proving "capable of so much help" from a teacher who is patient and wise.[74] Through a special kind of literacy, the eyes can be trained to serve as ears; writing and other sign languages can completely take the place of speech.[75] The circumvention of the mouth (with its problems of pronunciation) and the elimination of a vitiating oral transmission even lead to more accurate communication.[76]

"Arithmetick," it would seem, takes a special place in this linguistic utopia.[77] The capitalist economy being introduced into Scotland is based on the ability to do sums, to hold the decimal place; money unites all levels of the system, holding together the activities of brogue manufacturer, the entrepreneur, and the laborer. It levels by abstraction: "Money confounds subordination, by overpowering the distinctions of rank and birth, and weakens authority by supplying power of resistance, or expedients for escape" (p. 113). Like Scotland's new military roads, money will bind the disparate corners of the Western Islands (in which there is now "so little internal commerce, that hardly any thing has a known or settled rate" and "no appeal can be made to a common measurement" [p. 147]) into a single economic circuit. Across the Highlands and Islands, Johnson notes the lack not only of a standard written language but also of a standard currency and of a standard of measurement, vital impediments to the country's reformation.[78] Numbers themselves, he seems to argue, will form a kind of universal language, whose primarily written form allows it to be understood across cultural and linguistic barriers. Best of all, the teaching of arithmetic does not involve the forced suppression of a native language. Instead, it bestows bilingualism on the handicapped.

To learn the language of numbers is to enter the republic of letters as an apprentice to rationality, to leave behind differences of rank, class, and even gender, as an apparently insignificant episode, earlier in the *Journey*, makes clear in retrospect. In Anoch, a three-hut Highland village, Johnson offends his host by his visible surprise that the man owns a shelf of books and that his English (learned "by grammar") is spoken with "propriety" (p. 36). The daughter of the house was educated for a year at Inverness in reading and writing, as well as "the common female qualifications" of sewing, lace making, and pastry baking; "not inelegant either in mien or dress," she even prepares an English afternoon tea for the travelers. Like her father, Johnson notes with pleasure, she speaks "the English pronunciation. I presented her with a book which I happened to have about me, and should not be pleased to think that she forgets me" (p. 37).

The gesture excites "much inquiry" from the *Journey*'s readers—particularly from ladies who, "wishing to learn the kind of reading which the great and good Dr. Johnson esteemed most fit for a young woman, desired to know what book he had selected for this Highland nymph." Boswell's

Journal provides a comically disappointing disclosure, but Johnson as usual has the last word.

> The book has given rise to much inquiry, which has ended in ludicrous surprise. . . . My readers, prepare your features for merriment. It was Cocker's *Arithmetic*! Wherever this was mentioned, there was a loud laugh, at which Dr. Johnson, when present, used sometimes to be a little angry. . . . "Why, sir, if you are to have but one book with you upon a journey, let it be a book of science. When you have read through a book of entertainment, you know it, and it can do no more for you; but a book of science is inexhaustible." (B, p. 105)

Like the culminating deaf-and-dumb-school tableau, this episode sees mathematics as highly appropriate for the education of women, as an intellectual training to be added to domestic skills. The flip side of Johnson's insensitivity to ethnic difference is a genuinely enlightened refusal of—or at least a momentary obliviousness to—cultural codes of gender difference. Where Boswell describes the girl as a "Highland nymph," Johnson's gift recognizes her as an autonomous intellect who might well be able and eager to teach herself mathematics; the gesture reenvisions a tutorial relationship free of the power imbalances and gender struggles that proved the downfall of Jean-Jacques Rousseau's *Nouvelle Heloïse* (1761) and Jakob Michael Reinhold Lenz's *Hofmeister* (The tutor) (1774).

SAVAGE NOTIONS AND SECOND SIGHT

"My arithmetick left in Scotland": the memorial that Johnson sets himself to commemorate his journey differs in kind both from the national memorials he disparages throughout Scotland and from the Erse Bible he wishes to set in their place. The carrier of an Enlightenment faith in education, a book so abstract and utilitarian that it transcends any particular political ideology, the arithmetic apparently offers no difficulties of translation, no dilemmas of commemoration, no mandate for forced conversion. If we examine more closely the borrowed terms with which Johnson frames his final scene of mathematical enlightenment, however, his utopian faith in education begins to seem troubling again. Braidwood's school is an Enlightenment institution, and throughout the scene there, Johnson resolutely occupies the epistemological ground of the philosophes. Yet as everywhere in the *Journey*, he addresses classical Enlightenment problems and deploys Enlightenment theories, only to divert their political implications.

Both in Scotland and in France, the Enlightenment had long been interested in the cognitive consequences of deafness and blindness, in the mind's attempts to compensate for deficiencies of perception through a sharpening of other faculties. Denis Diderot's *Lettre sur les Aveugles*

(1749) points to numerous blind men who develop compensatory sensory powers. One blind contemporary shows a surprising memory for sounds, while for Nicholas Saunderson (1682–1739), mathematical theorist and author of *Elements of Algebra*, blindness apparently heightened, rather than decreased, an ability for abstract, especially mathematical, thinking.[79] Literary historians had long noted a similar virtuosity among blind poets: eighteenth-century postulations of oral tradition were often linked to the prodigious feats of bardic memory expected from blind poets such as Homer and Ossian. "He seemed by nature formed for his profession," writes Oliver Goldsmith in 1760 of "the last Irish bard," early-eighteenth-century poet-harpist Carolan, "for as he was born blind, so also he was possessed of a most astonishing memory."[80] Oral tradition was thus imagined as a kind of blind memory, functioning independently of the eyes.

In the popular imagination, the link between blindness and memory, physical handicap and sensory or mental compensation, appeared innate. Enlightenment philosophers, however, emphasized the development of compensatory skills, intriguing precisely as a provisional, improvised response to sensory deprivation. Physical impediments to perception, Hume argues in *An Inquiry Concerning Human Understanding* (1748), limit the cognitive abilities of the mind only provisionally. "A blind man can form no notion of colors, a deaf man of sounds. Restore either of them that sense in which he is deficient by opening this new inlet for his sensations, you also open an inlet for the ideas, and he finds no difficulty in conceiving these objects."[81] Their handicaps, in other words, may well exclude the blind and the deaf from linguistic or intellectual development. But in their underlying capacity for ratiocination, self-expression, or memory, they show no innate difference from the sighted or the hearing.[82]

The Enlightenment belief in their intellectual potential permanently altered the fate of the disabled, increasing both their social acceptance and their access to education. At the same time (and as always), the Enlightenment emphasis on equality and fundamental human commonalties is linked to an educational project that demands assimilation. If in the last sentences of his *Journey* Johnson draws a sudden analogy between the program of Braidwood's school and Enlightenment programs of improvement and anglicization, he is merely making explicit a parallelism implicit in Enlightenment thought.[83]

Johnson's turn from the epistemological to the geopolitical is overdetermined; the little fable of Braidwood's school braids together two distinct intellectual traditions, intertwining Enlightenment epistemological investigations with an English tradition of national and imperial allegory which takes shape in the early works of Daniel Defoe. During the early years of the eighteenth century, Defoe played a crucial part, as pamphleteer and government agent, in promoting the Union of Scotland with England. His pamphlets helped to establish both an iconographic repertoire for representing the new British state and an English discourse on the need for Scottish improvement. "When a Stranger comes into *Scotland*," Defoe writes in *Caledonia* (1706),

> Fill'd with thoße formidable Ideas which the Enemies of the Nation ignorantly and maliciously have form'd in him, he is confounded and asham'd of himself, the cultivated Lands, the Noble Harbours, the numerous Villages, the Seats of the Nobility and Gentry, and the Plenty of things all perfect Surprizes, and he is apt to enquire whether this be *Scotland* or no. . . .
>
> [W]hen I see the Politeness of the Scholars, the Courtesie of the Gentlemen, the Beauty of the Ladies, and at last the Grandeur of Your Grace's Court, the Illustrious Nobility, and all the Oeconomy of State and Government, Amaz'd at these Things . . . I go all along a Supposition of Improvment. . . . Why is she [Scotland] not Rich, Plentiful, and Fruitful? . . . 'tis in Your Power to put a new Countenance on the dejected Countrey Men, a new Prospect in the melancholy Surface, a new Treasure in the General Stock, and a new Face on the Whole Nation. . . . With or without a Union the Lands may be improved, the Tenants incouraged, the Fields inclosed, Woods planted, the Moors and Wastes fed, and *Scotland* recovered from languishing Poverty. With or without a Union, the Nobility and Gentry may plant, manure and enrich their Estates.[84]

Seventy years before Young or Johnson (and far more diplomatically than either), Defoe softens the prospect of Union by flattering Scotland on her cultivated airs, only to proffer hardheaded advice about clearances and the improvement of the country's "melancholy Surface."

A decade after the Union, Defoe is still writing for and about Scotland, but now, alongside his "improving" po-Union political pamphlets, working with a very different kind of Scottish material. In "The Highland Visions, or The Scots New Prophecy" (1712) and "The Second-Sighted Highlander, Being Four Visions of the Eclipse" (1713), he claims to deploy Highland powers of second sight, "an unconfin'd, celestial Ray of Light, empowering Nature . . . to discern of things to come," to predict Europe's political future.[85] And in works such as *The Dumb Philosopher, or Great Britain's Wonder* (1719), he begins a series of biographical studies of clairvoyants, many of whom claim the power of second sight as a compensation for handicaps of dumbness or deafness.

The economic deprivations and political future of Scotland, the Highland phenomenon of second sight, extrasensory compensations for physical handicaps: these preoccupations all come together in *The History of the Life and Adventures of Duncan Campbell* (1720), a book-length biography (traditionally attributed to Defoe, although the attribution is now in question) of a Highland clairvoyant who created a London sensation.[86] Unlike other contemporaneous accounts of Campbell's life, this biography gives a detailed account of his cultural and historical context, suggesting that second sight functions as a cultural compensation for endemic poverty and political persecution. As *Duncan Campbell* makes clear, early-eighteenth-century controversies over Highland claims to second sight and the possibility of culturally specific perception anticipate the vituperative controversy, at the end of the century, over Highland claims to oral tradition and the future of cultural specificity.

In this account, Duncan Campbell's gift of second sight is peculiarly bound up with his physical handicaps, with the cultural geography of the Highlands and Islands, and with the political history of Scotland. A descendant of the house of Argyll, Campbell's grandfather was driven by "some civil broils and troubles in Scotland" to take refuge on Shetland.[87] And Campbell's father, Archibald, spends years in Lapland, which reminds him of the islands not least because its inhabitants also claim second sight.[88] To its Swedish occupiers, however, Lapland is also "a nation so barbarous in its manners, and so corrupt in its principles" (p. 12), that they must legislate against local superstitions and clairvoyant powers. Archibald Campbell converts his Lap wife to Christianity, but she passes on to Duncan her powers of second sight.

After her death, the Campbells move back to the Shetlands. "Half a Highlander, half a Laplander," young Duncan delights in wearing a bonnet and plaid, that "antique and heroic" (p. 35) dress of the Highlands. But as Archibald eventually realizes, his son has been born deaf and dumb and will never regain the capacity either to hear or to speak. Luckily, a local clergyman masters a new sign language method, with the "charitable" object of teaching "the deaf and dumb to read and to write" (p. 19). Because sounds are "but token and signs to the ear" (p. 22), Duncan has little difficulty learning language through physical signs, and "in little more than two years, he could write and read as well as anybody" (p. 21). When the deaf-and-dumb learn to communicate, here as in the *Journey*, it recapitulates the civilizing and Christianization of whole "barbarous" nations. The clergyman who supervises Duncan Campbell's acquisition of literacy and who induces him to "leave off" the "savage motions" (p. 21) of his own improvised sign language thus reiterates Archibald Campbell's religious education, in Lapland, of Duncan's mother.

Duncan's clairvoyance is presented with similar suggestiveness: in Lapland the Swedish occupiers had attempted to civilize their subjects by outlawing second sight, yet this prohibition, as we saw in the case of Duncan's mother, could not suppress indigenous beliefs and powers. In Scotland we discover Duncan's clairvoyant powers at an unexpected juncture, immediately after the political upheavals that rob Archibald Campbell of his fortune and finally his life. Long ago, in Lapland, Archibald's wife predicted that her unborn son would become "one of the most remarkable men in England and Scotland for his power of foresight" but that Archibald would "meet with difficulties in [his] own country in the same manner as [his] father . . . and on the same account, viz., of civil broils and intestine wars in Scotland" (p. 14). In 1685, when the earl of Argyll and the duke of Monmouth rise up against King James II, clan loyalties draw Archibald Campbell into the struggle, against his better judgment; when their rebellion fails and Argyll is beheaded, Campbell, outlawed, exiled, and ruined like many of his clansmen, dies of a broken heart. "He perfectly pined away and wasted; he was six months dying inch by inch, and the difference between his last breath and his way of breathing during that time, was only that he expired with a greater sigh than he ordinarily fetched every time when he drew his breath" (p. 38). Left orphaned, Duncan discovers his powers of second sight.

Written only five years after the '15, *Duncan Campbell* seems preoccupied with the way clairvoyant powers function both as a resistance against imperial occupation and as a compensation for the handicaps and disfranchisements of history.[89] Sighing himself to death, Archibald Campbell might be said to mark, however preemptively, the death of Highland (oral) culture. Yet his speechless son is able to recover traditional Highland powers and even, anomalously, to remove them from their indigenous setting, to take them with him to London. *Duncan Campbell* functions as a historical and political parable, whose sympathies with Scottish particularity, with the exigencies of clan loyalty, and with the fate of the outlawed Scottish rebels counteract the discourses of improvement and assimilation that dominated Defoe's earlier propagandistic writings on behalf of the Union.

In the *Journey*, in contrast, the parable of Braidwood's school and the compensations of literacy drive home Johnson's long-standing advocacy of improvement and assimilation. The real imperialism of the *Journey*, arguably, lies in its insistent appropriation, occupation, and emptying out of both Enlightenment and nationalist positions. Positioning himself between a philosophical tradition that stresses both human equality and cultural relativism and a literary tradition that stresses the suffering singularity of Scotland, Johnson attempts to undo their work of cultural differentiation, to insist on human communality at the price of cultural tradition.

Literary Landscapes

If Young's *Tour* enjoyed a complicated novelistic posterity, Johnson's *Journey* and the Ossian debate had an even more profound effect on the development of the novel, shaping both content and form. A long series of novels rebut Johnson directly. Owenson's *O'Donnel: A national tale* (1814) devotes ten pages to a sustained demolition of his literary and political judgments, and Susan Ferrier's *Destiny, or The Chieftain's Daughter* (1831) opens with a sarcastic refutation of his pronouncements about the

Highlands. In Thackeray's *Vanity Fair* (1847–48), social upstart Becky Sharp throws Johnson's *Dictionary* out the window, in a gesture of calculated disrespect for the code of class and classics. And in Mrs. Gaskell's *Cranford* (1853), differing social philosophies are expressed in a heated debate between a pretentious Johnsonian and a populist Dickensian. Johnson is a "rude old thing," summarizes the young Edinburgh suffragette in Rebecca West's *The Judge* (1922), noteworthy mainly for "hating the Scotch and democracy, and saying blunt foolish things as if they were blunt wise ones."[90]

The second half of this chapter will trace a more indirect pattern of novelistic engagement with the legacies of Johnson and Ossian, as early-nineteenth-century novelists remain preoccupied with *Ossian*'s integrative vision (as it works to reconcile landscape and history, oral performance and literary tradition), with Johnson's skepticism (as it demystifies local traditions and points up the conjectural aspects of historical reconstruction), and with the necessary clash between these positions. As the next chapter will argue, the novel's development over the first decades of the nineteenth century centers on two new genres, the national tale and the historical novel, and on the constitutive influence, stimulus, and competition they offer one another. Neither genre is conceivable without the investigative journeys of the Enlightenment or the controversies around Ossian, for together these stimulated important novelistic experiments with the representation of place and history, with the problem of narrative perspective, and with the representation of intellectual debate.

Written on the eve of Johnson's journey to Scotland and concerned with defending Scottish scenery, manners, and civilization against a chauvinistic South, Smollett's *Expedition of Humphry Clinker* (1771) contains one of the earliest and most elegant defenses of Macpherson: the proof of Ossian's poetry resides self-evidently in the Scottish landscape. As Jery Melford writes from Argylleshire,

> We have had princely sport in hunting the stag on these mountains; these are the lonely hills of Morven, where Fingal and his heroes enjoyed the same pastime. I feel an enthusiastic pleasure when I survey the brown heath that Ossian was wont to tread, and hear the wind whistle through the bending grass. When I enter our landlord's hall, I look for the suspended harp of that divine bard, and listen in hopes of hearing the aërial sound of his respected spirit. The poems of Ossian are in every mouth. A famous antiquarian of this country, the laird of M'Farlane, at whose house we dined a few days ago, can repeat them all in the original Gaelic.[91]

In traversing the land about which Ossian sang, the Welsh tourist finds himself caught up in an Ossianic mode of seeing, hearing, and experiencing the countryside. Smollett's prose manifests an apparently effortless

Ossianic organicism both in its individual tableaux and in its seamless movement. The passage opens with a hunt through Ossianic terrain, and the hunters' sense, in reenacting a central activity of Fingalian society, of rein-habiting its ethos as well. Smollett meditates briefly on the way the sights and sounds of the landscape engender a sense of absorption, then notes how much the inn's decor, the local people, and the conversation of the local intelligentsia seem permeated by the spirit of Ossian's poetry. The culmi-nating proof of Ossian's authenticity at the end of the passage—the recita-tion of the poetry by a local antiquary, the evidence that an oral tradition does and can exist, for it is still alive—is almost gratuitous, for it merely reiterates the evidence already offered by the culture and the landscape.[92]

Taken as a whole, the *Expedition* seems resistant to so organic a view of landscape. The very form of Smollett's novel—a collection of letters writ-ten by a party of Welsh travelers as they tour England and Scotland—underlines the difficulty of an authoritative account of any locale, given the radical disjunctions in the way different travelers view the same landscape or the same culture: where Melford notes the picturesque character of local ruins or customs, Matthew Bramble ponders the region's political econ-omy. Scotland provokes the travelers' greatest admiration and strongest consensus. The rest of Britain, however, evokes highly variegated re-sponses: the imaginative sympathies of one traveler are thrown into high relief by the utilitarianism of another.

Throughout the eighteenth century, both picaresque and epistolary fiction explore the plot situations generated by travel and by the separation of characters. The emphasis and purpose of these plots change in the sec-ond half of the century, with a new focus on place, as well as on the episte-mology and sociology of travel. The locales through which the traveler passes now begin to be described with an ethnographic sense of their cul-tural specificity and of the contrasts offered by the itinerary. The worldview of the locals (presented either positively, as rooted in a deep local knowledge, or negatively, as narrowly provincial) is contrasted with the cosmopolitanism or the superficiality of the traveler's gaze, as he or she undertakes a comparative reading or performs an imperial conquest of the eye.

Eighteenth-century attempts to locate Homeric poetry influence this new interest in travel on several levels. According to Blackwell's *Inquiry*, the genius of epic poetry was inseparable from the peripatetic life of its creator, for it reflected the breadth of experience gained in traveling: "*[M]uch Trav-elling*, and wide *personal Observation*, has been the lot of the greatest *Epic Poets*." In his travels through the Greek city-states, "Homer stayed so long in each as was necessary *to see*, but not to be *moulded* into *their* manners," and the very act of "*stroling* from one little State to another" enriched the contemplative powers of the poet.[93] At the same time, as Wood argues, the power of the epic tradition was most visible in its performance; the genius of Homer and other traveling rhapsodes lay in their ability to carry their songs into a variety of locales, molding each performance to its new circumstances.[94]

> I have often admired the spirited theatrical action of Italian and Eastern poets, when they recite in the open air, pointing out each object of description in an imaginary scenery of their own extemporaneous creation, but availing themselves at the same time of every real appearance of Nature within view of their Audience that is applicable to their subject, and connects it, in the same degree, with the spot, where the recital is made.[95]

Despite his insistence on the transportability of epic poetry, Wood feels that Homer's own achievement can be fully grasped only by those who have visited the sites that Homer visited and described (and his own travels in Homer's footsteps inaugurate a new mode of literary tourism). Homeric poetry, to Blackwell and Wood, speaks from a variety of places, giving them new definition and cohesion in the act of performance. Macpherson's *Poems of Ossian* similarly understands oral epic poetry as emanating from, yet rooted in, a specific sense of place.

Under the influence of these poetic theories, some late-eighteenth- and early-nineteenth-century novelists trace the path of bardic or antiquarian travelers, describing the way their circuit of performance or observation gathers together the disparate locales of the nation. Others work, along more strictly Ossianic and antiquarian lines, to reanimate the ruined landscapes and object traces of the past. Ann Radcliffe's *Gaston de Blondeville, or The Court of Henry the Third, Keeping Festival in Arden* (written in 1802 and published posthumously in 1826) does both at once. In the novel's frame narrative two literary travelers traverse the Forest of Arden. Willoughton is poetically inclined and particularly susceptible to the atmosphere of the places they visit; his companion is consistently more skeptical. Between them, they decide, they possess the crucial attributes of an antiquary, who must continually balance the capacity for imaginative sympathy with the ability to hunt for facts and determine probabilities. In the meantime, at every stage of the journey, they quarrel happily over Willoughton's imaginative historical reconstructions.[96]

In traversing the Forest of Arden, both travelers are conscious not only that they are on "the ground of Shakspeare" but that they see its landscape much as the Bard himself may have seen it. A specific oak "'may have been of Elizabeth's time'": perhaps "Shakspeare's eyes have dwelt on it; perhaps he has rested under its shade." Past and present meet in landscape, and their coincidence makes Willoughton feel taken out of time: "Sunk in reverie, he was no longer in the living scene, but ranging over worlds of his own."[97] So, too, when an "aged historian" (1:27) guides the travelers through Kenilworth, Willoughton seems to hear the ruins speak.

> Those walls, where gorgeous tapestry had hung, showed only the remains of door-ways and of beautiful gothic windows. . . . Those walls seemed to say— "Generations have beheld us and passed away, as you now behold us, and shall pass away. They have thought of the generations before their time, as you now think of *them*, and as future ones shall think of you. The voices, that revelled beneath us, the poem of power, the magnificence of wealth, the grace of beauty, the joy of hope, the interests of high passion and of low pursuits have passed from this scene for ever; yet we remain, the spectres of departed years and shall remain, feeble as we are, when you, who now gaze upon us, shall have ceased to be in this world." (1:21)

In Radcliffe's Ossianic redaction of Volney's *Ruins*, Kenilworth evokes a swooning contemplation both of the long carrying power of tradition and of the nullity of each generation, faced with the obliterating power of time. This state of mental fugue, the characters' meditations on the vast scale of human history, and their discussions of antiquarian research as a mode of poetry all prepare the reader for the novel's subsequent plunge back into English history and thus for its central narrative, a tale of court life (and bardic performance) at the court of Henry III.

Macpherson's *Poems of Ossian* used a comparable technique to create an almost seamless dissolve between the narrative frame of a particular poem and the epic material (or bardic recitation) at its core. In the first lines of many of the poems, the blind bard is visible in the landscape of the present day, conscious of his infirmity and loneliness. But as the emphasis shifts first to the sounds of the landscape, then to memory, and hence to reverie, the concrete contours and mental anchoring points of the present become progressively dematerialized, until both Ossian and the reader find themselves in the past. The opening pages of *Gaston de Blondeville* echo this Ossianic effect. Yet Radcliffe also utilizes a much more literal means of transport through time. The guide shows the travelers an early printed chronicle, an illuminated manuscript, and a "Trew Historie of Two Mynstrells" recently dug out of the ruins; with its recapitulatory illustrations and interpolated minstrel's songs, the chronicle then provides the main bulk of Radcliffe's novel.

The Ossianic means of retrojection, then, is not allowed to stand alone but must be reinforced by antiquarian scholarship, a printed source, a literary source of evidence about the past. In the end, even all this cannot stand by itself. In the novel's final pages, as Willoughton finishes reading the story of Gaston de Blondeville, we learn that there were moments, in reading, when he doubted the full authenticity of his source. The narrator of the frame story adds further antiquarian scruples: the ceremonies described in the chronicle seem to date from a later period than the one ascribed, and the chronicle as a whole presents problems of attribution. Yet it also seems written from firsthand experience, and Willoughton, at least, is determined to be satisfied, "so willing to think he had met with a specimen of other times, that he refused to dwell on the evidence, which went against its stated origin" (3:53). Radcliffe's novel moves, then, from an initial spirit of Ossianic rhapsody to a final mood of Johnsonian skepticism, and from an initial invocation of landscape as the most privileged source of historic empathy to a closing discussion of manuscript problems (supplemented by almost thirty pages of appended antiquarian notes).

Throughout the later eighteenth-century novel, we find similar slippages from landscape to text, from bardic reverie to antiquarian debate. They are nowhere so dramatically and self-consciously staged as in two midcentury Anglo-Irish noves; together, Thomas Amory's *Memoirs: containing the Lives of several ladies of Great Britain. A History of Antiquities, Productions of Nature, and Monuments of Art* (1755) and *Life of John Buncle, Esq.* (1756 and 1766) explore the discursive construction of place in a spirit of radical playfulness similar to the subsequent explorations of the discursive construction of time in Laurence Sterne's *Tristram Shandy* (1760–67). As they recount their picturesque rambles through the Hebrides or along the northern coast of Ireland, Amory's narrators move at will—often without warning or narrative transition—in and out of different discourses as well as different locales. And as they alternate between geographical and ethnographic description and double-footnoted antiquarian commentary, Amory's narratives in turn evoke complex cultural landscapes and swathe them in discursive layers so thick that they are completely dematerialized. The effect is to subject the reader to constant epistemological uncertainty; in his technique, as in his mixture of cultural and theological obsessions, Amory anticipates the surrealism of a Flann O'Brien.

The *Memoirs*, its narrator informs us, was originally planned as a huge historical compendium, to include "a summary of his country's story ecclesiastical and civil; an abridged account of its constitution and church; its laws and monarchs; and the great men in each reign, who were friends to *liberty* and *property*, or slaves to the tyrants who have oppressed with intolerable servitude this land; a defense of the present happy establishment, the glorious revolution upon which it subsists," and so on. When this compendium is "all burnt to bits," the narrator is forced to compile a substitute book, which now focuses on "antique and natural enquiries and meeting in travels over England and Scotland with excellent and ingenious women."[98] A magisterial historical survey of great men and important battles, then, is to be replaced by an anecdotal account of remarkable women and local history, ongoing antiquarian researches, and travel narrative. Over brief stretches, the *Memoirs* does indeed deliver cogent pieces of ethnographic and antiquarian information, some recycled from extant textual sources (such as Mrs. Benlow's chronicle of her 1741 voyage to the Hebrides, which juxtaposes notes on the islands' bird life with notes on their religious institutions) and others ostensibly gathered by the narrator while perambulating in England and Scotland. And at moments, these descriptions seem genuinely ethnographic. On the Outer Hebridean island of Lewis, to cite one proto-Johnsonian passage, the natives

> are extremely sprightly and sensible. They have a surprising understanding for such poor people. Many of them are bards, that is natural Irish poets; and compose extempore the prettiest songs relating to the heros of former times, who lived in those isles; and to the bravery of the present race in climbing the rocks for eggs, and such like feats; and their own chast amours. They sing those songs extremely well, and many of them play the fiddle by the ear. They have not the least notion of art in music, but some of them perform in a wonderful way. I believe they had never heard any one that played by notes til I came among them, and they were so transported with such music as I could make on the fiddle, that they seemed as it were distracted by ravishments. (P. 157)

Over the long run, however, the *Memoirs* presents a wild, unassimilable jumble of natural and literary history, religious treatises, and antiquarian speculation. What began as a travelogue has turned into a bewilderingly heterogeneous miscellany, the landscape (and any trace of a narrative line) vanishing beneath an accumulation of learned detail.

John Buncle poses similar hermeneutic challenges, as a meager but endlessly repeating plot of travel, courtship, bereavement, and religious consolation is buried, every time it comes around again, under a new avalanche of learned disquisition, on subjects from philology to algebra. From its beginnings, the European novel has frequently disguised its own fictions under the guise of documentation, and it has proven itself an unusually protean and capacious genre, able to absorb many kinds of discourse. Here, however, its central tenets—plot, character, movement through time or space—are completely overwhelmed by the writing of fact, as by the flattened form and static temporality such writing inhabits. Narrative episodes are repeatedly overshadowed by the huge (and frequently digressive) editorial apparatus suspended beneath them; at many points, the novelistic narrative becomes quite literally attenuated, slowly snaking its way along, a sentence or two per page, while beneath it, two distinct layers of footnotes occupy the bulk of the page. An account, in the main text, of the lively music making of a latter-day bard in the household of an elderly descendant of the king of Munster is thus overwhelmed by antiquarian disquisition, in the footnotes, on the surviving manuscript records of ancient Milesian court life and on the parameters of conjecture they make possible.[99] And a novelistic passage through a sublime mountain landscape becomes the occasion primarily for a long footnoted guidebook discussion of the area's towns, sights, and inns. In turn, this information is glossed by a further layer of footnotes below, impugning the information given by previous antiquarian travelers: a particular published description of a local ruin, we are told, is based on the surveyor's report, rather than on firsthand observation.

The world of the living is overwhelmed by antiquarian conjectures about the dead; the natural world is overwhelmed by the library, by an ongoing discourse of place, and by previous scholarly debates. The Ossianic hero of M. Maskell's *Old Tapestry, A Tale of Real Life* (1819) literally turns the wilderness into a library, storing his books outdoors in "almost inaccessible recesses," caverns that had "never been entered by men since the days of Wallace and Bruce."[100] Worn out by reading "ponderous tomes of ancient and modern learning," Mr. Derrydown in Peacock's *Melincourt* (1817) comes across a volume of Thomas Percy's *Reliques of Ancient Poetry* and finds, "or fancied he found, in the plain language of the old English ballad, glimpses of the truth of things, which he had vainly sought in the vast volumes of philosophical disquisition." Resolved to undertake an annual peregrination of the countryside, he fits his traveling carriage with bookshelves, stocking them with volumes of ballads and popular songs, so that he may "study together poetry and the peasantry, unsophisticated nature and the truth of things."[101] The tourifications of Buncle and Derrydown expose them to a world outside the library. Yet their libraries continue to travel with them, carried in their heads if not literally in their carriages, and the printed page continues to block their view.

All scholarly attempts to describe a culture or a place remain caught within text-based modes of knowledge, dependent on textual sources for their investigations and on textual forms for the transmission of their discoveries. Written on the eve of the publication of Macpherson's Ossian fragments and a series of nationalist antiquarian revivals dogged by methodological and political controversy, Amory's novels identify a contradiction that will become even more acute in their wake. For the rest of the century and into the next, the tension between the experience of place and the textual descriptions of it, the experience of history and its textual recording, remains a primary source of antiquarian anxiety and a primary preoccupation for sentimental, Gothic, and historical fiction.

Ossian's power lies partly in its promise to provide unmediated access to nature and to the past; in his state of poetic rhapsody, the unlettered bard is able to immerse himself completely in memory, even while his poetry echoes in the natural sounds and songs of the landscape. But this rhapsodic state is potentially solipsistic; if the antiquary's quixotism lies in his inability to distinguish the landscape around him from what he has already read about it, the bard's madness lies in his inability to distinguish the landscape around him from his own subjective memory processes. Unhinged by the traumatic memory of "that day of blood and death" on which his master's family was murdered and their castle laid to ruin, the mad minstrel in Maturin's *Albigenses* (1824) "refused all solicitation to sing the songs that his companions called for, and persisted in chanting the wildest and loosest lays that ever minstrel uttered," to memorialize the dead: performed on a "dismantled" harp, his discordant songs eulogize the ruin of their ancestral home.

> "The stones of that castle," he cried, pointing to it, —"the weeds that burst through its walls—the very waters of its moat—the rugged battlements of its walls, are dearer to me than all or aught but *this*"—and with enthusiastic expression he kissed his harp as he spoke. "With this," he cried wildly, "I can raise palaces of amethyst and rivers of silver, and flowers of hue and odour that shame paradise.—But such visions mock me," he continued in a dejected tone;—"give me the dark-grey stone, the heavy water, the weeping and tufted weed, and the dim twilight that sheltered me as I sung of themes then praised, now forgotten—give me my dreams of childhood back again, when my harp and I were alone the tenants of a world of vision and felicity. Nay, were only one stone of those walls left on another—were the streams flowed away, and the trees rooted from the hills, this spot would still be populous with forms and sounds—would still have tenants for me. . . . The dead . . ."[102]

In his extremity, Maturin's minstrel exemplifies the fundamental tendency of Ossianic poetics: its desire to block out the transformations of the present, taking refuge in memory and poetry.

William Godwin's *Imogen: A Pastoral Romance from the Ancient British* (1784) tries to reimagine a new kind of literary history in which Ossian, not Homer, is the foundational figure.[103] This romance, as its preface announces, is a translation from the Welsh of a composition attributed to the ancient bard Cadwallo, probably active "at least one hundred years before the commencement of our present aera."[104] The editor and translator harbors doubts about the authenticity of his manuscript source: although it is not a work that "mixes together the different stages of civilization" (p. 171), it still bears a troublingly strong stylistic resemblance to a particular Miltonic masque. Yet rather than reject the romance (or Ossianic poetry) on this ground, the editor prefers to use "that license of conjecture, which is become almost inseparable from the character of an editor" (p. 170), and reverse the course of literary history as we know it, to hypothesize that its influence may work backward.

Macpherson presented the poetry of Ossian to an ecstatic—and then increasingly skeptical—public, as if its provenance were quite straightforward. Godwin and Radcliffe refuse to make the same mistake; their historical fictions are presented as if they derive from recently recovered manuscript sources (and are thus truly antique) *and* as if they are not quite to be trusted (bringing with them intractable manuscript problems). Ironically, the result of such qualifications, which force readers to consider the provenance of what they are reading, is that they are then more ready, once the main story begins, to suspend their disbelief; by raising the problems of authenticity, probability, and believability from the outset, these novelists are also able to contain them. Thus Godwin's antiquarian framing of *Imogen*, his insistence on raising the problem of literary historical lineage and influence from the outset of his novel, prepares the reader to enter its Ossianic world, to visualize the natural and social landscape of ancient Britain, to absorb at first hand its bardic strains. This is, indeed, the trick with frame narratives: whatever appears in a frame story or novelistic preface is accorded pride of place in the book, yet it remains external to the central narrative. In *Imogen* an antiquarian framing device that at first appears as a skeptical questioning and narrative containment of ancient romance actually helps the bardic performance of the inner story come to life. The eighteenth-century novel, then, internalizes Johnson's critique of Ossian by anticipating, and forestalling, criticism of its own procedures. In conceding the necessity and appropriateness of Johnsonian skepticism, novelists free themselves and their readers to indulge in Ossianic fantasies.

Conjectural Histories

"The *Hieroglyphic Tales*," explains the antiquarian narrator in the preface to Horace Walpole's 1785 tale collection,

> were undoubtedly written a little before the creation of the world, and have ever since been preserved, by oral tradition, in the mountains of the Crampcraggiri, an uninhabited island, not yet discovered. Of these few facts, we could have the most authentic attestations of several clergymen, who remember to have heard them repeated by old men long before they, the said clergymen, were born. We do not trouble the reader with these attestations, as we are sure every body will believe them as much as if they had seen them.[105]

Walpole's preface follows Johnson in satirizing Macpherson's "inventive" account of his recovery of the Ossian poems and lampooning Macpherson's attempt to convert his work's dubious provenance into a scholarly problem of authorship and dating. Ostensibly the pure products of a third-century Gaelic culture with only minimal contact with the rest of Europe ("the mountains of Crampcraggiri, an uninhabited island, not yet discovered"), both the poems and Ossian's persona appear suspiciously influenced by the example of Homer. Macpherson's own subsequent

Ossianic translations of Homer are an attempt, Walpole argues, to twist historical causality, to insinuate the literary priority of Ossian over Homer.

Macpherson's literary and historical improprieties are only possible, Walpole suggests, because antiquarians are already oriented toward hieroglyphic problems, so willing to launch conjectural reconstructions of specific texts—and entire historical epochs—on the basis of fragmentary or indecipherable evidence. Walpole's own shaping of the *Hieroglyphic Tales* can be seen to "confound" disparate elements—caricatures of contemporary politicians and events; literary references; flights of personal whimsy—by turns timely and timeless, historically representative and genially idiosyncratic.[106] The same mix of elements forms the basis for Macpherson's creative translations and his traverse of literary history, from the Homeric Erse of Ossian into eighteenth-century sentimentalism, then back again from Ossian to Homer. With its own wild swings of historical probability, the mock-antiquarian framework of Walpole's *Tales* jabs satirically at Macpherson's implausibility, and with it, at the frequent silliness of antiquarian speculation.[107] Yet because the preface works both with and against historical limits to the imagination, it also creates a fully appropriate framework for the fantastic fables that follow it. Walpole's apparent dismissal of antiquarian methods, and of Macpherson's literary-historical fantasias in particular, should not occlude his indebtedness to the historical speculation they make possible.

Twenty-five years earlier, Walpole prefaced *The Castle of Otranto* (1765) with a pseudoantiquarian account of his story's provenance: his narrative as an Italian tale "printed at Naples, in the black letter, in the year 1529," and found only recently in the library of "an ancient Catholic family in the north of England."[108] As the tale's translator and editor, Walpole embarks on several pages of antiquarian conjectures, work that involves both the enumeration of the narrative's historical referents and an even more sustained consideration of the text as a historical document in its own right. Although the preface then goes on to review the book's virtues and shortcomings, it ends by stressing again the probable material and historical basis of the main story; the novel's detailing of architectural space, in particular, suggests that the unknown author had a specific Italian castle in mind.

Like the preface to *The Hieroglyphic Tales*, this original preface to *The Castle of Otranto* suggests an ambivalence toward antiquarian activity. Like any late-eighteenth-century antiquarian, this editor-narrator insists on the archaeological basis of editorial activity, raising the tantalizing possibility that ancient texts and buildings can be checked against one another. And like Macpherson, he promises that if this translation is a commercial success, it will be followed by a modern edition of its original source. The success of *Ossian* created an increasingly uncomfortable pressure to produce the promised originals. Walpole, too, would have had no originals either, had they been demanded of him. Instead, in the preface to the second edition of *The Castle of Otranto*, he retracts all the claims he made in the first, exposing them as fictional and apologizing for his timid attempt to hide his work under the guise of antiquity.

The novel's original readers were never really in danger of reading Walpole's preface literally, of mistaking *The Castle of Otranto* for an Italian original, or of accusing Walpole of literary forgery. Neither his "historical" narrative nor his historicizing framework is particularly convincing as a period effect. Unlike Macpherson, who used *Ossian* to mount a new historical theory of the ethnic settlement of the British Isles, Walpole's antiquarian apparatus makes only local claims, without larger historiographical stakes. Both preface and subsequent amendment are framed as experiments in historiographical form, self-conscious performances in which a new formal vocabulary, method, and scholarly perspective are tried on for size.

By 1760 the British novel already had a long history of pseudodocumentary fictions framed, in their prefaces, by pseudoeditorial authenticating devices, and on one level, Walpole's novel merely represents an updating of novelistic conventions, to bring it in line with current intellectual trends. Yet the particular structure of its antiquarian imaginings also depends on Macpherson's highly literary way of conceiving the past: *Ossian* and the Ossian controversy mark a caesura for novelistic treatments of time as of place. With its emphasis on the melancholy weight of tradition, its presentation of experience as continually, claustrophobically mediated by textual precedent, and its compression and concretization of historical time in particular haunted places, the Gothic novel builds on the conjunction of *Ossian*'s particular historical vision (at once fixated on historical details and oddly anachronistic in its generalized historical melancholy) and a highly stylized and textualized mode of representing Britain's landscapes. Obsessed with the status of all written records as historical and cultural artifacts, the Gothic novel knows itself as an artifact of its own moment, even as it attempts to recuperate the lost sensibilities of the past. It is thus both historically expressive and historically evasive.

The Gothic novel typically frames well-established novelistic plots—the investigation and clarification of family lineages, the restoration of identities and inheritances—with meditations on textual accuracy and transmission as central problems of historical retrieval. Sophia Lee's *Recess: A Tale of Other Times* (1783) recounts the struggle of two unknown daughters of Mary Queen of Scots for official recognition by the British court, and thus for their rightful place in English history. Their hope of political restoration rests on the preservation of family records, important documents of state that Elizabeth manages to suppress and that James finally manages to destroy. The novel claims to be the transcription of a fragmentary historical document. The document's—and the novel's—presentation of a forgotten episode in the history of the English succession is redoubled by its insistence on its own fragmentation as proof of its historical authenticity; the lacunae in the manuscript mirror the lacunae in the historical record.[109] "Not being permitted to publish the means which enriched me with the obsolete manuscript from whence the following tale is extracted," writes Lee's narrator,

> its simplicity alone can authenticate it.—I make no apology for adapting the language to the present times, since that of the author's would be frequently unintelligible.—A wonderful coincidence of events stamps the narration at least with probability. . . . The characters interwoven in this story agree, in the outline, with history. . . . The depredations of time have left breaks in the story, which sometimes only heightens the pathetic.[110]

The attempt of Gothic fiction is at once to personalize history and to mimic the process of textual collection, collation, and comparison through which the antiquarian tries to establish an objective historical record. Sentimental fiction is similarly, if less directly, linked to antiquarian preoccupations; the crisis of historical thinking around the publication of *Ossian* helps to precipitate a significant change of direction in the genre. Oliver Goldsmith's *Vicar of Wakefield* (1766) is still structured by a cyclical, organic sense of temporality.[111] Written only a few years later, in the wake of *Ossian*, and in reverent parody of its controversial transmission mythology, Henry Mackenzie's *Man of Feeling* (1771) frames *its* sentimental story as a series of reconstructed fragments. As in *The Recess*, the form of *The Man of Feeling* is reinforced by, yet also played off against, its content. The transmission problem of the manuscript (its partial destruction, fragmentation, and survival against all odds) mirrors the explicit thematics of the novel: the inability of the man of feeling to ensure his psychic survival in a world of cruelty and indifference, and yet the survival, in trace form, of his memory and his example. Like Goldsmith, Mackenzie uses his narrative to display the siege of moral rectitude. For Goldsmith, however, such rectitude depends on the preservation of naïveté and innocence; its reward, the narrative implies, is a return to pastoral harmony. For Mackenzie, in contrast, the sentimental is a mode of reaction against, of retreat from, the world; the very mode of his narration emphasizes the belatedness and fragility of moral victory. In framing the problem of morality with the long perspective of the antiquary, Mackenzie begins to move beyond Scottish Enlightenment discussions of the sentiments toward a Schillerian and romantic sense of the sentimental, as a postlapsarian mode whose retrieval of a lost past is always partial and imperfect.

Mackenzie's antiquarian redefinition of the sentimental—and in his wake, Lee's links between the possibilities of historical retrieval and political restoration—helps an emerging local-color fiction develop a new way of approaching and describing place. It also provides Gothic and historical fictions with their central models for thinking about historical time and contingency, an inheritance acknowledged in Scott's dedication of his first historical novel to Mackenzie. Working in an explicitly Mackenziesque vein, Elizabeth Ryves's *Hermit of Snowden, or Memoirs of Albert and Lavinia, Taken from a faithful copy of the original manuscript, which was found in the hermitage, by the late Rev. Dr. L—, and Mr. —, in the year 17*** (1789) repatriates Mackenzie's Ossianic and antiquarian influences. In the way it reconnects the sentimental novel to the land of the bards, and in the way it pays explicit homage to antiquarian retrieval (laboring to fit the fragments of the past back into the landscape from which they originally came), her preface might be read as a model for a new national picturesque, to be built out of the convergence of bardic traditions and antiquarian activities. "In the summer of 17**," the novel begins,

> two gentlemen, well known in the literary world, made an excursion into *Wales*, not merely to view the country and those monuments of Druidical Superstition which have so frequently been examined and described, but to visit the villages in the neighbourhood of every Place which is supposed to have been a seat of the Druids, and where they thought it probable the peasants might retain many traditions, and customs which would throw light upon the imperfect account transmitted to us of their religious rites and ceremonies, and explain some points in the history of those early ages, which are at present exceedingly obscure.[112]

Just as Wood undertook an expedition through the Mediterranean, looking for the material correlatives of Homer's epics, so Ryves's antiquaries explore the Welsh mountains, in search of the traces of Druids and bards. What they find instead is a dead hermit, the verses he carved in the rock, and the autobiographical manuscripts that form both his legacy to the world and the novel's central, sentimental narrative. When the antiquaries take up the manuscripts, they find themselves "obliged to open [them] with great care, as the damps of the cell had injured the paper so much that it would scarcely bear to be separated; and in some parts the writing was almost defaced by mildew" (p. xxii).

Instead of retrieving the history of a national culture, the antiquarian travelers retrieve a single, poetic heart. Yet their mode of retrieval transforms even this recent, personal narrative into an antiquarian property, with its own preservation and hermeneutic problems, and thus in need of scholarly editing. *The Hermit of Snowden* demonstrates the overlap between antiquarian reconstruction and sentimental memory work, between the historical traces left by a lost civilization and the smaller traces left by an individual life.

As Mary Shelley argues in "Roger Dodsworth, the Reanimated Englishman" (1827), the effects of an epoch are most legible in the shape of an individual consciousness. The son of a well-known seventeenth-century antiquary, Roger Dodsworth inadvertently becomes a living antiquity; trapped in the snows of Saint Gotthard's Pass in 1654, he enters a state of suspended animation and is roused only in 1826. Like Walpole or Lee before her, Shelley frames her narrative as a conjectural editorial reconstruction of the gaps left in the story, as reported in the British press. Yet she imagines her object of investigation as singularly and supernaturally intact: suspended in ice for 172 years, with nothing added or taken away, Dodsworth must have remained similarly intact in his formation, worldview, and sense of historical horizons; the shock of his awakening is to find the world utterly changed around him, to the point of unrecognizability. His first real conversation with his rescuer is necessarily at cross-purposes; not only has the English language changed considerably since his fall into the crevice, but so has the political landscape of Europe. When he asks after the fate of England and the (Cromwellian) revolution, his rescuer mistakes him for a Jacobin or a Chartist; Dodsworth, in turn, is amazed to hear that the king is on the throne again. What this miscommunication suggests is that the course of English history between 1654 and 1826 has been one of repetition and reversal, with the eighteenth century reacting to and reprising the seventeenth, and the nineteenth century repeating what has come before. From Roger Dodsworth's perspective, however, everything that once anchored his world has vanished or become unrecognizable, and "every voice he had ever heard is mute" (p. 276). Like Ossian before him, Dodsworth embodies the pain of becoming a historical anachronism within his lifetime.

"He lived at the most interesting period of English History—he was lost to the world when Oliver Cromwell had arrived at the summit of his ambition, and in the eyes of Europe the commonwealth of England appeared so established as to endure for ever" (p. 276). Immured in the midst of the civil war, Dodsworth awakes to find its passions completely forgotten; he anxiously catches himself singing a royalist ditty, then realizes that any present-day auditors will be completely indifferent, whether he sings for the Roundheads or the Cavaliers. As the relic of a now-historical epoch, the only line of work left to him is to follow his father's lead and become an antiquary; as a living antiquity, he has firsthand, casual knowledge of the past that even the most learned scholars could never attain. From the first announcement of his disinterment, the antiquarians of England have been considering what they "could afford to offer for Mr. Dodsworth's old clothes, and to conjecture what treasures in the way of pamphlet, old song, or autographic letter his pockets might contain" (p. 274). And Shelley jokingly announces her own eagerness to meet him, to get answers to many long-standing queries about the past.

The real concern of her essayistic story is with three more fundamental questions: the problem of antiquarian objectivity, given the inherent pathos of antiquarian activities (although motivated by the loss of the past, antiquarian activity only exacerbates that loss); the problem of the historical specificity of human identity (how would the same personality take shape, Shelley wonders, if placed in radically different historical contexts?); and the possibilities for historical conjecture and speculation which antiquarian activity (and even antiquarian satire) makes possible. No more has been heard about Roger Dodsworth since his disinterment, Shelley surmises at the end of the story, because in the interim he has simply died again, this time for good. She goes so far as to imagine his tombstone—with his odd span of life on it—then begins to speculate on the retrieval of this monument of nineteenth-century culture by the antiquaries of the distant future, who might, on its basis, conjecture his life span of 172 years as the early-nineteenth-century norm. In the last paragraph of the story, then, readers find themselves flung forward in time, in order both to close off and to reopen the tale's speculations on evidence, historical situatedness, and historical relativity.

Shelley's novel *The Last Man* (1826) suggests a relative perspective on England's national character; "Roger Dodsworth" suggests a historical perspective on the present. Like *The Last Man*, the story is framed as a meditation on history rather than on scientific probability. Yet what both pieces of fiction help to establish, quite as much as *Frankenstein* does, is the conceptual reach of science fiction and the modernist literature of time travel, from Wells's *Time Machine* to Woolf's *Orlando*. Antiquarian work, as "Roger Dodsworth" makes clear, is fundamentally a speculative activity. Full of a utopian potential, it makes possible a reimagination of history in the image of the present, or a reimagination of the present as the outcome of a counterfactual past.

BARDS AND ANTIQUARIES

If late-eighteenth- and early-nineteenth-century novels absorb many of the *Poems of Ossian*'s distinctive structural features, they also internalize the structure of the Ossian controversy and remain preoccupied with the mutual implication of apparently opposed and fundamentally incompatible positions. Late-eighteenth-century novelists tried to represent this dialectical principle on the level of narrative form, developing framing strategies that at once held opposing positions in tension with one another and held them out of each other's way. Early-nineteenth-century novelists stage this tension more directly.

Already in *The History of John Juniper, Esq. Alias Juniper Jack* (1781), Anglo-Irish novelist Charles Johnstone systematically conflates Johnson with Macpherson, to produce the satirical portmanteau figure of the Scottish tutor. Educated, like Macpherson, in Aberdeen, Dr. Melchizedech Bocardo transmits a strong Scottish accent to his pupil along with his lessons. The organizing principles of his life are a "patriotic nationality" and a deep reverence for classical culture.[113] Where literature is concerned, these two principles come into conflict, for there he invariably "gave the precedence to his own dear country in every instance, allowing even to his favourite ancients only the honour of priority. He insisted that *Fingal* was a more perfect epic poem than the *Iliad, Allan Ramsay* a better lyric poet than Horace" (p. 86), and William Robertson and Hume superior to Thucydides and Livy. His mode of life, however, is guided by the precedent of the ancient world. Thus he eschews both shoes and linen, "because unknown to the ancients, and consequently unnecessary to man: and he held breeches to be such a vile encumbrance, such an impediment to the operations of nature, that he had never once put them on . . . when he could avoid it, or without a curse" (p. 86).

In most respects, then, Bocardo represents a principle of Ossianic "naturalness" elevated to the status of a classical precedent and extrapolated to a logical (and ridiculous) extreme. Yet Johnstone's satire on Macpherson eventually shades into a Fergussonian satire on Johnson. For if Bocardo is the author of a ten-volume history of Britain, which establishes the mythic origin of Highland second sight and "in which the errors of all former historians are confuted, and the whole island proved to have been originally enlightened from the northern end"—Macpherson was the author of *An Introduction to the History of Great Britain and Ireland* (1773) and *Original Papers, containing the Secret History of Great Britain* (1775)—he is also, "as tradition says," the proud author of an Aristotelian *Philosophical Enquiry into the Origin of Eating*, which argues that in satisfying his hunger, man proves himself "*by nature a solitary animal, eating only for himself*," with an appendix to show "that *oaten cakes are the food most favourable to genius*" (p. 99).

What Johnstone's portmanteau makes clear is the derivative character of both the Johnsonian and the Ossianic position. When Johnson surveys Scotland, his critique involves the continual appropriation of Ossianic and Scottish Enlightenment tropes. And when the illustrator of the 1805 Edinburgh edition of *The Poems of Ossian*, clearly in some doubt as to how to situate and dress Macpherson's characters, mixes Grecian dress and Gothic architecture, oak trees and Roman legionnaires, he merely underlines the fact that the Ossianic aesthetic is built from an amalgam of different heroic, pathetic, and poetic styles.[114]

To *Ossian*'s detractors, the poems' eclecticism and anachronism appear the very marks of inauthenticity. Yet novelists remain fascinated by Macpherson's attempt to represent the clash of world orders. Preoccupied with describing periods of epochal or ideological overlap, they derive both of their principal representational strategies, directly or indirectly, from aspects of the Ossianic tradition.[115] In *Ossian* the effects of historical dislocation are visible both in the mental state of the bard and in the fragmentary state of the text. In Ireland, however, as Charlotte Brooke demonstrates in *Reliques of Irish Poetry* (1784), the Ossianic tradition also included poetic dialogues in which Oisin and Saint Patrick debated their differences of belief and worldview. [116]

One legacy of Macpherson's *Ossian* is a new way of conceiving the unevenness of character, and of textuality, as historical testimony, as an inadvertent record of historical upheavals and endurance, survivals and extinction. This model understands witnesses to history, whether human or textual, as inherently passive, mute on the subject of their sufferings; it is the visible psychic dislocation of the characters, the tattered physical appearance of the manuscripts, rather than their direct utterances, which testify to their experience. The broader Ossianic tradition—and the Ossian controversy itself—makes available a rather different model, in which the representatives of the old order loudly challenge the representatives of the new; their way of life may be doomed, but they will go down fighting.

In practice, these possibilities are not mutually exclusive; Sydney Owenson's *Novice of St. Domnick* (1806) presents the clash of periods and worldviews both within individual characters and in their dynamic of interaction. In the "scriptorium" she has erected in a Dominican convent library, an eccentric elderly antiquary happily collates a history of church-sponsored genocide. In her relationship both to the world outside the convent and to her own scholarly material, she exemplifies antiquarian dissociation, composing her "voluminous History of the Crusades, whether foreign or domestic, against infidel or apostate, from the first instigation of Peter the hermit in 1104 to the massacre of St. Bartholomew in 1572" (1:194), which she herself has personally witnessed, with "learned dullness" (1:5) and profound detachment.

She is internally dissociated as well, for reasons that are partly historical. Like other Renaissance scholars, she identifies both with the patristic tradition and with the sedimentary layers of classical humanism beneath it. Emotionally, too, she is "half-heathenish, half-Christian" (1:194), torn between lust and piety, Ovid and Saint Bonaventure, Sappho and Saint Theresa. But whereas Magdelaine's continuing devotion to two competing

belief systems leads her into hypocrisy, Imogen, her genial young amanu-
ensis, uses *her* reading to free herself, quickly and irrevocably, from the
church and its superstitions.

> Poor Saint Gregory was the first who felt the effect of this intellectual revolu-
> tion; and departed, with his pious phalanx, between the victorious arms of the
> two Plinys; a few verses of the elegant Tibullus were equal to the defeat of the
> Sixty-two decades of saint Ely the Angelic: Plutarch's heroes overthrew the
> Golden Legend; and one book of Virgil completed the conquest of the whole
> army of martyrs! (1:68)

Owenson juxtaposes the aging, pedantic, mentally bifurcated, and "exhausted memory" of scholarship with the youthful spirit of poetry, pursu-
ing "through regions of impossibility . . . the glowing phantoms of fancy's
creation" (1:4–5). The allegorical contrasts become even more pointed
when a young minstrel arrives at Saint Domnick, to find himself an object
of intense erotic and scholarly interest, both to Magdelaine and to *The Novice*'s narrator; his arrival in the novel is greeted by an editorial footnote,
and his subsequent account of himself receives an immediate gloss from
the antiquary in the text.

> "The genius of my country found me, while yet a boy, tuning my rustic reed
> on the delicious banks of the Durance; and taught me to raise my humble lay,
> and emulate the bards of my native province, who diffused the light of poetry
> and song o'er the wide dominions of France, then involved in Gothic dark-
> ness. . . . Thrice have I carried off the golden violet at Thoulouse from my
> competitors; thrice have I . . . sung through the wide domains of France the
> superiority of my native province. . . ."
>
> "Neither am I ignorant [replies Lady Magdelaine] of the reverence in which
> thy sacred profession was held by the ancients: the king Alcinous is described
> by Homer as paying the highest honours to his inspired visitor; Ulysses, that
> wary chief, treated with profound respect the tuneful Dimondocus; the Athe-
> nians sent a minstrel to command the Spartans, who conquered under his in-
> spiring influence; Anacreon was caressed at the court of Polycrates, the tyrant
> of Samos." (1:23–25)

The minstrel evokes the adventurous life of the strolling poet; the antiquary
immediately provides a pedantic gloss. On the face of it, the contrast between the two personae and the two modes of literary work could not be
more extreme. Yet as the antiquarian attempts to echo the bardic register,
to court the minstrel by reflecting back to him the accolades bestowed on
poets throughout history, we glimpse the central paradox of eighteenth-
century antiquarian scholarship: the constant yearning of antiquaries to become the bards they translate and edit (Thomas Chatterton wanting to be
Rowley, Macpherson wanting to pass as Ossian), to believe that their own

conjectural reconstructions follow a bardic tradition of improvisation, and the tendency of their work, therefore, to drift into various degrees of forgery. As we have seen, there is a similar mimetic desire at the heart of the Ossian controversy: if the translator wants to fill in for the poet, Johnson's own polemics of feud mask a comparable sense of filiation and inheritance.

What is argument for? Does it lead toward a final melding or marriage or mirroring of positions, or does it merely confirm each disputant in an already-held view? The "literary antagonists" of the Ossian controversy, Robert Couper argues in *Tourifications of Malachi Meldrum*, "were within half an inch of one another, but they did not meet—perhaps they did not intend it . . . these are not the regulations of controversy."[117] So too, in Owenson's first novel, *St. Clair, or The Heiress of Desmond* (1802), the restaging of an already-standard argument about the national provenance of Ossian gives the reader a quick overview of its key stakes, positions, and pieces of evidence, while proving completely circular from the perspective of its participants. The narrator and his host, Sir Patrick Desmond,

> both displayed as much warmth in fixing the native place of Ossian, as the commentators of Homer, the spot which had the honour of giving him birth. Every mountain in the province was enriched by a feat of Fingal; not an old woman in the country, but could recite a poem of his inspired con; and he pointed to a promontory, which distance almost reduced to a shadow, the extreme point of which is still called the seat of Fingal (of which the lower order of Irish repeat many improbable tales.) To all these demonstrative proofs, I could only recapitulate the opinions of Blair, the arguments of Hume, and the sentiments of Gibbon! and we both arrived at Desmond Abbey, in the same mind with respect to Ossian as we set out.[118]

Owenson's *Wild Irish Girl* will repeat the same quarrel at much greater length. Guiding an English visitor through his collection of historic weapons, the Milesian prince tries to explain the connection between these material artifacts of the past and the tradition of Ossianic poetry; backed by his antiquarian priest, he ends up arguing his way through the whole Ossian controversy, over some dozen pages: the beauty and unfaithfulness of Macpherson's book, Johnson's skepticism, the conjectural colonization history of Ireland and Scotland, textual evidence and historical evidence, the proofs of Ossian's historical existence, and Irish origins in local place-names and oral traditions.[119] His guest, in turn, goes "over the arguments" as they have come down to him, but his secondhand knowledge of the controversy is no match for firsthand local knowledge. Finding himself "routed," he negotiates an "amnesty," made sweeter when the prince's beautiful daughter joins the party, to testify that she learned the songs of "our national bards" long before she could read, "in the bosom of my nurse, and in my father's arms" (pp. 106–7). One significant outcome of this scene is that the English visitor (and hopefully the English reader as well) has changed his mind about Irish claims to Ossian. Yet as the passage's sustained metaphors of warfare suggest, the argument is equally important as a way of displacing the contest of nations onto a symbolic plane: to refight the Ossian controversy is at once to address many of Britain's most fundamental cultural and political differences and to diffuse the ethnic hatreds they feed.

The showdown between bard and antiquary in Walter Scott's *Antiquary* (1816), in the skirmishes between the illiterate beggar Edie Ochiltree and the gentleman of letters Jonathan Oldbuck of Monkbarns, illuminates both the nature of political community and the problems of historical (and fictional) method. Once soldier, tinker, ballad singer, and traditional healer, Ochiltree is in old age a member of a royally chartered guild of beggars, said to be descended from the race of bards. He is thus "a sort of privileged nuisance—one of the last specimens of the old-fashioned Scottish mendicant, who . . . was the news-carrier, the minstrel, and sometimes the historian of the district. That rascal . . . knows more old ballads and traditions than any other man in this and the four next parishes."[120]

If Ochiltree is a vestige of the feudal order and the bearer of oral tradition, his antagonist represents a different inheritance. Monkbarns's ancestors include Johannes Faustus, Wolfbrand Oldenbuck (one of the first printers of Germany and printer of the 1493 *Chronicle of Nuremburg*), and Aldobrand Oldenbuck, who set into type the *Augsburg Confession*, "labouring personally at the press for the diffusion of Christian and political knowledge" (5:155). The antiquary traces his descent, then, from the Reformation, here imagined as a Protestant Enlightenment spread through the printed word, reclaiming and disseminating the sources of a national and religious history to free the people from the despotism of tradition and superstition. Yet Monkbarns is also the successor of the monastic scholars who inhabited his estate in the Middle Ages, and whom he resembles not only in his reverence for the traditional but also in his celibacy and misogyny. His obsessive study of the past is a compensation for disappointed love; when not engaged in writing denunciations of Ossian and Macpherson (or hectoring about the Ossian controversy to other characters), the antiquary studies castrametation, the walled fortifications that protected Roman fortresses from barbarian attack. His studies, published under the pen name Oedipus, serve to protect him from the threat of emotional involvement and from the castrating grasp of female chatterboxes.

Although scholarship is often concerned with the past, it also proves the best bulwark against it, against the flooding "mare magnum" of memory and loss. Yet if collected too assiduously, the artifacts of the past can, as in the antiquary's study, become an equally oppressive "*mare magnum* of miscellaneous trumpery" (5:34). The destruction of monastic libraries and of many monuments of the past, indeed, "may have saved the rationality of some modern antiquaries, which would certainly have been drowned if so vast a lake of learning had not been diminished by draining" (5:239). Antiquaries, then, need the world to be fragmented in order to feel that they have mastered those fragments. They endeavor to contain the past by overwhelming it with their meticulous attentions. They write "essays on medals in the proportion of twelve pages to each letter of the legend" (5:21).

Edie Ochiltree embodies a more rooted and less mediated local knowledge; his very name proves Johnson wrong: there are oak trees in Scotland. When Monkbarns decides, on slight etymological evidence, that a dike on his property is the trace not only of an ancient fortress but of the final battle between Agricola and the Caledonians, it is left to Ochiltree to reveal that this purported trace of Roman "Castrametation" (5:48) is nothing more than an earth wall he remembers being piled up twenty years before as a rain shelter for a wedding reception.[121] For all his learnedness and professed commitment to the unbiased reconstruction of the past, Monkbarns repeatedly proves unreliable as an antiquary and as a historian. He is quite willing to discredit the authenticity of an excavated coin hoard, on the grounds that it contains coins from too many different places and centuries (6:17). And he complains of the taste for a "modern Gothic" (5:218) architecture that will juxtapose a monument of a Knight Templar with a Grecian porch. Yet he embellishes a medieval Flemish tapestry in his possession by attaching to its base a sort of intertextual, textile footnote: a modern border with a quotation from Chaucer woven in Gothic letters (5:137). And he indulges constantly in the "creative interpretation" of a Percy or a Macpherson, deducing the tribal settlement of Scotland on the basis of the one remaining Pictish word and arriving at definitive readings of illegible inscriptions, of sites without landmarks.

As he reveals to his young visitor Lovel, his antiquarian activities conceal a secret desire to be a belletristic author, and he proposes an ambitious collaborative literary project: together they will write an epic poem, "The Caledoniad; or Invasion Repelled. . . . It will suit the present taste, and you may throw in a touch of the times" (5:195). All historical evidence to the contrary, the Caledonians of this poem will succeed in driving out the Romans.[122] The literary venture, intended to revitalize Scottish letters, will be a true compromise between the historically accurate and the fictionally expedient, and a true collaboration between authors of different generations, between antiquary and bard. Lovel is to write the actual verses, and Monkbarns will supply the footnotes.

In its recasting of old debates, Scott's novel goes beyond the old opposition/elision of antiquary and bard, of Johnson and Macpherson, to represent eighteenth-century positions in many other permutations and combinations. The antiquary does battle with his nephew Hector over the authenticity of Macpherson's Ossian, in the terms Dr. Johnson used in 1773 to interrogate the Highland gentlemen.

> "I assure you we are by no means insensible to the memory of our fathers' fame; I used often of an evening to get old Rory M'Alpin to sing us songs out of Ossian about the battles of Fingal and Lamon Mor, and Magnus and the spirit of Muirartach."
>
> "And did you believe," asked the aroused Antiquary—"did you absolutely believe that stuff of Macpherson's to be really ancient, you simple boy?"
>
> "Believe it, sir?—how could I but believe it, when I have heard the songs sung from my infancy?"
>
> "But not the same as Macpherson's English Ossian; you're not absurd enough to say that, I hope?" said the Antiquary, his brow darkening with wrath.
>
> But Hector stoutly abode the storm; like many a sturdy Celt, he imagined the honour of his country and native language connected with the authenticity of these popular poems, and would have fought knee-deep, or forfeited life and land, rather than have given up a line of them. (6:121–22)

Monkbarns has had similar arguments, over many years, with his Jacobite neighbor Sir Arthur Wardour, an amateur antiquarian driven by nostalgia for feudal society, a passion for heraldry and the "sacred list" (5:65) of the ancient Scottish kings. As a Germanic rationalist and an amateur archaeologist, Monkbarns also opposes the Germanic mysticism of the mountebank illuminato Dousterswivel, whose frauds have reduced the credulous Sir Arthur almost to bankruptcy, and who is finally brought down by the connivance of Ochiltree, his claims to second sight proving useless against the beggar's knowledge of local sites and command of local conditions. As genial representative of an uncontaminated and unconstrained folk tradition, Ochiltree is also needed to mediate and to reclaim the narrative of senile Elizabeth Mucklebait, who represents the feminine and aristocratic corruption of a virile folk tradition.

Like many of the novels discussed over the last few pages, *The Antiquary* is organized around symbolically fraught narrative encounters that reiterate British aesthetic and political debates. The novel depicts a society whose hierarchies are demarcated with exceptional clarity: when Sir Arthur's daughter wants to speak with Edie Ochiltree the morning after he has helped to save her life, she has him stand in the courtyard while she communicates with him through a barred window.[123] Yet for all its rigidity of social structure, this society is on the verge of toppling completely. Scotland is under threat of invasion from France, where a bourgeois revolution has turned radical and menacing. Stranded on the cliffs and endangered by unusually high tides near the beginning of the novel, surveying the coast in fear of invasion at the end, the novel's characters have reason to fear a rising sea, which in the course of the book drowns even professional fishermen. There is fear of Jacobinism and mob violence within the community as well; at various points in the novel, Dousterswivel, Ochiltree, Lovel, and Monkbarns are all suspected of spying or of radicalism. Even Monkbarns's archaeological excavations are seen as possessing an undermining potential: like the projected *Caledoniad* itself, they aim to uncover old foundations, perhaps to erect a new order on the ruins. More dangerous still are his textual excavations; trained as a lawyer, Monkbarns delights in uncovering the historical determination of legal texts, an investigation that potentially puts the investigator before and beyond the law.

Meanwhile, the beggar uses his royal charter to gain partial immunity from the law, and Sir Arthur, the local justice of the peace, is almost jailed for debt. Lovel, who in the beginning of the novel is mistaken for a strolling actor, ends it as the nephew of an earl. A hierarchical social structure conceals a frightening potential for social flux. What then ensures the cohesion of society, given the bankruptcy of the aristocracy, the neurotic alienation of the intellectuals, and the virtual extinction of the bards who once, in their epics, sang the praises and enshrined the legitimizing genealogies of the ruling classes? In moments of acute crisis the threat of invasion from without or mob violence from below can cause class differences to cede temporarily to a national solidarity. Trapped on the cliffs by the rising tide, Sir Arthur and Edie Ochiltree thus find themselves in "a neutral field, where even a justice of the peace and a strolling mendicant might meet upon terms of mutual forbearance" (5:97). The everyday life of the community, however, is held together by something different, the last survival of bardic functions, as Ochiltree's ceaseless circulation and news bearing connect locality to locality, fish hut to manor. Apparently a parasite on the community, Ochiltree actually binds it together, not least by his disrespectful jesting, a public, playful transgressiveness that contains and defuses the tensions between classes.[124]

The constitution of society in indignant laughter, in reaction to the controversial jokes of the minstrel, or the constitution of society in annoyed argumentation, in reaction to the controversial proclamations of the Antiquary: what unites community members most firmly, in Scott's novel, is the mode of their very differences and disagreements, their common longing for a lost past that they remember, mourn, and re-create in very different ways. In Scott's narrative, the debates of the eighteenth century are taken up and argued on to infinity. Bard and antiquary, Johnson and Macpherson stand side by side, linked by well-worn, comfortably familiar paths of argumentation. Apparently destructive and disruptive arguments about the interpretation of tradition have themselves become a solidified, solidifying tradition.

For Scott, the bard's function is to bind the community together, to harmonize a range of voices and classes into a single polyphonic chorus. The artist appears here as a figure between and beyond class categories, an embodiment of tradition who must use his repertoire of consonances and dissonances to create a social order even as he creates and performs his own works. Scott's formulation at once insists on the social meaning of art and on the social autonomy of the artist, suggesting that his social (and economic) dislocation is a precondition for his indispensable role in guaranteeing social (and economic) stability.

Not all of Scott's contemporaries, however, reached the same satisfying conclusions either about the politics of argument or about the politics of the bard.[125] *The Antiquary* derives its centerpiece debate over the provenance of the Roman camp from a scene in Robert Bage's *Hermsprong* (1796). There, however, the exchange is far from conciliatory; the Reverend Doctor Blick, "a profound antiquarian" who is fond of visiting the local "remains of the castle, the convent, or a remarkable place which had much the appearance of an encampment," is shown to be self-important and finally bullying, as he tries to persuade a gentleman tourist that the "remarkable place" before them was the site of a Roman camp.[126] When his interlocutor remains unconvinced, the rector challenges his credentials as a judge and finally questions his very presence in the parish. But the stranger has the last word, ending the scene with a denunciation of clerical self-importance and privilege.

> "I fear, reverence for the clergy,—I rather mean implicit obedience, —does not stand so high now, as when the castle and the convent now in view, were filled by illustrious barons and holy monks."
>
> "A little more reverence for the clergy would be no dishonour to these times, I presume."
>
> "They have less, in your opinion, than they merit."
>
> "Yes, Sir,—do you say the contrary?"
>
> "Oh, no! —I have no inclination to be libelled for heresy; Sir, I wish you a good morning." (Pp. 44–45)

The stake of this debate is not so much the putative Roman camp as the question of fundamental political rights—freedom of movement, the right to disagree—and the politics of antiquarian attachment. The rector's reverence for the ruins of the castle and the convent, the stranger suggests, is not disinterested at all; it conceals a nostalgia for a lost feudal order and a lost feudal absolutism.

Scott's notion of bardic poetry, argues Peacock in *Crotchet Castle* (1831), is distinctly upper class, and it functions as an ideological rallying point against working-class interests. In *The Misfortunes of Elphin* (1822), Peacock criticized antiquaries for their nostalgic simplification of bardic culture. Already in ancient Wales, his own tale argued, traditionalists and ruin worshipers worked to impede genuinely progressive cultural forces. And even when a particular king or bard managed to embody courtly or bardic ideals, he was still forced to operate in a world of venality, barbarity, and corruption; the utopian promise and the debased realities of the bardic system always existed side by side.

The Misfortunes of Elphin attempts to reconstruct a progressive and counterantiquarian account of bardic society. *Crotchet Castle* goes on to dissect present-day antiquarian conservatism. More pointed in its social allegories than *The Antiquary*, *Crotchet Castle* explicitly mirrors many of its central concerns, both in its symbolically charged plot and in the particular debates it stages. Like other works by Peacock, this novel consists of endless dialogues (or simultaneous monologues) between allegorically named representatives of the most important contemporary intellectual, political, and social currents. Many of the novel's most important debates take place between Scottish Enlightenment philosopher Mr. Mac Quedy (that is, MacQ.E.D., Quod Erat Demonstrandum, whose conversation blends utilitarian sentiments, belief in the environmental determination of character, and defensive praises of Scottish culture), the Reverend Dr. Folliott (who embodies classical learning, patristic authority, and a belief in government by the intellectual elite), and Mr. Chainmail (whose antiquarianism is based on utopian medievalism and an idealization of feudal "community").

The most explicit parallel to Scott's novel is a scene in which Mr. Crotchet (formerly Mr. Mc Crotchet, of Scotland) shows his guests around his grounds, leading them to "the Roman camp, of which the value was purely imaginary." Whereas Mr. Mac Quedy declares the camp "just a curiosity," Mr. Skonar (the representative of German metaphysics) is thrown into rhapsody. The camp, for him, summons up "the days of old, when the Roman eagle spreads its wings in the place of that beechen foliage," and the beech tree leads him to swooning meditation on "duration": it "must have sprung from the earth ages after this camp was formed." The company then becomes engrossed in calculating the age of the beech tree. Once again, Mac Quedy insists that "you get a clearer idea out of the simple arithmetic, than out of your eagle and foliage," whereas Mr. Skonar advocates a more poetical and philosophical "mode of viewing antiquities." Contemplated "in the ideality of space and time," both tree and eagle "become subjective realities, that rise up as landmarks in the mystery of the past." But as Mac Quedy insists in the final round of this particular argument, men "never begin to study antiquities till they are saturated with civilization," and civilization itself, in his opinion, is merely "just respect for property."[127] The scene echoes elements of *Hermsprong*'s and *The Antiquary*'s "castrum" scenes, with hints of the Johnsonian and Enlightenment discussions of Scottish forestation as an index of cultural tradition; its closing lines locate patriotic discussions of culture very firmly within a framework of property and class interests.

The links between antiquarian nostalgia, political economy, and the sanctity of property are even more explicit at the end of the novel. When Chainmail declares his intention to hold a medieval revel, a Christmas Day festival "after the fashion of the twelfth century," Reverend Folliott anticipates "old songs and marches" played by "an old harper": "[O]ld hospitality; old wine; old ale; all the images of old England; an old butler . . . old chairs, round an old table, by the light of old lamps, suspended from pointed arches, which Mr. Chainmail says, first came into use in the twelfth century; with old armour on the pillars, and old banners in the roof" (pp. 748–49).

Lord Bossnowl adds, somewhat less reverently, that the only way the present-day guests can match the "antiquity" of their settings will be to "all go in our old clothes" (p. 749). Accompanied by "the old harper playing . . . the oldest music in his repertory" (p. 753), the revels finally get under way, only to be interrupted by a surprise visit from "Captain Swing" and a Swing mob; suddenly the pageantry meant to stage and to enshrine traditionalist, feudal notions of community is interrupted by a threat of violence from a mass of nameless menials, protesting their exclusion from economic and political life.

Unnerved by this intrusion into their world of principles and fancies, the intelligentsia's first reaction is to keep debating: Reverend Folliott and Mac Quedy argue back and forth about the connection between Enlightenment progress and mob rule, disagreeing as to whether "the Jacquerie" is the modern equivalent of "the dark ages" or whether it is the result of "the march of mind" (p. 753). "The way to keep the people down," Mr. Chainmail contributes helpfully, "is kind and liberal usage" (p. 754). Yet when the crowd demands that the ancient weapons decorating the hall be handed out, the intellectuals are finally catalyzed into action. Arming himself in the twelfth-century armor, the Rev. Dr. Folliott charges the crowd in psychomachian attack, to "see what the church militant, in the armor of the twelfth century, will do against the march of mind" (p. 755). Dressed in their own medieval garb, Mr. Chainmail and his guests follow suit and promptly put "the rabble-rout" to flight (p. 756). "The twelfth century has backed you well," Mr. Chainmail concludes, as the heroes drink a bowl of punch after the battle is over. "Its manners and habits, its community of kind feelings between master and man, are the true remedy for these ebullitions" (p. 756). In the same triumphal spirit, the cooperationist Mr. Toogood (who has fought on the side of the intelligentsia rather than the rural laborers) devises a new slogan for the company: "arts for arms" (p. 756). Where Scott's novel used the debates around the medieval heritage of Scotland to defuse class struggle, Peacock's novel analyzes these same debates as the emblem of upper-class victory. "The twelfth century has backed you well": the Swing mob is utterly routed, so the intellectuals can return to their party and to their ceaseless and recursive argumentative loops. The real world of social conflict is left outside the castle, and inside, above the squabbling voices of the guests, the "oldest harper" plays on, as loyal retainer, entertainment, and alibi.

NATIONAL CHARACTER, NATIONALIST PLOTS: NATIONAL TALE AND HISTORICAL NOVEL IN THE AGE OF *WAVERLEY*, 1806–1830

But if the Union be an Incorporation . . . to the extent of the Letter, it must then be a Union of the very Soul of the Nation, all its Constitution, Customs, Trade, and Manners, must be blended together, for the mutual united, undistinguish't, good, growth and health of one whole united Body; and this I understand by Union.

—Daniel Defoe, "An Essay at Removing National Prejudices Against a Union with Scotland"

Ireland is a small country, connected by a mysterious bond of union with a larger, a poor country with a richer. . . . She is governed by men sent from England, to do the business of England, and who hold the honors, the emoluments, the sword, and the purse of Ireland. . . . England has 8,000,000 of united people, and they are free; Ireland has 4,000,000, of whom much above half are degraded, and ought to be discontented slaves. Instead of watching the insidious arts of our Government here, we are watching each other. . . . The English Government here was founded, has been supported and now exists but in the disunion of Ireland. . . . Ireland is paralytic; she is worse; she is not merely dead of one side, whilst the other is unaffected, but both are in a continual and painful and destructive struggle, consuming to waste and to destroy each other.

—Theobald Wolfe Tone, "Essay on the Necessity of Domestic Union"

A VERY CURIOUS EMPTINESS

A year before the 1937 publication of Georg Lukács's *Historical Novel* (whose famous first chapter on Walter Scott's *Waverley* argues for the so-ciohistorical genesis of the genre), Scottish modernist Edwin Muir published his controversial and influential *Scott and Scotland: The Predica-*

ment of the Scottish Writer, which in striking ways anticipated Lukács's use of Scott to postulate a reflection theory of literature. "The riddle," Muir argues,

> in approaching Scott himself, by far the greatest force in Scottish literature as well as one of the greatest in English, was to account for a very curious emptiness ... behind the wealth of imagination ... to account for the hiatus in Scott's endowment by considering the environment in which he lived. ... [H]e spent most of his days in a hiatus, in a country, that is to say, which was neither a nation nor a province and had, instead of a centre, a blank, an Edinburgh, in the middle of it. But this Nothing in which Scott wrote was not merely a spatial one; it was a temporal Nothing as well, dotted with a few disconnected figures arranged at abrupt intervals ... with a rude buttress of ballads and folk songs to shore them up and keep them from falling. Scott, in other words, lived in a community which was not a community, and set himself to carry on a tradition which was not a tradition; and the result was that his work was an exact reflection of his predicament. ...
>
> A people who lose their nationality create a legend to take its place. The reality of a nation's history lies in its continuity, and the present is its only guarantee. ... But where national unity is lost, the past is lost too, for the connection between past and present has been broken, and the past turns therefore into legend, into the poetry of pure memory.[1]

Concurring in a symptomatic reading of Scott, Muir and Lukács differ about what he represents: Lukács stresses his historical position, Muir his links to a country with a static relationship to its own history. For Lukács, Scott is an "English writer," who mirrors the cumulative history of the English novel, the protoindustrial state of English society, and a new European consciousness at the end of the Napoleonic Wars. Muir sees Scott as an ambivalent Scottish nationalist, suffering from and reflecting Scotland's intellectual unevenness and linguistic dividedness. Directly shaped by recent history, Lukács's Scott develops a historical consciousness that outstrips his class consciousness. Muir's Scott, like Scotland itself, is engaged in a mythologizing reinvention of the national past, his traditionalism expressing, in its negativity, the felt absence of continuous national traditions. Muir sees an unconsciously regressive Scott, caught in contradictions. Lukács posits an unwittingly progressive Scott who embodies his contradictions transformatively, as the Waverley novels' dynamic notion of representative character initiates new modes of registering historical change and links social processes to psychic development in ways that anticipate Lukács's and Muir's sociobiographic approaches to literary history.[2]

Together, Lukács's and Muir's claims for Scott represent an influential conjunction in the formation of a Marxist literary method and in the historiography of romantic fiction. Their exploratory attempts to link literary, political, and national transformations remain stimulating (Muir's nuance and acuity, in particular, seem newly useful for current discussions of literary nationalism). Yet the long-term effect of their work was to reinforce the underlying assumptions of a conservative historiography: historical determinism, the coherence of national traditions, a belief in great men who embody and shape their epochs. With its foregrounding of Scott's singular representative status, and its displacement of formal or generic analysis in the service of a national-historical reflection theory, the work of Muir and Lukács helped to foreclose not only contextual accounts of Scott's relationship to his contemporaries but with them serious study of the body of romantic fiction. Muir's Scott is a figure in a vacuum, alone in his stretch of literary-historical landscape, whereas Lukács polemicizes against all "fashionable" attempts to place Scott in relation to "a long list of second and third-rate writers . . . who were supposed to be important literary forerunners of his. All of which brings us not a jot nearer to understanding what was *new* in Scott's . . . historical novel."[3]

Following Lukács and Muir, most modern Scott scholarship has placed the Waverley novels above and outside the fiction writing of their time, seeing Scott as the sole inventor of the historical novel, at once the adjudicating biographer of his novelistic predecessors and the kindly patron of "lesser" novelists.[4] Yet most of the conceptual innovations attibuted to Scott were in 1814 already established commonplaces of the British novel. Even Scott's notion of historically representative character (for Lukács, his greatest innovation) is adapted from the novels of his contemporaries, from their experiments with characterological allegory and their attempts to represent the psychosocial effects of historical experience.[5] Equal to Scott's in formal and political complexity, their novels in fact give us radically different political perspectives—Enlightenment, Jacobin, feminist, and anti-imperialist—on the same historical processes. Yet because of Lukács's influential claims for Scott's influence—that *Waverley*'s mode of depicting social totality and dramatizing historical change shaped nineteenth-century realism, narrative history writing, and modern historical thinking as we know it—Marxist critics have spent the last fifty years continuing to explicate the Waverley novels as the major novelistic record of the political transformations of their era. So there are high stakes in displacing *Waverley* as a singular yet symptomatic event, to recover alternative forms of historical explanation that emanate from the same historical moment.

As a corrective to Muir and Lukács, this chapter takes a primarily formal approach. It reopens old-fashioned matters of influence, character, setting, and plot as problems with important political ramifications. As a corrective to previous, nationally focused accounts of the romantic novel, it establishes a more precise generic genealogy for Scott's first novel, and it traces the course of generic transformation by examining the intertwined history of the novel in Scotland and in Ireland, and the intertwined development of the historical novel and the national tale (a genre developed in Ireland, primarily by women writers, over the decade preceding the publication of *Waverley*). In this case, as one genre crystallizes out of another, authors, publishers, and reviewers mark (and market) distinct developmental phases by shifts in their use of generic designations.[6] The emergence of the national tale out of the novels of the 1790s and the subsequent emergence of the historical novel out of the national tale can be plotted quite precisely, book by book, through the 1810s. Yet the two genres remain interdependent, still almost identical in plot and characters, but already highly polarized in their overall novelistic strategies and political implications. The transition from the first genre, with its thick evocation of place, to the second, with its plot of loss and growth through historical change, may seem, in retrospect, to render irrevocable the movement away from an eighteenth-century novel of passage through place, a "traveling fiction" of picaresque and epistolary motion, into a nineteenth-century novel in which a society and a place pass through time together. Yet the further development of the realist novel depends not only, as Lukács argues, on the ascendance or "victory" of the historical novel over earlier novelistic types but also on an ongoing interplay and friction between two successive, related, and increasingly enmeshed generic forms. The national tale and the historical novel demonstrate both the fluidity and the stake of generic convention. Names, characters, set pieces, and plots are constantly borrowed back and forth between the genres, even among writers of sharply divergent political views who claim to disapprove of each other's work; in many cases, in fact, they mark their political differences in the way they order and recombine the same generic repertoire.

The national tale continued to evolve in the wake of *Waverley* and in reaction to it, as its authors historicize, politicize, and hybridize the tale, incorporating Gothic and annalistic elements and developing alternative models for representing historical processes.[7] Most histories of the novel, with teleological hindsight, have either ignored the genre altogether or mentioned it only as a historical "experiment" without issue or consequence. This chapter argues its importance at once on teleological and on nonteleological grounds. National tales were widely influential in their own right and of formative importance for nineteenth-century realism. As they evolved along with the historical fiction they spawned, they continued to offer a critical alternative to it; their noncanonization is therefore of historical and political interest.

The national tale is a genre developed initially by female authors, who from the outset address questions of cultural distinctiveness, national policy, and political separatism; when the genre shifts tack, it is due partly to their growing self-confidence in their ability to theorize political complexities. With its ambitions both to reflect and to direct national sentiment, the national tale considerably complicates that traditional account of Regency fiction which saw novelistic production polarized between Jane Austen—and other "lady novelists" preoccupied with female socialization, domestic dynamics, and the morality of novel reading—and Walter Scott, who repoliticized (and masculinized) the novel by reinserting it into the larger social field it had occupied with Defoe, Fielding, and Smollett.[8] For Scott derives much of his impetus and many of his strategies for dramatizing political struggles from his female contemporaries. In their main authorship, implied readership, and political perspectives, the national tale and the historical novel might seem to represent differently gendered ways of situating characters, cultures, and history.

The interconnection of the genres instead suggests a dialectical relation between the spheres of male and female authorship, as between Scottish and Irish literature.[9] For a brief moment in the early nineteenth century (as Edinburgh becomes a major center for novel publishing and reviewing) the intense mutual influence of Scottish and Irish novelists and their influence on novel readers of both nations begin to constitute a transperipheral Irish-Scottish public sphere. As genres, nonetheless, the national tale and the historical novel reflect their respective origins in differing historical and cultural experiences. In the Dublin of 1806 and the Edinburgh of 1814, the intensity and immediacy of political sufferings are quite different: the Lowlanders' carefully sentimentalized relationship, sixty years after Culloden, toward Highland culture has no easy parallel in Ireland.[10] There, in the wake of the 1798 United Irishmen rebellion and the 1802 Union with Britain, as many national tales record, the relationship of an Ascendancy intelligentsia to the Gaelic-Catholic culture outside the pale remained unstable and ambivalent; if Irish historical novels and national tales alike return repeatedly to the national trauma of the United Irishmen rebellion, this is because it is both an exemplification and a culmination of many decades of civil unrest.[11]

If Muir and Lukács had analyzed Ireland and the national tale instead of Scotland and the historical novel, they would have seen in Ireland's political turbulence a sufficient explanation for the genre's intermittent political radicalism, instability of tone, and alternation between formula and formal experimentation. Still affected by the desperate unrest of the 1790s, Ireland—Lukács would have argued—proved inauspicious for the birth of realism but sufficiently tortured for the birth of a novelistic protomodernism instead.[12] As Elizabeth Bowen put it in *Bowen's Court* (1942), an annalistic history of Ireland through the history of her own family, "[I]t is not lack of people that make the country seem empty. It has an inherent emptiness of its own."[13]

THE MYSTERIOUS BONDS OF UNION

In "The Story of an Injured Lady, Being a True Picture of Scotch Perfidy, Irish Poverty and English Partiality" (written circa 1706 but published only in 1748), Jonathan Swift uses sustained personification allegory to recount the historical woes of Ireland, the injured lady, at the hands of England, her heartless seducer, and to describe Irish jealousies toward an apparently more favored Scotland, about to enter an official Union with Britain. In Swift's epistolary tale, matters of state are presented as private, familial, and sentimental problems.

> Being ruined by the inconstancy and unkindness of a lover, I hope, a true and plain relation of my misfortunes may be of use and warning to credulous maids, never to put too much trust in deceitful men. A gentleman in the neighbourhood had two mistresses, another and myself; and he pretended honourable love to us both. Our three houses stood pretty near one another; his was parted from mine by a river [the Irish Sea], and from my rival's by an old broken wall [Hadrian's Wall]. . . . Some years ago, this gentleman taking a fancy either to my person or fortune made his addresses to me; which, being then young and foolish, I too readily admitted . . . and, to dwell no longer upon a theme that causeth such bitter reflections, I must confess with shame, that I was undone by the common arts practised upon all easy credulous virgins, half by force, and half by consent, after solemn vows and protestations of marriage. When he once had got possession, he soon began to play the usual part of a too fortunate lover, affecting on all occasions to shew his authority, and to act like a conqueror.[14]

Now he plans to marry his other neighbor instead of herself. What is surprising is that she has not joined forces with her rival; the most inexplicable part of this story is that two women betrayed by the same scoundrel should continue to compete with one another for a man who "pretended honorable love to us both" and deserves neither.[15]

His courtship, complains the injured lady, was a long series of persecutions, which have turned her "pale and thin with grief and ill-usage."[16] He used false promises and physical threats to make her his mistress, then seized control of her household, sapped her domestic authority (insisting that his own "stewart" [Stuart] govern her house), and robbed her blind, forcing her to pay the wages of many of her servants, even those (the absentee landlords) who remain living with him.[17] She has met all of these insults with long-suffering patience. Her rival, however, has met their suitor's bad behavior with rebellious and demanding behavior of her own. "Tall and lean, and very ill-shaped," with "bad features, and a worse complexion," this "infamous creature" has set thieves and pickpockets (the Scottish Highlanders) to rob and to beat him.[18] Yet she is still the one chosen for matrimony.

Recasting the political relations of Ireland, Scotland, and England as a courtship drama, Swift sketches a colonial psychology dominated by envy, passivity, self-reproach, and a tragic inability to see beyond one's own blighted chances. "I am sure, I have been always told," the injured lady says plaintively, "that in marriage there ought to be a union of minds as well as of persons."[19] To many of Swift's Scottish contemporaries, the Act of Union appears as a forced marriage, undertaken against the bride's better judgment. "Why Should I Be So Sad On My Wedding Day?" played the carillon of Saint Giles, Edinburgh, on the day the Treaty of Union was signed. In Ireland, however, many view the Union with envy: Scotland will be Britain's true partner, rather than merely its exploited colony.

Almost one hundred years later, in the wake of the United Irishmen rebellion, a short-lived Irish satirical newspaper, *The Anti-Union* (1798–99), offers two updated versions of Swift's "Injured Lady," to protest the plans for Ireland's Union with Britain. The governing sentiment here is antimatrimonial, and the magazine's masthead quotes an excerpt from the marriage service: "If any of you know any just cause or impediment why these two may not be lawfully joined together, let him now speak, or else hereafter for ever hold his peace." In the first story, a young orphan describes the efforts of her elderly relative, John Bull, to take over her shop, then force her into marriage. "I to marry Mr. Bull!" Sheelagh recoils with horrified scorn. Even "in the year 1783, when he was tolerably vigorous, and reasonably wealthy and well reputed, I would have rejected [him] with contempt!" Now his impending bankruptcy and "repeated fits of the falling sickness" make him less desirable than ever.[20] And the settlements he proposes are ridiculous: "There is to be no cohabitation, for we are still to continue to live on different sides of the water—no reduction of expenses, for our separate establishments are to be kept up—all my servants to be paid by me, but to take their orders from him. . . . He tells me . . . that I am to reap great advantages, the particulars of which he does not think proper to disclose."[21] He even has another wife still living, "who, though of harsh features and slender fortune, was of honourable parentage and good character" and has been shamefully treated by her husband, "with every mark of slight and contumely," with many of her marriage articles "scandalously violated."[22] Mr. Bull, then, is both bigamist and bully; the example of his first marriage makes his current promises impossible to believe. A century after the Union with Scotland, Ireland sees the neglect, bad faith, and condescension she can expect from a Union of her own—and the sight of Scotland's sufferings, over the course of the eighteenth century, has rendered this first consort more sympathetic than she appeared in 1706.

Realizing that he can no longer play his mistresses against each other or force Ireland to his will by exciting her jealousy, Mr. Bull plants a servant in Sheelagh's household to embezzle her money and foment discord among her other servants.

> Some of my servants he has persuaded (by infusing groundless fears and jealousies into their minds) to put on orange liveries, and to threaten death and destruction to the rest; those others again, by similar misrepresentations, he has induced to array themselves in green, and to commit the most horrible excesses, and others he has actually and openly paid with my own money, to aggravate and perpetuate the quarrels between the two former . . .[23]

What appears as an insoluble internal discord within Ireland is actually trouble created by an outside agitator, for John Bull's ends. The influence of United Irishmen rhetoric (particularly Wolfe Tone's argument for a *domestic* union, and a joint fight by Irishmen of all creeds against their English oppressors) is evident here: the refusal of a Union with Britain must be accompanied by an attempt to promote internal unity, by emphasizing a commonality of interests that transcends livery color.

Yet as another "True Story" argues only two weeks later in the same journal, the restoration of domestic harmony is no simple matter: the French invasion of Ireland, under Wolfe Tone's leadership, has shattered Ireland's peace of mind. In this story, the depraved Mr. Britton lusts after the beautiful young Ierne: "[T]ho' in every respect she would have been an eligible match, yet his pride would not suffer him to think of an honourable connexion." His ambitious steward Henry encourages him in "vicious schemes," and Britton finally conquers Ierne by raping her. "[O]ver-power[ing] her defenseless innocence, and invading the rights of hospitality and honour," he forces "the unfortunate and degraded lady" to acquiesce to "a life of dependent concubinage."[24]

Yet Britton is an amiable man, under more ordinary circumstances, and Ierne a woman of sensibility. To Britton's great fortune, then, his victim grows "fond of her violator; and to the first emotions of resentment, and wounded pride, succeeded those tenderer sentiments."[25] Ierne bears him several children, and the family develops an increasingly harmonious domestic life; eventually Britton resolves to "make her his wife." The "ill-adviser" Henry is long dead; his successor, George, concurs in Mr. Britton's plan; and Britton's sentimental attachment toward Ierne is heightened when his ward, Columbia, elopes to America with a Frenchman. In 1782 (at the beginning of Grattan's Parliament) he marries "his old and attached friend" with chastened heart, and for more than ten years, the couple is very happy. Then, the libertine younger brother of Columbia's seducer arrives in the neighborhood and lays siege to Britton's wife, bribing family servants to his cause and trying to stir up Ierne's memories of past resentments. Her response is to arm "the most able of her domestics and the most respectable of her tenants, with orders to horsewhip the intruder, whenever he should have the insolence to approach her," and then to reveal the full plot to Britton.[26] Far from praising his wife's loyalty, however, Britton blames her for what has happened, and his unjust suspicion and misdirected anger disillusion Ierne forever. Although she eventually agrees to a formal reconciliation with her husband, they face permanent emotional estrangement. Their former happiness is irretrievable.

> The loving, ardent, faithful wife had vanished; and the injured, abject, cold and reluctant slave remained. Love was for ever fled. She returned not caresses which she loathed, and submitted to, rather than participated. . . . Mr. Britton, conscious that he could not be loved, precipitated into the usual corruption of the human heart, and determined that he should be feared.[27]

Now, when the profligate Frenchman renews his addresses, his chance of success seems greater, given Ierne's "pitiable and alarming" condition.

> She often exclaims—"Foolish and unprincipled man, how happy might we have been together! I plighted thee my troth, and would have been proud to be thine to my latest hour, but I am abandoned, betrayed and forlorn, and it little matters what becomes of an injured spirit, and a broken heart."[28]

If "A True Story" resembles the previous "Injured Lady" stories, the loyalties it describes are new and newly complex; its tone is no longer that of political satire but of female domestic tragedy, from Richardson's *Clarissa* (1747–78) and Frances Sheridan's *Memoirs of Miss Sidney Bidulph* (1761) to Elizabeth Inchbald's *Simple Story* (1791). Its political message is more ambiguous as well: under bad influence, Britton is capable of rape and, later, of misdirected anger and inappropriate cruelty. Yet in the interim, he is lovable and beloved; it is impossible to dismiss him or his marriage. Ierne, too, shows a complexity and a complicity beyond any previous allegorical embodiment of Ireland; capable of forgiving the original violation of her person, she cannot forgive Britton's subsequent violation of her trust.

Perhaps it is in the nature of marriage that the smaller betrayals prove most damaging and most lasting. In "A True Story," the French invasion of Ireland, and even the United Irishmen rebellion, are less culpable than the original, far more brutal conquest of Ireland to which they offer belated, indirect response. Yet what is most damaging, in the face of overall Irish "loyalty," is the contempt and distrust these events inspire in Britain. There can be no union now, "A True Story" argues, because the marriage has already irrevocably failed.

During the first decades of the nineteenth century, novelists in Ireland, then in Scotland and England, continue to rewrite this national marriage plot. In its initial post-Union reincarnations, in the early novels of Owenson, Edgeworth, and Maturin, the national marriage plot gives the deceptive appearance of allegorical—and therefore political—transparency, stepping back from the emotional ambiguities of "A True Story," to present the Union as a happy ending. Yet these novels are also engaged, from the outset, in a complicated political reconciliation process. What they attempt is not only the cultural rapprochement of a colonizing nation and a colonized one, separated by a huge power differential and a bloody history, but also, more paradoxically, the reconciliation between the imperialist project of a United Kingdom and Wolfe Tone's vision of an internally united Ireland, in which shared purpose transcends differences of creed and culture. The novels of Owenson's and Maturin's middle periods envision crosscultural marriage as a form of countercolonization: when the English fall in love with the natives of Ireland, their courtship and union become occasions for proselytizing and revelation. In learning to live with those scarred by a history of English contempt, English characters are forced to see their own country from the perspective of its victims. Such stories may represent a retrenchment from the revolutionary goals of the United Irishmen (in almost all cases, their authors carefully distance themselves from armed revolution), but their political vision is radical nonetheless, as they imagine a union able to widen the worldview and the historical understanding of *both* partners equally.

From Waverly to *Waverley*

Conceptually, both the national tale and the historical novel develop out of Enlightenment comparative political analysis, from Montesquieu's contrasted cultural geographies to the Scottish Enlightenment's four-stage theory. Throughout the eighteenth century, the picaresque novels of Defoe, Swift, and Fielding, of Smollett and Goldsmith, of Anglo-Irish novelists Thomas Amory, Charles Johnstone, and Elizabeth Hamilton developed parallel modes of social scansion, from the fluid survey offered by picaresque and picturesque travel to the juxtaposition of perspectives made possible by epistolary exchange and the framing conceits of the Oriental satire.[29] During the era of the French Revolution, the novel is influenced directly by political theory: the heated exchanges between supporters and opponents of the Revolution (such as Burke, Paine, and Wollstonecraft) established influential rhetorics with which to present conservative and radical visions of society, and the shape and vehemence of the Jacobinism debate helped to enshrine the polemical contrast of alternative social forms as a major mode of political discussion. Already in 1789 Ann Radcliffe's first novel, *The Castles of Athlin and Dunbayne*, organized its Gothic plot and political analysis around the schematic juxtaposition, in the castles of two warring Highland chiefs, of good and bad variants of feudal life: Castle Athlin is a despotic dungeon, Castle Dunbayne a well-run civitas. By 1792 Charlotte Smith's pro-Jacobin *Desmond* used the same comparative framework much more elaborately, using a travel plot to anchor sustained political and social analysis.

Lionel Desmond accompanies a flighty youth on a pleasure trip into revolutionary France and, as this is an epistolary tale, is soon sending long letters home to his conservative friend Bethel, describing the social conditions that led to the Revolution and the unfolding of the Revolution itself. Bethel's letters, in return, counter Desmond's growing Jacobin sympathies with a Burkean skepticism; the reformers, he argues, appear "wavering and divided in their councils . . . which occasions me again to entertain some doubts of the permanency of the revolution."[30] The novel's first volume thus focuses simultaneously on the transformations in France, on the process of political conversion, and on the growing gap between a progressive political rhetoric based on a firsthand knowledge of social conditions and a reactionary rhetoric grounded in abstract political sentiment. In matched set pieces, furthermore, which reiterate both Third Estate polemics and Radcliffe's two-castle contrast, Desmond visits a democratic aristocrat-reformer, whose pleasant estate is being improved, cultivated, and drained, and then the reformer's despotic uncle, whose estate, still run according to feudal principles, shows signs of wastefulness, corruption, and want.[31] Here the peasants do not sing cheerfully at their work, the landscape is despoiled, and even the ceremonial avenues of trees are ragged from ill-considered chopping.[32]

This contrast between the feudal order and a new social contract implicitly grounds the novel's main story, a platonic but adulterous love that raises the question of women's rights in marriage. In the longer term, the succession and combination of Radcliffe's Highland castles, juxtaposed as discrete political systems, and Smith's plot of travel, cultural comparison, and marriage provide the national tale with its central plot device: the spatialization of political choices, as a journey of discovery and homecoming through the British peripheries.[33] Both the main political bifurcation within the national tale—Edgeworth's pro-Union Irish novels, Owenson's Jacobin-feminist national tales of Ireland, Greece, India, and Belgium—and the political thrust of Scott's historical novel can be measured by their differing adaptations of the novels of the 1790s.[34]

Edgeworth's Irish novels reiterate the Enlightenment critique of feudalism. If *Castle Rackrent* temporalizes Radcliffe's juxtapositions (as an elderly retainer chronicles the successive variants of feudal lordship the same castle has experienced over his lifetime), Edgeworth's subsequent novels respatialize them into discrete, if synchronous, social stages and political states between which her aristocratic characters move and among which they choose. Following Enlightenment discussions of improvement and modernization, *Ennui*, *The Absentee*, and *Ormond* see pre-rebellion and pre-Union Ireland as embodying numerous developmental stages, economic systems, and thus political and moral possibilities for the ruling Ascendancy. For Edgeworth, as for Radcliffe, the choice is between good paternalism and bad feudalism. Yet the Irish situation is complicated: a peasant culture, already formed and deformed by centuries of feudalism and religious strife, is now suffering anew under capitalist landlords, who exploit their political monopoly of power, rack rents, and expect feudal obedience without assuming feudal responsibility. The country's governors can either allow Milesian and Anglo-Irish castes to continue to grow apart or try, through improvement, to forge a new Union between landlords and tenants.

Scott's *Waverley* redacts Smith's *Desmond* both directly and indirectly, under the influence of the national tale genre that Smith's novel helps to shape, as well as of Jane West's antirevolutionary redaction of *Desmond*, *The Loyalists: An Historical Novel* (1812). Throughout his novelistic writing, Scott systematically plays down all of these influences, acknowledging only Edgeworth as a precedent. In the introduction to his first novel, he distances himself from chivalric, sentimental, Gothic, and women's fiction, by pointing to his "neutral" choice of name for his title character: "WAVERLEY, an uncontaminated name, bearing with its sound little of good or evil, excepting what the reader shall hereafter be pleased to affix to it."[35]

To the reader of Charlotte Smith and Jane West, however, this name is already occupied, in a way that sheds an important intertextual light on Scott's political project. Desmond's light-headed charge and travel companion, Waverly, is true to his name in his perennial inability to decide where he should travel and which woman he should marry. Put drunk into the packet boat, Smith's Waverly is so preoccupied with his own confused dissipations that unlike Desmond he is unable to grasp the significance of the political events going on in France. West's *Loyalists* (a tale of the English civil war, as "the reign of terror in England") is even more critical of its character, Sir William Waverley, and his political wavering; during a national emergency that calls for a decisive stand, Waverley is trapped into repeated double crossings, until he has "turned, and trimmed, and cut in, and cut out, till nobody knew whether he was of any side at all."[36] Forced to hide from both sides, he takes refuge in the ruins of his ancestral home, destroyed by the "ravages of civil war."[37]

> Waverley Hall was a complete ruin. A few of the meaner offices, and a part of the walls, marked where the residence stood, which once sheltered crafty selfishness. . . . [T]he unclaimed demesne, [was] once guarded even from the intrusion of admiring curiosity, by the secluding jealousy of a cold-hearted worldling, whose pride counteracted his ostentation, and whose timidity was even greater than his self-love. . . . The streets of the village were silent and deserted. Neither the loom, the flail, nor the anvil were heard.[38]

If West's extended description of the despoiled estate echoes Smith's description of the ill-managed aristocratic estate of midrevolutionary France, it anticipates Scott's description, at the end of *Waverley*, of the stately home despoiled during the Jacobite Rebellion, its outlawed aristo-cratic owners hiding in its ruins, and its blasted oaks marking the end of an epoch. Twenty years after *Desmond* and two years after *The Loyalists*, *Waverley* wavers between Smith's and West's visions of revolution. In contrast to West, Scott narrates a hapless journey into civil war from a perspective sympathetic both to the forces of rebellion and to Waverley himself: in a time of historical upheaval, loyalty is not a simple duty but requires repeated adjudications as circumstances shift. Like *Desmond*, *Waverley* uses set-piece comparisons to describe the collapse of aristo-cratic authority. Yet its political inferences end up reversed, Tory rather than Jacobin; a conservative rebellion, not a progressive one, receives the author's partial endorsement, and the feudal world of the Highland clans commands the deepest allegiance and easiest loyalty.

If Scott's first novel adapts both Jacobin and anti-Jacobin novelistic forms while disavowing the Jacobin political legacy, the title of Sydney Owenson's first novel announces its redaction of Smith with perhaps un-conscious force. Like *Desmond*, Owenson's *St. Clair, or The heiress of Desmond* (1804) is an epistolary novel that juxtaposes a travel plot with a plot of adulterous longing. It is preoccupied with the politics of redaction, transposing the plot of Goethe's *Werther* to Ireland, so that its ubiqitous Ossian references are not only sublime rhetorical tags but have geopolitical correlatives. Owenson's second novel, *The Novice of St. Domnick*, histori-cizes the redaction process in order to examine the surprising overlap be-tween historical epochs and discursive systems. Compared with Owen-son's later oeuvre, these early novels are striking for their grasp of how the contrastive plots of the 1790s can be used to launch a discussion of literary history—and for the way their preoccupation with the politics of writing preempts a more extended discussion of contemporary or national poli-tics.[39] Developing a still more complex variation of the same romance plot, Owenson's third novel, *The Wild Irish Girl*, juxtaposes the concerns of her previous novels to explore the tension between a literary, antiquarian sense of Ireland and a nationalist, bardic one. This suddenly recovers the political implications of Smith's traveling plot and the political analysis of Edgeworth's Irish chronicle.[40]

Banished by his father to his Irish estates, the English hero of *The Wild Irish Girl* is delighted to find picturesque scenery and customs: the dispossessed Princess Glorvina, singing to her harp; the priest's explanation of the antiquity and venerability of Irish traditions; and the eerily keening voices of the peasant funeral procession. A landscape assumed to be barren and backward reverberates with the sounds of an ancient culture. Growing to love Ireland, the hero ends the novel by marrying Glorvina, its allegorical embodiment, and settling on "their" joint estate. For the next ten years, the national tale will present increasingly stylized repetitions of this basic plot: the contrast, attraction, and union of disparate cultural worlds. In each subsequent version, an English character again travels to a British periphery, expected to be devoid of culture. Instead, under the tutelage of an aristocratic friend, he or she learns to appreciate its cultural plenitude and decides to settle there permanently. Each national tale ends with the traveler's marriage to his or her native guide, in a wedding that allegorically unites Britain's "national characters," or, to quote the title of an 1814 national tale by Christian Johnstone, *The Saxon and the Gaël*.[41]

Developed by Owenson and Edgeworth, influencing and influenced by Madame de Staël, the national tale reaches generic turning points first with Maturin's brilliant 1812 *Milesian Chief* (arguably the single most important source for *Waverley*) and then with the 1814 publication of *Waverley* itself; together, these two novels reiterate and transform the national tale's generic premises by historicizing its allegorical framework. The national tale before *Waverley* presents late-eighteenth-century culturalist assumptions, the influence of geography on character, setting, and events, in particularly concentrated and politicized forms, upholding the distinctiveness and autonomy of place. And from *Waverley* onward, the historical novel shows the collapse and transfiguration of place, as an annalistic accretion of time within the stability of place gives way to the phenomenological development of places. The national tale before *Waverley* maps developmental stages topographically, as adjacent worlds in which characters move and then choose between; the movement of these novels is geographical rather than historical. In contrast, the historical novel (which still, at the outset of *The Milesian Chief* and of *Waverley*, relies on a schematic juxtaposition of stratified cultural zones) finds its focus in the way one developmental stage collapses to make room for the next and cultures are transformed under the pressure of historical events. With their respective focuses on the domestic and political spheres as the sites of national and historical formation, on the stability of culture in place and the fragility of culture over time, the two genres develop dialectically opposed ways of situating culture. The national tale before *Waverley* presents national character as a synecdoche of an unchanging cultural space; here nationalism is a self-evident legacy, the result of unbroken continuity and a populist community that unites aristocracy and folk. The historical novel draws heavily on this vision of national continuity, but it posits the moment of nationalism at a further stage of historical development: only through the forcible, often violent, entry into history does the feudal folk community become a nation, and only through dislocation and collective suffering is a new national identity forged.

National Journey, National Marriage, National Character

As the national tale moves toward and past the historical novel, its key generic features change in emphasis. Focusing on the genre's three most distinctive features—the journey, the marriage, and the national character—this section will sketch its overall development, describing the shifting relationship in Owenson's work between tourism and textual tradition, the movement of the marriage plot from a comedy of national reconciliation toward a tragedy of doomed love in Maturin's *Milesian Chief*, and the transformation of an allegorically flattened national character, over the history of the genre, into one torn apart by the contradictions of uneven development. As it moves from the unchanging national world toward the dislocations of the historical novel, the national tale (as a genre centered on an allegorical equation of personal and cultural identity) becomes the birthplace of a new literary schizophrenia.

Throughout the nineteenth century, complains Daniel Corkery, Anglo-Irish writers create a self-consciously "Colonial" literature, their "account of this strange country they are condemned to, written not for their brothers and co-mates in exile . . . but for their kinsfolk in England . . . for what are all their books but travellers' tales?"[42] The national tale is at once traveler's tale and anticolonial tract; it sets out to describe a long-colonized country "as it really is," attacking the tradition of imperial description from Spenser to Johnson and constructing an alternative picture. The physical and cultural landscape of the periphery has its own beauty; as it arises organically from specific historical and geographical circumstances, a national art must be understood on its own terms, not forced into a prior aesthetic mold it can never fit. Yet nationalist authors also embrace all aspects of the national culture with even a remote resemblance to Mediterranean cultural prototypes, for such similarities provide a particularly powerful means of establishing cultural legitimacy.[43] The footnotes to *The Wild Irish Girl* labor to establish connections or analogies between the customs, religious rituals, music, dancing, and literature of ancient Greece and those of present-day Ireland; they also point out more esoteric resemblances between Hibernian and ancient Egyptian dress.[44] Already, then, the impulse to develop original, indigenous criteria for cultural evaluation is matched, or checked, by the resort to precedent.[45]

Owenson's next novel, *O'Donnel*, focuses explicitly on problems of cultural interpretation and the difficulty of ensuring that the English tourists who begin to visit Ireland after the Act of Union will be properly sensitive to Irish culture. The novel opens with a collective journey of national exploration; the boorish behavior of aristocratic Londoners as they traverse "the wilds" of northern Ireland, more interested in each other than in where they are, provides a negative exemplum for real-life English tourists.[46] Even in the presence of the most "venerable ruins," these travelers remain offensively "flippant," sprawling on ancient tombstones and treating all natives (including their social equals) with insulting condescension. They neither accord to Ireland the respect due to an ancient civilization ("It is totally impossible that an *Irish* scene could resemble anything in *Italy*: the comparison is really quite comical") nor take notice of its current efforts to modernize itself.

> [W]e happen to have no taste for coal-mines:—besides I don't give any credit to your knowing how to work coal-mines in Ireland. You had better stick to your bogs. . . . But have you nothing about Fingal here? No place that Ossian mentions? We are told that this is the spot for that sort of thing.[47]

O'Donnel at once parodies and promotes a touristic view of Ireland. For although it criticizes the way literary tourism blinds the visitor, ever searching for the ancient site, to the lived connections between past and present, the novel sets itself up as a literary guidebook to the north of Ireland, setting an agenda for future tours.[48] This is a growing double bind for the national tale: it uses Irish and Scottish picturesqueness to buttress claims to inherent worth and to English attention while trying to keep its own antiquarianism from obscuring either the peripheries' current problems or England's historical responsibility for them.[49]

In Owenson's *Florence Macarthy*, the literary mediation of Ireland not only accompanies but overshadows the journey of national exploration. As *Il Librador* lands in Dublin harbor, the vessel's passenger (actually Lord Fitzadelm, returning Anglo-Irish absentee) and its captain (actually General Fitzwalter, hero of South America's wars of liberation and rightful heir to Fitzadelm's estate) argue about Spenser's *View of the Present State of Ireland* and Volney's *Ruines des empires anciens* (1791); political differences can be restated as hermeneutic and aesthetic ones.

> "[I]n viewing Ireland through Spenser's pages, you will see it, as children do an eclipse, through a smoked glass. He was one of those, whose policy it was to revile the country he preyed upon, to spoil, and then to vituperate. . . . Spenser, the deputy of a deputy[,] . . . is no author for impartiality to judge by;

and when he stoops to eulogize the '*dreadless might*' of his ferocious patron, Grey, one of Ireland's Herods . . . however he may please as a poet, he is contemptible as an historian, and infamous as a politician."

"Oh! as a historian or politician I give him up, because both characters are equally ridiculous. . . . The imagination alone is always right; its visions are alone imperishable. The *Fairy Queen* of Spenser will thus survive, when his State of Ireland shall be wholly forgotten: and, for my own part, so much do I prefer the visions of his fancy to the historical relations of any period connected with the history of men, that I would go a thousand miles to visit the ruins of his Irish *Kilcoleman*. . . . But I am not sure that I would turn one point out of the way to tread upon the spot where legitimate despotism signed the fiat of its own destruction, and gave Magna Charta to an emancipated nation."[50]

Entering an impoverished, bedraggled Dublin, Fitzadelm and Fitzwalter gaze at the former Irish Parliament, turned into the Bank of Ireland in the wake of the Union.

"It is a beautiful thing of its kind [says Fitzadelm] . . . what will it be centuries hence, touched by the consecrating hand of time, when its columns shall lie prostrate, its pediments and architraves broken and moss-grown, when all around it is silence and desolation? Then haply . . . may cast some future Volney of the Ohiho or the Susquehanah upon the shores of this little Palmyra, and he may surmise and wonder, may dream his theories, and calculate his probabilities; and, bending over these ruins, see the future in the past, and apostrophize the inevitable fate of existing empires."

"Or an American freeman," observed the Commodore, "the descendant of some Irish exile, may voluntarily seek the bright green shores of his fathers, and, in this mouldering structure, behold the monument of their former degradation." (1:49–50)[51]

"The one spoke in epic, the other in epigram" (1:78); the Anglo-Irish proponent of Spenser and literary autonomy, scorning any connections between literary representation and political life, reads post-Union Ireland, too, in "aesthetiquarian" terms: the more ruins, the more beautiful. His Irish nationalist interlocutor condemns Spenser's imperialism and reads Ireland's ruins politically rather than aesthetically, as evidence of British oppression. Fitzadelm evokes the famous opening of Volney's *Ruins*: as a traveler contemplates the ruins of an ancient temple and mourns the destruction of past greatness, the genius of the ruins—the spirit and voice of the past—addresses him. Imagining his own present as some future traveler's tragically lost cultural past, Fitzadelm is affected by the melancholy and pathos of history. In his philosophy, the ruin of successive cultures is a recurring historical necessity as much as a recurring historical tragedy;

contemplating a ruined Irish abbey (and recalling a Spanish convent, whose cloisters adjoined a Moorish ruin), he muses "on the course of things, from the fragments of Arabic taste and Mahometan superstition, into the temple of Christian rites" (1:113).

This model of historical transubstantiation, in which one culture is wholly, inevitably, subsumed into the next, informed Owenson's *Novice of St. Domnick*. Now she condemns it for feeding political resignation; the Moors' conquest of and expulsion from Spain, the English conquest of Ireland, and the Spanish conquest of South America, with all their accompanying bloodshed, are in this worldview unalterable facts of natural history. When General Fitzwalter discusses the South American wars of liberation, Fitzadelm argues that any revolutionary struggles will prove futile in the end, as the forces of liberation become identical to the forces of oppression.

> Man . . . in whatever region he is found, may best be typified by a squirrel in a cage. . . . His little sphere is so planned . . . that he can be nothing but what he is, do nothing but what he does. He goes round his circle, and repeats his rotations, with no difference in the performance, but a little acceleration or a little retardment. These South Americans, therefore, but repeat an old story: they are savage and unprotected, they are conquered;—they are slaves, and degraded, they endure;—they are pressed to the quick, they turn and resist;—they struggle and succeed, become great, properous, illumined; conquer and oppress in their turn, moulder away. (3:143–44)

If Fitzadelm glorifies the ruin as an emblem of political futility, Fitzwalter, "the brave Guerilla Chief," refuses the ruin as an aesthetic spectacle to claim it instead as the evidence of historical crimes: his Volney laments the enslaving subjection of empire to proclaim the universal rights of man in its stead; his genius of the ruins appears not to mourn the past but to call for liberation. If Fitzadelm enthusiastically anticipates a distant age in which Ireland's ruin becomes picturesquely complete, Fitzwalter is impassioned by the signs of ruin visible already in the present day, in a parliament turned into a bank, a nation destroyed by its transformation into an economic colony. With such contrasts, Owenson implicitly refuses literary modes of reading culture, along with a colonizing tradition of literary depictions: from Spenser to Johnson, the great English poets are politically complicit with the imperialist expansionism of the English government. At the same time, like Jane Austen and other contemporaries, she continues to use literary judgments as touchstones of character and metaphors of reading to describe the problem of deciphering Ireland, that "text, whose spirit and whose letter were mis-rule and oppression" (1:94–95).

From its original didactic attempts to educate English readers (by providing them, in *The Wild Irish Girl* and *O'Donnel*, with picturesque and polemical guidebooks) the national tale moves toward critical sociologies of colonial society (*Florence Macarthy*, *The Absentee*, and *Ormond*), then militant histories of colonialism (*The Milesian Chief*, *The O'Briens and the O'Flahertys*, and *The Anglo-Irish of the Nineteenth Century*).[52] In parallel, its central political tendency shifts gradually from a celebratory nationalism, which both recognizes cultural distinctiveness and believes in the possibility of transcultural unions, toward a more separatist position; continuing meditation on a history of cultural oppression makes rapprochement and reconciliation increasingly inconceivable.[53]

These shifts deeply affect both the national tale's marriage plot and its national characters.[54] The culminating acts of union become fraught with unresolved tensions, leading to prolonged courtship complications, to marital crises, and even, in two of Susan Ferrier's novels, to national divorce.[55] The resulting traumas erode the mental stability of national characters, where they do not tear them apart. Owenson's 1811 *Missionary: An Indian Tale* (whose seventeenth-century Indian setting highlights the thematics of colonialism, domination, and forced modernization beginning to emerge in the genre as a whole) evokes the tragedy of Westernization through the ill-fated love of Hilarion, apostolic nuncio to India, and Luxima, Kashmir princess and priestess of Brahma. His attempts to convert her to Christianity and their subsequent romance result in her banishment and loss of caste and his defrocking and trial by the Inquisition.[56] Deeply irreconcilable, the two cultures of India and Rome can meet only when the analogous despotism of their respective superstitions becomes visible: the moment when Luxima attempts to perform suttee at the very stake on which the Inquisition has condemned Hilarion to be burned. Luxima's increasing self-alienation, as her thoughts are pulled back and forth between old cultural alliances and new emotional ties, suggests a sociohistorical genesis of mental illness.

> Her mind was wandering and unsettled; the most affecting species of mental derangement had seized her imagination, the melancholy insanity of sorrow: she wept no tears, she heaved no sighs—she sat still and motionless, sometimes murmuring a Brahminical hymn, sometimes a Christian prayer—sometimes telling of her grandsire, sometimes of her lover—alternatively gazing on the mantras she had received from one, and the cross that had been given her by the other.[57]

The madhouse scene in Maturin's *Melmoth the Wanderer* (1820) suggests a vertiginous proliferation of such divisions, as the imprisoned narrator is surrounded on both sides by men driven into alternative forms of schizophrenia by different aspects of the English civil war. On one side, a Loyalist tailor, ruined by giving credit to Cavaliers, spends his days reciting "fragments of Lovelace and Aphra Behn" in "a voice half in exultation and half in derision." On the other side, a Puritan weaver is driven mad by religious enthusiasm: "[H]alf the day he imagines himself in a pulpit, denouncing damnation against Papists, Arminians, and even Sub-lapsarians. . . . At night his creed retaliates on him: he believes himself one of the reprobates he has been all day denouncing, and curses God for the very decree he has all day been glorifying him for."[58] The early national tale's timeless, flatly allegorical characters are here transformed into tormented, bifurcated characters who wage a perennial civil war within themselves; entering violently into history, such characters are at once forced into rapid change and have a part of their psyche permanently numbed by shock, remaining behind in a state of arrested development.[59]

As Maturin's *Milesian Chief* demonstrates, the national tale becomes increasingly sophisticated in representing the link between cultural/character formation and a complex historical temporality. With its journey of national discovery, its national characters (Armida, the harp-playing Anglo-Italian aristocrat who returns from the Continent to her father's newly acquired Irish estates, and Connal, the fiery, dispossessed Irish prince), and its allegorical love story, on the one hand, and its setting in recent history, on the other hand (as its hero becomes unwittingly entangled in the United Irishmen rebellion), *The Milesian Chief* straddles the divide between *The Wild Irish Girl* and *Waverley*, national tale and historical novel. The novel also reiterates every Ossianic, sentimental, and Gothic trope of the last fifty years—in the moment before the paradigm shift, before the birth of a new genre, the concentration of sheer literariness results not only in many passages of great rhetorical intensity but in a powerful evocation of the need for tradition.

The novel's love story stages the meeting, mingling, and suppression of two adjacent, dialectically opposed cultural traditions, Greco-Roman and Greco-Hibernian, antiquarian and bardic, neoclassical and sentimental.[60] Over performances of respective national song and harp traditions, and an argument over Volney in a ruined cemetery, the Continental artistic genius and ruin enthusiast falls in love with the Irish genius loci and comes to see Ireland as a ruined and desolate country.[61] The diametrically opposed positions that Owenson develops, six years later, between Fitzadelm and Fitzwalter here confront each other, then begin to merge, as Connal adopts Armida's habit of classical allusion and as Armida learns to appreciate Ossianic poetry not just as "primitive" artistry but as sophisticated cultural expression and testimony. As in previous national tales, universalizing judgments and standards are replaced with a political energy based on local attachments. A decorative, scholarly neoclassicism becomes infected with the "wild energy" of national feeling; antiquarianism gives way to revolutionary romanticism.[62]

The Milesian Chief thus begins to allegorize historical development along with cultural essence, dramatizing the process by which one cultural episteme overlaps with, and gives way to, the next—only then, in its almost apocalyptic ending, to suggest the end of culture and of developmental history under the crushing forces of the modern state. The national revolution fails, brutally suppressed by the armies of the new English property owners; Connal is executed by a firing squad; Armida takes poison; and the cultural and aesthetic principles they stand for die. In comparison, the ending of *Waverley* (with its love in the ruins and its marriage of English and Lowland aristocracies, a private happiness that sublates the historical dislocation of Highland culture) comes to look unduly optimistic, giving the violence of history a retroactive meaning, purpose, and alibi.[63]

In other respects, it is but a small step from *The Milesian Chief* to *Waverley*, from Armida (herself a descendant of Glorvina and Corinne) to Flora, from national tale to historical novel. Scott's novel simultaneously traces and reverses the national tale's journey of discovery and homecoming, deposing and eulogizing its hero's romantic fantasies; while Waverley is moving northward and backward in cultural time (leaving the eighteenth century and traveling by way of the fourteenth century to discover what is left of the third), historical forces are beginning to move Highland culture toward modernity. The wavering of Waverley; the madness of David Gellatney, appearing first as regression and then as timely elegy; the fading of Flora as her culture withers and the second blossoming of Rose as the fortunes of her house recover: Lukács sees in *Waverley* an emerging characterological roundness or psychological realism, as the behavior or meaning of characters changes with their historical situation. But this increasingly phenomenological notion of character (which he sees as particularly suited to demonstrating the subtleties of historical change) has clear continuities with the ancient forms of personification allegory found in the early national tale and with the historically induced neurosis studied in the later national tale. The idea of representative character comes full circle.

GENERIC INNOVATION AND LITERARY HISTORICAL RECAPITULATION

One purpose in studying the history of genre is to trace how specific intellectual-historical formations within which new genres are forged and flourish become subsumed, over the course of the genre, into its formal and tropic vocabulary and thus live on long after this original context is forgotten, perhaps long after the genre is defunct. Even today, the haunted house of horror fiction and horror films horrifies because of its antiquity, the layers of memories and lives entombed within it. This horror of the past is the product of a long-distant historical moment, born of the obsessions of the eighteenth-century antiquarian revival and the Gothic fiction to which it gives rise. Both of these, in turn, have their roots in specific national histories. In the wake of the Reformation, the Elizabethan campaigns in Ireland, and the reign of Cromwell, eighteenth-century Britain and Ireland were full of historically resonant ruins, full of abandoned abbeys and desolate manor houses, in a way that the fifteenth century was not. The eighteenth century's new awareness of period is due not only to the increasing pace of economic modernization and cultural change but also to the lasting sense of historical rupture caused by the political and religious developments of the sixteenth and seventeenth centuries.[64] "Tonight the walls are lonely," writes one seventeenth-century Irish bard, lamenting the ruin of his master's ancestral home, "where we once heard harps and poets . . . sounds of soldiers sharpening weapons . . . wise men's voices over old books"; if, as translator Thomas Kinsella notes, a "catalogue of beloved sounds . . . which once enchanted the poet is a feature of Irish poetry from the earliest times," that cataloging tradition echoes very differently, with almost Ossianic resonance, from the walls of the abandoned castle.[65] So, too, the Gothic topos of the haunted house resonates with the half-repressed memory of these cultural defeats. The seventeenth-century Irish bard and the memorializing bard imagined by eighteenth- and nineteenth-century literari are equally obsessed with memorializing a lost cultural moment as a way of holding on to its fragments. The memory of genre functions both in parallel and in contrast to such bardic memory.

Literature's (involuntary) historical expressiveness, argues Owenson in the preface to *O'Donnel*, exists in tension with its recurring crisis of conventionality.

> Literary fiction . . . has always exhibited a mirror of the times in which it is composed; reflecting morals, customs, manners, peculiarity of character, and prevalence of opinion. Thus, perhaps, after all, it forms the best history of nations; the rest being but the dry chronicles of facts and events, which in the same stages of society occur under the operations of the same passions, and tend to the same consequences. But, though such be the primary character of fictitious narrative, we find it, in its progress, producing arbitrary models, derived from conventional thinking amongst writers, and influenced by the doctrines of the learned, and the opinions of the refined.[66]

The relationship between the genres of the national tale and the historical novel could be described in comparable terms. Throughout Britain and Central Europe, national literary histories were established or reestablished, during the late eighteenth and early nineteenth centuries, through the publication or republication of representative literary works in a few key genres. Some of these genres are philological and scholarly (including dictionaries, collections of folk songs, and editions of oral narratives and medieval literary "monuments"); some (national epics from *Ossian* to the *Kalevala*) are semi- or pseudoscholarly. The national tale and the historical novel belong to the few genres that are openly imaginative, although they too incorporate scholarly elements and many of the key features of the nationalist genres that precede them. This recapitulation is self-conscious, an accretion of literary conventions that corresponds on a formal level to the accretion of national characteristics, conventions, and experiences that forms the setting or subject of their narratives. For both the national tale (with its stress on the thick accretion of cultural life-forms) and the historical novel (with its stress on the fragility and malleability of cultures in the face of historical crisis), cultural memory and "genre memory" come to seem intimately linked.

The transition from national tale to historical novel, as a moment of generic accretion and generic rupture, offers an interesting place to examine how this process of recapitulation and repertoire sorting takes place. It also offers the opportunity for a second kind of theoretical speculation, about our ability to model the origins, development, standardization, and metamorphosis of generic forms. Where do genres come from? Why and how do they change? They arise, we might argue, in response to historical crises.[67] The growing inadequacy and obsolescence of social paradigms and thus also of literary forms used to represent a changing world leads at a particularly charged historical moment to the creation of a new genre; this literary equivalent of a paradigm shift gives expression to a new epistemology, a new constellation of social concerns. Thereafter, however, as it develops its own conventions, the genre may drop out of history again, become increasingly literary in its reference and models, and grow increasingly detached from the new social, historical, or national situation it was designed to describe, until the gap between literary representation and lived reality reaches crisis proportions and the cycle begins again.

This description of generic metamorphosis, like much of the modern vocabulary used to discuss historical change, is derived (at least indirectly) from the Waverley novels, with their depiction of clear historical thresholds and their related notion that those moments of transition, those breaking points, are the moments that are most historically charged, moments in which history is "entered" dramatically and irrevocably. But there are things this model cannot account for, given the fixed relationship it assumes between historical reality and representational form, between original, pathbreaking generic prototype and increasingly convention-bound copies. If literary works group themselves into genres, they do so by a number of means: through their methods of establishing narrative voice, perspective, and tone; their techniques of characterization; their demarcation of the narrative and sociopolitical space through which the characters move; and the range of social and literary concerns they address. But they are also patterned by their conscious recycling of a preexisting range of plot patterns and moves, the way they borrow and deploy tropes, themes, and characters from earlier works and announce their literary consanguinity with other works of the same genre. Literariness, conventionality, can express a powerful relationship to tradition. And the development of genre, seen from inside, can seem dynamic as well as static, as its conventions are worked over, tried out, discarded temporarily, fought over, and realigned from work to work.

If the national tale before *Waverley* habitually presents a regionalist chronotope so strong that it pulls cosmopolitan modern travelers back into it, the historical novel presents a violent struggle between different possible future worlds derivable from the same past, a process complete only when a particular present subsumes the past, with all its historiographical and narrative possibilities. Lukács and subsequent historians of the novel have seen the Waverley novels (immediately, rightly, and inevitably) supplanting or subsuming other narrative forms because they represented the most historiographically complex, politically nuanced, and psychologically sophisticated account of historical forces available in the British novel of its time. But if, with the historical novel, a progressivist history of linear progressions, paradigm shifts, and epistemic breaks seems to have gained a clear victory over other, more accretive models for representing temporality and change, its triumph was by no means so absolute in the historical moment in which it was apparently consolidated.[68]

After 1814 (while a late national tale is developed in interesting and diverging directions by Edgeworth, Ferrier, and the Banims) the Waverley novels are challenged by Galt's "theoretical histories" (his Tales of the West), on the one hand, and by the late work of Maturin and Owenson, on the other.[69] With the national tale as one starting point, these authors begin to explore the coexistence of multiple layers of time in place and the discontinuities of place in time. Problematizing schematic or totalizing explanations of historical causation, they approach history instead as a network of synchronous and nonsynchronous causes, effects, and processes.

Their most important divergence from Scott lies in their attention to the long-term effects of historical trauma, the deliberate or amnesiac repression of historical memory, and the neurotic mechanisms developed to contain its explosiveness. The historiographical structure of the Waverley novels depends on an important paradox. Continuously, omnisciently, and for the most part unobtrusively narrated, their central narratives represent the triumph of a single-focus narrative history; they thus point forward, toward the realist novel. At the same time, their elaborate documentary framework of footnotes and pseudoeditorial commentaries echo the footnoted debates among late-eighteenth-century antiquarians, foregrounding the retroactive, antiquarian production of historical knowledge out of a myriad of experiences, records, and possible reconstructions. Such framing lends density to Scott's historiographical survey. Yet it also privileges the perspective of antiquarian narrators over that of historical participants, for the intellectual complexity of the act of historiographic assembly potentially exceeds the psychological complexity of historical experience itself.

United in their criticism of this textualist vision of history, Galt, Maturin, and Owenson develop differing strategies, in the wake of *Waverley*, to recapture the thickness and jaggedness of lived history. Ironically, they choose to refigure the relationship between experience and text by appropriating elements from the Gothic novel and from annalistic history, although these represent even more extreme forms of textualism than the historical novel. The Gothic, with its self-conscious nesting of narratives, its chapters overshadowed by poetic epigraphs, and its plots matching characters to ancestral portraits or prophecies to fix their identities, is often textually as well as psychologically claustrophobic, presenting a real world overshadowed by textual tradition, a history mediated by previous representations.[70] The annal, conversely, with its apparently naive listing of narrated events in an order dictated only by chronology, levels banalities and catastrophes in a single dead-pan narrative voice.[71]

Yet the fusing of these genres with each other and with the national tale produces an alternative historical fiction of enormous psychological and political power. If Scott's novels depict the process of cultural erasure under the violence of history, Maturin's and Owenson's historical Gothics describe a historical and political repetition compulsion. And where Scott's novels telescope long-term historical processes into single dramatic events, played out by small groups of major and minor actors, Galt and Owenson refashion the annal form to explore the temporal unevenness of development and the otherwise invisible connections between local occurrences and long-term processes, local agency and centralizing institutions. Owenson's panoramic *The O'Briens and the O'Flahertys* (1827) demonstrates how the cumulative weight of Irish history affects individual historical players. The very names of the O'Briens and the O'Flahertys are saturated with historical meaning: "Every thing in Connaught is the sign of the feuds and alliances, of hatreds and loves, of ancient inheritances, and recent usurpations. What an abridgement of the history of the land. . . is the story of the O'Briens and the O'Flahertys."[72]

In a novel littered with historical namesakes, revenants, and reincarnations, the culminating union of Murrough O'Brien and Beauvoin O'Flaherty cannot provide a unifying resolution so much as suggest (because another Murrough O'Brien married another Beauvoin O'Flaherty several generations earlier, in an Ireland just as divided in her sufferings) the repetitive loop in which the Irish people are caught.

Despite its concern with revolutionary upheaval (culminating in the United Irishmen rebellion), the novel's sense of historical breakthrough is relativized by the interpolation of an illuminated chronicle of the two families, the *Annals of St. Grellan*, which details the history of Ireland from its first settlement through various waves of English conquest and occupation, breaking off with the unbearable horrors of the recent past.

> 1691. King William's army plunder and murder the poore Irish at pleasure . . . what sport they made to hang up poore Irish people by dozens, without pains to examine them; they scarcely thinking them human kind: so that they now began to turn rapparees, hiding themselves . . . in glens and crannies of O'Flaherty's mountains . . . nothing was commoner than to find many, who from too much melancholy, grief, fear of death, and constant danger, subsisting upon herbs . . . and the like. . . . And wild indeed were they, in these troubleous times, and down to the present; and when one of them was taken . . . it would be with long and extraordinary care and management that they were brought to their senses, and sure were they ever to remain affected or light. (Pp. 241–42)

The continuation a century later of a subculture of political outlaws and guerrilla fighters, based in the same hills and engaged in the same struggle, makes it difficult to dismiss the chronicle's portrait of the "rapparee, or wild Irishmen, Of the 18th century" either as mythology or historical aberration (p. 243). We are a long way, suddenly, from the "maddening" charms of the wild Irish girl and from an Ireland whose history of conquest poses a picturesque and empathy-inducing picture. The disconnected, repetitive nature of the family chronicle bears witness to the unassimilable nature of the violence done to Ireland: to become "wild," to go mad, is the only sane response. The annal both offers an enormously complex account of Ireland's religious and political conflicts and mournfully records the constancy of her woe. It "was curious," the hero remarks understatedly, "to observe the same system still reproducing the same effects" (p. 232).

In *The Entail* and *The Provost* (both 1822), John Galt emphasizes the nonsynchronicity of historical change and the increasing invisibility of historical agency. A family chronicle that ends as a romance, *The Entail* offers an indirect intellectual, political, and literary annal of eighteenth-century Scotland, presented as a complex tissue of innovations, survivals, nostalgias, and throwbacks. Its form reflects the shifting Zeitgeist of Scotland through a slow metamorphosis of literary genre and stylistic register, opening at the beginning of the eighteenth century with a hard-edged Defoean realism and closing late in the century in Ossianic elegy and Mackenziesque sentimentalism. The novel also offers a psychologically nuanced

picture of how historical change is internalized by a succession of characters, fundamentally affecting their self-perception and moral choices; although the basic pattern of family history repeats itself, the changing social
and economic context renders successive generations of the family mutually unintelligible. Galt's foregrounding of economic factors as the most
important long-term motor of plot and character development not only lets
him escape cultural nostalgia but places its euphemisms historically and
politically. In 1711, Joseph Addison's essay on the Border ballad "Chevy
Chase" inaugurates the ballad revival, in London. In Scotland, however,
during the same year, eleven-year-old Claud Walkinshaw (born, orphaned,
and impoverished during the failed Darien Expedition, which paved the
way for the 1707 Union) prepares to travel the Borders as a peddler, es-
chewing "Chevy Chase" (and the heroic tales that inspired his father to his
fatal patriotic adventure) for Dick Whittington's story of economic ad-
vancement. Even decades later, when he has become a prosperous landowner, the remembered weight of his pack and of his early poverty makes
Walkingshaw hunched, pinched, and pathologically stingy, obsessed with
reassembling his lost estate and passing it down intact, so that at least one
descendant will escape the curse of recent Scottish history.

And so, in the 1760s, while his neglectful elderly relative, Miss Chris-
tiana Heritage, draws up a codicil to her will "for the purpose of devising,
as heir-looms, the bedstead and blankets in which Prince Charles Edward
slept, when he passed the night in her house," Walkinshaw is in the next
room, disinheriting his beloved oldest son, Charlie (namesake of the
Young Pretender and "ay [his father's] darling chevalier"), out of a fear of
historical repetition that actually compels him to repeat history. "Ye ken
how I was defrauded," Walkinshaw explains to his lawyer in a greedy
voice, "of my patrimony, by my grandfather."[73] The middle-class nostalgia
of the 1770s for the heroic events of the '45, the cult being built up around
the Heritages of Scotland, is historically synchronic yet emotionally
nonsynchronous with Walkinshaw's sharp voice, with the long-term economic fears, the indelible trauma of class displacement inflicted by the
Darien disaster seventy years earlier.

The Provost is Galt's most bravura handling of the motor, mechanism,
and force of historical changes, as well as of the narrative voice that filters,
explains, and trivializes them.[74] Framed as the provost's reminiscences at
the end of a personally profitable career in public office, the novel gradually makes visible (under the annalistic accumulation of incident and anec-
dote) the equally gradual transformation of small-town society from the
1760s to the 1820s, the establishment of a new middle-class hegemony
under the guise of improvement, and the disfranchisement of the new Scottish working class. Like its most important model, Tacitus's annals of the

erosion of Roman republicanism, Galt's account of the consolidation of power by a new ruling class does not focus on consequence-laden historical turning points, dramatic psychomachian struggles in which old and new forces battle to the death. Instead we watch the unnoticed, almost imperceptible leaking away of one age, one political system, while another is slowly and deliberately constructed in its place, an accumulation of small but decisive incidents (the enclosure of the town moor; the repair, enclosure, and leasing of the Kirk pews to introduce a new hierarchy of property into the congregation; the suppression of the traditional fairs and of a meal mob protesting prices) that lend power to the new forces of bourgeois self-interest and erode the participatory power of everyone else.

The motors of historical change, here, are neither abstract historical forces nor larger-than-life world-historical agents. Historical change appears to be partly the result of deliberate attempts to alter the organization and character of social life and partly the indirect effect of such manipulations, the self-perpetuation and proliferation of changes once they have been introduced. On the most visible level, change appears as an incidental (even unintended) byproduct of the growing ambition and insecurity of small-time operators, who find themselves reorganizing social life to protect the economic interests of an already-prospering middle class. The provost suppresses the traditional fairs on two indirectly related grounds. With their inexpensive goods and low overhead, the traveling peddlers might challenge or break the growing monopoly (and rising prices) of village shopkeepers. And in the face of growing economic disparities, it seems best to abolish quietly any forum where a potentially mutinous lower class might assemble.

The attempt to set aside local traditions and to silence oppositional ones at first requires direct (if covert) intervention by the city's governors. But once they have set in motion the new social apparatus, it not only maintains and perpetuates itself, constantly justifying the expansion of its own scope of operations, but also renders increasingly invisible the human agency that put it in place. Once a few measures of improvement have been pushed through, they can be used to justify a virtually endless and increasingly repressive series of changes: once the road has been widened and sidewalks erected, a whole set of laws, surveillance procedures, and self-regulating "habits" follow quite naturally.

> New occasions call for new laws: the side-pavement, concentrating the people, required to be kept cleaner, and in better order, than when the whole width of the street was in use; so that the magistrates were constrained to make regulations concerning the same, and to enact fines and penalties against those who neglected to scrape and wash the plainstones fornent their houses, and to

denounce, in the strictest terms, the emptying of improper utensils on the same, and this, until the people had grown into the habit of attending to the rules, gave rise to many pleas, and contentious appeals and bickerings, before the magistrate.[75]

If in Scott's novels the motor of history is strangely impersonal, Galt's novel masterfully presents both the human agency by which social change is effected (demonstrating clearly whose interests are served and whose repressed) and how the machinery of change, once put into operation, camouflages this agency as the movement of history, freeing the manipulators to appear, even to themselves, as public benefactors.

If read backward from Galt's *Provost*, the first three Waverley novels (*Waverley*, *Guy Mannering*, and *The Antiquary*) might look annalistic as well. Set in the 1740s, the 1770s, and the 1790s, they together form a chronicle whose complicated continuities and discontinuities palliate the force of the specific historical ruptures of each novel. In *Waverley* the oral world of the Highland clans breaks apart under external pressures and a failed rebellion. In *Guy Mannering* the gentry's impulse toward improvement and domestic enclosure (synchronous with imperialist expansion abroad) intensifies the gap between property holders and the propertyless, erases feudal allegiances and aristocratic memory, and dislocates the people forever. Twenty years later, faced with the threat of foreign invasion, the community of *The Antiquary* (gentry, middle classes, and wandering beggars) are reunited precisely through an interpretive struggle over the past, the reconstitution of lost traditions.

Scott's novels as written by Galt would produce the Waverley novels as radical critique; the modernization of Scotland, this first trilogy would then suggest, was effected in three stages, each of which manages successfully to conceal its connection to those which preceded it. First the remnants of Highland clan society are decimated and dispersed *militarily*, in open warfare. Then the introduction of new *economic* principles and pressures weakens the traditional bonds of Lowland society as well, creating a new caste of pariahs and outlaws. And finally, the threat of Jacobin uprising and invasion can be used *ideologically* to consolidate the changes of the previous forty years, as a new patriotism and a new cultural nostalgia for a distant age of social harmony blunt the edge of popular protests, erasing more recent, vengeful memories and effectively occluding the human agency that produced present social inequities.

These are not quite the Waverley novels we know. The historical novel and the postcolonial novel, the politically quietistic realism of Scott and the politically seismographic protomodernism of Maturin, Owenson, and Galt were invented almost simultaneously, from the same peripheries and the same novelistic genealogy.[76] Yet despite these intermeshed histories, they point in crucially different directions. Lukács's championing of Scott's magisterial historical survey and his lack of interest in exploring the historical paranoia and neurosis of Scott's contemporaries are not accidental, in view of the political climate of his own writing. As Galt's provost instructs us, the reconstruction of how apparent historical breakthroughs actually occur is often the only way to understand how and why this "progress" is retroactively constructed, what it suppresses, what used to be there instead—in short, to understand how, in Muir's phrase, "the past turns to legend." So the traverse, here, of a more agitated fiction previous and parallel to Scott's own, can suggest what a still monolithic "Scott legend" continues to conceal, all that is hidden in Scott's "very curious emptiness."

PART TWO

National Memory, Imperial Amnesia

Little Henry and his bearer

Mary Martha Sherwood, *Little Henry and his Bearer* (1814). 1834 ed.
Courtesy of the University of Virginia Library.

Chapter 4

COMING HOME: IMPERIAL AND
DOMESTIC FICTION, 1790–1815

[M]y intended Journal commences immediately after we had
terminated a residence of some years in Ireland, of which we were
both heartily sick, tired, and disgusted; having witnessed during the
Rebellion, which broke out in 1798, all the horrors of civil war, during
which my dear husband had the command in the north; so that he was
not only obliged to meet the poor, infatuated, misguided people in the
open field, but, after defeating them there, also had the very distressing
task of holding court martials, and signing the death warrants of very
many, which was indeed heart-breaking to us both. . . . A few days
after our return [to England], General Nugent was surprised by his
appointment as Lt.-Governor and Commander-in-Chief of the Island
of Jamaica. We were neither of us over well pleased, but, like good
soldiers, we made up our minds to obey.

[Government Pen, Jamaica] Jan. 23, 1802. Set all the blackies to
scrape and clean all round the house, the lawn, &c. Treated them with
beef and punch, and never was there a happier set of people than
they appear to be. All the day they have been singing odd songs, only
interrupted by peals of laughter . . . they have reason to be content,
for they have many comforts and enjoyments. I only wish the poor
Irish were half as well off.
—Diary of Lady Maria Nugent

The peasant, once a friend, a friend no more,
Cringes, a slave, before the master's door;
Or else, too proud, where once he loved, to faun,
For distant climes deserts his native lawn.

. . . .

So the red Indian, by Ontario's side

. . . .

As fades his swarthy race, with anguish sees
The white man's cottage rise beneath his trees.

. . . .

Long may the Creek, the Cherokee, retain
The desert woodlands of his old domain,
Ere Teviot's sons, far from their homes beguiled,
Expel their wattled wigwams from the wild!
—John Leyden, *Scenes of Infancy*

THAT OTHER SETTING

In *Culture and Imperialism* Edward Said uses an evocative reading of Jane Austen's *Mansfield Park* to suggest the advent of an imperialist unconscious (which will structure all of nineteenth-century English literature) and to justify his own choice of methodology. Conventionally enough, Said sees Britain's "age of empire" as beginning only in 1800 and situates the rise of British fiction about the empire only in the later nineteenth century. *Mansfield Park* thus appears, in 1814, as a remarkable, even prophetic, anticipation of imperial false consciousness. Although profoundly analytic about the micropolitics of space, Austen's novel presupposes the macropolitical and macroeconomic basis for English gentry culture: Sir Thomas Bertram's rule over Mansfield Park depends on his simultaneous rule over an Antiguan slave plantation; the raw materials and mercantile revenues of the British overseas colonies are the direct source of his wealth and that of his class. To Said, Austen fails to perceive the incongruity between Bertram's two sites of control, between what he stands for domestically and what he stands for internationally. Fanny Price does raise the question of the slave trade with Sir Thomas. But her question is followed by a most embarrassed silence, which Said reads as the silence, the false consciousness, of Austen and her entire society.

> In order more accurately to read works like *Mansfield Park*, we have to see them in the main as resisting or avoiding that other setting, which their formal inclusiveness, historical honesty, and prophetic suggestiveness cannot completely hide. In time there would not longer be a dead silence when slavery was spoken of, and the subject became central to a new understanding of what Europe was.[1]

"It would be silly to expect Jane Austen to treat slavery with anything like the passion of an abolitionist or a newly liberated slave" (p. 96); instead, she reflects contemporary consciousness and denial about the empire.

For Said, the dense texture of admissions, attentions, and aporias that make up British society can be made visible only in the course of detailed work with complex, canonical texts. "A lesser work wears its historical affiliation more plainly; its worldliness is simple and direct, the way a jingoistic ditty during the Mahdist uprising or the 1857 Indian Rebellion connects directly to the situation and constituency that coined it. *Mansfield Park* encodes experiences and does not simply repeat them" (pp. 96–97).

Much of Said's book performs careful readings of *Heart of Darkness*, *Kim*, and *Passage to India*, texts already read many times before to explicate imperial contradictions. No time or energy remains to consider either a broader and longer spectrum of European writing about empire or the large body of indigenous writings about life under imperial rule. As a result, the individual readings, though internally persuasive, are neither broad nor narrow enough in their scope. Oddly foreshortened, they lack historical, political, and generic context; Said's *Mansfield Park* continues to stand in splendid isolation from its immediate surroundings.[2]

The novel's mapping of social space looks very different if read against contemporary fiction. A historicizing reading of *Mansfield Park* might well see its moment of silence about the slave trade as politically hard-hitting rather than evasive, a moment at which Austen's reader will know to fill in contemporary debates about abolition.[3] From the American Revolution onward, Robin Blackburn has argued in *The Overthrow of Colonial Slavery*, abolitionist attention to the empire automatically invoked the problem of domestic freedoms and political institutions. In the 1790s, while the conservative wing of the British abolitionist movement slowed its pressure on the government in the interests of domestic stability, radical abolitionists helped to establish the Corresponding Societies and modeled them on abolitionst organizations. In their admiration of the political independence effected by the American Revolution (despite its concessions to slaveholding interests), as well as in their deployment of a Painite rhetoric of the rights of man, British Radicals often drew parallels between domestic and imperial despotism.[4] Addressing an 1816 public meeting in Ayr, Scotland, one Radical speaker thus compared the situation of Ireland to that of a colonized British India:

> If the calamities of Scotland are not sufficient to wake the people to the need of Reform, let them glance for a moment to those scenes of blood and horror committed in India. There English dominion is founded on tyranny, on violence and terror. . . . But such deeds are not confined to distant possessions, they are sufficiently gloomy at home. . . . [In Ireland, the spirit of the people] is broken down, they are in a worse condition than the slaves of any country. . . . And who are the oppressors of Ireland? Even the same detestable faction who now seek our ruin and with rapid stride are now hurling us to the same abyss.[5]

Many contemporaries were forceful in advocating fair and equal treatment throughout the empire. "The great and fundamental principle of our government," writes the *Edinburgh Review* in 1804, is

> that the people inhabiting those kingdoms and provinces which have been reduced under our dominion in Asia, are become in every respect subjects of the same government under which we ourselves live, and are consequently entitled to all those blessings of security and protection which that condition implies. The improvement of the provinces of Bengal and the Carnatic ought

therefore to be as much an object of attention, as the cultivation of the counties of Middlesex and Dublin; and the personal rights and civil liberty of the inhabitants of India are in every respect as much under the paternal government of the King, as the rights and privileges of the people of the United kingdom.[6]

And the author of *Letters from the Irish Highlands* (1824), writing to call attention to the plight of Ireland, expresses a sentimental faith that "our English friends" will not forget Ireland but treat it with

that humanity which has so often penetrated even to the farthest corners of the globe, to seek out the objects of her care; and which regards no obstacle where the happiness of a fellow-creature is at stake. Look upon us with the same benevolent eye that you regard . . . the negro in your West Indian plantation, and we will forgive all past injuries. . . .[7]

The rhetoric of the interdependence of domestic and colonial interests, then, is much used throughout Austen's period, and across the political spectrum, by defenders of plantocracy as well as by radical abolitionists.

EXPANDING CHRONOTOPES

From the 1790s to the 1820s, the British novel remains preoccupied with the integrity and interpenetration of cultural spaces: successive novelistic genres establish a dialectical relationship between nationalist ways of thinking about place and the consciousness of empire, a dialectic crucial not only to romantic nationalist, regionalist, and local-color writing but also to early colonial literature. During this period, the British novel is both caught up in a wide-reaching experiment with new and old narrative coordinates and engaged in an unprecedented reflection of extranovelistic intellectual and political trends, especially the expansion and consolidation of a worldwide British Empire. In 1746 the British Army defeated the Jacobite Army at Culloden, occupied the Highlands, and began the Highlanders' forced anglicization. The conquest of Quebec (1759), followed by the loss of the American colonies in the 1780s, caused the reorganization of British colonizing efforts in North America. Pitt's 1784 India Act established British government control over the East India Company, and in 1787 Britain opened its Australian penal colony. The suppression of the 1798 United Irishmen rebellion in Ireland was followed by the 1801 Union of Ireland with Britain. During the first two decades of the nineteenth century, the British occupied and colonized the Cape of Good Hope (1806–14), made Sierra Leone a Crown Colony (1807), and captured French Senegal (1809); the East India Company established a British settlement in Singapore in 1819. In the meantime, in ongoing struggles with France over the control of the West Indies, the British captured Curaçao (1809), Marie

Galante and Desirade (1808), Martinique and Cayenne (1809), and Guadeloupe (1810). As we will see, the advent of a new epoch of British imperialism has both immediate and cumulative effects on the generic structure and cultural understanding of the romantic novel.

Late-eighteenth-century British imperial expansion contributes to the formulation of new chronotopes and thus exacerbates antilocalizing tendencies already present in British fiction. Or, to assign a different kind of causality: in the age of the French Revolution, even anti-Jacobin novelists manifest some internationalism. By the first decades of the nineteenth century, however, the new fictional genres of the national tale and the historical novel influentially reinstate the national chronotope as the primary framework of political analysis; the problem of empire is apparently put on hold. (A second wave of fiction about the empire will appear from the 1820s to the 1840s, along with a first wave of colonial fiction, itself heavily reliant on the imperial discussions of the 1790s.)

In the early nineteenth century, then, the British novel enters a period of renewed and intense interest in local color, customs, and attachments. This development might appear to negate the cosmopolitanism, relativism, and the radicalism of the 1790s. Yet both formally (in their modes of narration, allegorization, and emplotment) and politically (in their relational understanding of national culture as in a sometimes militant sense of cultural oppression) the new, early-nineteenth-century national novels subsume key elements of the imperialist and anti-imperial fiction of the 1790s.

Maria Edgeworth herself wrote several works concerned with abolition. As critics have recently suggested, her views of Britain's Caribbean colonies inform and are informed by her analysis of colonial Ireland.[8] In turn, her affirmative account of paternalistic slavery in "The Grateful Negro" and her negative depiction of slaves' agitation for their emancipation result partly from the way she has superimposed the economic and political situation of the Irish estate onto the more extreme conditions of the Jamaican slave plantation. In a more Gothic vein, Maturin's *Melmoth the Wanderer* (1820) begins in contemporary Ireland, only to open onto several geographically and temporally distant sites of European history, moving from the local gloom of Ireland to the traumas that accompany the Spanish conquest of the New World.

John Galt's local-color novels link the shape of Scottish national life to the development of imperial ideologies and economies: in *The Entail* a hundred years of post-Union Scottish history is built on the financial failure of the Darien Expedition; in *The Last of the Lairds* the return of a Scottish nabob to his native land has a deleterious effect on its social and political fabric; and in *Bogle Corbet* the rise of industrial culture and class struggle in the Scottish Lowlands is linked to the modernization of the Highlands, the Jamaican plantation system, and the colonization of Canada. As Galt's case demonstrates, the traverse between empire and nation can be visible in the shape of novelistic careers as much as in individual novels. Scotch-Irish novelist Elizabeth Hamilton is now remembered (if at all) for her last novel, *The Cottagers of Glenburnie* (1808), a didactic novel of Scottish rural life. Yet her novelistic career begins very far afield: her *Translation of Letters of a Hindoo Rajah* (1796) reformulates eighteenth-century epistolary travelogues and utopian reports by Oriental travelers (Montesquieu, Goldsmith) under the more acute pressures of imperial contact, describing the conversion of an Indian rajah to British and imperial ideals at the hands of a noble British officer, then his disillusioning journey of discovery to England. A tour de force of cross-cultural comparison, the novel is an apology for the British conquest of India, but it is also an attempt to rethink British society (particularly the state of female emancipation) from a Hindu cultural perspective and to think about Indian society from the perspective of a bardic nationalism.[9] Hamilton's novelistic career continues with *Memoirs of Modern Philosophers* (1800), an anti-Jacobin satire that undercuts the delusions of a circle of freethinkers by detailing their plans to found a utopian community among the Hottentots. Her turn to regionalist pastoral and to the problem of "national reconstruction" (Gary Kelly) is thus preceded—and informed—by the contrast between British political ideals and the cultural forms of the societies under British colonization.[10]

Owenson's novelistic career moves in the opposite direction, developing the national tale first as a genre to describe the cultural contests within Ascendancy Ireland, then (while still deploying the same basic plot) moving to describe struggles for national liberation in locales from present-day Greece and Belgium to seventeenth-century India. If the individual novels present a kind of counterweight to Scott's, in their attention both to the deeply traumatic character of the colonization process and to the deep cultural resistances left under the surface of imperial "normalization," the obviously parallel structures of Owenson's diverse national investigations suggest at once a limitation of novelistic imagination and the beginnings of a transnational model of imperial dynamics.[11]

The localism of early-nineteenth-century fiction represents not only a continuation of the nationalist preoccupations of the previous century but also a retrenchment from a more cosmopolitan literary self-understanding. Yet the 1790s' sense of the systematic, dialectical relationship between local investments and a global imperial economy does have a submerged afterlife in these novels. The remaining chapters of this book will explore the consequences of the novel's dialectical alternation between a resolutely localist framework and a self-consciously imperial framework, between the suppression and the retrieval of political consequences.

During the late eighteenth century—an era of intense discussion about the nature of Britain, British overseas expansion, and the developmental pattern of national characters and histories within an imperial framework—the formal development of the British novel becomes linked to new modes of national and imperial perception. As Irish and Scottish nationalists argue for the separate historical development of their cultural traditions (and as apologists for the British Empire argue along opposite lines, seeing this distinct character as a symptom of backwardness), the novel begins to codify the different British peripheries and colonies as distinctive chronotopes.

Already in the late eighteenth century, a new materialist picaresque traces the circulation of animals and objects—dog, coin, or carriage—to make visible a social and economic exchange as it connects nations and empires.[12] In the 1780s and the 1790s, the British intelligentsia begin to understand the new British Empire as a single, internally connected political system, and the novel tries to demonstrate the imbrication of national and imperial concerns, often through parallel, shadowing, or crossing narrative lines. During the early nineteenth century, the national tale and historical novel model a different dialectical relationship between nationalist ways of thinking about place and the consciousness of empire. As I argued in the last chapter, the historical novel develops out of the national tale; a genre obsessed with the political (or at least narrative) recuperation of historical processes that irrevocably alter and uproot traditional cultures has its basis, paradoxically, in a genre obsessed with the stability of a national/cultural life world; a genre obsessed with how time and change transform national places emerges out of a genre equally obsessed with how such places gain their plenitude by absorbing the cultural transformations of successive historical epochs. Yet if we move even further back, to look at the novels that establish the national tale's central generic repertoire and coordinates, we see that it, too, has a highly paradoxical genealogy, and that its short-lived idylls of national plenitude, stability, or progress subsume some highly unsettling elements.

Most early-nineteenth-century local-color fiction describes the self-understanding of an Irish, Scottish, or Welsh culture rendered economically and politically marginal by incorporation into Britain, and all the more concerned with establishing its own internal cohesion, integrity, and stability. At the end of the eighteenth century, however, the famous temporal vicissitudes of the novel—the Shandyesque confusion of narrated time and narrative time, narratives framed as fragmentary antiquarian retrievals, and Gothic novels that waver between historical and cyclical time—are matched by parallel vicissitudes in the novel's spatial locatability. Sterne's explorations of the discursive construction of time builds on Amory's work on the discursive construction of place; Amory's narrators move between narrative locales, between landscape description, antiquarian annotation and philosophical digressions, creating epistemological uncertainty in the narrative and rendering place by turns tangible and elusive. Writing in the wake of nationalist antiquarian revivals dogged by political and methodological controversy, the subsequent generation of antiquarian and Gothic novelists find their attempts to describe national places and their archaeological reconstruction haunted by comparable epistemological uncertainty.

BETWEEN NATION AND EMPIRE

An equally unsettling group of novels, shaped by the conjunction of Gothic and Jacobin influences, structures a plot of cultural comparison around the traverse between Britain and its colonial possessions. Implicitly critical of the empire and often explicitly abolitionist, these novels juxtapose a secluded, protected English, Scottish, or Welsh domesticity with the violence that accompanies British imperial expansion; Robert Bage's *Mount Henneth* (1782), *Barham Downs* (1784), and *The Fair Syrian* (1787) thus move between the self-absorbed Welsh or English village life of Mount Henneth or Barham Downs and the British Army's campaigns in Bengal and the Middle East. The very title of Agnes Maria Bennett's *Anna, or Memoirs of a Welsh Heiress, Interspersed with Anecdotes of a Nabob* (1785) makes clear this parallel structure. Although these novels foreground their ability to depict the simultaneity and interpenetration of apparently incommensurate worlds, they often question the desirability of reimporting colonial goods, modes of knowledge, and social attitudes back into Britain or, conversely, use their distant imperial retrospect to interrogate British society.

Forced into exile in various corners of an emerging Elizabethan empire, the heroines of Lee's *Recess* look back from their West Indian slavery or their frightened proximity to the English campaigns in Ireland to the protected seclusion of their subterranean childhood hiding place, "recessed" from the pressures of a historical and political world.[13] The first half of Charlotte Smith's *Old Manor House* (1793) is romantic and Gothic: two lovers, dependents of the old manor's despotic mistress, endlessly attempt to find uninterrupted trysting places; the plot rests on minute details of architectural space and household timetables. The second half of the novel abruptly sends the hero to fight in the American Revolutionary War. Dislocated from the world to which he once belonged and increasingly unsure of the justice of the imperial cause, he falls into Indian captivity, treks alone across much of North America, and returns home to find the manor deserted. In the movement from its first to its second half, *The Old Manor House* relativizes the worldview of the English aristocracy, even as it demonstrates their inability to grasp their place in and impact on the rest of the world, given their resolutely local and provincial perspective.

> They saw not the impossibility of enforcing in another country the very imposts to which, unrepresented, they would not themselves have submitted. Elate with national pride, they had learned by the successes of the preceding war to look with contempt on the inhabitants of every other part of the globe; and even on their colonists, men of their own country.[14]

Smith's hero and novel can only attempt, then, to bring the war home, to explain the wide-ranging consequences of domestic politics.

Abolitionist tales of infant education, from Thomas Day's *History of Sandford and Merton* (1783) to Barbara Hoole Hofland's *Matilda, or The Barbadoes Girl* (1816)—and beyond it, to Frances Hodgson Burnett's 1911 *Secret Garden*—describe the reimportation into Britain not of hard-won self-knowledge gained in the empire but of the ignorance and corruption endemic to the imperial system. When planters' children born and raised in the West Indies are sent to England to be educated, their wish to transplant the values and behaviors of the plantation system back into the home country catalyzes lasting social conflicts.[15] At first these colonial children dismay their English peers by their self-absorption, their abominable manners, and their wanton cruelty toward household servants: the Barbadoes Girl disgraces herself by flinging a scalding cup of tea at her long-suffering black attendant.[16] As they come under the influence of their English playmates, however, these children gradually absorb more egalitarian values and therefore can be absorbed into English society; once they learn to treat everyone, even social inferiors, with respect and affection, they become capable and worthy of real friendship. Optimistic about the chances of personal and thus of imperial reform, this children's literature stresses individual transformation over systemic change, abolitionist sentiment over abolition. *Sandford and Merton*, for instance, ends with the social reclamation of the planter's son Tommy Merton through his friendship with the farmer's son Harry Sandford. England has inculcated a rising generation of leaders with its characteristic democratic spirit. Yet the income and affluence of the Merton family, presumably, is still supplied, as at the beginning of the story, by the distant and now-forgotten plantation: a "large estate in the island of Jamaica," where the many Merton "servants" "cultivate sugar and other valuable things for [the planter's] advantage."[17] In such works, despite their explicitly abolitionist sentiments, the West Indies become the kind of "other setting" that Said describes; suppressed from British consciousness and conversation, they nonetheless continue to finance the operation of English culture.

Barbadoes Girl.

Miss Hanson, throwing a glass of Beer in Debbys face. See page 14.

Barbara Hoole Hofland, *Matilda, or The Barbadoes Girl* (1816). Courtesy of The Osborne Collection of Early Children's Books, Toronto Public Library.

A parallel cluster of novels about female liberty and education, written by women authors during the 1780s and 1790s, explore the links between colonial and domestic slavery much more fully. Once repatriated, small children may outgrow the deleterious influence of an empire built on slavery and exploitation, but when grown men who have exploited the empire to make their own fortunes return to Britain to marry and settle, these novels argue, not even the most saintly wife can convert them from the habit of despotic power, from the imperiousness, immorality, and ruthlessness that have marked their business lives. When two characters in Austen's "Catharine, or The Bower" (1792) discuss the "lucky" girls who are sent out to "Bengal or Barbadoes" in quest of husbands, one refuses to consider such girls fortunate: no girl in that position will have the opportunity of judging whether her new husband is "a tyrant, or a fool, or both" until "her judgement is of no use to her"; a girl would be luckier and happier were she simply allowed to remain in England.[18]

In Bennett's *Anna*, a villainous Anglo-Indian nabob who has returned to Britain attempts to seduce an innocent Welsh heiress and fantasizes about murdering her chaperone; if only he were back in India, free of Britain's legal and moral constraints—"Rude, inconvenient *English laws* were the dread of his soul"—both deeds would be easy to arrange.[19] Colonel Gorget represents at once the continuation and the imperial intensification of a long tradition of domestic entrapment. As the eighteenth-century novel documents, Britain's national disfranchisements and domestic penury created generations of predatory fortune hunters; Gorget's own father was an Irish adventurer, who managed to marry a woman of fortune and good family. At the beginning of the nineteenth century, as the same national inequities continue unabated, the disfranchised find in the empire a new arena of compensation and displaced revenge. To judge from their domestic behavior, the fortune hunters produced by the overseas empire are even more predatory, ruthless, and venal than those produced by the internal empire. Yet their misbehavior, argues Amelia Opie in *Adeline Mowbray* (1804), underlines the fundamental contradictions of British rule. When domestic relations are structured in imitation of imperial ones, when British marriages mirror the relations between slaves and masters, when British family life resembles an indentured servitude, two things are clear simultaneously. The empire and its subject peoples are governed by a rule of violence that British citizens would never find tolerable for themselves. Yet many of Britain's married women are forced to tolerate analogous conditions in their own homes, with almost no legal recourse: the domestic institution of marriage permits legal relationships of such fundamental inequality that they are little more than bondage.

Adeline Mowbray explores the shortcomings of Jacobin ethics and the insoluble conflicts they engender in idealistic and well-intentioned

freethinkers; on a deeper level, the novel also moves from an implicit allegorization of the internal union of Britain to an explicit allegorization of the
problems of Britain's overseas empire. Initially, the novel revolves around
a choice between competing suitors, who (as in Swift's "Injured Lady" or
in Frances Burney's 1796 *Camilla*) represent the constituent national characters of Britain: the English heroine sidesteps the seductions of the Irish
fortune hunter, then enters an idealistic but increasingly guilt-ridden liaison
with the Scotch philosopher. The first half of the novel centers on a problematic (because unsanctified) domestic union, the second on a dysfunctional (and legally binding) imperial union: Adeline Mowbray marries a
despotic West Indian slaveholder whose moral fiber has been eroded by the
plantation system. If the colonial empire functions as an explicit model for
British domestic inequities, it also structures the novel's traverses and
moral transformations at a more subtle level, as Opie's characters disappear
to and reappear from the East or West Indies. The centrality of imperial
exigencies, behaviors, and experiences for the domestic world of England
is just what Said finds in *Mansfield Park*. Only here, ten years before
Austen's novel, the price of imperial knowledge and prosperity is made
explicit.

If *Mansfield Park* is read against an abolitionist-feminist novel such as
Adeline Mowbray, it may appear as a conservative retrenchment from the
political issues that slavery raised. Yet it can also be read as an abolitionist
novel in its own right, with considerable resemblance to works such as
Adeline Mowbray, not least in its attempts to advocate gradual abolition
and moderate feminism as in its effort to disengage these causes from their
Jacobin origins. Austen's understated treatment of the imperial problematic has important precedent in the manifestly proabolitionist novels of the
1790s. Although slave plantation and empire form the unspoken basis for
the Bertrams' social standing, *Mansfield Park* contains only one explicit
discussion of the slave trade. Not long after Sir Thomas Bertram's return
from Antigua, Fanny Price raises the question during a family evening. So
too in Mary Hays's *Memoirs of Emma Courtney* (1796), the subject of
slavery surfaces at a family party, with similar singularity (given the focus
on women's rights in the rest of Hays's novel) and even more social
awkwardness.

The dinner is a family reunion, at which Emma Courtney and other family members welcome home to England a cousin

> who had, when a youth, been placed by his father in a commercial house in the
> West Indies, and who had just returned to his native country with an ample
> fortune. . . . We were little aware of the changes which time and different situ-
> ations produce on the character, and, with hearts and minds full of the frank,
> lively, affectionate, youth, from whom we had parted, seven years since, with

mutual tears and embraces, shrunk spontaneously . . . from the cold salutation, of the haughty, opulent, purse-proud, Planter, surrounded by ostentatious luxuries, and evidently valuing himself upon the consequence which he imagined they must give him in our eyes.[20]

If Hays's heroine is dismayed by the changes a West Indian sojourn have wrought in her cousin, she is even more vexed by the companions whom Melmoth has brought back from Jamaica with him: his ill-bred wife and the arrogant Mr. Pemberton, a militia officer who has just come into possession of a Jamaica estate. All three West Indians are so deeply permeated by plantation ideology that their London guests feel compelled to refute even their polite small talk.

The dinner conversation thus becomes an occasion for political interventions, sallies, and rebuttals. It begins trivially enough. Mrs. Melmoth expresses her admiration for soldiers, prompting Emma to the impolitic but truthful rejoinder that their profession is murder. Melmoth defends the operations of the military, "wishing, 'that they had some thousands more of these *murderers* in the West Indies, to keep the slaves in subordination, who, since absurd notions of liberty had been put into their heads, were grown very troublesome and refractory, and, in a short time, he supposed, would become as insolent as the English servants'" (p. 114). When Mrs. Melmouth takes this cue to complain of the impossible self-assertiveness of English servants, Mrs. Denbeigh, her new sister-in-law, feels compelled to remind her that "[t]his is a land of freedom . . . servants, here, will not submit to be treated like the slaves of Jamaica" (p. 115). Mr. Melmoth objects both to servants and to women who do their own thinking—and Emma Courtney, in turn, challenges his slight to female intelligence. From the servant problem, Mr. Melmoth passes to the slave trade, prompting yet another guest to argue against "the inequity as well as impolicy of so accursed a traffic" (p. 115). The debate has become both engrossing and instructive to all attentive participants; in its final round, Mr. Pemberton charges that abolition would cause temporary political unrest and economic instability, and he is once more firmly argued down, with the reassurance that any abolition would be implemented gradually, after the "oppressed Africans" (p. 116) had their minds prepared for their new condition.

When the ladies retire to the drawing room, Mrs. Melmoth scolds Emma Courtney for her "ill-nature" and her rudeness to Mr. Pemberton. The other guests regard the conversation quite differently, as the beginning of a necessary dialogue between plantation owners and abolitionists on the fate of the slave colonies. The reader has been even more edified by the exchange, for its logic has demonstrated on several levels the interconnection of the imperial and the domestic. The parallels between West Indian slavery and the domestic oppression of European women, as between the situation of "oppressed Africans" and the more mundane oppression of the British servant classes, are implicit in the conversational logic of the plantocratic patriarchs—and the first task of the abolitionists at the dinner table is to make this logic explicit, to refute their opponents' underlying assumptions.

The clear mandate of the abolitionist, then, is to speak out for what is right: to bring hidden connections to light, to break a tacit silence about the subject of slavery, and to break the more general taboo against political argument in mixed company. If this scene argues for a new literature of commitment, the rest of the novel is intent on investigating female desire and self-liberation, and it is far more ambiguous in its stance toward empire. Like many other feminist abolitionists, it could be argued, Hays finally subordinates the distant problem of Caribbean slavery to the problem of women's emancipation in Britain.

With a sketchy suggestiveness typical of the radical novels of the 1790s, *Emma Courtney* places its English, feminist heroine within a social and familial milieu defined by overseas trade and transatlantic traverses. Emma's foster father, Uncle Melmoth, owns a West India ship, and his prosperity eventually "enabled him to leave the sea, and to carry on an extensive mercantile employment in the metropolis" (p. 9). Emma finds a place to live in London only because her cousin Mrs. Denbeigh (sister of the West India planter) is married to an East India officer; when he is stationed in Bengal for three years, Mrs. Denbeigh remains behind and decides to lease out part of their London house. The question such details raise is the degree of *Emma Courtney*'s narrative consciousness and Mary Hays's political consciousness. How can the heroine's outburst against Jamaica slavery be reconciled with the matter-of-factness with which her Melmoth relatives pass in and out of the novel on colonial business, supporting her directly and indirectly with its profits? Are these details brought into the novel only incidentally, as a note of realism (as everyone in Britain begins to be affected, in quotidian but important ways, by colonial comings and goings, profits and losses, and by the changes of situation and character they produce), or do such details suggest, however sketchily, an indictment of the heroine's whole domestic world?

The Silence of the Bertrams

With such questions, we are back at *Mansfield Park*. From Mansfield Park, the West Indies seem virtually invisible; although two characters visit Antigua, the narrative never reports at any length what Sir Thomas and Tom Bertram saw or experienced there. But does the novel's dematerialization of Antigua necessarily announce a refusal to address the problem of British imperial domination? Might it not signal, instead, the replacement of an old, site-specific critique of particular imperial operations with a new, overarching critique of imperial ideology, which locates the operations of power at once more diffusely and more ubiquitously than previous analyses?

Over the last fifteen years, literary scholars have uncovered considerable evidence of Austen's personal interest in the subject of slavery. Her brother Francis (clearly one model for Fanny Price's brother William) was a firmly committed abolitionist; stationed in the West Indies as an officer of the British navy, he "wrote letters home deploring the conditions of slaves in Antigua."[21] Austen read Thomas Clarkson's *History of the Abolition of the Slave Trade* while working on *Mansfield Park*, and she jocularly declared herself "in love" with Clarkson.[22] The very name of Mansfield Park, several critics have argued, invokes Austen's meditations on the slave trade: in 1722 Lord Chief Justice Mansfield wrote the legal decision that "stipulated that no slaves could be forcibly returned from Britain, which was widely interpreted to mean that slavery in Britain had been legally abolished." Austen met Mansfield's niece on a number of occasions.[23]

If this is indeed the reference behind Austen's nomenclature, then Mansfield Park and *Mansfield Park* are haunted by the specters of abolition and emancipation. The novel used to be read rather differently, as the coercive socialization of a timid heroine (less assertive and more masochistic, it was often said, than any of Austen's other heroines) who finally wins the respect of her rich relations and the hand of her beloved cousin. Early feminist critics saw Mansfield Park as an explicitly patriarchal institution and *Mansfield Park* as the most socially quiescent of Austen's novels. Yet once its colonial subtext is considered, *Mansfield Park* appears not only as a novel of female education but also as a more wide-ranging meditation on the reproduction and transformation of power relations. Although it is Fanny's story that is foregrounded, and her dilemmas, doubts, and deserts that engage the reader's attention, the collective story of the Bertram family and the story of Sir Thomas's moral reeducation run parallel to Fanny's. Read against the background of abolitionist fiction, the infant literature and marriage novels of the 1790s and 1800s, *Mansfield Park* appears preoccupied with the indirect effects of slavery and the long reach of the plantation system into the heart of England.

Indirection, it must be stressed, is the key to Austen's treatment of abolitionist concerns and what gives the novel its subtlety and its power.[24] At Mansfield Park there is no Barbadoes Girl, throwing tea at a servant, advertising her immaturity and intemperance; instead, there are the Bertram daughters, polite and superficially decorous. At Mansfield Park there is no sinister nabob or slave trader, come back from the colonies to wreak his will upon the helpless body and mind of the unsuspecting English heiress. Even at the beginning of the novel, Sir Thomas Bertram is neither despot nor demon. He is only, like General Tilney before him, obsessed with small distinctions of rank, forbidding in his manner, harsh in his judgments—all of which are frightening enough to a young dependent.

The abolitionist fiction of Austen's day depends on a high degree of moral clarity and characterological transparency. Austen's rewriting of a central abolitionist plot involves a critique of its epistemological presuppositions, in a register at once less harsh and less comic than her critique of Gothic conventions in *Northanger Abbey*. For what if the effects of slavery and colonialism are not so easily visible, either on the faces of their beneficiaries or on the surface of British social life? What if those who return from the colonies to Britain with their ill-gotten fortunes cannot be clearly identified, even on longer acquaintance, as moral monsters, and cannot simply be avoided by those of rectitude and conscience? What if their lives appear unchanged, and yet, like Blake's rose, they are hollowed out imperceptibly from within, by an insidious moral decay? What we eventually witness, at Mansfield Park, is the sudden collapse of the house of Bertram, as most of Sir Thomas's family succumbs to a slow rot. Such social cataclysm is a recurring plot device in Austen's novels as in those of Burney and other contemporaries; here, it represents the collapse of an entire corrupt social order. Fanny's elevation at the end of the novel can take place only because her contemporaries and playmates have been swept away, dishonored, disgraced, and banished forever. Yet for all that, the end of the novel is happy: the vindication of Fanny, the salvation of Edmund, and the confirmation of Sir Thomas's moral reclamation, which we have seen developing, subtly but perceptibly, since his return from Antigua.

Just as Austen supplies us with no exhaustive account of Sir Thomas's activities abroad, she gives us no direct explanation for what has changed him, and only very gradually can we piece together an explanation for his transformation. A year earlier, when he leaves for the West Indies, his unkind brusqueness toward Fanny expresses his generally harried state of mind: he is worried by a spendthrift son and by unspecified political upheavals in the Caribbean which threaten the economic stability of the Bertram fortune. Understanding his journey to Antigua as a voyage into danger, his family feels uncertain whether they will ever see their father again. Yet the true pathos of his departure, as Fanny considers at length, is that no one will really miss him. A year later, when he arrives home unexpectedly, into the midst of the rehearsal of *Lovers' Vows*, everyone is dismayed, not jubilant, at his return. Yet as they eventually learn, some to their chagrin and others to their pleasure, they now face a rather different Sir Thomas. The most easily perceptible changes are physical ones—he is thinner, tanned, and exhausted. Beneath this surface lie more fundamental psychic changes that reveal themselves only gradually: the beginning of a new moral stance, stature, and firmness of judgment; the replacement of an indifferent paternalism with a more active and egalitarian conception of fatherhood. Already on the night of his return, he greets Fanny "with a kindness which astonished and penetrated her. . . . He had never been so kind, so *very* kind to her in his life. His manner seemed changed . . . all that had been awful in his dignity seemed lost in tenderness."[25]

Is it merely the ardors of the journey, the long absence from home, that have catalyzed this transformation, or has something occurred in Antigua to make Sir Thomas more responsible, responsive, and contemplative?[26] Moira Ferguson's summary of the political history of the plantation system gives one kind of answer. Writing *Mansfield Park* in 1811, Jane Austen sets her novel in 1808–9; Sir Thomas travels to Antigua in the immediate wake of the 1807 Abolition Bill, which outlawed the slave trade in the British Empire, and at the very beginning of a new period of political turbulence for the West Indies.

> After a brief, quiescent period following the passage of the abolition bill in 1807, however, fierce contestations over slavery began anew at home and abroad. As the British press reported news of increasing atrocities in 1809, 1810 and 1811, it became obvious that the abolitionists' utopian vision of a Caribbean plantocracy committed to ameliorating the conditions of their only remaining slaves was transparently false. . . .
>
> Sugar prices had plummeted as a result of a major depression after 1807. The ensuing urgency to diversify the imperiled sugar monoculture made the physical presence of customarily absentee landlords expedient. . . The task at hand was to maintain his estates at a profit and, since trading was now illegal, to ensure in the process the survival of his slaves as steady, well-nourished workers. Sadistic overseers, with whom Sir Thomas may have been content in the past (provided returns were satisfactory), would no longer do. His appearance when he returns to England suggests not only an exhausting engagement with his overseers and a severe reaction to noisome conditions but also emphasizes through metonym his affiliation with the creole class. He "had the burnt, fagged, worn look of fatigue and a hot climate."[27]

Mansfield Park reconstructs the moral texture of a transient historical moment, just after partial abolition has decisively changed the conditions of plantation society and just before political unrest destroys the hopes that abolition engendered. When Sir Thomas departs for Antigua, his irritation may express itself as anger at the probable effects of partial abolition on his livelihood and squeamish dislike at the prospect of confronting, in person, the repulsive sources of his wealth, after years of absence have protected him from an intimate knowledge of plantation conditions. And he comes back a changed man, we can infer, because the end of the slave trade has

changed the nature of the plantation, because the ensuing amelioration in
the conditions of slave life has meant the easing of a long-standing burden
of guilt he did not even know he carried.[28]

Abolition brings with it the end of a deep-seated moral hypocrisy long
part of the fabric of daily life, both on the Antiguan plantation and in Mansfield Park. Several decades before the manumission of Sir Thomas's Antiguan slaves, then, the end of the slave trade signals the moral emancipation
of the slaveholder. "To our own country," writes Thomas Clarkson, abolition "is invaluable."

> We have lived, in consequence of it, to see the day, when it has been recorded
> as a principle of our legislation, that commerce itself shall have its moral
> boundaries. We have lived to see the day, when we are likely to be delivered
> from the contagion of the most barbarous opinions. They, who supported this
> wicked traffic, virtually denied that man was a moral being. They substituted
> the law of force for the law of reason. . . . Nor is it a matter of less pleasing
> consideration, that, at this awful crisis, when the constitutions of kingdoms are
> on the point of dissolution, the stain of the blood of Africa is no longer upon
> us, or that we have been freed (alas, if it not be too late!) from a load of guilt,
> which has long hung like a mill-stone around our necks, ready to sink us to
> perdition. . . . [W]hat is physical suffering compared with moral guilt? The
> misery of the oppressed is, in the first place, not contagious like the crime of
> the oppressor. Nor is the mischief, which it generates, either so frightful or so
> pernicious.[29]

Austen's novel reflects Clarkson, the mainstream abolitionist movement,
and the tradition of abolitionist literature not only in its gradualism but in
its greater interest in the moral salvation of the slaveholders than in the fate
of the slaves.

If Lord Chief Justice Mansfield's landmark legal decision is the founding charter of Mansfield Park, then Sir Thomas's house is founded on the
principle of the categorical separation of the West Indian plantation, where
slavery is still legal if immoral, from a British estate populated by freemen.
Yet the late-eighteenth-century abolitionist movement won its victory
partly, as we saw at Mary Hays's fictional dinner party, through its tireless
emphasis on the domestic consequences of slavery. As Maaja A. Stewart
has put it, abolitionists made ceaseless efforts

> to deconstruct the separation between the metropolitan and the imperial
> spheres by bombarding the Parliament and the nation with extensive statistical
> evidence that the negative effects of slavery could not be contained in the
> Caribbean but must inevitably effect interactions among Englishmen them-
> selves. Specifically, Clarkson argued that the brutal and brutalizing relations

between the captains and sailors on slave ships duplicated the interactions between planters and their slaves in the Caribbean, thereby incalculably weakening British sea power and the British economy.[30]

During the first part of Austen's novel, the owners of Mansfield Park, despite their strategic silence on the subject of the West Indies, do not succeed in separating and freeing themselves from the slavery that maintains them: a new rhetoric of democracy is contradicted both by many vestiges of feudal privilege and by the colonial habit of command. As Ferguson points out, the word *plantation* is used repeatedly to designate Sir Thomas's British as well as Antiguan property; Mrs. Norris is set up, in Sir Thomas's absence, as overseer of the Bertram family, and Fanny is often treated not only as a servant or paid companion but also as movable chattel, to be uprooted and relocated at the master's convenience. Over many years, the legacy of the slave trade has made itself visible in the Bertram family's human relationships. Yet when Sir Thomas returns from the West Indies to Mansfield Park in 1809, his arrival from the site of slavery no longer reinforces these effects but begins to undo them. "Under his government," we are told soon after his return, "Mansfield was an altered place" (p. 196). For decades, the slave trade's traffic in human lives and flow of profits bound together a global mercantile network. But if the slave trade rendered impossible any disengagement of one site of British life from the others, its abolition creates a first opportunity for domestic reform.

For radical emancipationists, the Mansfield decree and the Abolition Bill of 1807 signal only the beginning of the end of slavery. So too for Sir Thomas, and for Fanny, the return from Antigua, at the end of the first volume, marks only the beginning of the end of the old order. The effort to leave slavery behind is not yet the inauguration of a new social contract, though one development may eventually be followed by the other. For three out of four Bertram children, their father's reforms come far too late to save them. Even Sir Thomas finds the effort to live a new life quite strenuous, as we see by his moments of backsliding. Although his attitude toward Fanny becomes steadily more appreciative and conciliatory, his counsel about Henry Crawford still feels like "the advice of absolute power" (p. 280), and he condemns what he sees as her "independence of spirit" (p. 318).

Yet by playing Sandford to his Merton, Fanny finally effects the permanent reorientation of Sir Thomas's values. It is she who shows the most interest when Sir Thomas tells of the West Indies, and it is she who raises the question of the slave trade in the course of family discussions. The question, as Said underlines, is met with silence, but it is not quite the silence he suggests. As with everything concerning the West Indies in this novel, we learn of the discussion very indirectly, the day after it has taken place, when Edmund encourages Fanny to engage her uncle more often in conversation, so that his heightened appreciation of her outward appearance can be matched by an appreciation of the powers of her thought and personality.

> "Your uncle is disposed to be pleased with you in every respect; and I only wish you would talk to him more.—You are one of those who are too silent in the evening circle."
>
> "But I do talk to him more than I used. I am sure I do. Did not you hear me ask him about the slave trade last night?"
>
> "I did—and was in hopes the question would be followed up by others. It would have pleased your uncle to be inquired of farther."
>
> "And I longed to do it—but there was such a dead silence! And while my cousins were sitting by without speaking a word, or seeming at all interested in the subject, I did not like—I thought it would appear as if I wanted to set myself off at their expense, by shewing a curiosity and pleasure in his information which he must wish his own daughters to feel." (P. 198)

The silence following Fanny's question is not general at all, but very particular: Julia and Maria Bertram remain silent, resolutely uninterested in the source of their own fortunes and in the history of the human suffering behind it. What Edmund's words suggest, at the same time, is that Sir Thomas is *pleased* to be asked about the slave trade. A year earlier, we suspect, the same question from his pious niece would have embarrassed and shamed him—and therefore would never have been asked in the first place. Now Fanny's question is neither a social gaffe nor the opening of a moral abyss. Sir Thomas would have liked to talk on the subject at greater length; he recognizes Fanny's interest as a mark of her engagement with his interests and with his moral standing. He now has nothing to hide from her on either score; his more general change of manner, as his attitude confirms, is due to the changed political situation of Antigua.

For Fanny, at the same time, the question and the discussion mark the beginning of intellectual emancipation. For years, her shyness and awkwardness have made her a perennial target of fun among her cousins, prevented her from full participation in family life, and made it impossible for her to stand up either for herself or for her principles, even when she might ward off moral danger to the household. Where slavery is concerned, however, the moral stakes are so high and so clear-cut that she questions without hesitation and, at least for the moment, without self-consciousness. An instant later, she feels hesitant again, worried lest her concern on behalf of those far more powerless and helpless than herself be mistaken as self-assertion. Yet her impulse is still to question further. Driven by a moral worry of real magnitude, she asserts herself publicly for the first time, demonstrates to Sir Thomas that she has a thinking, feeling mind, and begins to throw off the crippling bonds of her own undue deference.

Her subsequent resistance to Henry Crawford shows a new moral fortitude—and the refusal of the false freedom embodied by the libertine. As many commentators have pointed out, Austen's novel aligns both Crawfords—with their French connections, open disrespect for organized religion, and private willingness to flout moral rules—with the false allures of Jacobinism. The charm of the Crawfords seems undeniable, yet it must be resisted. When Henry Crawford visits Fanny in Portsmouth, she is impressed by his kind, egalitarian attitude toward her uncouth family. Yet his rhetoric of personal emancipation, as he laments her "confinement" in a plebeian and physically noxious milieu and advocates her return to "the free air, and liberty of the country" (pp. 410–41), merely masks his belief in his own right to aristocratic and masculine privilege. As his subsequent libertinism shows, he subscribes to a social philosophy that puts his pleasure and the exercise of his freedom, the momentary excitement of amorous pursuit and the transient joys of seduction, above any sustained personal or social commitment, above family order or domestic harmony.

Mary Crawford's version of moral lightness is less overtly sexualized than Henry's, but nonetheless selfish—and as with the Bertram daughters, nonetheless dangerous for its pleasing surface of sensibility and politeness. Accustomed to getting her own way and being able to buy anyone whose services she needs, Mary is openly irritated at the "sturdy independence" of the local farmers. If her inability to recognize the needs or autonomy of others identifies Mary with the unprincipled selfishness of the slaveholder, her persistent desire that the harvest be brought to a halt, if necessary, so that her harp can be transported identifies her with the French aristocrats of the ancien régime insisting on their droits du seigneurs. Ostensibly committed to a new intellectual, moral, and political order, both Crawfords represent the vestiges of an aristocratic libertinism equally uninterested in the activities or rights of the common man and in the claims of the past. Fanny, in contrast, is aligned with the forces of tradition and memory.

If *Mansfield Park* can be read as an abolition novel, it labors, like *Adeline Mowbray* before it, to link the causes of gradual abolition and moderate feminism and to disengage both causes from a Jacobinism that has, among its other misdeeds, betrayed abolitionist and feminist interests.[31] Mansfield Park embodies the principle of gradual reform and a limited abolition, which begins by banishing all vestiges of slavery from Britain.[32] Set at a historical turning point in the West Indies, a moment of utopian visions of a new plantocratic society, *Mansfield Park* begins to envision the social transformation of Britain as well, along lines simultaneously reformist, gradualist, and traditionalist. Characterized by a new kind of lived equality, between and within still sharply divided ranks, the new British estate will be overseen by a new breed of altruistic and nonpatriarchal paternalists.

Between overseers and paternalistic governors, ironically, Austen's political imagination remains firmly circumscribed by the model the plantation offers. From the perspective of the present day (in which the principles of civil and human rights, self-determination, and equality before the law are held to be self-evident), an abolitionist movement that works gradually toward a limited abolition, first of the slave trade, then of slavery itself, seems not only intolerably compromised in its conciliation of slaveholder interests but internally inconsistent as well. For until all slaves are actually manumitted and enjoy full citizenship and social integration, true emancipation has not yet taken place, and anything short of this only assuages the British conscience prematurely.[33]

Most early-nineteenth-century abolitionists, however, were committed gradualists. In her 1802 abolitionist story "The Grateful Negro," Maria Edgeworth champions Mr. Edwards, the benevolent slaveholder, who

> treated his slaves with all possible humanity and kindness. He wished that there was no such thing as slavery in the world; but he was convinced, by the arguments of those who have the best means of obtaining information, that the sudden emancipation of the negroes would rather increase than diminish their miseries. His benevolence, therefore, confined itself within the bounds of reason.[34]

Edwards and Edgeworth argue strongly against the slave trade, but *for* the continuation of a paternalistic slaveholding; to them, these positions do not appear incompatible. In its "second wave," from 1804 to 1815, the mainstream British abolition movement "concentrated on the slave trade, explicitly disavowing any intention of pressing for slave emancipation in the British colonies." When a young member of Parliament proposes gradual emancipation, amid "the enthusiasm of the passage of the 1807 Act," he is opposed by Wilberforce himself,

> who declared that, although he looked forward "with anxious expectation to the period when the negroes might safely be liberated," he did not feel that they were yet "fit . . . to bear emancipation." Together with most other abolitionists Wilberforce hoped that the ending of the slave trade would itself bring about an amelioration of the slaves' condition. Brougham . . . was even more categorical on the imprudence of moving to a "free negro" system until the slaves had been thoroughly exposed to civilizing influences. Most abolitionists hoped that the ending of the slave trade would itself encourage an improvement in slave conditions, obliging slave-owners to foster the natural reproduction of their plantation labour force.[35]

Many British abolitionists held their beliefs about slavery to be fully compatible with profound domestic conservatism; since the 1790s, mainstream abolitionism had been explicitly anti-Jacobin. Abolitionist literature evokes the excesses of the West Indian overseer, the abuses of the plantation owner served, and the wretched trade in bodies and souls in part to confirm the relative uprightness and rectitude, freedom and egalitarianism, of British life and to urge the greater influence of these virtues on the government of British plantations and colonies.

Working out of this literature of moralizing contrast and of pathetic set pieces, Austen chooses a strategy of indirection instead.[36] If Sir Thomas's plantation is never shown to us directly, it is also never wholly out of mind, either for the novel's author or for its principal characters. The silence that greets Fanny Price's question about slave trade is much more than a dumb, doomed innocence, whether that of Sir Thomas, Austen, or Britain. The moment, instead, is one in which Austen recognizes—to acknowledge more than to repress—a legacy of political thought and abolitionist fiction whose achievement is to link the British manor, and the fate of national life, to that distant "other setting" of British rule. Austen's novel describes not an unacknowledged connection between two incompatible places but a moment at which the relationship of the domestic and the imperial shifts profoundly, even if most domestic spectators are oblivious to what is occurring. As a meditation on the texture of recent history, Austen's novel is most intelligent and most arresting precisely in the way its narrative consciousness evokes the operations of ideology, holding assumptions and analyses just under the surface of every conversation, and yet showing us, at the same time, the subterranean influence of specific political rhetorics and debates.

Had she lived longer, Austen would almost certainly have written more, and probably more directly, about the imperial legacy of the West Indies. *Sanditon* (begun in January 1817 and left a fragment at Austen's death in July) announces a West Indian heiress—"17, half Mulatto, chilly & tender"—as one of its main characters, and the novel's ten completed chapters explicitly question the effects of imperial fortunes, homecoming colonials, and their "diffusion of Money" on Britain's domestic economy.[37] With its emphasis on economic forces, on the social changes wrought by improvement and speculation, entrepreneurial thinking and the rise of tourism, *Sanditon* represents both a new departure for Austen and the promise of a return to the problem of empire that *Mansfield Park* raised, to be linked quite explicitly this time to the economic, cultural, and moral transformation of British society.

THE AMNESIA OF THE BERTRAMS

In *Mansfield Park* we see a provisional means of representing the imperial underwriting of British self-knowledge. In describing what he sees as Austen's aporias, Said actually identifies Austen's mimetic strategy: her use of ellipses and undertones to describe the indirect moral and ideological effects of empire, her evocation of the West Indies as that "other setting" suppressed from the everyday consciousness of the characters and thus from the narrating consciousness as well. Although this is not the usual current reading of Austen, it informs a virtually contemporaneous novel, similarly preoccupied with the alternating consciousness of nation and empire. Almost certainly written under Austen's influence and in imitation of her narrative strategy, Walter Scott's 1815 *Guy Mannering, or The Astrologer* nonetheless seems a peculiar point of comparison with *Mansfield Park*, for it appears both to belong to a different genre and to inhabit a very different social universe. Austen's novel is a domestic tragicomedy of marriage set in contemporary England; Scott's is an adventure story and a historical novel set in Enlightenment Scotland; whereas Austen's novel is a canonized classic, Scott's, although a sensation at the time of its publication, is now usually considered something of a botch.[38] *Mansfield Park* represents the relationship between local and imperial knowledge, using a strategy of indirection; *Guy Mannering* explores the mechanisms of repression more actively and more visibly. Between them, they inaugurate a new analytic model (more ideological in one novel, more psychological in the other) for describing the workings of the imperialist unconscious.

Both novels describe the collapse and moral redemption of an aristocratic family named Bertram. In *Mansfield Park* Sir Thomas Bertram, English aristocrat and West Indian slaveholder, contaminates his family with the taint of the slave trade. Although Sir Thomas returns from Antigua fatigued, tanned, and repentant, to lead a better life, only the dislocation and reconstruction of the family line can expiate the collective and cumulative sins of Mansfield Park. The generational pattern is reversed and the apportionment of guilt works differently in *Guy Mannering*, but the plot remains the same. Godfrey Bertram, Scottish laird and great landowner, descended from an Edgeworthian line of corrupt, self-serving masters of Ellangowan, causes the collapse of the feudal economy and thereby the downfall of his family. In the mid-eighteenth century, under the guise of improvement, landowner Dunbog begins clearing tenants and enclosing previously common lands.[39] Following his neighbor's example, Bertram evicts the Gypsies and other "banditti" (3:64) from his estate, incarcerating some in the asylum and the house of correction. The displaced resist this treatment with escalating violence, and their acts of retribution destroy the Bertram family. When the Gypsy leader, Meg Merrilies, kidnaps Bertram's five-year-old son and heir, the laird's pregnant wife goes into premature labor and dies giving birth to a daughter.

From the narrative retrospect of the 1810s, Harry's kidnapping and the collapse of the Bertram family are at once the outcome of a long series of

moral and political misjudgments and the product of historical forces—
improvement, modernization, enclosure, *enfermement*—larger than any individual players.[40] From the more immediate perspective of the 1750s and
the 1770s, however, these developments appear preordained and unalterable. Harry's kidnapping was forecast at birth by two different kinds of
transient necromancers, by Guy Mannering, scholar and passing traveler,
and by Meg Merrilies, the witchlike Gypsy. Guy Mannering later predicts
the mortal endangerment of his wife to be almost twenty years before it
occurs. Although neither danger is supernatural in cause (Merrilies directs
the kidnapping, Mannering endangers his wife through his own rashness),
this does not explain away the accuracy of the astrological predictions.

Guy Mannering's bifurcated historical consciousness (and concomitant
generic dividedness) makes it seem failed as a historical novel. Yet this
strategy of narrative bifurcation, here as in *Mansfield Park*, reveals the
novel's ambition. Along with *The Recess*, *Guy Mannering* is one of the first
historical novels in which characters receive their fates as private, individualized tragedies, as random bad fortune, or as foreordained destinies, without a larger vision of themselves as pawns or actors in a larger historical
process.[41] *Mansfield Park* anticipates a long line of Victorian and postcolonial novels concerned with imperialist consciousness; *Guy Mannering*
stands at the beginning of a long line of historical novels, stretching from
Alessandro Manzoni's *Betrothed* (1821–27, published in 1840), Dickens's
Tale of Two Cities (1859), and Tolstoy's *War and Peace* (1863–69) to
Junichiro Tanizaki's *Makioka Sisters* (1957) and Abdelramin Munif's *Cities of Salt* (1984), whose descriptions of historical process are filtered
through the uncomprehending consciousness of history's unwitting victims, who do not understand what they experience, the forces that surround
and carry them.

More locally, *Guy Mannering* links the early nineteenth century's new
sense of the dissociations of historical consciousness to the problem of the
bifurcated or dissociated imperial consciousness delineated in the novels of
the 1790s. The effect of the juxtaposition is odd. Scott relocates the abolitionist, Austenesque plot of expiation, restitution, and resocialization, with
its carefully calibrated course of internal transformation, to the rugged terrain of the adventure story; the result is the profound disorientation of all
the characters.

On the surface, *Guy Mannering*'s multilayered plot resolves itself quite
locally, on the Bertram estate. Seventeen years after Harry Bertram's disappearance, the initial cast of characters reassembles at Ellangowan, joined
by Guy Mannering's daughter, Julia, and her lover, Captain Vanbeest
Brown. The family tragedy begun so long ago must play itself out to the
end: flanked by his land surveyor, Gibbie Glossin (a *Rackrent*ian former dependent turned heartless creditor) drives Godfrey Bertram (now a

helpless paralytic) and his young daughter from "the house that has shel-
tered us and ours for a thousand years" (3:141).

Bertram's subsequent death seems to mark the end not only of the family
line but also of estate ownership by aristocratic inheritance and the beginning of a tradition of estate ownership by a rising middle class and colonial
cadre; Glossin's application to matriculate his arms, as the new laird of
Ellangowan, coincides with applications from "two commissaries from
North America, three English-Irish peers, and two great Jamaica traders"
(4:167). On a local level, however, the final fall of the house of Bertram is
postponed by the joint efforts of those who predicted it. Guy Mannering
adopts Bertram's orphan daughter and initiates a legal investigation into
the seizure of Bertram's property, while Meg Merrilies attempts to undo
the harm caused by her kidnapping years before: she watches over Brown,
extricates him from various scrapes, and finally reveals him to himself and
to the community as the long-lost Harry Bertram. The fortuitous advent of
Harry's unknown illegitimate stepbrother, "Godfrey Bertram Hewit, arrived last night from Antigua *via* Liverpool, mate of a West Indian"
(4:353), foils the last attempts of local villains to discredit Harry's identity.
And so, in the final scenes, Harry Bertram is restored to his name and his
estate, his sister and his beloved, and above all, to the approval of Guy
Mannering, his former commanding officer and future father-in-law.

The novel ends with the reconstruction of the Bertram family, now
jointly headed by Guy Mannering and Harry Bertram. Yet the principal
focus of *Guy Mannering* (as of Austen's and Edgeworth's novels before it)
is the moral regeneration set in motion when long-time absentees return
from the outposts of empire to a domestic sphere that has virtually collapsed during their absence. When Godfrey Bertram cleared his lands and
displaced long-standing Gypsy residents, he created a new diaspora and
inadvertently sent his son into a long exile. Twenty years later, when Guy
Mannering, Julia, and Harry Bertram return to Britain from India, they can
come home only by a long process of mental and moral readjustment. Once
a humble scholar, Guy Mannering has become a famous war hero; he "relieved Cuddieburn, and defended Chingalore, and defeated the great Mah-
ratta chief, Ram Jolli Bundleman" (3:122). He and those around him regard
these achievements with pride; his duty as a colonel of the British Army in
India was to subdue rebel armies and native populations alike, and he succeeded superlatively.

Yet in private he suffers from the same unassuageable guilt as Godfrey
Bertram; through misplaced jealousy and a series of misjudgments, he indirectly caused the death of his wife and the orphaning of his daughter. At
what he later recalls as "a moment of peculiar pressure (. . . how hard we
were sometimes run to obtain white faces to countenance our line of battle)," his regiment takes on "a young man, named Brown" (3:128), who

distinguishes himself in battle, wins Mannering's esteem, and arouses the envy of the Iago-like Archer, who poisons Mannering's mind with allegations that the cadet is courting Mannering's wife. The commander cannot really suspect his wife of misconduct, although India's insalubrious atmosphere has weakened her morally and physically. But the accusations heighten his own haughtiness, until he begins to act the part of "an oppressive aristocratic man, who made my rank in society, and in the army, the means of galling those whom circumstances placed beneath me" (3:130).

Finally, Mannering seeks a flimsy pretext to challenge Brown and wounds him badly in a duel outside the British fortress. Busy fighting one another, the duelists are set upon by native banditti, who wound Archer, carry off Brown, and almost capture Mannering's wife. Although Archer subsequently clears Brown's name, Brown has vanished for good, and neither Mannering's wife nor his daughter, Julia, ever recovers from their shock. Mannering's wife dies eight months later, and his daughter is left so ill that Mannering resigns his commission to bring her back to Europe, "where her native air, time, and the novelty of the scenes around her, have contributed to dissipate her dejection and to restore her health" (3:131). Yet as her inconsiderate and immature behavior through most of the book suggests, it takes a long time before Julia, the India Girl, has fully gotten the corruptions of the colonies out of her system.

If this episode is strongly reminiscent of *Othello*, the racial tensions of Shakespeare's plot find displaced expression in their new Anglo-Indian setting. Appearing in Guy Mannering's regiment at a moment when the British are winning India, with an army largely made up of natives, Brown is a figure around whom Mannering's fears of racial and social miscegenation can crystallize. Yet when he is captured by the Indians, he leaves Mannering with a guilt that must be expiated, upon the colonel's return to Britain, by good offices to the remaining members of the Bertram family. At the same time, the episode somehow expiates the inherited guilt of the Bertrams for the violence of Godfrey Bertram's clearances. Guy Mannering's domestic tragedy in British India oddly parallels Godfrey Bertram's domestic tragedy at Ellangowan twenty years earlier, with Harry Bertram playing the same role in each performance. The symmetry of these events is reinforced by the novel's persistent metaphoric associations of the Scottish Gypsies with the natives of India, similar in appearance and dress, in language, and in their alternation between submission and rebellion. Bertram's displacement of the Gypsies leads to Harry's kidnapping by Gypsy ruffians and thus to his wife's death; Mannering's displacement of the Indian natives leads to Harry's kidnapping by native banditti and thus to *his* wife's death.

What happens in the course of this repetition, and in Harry's second victimization, is the canceling out of Godfrey Bertram's original sin, the

beginning of the end of the curse on the Bertram family, and the commencement of a new cycle of atonement for Guy Mannering. Domestic
mismanagement is repeatedly linked to imperial mismanagement; imperial
misdeeds are restituted by a process of domestic atonement and rebuilding.
The domestic expands into the imperial; the imperial folds back into the
domestic. And by a sleight-of-hand, the sins of Scotland are eclipsed and
righted by the sins of the empire: Gypsies become Indians, domestic victims become imperial enemies, and battle-stained imperial heroes replace
ineffectual domestic despots as Britain's new leaders; Guy Mannering replaces Godfrey Bertram as the figure who can expiate the political sins of
the past, by taking over parental responsibilities for Bertram's orphaned
children, as well as for his own spoiled daughter. By the end of the book,
Guy Mannering's close parental supervision has begun to compensate for
Julia's flawed moral formation and for the lasting influences of India; Julia
finally seems capable of reciprocating his affection. Although her marriage
will soon transform her into Julia Bertram, she will behave differently from
her unredeemed namesake at Mansfield Park, who sat through family life
with no interest in her father's affairs.

Taking its cue from its West India sailor Godfrey Bertram Hewit, *Guy
Mannering* might well be seen as an illegitimate son of *Mansfield Park*,
born onto the estate of *Castle Rackrent*; although it inherits many of its
parent's lineaments, it achieves neither the social grace nor the political
acuity of its progenitor. Scott's rewriting of Edgeworth simplifies her account of long-standing cultural differences *within* a colonial culture by
introducing the Gypsies, nonindigenous and nonwhite, as his figures of
difference. And Scott's rewriting of Austen flattens her characters and
nominalizes her implied connection between the imperial and the domestic: where Sir Thomas Bertram returns home from Antigua tired, tanned,
and somehow transformed, Harry Bertram returns home from India simply
as Brown.

Yet Scott also goes beyond Austen in exploring the intellectual dissonances that plague those who pass between the parallel yet incommensurate worlds of the imperial and the domestic. The second half of *Guy
Mannering* is devoted primarily to a lengthy and quite extraordinary psychological study of Harry Bertram, presented at once as a recovering amnesiac and as a colonial adventurer, who now, after a long physical and psychic passage that has transformed him quite literally into another person,
must try to leave the empire behind him, recover his earliest self, and fit
himself back into his ancestral home. With Austen's Sir Thomas, we occa-
sionally glimpse a sign of inner transformation; here, we follow the process
step by step, as Bertram attempts to reconstruct his own hazy memories and
fit together the two disjunctive pieces and sites of his life.

What Scott presents is a pioneering account of the working through of psychic materials. Yet the psychologizing of the specific problems empire raises also creates new problems. First, the displacement of geopolitical struggle into mental conflict transforms public, political, and moral problems of power and of collective destiny into merely private neuroses, subjective mental states, and problems of emotional health. (The question is one of scale and proportion: the feminist appropriation of abolitionist rhetoric, similarly, remained powerful where it explicated institutional continuities and structural similarities of oppression, and callous where the collective fate of the whole black Caribbean was evoked opportunistically, to add a new shock value or moral weight to female marital difficulty.) Second, the model of working through assumes the finitude, efficacy, and sufficiency of a psychic coming to consciousness, that a brief phase of self-examination, expiation, and reconciliation will be followed by forgiveness and lasting inner peace. To work through the legacy and guilt of empire is to assume that the burden can be gotten rid of altogether and forever, that Mansfield Park and Ellangowan can eventually subsume, cover over, and in good conscience forget the West Indian plantation, the Anglo-Indian fortress, and the cleared Gypsy settlement.

Throughout its modern history, European literature has displaced widespread European anxieties about progress and cultural memory onto the figures of the Gypsies as a way of externalizing and banishing these fears; chased out, sent on their way, the Gypsies, it is hoped, will carry the problem of memory away with them.[42] On one level, *Guy Mannering* reverses this trend. Kidnapped by Gypsies intent on eradicating the Bertram family, and ordered to forget his origins, Harry Bertram eventually struggles back toward his beginnings, managing to close a personal circuit of memory, to be remembered in turn by those he left behind, to reclaim his rightful inheritance, and to be reinstated as laird of Ellangowan. Yet on another level, it is left to the reader to grope toward a larger set of geocultural and geopolitical connections, which the novel makes only partly explicit.

Taken together, the laird's originary administrative violence against his former tenants and the retributive violence of those displaced by improvement amount to a small-scale civil war over progress. The novel's narrator, significantly, dubs this struggle "the Scottish Maroon war" (3:72). If this reference evokes the ongoing political unrest in Britain's West Indian colonies, the chapter epigraph immediately above it in Scott's text, from John Leyden's *Scenes of Infancy, Descriptive of Teviotdale* (1803), evokes the expulsion of Native Indians from the British colony of Upper Canada.[43] The expelled Gypsies of Ellangowan, displaced in the domestic reconfiguration of Scotland, are associated with several different dark-skinned "Indian" peoples conquered, enslaved, or displaced in different, distant corners of the British Empire: the West Indian slaves, the North American Indians, the Indians of the South Asian subcontinent.

In Jamaica the "Maroons" (so called by the British) were plantation slaves who escaped their Spanish masters during the 1655 British conquest of the island, united into guerrilla bands, and attempted to undermine British plantation society through repeated acts of terror.[44] At Ellangowan the Scottish Maroons function at once as general signifiers of cultural and racial difference and as symbols for specific domestic and imperial struggles. To their eighteenth-century Scottish compatriots, their tawny skin and unusual clothing make the Gypsies simply "Egyptians," whereas the more sophisticated early-nineteenth-century narrator, narrating with the benefit of hindsight, associates them both with the emancipationist struggles of the West Indies and with the British conquest of India under Guy Mannering's command. Scott links the Gypsies to India's native populations partly because early-nineteenth-century linguists had begun to realize that the Gypsies were of Indian origin; at the same time, Scott's scenario of Gypsy displacement in Scotland recapitulates contemporary political debate over the deleterious consequences of the Western property laws forcibly introduced into British-ruled Bengal.[45]

Scott's intertextual reference to *Scenes of Infancy* evokes similar moral anxieties. Leyden's poem is at once a patriotic description of the physical glories of the Borders, a nostalgic invocation of Scotland's past martial glory, and a worried prognosis of the country's precarious economic, cultural, and political situation: the dissolution of an organic agricultural society formerly bound by clanlike ties of loyalty and the threat that the region's agricultural laborers, discontented with their new disenfranchisement, will emigrate en masse to some other part of the British Empire. Emptying Teviotdale, they will, as they settle in Upper Canada or other colonies, drive the native population there out of *its* traditionary homes. The displacements of domestic modernity, Leyden argues, feed even more violent displacements of empire.

At least on a subterranean level, this is the argument of *Guy Mannering* as well. But although the metaphoric system of Scott's novel carefully traces the entire colonial circuit and points to the empire's economic and political consequences, the novel's characters do not understand the size, coherence, or meaning of the imperial framework. They believe themselves to be expiating personal or familial transgressions and cannot see the political resonance of their actions; they think themselves in a corner of rural Scotland and cannot see that they are in the middle of the empire.

From the national-imperial novels of the 1790s *Guy Mannering* and *Mansfield Park* inherit the novelistic, ideological, and moral problem of how to fit the domestic to the imperial setting. Of the two novels, *Guy Mannering* gives both the more explicit and the more evasive rendering of the problem. Like *Mansfield Park*, its main strategy is to dematerialize the "other setting" and to rematerialize it only as a kind of memory theater, which is entered indirectly: in Harry Bertram's efforts to remember the other setting of the past, in the confessional letter in which Guy Mannering recounts the fatal effects of his Indian jealousies, and in the sentimental letters in which Julia Mannering reminisces about India and the atmospheric stories of her ayah.

Like the astrological predictions of the astrologer and Gypsy fortune-teller which open the novel, these subjective, indirect, and veiled memory processes find themselves suspended within the apparently omniscient consciousness of the narrative, just as the events of the novel, the experiences, emotions, and memory work of Guy and Julia Mannering, Godfrey and Harry Bertram, are subsumed and explained within the retrospective historical framework of the Scottish Enlightenment. Scott is justly famous for his detailed attention to epoch as a determinant of character and of plot, and *Guy Mannering*, perhaps even more than *Waverley*, represents a new attempt to historicize the problem of memory, correlating layers of personal and collective memory with the different cultural spaces of the empire and (following the logic of Enlightenment four-stage theory) with its uneven layers of intellectual and material development. What this produces, paradoxically, is an amnesia in memory, a regression in retrieval. As Guy and Julia Mannering grow morally, and grow into Scotland, their ambivalent memories of India recede and grow dim; as Harry Bertram unconsciously prepares to assume the rule of Ellangowan, his memories of Scotland grow stronger, and the memory of the Gypsy clearances is painstakingly reconstructed in order to be gotten over forever. "I come, to trace your soothing haunts again / .... To lose, amid your winding dells, the past"; thus Leyden explains his rationale for reconstructing, in memory, a Teviotdale now changed forever by capitalization, dislocation, and the shadow of empire.[46] *Guy Mannering*, too, commemorates in order to forget, politicizes the memory problem only to subjectivize it, and retrieves the problem of empire in order to relegate it to the realm of infantile memory.

Like the novels of the 1790s, *Guy Mannering* works to expand the coordinates of the chronotope. Yet Scott's experiments with narrative time ultimately erase his experiments with narrative space. The novel's temporal relativizing of its two layers of historical events through an even later narrative perspective makes possible a nuanced account of the possibilities and limits of historical consciousness. *Guy Mannering* presents simultaneously a historicist sense of the past and a sense of historical contingency, a people's sense of absolute enclosure or boundedness in their own particular historical moment and the retrospective historical relativity of all human belief systems. At the same time, as in many of the Waverley novels, Scott explores the nonsynchronicity of historical development, as characters still held within the distinctly premodern political and cosmological worldview of early modern Scotland are shown to coexist with a Scottish Enlightenment culture, with a different (and in Scott's view, more advanced) sense of world order, social systematicity, and probability. Scott's identification of synchronous, coexisting, and successive historical frameworks serves to establish a more nuanced, complicated, and contradictory sense of historical temporality than the British novel had deployed heretofore. Yet *Guy Mannering*'s parallel experiments with the novel's spatial coordinates— with the coexistence, connection, and dissociation of geographically distant imperial spaces—finally give us a much more disconnected sense of political causality and imperial responsibility than the novels that precede it.

In representing *Guy Mannering*'s events as historical, as located in and created by the conditions of a now-historical past, Scott works to place his characters' ignorance in high relief, so that we understand their now-alien construction of the world while feeling our own distance from it. In representing *Guy Mannering*'s events as political and geographical, as created by and located within the condition of modernity and imperial expansion, Scott takes advantage of his characters' obliviousness to retard the narrative's—and the reader's—ability to make intellectual and moral connections. From the imperial novels of the 1790s, from Edgeworth, and from Austen, *Guy Mannering* inherits not only an interest in the synchronicity of space and of cultural development but the narrative means to represent several places at once, in their interpenetration. Its final effect, however, is to allow domestic concerns to drown out imperial ones. When Harry Bertram comes home to become a local authority figure, the wide world and its problems disappear behind him.

Chapter 5

THE OLD WIVES' TALE:
THE FOSTERING SYSTEM AS
NATIONAL AND IMPERIAL EDUCATION

It is from the lips, as it is on the knee of a *Mother*, that childhood
is nursed, and instructed. . . . But it is more immediately under the
tradition of the Patriarch, or Nation, of the Aunt, or Grandsire, that
in Scotland, in particular, a decided, and over-ruling bent is given to
the character of children. . . .

Scotland has been, at no very remote period, a pastoral country, a
land of shepherds and shepherdesses—an Arcadian scene of loves and
affections, fostered on the mountain, and expressed by the stream of
the valley. She is, accordingly . . . possessed to this hour of a national,
most powerful and tender music. . . . Although the names of those . . .
whose simple, but eminently impassioned strains, have given body and
immortality to our "national song," have, in many instances, perished,
amidst the darkness of the unrecorded past, although the shepherd poet
. . . has in the "lapse of ages, perished from the way" . . . yet powerfully
does he still continue to speak in the "ballet" and "tender ditty" of her
who, to soothe and to gratify our childish desire, of entertainment, and
of story, hangs upon her lips, and models, though imperceptibly to
herself and us, our early taste. . . How often have we listened with an
interest of which we now retain little more than the recollection, to the
"Flowers of the Forest," "The Braes o' Yarrow," "The Fair Helen of
Kirkconnel," or to the still more eventful history of "Young Tam
Lean," as they fell upon our ears in all the soft and penetrating cadence
of an aged and tremulous voice . . . ? Can England!—but England has
no natural music—nor is she at present, nor has she for ages past, been
possessed of *the means*, of transmitting from the age that is past, to that
which is to come, any deep or sacred feeling connected with national
song. In England, the peasant child acquires its habits, and receives
its prepossessions, directly from its parents. In Scotland, the past
generation, the venerable and experienced—the legendary veterans
of a former day, cast a mantle of inspiration, and a hue of poetry, over
their grandchildren. Our national character and our national prejudices
if you will, die thus more slowly away; and the tastes and the views,
and the prepossessions of earlier times, are thus transmitted, warm
and unqualified, through many successive ages.
—Anonymous, "Essay on the Present State of Education in Scotland"

A single tree stood alone on this bank; under it sat a native [Bengali]
woman, and by her lay several gaudy toys. Alas! it was the nurse of
my departed child. She had been aware of our approach, and had sat
waiting there to see her boy. . . . There are moments of intense
feeling in which all the distinctions of nations, colours, and castes
disappear, and in their place there only remains between two human
beings one abiding sense of a common nature. When I saw the beloved
nurse of my Henry brought into the boat, and unfeignedly weeping
for her boy, I felt in truth that she was a human being like myself,
and as dear to him that made her as the most exalted saint that ever
existed in the Christian world.
—Mary Martha Sherwood, *The Life of Mrs. Sherwood*

Oedipus's Scar: The Revolution in the Nursery

In Samuel Richardson's *Pamela* (1742), Pamela's infant contracts small-
pox from its nurse, with almost fatal results. The novel's deepest anxieties
about nursing, however, lie elsewhere: maternal breast-feeding threatens
marital harmony by abrogating the husband's conjugal pleasures, yet wet-
nursing threatens the nursling's moral development, by exposing it to servant life during a formative period. When early-nineteenth-century reformers denounced the practice of putting children out to nurse, their favorite
arguments were hygienic: the wet nurse's cottage was conducive to the
transmission of disease, and wet-nursing decreased the chances of survival
both for the nursling and the nurse's own child.[1] Yet the debate over nursing had long involved cultural and social questions as well as medical ones.
Since antiquity, wet nurses were believed to transmit physical and social
traits to their sucklings in their milk.[2] Now, in a period of escalating class
conflicts, and in a society obsessed with the mechanisms of social reproduction, nurses pose a threat to infant acculturation.

As Rousseau argues in *Emile* (1762), wet-nursing weakens the state in
its foundation by preventing the consolidation of the family. A wet nurse is
"a bad mother," abandoning her own child to suckle a stranger, so "how
can she be a good nurse?" If she develops maternal feeling for her nursling,
this new bond endangers parental authority; unless the "ties of nature" are
"strengthened by habit," family members will become virtual strangers,
and the roles of "fathers, mothers, children, brothers, and sisters cease to
exist."

Every evil follows in the train of this first sin; the whole moral order is disturbed, nature is quenched in every breast, the home becomes gloomy. . . But

when mothers deign to nurse their own children, then there will be a reform in morals; natural feeling will revive in every heart; there will be no lack of citizens for the state; this first step by itself will restore mutual affection. (P. 13)

For Rousseau "there is no substitute for a mother's love." If, out of selfishness, a mother puts her infant out to nurse, she must be

prepared to divide her mother's rights, or rather to abdicate them in favour of a stranger; to see her child loving another more than herself; to feel that the affection he retains for his mother is a favour, while his love for his foster-mother is a duty; for is not some affection due where there has been a mother's care? To remove this difficulty, children are taught to look down on their nurses, to treat them as mere servants. When their task is completed the child is withdrawn or the nurse is dismissed. After a few years the child never sees her again. The mother expects to take her place, and to repair by her cruelty the results of her own neglect. But she is greatly mistaken; she is making an un-grateful foster-child, not an affectionate son; she is teaching him ingratitude, and she is preparing him to despise at a later day the mother who bore him, as he now despises his nurse. (P. 13)

The affection of nurse and child can create a fostering bond almost as strong as the maternal bond. Yet this relationship remains socially vulner-able, and its forced dissolution, so that the maternal relationship can regain its primacy, is morally damaging to child and nurse; the mother's dismissal of the nurse is a first sin from which all other social injustices follow.

By 1800, bourgeois mothers began to breast-feed their own children as a matter of course, and the nurse, once the dominant figure of early child-hood, all but vanished, replaced by the nanny and the governess.[3] Yet as Rousseau predicted, the nurse's banishment gave rise to new anxieties, with far-reaching effects on the bourgeois psyche. The rise of maternal child care around 1800, argues Friedrich Kittler, marked a new epoch for European cultural life, as the bourgeois family and literary life were re-structured around a new, Oedipally driven psychic economy.[4] Even the romantic notion of genial authorship, with its emphasis on the inspiring voice, was grounded in the new maternal teaching of the "mother tongue."

In late-eighteenth-century Germany, a new pronunciation machine taught mothers proper articulation, helping them to purify their vowels from the contaminations of dialect, to pass on to their children a pure ver-sion of their native language. Pedagogical treatises for mothers placed sim-ilar emphases on maternal self-improvement, self-censorship, and self-discipline. As the responsibility for education was shifted from fathers onto mothers, Kittler argues, the social role of women was correspondingly re-duced, until they saw themselves as mere conduits of information. Mothers were reduced to their reproductive function, to pure vessels of transmission, and asked to remain permanently in labor, struggling endlessly to bring their children into the world. The German title of Kittler's chapter, "Der Muttermund," signifies both the mouth of the uterus, through which the infant passes to be born, and the mother's mouth, through which she teaches her children to speak. Together, Kittler argues, the new ideology of motherhood and the maternal self-cancellation that it necessitated intensified and Oedipalized the relationship between mother, child, and father. And poetic inspiration came to depend on a new maternal muse: in the act of writing, the adult poet simultaneously remembers and represses the memory of his primal encounter with language, in his mother's lap, in her alphabetizing breath. Written to recapture the mother's voice, German romantic poetry both works to reverse her self-abnegating silence and celebrates her self-sacrifice.

British romantic literature, however, links poetic inspiration and cultural memory to the banished nurse as much as to the self-effacing mother.[5] The diary of Lady Nugent, wife of the governor of Jamaica, bears witness to the intensification, during this period, of a triangular relationship between mother, child, and nurse.

> Sept. 16, 1802. . . . Mrs. Hamilton, the wife of one of the Irish soldiers . . . has come to offer herself as my nurse. I like her appearance very much. She is pretty and very good humoured . . . and [Dr. L] has persuaded General N. that it will be such a good thing to have her in the house, in case I can't take charge of the dear baby myself. I have consented, if her character answers, to receive her, and to give up the delightful idea of nursing, if it should be found best for the darling child . . . my mind is so agitated all day, that I am quite unwell, and good for nothing. . .
>
> Sept. 17, 1802. Don't sleep all night thinking of nurse Hamilton and the future. . . [My husband] consoles me very much; for he says it would be impossible for me to do justice to my dear baby in this horrid climate . . . and that Mrs. Hamilton's fair and fat little boy shews what a good nurse she really does make. Try to be satisfied. . .
>
> Oct. 1, 1802. Nurse Hamilton came; feel half angry at her superseding me in what is one of the most precious parts of my expected duty, but play with her fair little boy, till I was quite in good humour with the mother. . . . Still full of jealousy and worry about nurse Hamilton, for why should I not be a mother indeed?. . . .
>
> Nov. 23, 1802. Received an express from Stony Hill, giving an account of the death of poor nurse's husband. Poor creature, I don't know how to tell her, and am much distressed on her account . . . and do all I can to comfort her. She has promised to feel as little as possible, on account of the baby, and I will do all I can for hers.

Nov. 24, 1802. Out early in the sociable, with nurse and dear baby.—Poor nurse, trying to look cheerful, not to distress me. . . .

April 18, 1803. Heard this evening of the death of poor nurse's child; poor soul! I am indeed distressed for her, and don't know how I shall be able to break the sad news to her. . . .

April 20, 1803. Nurse came to my room early to-day, with a much more cheerful countenance than I had dared to expect, and I am really grateful to her for the effort she evidently makes, to conquer her own feelings, on account of my precious boy.[6]

The mother's initial jealousy is displaced by almost ghoulish pity for the "poor nurse"; successively losing most of her family, the nurse is forced to sublimate her grief into her nursing. Here, as in contemporary antinursing polemics, the death of the nurse's own child appears as divine retribution for her social presumption, her usurpation of the maternal role.

As bourgeois mothers gripped by the new maternalism become increasingly possessive of their children, they try to restrict the nurse's role in the household, instituting a class divide between mind and body.[7] They themselves are to guard their children's souls, train their minds, and fill their mouths with (well-pronounced) words; the nurses merely will care for the children's bodies, filling their mouths with food and milk. Yet this absolute divide is impossible to maintain; as long as children are cared for by nurses as well as by their mothers, they are acculturated, for better or worse, into two very different linguistic, cultural, and literary worlds, and receive formative exposure to lower-class dialects, stories, and songs. British romantics, interested in reconciling learned and popular tradition, often defend this tradition of secondary acculturation: the nurse embodied oral abundance, and her rhymes and tales inspired a lifelong love of literature.

As romantic novelists argue contra Rousseau, the nurse's disappearance from the early-nineteenth-century household fundamentally alters children's relationship to language and the day-to-day texture of class traditions. Once under official prohibition, indeed, the nurse (like the bard or the bog before her) begins to represent a repressed collective unconscious; her persistent return in fiction and in dreams (and a new cult, elegiac and sentimental, around the memory of the dead nurse) represents a collective resistance against the order of banishment.[8] Once a most ordinary and familiar presence, the nurse is transfigured into a mythic personage, bathed in nostalgia and longing. As British intellectuals begin to conceptualize cultural tradition as a series of developmental layers, they come to see literature too as evolving out of an oral tradition that becomes its repressed prehistory.[9] If the nurse is remembered ontogenetically, by individual adults, as the object of their earliest, most fragmentary memories, she is also remembered phylogenetically, as the embodiment of an earlier, now-lost cultural epoch, which can be reconstructed only fragmentarily. Initially, she is the molder and witness of childhood development, and later, an absent, lamented figure, whose prohibition stimulates new reconstructive memory processes. She is at once a figure for the persistence of memory (her own memory shores up the past; the memory *of* her is a triumph over the forces of amnesia) and, like the bard before her, an emblem of how much is irrevocably forgotten.[10]

When the emphasis of European memory work shifts over the course of the nineteenth century, the nurse's role as a placeholder of memory shifts as well. Reminiscing about an 1818 visit to Abbotsford, Washington Irving evokes an ancestral landscape that resonates, bardically, with the remembered songs of the nursery.

> What a thrill of pleasure did I feel when first I saw the broom-covered tops of the Coaden Knowes . . . and what touching associations were called up by the sight of Ettrick Vale, Galla Water, and the Braes of Yarrow! Every turn brought to mind some household air—some almost forgotten song of the nursery, by which I had been lulled to sleep in my childhood; and with them the looks and voices of those who had sung them, and who were now no more. It is these melodies, chanted in our ears in the days of infancy, and connected with the memory of those we have loved, and who have passed away, that clothe Scottish landscape with such tender associations. The Scottish songs, in general, have something intrinsically melancholy in them; owing, in all probability, to the pastoral and lonely life of those who have composed them. . . . Many of these rustic bards have passed away, without leaving a name behind them; nothing remains of them but their sweet and touching songs, which live, like echoes, about the places they once inhabited. Most of these simple effusions of pastoral poets are linked with some favorite haunt of the poet; and in this way, not a mountain or valley, a town or tower, green shaw or running stream, in Scotland, but has some popular air connected with it, that makes its very name a key-note to a whole train of delicious fancies and feelings.[11]

So too, in Mary Shelley's *Matilda* (written in 1819), the nurse assists in the Ossianic sublation of an individual poetic voice into a collective voice, which emanates from the national landscape.

> The care of me while I was a baby, and afterwards until I had reached my eighth year devolved on a servant of my mother's. . . . I was placed in a remote part of the house, and only saw my aunt at stated hours. . . . She never caressed me, and seemed all the time I stayed in the room to fear that I should annoy her by some childish freak. . . .
>
> Under my good nurse's care I ran wild around our park and the neighbouring fields. . . . I believe that I bore an individual attachment to every tree in our park. . . .

When I was seven years of age my nurse left me. I now forget the cause of her departure if I ever knew it. She returned [from Scotland] to England, and the bitter tears she shed at parting were the last I saw flow for love of me for many years. My grief was terrible: I had no friend but her in the whole world. By degrees I became reconciled to solitude but no one supplied her place in my affections. I lived in a desolate country where
—there were none to praise
And very few to love.[12]

A hundred years later, in her *Memoirs of a Revolutionist* (written in 1913–26, from prison), Vera Figner evokes her equally powerful childhood attachment to her nurse in the service of a very different notion of collectivity, to describe the source of her lifelong dedication to class justice and the emancipation of the serfs. Like other Russian anarchists, Figner sees the patriarchal aristocratic household in which she was raised as a microcosm of the state.

And in the midst of this deadly, soulless barrack atmosphere was a single point of light, our comfort and joy: our old nurse. All around us no one had the slightest understanding of the character of children, of childish ends. Absolutely no consideration for children's weaknesses, nothing but mercilessness and hardness. Only in the room of the nurse, where my father never came, only with her alone did we have the feeling that we were ourselves; we felt ourselves as human beings, as children and masters, but above all as beloved and spoiled children. This room was for us in a way a shrine, where the injured and downtrodden could stand up tall again. Here one could reveal all of one's childish suffering and find tenderness and sympathy. How good it felt, to hide oneself in the nurse's lap, to weep one's suffering out and to let the tears be dried by her kisses! The good-hearted, loyal soul! How lonely we would have lived without her! Here was a world full of warmth and tenderness, uninhibited happiness, love and devotion.[13]

In a family life built on oppression, the nursing relationship is a crucial counterforce; enabling the child to grasp the deep humanity of her "underlings" and her own dependence on a class of people she ostensibly "owns," it announces the need and suggests the means for revolutionary struggle.[14]

Yet during the same period, Sigmund Freud's influential psychoanalytic theories work to depoliticize infantile memory and minimize the nurse's role in the development of infant desires. Freud was deeply ambivalent about his own nurse; during his early childhood, she was sent away in disgrace for stealing, and as a result she lingers as a figure of desire and menace throughout his adult dream life.[15] In *The Interpretation of Dreams*, he argues that the "deepest and most eternal nature of man, upon whose evocation in his listeners the poet is accustomed to rely, lies in those impulses of the mind which have their roots in a childhood which has since become prehistoric." Then he recounts one of his own dreams, in which this "prehistoric old nurse" appears reincarnated.[16] For Freud, then, the nurse guards the "prehistoric," the ground of adult emotional and literary response. Yet his theories of infantile amnesia and the Oedipal complex transform the nurse into a figure of anachronism, who appears only dimly on the edge of adult consciousness, her memory, now disconnected from any important psychic affect, quite without psychoanalytic interest.

In case studies from *A Case of Obsessional Neurosis* (1909) to *From the History of an Infantile Neurosis* (1914, published in 1918), Freud details the complex, fraught relations between nurse and charge. Yet what is played out between them becomes significant only when the child attempts to replay the same scenario with the biological parents. The fostering relation is only an anticipation and a preparation, never an end in itself; although the nurse may shape the child's understanding of the world and serve as the first object of sexual attachment, experimentation, or frustration, inducing or intensifying infantile traumas, she is only a temporary stand-in, never a lasting object of cathexis in her own right.

Even Freud's influential reading of Sophocles' *Oedipus* misreads the play's central relationships to secure the primacy of biological parents: "It is the fate of us all, perhaps," he concludes, "to direct our first sexual impulse towards our mother, and our first hatred and our first murderous wish against our father."[17] Yet if Sophocles describes the rediscovery of blood relations, the childhood that Oedipus reconstructs is dominated not by an intense relationship with his biological parents but by their abandonment, and by the disconnected relay of foster parents who adopt him in their stead. His murder of his father and his desire for his mother are rooted not in the tight emotional economy of the nuclear family but in his failure to recognize and to feel appropriate emotions toward parents who have become strangers. It is *this* psychic scenario which dominates nineteenth-century fiction and Freud's own case studies.

Nineteenth-century novelists see the nurse as the bearer of a cultural inheritance, able to rouse her grown-up charges from their disaffection with national life into a more committed engagement with its past and present. Freud, in contrast, develops an experimental science of memory retrieval in part to screen out particular memories, to legitimate the individual and collective obliteration of the memory of all the nurse once meant. Rejoining Rousseau in emphasizing the primacy of the biological parents, Freud works to displace the nineteenth century's counter-Rousseauian model of collective memory. By reconstructing the historical development and political implications of this alternative model, this chapter will suggest what Freud loses in his attempt to dissociate psychic development from cultural tradition.[18]

Enlightenment Memory: Recapitulation and Progress

"Nothing has of late been revolutionized so much as the nursery," writes cultural and natural historian Robert Chambers to introduce his *Popular Nursery Rhymes of Scotland* (1841). The preeminent Scottish antiquary of his day and one of the main pre-Darwinian theorists of biological evolution (*Vestiges of the Natural History of Creation*, 1844), Chambers wishes to reconcile conservation and improvement. Human development appears to him simultaneously as a cycle of reproduction and self-recapitulation, as a process of biological and cultural accretion, and as a line of evolutionary transformation. The nursery makes visible all three tendencies. There, the process of cultural formation constantly begins anew. As a domain ruled by loquacious women, who divert, punish, and teach through a vast oral reper-toire, the nursery serves as a site of cultural transmission, where the literary legacy of past ages is handed down to a new generation. Yet the nursery is also a cultural institution, and subject, as such, to historical mutability; writing in an age of intellectual and political revolutions, Chambers views the nursery as the most important, and most vulnerable, site of cultural reproduction.

> The young mind was formerly cradled amidst the simplicities of the unin-structed intellect; and *she* was held to be the best nurse who had the most copious supply of song, and tale, and drollery at all times ready to soothe and amuse her young charges. There were, it is true, some disadvantages in the system; for sometimes superstitious terrors were implanted, and little pain was taken to distinguish between what tended to foster the evil, and what tended to elicit the better feelings of infantine nature. Yet the ideas which presided over the scene, and rung through it all day in light gabble and jocund song, were simple, often beautiful ideas, generally well expressed, and unquestionably suitable to the capacities of children. In the *realism* . . . now demanded in the superiors of the nursery, and which mothers seek to cultivate in their own intercourse with the young, there are certain advantages; yet it is questionable if the system be so well adapted to the early state of the faculties, while there can be little doubt that it is too exclusively addressed to the intellect, and almost entirely overlooks that there is such a thing as imagination, or a sense of fun, in the human mind. . . . I cannot help looking back with the greatest satisfaction to the numberless merry lays and *capriccios* of all kinds, which the simple honest women of our native country used to sing and enact with such untiring patience, and so much success, beside the evening fire in old times, ere yet Mrs Trimmer or Mr Wilderspin had been heard of. There was no philoso-phy about these gentle dames; but there was generally endless kindness, and a wonderful power of keeping their little flock in good-humour. It never oc-curred to them that children were anything but children—"bairns are just

bairns," my old nurse would say—and they never once thought of beginning to make them men and women while still little more than able to speak. Committed as we were in those days to such unenlightened curatrixes, we might be said to go through in a single life all the stages of a national progress. We begun under a superintendence which might be said intellectually to represent the Gothic age; and gradually, we waxed in years, and went to school and college, we advanced through the fourteenth and sixteenth centuries; finally coming down to the present age, when we adventured into public life. By the extinction of the old nursery system, some part of this knowledge is lost. (Pp. 11–12)

The nursery has been "revolutionized" by utilitarian pedagogical theories, and this process threatens the old, egalitarian sense of a cultural tradition shared across classes and epochs.

The Enlightenment emphasizes social and intellectual progress at the expense of cultural replication. For Chambers, each stage of a child's individual development and the collective development of each generation build on and recapitulate a long series of previous developmental stages. Every tale or song of the "old Scottish nursery" makes newly visible the vestiges of premodern social and literary forms.

> What man of middle age, or above it, does not remember the tales of drollery and wonder which used to be told by the fireside, in cottage and in nursery, by the old women, time out of mind the vehicles for such traditions? These stories were in general of a simple kind, befitting the minds which they were to regale; but in many instances they displayed considerable fancy, at the same time that they derived an inexpressible charm from a certain antique air which they had brought down with them from the world of their birth—a world still more primitive, and rude, and romantic, than that in which they were told, old as *it* now appears to us. They breathed of a time when society was in its simplest elements, and the most familiar natural things were as yet unascertained from the supernatural. It seems not unlikely that several of these legends had been handed down from very early ages—from the mythic times of our Gothic history—undergoing of course great change, in accordance with the changing character of the people, but yet, like the wine in the Heidelberg tun, not altogether renewed. (P. 48)

To foster children's burgeoning rationality, utilitarian nursery reformers ignore—or actively suppress—their intuitive, imaginative forces. If reformers cleanse the nursery curriculum of traditional ballads and implement didactic texts in their stead, future generations will lose their literary birthright. For Chambers, the nursery is therefore the site of a crucial cultural struggle, between realism and romance, present and past.

"If, in advanced years, we would form a just notion of our progress from the cradle," writes Adam Ferguson in *An Essay on the History of Civil*

Society (1767), "we must have recourse to the nursery, and from the example of those who are still in their period of life we mean to describe, take our representation of past manners, that cannot, in any other way, be recalled."[19] The Enlightenment sees childhood as a fascinatingly paradoxical state and the nursery as a workshop in which to test basic learning processes and to fathom human origins.[20] Epistemologically, the child begins life as a tabula rasa, accumulating knowledge through direct experience. Yet the course of ontogenic development also recapitulates the entire phylogenic developmental history of mankind. Unfortunately, during the early years of life, children are unable to communicate their experiences with any precision; once their capacities for language and thought have developed sufficiently to make such communication possible, they have already begun to forget their earliest perceptions. The nursery is thus a space both of singular pedagogical transparency and uncanny opacity.[21]

If the interaction of nurse and child makes visible the mechanisms of cultural transmission, the nurse's stories can also appear as threatening throwbacks to more primitive epochs. Edgeworth's *Harrington* (1817) describes the long-term evil unleashed by one superstitious nurse to make clear what is at stake, epistemologically and politically, in the battle for the nursery. When a malicious young nurse threatens her charge with a bloodthirsty Jewish bogeyman, she infects young Harrington with her own irrational anti-Semitism. From one perspective, she merely repeats and transmits an age-old hate story. But these teachings fall on impressionable ears, becoming an integral part of Harrington's knowledge of the world, and he will spend years struggling to rid himself of the primeval fears they induce.[22] Edgeworth presents an epistemological Garden of Eden, in which the child's innocence, at the dawn of life, is poisoned at the source by an ancient, vicious, and false cultural "knowledge," which transforms strangers into ogres, the unfamiliar into the uncanny.[23] Individual and collective progress can be ensured only by suppressing the transmission and reproduction of premodern beliefs: only a revolution in the nursery can give children an unencumbered start in life.

"ALL THE HILLS ECCHOED": FROM BARDIC INSTITUTION TO FOSTERING SYSTEM

Romantic writers inherit from the Enlightenment a deeply divided view of the nurse, and some explain this dividedness in historical terms. As William Blake argues in the paired "Nurse's Songs" of *Songs of Innocence* (1789–90) and *Songs of Experience* (1793–94), the sociological reconfiguration of the nursery (as well as of other British institutions) has profound political and aesthetic implications, for it marks the transition from an unselfconscious culture based on shared traditions, collective experience, and bardic memory to an intensely introspective and individualistic culture, whose sentimental or neurotic obsession with its failing abilities to remember a lost communal past only highlights its sense of fragmentation and loss. *Songs of Innocence* shows the nurse invested with bardic functions and situated within a recognizably bardic landscape. Some copies of the first edition are framed by the linked pair of nurse and bard: the title engraving shows a nurse seated under a tree, reading aloud to two children, and the final illumination for "The Voice of the Ancient Bard" shows the bard, under a tree, playing a large Celtic harp to a considerable audience.[24] From the earliest portrayals of Ossian through the 1818 edition of Joseph Walker's *Historical Memoirs of the Irish Bards* (the source of the frontispiece/cover illustration for this book), the bard was often shown playing under a tree (preferably a Druidic oak), with the national landscape and national audience behind him, at once context, subject, and object of his song. In the cover image for *Songs of Innocence*, as in the engraving for the "Nurse's Song," Blake places the nurse in this bardic posture, linking her stories to the regenerative forces of nature and of childhood and grounding the *Songs* in a tradition of bardic and nursery songs.[25]

The two contrasting "Nurse's Songs" reiterate these connections: both place the nurse's voice within a natural and aural landscape to evoke a specifically Ossianic crossing of voice, echo, and memory. In some early copies of *Songs of Innocence*, the "Nurse's Song" appears immediately after "The Ecchoing Green," echoing the childhood pastoral it has established.

> When the voices of children are heard on the green
> And laughing is heard on the hill,
> My heart is at rest within my breast
> And everything else is still
>
> Then come home my children, the sun is gone down
> And the dews of night arise
> Come come leave off play, and let us away
> Till the morning appears in the skies
>
> No no let us play, for it is yet day
> And we cannot go to sleep
> Besides in the sky, the little birds fly
> And the hills are all coverd with sheep
>
> Well well go & play till the light fades away
> And then go home to bed
> The little ones leaped & shouted & laugh'd
> And all the hills ecchoed.

Whereas "The Ecchoing Green" suggests an instinctual logic behind—and diurnal or seasonal limitations to—children's play, the "Nurse's Song" reflects the nurse's consciousness and emphasizes the institutional framing

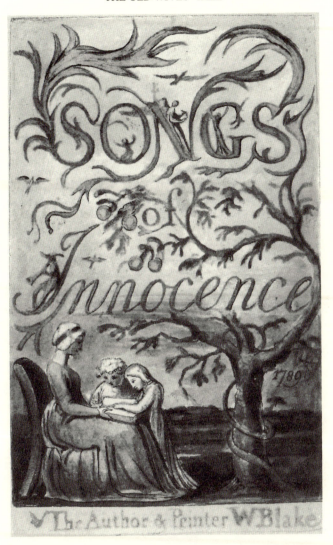

William Blake, *Songs of Innocence* (1789–90). Courtesy of The
Huntington Library, San Marino, California.

of childhood by the nurse's supervision and nursery schedules. As yet,
nursery rules are open to negotiation, and play still takes precedence over
duty; when "all the hills ecchoed" at the end of the poem, they resound with
the children's delighted laughter, not adult shouts of command. As yet, the
nurse's guardianship is benevolent and self-effacing; her song reflects not
her own authority so much as her determination to watch over the space of
childhood innocence as its genius loci and recording spirit, much as the
ancient bard presides over the *Songs of Innocence*.

William Blake, "The Ecchoing Green," in *Songs of Innocence* (1789–90). Courtesy of The Huntington Library, San Marino, California.

The illumination of the "Nurse's Song" in *Songs of Experience* depicts a younger, more modern, and less maternal figure; its scene of nursing conveys a brittle new sense of hierarchy. The nurse still frames the scene, but her body no longer touches her charges, and her hands, brandishing a comb over the boy's head, betray her desire for control. When this nurse sings, she echoes the earlier nurse's song, but to a very different effect.

> When the voices of children, are heard on the green,
> And whisprings are in the dale:

The days of my youth rise fresh in my mind,
My face turns green and pale.

William Blake, "The Voice of the Ancient Bard," in
Songs of Innocence (1789–90). Courtesy of The Huntington Library, San Marino, California.

The days of my youth rise fresh in my mind,
My face turns green and pale.

Then come home, my children, the sun is gone down
And the dews of night arise
Your spring & your day, are wasted in play,
And your winter and night in disguise.

This nurse calls on the children to abandon their play: children's lives,
she moralizes, are wasted where they seem joyous, hollow where they
seem dutiful. From her bitter vantage point, there is no possibility, even in

William Blake, "Nurse's Song," in *Songs of Innocence* (1789–90). Courtesy of The Huntington Library, San Marino, California.

childhood, for autonomy or resistance. Like the song of the old nurse, her poem opens by invoking the "voices of children . . . heard on the green, / And whisprings . . . in the dale," but only six lines later, the children have become completely silent, and the echo of their play has died out of the landscape.

More concentratedly than anything in the older nurse's song, her opening lines evoke the Ossianic memory effect. An echo in the landscape gives rise, then gives way, to a mental image of the past; a reverie begun in

When the voices of children are heard on the green
And whisprings are in the dale:
The days of my youth rise fresh in my mind.
My face turns green and pale.

Then come home my children the sun is gone down
And the dews of night arise
Your spring & your day are wasted in play
And your winter and night in disguise

William Blake, "Nurse's Song," in *Songs of Experience* (1793–94). Courtesy of The Huntington Library, San Marino, California.

contemplation of natural surroundings ends in the melancholy contemplation of what is past and lost, the sufferings of experience. The older nurse sat resplendent amid the children's echoing laughter. Preoccupied with her own cares, the younger nurse hears little more than "whisprings" and has soon turned away from the children altogether, to the bitter contemplation of her own lost youth; surrounded by her own ghosts, the nurse reduces her living charges to shadows.

Blake's two songs contrast not only the traditional and modern variants of the nursery, as they vied for supremacy at the end of the eighteenth

Mary Martha Sherwood, *Social Tales for the Young* (1835). Courtesy of The Osborne Collection of Early Children's Books, Toronto Public Library.

century, but the two faces of traditionalism, as seen by its nationalist defenders and by an Enlightenment consecrated to its effacement. In the first song, the old nurse is the source, protector, and renewer of tradition; the resounding, unending echo of the children at the poem's end guarantees the continued transmission and vitality of her culture. In the second song, sentimental rather than naive, the young nurse blocks the children's voices for the sake of her own memories. Here the reverberation of the echo no longer signals a robust refusal to desist; instead, it enacts a gradual vitiation and diminution, a slow dying away.

In the modern nursery, Blake suggests, the nurse has begun to lose her bardic powers and her bardic authority. In Mrs. Sherwood's "Mail Coach" (1835), the old Welsh nurse is unable, of her own accord, to guide her young charge into the ways of righteousness. She does bring him to a place of meditation and reflection—the village churchyard—but that is the extent of her philosophical or religious guidance. When the boy asks there about the nature of death, he is answered not by the nurse herself but by an old Welsh bard ("one of the last remaining specimens of those ancient bards who used to pass from one gentleman's house to another, carrying his harp on his shoulders, and being well assured of a joyful welcome") who has entered the churchyard unnoticed, and now steps forward to offer his auditors an improvised Christian catechism on death and resurrection, and a final "hymn about going to heaven," accompanied on his harp.[26] When "old David" dies, soon afterward, he bequeaths his copy of *Pilgrim's Progress* to the young boy. Together, this book and the old harper's personal influence lead the boy into new piety; the boy's example, in turn, eventually leads his wayward father, a religious skeptic and misguided social reformer, to a new acceptance of God and of the inevitability of social divisions. Between the psalm, the book, and the conversion of the social reformer, Sherwood's story modernizes—and Christianizes—the role of the bard in cultural reproduction, yet it insists on the primacy of the bard as the bearer of cultural meaning; the nurse, his modern, secular substitute, is inadequate on her own.

Irish and Scottish novelists, in contrast, insist on the successful transfer of bardic authority to the nurse; for them, she is the final carrier of bardic values. In content and etymology, argues Sydney Owenson in an antiquarian footnote to *The Wild Irish Girl*, the nurse's tales are linked to bardic chronicles.

> [The nurse] hums old *cronans*, or amuses me with what she calls a little *shanaos*,[1] as she plies her distaff. . . .
>
> . . . . .
>
> [1] *Shanaos* pronounced, but properly spelt *Sheanachus*, is a term in very general use in Ireland, and is applied to a kind of genealogical chit-chat, or talking over family antiquity, family anecdotes, descent, alliances, &tc., &tc., to which the lower, as well as the higher order of Irish in the provincial parts are much addicted. I have myself conversed with several ladies, in Connaught and Munster, who were living chronicles of transactions in their families of the most complicated nature. *Senachy* was the name of the antiquary retained in every noble family to preserve its exploits, &tc., &tc.[27]

Ellinor, the old Irish nurse in Edgeworth's *Ennui*; Mor ny Brien, the foster mother in Owenson's *O'Briens* (1827); and Moome, the old Highland nurse in Christian Johnstone's *Clan-Albin* (1815), demonstrate the same genealogy. "At making Gaelic rhymes, none in the glen—in a glen where all were poets—excelled Moome; and a more extensive collection of the tales of *Ossian Mach-Fingal*, and every ancient bard, was in the possession of no person in the highlands. With the genealogy of all the neighbouring clans she was intimately acquainted."[28] Possessed of a "miraculous" memory and a "most melodious voice," Mor ny Brien was known "far and near" as "*clarsagh na vallagh* . . . the *harp of the village*," and her voice is heard "in the mountains to this day, when the wind is asleep, keening th'ould moan." And even years later, her foster son treasures the memory of her recitations of "the feats of the heroes of our family," of "Fionne Mac Cumhal" (the Irish name for Fingal), of "Angus Ossin," and of "a spirited controversial dialogue" between Saint Patrick and Ossian, "which she used to sing to a wild strain."[29]

Like the bardic recitation they are descended from, Ellinor's historical legends, stories, and genealogies stoke family pride, strengthening feudal loyalties in their aristocratic auditor.

> She was inexhaustible in her anecdotes of my ancestors, all tending to the honour and glory of the family; she had also an excellent memory for all the insults, or traditions of insults which the Glenthorns had received for many ages back, even to the times of the old kings of Ireland; long and long before they stooped to be *lorded*; when their "names, which it was a pity and a murder, and moreover a burning shame, to change, was O'Shaughnessy." She was well-stored with histories of Irish and Scottish chiefs. . . . Then she had a large assortment of fairies and *shadowless* witches and *banshees*; and besides, she had legions of spirits and ghosts, and haunted castles without end, my own castle of Glenthorn not excepted, in the description of which she was extremely eloquent; she absolutely excited in my mind some desire to see it.[30]

The movement from bard to nurse involves the domestication, feminization, and popularization of tradition. The bard remembered and repeated national narratives to resist imperial occupiers; the nurse transmits culture and reconciles different classes. Adviser to his lord, muse to his clan's military campaigns, the bard helps to create a national-feudal courtly culture; he is the creation of aristocratic patronage, feudal loyalties, and early national institutions. The unlettered nurse, in contrast, represents the robustness of common knowledge.

If the nurse evokes the bards' traditional strengths—their prodigious memory, their narrative powers, and their loyalty to their masters—she also recapitulates their legendary weaknesses: their credulity, their partisanship, their uncritical allegiance to the ruling house, and their willingness to fabricate mythic histories in the service of an oppressive feudal order.[31] The bards sang their lays, in public, to a large audience, on ceremonial occasions. The nurse recounts her stories, day after day, to a small and impressionable audience of children, in the intimate (or claustrophobic) setting of the nursery. As Charles Dickens argues in his autobiographical "Nurse's Stories" (1861), about the grisly tales that blighted his childhood, the nurse's power is greater than that of any bard, for her stories can blast young lives forever.

> If we all knew our own minds (in a more enlarged sense than the popular acceptation of that phrase), I suspect we should find our nurses responsible for most of the dark corners we are forced to go back to, against our wills. . . . The same female bard—descended, possibly from those terrible old Skalds who seem to have existed for the express purpose of addling the brains of mankind

when they begin to investigate languages—made a standing pretence which greatly assisted in forcing me back to a number of hideous places I would by all means have avoided.[32]

The modern child struggles to be free of the stranglehold of the past, only to find him or herself sucked back into its darkness. Here, as in *Harrington*, oral tradition perpetuates the bloodthirsty violence of an archaic world. [33]

Yet Dickens's association of tale-telling nurses with the scalds studied by antiquarians also suggests a subterranean link between the cultural anxieties once associated with the antiquary and those now associated with the nurse. Filled with a misogynist phobia of the female body, Scott's antiquary fears the "mare magnum" of the historical record, the vastness of what has already been, and the number of material artifacts that survive to aid in reconstruction. To remember or imagine too much, argues Dickens, is to risk overwhelming all psychic defenses. The coherence of a personality or culture depends on the ability to winnow and assemble the memories of the past. Any breakdown of this filtering process threatens the breakdown of meaning. What the antiquarian process of imaginative reconstruction and the nurse's tales threaten equally is an overwhelming by narrative, a drowning in memory.[34]

Dickens's essay hinges on an important irony. If the nurse, as "female bard," holds her childish listener in narrative captivity, she also prefigures Dickens's adult career as an author. In the nineteenth century, literature is defined at once by the struggle of individual voices against the tradition and by their need to recapitulate its effects.

Odysseus's Scar

At least since Homer's aged nurse, Euryclea, recognized the long-absent Odysseus by his scar, Western literature has been intrigued by the bond that unites child and nurse.[35] Two related fostering plots recur in British fiction. In one, the genteel but impoverished orphan is raised by a devoted foster mother and grows up with a divided class consciousness; although bound by loyalty to the humble world of the foster parent, he or she must eventually leave it behind, to reclaim a place in the upper classes.[36] The other story is of children switched in the cradle.[37] Recognized and reclaimed by blood relations, the hero or heroine bids a grateful farewell to the cherishing foster parents, and henceforth the world of childhood disappears from the story.[38] The happy ending in which these changelings are restored to their proper station is happy partly because it rights the plot's long-standing characterological anomalies. In a fictional world where character traits are stratified along class lines, the unusual beauty or intelligence of a child of the people threatens to disrupt this economy, and the discovery that the character is actually a member of the aristocracy renaturalizes class divisions.

The rise of modern nationalism gives new life to this formulaic story. A series of early national tales vary it to striking effect; not only is the final discovery inverted (the seeming aristocrat is actually the child of the nurse, changed at birth to secure an inheritance), but this denouement is as happy as its reverse would have been fifty years earlier: through their class demotion, and the loss of the lands to which they now have no "natural" claim, the "aristocratic" characters come for the first time to understand their own deep connection to the people. The path from the castle back to the nurse's cabin repeats the passage of the national tale's absentee heroes from the metropolises of Europe back to their native land, with the nurse/mother serving as the national initiator. Hurt by her rich mother's lack of affection, the heroine of Susan Ferrier's *Inheritance* (1824) is relieved to learn that she is really the daughter of a poor but affectionate peasant woman, the long-dead nurse of whom she treasures warm if fragmentary memories. As a small child, she was deeply loved by her "real" mother; as a grown woman, she loses her mercenary lover when she loses her fortune but wins the uninterested love of a poorer man.

The work that initiates the nationalist reclamation of the fostering system, Edgeworth's *Ennui*, makes clear the full political potential of this ending. Edgeworth undertakes a groundbreaking redaction of seventeenth-century Anglo-Irish polemics about Ireland, trying not only to undermine the paranoia that has long governed Anglo-English attitudes toward Ireland but to reverse the whole direction of Anglo-Irish relations. During the colonization of Ireland, English polemics against the Milesian fostering system express the fear that Irish custom will influence and contaminate Anglo-Irish culture. When English settlers enter into relations of trade, marriage, and fosterage with the indigenous inhabitants, argues "E.S." in *Survey of the Present Estate of Ireland, anno 1615*, these new ties erode their loyalty to their countrymen and lastingly threaten English security.[39]

With *Ennui*, Edgeworth gives such fears a sustained rebuttal, defending the fostering system as a means of transcultural reconciliation. Ellinor's legends and stories rescue the Anglo-Irish absentee from the deadly ennui of his caste, teach him the nature of his attachments to Ireland, and create a new unifying national culture. At Glenthorn's sickbed, the nurse's mediation between a cosmopolitan aristocracy and an indigenous population is evident in her transitionless passage from the "histories of Irish and Scottish chiefs"—tales of the greatness of the Glenthorns, recounted with fierce pride by their loyal retainer—to popular tales of witches and ghosts.[40]

In a long footnote to this scene of nursing and national reconsecration, Edgeworth quotes Sir John Davies' 1612 treatise on Irish discontents, *A*

Discoverie of the True Causes why Ireland was never entirely subdued, nor brought under Obedience of the Crowne of ENGLAND, *untill the Beginning of his Majesties most happie Raigne.*

> For fostering, I did never hear or read, that it was in use or reputation in any country, barbarous or civil, as it hath been, and yet is, in Ireland. . . . In the opinion of this people, fostering hath always been a stronger alliance than blood; and the foster-children do love and are beloved of their foster-fathers and their sept (or *clan*) more than of their own natural parents and kindred; and do participate of their means more frankly, and do adhere unto them, in all fortunes, with more affection and constancy. . . . Such a general custom in a kingdom, in giving and taking children to foster, making such a firm alliance as it doth in Ireland, was never seen or heard of in any other country of the world besides.[41]

English-born and Oxford-trained, Davies was solicitor-general, then attorney-general, for Ireland. From the perspective of an Elizabethan imperial administrator (who had enforced the banishment of Catholic priests from Ireland), the fostering system—like anything that reinforced the social cohesiveness of the Milesian peasantry—posed a threat to English hegemony. Fostering not only created "strong parties, and factions . . . Combination and Confederacy punishable in all well governed Common-weales" but encouraged a mode of going native imagined as a reversion to an animal existence.

> These were the Irish Customes, which the English Colonies did embrace and use, after they had rejected the Civill and Honorable Lawes and Customes of *England*, whereby they became degenerate and metamorphosed like *Nebuchadnezzar*: who although he had the face of a man, had the heart of a Beast: or like those who had drunke of *Circes* Cuppe, and were turned into very Beasts; and yet tooke such pleasure in their beastly manner of life, as they would not returne to their shape of men againe: insomuch as within lesse time than the Age of a man, they had no markes or differences left amongst them of that Noble nation, from which they were discended. For, as they did not only forget the English Language, and scorn the use thereof, but grew to be ashamed of their very English Names, though they were noble and of great Antiquity.[42]

When Anglo-Irish children drink from the breasts of their Irish nurses, the English colony drinks from Circe's cup; to Davies, writing on the eve of the Ulster Plantation Uprising, cultural hybridization involves a renunciation of civilization. Yet to Edgeworth, writing in the immediate aftermath of the United Irishmen rebellion and the Act of Union, the need for religious and ethnic reconciliation is paramount, and the nurse the figure best able to effect it.[43] To assist in the improvement and education of Ireland, the Anglo-Irish must first allow themselves to be educated by their own native nurses.

Yet if Glenthorn is lastingly reclaimed by Ellinor, he is unable to educate her in turn, and he eventually discovers that her efforts on his behalf are less altruistic than he first believed: he is actually her biological son. Switched in the cradle and raised in her household as her son Christy, the real lord of Glenthorn has grown up to be a blacksmith, a man so ignorant and credulous, under Ellinor's lifelong tutelage, that he is incapable of managing his recovered estates. *Ennui* at once travesties the claims of feudal loyalty and suggests the primacy of nurture over nature. Over hundreds of years, the character of the Irish has been fatally shaped by ignorance, unrelenting poverty, political disenfranchisement, and a compensatory faith in tradition. Edgeworth favors the continuation, for the present, of Ascendancy rule in Ireland: the Anglo-Irish aristocracy are entitled to power neither by right of conquest nor by right of birth, but by right of education. Although they have not yet learned to govern Ireland wisely, the Anglo-Irish are still preferable, for the moment, to their Milesian counterparts; the Irish people are not yet ready, because they have not yet been educated, to govern themselves.

Edgeworth's argument echoes imperial rhetoric. And if British discourse about the fostering system originates with the English colonization of Ireland, and is then analyzed and rethought in nationalist fiction, it gradually comes to dominate political and literary discussions of the British imperial project as well, with the relationship of native nurse and young English charge modeling (whether critically or sympathetically) the domestic implications of imperial relations. What these repetitions of the nurse's story make visible are the crucial, if paradoxical, continuities between British nationalist and imperial fiction, the ways in which the cultural anxieties accompanying the internal colonization of Britain (particularly the subjugation of Ireland) are both displaced and reformulated once the arena of imperial conquest becomes the overseas empire. The nurse is not only a recurrent character in early-nineteenth-century Irish and Scottish fiction but helps to define fundamental distinctions between the two adjacent genres, the national tale and the historical novel, in their opposed theories of cultural memory. In the national tale, she represents the imperatives of cultural preservation, whereas in the historical novel, she at once absorbs the shocks of history and proclaims as unforgettable the traumatic dislocations that form the nation. In the early colonial fiction of British India, Upper Canada, and Australia, she continues to represent both functions in turn: figuring emigrant cultural amnesia, colonial reacculturation, and imperial conscience, she helps to define the divide between affirmative and critical views of the colonial relationship, as quasi-familial or as inherently exploitative.

For writers worried about the morality of the imperial system, the mutual dependence of nurse and nursling demonstrates how the clear power imbalances of the imperial relationship might be counteracted in daily life. At best, colonial society (whether in Ireland or in British India) is dominated by paternalistic colonizers, who offend the natives with their self-satisfied condescension. Yet this is only the colony's public face. Inside the household, self-sacrificing nurses can set a very different, maternal tone. If British colonial expansion inevitably involves the erosion or proscription of native custom, the native nurse ensures not only the survival of native beliefs and practices but their formative influence on every generation of young colonials. In the empire as in Britain, the nurse and the fostering system guarantee simultaneously the survival of the indigenous, the promulgation of transcultural tolerance, and the emergence of a new hybrid imperial/national culture.

Johnstone's *Clan-Albin* opens with the Highland clearances and the shattering of a traditionary, kinship-based clan society; it ends by envisioning a new, multinational, and pan-British community, forged by shared experience. Johnstone describes two parallel modes of national bonding, one for each gender. The main, male plot describes the transnational friendships between Highland, Lowland, and Irish soldiers that develop in the Highland Regiment over several imperial campaigns, in Ireland and overseas. One byproduct of military campaigns for imperial expansion is the development of an expanded sense of nationality and shared Britishness within the British Army. On the domestic front, the women of Clan-Albin initiate a new, transnational social architecture based on fostering. As Johnstone explains, in a footnote like that in *Ennui*, fostering is the domestic equivalent of the clan system.

> The custom of fosterage still subsists in the Isles, and some parts of the Highlands, in primitive force. By the lower classes it is clung to with Hibernian zeal. It promotes their interests, flatters their pride, and forms the bond of very endearing connexion between the poor and rich.[44]

Yet because its bonds are based on milk rather than on blood, fostering offers a more inclusive, voluntary, and pluralist notion of community than the clan. While the men of the Glen are in Ireland, at once subduing and befriending its benighted inhabitants, the women work at home to make fostering the gentlest possible form of conquest: they adopt an Irish Catholic orphan, cure her of religious intolerance, and fit her to marry one of their own. She is not asked to renounce her national heritage, only to live with those different from her.[45]

Clan-Albin is politically contradictory; it begins by condemning mass deportation and ends by glorifying an imperial army as a site of self-realization and social transformation. Doubleness is built into the novel's very structure: Johnstone separates out male and female strategies for re-constituting the shattered community, to end with their reintegration. In the process, the narrative proposes a solution for Britain in the wake of the Union with Ireland as it works to reconcile competing national allegiances. It also proposes a solution for the dilemmas of the national tale in the wake of *Waverley* as it struggles to reconcile the allegory of national union and domestic stability developed by female authors with a male narrative of civil war and national dividedness. *Clan-Albin* transforms male bonding into a male fostering system. It also proposes the reconfiguration of patriar-chal institutions such as the British Army along similar lines, its traditional emphasis on conflict replaced or influenced by traditional feminine ideals of conciliatoriness, inclusiveness, and nurture.

The early national tale represents an ambitious attempt to map new polit-ical phenomena. Yet its emphasis on union, compromise, and coexistence, on the resolution of cultural differences within a family expanded and re-constituted by fostering or intermarriage, often means the stylization and simplification of political conflict. From *Waverley* onward, the historical novel describes how war divides loyalties and rends domestic harmony. In early historical novels such as *Guy Mannering*, James Hogg's *Brownie of Bodsbeck* (1818) and William Godwin's *Mandeville* (1818), the effects of civil strife—whether between landowners and cleared tenants, the Cove-nanters and Claverhouse's army, or Ulster's Protestants and Catholics—are concentrated in the schizophrenic loyalties, unbalanced mind, or scarred body of the nurse.

Like several other Scottish novels, *The Brownie of Bodsbeck* is written to rebut Scott's *Old Mortality*. Whereas Scott depicts the Covenanters as religious fanatics, Hogg presents them as national martyrs, whose fight for Presbyterian church government upholds a distinctive Scottish religious tradition against the forces of royalism and episcopacy. Hogg follows *Guy Mannering*, however, in studying this struggle on the most local level, re-cording the acts of resistance committed in a single Covenanter household and the martyrdom suffered by the household's elderly servant. Apparently half-deranged, Nanny Elshinder mutters fragmentary reminiscences and snatches of hymns at her work; together, these sketch a partial history of the Covenanter movement. Like the members of the household, we are initially uncertain of Nanny's loyalties: she sings Covenanter revenge songs to her-self, yet in public she avows "prelatic principles." During Nanny's most dramatic moment of mental bifurcation, we finally learn where her sympa-thies lie. In the course of her distracted yet detailed rendition of a cross-examination "in which two distinct voices were imitated," the voice of the military interrogator alternating with the voice of a woman accused of be-ing a Covenanter, we realize we are listening to a verbatim account of Nanny's traumatic interrogation, torture, and mutilation, in which her cheek was branded and her ears were cropped. "I have suffered for that cause *in this same body*," she says, showing her scars as irrefutable evidence of her principles, "for there is but one half of my bone and my flesh here."[46] A civil war of religion has passed right through Nanny's body, dividing it in two and dividing her from herself.

In Nanny's literary forebear, Meg Merrilies, Scott traced this process of bifurcation in slow motion. The mother of twelve children (all subsequently lost to her), Merrilies becomes honorary nurse to the children of Ellangowan. She attends Harry Bertram's birth, casts Harry's fortune, and spends afternoons sitting, with Harry on her knee, under the willow tree, singing him "sangs of the auld barons and their bloody wars."[47] When Godfrey Bertram clears Meg's people from his land, leaving previous loyal retainers unsure of their allegiances, this nursing idyll is irrevocably shattered. In a state of domesticated civil war, the nurse suffers her divided loyalties with particular acuteness, under careful scrutiny from both camps. Godfrey's actions, Meg notes angrily, have particularly cruel consequences for nursing mothers and children, yet her response is to *increase* her attention to Godfrey's son, as an act both of protest and of symbolic compensation.

> This woman's ancient attachment to the family, repelled and checked in every other direction, seemed to rejoice in having some object on which it could yet repose and expand itself. . . . On one occasion, when the child was ill, she lay all night below the window, chanting a rhyme which she believed sovereign as a febrifuge, and could neither be prevailed upon to enter the house, nor to leave the station she had chosen, till she was informed that the crisis was over. (3:73)

Yet soon afterward, she assists at his kidnapping, robbing him of his identity and his home.

Twenty years later, attempting to undo her earlier acts, she will work to restore him to his rightful inheritance, presiding over his amnesiac rebirth into his true self. The eventual restoration of Harry to Ellangowan enacts not only a popular reinvestment in an essentially unchanged system of Scottish feudal loyalties but a simultaneous aristocratic disengagement from the British Empire as an international arena in which a now-familiar drama of modernization, guerrilla warfare, divided loyalties, and cultural schizophrenia continues to play itself out. The book's parallel plots, the imperial replication of traumas initially experienced in the domestic sphere, raise the possibility that the tragedy of development may proliferate infinitely, moving from Scotland to India and beyond; Scott's final return to the domestic sphere, and his attempt to work out, in very local terms, a symbolic resolution for the novel's initial disruptions, cannot put to rest the larger specter of escalating displacement.

A Gypsy, an eternal wanderer, a madwoman, Merrilies sometimes appears (like the "untuned," wandering bard before her) to represent the dislocation of culture—except that (like the exiled bard) she is also a prophet, Sibyl and Fate, the restorer of cultural memory. "Equipt in a habit which mingled the national dress of the Scottish common people with something of an Eastern costume" (3:41), she embodies not only the contradictions of a traditionalist cultural nationalism born of modernization and imperialism but also the traditional magical cultures of Europe and, at least in trace form, the diverse Eastern cultures under the threat of European colonization. She thus makes visible the structural similarity between European struggles over development (and the cultural nationalism it spawns) and imperial struggles over colonization (and the cultural resistance it strengthens). Although Scott ultimately attempts to displace the political, cultural, and moral problems raised by the British imperial campaigns through the elaborate and prolonged homecoming to Ellangowan, even the recognition scene between the homecoming wayfarer and his old nurse—a scene that from Homer onward marks the beginning of true cultural reabsorption—remains tainted by exoticism and estrangement.

When Odysseus returns home from the Trojan War, he rids his home of the strangers who have invaded it in his absence by reinstating clear distinctions between the foreign and the familiar. His real moment of homecoming is the nurse's leap of instinctual recognition as she glimpses, beneath a surface grown strange, the deeply familiar body of the foster child.

> *You are Odysseus!* Ah, dear child! I could not
> see you until now—not till I knew
> my master's very body with my hands. . . .
> Child, you know my blood, my bones are yours.[48]

What is recapitulated here is the long-ago, half-forgotten moment when the nurse watched an infant sucking or sleeping at her breast, felt a surge of proprietary emotion, and silently claimed the strange child for her own.

Those who return home from the British imperial wars, however, have habits of objectification and distantiation fused into the structure of their thinking. When Meg and Harry meet again after seventeen years, they cannot quite recognize each other; Harry will take almost two hundred pages more to achieve full recognition. In the meantime, "he was surprised to find that he could not look upon this singular figure without some emotion. 'Have I dreamed of such a figure?' he said to himself, 'or does this wild and singular-looking woman recall to my recollection some of the strange figures I have seen in our Indian pagodas?'" (3:231–32).

The sight of Merrilies evokes not a deep sense of familiarity but the occupying soldier's familiar reflex of wariness and disquiet at any sign of native singularity. What makes Harry's full retrieval of childhood memory—and with it, the restoration of his real identity—so difficult and protracted is the defensive mental habits acquired over the course of his two captivities and from life in a British India where unrest or revolt are daily anticipated.

As a woman born into the same colonial society and suffering her own "[m]isfortune from the cradle" (3:169), Julia Mannering experiences her imperial alienation in a different, yet finally parallel, modality. Surrounded by native attendants from infancy onward, she imbibes the atmosphere of Indian culture, yet the pervasive distrustfulness of colonial society prevents the development of real bonds with her nurses. When she reminisces about her infancy, her description is at once full of local color and oddly depersonalizing.

> You will call this romantic: but consider I was born in the land of talisman and spell, and my childhood lulled by tales. . . . I wish you could have seen the dusky visages of my Indian attendants, bending in earnest devotion round the magic narrative, that flowed, half poetry, half prose, from the lips of the tale-teller. No wonder that European fiction sounds so cold and meagre after the wonderful effects which I have seen the romance of the East produce upon their hearers. (3:170–71)

The chill and meagerness of European narrative are replicated in Julia's inner life; caught from childhood between a forbidden desire for immersion in native life and the self-conscious detachment that allows her to resist its "magic," she grows up a coldhearted sentimentalist, overcompensating for inner distance and missing emotions by excessive effusion. Engaged, by the end of the novel, in the prolonged search for new personalities, as much as to each other, Julia Mannering and Harry Bertram are linked not least because, in some metaphoric sense, they have shared—and lacked—the same nurse.

Guy Mannering is structured around retrospection and amnesia, and the novel enacts these processes as it describes them.[49] Drawing back from the events it narrates, and the now obsolete belief system it describes, the narrative uses its position of historical retrospect as a distancing mechanism— only then, in allowing the characters' prophecies to determine the plot's unfolding, to lose or forget its historical detachment. Its handling of space is just as controlled and contradictory as its handling of time. Drawing back from a late-eighteenth-century self-understanding, the novel understands the relationship between national and imperial history in ways its characters do not: whereas they themselves view their life in Britain as fundamentally disconnected from the life they lived in British India, the plot underlines the parallels between domestic clearance and imperial expansion, between a British childhood in the care of a national nurse and a colonial childhood in the care of native attendants. Yet as Harry Bertram reconstructs his British infancy only to lose track of the intervening Anglo-Indian years in the process, the narrative replicates this new amnesia, losing its earlier interest in the connections between India and Scotland. As the time of the distant past and the time of the present are knit together into an organic narrative, and as personal histories, once seen in contiguity with the historical development of Britain, are shown to be internally continuous, the mental horizons of the novel shrink as well; in the drama of homecoming, India is forgotten, and the Indian interlude comes to seem irrelevant.[50]

As the dominant figure in the novel (and for nineteenth-century readers, Scott's most memorable character), Meg Merrilies plays a central role in the novel's enactment of memory and forgetting, as well as in its attempts to establish parallels between domestic and imperial spheres.[51] It is Merrilies who makes explicit the links between displaced Gypsies in Scotland and displaced natives in India, who sets in motion the novel's passage from Scotland to India, and who raises the political questions that haunt the rest of the novel. Yet in her attempts to goad conscience, spur memory, and force the characters to link the several sites and times of the novel's plot, she serves the ends of amnesia, dissociation, and forgetfulness. Even more than Guy Mannering's astrological predictions, Meg Merrilies' prophecies and curses shape the plot of the novel and thus mark the final move away from historical relativism, its narrative capitulation to the worldview it initially claimed only to reconstruct. As the figure who presides over the reintegration of memory, helping Harry find his way out of his paralyzing amnesia, Meg indirectly precipitates the novel's final amnesia about India.

Compared with the national nurse's tales that precede it, *Guy Mannering* at once expands and undermines the equation between nurse and national memory. If Ellinor and Moome represent reproduction of national culture, Meg represents a new consciousness—and conscience—about the links between nation and empire. Yet even in Meg's most cogent moments of political analysis, her credibility is undermined as the narrator stresses her erratic temper or her fits of madness. Scott's narrative deployment of Merrilies ultimately evacuates the force of her message, to protect characters, readers, and the narrative consciousness from its political implications. And by the end of the novel, Meg's criticisms are no longer directed at the blatant social injustices of a nascent capitalism, but rather at Glossin, social upstart and usurper of Ellangowan. Like Ellinor before her, Meg has come to stand for the forces of conservatism, the restoration of feudal loyalties.

In its sustained attention to the problem of infantile memory, its depiction of remembering and forgetting as linked, sometimes simultaneous, psychic processes, and its concurrent efforts to extend and cancel a new analysis of imperial ideology, *Guy Mannering* breaks new ground for the British novel and represents an important bifurcation point for the nurse's tale. One way to go on from *Guy Mannering* is to develop a new Gothic fiction that explores the effects of historical repression in a supernatural register (Charles Maturin's "Leixlip Castle," published posthumously in 1825) or in a psychological one (Godwin's *Mandeville*). The opening sentence of "Leixlip Castle" ponders the apparent "tranquillity of the Catholics of Ireland during the disturbed periods of 1715 and 1745," only to underscore the difficulty of reconstructing "their probable motives."[52] For many Catholics did, in fact, manifest "a kind of secret disgust at the existing state of affairs, by quitting their family residences and wandering about like persons who were uncertain of their homes, or possibly expecting better from some near and fortunate contingency" (p. 272). In 1720 Sir Redmond Blaney, a Jacobite baronet grown "sick of his uncongenial situation in a Whig neighbourhood, in the north, where he heard of nothing but the heroic defence of Londonderry," removes his daughters from their "paternal residence" to settle near Dublin (p. 273).

Yet Leixlip Castle, too, proves a living tomb for the Blaney family. Its solitude "tranquillize[s]" and calcifies Sir Redmond's political beliefs; when a Jacobite friend offers a toast to "the King over the water," when the parish priest speaks of "the final success of the *right* cause, and the old religion," when a Jacobite servant whistles "Charlie is my darling," Sir Redmond still responds "involuntarily"—but his sense of political urgency and grasp of political events gradually die away (p. 274). His youngest daughter vanishes mysteriously in the woods, apparently lured away by "an old woman, in the *Fingallian* dress," and is never again seen alive; ten years later, she reappears to the terrified household as a ghost, "shrunk to half her usual size" (p. 275). The eldest daughter marries an "unexceptionable" Catholic gentleman who murders her on their wedding night, seized by "a sudden and most horrible paroxysm of insanity" (p. 276). And the middle daughter, Anne, left to the company of servants, "among whom she increased her taste for superstitious and supernatural horrors, to a degree that had a most disastrous effect on her future life" (p. 276), is fatally influenced by her mother's old nurse.

> This woman was called *Colluge* by the family, a name equivalent to Gossip in England, or Cummer in Scotland (though her real name was Bridget Dease); and she verified the name, by the exercise of an unwearied loquacity, an indefatigable memory, and a rage for communicating and inflicting terror, that spared no victim in the household, from the groom, whom she sent shivering to his rug, to the Lady of the Castle, over whom she felt she held unbounded sway. (P. 277)

On All-Hallow's Eve, under the nurse's malevolent influence, Anne performs an impious ceremony meant to reveal her future bridegroom; instead, she sees a "vision of indescribable horror" (p. 284), which leaves her more dead than alive. A few days later, a bridegroom appears at Leixlip: the corpselike Scottish baronet, Sir Richard Maxwell, who plans to settle permanently in Ireland, driven from his own country by family misfortune. After his marriage to Anne, he continues to manifest two oddities of behavior: he shuts himself away every year, on October 31, and anytime there are Scottish gentlemen in the neighborhood.

Given the story's opening, the reader may think that Sir Richard Maxwell hides some political secret; he is, perhaps, an outlawed Jacobite or a traitor to the Jacobite cause. Yet his secret is something different: he has murdered his own brother, with whom he had long been "at deadly feud." The family tried to stage a reconciliatory feast. Yet because

> the use of knives and forks was then unknown in the Highlands, the company went armed with their dirks for the purpose of carving. They drank deeply; the feast, instead of harmonizing, began to inflame their spirits; the topics of old strife were renewed; hands, that had at first touched their weapons in defiance, drew them at last in fury, and in the fray, Sir Richard mortally wounded his brother. His life was with difficulty saved from the vengeance of the clan. (P. 285)

Fleeing to Ireland on the night of October 31, he flung his murderous dagger into the sea. On that same night, Anne performed her "unhallowed ceremonies" and received his bloody dagger, as a token by which to know her future husband. When Maxwell finally finds it in her possession, he recoils from their marriage as a devil's pact—and their union is blasted forever.

In "Leixlip Castle" Maturin's initial preoccupations with the displaced effect of a Scottish uprising and an abortive civil war on Irish Catholics, the inhabitants of another deeply divided country, are both displaced into a supernatural register and intermittently visible in the devil's pact. The failure of the Jacobite cause forces the Blaney family into various modes of suspension or regression: the father's political sentiments begin "to rust" (p. 274); lured away by a Fingallian spirit, the youngest daughter becomes a ghost, "as diminutive in form, as though she had not grown an inch since she was ten years old" (p. 275); the eldest daughter is killed at the moment she is to become a full adult; the middle daughter succumbs to superstition, and her husband, intending to mend a family feud, falls back into it without fully meaning to, because his clan is drunk and because "the use of knives and forks was then unknown in the Highlands." In Scotland as well as in Ireland, then, the regression of Jacobite aristocrats reflects a cataclysmic political defeat and the latent regressiveness of Highland and Milesian culture, visible equally in the feast of the Highland clan and the tales of the Milesian nurse. The Irish and the Scottish baronets try in vain to flee the political fallout from the '15 and the bellicosity of clan society.

"Leixlip Castle" hinges on an important contradiction. Maturin evokes the supernatural to demonstrate what needs to be rooted out of a culture if it is to advance, yet he himself deploys supernatural forces to suggest the impossibility of such suppressions and to stage the inevitable return of the repressed. The Godwinian novel follows the long-term effects of historical repression in a more purely psychological register. In *Mandeville* the repressed trace memory of the 1641 Ulster Plantation Uprising surfaces again during the first phases of the civil war to cause complete mental collapse. Galt's *Entail* and John Gibson Lockhart's *History of Matthew Wald* (1824) transpose Godwin into Scotland; beginning with the national traumas of the Darien Expedition, the Union, and Culloden, they build the rest of their plots—tragic disinheritance, disasters, and insanity—on the buried legacy of those events. These novels work by holding in suspension a fore-grounded psychological narrative and an implicit historical chronology that allows the reader to date plot developments and thus to explain the characters' mental states.

Mandeville hypothesizes about the way psychological disorders arising from the experience of historical disorder work in turn to shape a neurotic philosophy of history.[53] In Godwin's novel the violence of history and the childhood traumatization result in the malfunctioning of all memory functions into adult life. Building on *Guy Mannering*, *Mandeville* prepares the way for a new psychological novel, which studies the historical formation of a personality and in which the nurse's role continues to be formative, for she shapes the most impressionable years of infancy and links a cumulative, communal time to the psychic time of a unique personal history.

Mandeville opens with the background to the 1641 Ulster Plantation Uprising. The Irish will not "wean" themselves from their traditional way of life, and so the English try to outnumber them in their own country, by planting large numbers of settlers among them.

> No people were ever more proud of their ancestry and their independence than the Irish, or more wedded to their old habits of living;—and the policy of the English administration had not been such as to wean them in any degree from the partialities to which they were prone. . . . [James I's] system in Ireland, was that of colonization, of placing large bodies of civilized strangers in every great station through the country, and undertaking, by a variety of means, to reclaim the wild Irish from what might almost be called their savage state. The government of his lieutenants and deputies was not exactly that of benignity. . . . The party, or rather the great mass of the population of the country, who were in opposition to the government, felt that they were the ancient proprietors of the soil. Irish manners and Irish sentiments, every thing that was local in human society, was with them; the party that, in the great majority of cases, lorded it over them, they regarded as aliens. And when we add to this

general view of the case, the recollection that must necessarily accompany it, of all the individual circumstances, and all the bitter aggravations that attended each act of oppression, we may easily conceive what must have been the state of the Irish mind.[54]

In the face of English efforts to annihilate their cultural memory, religious traditions, and legal rights, the Irish plan a rebellion against their English oppressors, taking their cue from the Scottish Covenanters: "The period was favourable; and if they neglected to improve it, they would deserve to be slaves" (p. 11).[55] Ulster chieftain Phelim O'Neile gives the cue for the uprising by bringing his followers to a "sociable meeting of the ancient Irish and the English settlers" at Charlemont Castle and taking as prisoner the entire English garrison, reminding them *they* are the true guests and trespassers in Ireland.[56] The uprising thus exposes the founding contradictions of the Ulster Plantation. The English settlers

> had lived among their Irish neighbours with every appearance of good fellowship; and the demonstrations of love and affection on either part had been mutual. Hostilities between them had ceased, for almost as long a time as the memory of any one living could reach; and nothing could exceed the quietness and security with which the new settlers enjoyed their possessions. (P. 15)

Led unsuspecting into the rebel ambush, the English are the victims of their own confidence: their belief that they possess Ireland has made them oblivious to prior Irish claims.

Mandeville presents the uprising as the response to patent injustices, yet condemns its brutalities; caught in its cross fire, English settlers are driven from their homes, left to die on the roads or murdered at random, with "children at the breast, women far advanced in their pregnancy . . . often . . . made the preferred objects of destruction" (p. 17). In a climate of escalating reprisals, O'Neile breaks his promise of safekeeping to the Charlemont prisoners, and they are all put to death, men, women, and children. Mandeville's father and mother are among the dead; Mandeville records the massacre both as its only eyewitness survivor and as his own earliest memory.

> I was a little more than three years of age, at the time when this tragedy was acted. I do not remember the scene distinctly in all its parts; but there are detached circumstances that belong to it, that will live in my memory as long as my pulses continue to beat. . . . [They] fired vollies into the midst of us. Every shot told. . . . From the general massacre of the English within Sir Phelim's residence this day, I was the only one that escaped. My preservation was owing to the fidelity and courage of an Irish woman-servant, to whose charge I had been committed. Her mistress and family she could not save; but me she caught up in her arms with a resolution that nothing could subdue. "What have

you there?" said one of the murderers; "that child is an English child." "By the Virgin," replied the woman, "it is my own flesh and blood; would you go for to confound this dear little jewel, as true a Catholic as ever was born'd, with the carcasses of heretics?" "Let the child speak," answered the ruffian, "he is old enough; who do you belong to?" "To me! to me!" shrieked the woman, in an agony of terror. "Speak!" repeated the assassin, and lifted over me the instrument of death. I hid my face in my nurse's bosom. I did not comprehend the meaning of the question, but I felt that the faithful creature who embraced me was my protector. "To Judy," said I; "Judy is my mammy." "Begone," said the murderer sternly, drawing back his skein, "and mix no more with this dunghill of Protestant dogs."

  Judith carried me away, with the intention of retiring with me to her native village and bringing me up as her own child. (P. 20)

The uprising was caused by imperious attempts to wean the Irish from their culture and their property and by Irish attempts to repossess what was their own. Yet what we see in the midst of the massacre, beside the corpses of Mandeville's parents, is the sudden forging of a familial bond between Irish nurse and English child. In an Ireland that gave the English sanctuary, only to deliver death, Judy's compassion suggests the paradoxical survival of the Ulster Plantation's official ideals, even in the midst of a civil war.

As nurse and child travel across the dangerous terrain of the uprising, indeed, their bond grows in intensity. All around them, however, the sense of grievance and outrage grows hourly. By the time Judy and Mandeville reach the expected safety of the English lines, the Protestants are so filled with religious hatred that they are maddened by any vestige of fraternization; they forcibly remove Mandeville from Judy's care.

My life, indeed, was now in safety. In that thought she truly rejoiced. But was it to be endured that she, who had nursed and fed me from her own breast from the hour of my birth, and who had just brought me hither unhurt through a thousand hair-breadth escapes, should now be thrust out from me with contumely, as one whose touch henceforth would be contamination and pestilence to me? She raved; she intreated. "And was not it myself that saved him? And has not he owed his life to me times without number? And am not I ten times his mother? Jewel, dear, you have no mother; you have no father; suddenly, fearfully, they have been taken from you; there is nobody now in all the world that can do for you but Judy. . . . Who shall take care of the poor helpless wretch, if I am put away from him, who am his natural fosterer? You do not mean to be the death of him! Kill me, cut me to pieces, but do not ye, do not ye, be so barbarous as to put me away from him, and leave me alive. My child! my child! my child!"

  It will easily be imagined, that I was moved to the utmost degree with the agonies of my nurse, and that I joined my anguish, my tears, my cries, my intreaties, to hers. But this was a portentous moment, in which all human emotions, except within a certain definite limit were utterly extinguished. . . . [I]n the street of Kells, she was wholly surrounded by British,—with creatures who had just, through every degree of hardship and misery, escaped with life, who had each one left behind a husband, a wife, or a child, the prey of this bloody pursuit, and to whom it was agony to see among them for a moment a being of the race of their destroyers. The more clamorous the unhappy woman showed herself, the more importunately she forced her intreaties and her shrieks upon their hearing, by so much the more inexorably were they resolved to expel her. Was a woman of this accursed, savage, Irish, Popish brood, to be supposed to have any feelings, or any feelings entitled to the sympathy and favour of a Protestant heart? They repelled her with every degree of contumely; and, when at length she sunk senseless under the protracted contest, they flung her out of the town, like some loathsome load of contamination, too pestilent for wholesome British senses to endure. (Pp. 21–22)

Religious fanaticism, for Godwin, results from a failure of historical perspective. The murderous nationalism of the Irish Catholics and the inhuman bigotry of the Ulster Protestants are positions explicable by historical circumstances; they become dangerous when each group becomes unable to remember the historical contingency of its struggle and sees its opposition as historically immutable. Any survival of the fostering system threatens this new ideological economy, by demonstrating that transcultural affections can and do exist, that cultural differences can be successfully absorbed into a structure of family alliances, that there is no inevitability to present antagonisms. When the hate-crazed Protestants of Kells separate Mandeville and Judy forever, expelling her and sending him off to England, the violent sundering of the fostering bond marks an epoch not only in Mandeville's psychic development but also in Irish political history, annihilating the last reminder of peaceful coexistence and announcing a perpetual state of civil war.

During his first fourteen years in England, Mandeville seems to repress the memory of Judy and of Ireland. Then England enters its own civil war. During the Penruddock Uprising, Mandeville is accused of disloyalty to the royalist cause and collapses completely, overwhelmed by the unexpected resurfacing of memories of Ulster. Hieronymo's mad again: as Mandeville breaks down, different historical moments, layers of personal and historical experience, become fused inside his head.

All that had ever occurred to me of tragic in the whole course of my existence, had beset me. Ireland, and its scenes of atrocious massacre, that one might have expected to be obliterated from the tablet of my memory, presented themselves in original freshness. My father and my mother died over again. The shrieks, that had rent the roofs of Kinnard fourteen years before, yelled in my ears, and deafened my sense; and I answered them with corresponding and responsive shrieks. I forgot the lapse of time that had passed between; I did not advert to the circumstance, that I had then been a child; and I put forth my virile strength, and uttered my firmer expostulations and threats, to save the lives of him who begot, and her who bore me. The scenes of unspeakable distress that I had witnessed in my journey from the north of Ireland to Dublin all assailed me, in their turn. The cries and struggles even of the poor Judith, from whose arms Hilkiah had so unjustifiably torn me, were once more heard and seen by me, in their original Hibernian energy. Then came Penruddock and Grove, and the many victims that had fallen by the sword of the law. . . . I saw their heads roll on the scaffold; I saw the blood spouting from the dismembered trunk; I saw the executioner. (P. 144)

Throughout *Mandeville* Godwin shows both the entwining of psychic and public history and the distance between them. The English civil war repeats some excesses of the Ulster Plantation Uprising, but only within Mandeville's mind is the overlay of events complete. Mandeville's disorienting flashbacks and his repressed longing for Judy do illuminate the political and cultural dilemmas of seventeenth-century Ulster: not even the most active efforts at repression can wean anyone from the memory of what was cherished and lost or cure him or her of the traumas that the separation produced. Yet Mandeville's psyche, Mandeville's story, matches a collective psyche, a national narrative, only intermittently and by chance.

In the eighteenth century, picaresque novels often began with the birth of the hero or antihero, so that his subsequent ascents, declines, and falls would be easily legible in succession. Now, under the pressures of a new historiographical consciousness and a new developmental sense of the human personality, the British novel finds a new reason to begin its case studies in the nursery. Psychic life is cumulative and continuous, with individuation commencing already in infancy, influenced by many different stimuli, relationships, and experiences. From *Guy Mannering* onward the new psychological and historical novels describe the effect of historical forces on the development of emotional reflexes, illuminating the way individual patterns of psychic investment and cushioning, desire and repression, form in response to specific social constellations.

THE NATIONAL NURSE AND THE NATIVE ATTENDANT

A long series of imperial nurse stories emphasize a different aspect of *Guy Mannering*: its attention to the mental texture of imperial experience. In Scott's novel the relationship of Bertram and Merrilies forms the implicit, affective center of the story. The imperial nurse tales focus quite explicitly on the relationship of colonial child and imperial domestic; here too the nurse is a figure simultaneously of cultural alterity and (as she assists in the process of transculturation) of cultural rapprochement. This formulation suggests an optimistic view of the possibilities for reconciliation between colonizer and colonized. Yet over the course of the nineteenth century, under the influence of a Godwinian historical psychology, a more dystopic version of this story describes colonial false consciousness about empire and the pervasive dissociation it causes, tracing the long-term psychic strains caused by its repressions and its willed amnesias.

Generically, the imperial nurse's tale is shaped by the pressures of the historical novel on the fostering plot of the national tale. The national tales of Edgeworth and Johnstone celebrated the fostering system as a crucial means of uniting a divided Ireland, a divided Scotland. Scott's and God-win's historical novels meditate rather on the fragility of the fostering bond. A relationship both rooted in and inclined to perpetuate local tradi-tion, it is threatened by the encroachments and displacements of modernity. And as a relationship that joins families of differing class, religion, and ethnicity, it is threatened by any nationalist or separatist resurgence. In *Ennui* and *Clan-Albin* the fostering system is powerful enough to deflect the pressures of history, or to adapt itself without losing its essence; in *Guy Mannering* and *Mandeville* the same system appears under such acute pres-sure that the relationship between nurse and child breaks apart, with far-ranging psychological consequences.

On the terrain of the British novel, the national tale and the nursing idyll are supplanted by the historical novel and a nurse's tale fraught with his-tory. Yet both nurse's plots persist in early imperial fiction. One kind of imperial nurse's tale, influenced by the national tale, is essentially optimis-tic. The conquest of a new colony inevitably involves bloodshed, brutality, and the attempt to suppress native culture. A colonial society necessarily remains scarred and divided. Yet the native nurse is able, through her milk, her love, and her influence, to heal the colony's scars and to effect a lasting rapprochement between the colonizers and the colonized. By raising the colonizer's children as if they are her own (or indeed, together *with* her own children) the nurse works to fuse the warring, seemingly incompatible cul-tures of the conqueror and the native. She presides over the formation of a new, creolized cultural identity. And she reconstitutes the colony as an extended family, in which the bonds of foster kinship and shared early memories will link colonizer and colonized forever more.

The other colonial nurse's tale is more pessimistic. Following Scott's and Godwin's historical novels in their emphasis on civil war and divided loyalties, this nurse's story uses a moment of acute crisis for the colonial system, and the nurse's struggle of loyalties, to illuminate the contradic-tions of the imperial status quo. Colonial societies, we learn, are permeated by a subterranean sense of fear, malaise, and moral compromise. To counteract their imperial guilt, they cultivate racist ideologies and enforce categorical racial taboos, but these measures can only increase the colonists' claustrophobia and emotional desolation, their sense of geographical isolation from the rest of the world, and their sense of entrapment in a cultural landscape that will never cease to be alien. What the slave revolt, the mutiny, and the civil war make clearer than ever is the colonists' fundamental estrangement from the native society around them, and the nurse's redemptive personal gestures of mercy and sympathy only underline the permanence of this gulf.

In its several variants, then, the colonial nurse's tale reflects a wide range of attitudes about the feasibility and the future of imperial life. Those stories set in the settler colonies of North America tend to be more optimistic than those about British India, and these, in turn, are more sanguine than those about the penal and slave colonies of Australia or the West Indies. Those stories in which nurse and child represent different nationalities, ethnicities, and classes are more likely to argue the possibilities of transcending cultural differences than stories in which the differences are manifest in race, language, or religion. In Catharine Parr Traill's *Lady Mary and Her Nurse, or A Peep into the Canadian Forest* (1856), Mrs. Frazer introduces Lady Mary Campbell, daughter of the governor-general of Canada, to the natural and national history of her new country; like Upper Canada itself, the transnational nursing relationship is utterly devoid of conflict, for no substantive cultural differences separate the Scottish-Canadian governess and the Scottish-Canadian child.[57] Similar absence of conflict marks the bond, in other Canadian nurse's tales, of English children with Indian or Inuit nurses. In Mrs. Mary Martha Sherwood's *Indian Chief* (probably published between 1840 and 1850), a young British boy, separated from his parents, is adopted into the benevolent tribe of his loving Indian nurse. Although Sherwood remains suspicious of the moral foundations of native life, the relationship of English nursling and native nurse remains one of mutual affection, respect, and influence.[58]

When Mrs. Sherwood writes of the more embattled colonial life of British India, however, she affirms the colonial bond as a form of voluntary servitude. Like *The Indian Chief*, Sherwood's *Little Henry and his Bearer* (1814) and *Little Lucy and her Dhaye* (1823) dwell on the deep love that English infants, helpless and dependent, inspire in their Indian caretakers.[59] Yet ultimately it is the English infants who proselytize, convert, and "save" their foster parents. Here acculturation—and dependence—runs in the opposite direction from the one in the British national tale. For here it is not the child who learns, from its nurse, to respect and cherish indigenous culture but rather the nurse who learns, through the colonial nursling, to leave behind indigenous practices and adopt "civilized" ways. Edgeworth's *Ennui*—and the Anglo-Scottish novels written in its wake—vindicated national character, honoring the nurse and the spirit of her love. Sherwood's Indian oeuvre, in contrast, insists on the essentially pagan character of native life and denounces the potentially corrupting influence of native servants.[60]

In a small group of abolitionist tales, set in the West Indies, Sherwood does examine the colonial relationship from the other side. Her most complex and balanced treatment of the master-servant problem, tellingly, is a nurse story that uses the civil war framework provided by the historical novel and that reaches its climax during a slave revolt. After the death of his mother, the boy narrator of *Babes in the Wood of the New World* (circa 1830) is raised in England by his aunts. When he rejoins his Dutch father on a Surinam slave plantation, he finds the system of slavery corrupting masters and slaves alike; although he makes friends with slaves of his own age, his spoiled younger stepsister (born and bred in the plantation system) treats her slave nurse so cruelly that Kowaree runs away.

Then some slaves revolt against their Dutch masters and threaten to slaughter all white inhabitants. The boy and his sister flee the plantation, and Kowaree must decide whether to aid their escape. She would willingly risk her own safety to save her son's friend, but she is still angry at her tyrannical child mistress, and for a moment, at least, she is tempted to abandon Catharine to her fate.

> "It is little Catharine, only little Catharine," I said; "you will not refuse to take little Catharine on board?" the poor child at the same time extending her arms, and addressing her nurse in some of these endearing terms which she had been accustomed to use to her. The old woman muttered something that I could not hear; and I never could discover whether the spirit of revenge had ever had such influence over her mind, as to have led her to wish the death of Catharine. But, be that as it might, it is certain that when she saw the child standing on the river's bank, all her old affection returned, and rushed in a strong tide to her heart; for she lost no time in helping us into the boat . . . and it was well that she was thus quick in her motions, for by the remaining light of the flames we saw the rebels scouring the lawn from around the house in every direction.[61]

In Sherwood's severe moral terms, death might seem a fitting punishment for Catharine's imperiousness.[62] Yet the nurse's fostering instincts win out, and she saves both children. Like Edgeworth's "Grateful Negro" (a likely source for Sherwood), *Babes* finally advocates Christian quietism as the appropriate attitude of the oppressed. But it does not sympathize with the masters any more than with the murderous rebels. In the colonial context,

Sherwood suggests here, the master-servant relationship is cemented by hatred and fear as much as superiority and servile love.[63]

COLONIAL AMBIVALENCE AND COLONIAL AMNESIA

The movement from national to imperial fictions of the nurse might be described as the move from a story about the danger of split loyalties in the children raised in the fostering system to a story about the lasting danger of split loyalties within the nurses themselves. The first story, with its emphasis on national continuities and personal loyalties, begins with Edgeworth's *Ennui*, evolves through the early wave of national tales, and lives on through the nineteenth century. The second story, launched with *Guy Mannering, Mandeville*, and Sherwood, remains visible in postcolonial fiction. Under imperial conditions, this second story argues, the nursing relation is psychically fraught both for nurse and for child—and the nurse becomes a figure of imperial fantasy.

As the next chapter will argue at length, Galt's last major novel, *Bogle Corbet, or The Emigrants* (1831), offers the most complicated instantiation of this plot. The autobiography of a depressive imperialist, who moves between the politically unstable plantation society of the West Indies, a Britain in economic and political transformation, and the wilderness of Upper Canada, *Bogle Corbet* begins with the irreparable early childhood loss of a Jamaican nurse. Like Mandeville, Bogle Corbet spends the rest of the novel mired in chronic depression, a displaced grieving both for a lost fostering and for lost imperial ideals. But where Mandeville's madness manifests itself as surges of overwhelming and disorienting historical memory, Corbet's manifests itself as a progressive erasure of all memories of the past. If Galt accounts for this amnesia in psychological and biographical terms—Corbet's loss of parents and nurse—-he also explains it sociohistorically, in terms of the historical formation of the empire.

In Susanna Moodie's *Roughing It in the Bush, or Forest Life in Canada* (1852), the most influential mid-Victorian chronicle of immigrant and settler life in Upper Canada, Canada is apostrophized as an allegorical nurse, who nourishes its foundling immigrants and serves as Moodie's muse. Moodie's pioneer sketches double as a spiritual autobiography, modeled on abolitionist conversion narratives and chronicling the author's personal transformation from an English lady obsessed with class distinctions into a more tolerant Canadian. Initially, Moodie disdains the lower-class Irish immigrants who enter Canada with her and is horrified by the vulgar, dishonest, and greedy American squatters who are her new neighbors. Yet her attachment to two successive Irish nurses who work as servants in her household gradually transforms her social vision.

The first nurse is an Irish serving boy, whose arrival on the Moodie homestead precipitates a domestic crisis of national loyalties. Although John Monaghan is an Ulster Protestant, the Scottish maidservant, afraid of "Papists," refuses to remain in the same house with him, and the neighbors, similarly prejudiced, bully Monaghan at every turn. The Moodies' protective toleration of Monaghan is amply repaid by his loyalty. Taking over the work of the departed maid, Monaghan becomes an indispensable family retainer.

> [H]e lighted the fires, swept the house, milked the cows, nursed the baby, and often cooked the dinner for me, and endeavoured by a thousand little attentions to show the gratitude he really felt for our kindness. To little Katie, he attached himself in an extraordinary manner. All his spare time he spent in making little sleighs and toys for her, or in dragging her in the said sleighs up and down the steep hills in front of the house, wrapping up in a blanket. Of a night, he cooked her mess of bread and milk, as she sat by the fire, and his greatest delight was to feed her himself. After this operation was over, he would carry her round the floor on his back, and sing her songs in native Irish.[64]

Monaghan is himself "a poor foundling from the Belfast Asylum, shoved out, by the mother that bore me, upon the wide wurld, long before I knew that I was in it" (p. 147). Brought up "by hand" in an impersonal institution, the orphan compensates for maternal deprivation by becoming a nurse to others and reconstituting a substitute family.

So, too, Moodie compensates for the deprivations of the bush by making Monahan, and then Scotch-Irish nurse Jenny Buchanan, members of her family; Moodie's relationship with her Irish nurses becomes her means of expressing solidarity with other classes of settlers.[65] Yet it is easy to accept, even reciprocate, the affections of nurses whose loyalty amounts almost to masochism, who are determined to take all work upon themselves. Abjectly grateful that he is no longer working for a master who beats him, Monaghan happily takes on women's work, runs the whole household, and makes maple sugar candy for "his nurse-child" (p. 275). Jenny Buchanan has spent a long life in selfless bondage to others. Rather than desert the family she has long served in Ireland, she emigrates to Canada with them. When they fall on hard times, she supports them by doing man's labor, finally hiring herself out to another family. There, a brutal master cheats her of her pay, beats her, and finally drives her from the house. Yet her maternal solicitude for his destitute family continues unabated.

> For five long, hopeless years she served a master from whom she never received a farthing of her stipulated wages. Still her attachment of the family was so strong, and had become so much the necessity of her life, that the poor

creature could not make up her mind to leave them. The children whom she had received into her arms at their birth, and whom she had nursed with maternal tenderness, were as dear to her as if they had been her own; she continued to work for them although her clothes were worn to tatters. (P. 442)

Her subsequent service to the Moodies is similarly self-sacrificing: skeptical of Moodie's efforts to earn money by her pen, Jenny undertakes to support the family through the home manufacture of maple syrup (the mother's milk, it seems, of all Canadian nurses).

Moodie's belated fostering teaches her a new class tolerance, yet the relationship of lady to Irish-Canadian servant remains comfortingly nonreciprocal.[66] When her family moves back into town from the isolation of the bush, in the last pages of the book, Moodie uncritically records their amusement at Jenny Buchanan's eccentric attire and their embarrassment at being seen in her company. On the eve of her reentry into colonial society, Moodie's momentary reversion to class discomfort suggests both how far she has come since her arrival in Canada and her danger of recidivism.

Although Moodie develops a warmer relationship to the people who surround her, she continues to feel a fundamental ambivalence about Canada, about the wilderness, and about the country's terrifying indifference both to privileges of birth and to the culture of letters. Yet it is the only home that remains to her.

> However the world has frowned upon me, Nature, arrayed in her green loveliness, had ever smiled upon me like an indulgent mother, holding out her loving arms to enfold to her loving bosom her erring but devoted child.
>
> Dear, dear England! why was I forced by a stern necessity to leave you? What heinous crime had I committed that I, who adored you, should be torn from your sacred bosom, to pine out my joyless existence in a foreign clime? Oh that I might be permitted to return and die upon your wave-encircled shores, and rest my weary head and heart beneath your daisy-covered soil at last! Ah, these are vain outbursts of feeling—melancholy relapses of the spring home-sickness! Canada! thou art a noble, free, and rising country—the great fostering mother of the orphans of civilization. The offspring of Britain, thou must be great and I will and do love thee, land of my adoption and of my children's birth; and oh—dearer still to a mother's heart—land of their graves! (P. 73)[67]

To a female writer preoccupied with her own maternity, emigrant home-sickness appears as maternal desertion.[68] When Moodie considers the prospect of spending the rest of her life in the colonies, she must, like the other mournful foundlings of the British Empire, strive to forget the beloved mother country that has inexplicably expelled her from its bosom and take comfort at the welcoming breast of the New World. Moodie's poetic epigraph to her 1853 *Life in the Clearings versus the Bush* insists on her gratitude to Canada.

> Dear foster-mother, on whose ample breast,
> The hungry still find food, the weary rest;
> The child of want that treads thy happy shore,
> Shall feel the grasp of poverty no more;
> His honest toil meet recompense can claim,
> And Freedom bless him with a freeman's name![69]

Yet her new home can never fully supplant the object of her first affections. As Anna Brownell Jameson puts it in *Winter Studies and Summer Rambles in Canada* (1838), "Canada is a colony, not a *country*; it is not yet identified with the dearest affections and associations, remembrances, and hopes, of its inhabitants; it is to them an adopted, not a real mother."[70] And although Canada is the most affectionate of nurses, she can also be a careless guardian. She nourishes her adoptive children as warmly as she can, but her underlying chill may still cause their premature deaths.[71]

In describing pioneer life in "that rural prison-house the Bush," Moodie suggests that no amount of native nursing can completely forestall the emigrant's feelings of abandonment and displacement.[72] Marcus Clarke's *For the Course of His Natural Life* (1870), the most influential nineteenth-century Australian novel, indicts the penal colony in terms that intensify those of Moodie. Transported for life and exiled without the hope of a reprieve, the convict feels his abandonment and displacement much more absolutely than any ordinary settler. Rufus Dawes, an English gentleman transported to Australia for a murder he did not commit, finds himself condemned to slave labor, in a colony whose social divisions, based on degrees of freedom or imprisonment, are as terrifyingly absolute as those of the slave plantation.

Far more than Moodie, Rufus Dawes runs the risk of being brutalized by the conditions of his exile. Like her, and like John Monaghan, he saves his sanity by improvising a fostering system in the wilderness. Escaping from the desert island on which he was left to die, Dawes helps to rescue the family of the commandant of Macquarie Harbor, taken hostage in a prisoners' mutiny and now close to starvation and madness. As Dawes nurses the governor's feverish child, trying to save her life, he remembers and regains his capacity for human emotion. As always, the act of nursing helps (here across class barriers that are more pronounced than usual) to restore a bond of common humanity.

Clarke's novel is structured around a melodramatic twist (influenced both by *Guy Mannering* and by Dickens's *David Copperfield*), which runs through the middle of the nursing plot. Dawes saves Dora Vickers's life and continues to love her from the unbridgeable social distance that separates convict from governor's daughter. (At the end of the book, he will save, nurse, and raise Dora's daughter as his own.) Dora, however, recovers from her fever unable to remember anything about her illness. The party's other survivor, Maurice Frere, has haunted Dawes as an evil nemesis throughout the novel, the usurper of his inheritance, the man responsible for his imprisonment. Now, Frere usurps Dora's gratitude and love as well, claiming that *he* was the one who nursed her. Although Dora had previously feared Frere, she awakes from her fever unable to reconstruct the grounds of her distrust.

Nonetheless, like Harry Bertram (whose encounters with Meg Merrilies leave him haunted by the sense of vital memories just out of reach), Dora is overcome by uncertainty every time she sees Dawes. As she hovers, for hundreds of pages, on the brink of being able to remember the traumatic events of her childhood, she decides it is not Frere but the convict, so threateningly savage in appearance, who is the source of her discomfort; shunning his gaze, she cultivates her attachment to Frere, as "you who have saved me and nursed me." Eventually, she marries him, without conscious suspicion of the real truth: "[W]hen you nursed me as a little child in your arms, and fed me, and starved for me—did you ever think we should be married?"[73]

The son of a man involved in the slave trade and ruined by its abolition, Frere makes his career in Australia as an administrative slave driver; as inspector general of penal establishments and commander of the Pentridge Stockade, his sadistic treatment of "his" convicts (and of Dawes in particular) finally leads them to murder him. In the meantime, Frere's harshness toward his convicts seeps into his marriage with Dora. In the abolitionist novels of the 1790s, slavers and nabobs prove intolerable husbands, as they attempt, to a man, to import the power imbalance of their daily work into the domestic sphere. In nineteenth-century Australia, as Dora points out, free men or women can marry convict spouses by having them designated their "assigned servants," then regulate any marital disagreements by having them punished for "insubordination" (p. 361).

As the daughter and then the wife of prison governors, Dora appears to enjoy particular immunity from the punitive practices of the penal colony. Yet her unhappy, inchoate longings for her lost nurse express unconscious guilt at her own complicity in the colonial system. If the nurse stories of *Roughing it in the Bush* help Moodie to work through her colonial ambivalence, the nurse story of *His Natural Life* tries to represent colonial false consciousness: the psyche protects itself from inevitable feelings of guilt over the empire's fundamental injustices by developing a phobic aversion to the sight of the colonized, whether natives, convicts, or slaves.

In the penal colony, the convicts learn docility in part through literary precedent; as Clarke notes sardonically, the prison library contains mostly Sherwoodian tracts such as "Henry, the little Anglo-Indian" (p. 585). Yet Clarke presents colonial self-conception and resistance in terms derived from the nursing and fostering tales as much as from the historical fiction of the early nineteenth century. Clarke's use of a case of amnesia to illuminate the shape of a whole political system in crisis depends on the example of Scott and Godwin. Yet his emphasis on blockage as a cornerstone of the colonial system draws on *Harrington*'s analysis of racism as an infantile disorder, just as his description of Dora derives ultimately from Sherwood's troubled colonial children.

Clarke's Dora is also the namesake of David Copperfield's child bride, Dora Spenlow, and functions, like her, as a blinkered, emotionally limited child wife. Yet when she broods about the emotional texture of her marriage, and unconsciously about the political system that underlies it, Dora Vickers also takes on (and gives political content to) David Copperfield's psychological state at the end of his first marriage. "The old unhappy feeling pervaded my life," writes Copperfield of his realization that his Dora will never change.

> It was deepened, if it was changed at all; but it was as undefined as ever, and addressed me like a strain of sorrowful music faintly heard in the night. I loved my wife dearly, and I was happy; but the happiness I had vaguely anticipated, once, was not the happiness I enjoyed, and there was always something missing.[74]

The passage could just as well come from *His Natural Life*, as Dora Vickers repeatedly attempts to give contours to a malaise whose source, at the same time, she carefully conceals from herself.

Like Clarke's Dora, David Copperfield's first childhood love is his nurse. "The first objects that assume a distinct presence before me, as I look far back, into the blank of my infancy," writes Copperfield,

> are my mother with her pretty hair and youthful shape, and Peggotty with no shape at all. . . . I believe I can remember these two at a little distance apart, dwarfed to my sight by stooping down or kneeling on the floor, and I going unsteadily from one to the other. I have an impression on my mind which I cannot distinguish from actual remembrance, of the touch of Peggotty's forefinger as she used to hold it out to me, and of its being roughened by needlework, like a pocket nutmeg-grater.
>
> This may be fancy, though I think the memory of most of us can go farther back into such times than many of us suppose; just as I believe the power of observation in numbers of very young children to be quite wonderful for its closeness and accuracy. . . .

> Looking back, as I was saying, into the blank of my infancy, the first objects
> which I can remember as standing out by themselves from a confusion of
> things, are my mother and Peggotty. (P. 61)

Copperfield's earliest memories are of his passage back and forth between
his mother, a differentiated, attractive, yet problematic figure, and
Peggotty, a singular yet undifferentiated figure, whose affections create a
whole encompassing world from which she is indistinguishable. The emotional pattern established here continues throughout childhood—and into
his bifurcated adult love for the giddy Dora and the self-abnegating Agnes.
Like Dora Vickers, David Copperfield feels buried alive in his marriage
because he is trying to love the wrong person; he somehow finds himself
married not to Agnes, the woman who recapitulates Peggotty's deep loyalties and quiet virtues, but to a woman who embodies the frivolous imma-
turities of his mother in intensified form.

This is the underlying emotional scenario of *His Natural Life* as well.
The callow product of shallow parents, Dora Vickers is emotionally and
spiritually awakened only when she is nursed in Dawes's arms. When
she recovers from her fever, however, she finds herself indebted and then
engaged not to her source of salvation but to a man who pursues her father's profession with intensified zeal, self-righteousness, and sadism.
For David Copperfield, the problem raised in his marriage with Dora
Spenlow is the maturity of his life choices and his wife's inability to aid
his mental and spiritual development. And it can be solved, tragicomi-
cally, with Dora's early death and a better, second marital choice. Dora
Vickers's hidden anxieties stem not merely from a misconceived marital
choice but from guilt about the whole colonial system and the psychic
investments, denials, and occlusions it occasions. If Dora does not find
belated happiness with Dawes, it is because of the scale of the social barriers that separate them; a whole penal colony has been instituted to keep
them apart.

Their separation is also the result of an incest prohibition more obvious
to Clarke than to Dickens.[75] If the fostering relationship suspends the divides of ethnicity and race, of class and generation, to replace them with a
willed bond of kinship, and if the success of the fostering system lies in its
ability to domesticate alterity, transforming its allures and threats into
household commonplaces, these transformations also enlarge the terrain
covered by incest taboos. To take comfort in the bosom of a nurse, male or
female, and to find there a new object of familial love, means necessarily
to forgo full physical union with the object of one's affections. The consequence of this incest taboo for all nineteenth-century political allegories
sustained by the nurse is that the bond between colonizer and colonized,
between convict and jailer, master and slave, becomes at once more

indissoluble and less able to serve as a permanent political solution than the culminating union of the national tale.

THE DUSKY VISAGE AND THE DARK CORNER

Throughout the nineteenth century, novelists describe the construction of makeshift colonial fostering systems to defend or criticize the dynamics of colonial life. In the late twentieth century, when Margaret Laurence attempts to set in motion the mental decolonization of Canada, she evokes the native nurse to serve both as the repressed conscience of imperialism and the figure of imperial repression itself. Set in mid-twentieth century Manitoba, Laurence's novel *The Diviners* (1974) centers on a comparison between the collective, traumatic history of the province's Scottish settlers (forcibly cleared from the Highlands to the Red River settlement, only to become colonizers in turn, clearing "their" land of its Indian and Métis inhabitants) and the history of the Métis community, outcasts because of their mixed race, their bilingualism, and their hybrid culture.

In the intermittent love story of Morag Gunn (an Anglo-Scottish orphan raised by loving but socially marginal foster parents) and Jules Tonnerre (a Métis schoolmate whom the local school refuses to foster as its own), Laurence compares these two ethnic heritages, exposing the radical inequities of political privilege they bestow. As it recasts the national tale's plot of political rapprochement through ethnic union, *The Diviners* tries to radicalize all of its terms. A true novel of the 1970s, the novel emphasizes sexuality as a primary site of cultural rapprochement, yet it understands sexual unions as unstable and impermanent: Morag eventually bears Jules's child, but the couple are unable to forge a life together, and their daughter continues to face all the prejudices of white, Anglo-Scottish Canada.

The novel's fostering relationships, in comparison, appear more sturdy, more able to produce lasting political energies. Morag's foster father, Christie, functions as a male national nurse, from his inherited Gaelic accent to his repertoire of epic stories. Both in his own defiance of social convention and his tales of clan heroism during the Highland clearances, he transmits to his nursling a cultural legacy of political resistance (even if, like Edgeworth's Ellinor, he at first works to capture Morag's interest by magnifying the heroic deeds of her own family). Christie's stories directly inspire Morag's life as a writer and her wish to give voice to the silenced; they also help her to transform a deep-rooted class shame into a principled resistance to social hierarchies.

In a novel populated by foster children, peoples abandoned by their governments and by history, the most neurotic character is an arrogant Anglo-Indian English professor who destroys his marriage to Morag by refusing to learn anything about her previous life. He is, of course, deeply scarred by his own past, by the authoritarianism of his schoolmaster father and by a clash, in British India, between colonial and indigenous cultures which leaves him traumatized forever. Decades later, continents away, he startles his wife by muttering brokenly, in his sleep, an exotic name: the name of his lost ayah.

> "Well, I may as well tell you, not that it's all that important. She was a Hindu woman. . . . She seemed old but she may only have been a girl. I was about five or six. She was my *ayah*. . . . She looked after me. She was very— oh, I don't know—very affectionate, and tender, I guess, and there was not much of that kind of feeling around our house. My mother spent nearly all her time lying in a hammock, suffering from migraine. Minoo used to play with me, and build little stone forts for me, and—"
>
> "Go on."
>
> "Well . . . actually, when I couldn't get to sleep she would get into bed beside me, and hold me in her arms, and stroke me. I mean, all over. I used to have an orgasm or whatever is the equivalent in a child, and then I'd go to sleep. It was quite a common practice there, I later learned. Not, however, among Europeans. . . . But one evening, my father came into the bedroom. . . . That was, as a matter of fact, the reason why, next day, he beat me, and tied me to the steamer trunk outside the gate, with the sign *I Am Bad* on me."
>
> "Brooke, that was terrible."
>
> "Not really. . . . It's a nuisance that it comes back to me, that's all. But it certainly strengthened my resolve. I hated him forever after, and I suppose as a child I must have wondered if he was right about it, but at least it taught me at an early age that life is tough and that one has to be pretty tough, as well, to stand up to it. I learned to run my life that way, to keep a firm control over things so that the external forces would batter at the gates as little as possible."
>
> "And yet, earlier tonight, when you were depressed, you said it was the human condition and nothing could be done about it."
>
> "Oh, that. Well, yes, I guess that's more or less fate, that kind of depression."[76]

Like Harry Bertram, Mandeville, Dora Vickers, and all the neurotic colonials before him, what haunts Brooke Skelton is the childhood loss of his native nurse, under circumstances that render him permanently unable to invest either in the imperial order or in domestic life. Like Bogle Corbet, Skelton is completely resigned to the perpetual depression he inhabits, accepting it as part of the human condition. Even a homemade "talking cure" does not puncture his shell. Yet the reader understands this lifelong despair as the product of a particular cultural conjuncture. The nurse, her disappearance, and the child's lifelong inability to recover from her loss derive their psychic importance from three very specific historical developments: the sociological transformation of the European nursery, the consolidation of the British Empire, and the developmental history of the nurse as conscience, as unconscious, and as literary memory.

Chapter 6

THE ABBOTSFORD GUIDE TO INDIA:
ROMANTIC FICTIONS OF EMPIRE AND THE
NARRATIVES OF CANADIAN LITERATURE

"The seasons in this colony," said the Judge, "are not only accompanied by the ordinary mutations of weather observed in other countries,
but present a constant and rapid succession of incidents and people.
From the opening of the ports to the close of navigation, everything
and everybody is in motion, or in *transitu*. The whole province [of
Nova Scotia] is a sort of railroad station, where crowds are perpetually
arriving and departing. It receives an emigrant population, and either
hurries it onward, or furnishes another of its own in exchange. It is the
land of 'comers and goers.' . . . New groups gradually fill the space
vacated by others. The new know not the old, and the old inhabitant
feels that he is in a land of strangers. Governors and their staffs,
admirals and their squadrons, generals and their regiments, come and
go, ere their names have become familiar to the ear. . . . At the capital,
all is change: it is the abode of the houseless, the wayfarer, and the
stranger, but home is emphatically England to the English, Ireland to
the Irish, and Scotland to the Scotch. To the Nova Scotian, the province
is his native place, but North America is his country. The colony may
become his home when the province has become a nation. It will then
have a name, the inhabitants will become a people, and the people have
a country and a home. Until that period, it would seem as if they
were merely comers and goers."
—Thomas Chandler Haliburton, "The Seasons, or Comings and
Goings" *The Old Judge, or Life in a Colony*

[Trinidad, t]he island of his birth, on which [Alistair Ramgoolan] had
grown up and where he had made his fortune, was transformed by a
process of mind into a kind of temporary home. Its history ceased to be
important, its present turned into a fluid holding pattern which would
eventually give way. . . . [He] could hope for death here but his
grandchildren, maybe even his children, would continue [in their own
immigration to Canada] the emigration which his grandfather had
started in India, and during which the island had proved, in the end,
to be nothing more than a stopover.
—Neil Bissoondath, "Insecurity"

THE VIEW FROM ABBOTSFORD:
COLONIAL, POSTCOLONIAL, AND TRANSCOLONIAL

In *The Abbotsford Guide to India* (1986), Canadian poet Frank Davey describes his travels through an India he constantly, involuntarily measures against his hometown of Abbotsford, British Columbia. Davey's gnomic poems meditate on the incomprehension of tourist perception, the gaps between cultures, and the literary-historical mediations of place. At once exoticizing and "Buddhistic," the poems empty out of their objects, noting, in transit, the blurring of the traveler's identity and suggesting how the vast descriptive literature of empire flattens India the referent behind India the historically charged system of signs. Yet *The Abbotsford Guide* suggests the historical encrusting of places along with their emptying out; Davey identifies the historical preconditions of the encounter of Canada with India, in their parallel, indirectly linked histories as British colonies.

In Abbotsford Davey finds a point from which to evoke a traditional bifurcation in colonial views of the empire. Located on the Canadian-American border and on the edge of the North American continent, Abbotsford (founded in 1889) would seem to afford only the most peripheral view of India—a small town reading a subcontinent—were it not that Abbotsford's large Sikh population demonstrates their long-standing, live connection. The imperial legacy of displacement, cross-pollination, and cosmopolitanism informs even present-day touristic journeys.

The name Abbotsford also suggests a more hegemonic imperial memory, evoking a literary memorial half a world away: the famous "baronial mansion" in the Scottish Borders, "which Sir Walter Scott built with the profits of his [Waverley] novels."[1] Scott's Abbotsford recapitulates his novels' antiquarian reconstruction of Scottish tradition. Designed as a monument to Scottish Britishness, it gathers memorials of ancient Scottish life, trophies of modern British military campaigns, and mementos of Scottish emigrant settlements throughout the empire. Throughout the nineteenth century and across the empire, Abbotsford remains an often-evoked symbol for the links between national, British, and imperial ideals. During Scott's lifetime, Abbotsford became a repository of empire, as friends and admirers involved in the colonization of Africa and Australia sent back a flock of emus, the skin of their first lion, and their pioneering works of colonial literature, dedicated to Scott.[2]

As late as 1909, an advertisement for Rev. W. S. Crockett's *Abbotsford* vaunts its appeal not only to "pilgrims to the home of the Great Wizard of the North" but also "to the great congregation across the seas who, although they know 'Abbotsford' as a household word, can scarcely hope to behold the original with their own eyes."[3] And as Canadian-Anglo-Indian satirist Sara Jeannette Duncan notes in 1903, the typical British official in the summer capital of British India still lives in "a ridiculous little white-washed house made of mud and tin, and calling itself Warwick Castle, Blenheim, Abbotsford! They haven't a very good hold, these Simla residences, and sometimes they slip fifty yards or so down the mountain side."[4]

Unlike Warwick and even more than Blenheim, Abbotsford is not a historically rooted national and public institution; instead, Scott's cobbled-together private home, purchased in 1811 as Clartyhole (muddy or dirty hole), renamed and rebuilt more splendidly as Abbotsford, was almost lost again after his bankruptcy in 1826.[5] Yet Scott himself guided visitors through Abbotsford as if through a sacred shrine or a museum of Scottish history.[6] Especially from a distance, Abbotsford evokes an idea bigger and sturdier than the building, even if, in its colonial reinstantiation, refashioned of necessity from native materials, the stately British-imperial edifice finds itself diminished, miniaturized, and transformed back into a bungalow, with only a precarious hold on the colony's unstable political terrain.

In present-day British Columbia, the Victorian monuments to the Scottish explorers who "opened up" the West Coast, and to the Native Indian cultures eclipsed in the name of the empire, are overshadowed by a ubiquitous suburban sprawl of drive-ins and drugstores; the Abbotsford ideal of empire (which masked inequities and disfranchisements) and the multicultural population assembled in every one of Britain's colonies seem increasingly submerged by a global monoculture. The American cultural empire both replaces and covers over the structures of an earlier empire. Davey's excavations of Abbotsford's imperial formation, and his insistent retracing of old imperial routes, are thus not only acts of postcolonial reclamation but a resistance against neocolonialism.

An empire lives from its peripheries; its economy and trade depend on their underdevelopment in relationship to the imperial center. Yet the large-scale social displacements that result from such economic unevenness, and from the need to anchor colonial authority with imperial armies and administrations, bind the peripheries to one another, as well as to the center. On one level empires function by fixing a hierarchy of place and by instituting laws that keep colonized subjects in their respective places; on another level they function only by perpetual motion. What Nova Scotia satirist Thomas Chandler Haliburton described in 1849 as the characteristic "comings and goings" of the colonies—the perennial movement of explorers, missionaries, traders, administrators, soldier, convicts, and immigrants between the empire's most "remote" places—brings with it a corresponding circulation of goods and customs, ideas and ideologies, languages and literary tropes. Davey's Abbotsford boasts Sikh temples more numerous than those of Madras, "larger than the Sikh temple of Bombay."[7] Due to its imperial history, Abbotsford is a place of deep provinciality and surprising internationalism, a place historically marginal yet of symptomatic historical significance. Davey's *Guide* is a manifesto from Abbotsford about the

connected perspectives and cultural cross-pollination of different peripheries, and about the emergence of a transperipheral view that bypasses or
actively opposes the empire's nominal center.

"Abbotsford and India," Davey suggests in the listlike introduction to
his *Guide*, are joined, as imperial locations, by deep historical and structural connections, yet they remain fundamentally self-centered and incommensurate.

> Abbotsford is the centre of Canada & India is the centre of the world.
> Both India and Abbotsford missed the Industrial Revolution.
>
> .   .   .   .
>
> Tourists from Abbotsford have travelled to every part of India.
> The Abbotsford Sikh temples are larger than the Sikh temple of Bombay.
>
> .   .   .   .
>
> Abbotsford & India were once agricultural societies.
>
> .   .   .   .
>
> Abbotsford & India are targets of multi-national corporations.
>
> .   .   .   .
>
> The Fraser River is wider but less holy than the Ganges.
>
> .   .   .   .
>
> In Canadian fiction there are more scenes set in India than in Abbotsford.
>
> .   .   .   .
>
> Some of the telephones of India were purchased from Abbotsford in 1953.
>
> .   .   .   .
>
> When Indians & Abbotsfordians dream of a common language they dream of
> their own language.[8]

If one effect of empire is to establish circuits of communication, transmission, and exchange, another is to hold in suspension competing imperial
service sectors. Two former "agricultural societies," both trying to catch up
on missed industrial revolutions, are only tangentially connected by the
British Empire, as later by multinational corporations. The telephone technology that links Abbotsford and India economically is not, for the most
part, used for calls between the two places; each remains the center of its
own world, couching its dreams of a common language in its own vernacular. If Abbotsford stands for a periphery from which other peripheries, and
the empire, can be seen in a new light, it also stands for a long history of
colonial insularity and accommodation to empire. Transcolonial thinking
is itself a colonial legacy, with imperial hierarchies and structures all too
easily replicated within it. If one historical precondition of the modern-day
encounter of Canada with India is their shared, separate pasts as British
colonies, another is the imperial history of comparison between them.

"The [British] colonial history of India," Davey reminds us, "is briefer
than the colonial history of Canada."[9] Yet from the nineteenth century
onward, Canada has continually needed India—at once the fabulous

centerpiece of the British Empire and a "possession" fundamentally resistant to its occupiers—to understand its own history. Canada is both a model colony and a highly unrepresentative one. Constituting, with the Australian colonies, the Cape and later New Zealand, the empire's small group of "settler" colonies, British North America was neither established as a penal colony nor (with the important exception of the Maritimes) based on a slave economy.[10] Unlike India or Britain's various holdings in Africa and the Caribbean, British North America was a cluster of colonies in which (with the important exceptions of Lower Canada and Acadia) British settlers quickly outnumbered both indigenous inhabitants and older settler groups, a trend consolidated, between the American Revolution and the War of 1812, by the large influx of United Empire Loyalists fleeing the "rebellious" United States.[11] Both in Nova Scotia and in Upper Canada, the proximity of—and constant self-definition against—the breakaway American colonies helped to form a colonial identity whose relationship to the empire, and to Britain behind it, seems the most unproblematic, least traumatized, and most intensely identificatory of all British colonies.

So why do Canadian intellectuals turn to India for national self-knowledge? Because what seems to structure Raj India is the clear separation between an imperial administration, imposed from outside, and the country's vibrant non-Christian, non-Western indigenous cultures. In comparison, Canada's relationship to imperial rule is less problematic but all the more enigmatic. Davey's poems point to the obvious vestiges of colonial consciousness in a still emphatically *British* Columbia (especially in the survival of imperial attitudes toward its own "Indians"), but they also identify more mysterious residues of colonial self-doubt and self-hatred. Davey's meditations on Abbotsford through India at once explicate and reenact Canada's historical difficulty in describing itself as a place except in relation to somewhere else, with the comparative vocabulary provided by British travelers and the models provided by British, especially Scottish, literature.[12] ("Canadian literature like Canadian history is largely Scottish," British Columbia writer George Bowering concludes sardonically in 1977. "To get into Canadian literature it helps to be . . . named Alex or Ian or Malcolm.")[13]

Along with the works of Shakespeare and then of Dickens, Scott's Waverley novels were the most widely circulated British literature in nineteenth-century Canada and, indeed, the whole English-speaking world. The empirewide influence of the Waverley novels lies in their ability to harmonize Scottish materials with British perspectives, as they reconstruct the historical formation of the Scottish nation, the simultaneous formation of the Britain that subsumes it, and a cultural nationalism that survives because it learns to separate cultural distinctiveness from the memory of political autonomy and can therefore be accommodated within the new imperial framework.[14] Scott's belief in the ideological capaciousness of empire, his ability to reconcile nationalist and imperialist mandates, made him popular at once with the British public, with imperial advocates and administrators, and with colonial readers trying to understand their own identity. His emphasis on the analogies between nation formation and empire building, and on national identity as a central component of imperial identity, lastingly influence the literatures and the self-understanding of the British Empire. "I know most of Scotts [*sic*] descriptive scenes by heart," writes Susanna Moodie, "while I scarcely remember his stories."[15] Moodie's fiction, in fact, echoes not only the figures but the narrative logic of Scott's plots; by midcentury, the Waverley novels are so deeply embedded in the colonial imagination that their full influence is not always understood.

Yet the scope and ramifications of the Abbotsford cult throughout the empire should not obscure the coexistence of alternative romantic modes of describing empire and of an oppositional current within colonial literature. While Scott's novels depicted the subsumption of nation into empire as as an inevitable, irrevocable process, other novelists developed new psychological models to describe the lasting psychic fragmentation of imperial occupation. Scott describes a moment of acute cultural suffering and loss, which gives way to a future of unexpected compensations; other novelists, however, insist that the trauma of colonization can never be exhausted or recovered from. Instead they describe the neuroses—obsessions, repetition compulsions, memory losses, and permanent difficulties in "settling" or in forming affective bonds—suffered in perpetuity by collective and individual "national characters." Scott's fiction describes the parallel formation of internal and overseas British colonies, aligning the modernization of Scotland with the conquest of India and interpreting these developments optimistically as harbingers of progress. Some of Scott's contemporaries, by contrast, see Britain and its empire as grounded in slavery and oppression. The two positions meet with very different literary-historical posterities. The Scott tradition feeds a new colonial-imperial nationalism, literature, and literary history. Equally rooted in Scottish regional writing but with a resolutely transnational vantage point and a much more acerbic view of the workings of empire, the countertradition is read primarily as satire during its own period and is then buried by nationalist literary historians determined to construct affirmative genealogies for each colonial literature.

In Canada, for instance, early colonial literature began to be rediscovered and republished in the 1960s and 1970s, under the influence of English Canadian cultural nationalism; the new canon builders constructed a literary history with a nationalist teleology and emphasized a tradition of Canadian fiction defined by Scott's influence.[16] As if the novelistic tradition of a modern nation could begin only with a Waverley novel, they hailed John Richardson's 1832 *Wacousta* (with its Highland subplots and its open derivation from Scott and Cooper) as the first "real" Canadian novel.[17] This chapter will argue for the importance of Canada's earlier fiction. The concerns of contemporary Canadian writing, indeed, are most strongly prefigured by Nova Scotia satirists Thomas McCulloch and Thomas Chandler Haliburton and by John Galt's *Bogle Corbet*. For these writers, Canada is imperially constructed and empire locked: McCulloch and Haliburton emphasize the cumulative, transmutative logic of empire, while Galt uses the backwoods as a place from which to reassess the whole imperial project and the British experience of modernity.

For Robert Barr, writing during the final weeks of the nineteenth century to assess Canada's literary prospects for the twentieth, it is still Scott who guides the view and provides the standard for judgment.

> Canada, from its position on the map, its hardy climate, its grand natural scenery, its dramatic and stirring historical association should be the Scotland of America. It should produce the great poets, which I believe it is actually doing, although I doubt if their books are selling in the Dominion. It should produce the great historical novelist; the Sir Walter Scott of the New World. Has the Sir Walter Scott of Canada appeared? And if so, is he unrecognized? If he has not yet come forward, what are the chances for his materialization? If Scott came to Canada . . . how long would it be before he starved to death? . . .
>
> Commercially, nothing pays a country better than lavishly to subsidize an author. A Sir Walter Scott would bring millions into Canada every year. Scotland could well have afforded to bestow on Sir Walter Scott a hundred million dollars for his incomparable Waverley Novels. His works have made Scotland the dearest district in the world in which a traveller can live, and have transformed it from a poverty-stricken land into a tourist-trodden country, rolling in wealth. . . . Now Sir Walter Scott was not writing for laurel wreaths; he wrote entirely and solely for cash. He began his Waverley Novels to support his lavish expenditure on Abbotsford. I doubt if he had any idea how good the books were . . . whether they were good or bad he resolved to write them if they would bring in money. He continued his output afterwards to pay his debts. . . . If Sir Walter had thought he could make more money by planting trees or raising stock he would undoubtedly have turned his attention to those pursuits, and the Waverley Novels would have been unwritten. . . .
>
> What chance has Canada, then, of raising a Walter Scott? I maintain that she has but very little chance, because she won't pay the money, and money is the root of all literature.[18]

From one vantage point, Barr performs the gestures of colonial self-abnegation before the literary institution of Abbotsford, acknowledging the literary standard that the Waverley novels set for a rising colonial literature and waiting for a Canadian Scott as for a cultural and fiscal Messiah. Yet Barr's attention to Scott's economic circumstances also suggests a more cynical attitude toward Abbotsford that anticipates Davey and other post-colonial critics. For if Scott's precarious financial situation demonstrates the need for state support for the arts, the national novels he composed *en grosse* to save Abbotsford from his bankruptcy succeeded in putting Scotland on the cultural map of Europe, stimulating a new cultural tourism and generating almost unending revenue. Like the empire, Abbotsford appears to Barr as a money-making operation disguised as a cultural mission, and its idealistic rhetoric only partly conceals the cash nexus.

GLEN TILT: FROM INTERNAL TO EXTERNAL EMPIRE

During the late eighteenth and early nineteenth century, Britain conquered, colonized, and consolidated a vast new empire in North America, Asia, Australia, and Africa. Its formation was anticipated by, then meshed with, the formation of Britain as the "United Empire of Great Britain and Ireland."[19] The modern British state, as Michael Hechter has influentially argued, resulted from the internal colonization of Wales, Ireland, and Scotland, building its economic strength on the systematic underdevelopment and impoverishment of these domestic colonies.[20] One British imperialism produces another. The conquest and administration of domestic colonies served as a trial run for the colonization of the overseas empire and caused the disproportionate representation of Scots and Irish in the British Army that conquered the empire, as among the colonists who settled it.[21] "Here was a whole company of Scotch people," writes Janet Schaw in 1774 upon her arrival in Antigua from Edinburgh, "our language, our manners, our circle of friends and connections, all the same. . . . We were intimates in a moment." Even the local graveyard is full of Scottish names; for Schaw, the presence of her countrymen in the new colonial setting means that a very unfamiliar landscape feels like home.[22]

Yet the strong presence of Scots and Irish in the British colonies also resulted in the export of intranational tensions into a new setting, particularly when their forced emigration—as with the tens of thousands of Irish whom Cromwell "evicted" and sold into slavery in the West Indies, with the Highlanders "cleared" to the Maritimes, the tens of thousands of United Irishmen transported to New South Wales, and the hundreds of thousands of Irish starved out of Ireland over the course of the nineteenth century—had clear ethnic or political causes. These emigrations also transplanted nationalist plots and tropes into the colonies, where they shaped early colonial literature.

In the mirror of these nascent literatures, the model of cultural and literary nationalism developed in Ireland and Scotland demonstrates its potential both for radical anti-imperialist critique and for political accommodation. Many emigrants from Britain's internal to its external colonies retained a sense of aggrievement, seeing the colonial situation as a replication of Britain's own structural injustices.[23] For exiled Fenian leader John Mitchel, transported in 1848 to the West Indies, the Cape Colony, and Australia, this perception of systematic parallels intensifies an already militant nationalism and creates a sense of international solidarity. Insisting on Ireland as the original British colony, where genocidal tactics of empire continue to be tested, most recently in the "artificial" potato famines, Mitchel's *Last Conquest of Ireland, (Perhaps)* (1860) ends by denouncing the British Empire as a worldwide system of domination and predicting the ultimate victory of nationalist interests.

> Now, that million and a half of men, women, and children, were carefully, prudently, and peacefully *slain* by the English government. They died of hunger in the midst of abundance which their own hands created. . . .
>
> The subjection of Ireland is now probably assured until some external shock shall break up that monstrous commercial firm, the British Empire; which, indeed, is a bankrupt firm, and trading on false credit, and embezzling the goods of others, or robbing on the highway, from Pole to Pole; but its doors are not yet shut; its cup of abomination is not yet running over. If any American has read this narrative, however, he will never wonder hereafter when he hears an Irishman in America fervently curse the British Empire. So long as this hatred and horror shall last—so long as our island refuses to become, like Scotland, a contented province of her enemy, Ireland is not finally subdued. The passionate aspiration for Irish nationhood will outlive the British Empire.[24]

As Mitchel records in absorbing detail in his *Jail Journal* (published serially in 1854), his own forced travels through much of the empire, as a "Prisoner in the Hands of the English," give him a firsthand grasp of the imperial system. Sentenced, after an openly rigged trial, to fourteen years of transportation for sedition, Mitchel is first sent to Bermuda, where he spends months in solitary confinement on a prison hull while his fellow convicts labor on shore. He is then moved to the Cape, but the prison hull is refused landing. The convicts have arrived in the midst of a crisis for the colonial system: the British plan to institute a penal colony at the Cape is resisted by English *and* Dutch settlers, joined for the first time against "a common danger threatening their country."[25] As the "colonists at the Cape come to regard Downing Street as a den of conspirators and treacherous enemies" (p. 271), their shared grievances and common cause begin to create a new "national spirit" (p. 194) across all ethnic divides.

Still imprisoned in their ship, the convicts are moved on to Australia. Van Diemen's Land, reports Mitchel, is "a realm of utter darkness" (p. 265), the free settlements a "small, misshapen, transported bastard England; and the legitimate England itself is not so dear to me that I can love the convict copy" (p. 263). But there are also Scottish and Irish settlements: a valley of the Clyde settled by Scotch colonists; an enclave of "Tasmanian Highlanders, trying to make a Ross-shire glen under the southern constellation" (p. 239); a farm whose isolation has preserved the "Munster accent" (p. 271) of its owners some thirty years after they emigrated from Cork. "Carthaginian 'civilisation' has been closer and more deadly in its embrace amongst the valleys of Munster, than it could be amongst the wilds of the Sugar-loaf forests" (p. 271); for the first time in centuries, and thousands of miles from home, the Irish (and Scots) in Australia are able to live among themselves, with less English influence than in Britain. Yet no Irish enclave or recess can fully substitute for a free Ireland: "Ireland without the Irish, the Irish without Ireland—neither of these can be our *country*" (p. 367). Refusing Australia's "narcotic lotus" (p. 279), which deadens the memory of the outer world, he and several other "Irish State Prisoners" make a daring escape and finally reach the United States, where they continue to agitate for Irish independence.

Recording a tour of the empire from the convict ship, the *Jail Journal* documents the evolution, in transit, of a new anti-imperial thinking. Mitchel experiences at first hand the full extent of the transportation system: all over the globe, the British government is erecting small hells, populated with those who oppose the British order. As Mitchel concludes from his encounters with the empire's administrative personnel, imperial operations depend on keeping the Scots and the Irish divided from each other, ignorant of nationalist agitation taking place at home, and unable to grasp the connection between their domestic experiences and the expansionist projects they help to carry out.[26] During his time in the navy, an Irish officer on Mitchel's ship has lost not only any sense of nationalist grievance but all grasp of Ireland's political situation; the Scottish hull chaplains seem oblivious to the moral contradictions of the empire they serve. In Bermuda, as Mitchel observes every evening from his window, the Forty-second Highland Regiment muster on the esplanade "and march up to their barracks with bagpipes playing 'The Campbells are Coming,' or some other kindred air. But upon the other side, upon the breakwater . . . is another muster, sad to see: many hundreds of poor convicts marched in gangs, some of them in chains" (p. 53).

As Mitchel argues in stinging denunciations of Macaulay and Clive, of the *Edinburgh Review*, and of popular imperial rhetoric, the "Carthaginian" ideology depends on its ability to engender false consciousness, to blind those in its service to what they are doing, to erase their conscience and their memory. Mitchel himself is deeply invested in the traditions of British intellectual life and in contemporary British literary culture; he is remarkable in his emphatic rejection of every premise of contemporary British political thinking and in his determination to lay bare the mechanisms of

British self-understanding. His nationalist ideology critique, indeed, parallels the new Marxist analysis emerging during the same period.[27]

During his long nights on shipboard, Mitchel hears the Irish convicts, from a distant part of the ship, singing mournful dirges, "some Irish air that carries me back to old days when I heard the same to the humming accompaniment of the spinning wheel; and then I curse, oh! how fervently, the British Empire" (p. 171). Throughout the nineteenth century, radical Irish emigrants from Australia to Canada will follow Mitchel in countering the ideological and political pressures of the British imperial system with a national memory work that insists on the connections between Britain's domestic and imperial repressions and that indicts the transportation of impoverished Irish to "New South Wails" and other imperial outposts.[28] Australian outlaw Ned Kelly condemns the penal colony as an extension of an enslaving Britain: "Port McQuarrie Toweringabbie Norfolk Island and Emu plains and in those places of tyranny and condemnation many a blooming Irish man rather than subdue to the Saxon yoke was flogged to death and bravely died in servile chains."[29] And in Canada, where thousands of Irish immigrants died of cholera in 1847 in immigration quarantine, the Ancient Order of Hibernians continues, into the twentieth century, to accuse the Canadian authorities of a deliberate genocide, which reiterated the effects of centuries of British imperialism in Ireland.[30]

For many Scottish emigrants, however, life in the colonies brought new prosperity, social mobility, and political influence. "The persons of greatest weight, in the Canadas," writes one 1795 correspondent,

> are the merchants, or storekeepers. Among these, the gentlemen from Scotland take a decided lead. I have been informed that they have the same ascendancy in the West Indies. They are sent out at any early period of life from Scotland, and, by the time they arrive at manhood, are perfectly conversant in a knowledge of the country. If superior industry and activity are grounds of pretension to affluence, I know no men whose claims are equal to those of the Scotch.[31]

Generalizing from their own experiences, such colonists were often transformed, morally, politically, and economically, into colonizers.[32] Subsuming their nationalist pride and their ambivalence about English culture into support for the empire, they embraced the compensatory cosmopolitanism it fostered; the Scottish engineers, doctors, officers, administrators, and missionaries so ubiquitous in Victorian imperial literature often worked actively to extend its spread.

Contemplating the hypocrisies of nineteenth-century Australia, Marcus Clarke describes an about-face that amounts almost to a somersault: "Glen Tilt—it was wonderful how Scotland was turned upside down in the antipodes!"[33] To still militant nationalists, the conversion to the imperial cause seems an unforgivable betrayal, the negation of a hard-won historical heritage. How, asks Nova Scotia politician Joseph Howe in 1839, "can an Englishman, an Irishman, or a Scotch man, be made to believe, by passing a month upon the sea, that the most striking periods of his history are but a cheat and a delusion[?]"[34] And "[h]ow was it," asks Canadian novelist Graeme Gibson in *Perpetual Motion* (1982), that

> common folk who'd fled tyranny in their homelands submitted here, embracing it at that moment when like their American cousins they might have driven it yelping from the land? And how the swine who celebrated the hangings of Lount and Matthews, Scots whose grandfathers died at Culloden, whose families were harried from the glens, and Irish too, men and women who should have known better, how they were then rewarded, advancing in leaps and bounds until now, not thirty years later, they minced and postured everywhere, comfortable arse-lickers, bum-faced servants of the Crown.[35]

This colonial tilt, this collective amnesia whereby Scottish (and Irish) settlers misplace in transit their age-old anti-English, anti-British, and anti-imperial hatreds, appears to be both the cornerstone and the central mystery of empire. It is also what gives the empire its structural instability—erected on a fundamentally wobbly, unsteady foundation, the edifice of empire threatens, in moments of storm, to topple over again.

For what would happen—asks Clarke in *His Natural Life*—if the colonists ever regained their collective memories and understood themselves to be replicating the injustices they once suffered? And what, asks Laurence's *Diviners*, are the psychic consequences of the settlers' continued repression of the structural parallels between their own traumatic experience of conquest and that of the native inhabitants they displace, in turn, through their settlement?[36] In Manawaka, Manitoba, the descendants of Highlanders forcibly cleared by the earl of Selkirk to the Red River settlement use stories and songs to commemorate the sufferings of their ancestors, first in the Highland and then in a New World of "Locusts. Hailstorms. Floods. Blizzards. Indians. Halfbreeds."[37] The local Métis community, however, has a parallel repertoire of legendary narratives, commemorating their own long-standing resistances to the Highland settlers who cleared them from their ancestral lands, and their own heroism during the Métis rebellions of the 1870s and 1880s. Although the novel's main character works to understand the structural similarities and long-standing historical entwinement of the two cultures, the other Anglo-Scottish characters remain in a state of denial, unable or unwilling to put the pieces together.

> (Did [the Highlanders] fight the halfbreeds and Indians, Christie?)
> Did they ever. Slew them in their dozens, girl. In their scores.
> (Were they bad, the breeds and them?)

What? . . .

"No," he says at last. "They weren't bad. They were—just there."[38]

What keeps the Scots "safe" from disturbing self-knowledge is a proprietary attitude toward historical suffering and a nationalist nostalgia that is too specific and too narrow in its objects of veneration, pity, and memorialization.

The ideology of the tilt presents itself not as a mode of repression but as a spirit of conciliation. The fundamental dynamic of empire is not displacement—as the displaced of Teviotdale displace the Creeks of Upper Canada from their "wattled wigwams," in John Leyden's careful phrase—but reconciliation; the empire is not a site of struggle and conquest but a place in which Britain is successfully reconstituted, in miniaturized form. "The Thistle, Shamrock, Rose entwine" to form a single national culture—and the problem of Britain's internal unity is solved, symbolically, thousands of miles away from Britain.[39] "In Canada," writes Susanna Moodie in 1853,

> where all religions are tolerated, it appears a useless aggravation of an old national grievance to perpetuate the memory of the battle of the Boyne. What have we to do with the hatreds and animosities of a more barbarous age? These things belong to the past: "Let the dead bury their dead," and let us form for ourselves a holier and truer present. The old quarrel between Irish Catholics and Protestants should have been sunk in the ocean when they left their native country to find a home, unpolluted by the tyrannies of bygone ages, in the wilds of Canada.[40]

Yet Joseph Howe's "Acadia" (published posthumously in 1847) argues for an ethnic politics based on nostalgia rather than cultural amnesia.

> O'er the stout hearts that death and danger braved,
> The flag of Britain soon victorious waved,
> And races, hostile once, now freely blend
> In happy union, each the other's friend;
> Striving as nobly for the general good
> As once their fathers strove in fields of blood.
>
> . . . .
>
> Here England's sons, by fortune led to roam,
> Now find a peaceful and a happy home;
> The Scotchman rears his dwelling by some stream,
> So like to that which blends with boyhood's dream,
> That present joys with old world thoughts combined
> Repress the sigh for those he left behind;
> And here the wanderer from green Erin's shore

> Tastes of delights he seldom knew before.
> He toils beneath no law's unequal weight,
> No rival parties tempt his soul to hate. . . .[41]

On the new terrains of Nova Scotia and British North America, all British emigrants share the same military interests and (compared with other indigenous and emigrant groups, at least) similar cultural assumptions. As long as they all grasp this fundamental truth, they should remain free to cultivate memories of home, with as much intensity as they wish. For as Scots and Irish band together to defend British interests in the colonies, their collective memory of past aggrievements will fade, of its own accord, into a nostalgic melancholy.

In Ireland and in Scotland elegiac nostalgia once fueled cultural nationalism; in the new context of the empire, nostalgia works primarily to enforce political quietism. Thomas Pringle's *African Sketches* (1834), the first work of African literature written in English (and dedicated to the memory of a recently deceased Walter Scott), attempts to depict a "new" colonial landscape in order to describe the "Progress of Colonial Encroachments and Reduction of the Aboriginal Race to Servitude."[42] Yet even as Pringle traverses and describes the countryside of southern Africa, he continually evokes the landscapes of Scottish literature. Set on the African veld, yet set to the air of "The Banks of the Clyde," "The Exile's Laments," for instance, rehearses its Scottish—and Scottian—details more overpoweringly than its African ones.

> By the lone Mankazàna's margin grey,
> A Scottish maiden sung
> And mournfully poured her melting lay
> In Teviot's Border tongue.[43]

In an odd extension and reversal of nationalist modes of imaginative seeing (in which the ruin is reanimated in the mind's eye), the living landscape of the veld here is overlaid and then effaced by the distant mental landscape of memory.

The true emotional center of Pringle's "Narrative of a Residence in South Africa," similarly, is in its carefully staged scenes of Scottish national recognition, as a Scottish settler, in Africa already for twenty years, encounters the new Scottish immigrants and is overwhelmed by the almost-forgotten sound of their Scots voices, or as the Highland Regiments of the British Army, on hand to help the immigrants land, hear Pringle hail them in "broad Scotch." "The name 'Auld Scotland' was a sufficient password to their national sympathies," and the Highlanders bring the Lowlanders' boat to shore with particular care.[44] Far from home, once-divisive ethnic, regional, and even linguistic differences melt away under the dulcet tones of "broad Scotch" and the naming of "Auld Scotland."

The dream of empire is that a long history of British ethnic strife (and the violence of imperial conquest) can be sublated into a new utopian community. Nowhere is the fantasy more powerful, poignant, and fragile than in the first fiction published in Australia. Henry Savery's *Hermit of Van Diemen's Land* (1828) presents the letters of an English man of leisure who is so impressed by Van Diemen's Land that he contemplates settling there.[45] The island's notoriety as a convict colony proves utterly undeserved; the territory is so well policed and governed that it is safer than many parts of Britain, and the convict laborers are nowhere in evidence. In physical appearance, the island recapitulates the most sublime scenery in Britain, offering prospects similar to those "so attractive to the Cambrian or Scottish traveller; I could have almost have fancied myself in the vicinity of Loch Tay."[46] And the society of Van Diemen's Land assembles a cross section of the best of the British people. Whether the Hermit travels the banks of the Derwent and Clyde or moves in the genteel yet tolerant society of Hobart Town, he is treated to an array of mellifluous British national accents. One gentleman "had a little of the brogue in his style of language, but only such as is met with in the best bred Hibernians—just enough to swear by; but it was not difficult to see that his birth and breeding had been good" (p. 61). Another gentleman, "evidently by [his] dialect 'fra north o'the Tweed" (p. 161), proves liberal minded and an excellent conversationalist; a lady has in her accent "just enough of the Emerald Island to be interesting" (p. 75).

Of all eighteenth- and nineteenth-century literature in English, *The Hermit of Van Diemen's Land* offers the most delicate and unpolitical treatment of its Scottish and Irish characters. Cultural differences appear in Savery's work only as the vestigial traces of a distant Britain in which such distinctions were still significant. When a hospitable Scotsman, encountered on the banks of the Derwent, issues an invitation to share a jug of whiskey—"and by Charlie, I hope ye ken me weel eneugh to believe ye'll be vara welcome" (p. 136)—the incidental invocation of Bonnie Prince Charlie (and thus of the Jacobite loyalties that divided Scotland and threatened the British Union throughout the eighteenth century) is nothing more than a picturesque detail from a lost world.

The trouble with Savery's Van Diemen's Land—and with the leveling colonial society in which national differences become merely picturesque—is that it does not really exist. Even more than early accounts of the Cape Colony or Upper Canada, the first literary description of Australia must be read as utopian fantasy. For the Hermit's paradise was simultaneously the most remote and stringent "convict's hell" of the entire Australian penal archipelago, "a disgrace to humanity, a leper spot on the face of creation!" as one 1848 commentator insists.[47] As Savery makes clear in his autobiographical novel *Quintus Servinton, a Tale founded Upon Incidents of Real Occurrence* (1830), he himself experienced Van Diemen's Land not as a visiting Oxonian but as a transported felon, convicted of forgery.[48] Denied his ticket-of-leave, deserted by his wife, and twice convicted of further financial crimes, Savery repeatedly attempted suicide. Sentenced, finally, to the dreaded maximum-security prison at Port Arthur, he succeeded in cutting his own throat. As *Quintus Servinton* makes clear, Van Diemen's Land is a place of extreme social hierarchy and harsh social anxieties.[49] *The Hermit*'s utopia of a colonial British commonweal functions, then, as the inverse reflection of a brutally degrading imperial reality.

The Thistle, Shamrock, and Rose Entwined

In 1840 Captain Maconochie, the reformist Scottish governor of Norfolk Island (hitherto the most feared prison in the Australian penal archipelago), purchased a set of Scott's Waverley novels for the edification of his Scottish inmates. He also purchased a set of Edgeworth's works for the Irish prisoners and the works of Robert Burns, George Crabbe, and Mary Mitford for the whole prison population. The reading of these works was to encourage patriotism, to restore a damaged or missing sense of national pride, and "to invest country and home with agreeable images and recollections [that] are too much wanting in the individual experience of our lower and criminal classes."[50]

The university study of English literature began in late-eighteenth-century Scotland; its school study began in the native schools of early-nineteenth-century colonial India, where it served as a secular substitute for both an overtly Christian curriculum (controversial among Hindu parents) and an "indigenizing," Hinducentric curriculum (equally controversial among Anglo-Indian colonial administrators).[51] In contrast to both, a course of English letters promised to convey the spirit of British culture and instill British values without overt proselytizing. On Norfolk Island Captain Maconochie's course of British literature promised similar effects in the rehabilitation of prisoners. When Scottish and Irish prisoners in Australia read their respective national literatures, the nostalgic homesickness this induces will make "England's Exiles" better, more loyal subjects of the British Crown.[52] Edgeworth's national tales and Scott's historical novels will excite a constructive national pride among the convicts, without any danger of inciting national rebellion against their British jailers.[53]

Like Maconochie, Anna Brownell Jameson, wife of the attorney general of Upper Canada, regards Scott (along with Shakespeare, Wordworth, and Goethe) as a "healing, holy influence."[54] And even John Mitchel, full of spleen and "tired to death of reading books" during his long transportation, finds rare solace in "devouring (for the fifth time) 'Ivanhoe' and 'The Heart of Midlothian.' My blessing on the memory of Walter Scott! Surely all prisoners and captives, sick persons, and they who are heavy of cheer, ought to pray for his soul. One is almost reconciled to 'popular literature,' because it has made the Waverley Novels common as the liberal air."[55] Colonial readers "from the Thames to the Neva, from the Ganges to the Mississippi," find the Waverley novels just as reassuring.[56] For Yasmine Gooneratne, the Singhalese discovery of the Waverley novels describes metonymically the colony's discovery of English literature and the novel itself as a literary genre. "With every year, the novel's popularity grew. A circulating library in the Fort of Colombo helped to encourage a popular taste, and even in Tangalle, where libraries were non-existent, the young Leopold Ludovici (later Editor of the *Ceylon Examiner*) discovered and read *Waverley*."[57] In the Australian outback of the 1840s, Annabella Boswell considered Scott the main representative of the British novel: "We were very much thrown on our own resources. . . . I read greedily such books as we possessed, chiefly the *Waverley Novels*, which then and now always interested me. I read most of them aloud as well as to myself."[58] And when Thomas M'Combie's bildungsroman, *Arabin, or The Adventures of a Colonist in New South Wales* (1845), describes the early English and Scottish education of a future colonist, he stresses Arabin's boyhood reading of the Waverley novels. In developing Arabin's imaginative capacities and desire to see the world, Scott's novels are directly responsible for his subsequent decision to emigrate to Australia. If Edward Waverley, before him, was led by *his* youthful reading of less worthy romances to an embrace of the wrong historical cause, Arabin finds in the Waverley novels a more appropriate guide to life and, in the development of the British settler colonies, a more worthy object for his enthusiasm.[59]

In an 1833 speech to raise funds for Abbotsford, Sir James Malcom argues that Scott is the most popular and important author of British India: "[I]n those places of the earth far away and under the British sway in the East, I have found the works of Sir Walter Scott more honoured, and more extensively read, than those of any other author, even in his own country: it is almost incredible to what an extent the writings of Sir Walter Scott are circulated in India."[60]

"We can, in Calcutta, command many of the requisites of good society," confirms Anne Monkland's novel *Life in India, or The English in Calcutta* (1828). "For those who chose literature there was Sir Walter Scott, Lord Byron's works, and the last Romances from Paris, in splendid morocco bindings": Scott symbolizes the ongoing cultural connection between imperial outposts and imperial centers.[61] The Waverley novels both entertain colonial administrators and educate them for their new duties; when

Anglo-Indians plan to act out Scott's *Kenilworth*, they do so primarily for amusement—but the novel's elaboration of pageantry and court life will also provide a model for their imperial role in India. Scott's poetry, finally, promises to have talismanic properties, evoking national nostalgia to keep alive memories of home and to forestall any emotional investment in the alien landscape of the colony. On "the plains of Hindostan," two Scots, a doctor and a major, express their gratitude "to our own bards [Byron, Campbell, and Scott] for the pictures of our native land they have given, though half the globe lies between" (3:24–25).[62]

Only twenty years earlier Scottish Anglo-Indian gentlemen had financed the publication of the fraudulent Gaelic "originals" of Macpherson's *Poems of Ossian*, for they "were anxious to see those poems, which they had so often heard recited in their youth, printed in the language of their ancestors."[63] As Benedict Anderson has recently argued, the "long-distance nationalism" that emigrants or exiles feel often involves the distillation, stylization, diminution, or falsification of collective cultural memories to meet present needs.[64] Monkland's characters also collapse the obvious political differences between Byron (famous as a critic of imperial despotism and a champion of national freedom) and Scott (whose *Guy Mannering* and *Surgeon's Daughter* celebrate the British conquest of India). In the same spirit, Captain Maconochie conjoins Edgeworth and Scott, Burns and Crabbe, as puveyors of national sentiment, despite obvious differences in their forms of nationalism. For Monkland, for Maconochie, and for early colonial authors writing under the sign of Abbotsford, the empire appears unproblematically inclusive, extending and enhancing national feeling and absorbing into itself even the most principled critique of imperialism.[65]

From *Blackwood's* to the Backwoods: Scottish Fictions of Canada

Of all early-nineteenth-century British periodicals, *Blackwood's Edinburgh Magazine* offered its readers the most sustained exposure to a nationalist literary culture: the magazine played a central role in publishing, launching, and promoting Scottish "regionalists" from Galt to John Wilson and David Moir.[66] Yet *Blackwood's* was also a key source of information about the new British Empire, including "debates regarding the efficacy of British territorial expansion, trade, slavery, on the phenomenon of displaced and mixed races and peoples and explorations in natural history and geography."[67] Several of *Blackwood's* leading writers, Pringle, Galt, and William "Tiger" Dunlop, spent part of their careers quite literally in the service of the empire; while leading parties of Scottish settlers to Upper Canada or to the Cape, each "Blackwoodian Backwoodsman"[68] also composed some of the first English-language literature of his respective colony.[69]

Beginning publication only three years after the appearance of *Waverley*, *Blackwood's* worked to diffuse Abbotsfordian ideas throughout the empire, both by providing a popularizing gloss of Scott's national-imperial thinking and by extending a Scottian analysis into new imperial situations.[70] As Scott describes in the 1829 general preface to *Waverley*, his younger brother Thomas, stationed in Canada during the publication of the first Waverley novels, planned to write his own historical novel, in which an Edinburgh emigrant to North America has adventures with the colonists and the "native Indians."[71] Thomas Scott died, however, before he could even begin the work, so the work of describing Canada was left to the *Blackwood's* circle, then to a long succession of Scott imitators. The second half of this chapter will describe the way Scott's contemporaries in Edinburgh and at *Blackwood's* develop Abbotsfordian narratives about the conquest and settlement of Canada—and the simultaneous development, in Nova Scotia and Upper Canada, of powerfully anti-Blackwoodsian, anti-Abbotsfordian narratives that situate Canada very differently.

As one of the most influential nineteenth-century French Canadian novels makes clear, the conquest of Quebec offers clear analogies with the '45 as a national conflict with novelistic appeal. Thematically and formally a close derivation of *Waverley*, Philippe Aubert de Gaspé's *Anciens Canadiens* (1862) opens as a French Canadian national tale, whose ethnographic excursuses and long historical footnotes provide a compendium of information about *Canadien* life. Its plot quite literally extends the *Waverley* plot: after Culloden, a Jacobite Highlander finds refuge in Quebec, is then forced as a British Army officer to participate in its military conquest, and finally, in the new British colony, is reconciled with his adoptive Canadien family after elaborate ceremonies of absolution. *Les anciens Canadiens* functions as a national allegory, describing the political conflicts and eventual unity of the two Canadas to create a foundational myth of the modern state.[72]

Aubert de Gaspé's story is, in many respects, the obvious application of *Waverley* to the situation of the Canadas. *Blackwood's* earlier Canadianizations of *Waverley* are all the more striking, then, for their lack of interest in the French Canadians as national or historical subjects. Instead, the problem of division and unity, of reconciliation and nation formation, is played out entirely within the British Army; Canada, and the struggle between Britain and France for control over North America, are only the backdrop to the drama of British national allegiance. The *Blackwood's* writers are particularly preoccupied with the career of the British Army's Highland Regiments, in their exemplary subordination of national loyalties to imperial ones. First raised in the years before the '45 as the first Catholic army units since the seventeenth century, the Highland Regiments ostensibly represented the British Army's renewed vote of confidence in the High-landers' trustworthiness and loyalty after the 1715 uprising. In fact, the raising of the regiments enabled the army to move militant Highlanders out of a precarious home front (where simmering resentment against the Brit-ish government might feed insurrectionary activity) and force them to do battle on Britain's behalf.[73]

Throughout the seventeenth and eighteenth centuries, as Chaigneau's *History of Jack Connor* reminds us, the British Army successfully de-ployed Scottish soldiers (and settlers) against the Irish, and Irish soldiers against the Scots.[74] Jack Connor is the son of a Scottish soldier, recruited from Inneskillen to fight in the Williamite wars. After the Protestant vic-tory, when many of the Scottish soldiers settled permanently in northern Ireland, Jeremiah Connor settles in County Limerick and marries an Irish Catholic. Twenty-five years later history enters the novel again: the news of the Jacobite Rebellion in the Scottish Highlands shocks Jack's pregnant wife into premature delivery, which kills both mother and child. The be-reaved widower enlists in the British Army to fight the Jacobite rebels. As his journal records, the army is eventually victorious.

> —They slipped by—We marched to—Missed again—Slipped again—Men much harrassed . . . The inhabitants of *** deserve encouragement, but the city of *** to be burnt . . . Our people in great spirits—Victory or death—Then followed in capital letters, CULLODEN 16TH OF APRIL 1746. THEY WERE WEIGHED IN THE BALANCE AND FOUND LIGHT.[75]

Yet if Connor (and "all England" with him) rejoices at the British victory, he shows himself a particularly compassionate victor, spending many hours with his defeated and imprisoned Highland counterparts in an at-tempt to show them the error of their ways.

> Such a conduct made Mr. Connor vastly beloved, and brought some, who were violent, to think with more moderation. He greatly pitied the poor Clans, as they were bred up in a blind and implicit obedience to their chiefs. He la-mented those gentlemen, who acted from conscience and principle. . . . Not content with this sort of behaviour, he endeavoured to remove our own preju-dices, and take off that acrimony and ill-nature, which some of us are too subject to.—He proved the injustice and cruelty of branding a whole kingdom, for the faults of a few. That, even those few were fallen brethren, and erred in their duty, but from their zeal to mistaken opinions. That, most deserved our pity more than our anger. That, so far from perpetuating animosity, all encour-agement and regard should be shewn to the good, and every scheme set on foot to convert the bad. (2:212–13)

Here, Connor models himself on Lord Truegood, the benevolent Anglo-Irish landlord who watched over his own youth, laboring ceaselessly to reclaim his rebellious Catholic tenants for the British Crown. Connor's life story suggests the Crown's success in deploying Scots and Irish to conquer and conciliate each other: after absorbing the paternalistic doctrines of the Anglo-Irish Ascendancy, the son of a Scottish soldier and a Milesian peasant proselytizes successfully among the Jacobites.

Divide, redeploy, and conquer: the ingenuity of the British strategy was apparent in the 1750s and the 1770s, when the Highlanders were sent to North America to fight first the French and then American revolutionaries, and again in 1798, when Highlanders were deployed to suppress the United Irishmen rebellion. Charles Hamilton Teeling, a member of the United Irishmen and a believer, therefore, in a united, multiethnic fight against common British oppressors, is disturbed to hear the occupying army addressing the rebels in a mutually comprehensible Gaelic, and he takes comfort only in the rectitude with which the Highland Regiments fight their fellow Catholics.[76]

Forty years earlier, the Highlanders were deployed in another part of the empire, against a different Catholic population.[77] After the '45, when the British Army occupied and demilitarized the Highlands, General James Wolfe participated in military atrocities against Jacobite soldiers and civilians.[78] Fifteen years later, laying siege in 1759 to a fortified Quebec, Wolfe could penetrate the French defenses only with the help of his Highland Regiments; it was a Scottish officer (and former Jacobite) who successfully answered the sentry's challenge, in a French perfected, perhaps, in Jacobite exile.[79] The next day, on the Plains of Abraham, Wolfe won Quebec from the French, dying in the course of the battle; well into the nineteenth century, Wolfe continued to be celebrated as a national hero, whose martyrdom brought into being a new empire.[80]

Yet for *Blackwood's* authors, attempting to mount a new literature of empire in the wake of the United Irishmen rebellion, it is Wolfe's Highland soldiers who are the real objects of interest, for their symbolic reintegration into the British military economy makes them the first real imperial subjects.[81] Already in 1762, to be sure, Tobias Smollett rebuted Wilkes's attacks on Scotland by pointing to the Highlanders' bravery in fighting for British causes, from Culloden to Quebec.

If Scotland is to be upbraided with the last rebellion, let it also be remembered, that not one hundredth part of the Scottish nation was embarked in that desperate scheme [of the '45]: that not one native of Scotland, employed in the service of the government, shrunk from his duty, or betrayed his trust on that occasion . . . that the Duke of Cumberland led the Scots by whole regiments against the rebels at Culloden; that the number of Scotchmen in his army on that auspicious day, was at least equal to that of their southern brethren, and every officer that fell on his side of the battle, was a native of North Britain. Let it be moreover remembered . . . that the survivors have since literally washed away their offences with their blood; witness their bones now bleaching in almost every quarter of the globe,—at Cape Breton, Ticonderoga, Fort du Quesne, and Quebec, in Guadeloupe and Martinique, before the walls of Pondicherry.[82]

Yet *The Expedition of Humphry Clinker* uses the Highlanders' role in the Canadian campaign to warn *against* imperialism and its cultural insensitivities. Smollett's novel is concerned both with Britain's internal heterogeneity and with the changing situation of Britain in relation to its new colonies. Matthew Bramble's invectives against the West Indians and Anglo-Indian nabobs who mob Bath invoke British fears about the economic restructuring and social mobility the empire brings with it. The parallel danger, as the book's most famous subplot makes clear, is that an imperial view of subject cultures will inform English views of Scotland. When a Scottish nationalist describes his army service in Quebec and his captivity among the Miamis, he dwells both on the Indians' physical ruthlessness toward their white captives and on the voluntary (and well-deserved) martyrdom of two arrogant French missionaries, who presume to convert them without understanding anything of their language or culture. Recounted to Anglo-Welsh travelers, on the eve of their arrival in a Scotland they expect to be backward and savage, Lieutenant Lishmahago's tale is cautionary, warning them not to recast the Scots in the role of militant primitives.[83]

For Lishmahago, as for Smollett, Scottish nationalism leads to a critique of imperial attitudes. The *Blackwood's* literati, however, take up the Lishmahago plot to reverse its values; following the example of *The Briton* and the early Waverley novels, they build a defense of empire out of Scottish nationalism. Canada becomes a site of Jacobite expiation, where nationalist alliances can be re-formed into imperialist ones.

Published in the same year as *Guy Mannering*, Christian Johnstone's novel *Clan-Albin* follows the lead of both *Waverley* and *Guy Mannering* in dramatizing historical change as dislocation, weighing its immediate evils against the possibility of long-term ameliorations, and amplifying Scott's ambivalence about modernization and empire.[84] *Guy Mannering* juxtaposed national and imperial plots, the modernization of Scotland and the conquest of India. What preoccupies Johnstone is the relationship between the homogeneous traditional societies of Ireland and the Highlands and the heterogeneous, multiethnic collectivity of the British Army, as it fights imperial wars at home and abroad. Especially in its initial Highland setting, Johnstone's novel deploys the generic tropes of the Irish-Scottish national tale, set in the traditional home of the clan of Albin and peopled with the stock allegorical figures of Irish and Scottish nationalist literature, representing the clan's bardic traditions, cultural memory, and cultural practices. The old nurse Moome (modeled on Edgeworth's Ellinor) is a female

bard and a traditional healer. And the elderly piper (a model for Edgeworth's King Corny) represents the economic self-sufficiency of traditional culture and "the universal talents of his countrymen."

> Hugh could brew ale, and distil whisky *con amore*; he could tan hides, and
> make brogues, and build boats and huts, and twist other baskets of all kinds.
> Indeed with any odd piece of wood and a knife Hugh could make any thing, or
> rather a substitute for any thing; and to the ingenuity of Robinson Crusoe be
> united the docility of his man Friday.[85]

The village of Dunalbin enshrines the unbroken continuity of past and
present generations, the cultural practices and collective identity of the
clan. As if to warn of the historical pressures on traditional societies, two
figures of a neighboring bardic tradition—a "blind, feeble and very aged"
Irish harper and his six-year-old granddaughter—seek refuge there, fleeing
the upheavals of the 1790s (1:196). One too young to take a real place in
the world, the other so old he has not long to live, these modern incarnations of Macpherson's Malvina and Ossian (at once Irish versions of Mig-
non and the Old Harper from Goethe's 1786 *Wilhelm Meister's Apprenticeship* and forerunners of Little Nell and her grandfather from Dickens's
Old Curiosity Shop) bring to Dunalbin not only Irish oral traditions but also
the elegiac tone of Ossian, exacerbated by Ireland's current civil war.

Soon after, the Highland clearances displace the clan of Albin to one of
the "many little colonies of Highlanders . . . scattered over the continent of
America" (1:90) or into the Highland Regiments.

> Torn at once from home and country—that delicate and mysterious union
> which connects the human mind with the scenes of its early joys, in a moment
> rudely dissolved!—every cherished association which had imperceptibly
> twined round the heart, binding it to home and happiness . . . driven forth from
> the place where the ashes of their fathers reposed, . . . exiled to a new world,
> a land of strange speech, in whose vast territory the remnant of Macalbin's
> clan would be swallowed up like a drop of water in the extended ocean!—
> Pride, patriotism, regret, home, and a thousand painful feelings, combined to
> agonize the bosoms of the wretched emigrants. (1:89)

The Highlands are "made grass parks for England" (1:131), and Dunalbin
is left a deserted village. The transformation of a deeply loved local landscape may be followed by a slow transformation and abandonment of the
Highland national character, once there is "no stone left to tell where Dunalbin stood" (1:130), once the community no longer has its traditional setting to contain and nurture it.

> "The patriotism of our countrymen is much stronger than that of any other
> class of the British public. What must be a feeble sentiment amid the bustle of
> crowded society, is a vehement passion in our insulated glens. But oppression

gradually weans the affections of our countrymen from that land from which it is driving them forth. One cannot help rejoicing that so many have reached another region, where the woods will afford that clemency and protection which are denied at home. There, I hope, they will long retain those ancient manners, which are so intimately connected with all their characteristic virtues. I trust they will ever preserve that prudent, and unsubdued spirit of independence, which has in every age been their ennobling distinction: the national tongue, and the warlike garb; fondly cherish the remembrance of their heroic ancestors, and yet teach the wilds of America to echo the songs of Selma." (1:130)

"It is extremely improbable that the generous wish you have expressed can ever be accomplished. The state of society which originally formed, and afterwards preserved, our national character, can never be realized in the new world. Our countrymen, I fear, will soon forget that 'Fingal has lived, or Ossian sung.'" (1:133–34)

Yet as the rest of the novel shows, the ultimate effects of dispersal, banishment, and service in the British Army are not the loss of indigenous cultural ideals so much as the expansion for a broader framework within which to imagine community, and the production of a new identification with the Irish people, whose collective sufferings the Highlanders come to see as comparable to (or more desperate than) their own. When the novel's hero enters the British Army,

[H]is first disappointment had been, to find that a Highland regiment, a name consecrated to glory, was composed of English, Irish, and Lowland Scots, and these not always the free-born, lofty-minded Englishmen of his fancy; and still seldomer the quiet, intelligent and amiable peasants that . . . Burns . . . had taught him to expect. It was in fact like many other regiments, a promiscuous horde. (2:103)

As Norman gradually makes friends with his fellow soldiers, however, and teaches several Irish soldiers to read (by exposing them, like Captain Machonochie after him, to Edgeworth's fiction), his feelings of alienation give way to camaraderie. Yet his outrage at his brutal Anglo-Scottish commanding officer (who is also the usurper of Clan-Albin's lands) prevents Norman from identifying completely with the British Army. His Irish friend, Phelim Bourke (named for Phelim O'Neil, who led the Ulster Plantation Uprising), protests army injustices more strenuously, deserting to join the French, and finally, in a one-man recapitulation of the 1798 United Irishmen rebellion, killing himself rather than undergo official execution at the hated hands of "*the English*" (3:127). This fate, and Norman's firsthand observations of Ireland's desolation, force him to acknowledge the Highlanders' relative privilege within Britain, clearances and all. The Irish are "a people treated as slaves, and punished because they then ceased to act like men" (2:178). Although Johnstone distrusts the long-term effects of revolutionary rhetoric and action on the Irish situation, she shows guarded respect for Bourke's "free and Irish spirit" (2:178) and for the intensity of Irish national feeling (3:127).

Her own effort, however, is to define a community of suffering and shared experience in ways that transcend both the feudalism of the clan system and nationalist resentments.[86] At the end of the novel, when Norman is revealed as the true chieftain of Albin, he repossesses Dunalbin's abandoned glens and brings them to new prosperity, through economic and agricultural reform. What is missing, however, is the old clan; transplanted to Canada, most clansmen are no longer able or willing to return to their old home. Dunalbin is repopulated instead by the soldiers from Norman's Highland Regiment; a refuge for Britain's other displaced peoples, it becomes home to a new transnational British community. Where once a series of clearances sundered an ancient community forever, Scottish, Irish, and English ex-soldiers and expatriates live in harmony. The clan of Albin has been shattered; a new Albion is born; and the genre of the national tale has been reforged, under the influence of *Waverley* and *Guy Mannering*, to depict the texture of emigrant and imperial experience.

Johnstone's arguments undergo conservative redaction in John Wilson's *Lights and Shadows of Scottish Life* (1822), an influential forerunner of Scottish "Kailyard" fiction. As one of the key literary presences behind *Blackwood's*, Wilson was personally responsible for much of the magazine's sentimental and reactionary tone, its intolerance toward aesthetic innovation, and as his story "The Shieling" suggests, its affirmation of the empire as an extension of or substitute for national feeling. The story evokes the victorious memory of the Battle of Quebec as a way of expiating the more ambivalent memory of the Battle of Culloden: for Wilson, the victories of empire retroactively redress and rewrite the traumas of national history. "The Shieling" centers on the deathbed of an old Highland solider who allegorizes Scottish military valor, ancient and modern. A veteran both of the '15 and of the '45 (the two military defeats that sealed the fate of the Highland clan system), he subsequently joined the British Army and fought in Quebec. Now, on the anniversary of the conquest of Canada, the old veteran lies dying, "like Ossian attended by Malvina"; his granddaughter watches over him, then summons the priest for the last rites.[87]

In the end not one cleric but three—local presbyter, Catholic priest, and Episcopalian minister—find their way to the shieling. With their arrival, the elegiac, Ossianic notes struck earlier in the story—the sense that this death dooms a whole cultural world—give way to happier reflections about the new cooperative work, in the Highlands, between Britain's three major churches. The military valor called forth in Scotland by the '15 and the '45 can be subsumed into the British cause of empire and a new set of imperial virtues; the death of the Gael is sublated by the spiritual union of Ireland, Scotland, and England.

For Johnstone, the British Army is both a morally problematic institution and the crucible of transnational British feeling; Canada is at once the exile and the new home of traditional Scottish culture. For Wilson, the British Army and Canada are sites where the veterans of national rebellion and defeat are transformed into British heroes. For William "Tiger" Dunlop, the British Army creates a new, rank-and-file, all-British alliance; settled after 1814 by a new breed of self-consciously British veterans, Canada is the lucky colony able to enshrine a new, transnational definition of British character.[88] Dunlop spent much of his life in Upper Canada, first as a British Army surgeon during the American War of 1812–14, then as a colonizer. His two books about these experiences, *Statistical Sketches of Upper Canada for the Use of Emigrants* (1832) and *Recollections of the American War* (1847), emphasize the continuities between life in the British Army and settler life in Canada.

During the War of 1812, British Army regiments had been sent to Canada to strengthen local garrisons against American attackers and protect United Empire Loyalists, still faithful to the British Crown, from American republicanism. Sensitive, as a Scot, to the ethnic heterogeneity of the British, Dunlop finds an overwhelming preponderance of Lowlanders, Highlanders, and Irishmen everywhere in Canada, beginning with his own regiment; his fellow officers are "a fine jovial unsophisticated set of wild tremendous Irishmen," and his commanding officer, Donald McB—, is originally from Invernesshire: born, during the '45, into a patrician Jacobite family driven into a long continental exile, McB— already had "thirty-seven years' hard service in the British Army (to say nothing of fourteen in the French) in North America, the West Indies, South America, the Cape of Good Hope, Java and India" before his posting to Canada.[89]

McB— begins life as an already outlawed, a Jacobite '45er, born into an acute crisis for a recently formed Britain and into a legacy of Scottish resistance to English rule. Through years of army service, he is transformed instead into a representative of empire, who has helped to consolidate British rule in every part of the world. For Dunlop, both the cause of empire and the multiply national British Army that wins and maintains it repair the historical fissures that divided Britain's different national groups and reconstruct, in less explosive form, a Britain long troubled by intranational conflicts. Faced with the discipline of the army and the hardships of the colony, each national group is forced to redirect its energies away from nationalist, anti-English struggles and to collaborate fully with the British authorities. This process also develops each group's proverbial national characteristics so that they serve—and become the shared strengths of—the entire British Empire. Observing the several British Army divisions staffed and commanded by Highlanders (as well as the local Glengarry Militia, made up of previous Highland emigrants to Canada), Dunlop sees traditional clan loyalties—and the Highlanders' proverbial bellicosity—rechanneled into army discipline and military bravery in the British cause.

The army also forces national or religious groups who have long been enemies to work together. From the seventeenth-century colonization of the Ulster Plantation with Scottish Protestants (and their subsequent slaughter during the Ulster uprisings) to the vituperative late-eighteenth-century debates over Ossian and the nationality of an oral Gaelic cultural heritage, the relationship between Irish and Scots had often been severely strained. Only under the aegis of new, romantic nationalisms does the cultural and literary life of the two British peripheries begin to be connected; racializing notions of a shared Celtic origin do not gain currency until the 1850s.[90]

Yet already in 1813, when Tiger Dunlop is quartered for the winter in the small Upper Canada town of Cornwall, he finds the allegorical signs of a completed Scottish-Irish national rapprochement in the humble "log hotel" (public house) where he is billeted.

> Peggy Bruce was the daughter of a respectable Irish farmer, and had made a runaway match with a handsome young Scotch sergeant. She had accompanied her husband through the various campaigns of the revolutionary war, and at the peace, his regiment being disbanded, they set up a small public house. . . . The sign was a long board, decorated by a very formidable likeness of St. Andrew at the one end, and St. Patrick at the other, being the patron saints of the high contracting parties over whose domicile they presided and the whole surrounded by a splendid wreath of thistles and shamrocks.[91]

Even in 1832, on the eve of the Upper and Lower Canada Rebellions, Dunlop continues to believe in the empire as a new arena in which historical quarrels can be set aside: the final chapters of *Statistical Sketches* praise the loyalty of Irish emigrants transplanted to British North America and predict the merger, in Upper Canada, of several competing factions of the Scottish Presbyterian Church. In this conciliatory climate, Dunlop notes the growth of his own religious tolerance.

> An elder of the Kirk, and bred in the most orthodox part of Scotland, I came to this country strongly prejudiced against Catholicism and its ministers; but experience has shown me that my prejudices were unjust. I expected to find both priests and people as violently opposed to the British government here as at home,—I found them the strongest supporters of the constitution.[92]

If Dunlop's retrospective account of his initial 1813 visit to Canada signposts a new, empire-derived sense of Britishness, his subsequent return to Canada in 1826 and his *Statistical Sketches* are occasioned by different imperial exigencies. In the interim, Dunlop spent several years in India (working as a newspaper editor and—hence his sobriquet—as the "super-intendent of a fantastic scheme to rid the island of Saugor of tigers"), then in Scotland (where he became a major *Blackwood's* contributor and a member, with Wilson, Hogg, and John Gibson Lockhart, of the "Noctes Ambrosianae" circle).[93]

In 1826, when John Galt moved to Upper Canada to supervise the colo-nization of the Huron Tract, Dunlop accompanied him as the warden of forests. Revisiting British North America after more than a decade, Dun-lop's perceptions of the Canadian landscape are now colored by his memo-ries of India (and the Cape), and he uses this new frame of reference to generalize about the function of colonies for British economic life. When Dunlop describes the rivers that traverse Upper Canada's Western Divi-sion, he shows no interest in the way their names—Thames, Ouse, Nith, Saint Clair, Aux Sables—recapitulate the area's various exploration and settlement histories. Instead, he is struck by the resemblance between the Saint Clair and the Ganges—and by the possibility that Upper Canada shares geological features with other British colonies, however geographi-cally remote: "My attention was first called to alluvial formations . . . on the banks of the Ganges, some fourteen or fifteen years ago . . . and I was surprised to find the St. Clair, where it issues from Lake Huron, presenting all the features of the sacred river of Hindostan."[94] Dunlop's stress on preexisting structural analogies between otherwise distant and disparate places undergoing colonization gives the ensuing uneven developments and cultural dislocations the status of a synchronized geological formation, an inevitable natural history.

In the wake of his sojourn in India, Dunlop's initial sense of a colony as a place where Scottish immigrants and other settlers can reforge their loyal-ties to Britain and bring into being a more truly united kingdom seems to be overlaid by a more abstract notion of a colony as an economic service unit for Britain, providing it with new markets and relieving it of su-perfluous population. Given a "superfluity of manufactures and a paucity of consumers," the poor and orphaned, those whose trades are supplanted by industrial processes or who are unable to "support themselves comfort-ably by their labour at home," should be sent to the colonies. Those who emigrate "go to Canada to restore the equilibrium between supply and de-mand," to offset the consequences of modernization.[95]

As the perspective of Scottish Canada is overlaid with that of British India, the Scottish apologist for empire as the rectification of British in-equalities appears transmuted into the Scottish imperialist. But the reverse is true as well. Only after the global spread of the British Empire, after a far-flung network of colonies has been fully subordinated to British rule, does Britain become acutely visible in the eyes of the world, its stability

and internal unity at once the mark of cultural superiority that justifies imperialist expansion and a model for all overseas colonies. Dunlop's works
form two different trajectories. Ordered by the events they describe—the
experiences of 1813 overlaid by subsequent colonial ventures—they suggest the movement from British to imperial identifications. Ordered, rather,
by the chronology of their publication—*Statistical Sketches* in 1832 and
Recollections in 1847—they suggest the notion of a unified Britain as a
nostalgic retrojection from the outposts of the empire. So too the wartime
and colonial rapprochements of Scots and Irish gain their full significance,
and their allegorical force, only from a distant retrospect. For Dunlop, then,
an imperial sense of the world is built on top of a sense of Britain itself as
a model empire, joining and fusing different nations—at the same time,
conversely, that the emergence of the empire puts increasing stress on ethnic conciliation within Britain.

Comings and Goings: Early Canadian Fictions of Empire

Taken together, the works of Johnstone, Wilson, and Dunlop suggest both
the scope and the range of Scott's influence, as the *Waverley* plot of conquest, historical transformation, and national reconciliation influences the
national tale, the local-color sketch, the colonial report, and the colonial
autobiography. They also suggest an internal transformation, from the
1810s to the 1840s, in Scottish literary thinking about empire, as Scott's
often ambivalent exploration of the nexus of nation and empire hardens
into a celebratory *Blackwood's* line.

In some respects, John Richardson's 1832 *Wacousta*—written by a British Army major and dedicated to his regiment—represents a Canadian extension of the *Blackwood's* tradition. But it also works to reconcile the
Blackwood's mode of allegorizing Canada with Scott's more indirect way
of allegorizing historical process; Richardson's juxtaposition gives new
complexity to the account of Canadian history. For the *Blackwood's* writers, Canada is significant as a site of displacement, so geographically distant from Britain (and so devoid of its own history) that its icy remoteness
can absorb and neutralize the most burning Scottish anger. Both *Waverley*
and *Guy Mannering* focus rather on a process of historical combustion, in
which long-standing political discontent is fanned to conflagration, then
gradually burns itself out.

Like the *Blackwood's* writers, Richardson sees Canada as a place of reconciliation. But he also sees it as possessing a complicated history of its
own: if its inhabitants now display an exemplary attachment to Britain and
to imperial ideals, this loyalty is the outcome of a particular historical process, not simply an originary state. In the 1760s, the period in which
Wacousta is set, the Canadas "had very recently been under the dominion

of France," changing hands only after "a long struggle," which continued long after the British victory on the Plains of Abraham. Long after the treaties had been signed, the French Canadians, "though conquered as a people," continued "to oppose obstacles to the quiet possession of a conquest by those whom they seemed to look upon as their hereditary enemies; and in furtherance of this object, paid agents, men of artful and intriguing character, were dispersed among the numerous tribes of savages, with a view of exciting them to acts of hostility against their conquerors."[96]

Richardson's novel describes how an entire British Army garrison became the target of this hostility. Yet in the end, as Richardson assures us at the outset, the Canadas will be fully pacified.

> [P]owerful as was the feeling of the hostility cherished by the French Canadians towards the English when the yoke of early conquest yet hung heavily on them, this feeling eventually died away under the mild influence of a government that preserved to them the exercise of all their customary privileges, and abolished all invidious distinctions between the descendants of France and those of the mother-country. So universally, indeed, has this system of conciliation been pursued, we believe we may with safety aver, of all the colonies that have succumbed to the genius and power of England, there are none whose inhabitants entertain stronger feelings of loyalty and attachment to her than those of Canada. (P. 11)

What *Wacousta* records, then, is the story of how Canada moves from a state of turbulence to a state of unmitigated peace. The novel's chief malefactor—and title character—as we learn in its final chapters, attacks the British Army out of a justified desire for personal revenge; because *Wacousta* ends both with his death and with the death of his principal target, the story closes at a moment in which lasting peace is suddenly conceivable. Yet if *Wacousta*'s action appears driven by a personal vendetta rather than by larger historical forces, the particular circumstances of Wacousta's early life, as he finally reveals them, make clear how much the novel *does* intend its particular plot to stand in for a broader historical process.

From beginning to end, Wacousta's confession seems deeply familiar, derived from *Duncan Campbell, The Recess,* and *Melmoth,* from Chaigneau, Godwin, Cooper, and Scott. Born and raised in England, Sir Reginald Morton joins the British Army. In the 1730s his regiment is stationed in the Highlands, and he falls in love with Clara Beverley, who has never before seen a man besides her own father. An English officer who fought with the Jacobites against the British Army during the '15 and who lost his wife during the uprising—her death "accelerated by circumstances connected with the disturbed nature of the times" (p. 463)—Colonel Beverley had resolved to retreat from civil society and had set up house, with his infant daughter, in the same mountains where he had hid from the British. Years later, Morton penetrates this Edenic recess and persuades Clara to elope with him. Before they can be married, however, he is called away on regimental business and leaves his best friend, Ensign de Haldimar, to watch over his fiancée. But de Haldimar betrays him, marrying Clara himself and persuading the military authorities to court-martial Morton. Abandoned, cashiered, and filled with murderous bitterness, Morton determines to avenge himself not only on his rival's family but also on the army he once served.

> The rebellion of forty-five saw me in arms in the Scottish ranks; and, in one instance, opposed to the regiment from which I had been so ignominiously expelled. Never did revenge glow like a living fire in the heart of man as it did in mine; for the effect of my long brooding in solitude had been to inspire me with a detestation, not merely for those who had been most rancorous in their enmity, but for every thing that wore the uniform, from the commanding officer down to the meanest private. Every blow that I dealt, every life that I sacrificed, was an insult washed away from my attainted honour. (P. 494)

When his old regiment, now commanded by de Haldimar, "participates in the expedition against Quebec under General Wolfe" (p. 495), Morton follows the British Army to Canada, disguises himself as Wacousta, and wages a one-man war against the British fort that de Haldimar commands.

The novel opens inside the fort, as Wacousta and his helpers besiege it. And until the very end of the novel (when we belatedly learn who Wacousta really is and what drives his actions), we see Wacousta as the British Army does, a mysterious menace to military order and British sovereignty. On one level, then, Wacousta's final confession radically alters the novel's meaning, both because it challenges the perspective through which we have seen the book's events and because it retroactively transforms an adventure story into a political parable. If the British presence in the Canadas, in the 1760s, is imagined as a garrison continually under attack, the most threatening enemy is not the French but rather a man who, hating everything the British Army stands for, has allied himself with the Scots as an expression of his hatred.

Yet these revelations come too late to change what the book is fundamentally about. Just as Scott could have written a *Guy Mannering* that worked out the implicit parallels between Scotland and India, so too Richardson (whose grandfather emigrated to North America as a result of the '15) might have written a *Wacousta* that fully worked out the impact of eighteenth-century Scottish history, in all its turbulence and unhappiness, on the formation of Canadian identity. Richardson gives us all the pieces of this analysis: Wacousta's move to Canada and his attempt to sabotage the operations of the British Army in its new territories clearly repeat his fight against it during the '45, and that, in turn, repeats Colonel Beverley's fight against it during the '15. The Jacobite cause, as we see, is not simply a Scottish affair, for it offers an important gathering point, again and again, for all those disaffected with British institutions and the British state. The repeated failures of the Jacobite campaigns, conversely, leave the disaffected more alienated than before. Colonel Beverley becomes a hermit, attempting to remove himself both from British society and from British history. And when another army officer stumbles upon his retreat, he too, in turn, becomes disaffected and rebellious. The loss of the '45 only makes Morton more determined to fight—and *his* life in the Canadian wilderness is marked by an escalating ferocity and ruthlessness. In this case, at least, Canada's distance and emptiness have no power to neutralize old angers or to dull the cause of vengeance.

What we glimpse in *Wacousta*, then, is the possibility of a very different view of Canada from the one proposed by *Blackwood's*: a Canada full of previous histories and undying hatreds. But like Scott before him, Richardson structures his novel so that it is finally evasive. Wacousta's vengeance fulfills itself and then is gone, leaving behind a country full of loyalists and the possibility of a historical fresh start. The emotions of the past give way to the (ostensible) tranquillity of the present. A novel that might, five years before the Lower and Upper Canada Rebellions, have explored Canada's continuing sources of political discontent and motivations for revolt, is content finally to view the colony from within the stockade, from the perspective of the British Army. Richardson, argues Gaile McGregor in *The Wacousta Syndrome* (1985), demonstrates the fortress mentality at the center of Canadian culture, caused by a fear of the Canadian wilderness. Yet there is a different Wacousta syndrome to be argued for as well, and it is equally central to the development of Canadian consciousness: the ability to repress resentment and rebelliousness, so that Canada appears a model colony.

The fiction of McCulloch, Haliburton, and Galt casts the emerging ideology of empire, and the *Blackwood's* model, in a more consistently ambiguous light. All three writers had complicated personal relationships with William Blackwood's publishing empire. Although Galt was the first and most influential of the "Blackwood novelists," he resented Blackwood's repeated alteration and censorship of his work.[97] And when Galt and McCulloch each wrote a historical novel to counter Scott's *Old Mortality* (1816), which they saw as biased against the Covenanters and as sympathetic to their Tory, royalist, and Episcopalian persecutors, Blackwood published neither novel.[98] Galt moved to Oliver and Boyd, a new publisher, for *Ringhan Gilhaize, or The Covenanters* (1823) and his two next novels.

McCulloch's *Auld Eppie's Tales* was offered to, and turned down by, Blackwood; the novel remained (and remains) unpublished. In return, when Blackwood asked to reprint his *Letters of Mephibosheth Stepsure* (originally published between 1821 and 1823 in the *Acadian Recorder*), McCulloch refused the offer, expressing his disapproval of both Blackwood's publishing house and his magazine, and thereby forwent British publication altogether.[99]

Thomas Chandler Haliburton, however, began his writing career as a member of a Halifax literary clique that fashioned itself explicitly on *Blackwood's* editorial circle. His first publications were in the group's collectively authored "Club Papers" (published from 1828 to 1831 in *The Novascotian*), modeled on *Blackwood's* "Noctes Ambrosiae"; their imitation was so successful that Blackwood proposed the club members as the new editors of *Blackwood's*.[100] Haliburton's first book, *A Historical and Statistical Account of Nova Scotia* (1829), quotes a famous line about Scotland from Scott's "Lay of the Last Minstrel"—"This is my own, my native land"—as the epigraph to its portrait of Nova Scotia.[101] In the very act of announcing his engagement with his own country, then, Haliburton performs an act of literary homage that links Nova Scotia once more to Scotland and that evokes Scott as the most powerful representative of national identity. But although Haliburton's earliest works take Scott and the Scottish regionalists as their literary models, his later works snipe repeatedly at Scott as a nostalgic sentimentalist.

Galt, McCulloch, and Haliburton all see the empire in distinctly non-Blackwoodsian terms, as a political structure whose enormous disparities of wealth, power, and freedom seem less likely to create a lofty new sense of joint cause than to forge bonds of slavery or dependence. The empire represents economic exploitation, moral disconnection, and psychic dislocation; each writer is particularly obsessed with one of these imperial effects, in accord with his own particular occupation. Minister; judge and parliamentarian; colonizer and territorial administrator: McCulloch, Haliburton, and Galt criticize the empire from different sectors of the colonial elite.

Sent from Scotland by the colonial missionary service of the Presbyterian Church, McCulloch helped to establish higher education in Nova Scotia and became the first president of Dalhousie College. As a man of learning and of God, McCulloch condemns slavery and commerce as sources of moral contamination. Now remembered as a first example of Canadian humorous writing, McCulloch's *Stepsure Letters* chronicles the life of a small Nova Scotia town, populated by Scots settlers, with a distinctly Scottish tone and annalistic perspective. Yet if such features suggest a simple transposition of Scottish literature into a Scotch-Canadian setting, the very first

letter—a cautionary fable about the way commerce breeds commerce, colonies colonialism, and slavery slaveries—insists that colonial life, even at
the most local level, is implicated in the imperial project.[102] With the help
of the West India merchant Calibogus (who trades in tobacco, tea, and
"West India produce," the goods of slavery and colonial oppression), Nova
Scotia settler Solomon Gosling sets himself up as a storekeeper, introducing credit, consumerism, and class division into his town. He also bank-
rupts himself, grows dissatisfied with Nova Scotia's economic opportunities, and resolves to emigrate to a more promising colony.

> "The truth is . . . the country does not deserve to be lived in. There is neither
> trade nor money in it, and produce gives nothing. It is fit only for Indians, and
> emigrants from Scotland, who were starving at home. It is time for me to go
> elsewhere, and carry my family to a place that presents better prospects to
> young folks. . . ."
>
> The whole family agreed that, then, with the rest of his property, they would
> go to a country better worth the living in. I found among them, however, a
> diversity of opinion about where this should be. . . . Miss Dinah preferred the
> Cape of Good Hope, but she was afraid of the Caffres, who sometimes carry
> off white women. To elope with a lord or a duke, she observed, would be a
> very pretty incident, but should any person ever write a novel about the Gos-
> lings, to be carried off by a Hottentot would appear so droll. Upon the whole,
> they seemed to think the opinion of Miss Fanny most feasible; that it would be
> best to go to Botany Bay, where every genteel family like the Goslings, re-
> ceives so many white niggers, sent out every year from Britain by Government
> for the supply of the colony.[103]

As the family rehearses its possible colonial destinations, it is most drawn
to those in which white settlers have automatic standing and privileges. In
Botany Bay, with its unending supply of indentured convicts to serve them
as "white niggers," their mastery will be complete. McCulloch's fable indicts an imperial economy built on, implicated in, and connected by slavery. Rather than seeing political domination (Caliban's struggle with Prospero over the possession of the colonized island) as the crux of empire,
McCulloch focuses on the economic complicity that empire creates; the
far-reaching trade routes of Calibogus double the routes of slavery.[104]

Like McCulloch, Haliburton is haunted by the specter of slavery. Born
into a prominent Nova Scotian family, he spends his working life as a
lawyer, justice, and supreme court judge, as Tory member of the Nova
Scotia legislature and of the British Parliament. Over many decades, his
fiction remains preoccupied with the nature, distribution, and self-
deceptions of political power. His earliest and greatest literary success, his
Sam Slick sketches (serialized from 1835 onward in the *Novascotian*),

travesties the young United States, whose insistent rhetoric of freedom and individual liberty cloaks the murderousness of its capitalist economy, which mixes Caribbean-style slave labor with brutalizing industrial wage labor. The Irish who flee famine by emigrating to the United States find themselves in a second death trap, paid starvation wages and literally worked to death.[105]

> "Upon my soul . . . the poor labourer does not last long in your country; what with new rum, hard labour, and hot weather, you'll see the graves of the Irish each side of the canal, for all the world like two rows of potatoes in a field that have forgot to come up."
>
> "[The United States] is a land, sir . . . of hard work. We have two kinds of slaves, the niggers and the white slaves. All European labourers and blacks, who come out to us, do our hard bodily work, while we direct it to a profitable end; neither rich nor poor, high nor low, with us, eat the bread of idleness. . . . An idle fellow . . . who runs away to us, is clapt into harness afore he knows where he is, and is made to work; like a horse that refuses to draw, he is put into the steamboat; he finds some before him and others behind him; he must either draw, or be dragged to death."[106]

In the British Empire, a similarly grandiose rhetoric of allegiance and meritocracy is belied by a civil service that runs on patronage and favors the English elite.[107] The empire harnesses indigenous talents but refuses to give colonials their due; it drains indigenous riches without giving enough back.

Epistemologically and formally, Haliburton's fiction is preoccupied with the centrality of a traveling perspective for colonial consciousness, given the empire's economic, administrative, military, and migratory circuits. In the first series of Sam Slick sketches (republished as *The Clockmaker* in 1836), the self-congratulatory rhetoric of the peripatetic Yankee peddler lays bare not only the ideological contradictions of American society but the fundamental instability of the traveling perspective. *The Letter-Bag of the Great Western, or Life in a Steamer* (1840) is a collection of letters written during an Atlantic passage by boat passengers, from cabin holders to servants, slaves, and sailors. The book's formal structure suggests the radically heterogeneous and rootless character of colonial life, with nothing holding it together; the boat's passengers, indeed, include emigrants who remain so restless they "cannot settle" and instead migrate continually between settler colonies.[108] *The Old Judge, or Life in a Colony* (1849) argues that colonial government is based on the interchangeability of postings, and that colonies therefore breed a perpetual motion, which renders impossible the development of a colonial national character. Somewhat surprisingly, then, Haliburton's last major work, *The Season-Ticket* (1860), pleads for a better imperial transport and communication network to link imperial outposts. A series of sketches ostensibly written during a rail journey through Britain, *The Season-Ticket* goes further than any of Haliburton's previous works in suggesting the loss, in transit, of a coherent sense of place.

> Everything has altered its dimensions, except the world we live in. The more we know of that, the smaller it seems. Time and distance have been abridged, remote countries have become accessible, and the antipodes are upon visiting terms. There is a reunion of the human race; and the family likeness, now that we begin to think alike, dress alike, and live alike, is very striking. The South Sea Islanders, and the inhabitants of China, import their fashions from Paris, and their fabrics from Manchester, while Rome and London supply missionaries to the "ends of the earth," to bring its inhabitants into "one fold, under one Shepherd."[109]

In *The Clockmaker*, twenty-five years earlier, Haliburton had seen in the American development of railroad technology the murderous advance and mechanization of American capitalism; here mechanized transport appears as an indispensable vehicle for imperial commerce, for cultural interchange, and for a new transcolonial cosmopolitanism.

For John Galt, the effect of economic modernization is to derail the political struggle for democratization, both within Britain and throughout the empire. Galt's parallel professional careers, as merchant and lawyer, colonizer and professional writer, at several imperial nodal points (Greenock, London, and Upper Canada) inform his annalistic case studies. A family chronicle that details eighteenth-century Scottish social history (*The Entail*); the annalistic "autobiographies" of a rural Presbyterian minister (*Annals of the Parish*) and a zealous Covenanter (*Ringhan Gilhaize*), of a corrupt, modernizing town councilor (*The Provost*) and a laird impoverished by the same modernity (*The Last of the Lairds*), of an optimistic businessman who emigrates to America (*Lawrie Todd, or The Settlers in the Woods*) and a depressive imperial trader who emigrates to Canada (*Bogle Corbet, or The Emigrants*), of a Tory member of Parliament (*The Member*) and a Chartist reformer (*The Radical*): these novels form a panoramic, historical survey of modern Scotland worthy of Balzac or Zola.

They also suggest the influence of the British imperial economy on Scottish history. *The Entail* sees the failure of the Darien colony as the beginning of Scotland's fiscal and political colonization. *The Last of the Lairds* traces the social displacement caused when the influx of new wealth generated from colonial revenues—personified by Mr. Rupees, the nabob who returns from Bengal to his native Renfrewshire loaded with ill-gotten gains and Anglo-Indian idioms—challenges the traditional political authority of the Scottish aristocracy. Although these "Blackwood's novels" of the 1820s are wary about the empire's influence on Scottish consciousness,

Galt's own career becomes inextricably bound, during the same decade, with imperial consolidation.

In 1824 a group of United Empire Loyalists hired Galt to obtain British government recompense for damages they sustained during the War of 1812. Galt proposed that the government raise the money by colonizing several large tracts of government land in Upper Canada—and found himself superintendent of the new Canada Company. Moving to Upper Canada, Galt founded several towns and supervised the settlement of the Ontario townships.[110] Yet when he ran afoul of the Family Compact, Upper Canada's powerful oligarchic clique, his career as a colonizer unraveled completely; in 1829 the Canada Company recalled Galt to Britain and fired him without his back salary, forcing him into debtors' prison. There he began two contrasting novels about his North American experiences—the optimistic *Lawrie Todd, or The Settlers in the Woods* and the sober *Bogle Corbet, or The Emigrants*.

For two volumes, the depressive Bogle Corbet recounts his failed industrial and mercantile careers in Britain and the West Indies; in the third, he emigrates to Upper Canada, oversees a new Scottish settlement in the forest, and struggles to maintain control over the settlers. He faces not only republican influences from the nearby United States (with its allures of economic and political liberty) but, more important, the old Jacobin ideals of the settlers, Glaswegian artisans with a shared history of struggle in the 1790s. Once a youthful Jacobin sympathizer, Bogle Corbet now echoes United Empire Loyalist rhetoric, extolling the oligarchic mode of Scotch-British settlement, in contrast to the anarchic and individualistic American settlements in nearby upstate New York.

The nationally inflected modern reception history of *Bogle Corbet* has enshrined this contrast between a loyally colonial Upper Canada and a rebelliously republican United States as the main point of the novel. In 1977, during a period of intense anti-American sentiment and equally intense literary nationalism in Canada, *Bogle Corbet* received its first modern and first Canadian printing, in the canon-forming New Canadian Library of McClelland and Stewart, "the Canadian publishers."[111] The reprinting, however, involved severe abridgment, omitting the first two-thirds of the novel, so that only Bogle Corbet's Canadian sojourn remained.[112] Apparently working from this abridgment—and often conflating Galt with his narrator—the novel's few subsequent commentators have read it as an affirmative account of imperial growth, as a settler colony transplants Old World virtues into a new colonial situation.[113]

The full novel deserves a more complex reading. Like Galt's other annalistic novels, *Bogle Corbet* uses the personal history of its first-person narrator to focus attention on the internal development and historical force of an ideological position, even though the shifts, breaks, and prevarications within the narrator's speaking voice point up internal inconsistencies, blind spots, and hypocrisies. This novel's extended comparative study of empire is framed by nuanced analyses of the historical relationship between capitalism and imperialism, describing the emergence of the British Empire in relation to both the Industrial and the French Revolution. Like McCulloch and Haliburton, Galt places British North America in relation to other parts of the empire (particularly the West Indian slave colonies) and to mercantilism. For the first half of the novel, Corbet's perspective on empire is primarily that of Glasgow. An early node of imperial trade (and therefore one of Britain's earliest industrial centers), Glasgow's boom periods were punctuated by recurrent, devastating crashes, often precipitated by events in the colonies. The tobacco trade, the first basis of the city's mercantile fortunes, collapsed in the wake of the American Revolutionary War, and the crash of the 1790s was precipitated by the collapse of a major Glasgow West India house. Attempting to corner the slave trade, Alexander Huston and Company transported thousands of Africans to the West Indies. There proved to be no market for so many slaves; many of them starved to death, the West India house declared bankruptcy, and the Glasgow banks failed.[114] As Glasgow's economic life made visible, the enormous financial gains of empire were matched not only by enormous financial risks but also by the erosion of social stability and moral values.

Corbet is a product of empire on every level. Born in Jamaica to a Scottish planter, his earliest and deepest bonds are to his Jamaican nurse, Baba. Orphaned while still very young, he undergoes a traumatic separation from Baba as well, and then is sent back to Scotland to be educated. He eventually enters the cotton business. Yet the mercantilist teachings of his new guardian, MacIndoe, a merchant who made his fortune in the East and West Indies, cannot replace the sympathies formed at Baba's breast. "When I heard the merchants talk of their West Indian articles, I used to speculate not in them, but on what, in time, would become of the islands when the Negroes got understanding. . . . [R]eflections of that kind were neither favourable to the making of money, nor to the attainment of eminence in Glasgow."[115]

At work in a Glasgow cotton mill during the 1780s and 1790s, Corbet watches the rise of large-scale manufacturing, the emergence of an industrial working class, and the growing influence of Jacobinism among the workers, a confluence of developments that leads him to reflect both on the uncontrollability of historical change once set in motion and on the apparent inevitability of revolution in the West Indies. Yet by the beginning of the nineteenth century, Corbet has become a West India merchant, fully involved in the business of empire. He mixes, in London, with a circle of repatriated Anglo-Indians, solicits the patronage of an India director, and marries his natural daughter.

When his business founders, he travels to Jamaica, but his native land disturbs him, reawakening his old doubts. Although the "degradation" of slavery is less harsh than he expected (especially compared with European wage slavery), Jamaica's slaveholding history has permanently undermined the colony's economic and political stability: living in fear of black uprisings and retributions, the white settlers see the island as "only a scene of temporary possession . . . [with] every thing . . . prepared for a sudden abandonment" (1:305). The colonization project, then, has already failed, emotionally and ideologically, in advance of any revolution—and this failure marks human relations on the island. Although happily reunited with his nurse, Baba, and an affectionate foster sister, Corbet also has an unnerving encounter with a modern Sycorax, a West Indian Meg Merrilies: a deformed old woman whose peculiar dialect proves to be a "Negro Scotch." In her youth, in captivity, she had been the slave mistress of a Scottish plantation overseer, until she and her "African lover" rose up against their master's authority, murdered him, burned down his house, and escaped to join the Maroons. In Corbet's continuing ties to his black foster family, the slaveholding system seems to keep its paternalist promises, forging familial bonds between master and slave women. Yet the Maroon woman's "wild mockery of language" (1:299), with its taunting traces of Scots, eerily evokes the coerced circumstances under which such affective and cultural transferences take place—and the rebellious violence beneath the colony's surface.

In slaveholding Jamaica, property relations underlie personal relations. Even in Scotland, Highland lairds who once defined themselves by their clan and its familial alliances are beginning to "stoop from their dignity to pick up commercial money" and send their youngest sons "into the armies as subalterns, or as cadets to India" (1:74). Traveling through the Highlands and Hebrides, Corbet meditates on the advent of capitalism and the collapse of clan culture, on the creeping "disease of depression and lassitude" and on mass emigration to the New World. "The Highlands," argues one local informant, "have seen their best days; the chieftains are gone, and the glory of the claymore is departed forever. . . . This country is now but for sheep—Men have no business here" (2:219–20). Captain Campbell, a Highlander who joined the British Army and then yearned for his native surrounding, "remembered in distant scenes as the pleasantest that the earth could contain," had returned to his old home after many years to find it deserted, an "empty place" in which "all that had endeared it in recollection existed no more." Depressed and "weary," he "resolved to seek another scene" (2:220), probably Canada. His reasoning echoes that in *Clan-Albin*. Because the British Army initially took him away from Scotland, the only community he has left is in Canada, in the company of fellow veterans.

> [A]ll countries are alike to me: it is one of the advantages of a military life that we lose local attachments. Before my return, every place had something about it inferior to my own house, but the delusion is gone. . . . Canada will probably have my bones; for several officers whom I knew in the army have settled with their families there. I have no comrades here, and it sweetens death to fall among companions. (2:221)

In light of this story and the overall situation of the Highlands, Corbet's immigration to Canada, immediately afterward, and his attempts there to reconstruct a traditional mode of Scottish settlement seem both compensatory and ambivalent.

Given Corbet's history of political doubt, his traumatic personal bankruptcy, and the moral bankruptcy he feels in Jamaica, in London's Anglo-Indian community, and in a rapidly changing Scotland, Upper Canada represents not so much a personal fresh start as a last chance for the entire imperial system. Settled there at the end of the novel, Corbet becomes a vocal defender of empire and of the British order. Yet he has sunk into recurring, almost suicidal depression, and the novel ends on a note of profound pessimism.

> But though many days are here blank leaves in the book of life, let me not be misunderstood; I have no cause to regret my emigration; I have only been too late. . . . Emigration should be undertaken at that period when youths are commonly sent to trades and professions: the hardships are too heavy an apprenticeship for manhood, and to riper years penalty and privation. (3:302; M&S, p. 198)

If Canada is meant to be the salvation of the imperial system, it fails utterly as the salvation of Corbet himself.

With its passage to Canada in the third volume, the novel offers not so much a new beginning as a restaging of all of its political and economic issues within a fresh colonial context. Mass emigration from Britain, as Corbet analyzes it, arises from industrialization, because "agricultural changes, and the introduction of new machinery, is constantly throwing off swarms of operatives who have no other resource" (2:234; M&S, p. 11). For such workers, now stripped both of economic self-sufficiency and artisanal identity, North America offers the hope of renewed economic and political agency. Corbet's real sympathies, however, lie with the smaller group of middle-class emigrants "in impaired, or desperate circumstances, unable to preserve their caste in the social system of this country, wrecked and catching at emigration as the last plank" (2:234; M&S, p. 11). Whereas British industrialization depends on the materials and the capital that the colonies produce, the colonies appear, for an impoverished gentry, as a final refuge from the economic transformation of Britain, as from an encroaching democracy that would deprive them of their last privileges.

Yet even in emigration the indignities of modernity cannot be evaded. When he founds his town in the forests of Canada, Corbet attempts to establish a genteel ascendancy. The majority of "his" settlers, however, have emigrated in search of new political freedoms and continue to agitate for self-government. On the eve of the passage of the First Reform Bills, and shortly before the Upper and Lower Canada Rebellions, this backwoods conflict over future political life reiterates the British class struggles, between Jacobins and property holders, fought throughout the 1790s. At stake now is nothing less than the political and social temporality of the new colony.

> On the one side rolled the majestic St. Lawrence . . . and on the other the primeval forest, with a narrow strip of cleared land between, stood like the arborous wall of Paradise, with, here and there at long intervals, a narrow vista into the green Eden of the new settlements beyond. The landscape is, however, solitary, and, to say the truth, is to the emigrant a little saddening. It lacks the social cheerfulness of villages . . . the gorgeous castle, the manorial hall, and the mouldering monastic piles of the olden time, which make the landscape of England, in the variety of its imagery, so like the associations of the English mind. (2:302; M&S, p. 45)

Trusting to the openness of its future, will the colony understand itself as a new Eden, an attempt to form a new social contract and a new social order? Or, as a last refuge from British modernization, will it insist, at all costs, on the transplantation and preservation of the old order?[116] Will the colony be a place of new beginnings, or will it be consecrated to the nostalgic worship of distant ruins?

A disgruntled, eccentric local doctor frames the problem with a different emphasis: "[F]ostering in himself absurd antipathies against the Celtic settlers" (2:11; M&S, p. 55), he insists that the new immigrants from Paisley, from the Highlands, and from Ireland should not stick together in the new colony but instead mix with other groups to form a new and more productive whole. If this formulation invokes, once more, the old allegory of British national reconciliation in the new context of the empire, the choice of mouthpiece here suggests considerable ironic distance. Galt's framing of the colonial situation of Canada, indeed, insists that the weight of history and of the imperial system make a new union, a truly fresh beginning, a virtual impossibility.

Already as Corbet and his family approach the Canadian coast, the immigrant ship encounters a huge iceberg, and it is saved from destruction only because the iceberg fissures internally and breaks apart. Corbet and his fellow passengers are overwhelmed not only by their mortal peril but by the iceberg's sublime scale and chilly radiance: they face the iceberg as if it were "a whole dreadful continent, for such it seemed" (2:256; M&S, p. 22). An ominous, frozen embodiment of North America threatens to crush them, before shattering into tiny pieces, rent by its own furious instabilities. Profoundly shaken by this glimpse of an alien and precarious natural world, Corbet tries to regain psychic stability through a predictive interpretation of the landscape around him, as the boat enters the Saint Lawrence; informed at once by the tradition of Calvinist hermeneutics, by superstition, and by deep-rooted personal neurosis, he anxiously studies a change in the color of the water.

> There was nothing in this which a very little reflection might not have explained; but my mind, naturally, perhaps, too apt to ponder on mysterious causes, regarded the phenomenon, so common where rivers diffuse themselves in the ocean, as a consequence of some great internal turbulence—an earthquake, or a deluge proceeding from the snows being suddenly melted by a volcano! (2:258; M&S, p. 23)

As we realize over the course of "A Shipwreck," the following chapter, Corbet is merely projecting his need for repression onto the landscape. For when the boat passes Anticosti Island (2:260; M&S, p. 24) and a tempest threatens to drive it onto the rocks, Corbet and his fellow passengers anxiously remember a horrible shipwreck on the same rocks, then succeed, for the moment, in suppressing what they have read of that accident. Yet the memory resurfaces repeatedly over the next pages, always still half-suppressed, always only half-articulated, as the boat approaches the "forbidden isle" (2:260–61; M&S, p. 24). Finally, in the crisis of the storm, we learn what has happened on the island to render it such a place of horror. "That dismal Anticosta, and the cannibalism of necessity by which its unblest shores had been rendered so frightful to the imagination, acted like sorcery upon me, warranting fancies wilder than the roaring tempest" (2:263; M&S, p. 26).

Although it appears concerned with present-day events, "A Shipwreck" proves preoccupied with an overshadowing past. With its cannibalism, tempests, and sorcery, this episode constantly conjures up the famous Renaissance works that describe first arrivals in the New World. In Christopher Columbus's *Diario* (the log he kept from 1492 to 1504), initial descriptions of an Edenic tropical landscape give way to a paranoid obsession with the threat of Carib cannibalism, as the Spaniards project their own acquisitive desire to absorb the whole New World onto its indigenous inhabitants.[117] So too in Shakespeare's *Tempest* (1611), the exiled Prospero, conjurer of the storms, secures a Caribbean island at the expense of its native inhabitant; this imperial takeover is implicitly justified by the native's name, Caliban, which invokes the savage cannibalism imputed to the Caribs from Columbus onward.

Two hundred years later, Bogle Corbet's first contact with Canada is still overshadowed by the imperial conquest of the Caribbean. As recently as 1796, when in the wake of the Maroon Wars, Jamaica's colonial government decided to deport the rebellious Trelawny Town Maroons to another part of the British Empire, they were first to be sent to colonize Upper Canada. Instead, the rebels were deported to Nova Scotia. There they spent several years on land previously assigned to discharged British soldiers and, once abandoned by them, by black American loyalists, ex-slaves who had deserted their American masters during the American Revolutionary War, fled to Canada (where they received their freedom from the British government), and later resettled en masse in the new colony of Sierra Leone. The Maroons would eventually follow them there, daunted by the Nova Scotia climate and disappointed that they were not, as they had hoped, enlisted in the British Army in India or at the Cape.[118]

Bogle Corbet's private history, as he moves from Jamaica to Britain to Canada, recapitulates this imperial history of economic, military, and political connection. To the transcolonial Corbet, as to the globe-trotting Dunlop, the empire's places and peoples come to seem superimposed on one other: Quebec appears as a reincarnation of Edinburgh, the habitants as Highlanders (2:269; M&S, p. 29). Corbet's suffering, as he himself realizes dimly, has historical and transcolonial sources. But he is also psychically committed to sociopolitical and historical repetition. Born into the plantation system and bred into mercantilism, Corbet's first and only assertion of intellectual autonomy is his youthful turn to Jacobinism. But he is gradually reabsorbed by British and imperial power structures, and by the time he comes to establish his own settlement in the Canadian wilderness, he is using a capitalist and feudal model derived from the plantation system. Despite his fundamental doubts, then, about the authoritarian forms of power that accompanied imperialist expansion in the Caribbean, and despite his wish to escape to a part of the empire not yet marked by them, he is compelled to reconstruct them afresh, in the Canadian forests, to build the new colony in the image of the old.

At first Corbet seems critical of the colonial administration: it appears fundamentally uninterested in the welfare of its new citizens, yet it is routinely engaged, through a bloated and overzealous judiciary, in "the irksome evil of excessive surveillance" (2:308; M&S, p. 48). Yet once he has established his own settlement, Corbet implements surveillance procedures to maintain his own authority: increasingly uninterested in the well-being of the other settlers, and increasingly annoyed by their "mutinies," their insistence on self-determination and freedom of movement, he watches over the settlement "with that constant and strict vigilance . . . , which every day rendered more necessary" (3:65; M&S, p. 82). Eventually, he assembles a sizable police force, empowered to enforce a military "discipline." "The advantage of an arrangement of this kind," argues his new police chief, "can only be appreciated by those who have seen it in the army, and compared its effects with the misrule and confusion which arise among the same men, when relieved by the accidents of war from the restraints of discipline" (3:73–74; M&S, p. 86). With this declaration of permanent martial law, the Jacobin hope of establishing a self-governing and self-regulating community in the New World seems sunk forever.

In the economic organization of the settlement, the Jacobin settlers are betrayed by the "gentleman magistrate," whom they once perceived as a sympathetic fellow traveler. As the area's major landowner, Corbet organizes the clearance of forests, the building of roads and houses so that they will enhance his property, trying to keep all farmland himself and to sequester the settlers in the new town of Stockwell. They demand their own homesteads, to become economically self-sufficient. Yet Corbet controls the food stockpile for the territory, and winter is coming; threatening starvation to anyone who protests, he blackmails the settlement into submission. Although the settlers have labored to fashion the wilderness into a new home, it is never to be truly theirs, any more than the factories of Glasgow, made prosperous by their labor, would ever have come into their possession.

> "Angus, I thought you not wanting in common sense; when a weaver in the Gorbals, had you any right to the webs [looms] you were employed to work?"
>
> "But there's a wide difference, Sir, between the Gorbals and this wild country, which was all ta'en from the Indians, who have the best right to the land, if any body has a right; and I am sure you would na go far ajee frae justice, if you would think of our request."
>
> "Depend upon 't, Angus, I shall think of it, and the reasons ye have stated to make me comply; for the King's law is here as well as in the old country; and I can assure you that I am as little disposed to indulge covetousness in Canada as I would have been in Glasgow, had you pretended such a right to any property of mine there." (3:46–47; M&S, pp. 73–74)

Caught in the tempest off Anticosti Island, Corbet seemed tormented by the memory of the imperial cannibalization of the New World. And when radical weavers, in the forests of Canada, challenge the reemergence of oligarchy, Corbet has a final chance to reverse the course of colonial history and to found a settlement marked by a new kind of justice. (As Angus M'Questin points out, the land they are settling has all been "ta'en from the

Indians," and the only way of expiating for that first appropriation is to insist henceforth on distributive justice.) Instead, citing biblical authority and British legal precedent, Corbet dismisses the Jacobin claim altogether.

As narrator of his own autobiography, Corbet's continual efforts to justify his position amount to an ideological filter, through which the reader is shown a particular vision of imperial and Canadian life. At regular intervals, however, Galt allows the reader to see the limits of the narrative perspective, how much it regularly omits. Corbet's exchange with M'Questin is one such moment. The problem of equality *within* the settler community raises the problem of conquest and settlement in the first place—yet it is only the old Jacobins, still in quest of freedom and justice, who make the equation. As Corbet recognizes, this question shakes the moral foundations of his settlement. But in public, at least, he refuses to acknowledge it, and the displacement and disfranchisement of the Indians is carefully suppressed from the remainder of his narrative.

Such suppressions structure the whole novel. Corbet starts his life in Jamaica, yet when he enters the mercantile world, he begins to forget the human price of the plantations. As a Glasgow industrialist and as a visitor to the Highlands, he watches the Industrial Revolution destroy Scotland's economic, social, and cultural life. Yet he departs for Canada extolling the imperial system and apostrophizing England as "my native land" (3:250; M&S, p. 19). It is as if his Caribbean birth and Scottish education had been replaced by a new life narrative, as if, by willful self-reconstruction, he could somehow make himself into a real Englishman, to become master of his destiny at last. In Canada, finally, as he sets up his own colony within a colony, the personal and political insights accumulated over the first two volumes of his autobiography become increasingly hazy and then irretrievable. Haunted by empire, the imperialist becomes a hollow man.

> By this time I was sensible of a curious change incrusting, if I may say, my mind; no doubt an effect of our sequestration in the forest. Every little occurrence, which in other circumstances would have passed unheeded, became important. ... In the same manner, remote transactions lost their interest, in proportion to their distance they became indistinct, and seemed to occupy no larger space in the mind, however consequential, than nearer trifles. (3:125; M&S, p. 112)[119]

If Corbet's final ideological resting point represents both the issue and the denial of the events of the previous thirty years, so too early-nineteenth-century British ideological investment in Canada and the other new settler colonies both subsumes and sublates the problems of the eighteenth-century empire. Upper Canada's success as a colony is to compensate for the perceived debacle of the West Indies. The West Indies were colonized already during the Renaissance, Upper Canada founded only in 1791. Its ideological formation, then, is the product of a later moment not only in imperial history but also in the development of imperial rhetoric.

Yet as Bogle Corbet's case shows clearly, there can be no new Edens after the Fall. Marked by an early exposure to Britain's most brutal colony, scarred by the political betrayals of the 1790s, Corbet arrives in Canada in the 1820s obsessed with cannibalism and class privilege and depressed by the cumulative weight of British history. This baggage makes any real fresh start fundamentally impossible; as he puts it at the end of his autobiography, "I have only been too late."

Both its own history and the ongoing operations of the empire lock Canada into triangulated relationships with its fellow colonies and with its British home base. Corbet's relationship to Britain (and even to Scotland) has been deeply troubled from the beginning, undermined by the buried attachments and memories of Jamaica. And even when Corbet seeks a fresh start in Canada, decades later, the half-suppressed, traumatic history of Jamaica (the love induced by Baba, the terror induced by the Maroons, and the moral dilemmas of slavery and exploitation) is carried along to a new setting, inducing recurrent, lingering bouts of depression, which prevent any real adaptation to Canadian life. Galt's depiction of the sociogenesis of mental illness follows both the abolitionist literature of the 1790s and the national tale of the 1810s: an early contact with Caribbean slavery leaves Corbet permanently contaminated, prey to a recurring, festering malaise.

Like Claud Walkinshaw, Corbet is formed by a particular, indelible historical trauma, which continues to paralyze and arrest his development while historical time goes on without him. At the same time, he is continually pushed forward—bruised, exhausted, frozen inside himself, and conscious of his own anachronism—through all the historical time that comes after his moment of formation. Corbet's depression is at once the cumulative product of two centuries of British history and the effect of a particular historical conjuncture, a specific moment of imperial crisis. With its complicated movement from old colonies to new, Corbet's story recapitulates the whole development of the empire. Yet it is also narrated in a psychic vocabulary produced by a particular moment of imperial self-delusion amd denial.

Read as a psychological novel (along the lines suggested by Defoe, Edgeworth and Sherwood, Lockhart and Godwin, as by the national fostering plot), *Bogle Corbet* recounts a traumatic early separation from a beloved (although enslaved) love object, the native nurse; the reinvestment of emotional energies in a political movement that fails; a series of unhappy romantic choices; the increasing replacement of human attachments by mercantile relations, of a settled emotional life by an accelerating circulation between places; and finally, in the Canadian forests, recurring bouts of despair. If these elements are read as intellectual history, the novel's progression—from an emotional attachment to an idealized noble slave and a political commitment to European and colonial emancipation, to mercantile ventures and commercial failures, to recurring crises of imperialist conscience, and finally to complete ideological and financial investment in the settler colony as a fresh start—chronicles the development, and growing false consciousness, of British attitudes toward the empire. The novel shows us how Corbet's personal repetition compulsions—and the British compulsion to repeat, again and again, the fundamental injustices of colonization—are accompanied by a profound amnesia that both fuels a neurotic sense of disorientation and imparts a temporary, stabilizing illusion that the contradictions of ideology and experience can be reconciled.

Bogle's odd first name has a double meaning in Scots usage: a bogle is either a haunting bogeyman or a scarecrow.[120] Appropriately, Bogle Corbet is both a figure haunted by a suppressed past, by the specters of slavery and revolution, and a tattered figure whose sense of subjectivity becomes hollowed out under the weight of repression and depression. The more Corbet repeats the false moves of empire, the less he seems able to remember what he is doing, let alone to reflect on its long-term consequences. Seized with a particularly virulent form of emigrant's amnesia, Corbet ends his autobiography without referring back to anything that happened before Canada, as if unable to remember anything about where he came from. This same amnesia informs the McClelland and Stewart abridgment and the subsequent Canadian reception of the novel: a "transcolonial" writing of empire is received and preserved so partially that only "national literatures" remain.

CALIBOGUS, CALIBAN

Contemporary discussions (and syllabi) of postcolonial literature often begin with the famous cluster of postwar texts that reexamined Caliban's struggle with Prospero to begin analyzing imperial power relations.[121] As this chapter has argued, such self-consciously postcolonial writing builds at least implicitly on a critical *colonial* tradition of writing about the empire, begun by writers such as McCulloch, Haliburton, and Galt. One of the first tasks of the new field of postcolonial literary studies must be to reexamine this relationship, to reread colonial literature itself, and to investigate a much broader and more varied body of work than discussed heretofore.

In the meantime, most depictions of imperial and colonial culture still work either from fairly static notions of the interaction between center and periphery, colonizer and colonized, or from nationalist developmental narratives that are equally problematic. The problem with the first model of imperial interaction is that its terms often seem fixed at the moment of conquest (if not, indeed, to follow imperial mythology and iconography, already at the moment of "discovery" and contact). Although it appears more dynamic, the nationalist model is problematic for different reasons. Even if the colony was not a self-contained political entity before its incorporation into the empire, argue Benedict Anderson and Partha Chatterjee, the experience of colonialism, paradoxically, creates a new sense of national cohesion and initiates the classic process of nation formation, which can culminate in a national liberation struggle, even in eventual autonomy from the empire. Thus European rule shaped Arab and African nationalism out of regional or tribal identities, and the empires of the Mughals and then the Raj shaped the multiethnic South Asian subcontinent into a single "India."[122]

The political analysis of colonial life tends to situate it between two moments: on one hand, its helpless or reluctant subordination to the directives of a distant imperial center; and on the other hand, its resistance to imperial efforts at homogenization, the revival of native leadership and indigenous social forms, and the launching of campaigns for national autonomy.[123] Very similar categories have been used to discuss and canonize colonial literatures. The colony's early literary production is thus characterized by its imitative, reactive, and subordinated relationship to the literature of the imperial center.[124] Then, as time and distance increase the separation between "home countries" and colonies, and as the colonial educational system produces an indigenous intelligentsia and reading public, the growing influence of indigenous material and literary forms begins to shape a distinctive, autonomous colonial literature. At some point, then, each colony sees a second literary beginning, with the emergence of a more clearly national literature. Literary historians have typically emphasized the Victorian period as the real imperial era, and they have replicated both strictly imperial and strictly national principles in their attention to the subordination and reemergence of nations in empires. Their investigations have left virtually unexamined a significant body of earlier literature, written both in Britain and in the colonies, which describes the experience of empire in terms of the transcolonial consciousness and transperipheral circuits of influence it creates.

The last thirty years have seen a new wave of self-consciously literary reckonings, throughout the former British Empire, with the legacies of imperialism. In parallel, the academic study of the English-language literature of empire has undergone a conceptual and political shift, moving away from Commonwealth literature, the shared colonial reception of imperial traditions, to the history of resistant, critical, and indigene literatures within each colony, and the contemporary postcolonial literature being written both within the nation-states of Africa, Asia, the South Pacific, Canada, and the Caribbean and by émigré writers living in Britain and elsewhere.

The old study of Commonwealth literature was often affirmative, implicitly sympathetic to the cultural mission of empire, and concerned primarily with what was either literally or metaphorically a "white writing" (Derrida and Coetzee); the bastions of such study, indeed, were the "white" settler colonies (Canada, Australia, and New Zealand, not Hong Kong or Pakistan).[125]

The postcolonial model has different emphases—and comparable, if different, problems.[126] Its dual preoccupations have been the indigenous and the creolized, which in some ways are collapsed into one another, as the historical problem of national political autonomy becomes merged with the quest to identify the situated specificity of new colonial cultural forms. Under the sign of postmodernity, at the same time, the new field of postcolonial literary studies has also begun to address the diasporic, internationalized character of contemporary postcolonial writing, often the work of émigrés, exiles, or deterritorialized intellectuals, and often read not only by local readers but also by a worldwide audience of émigrés. The danger of this emphasis is that the patently transcolonial and international character of much writing from the Third World will be read as a *new* development, an effect of the present globalized, postcolonial moment, rather than as a constituent feature of empire.

The parallel danger is that in each individual postcolony, literary interpretation will proceed much as usual, with parochially "historical" procedures (still territorialized searches for "indigenous voices" to claim for the national canon or countercanon) alternating only with cosmopolitan "theoretical" ones (deterritorialized intertextual readings that emphasize the sophistication, Europeanization, and mutual influence of postcolonial writing). But it is rather the *longue-durée* pull of nation against empire, the recurrent gap between the experienced specificity of culture or place and the rhythm of comparison in the traverse of "parallel" places, that gives colonial and then postcolonial literatures their particular texture. Arjun Appadurai has persuasively described the global flow of population, knowledge, tastes, and goods as a quintessential condition of late capitalism and postmodernity.[127] Such flows tend to traverse the former British Empire (as through the residual "alluvial formations" of other former empires) not only in straight lines back and forth between periphery and center but also through a large number of thoroughly transcolonial circuits or conduits, many as old as the fact of colonial settlement.

In Canada, as in other parts of the former British Empire, much of the most interesting English-language literature written over the last fifteen years has been the work of immigrants, often from other British postcolonies, such as Barbados and Sri Lanka. Their pathbreaking work in calling attention to Canada's structural racisms as an explicitly imperial and colonial legacy seems rooted in transcolonial transits and consciousness.[128] "In

Canadian literature," as Davey noted sardonically in 1986, "there are more scenes set in India than in Abbotsford," a comment simultaneously on Canadian exoticism, on the uneven distribution of literary attentions to the peripheries, and on the proverbial historical and institutional weaknesses of Canadian literature. Today the fact of a Canadian literature as interested in India and Indians (West, East, and Native) as in the imperial legacies of Abbotsford seems thoroughly unsurprising. But now, instead, it may be the historical roots of this transcolonial perspective, in the functioning of the empire, that threaten to be lost, as the present sense of globalization is misunderstood as a phenomenon without historical precedent. The danger of a postcolonial literary history is that, as its name implies, it will emphasize temporal caesuras between the empire and the postindependence life of the individual nation-state, as if the process of nation subsumed into empire, which Scott enshrines at Abbotsford, can simply be reversed and run backward. Davey's *Abbotsford Guide to India*, and the transcolonial and immigrant literatures being written throughout the former English-speaking world, ought to help us see instead how thoroughly the English view of India—and Canada, New Zealand, and Jamaica—has been guided by the novelistic institution of Abbotsford.

What a geopoliticized investigation of romantic fiction reveals is not only Scott's centrality in establishing a novel of imperial expansion but also how differently some of Scott's contemporaries imagined a critical, cosmopolitan fiction of empire. The study of their novels not only gives us an important prehistory of postcolonial perspectives but simultaneously, in the way they add Calibogus to Caliban as symbols for imperial experience, should open new ways of describing the formation of colonial consciousness.

NOTES

PREFACE

1. Bakhtin, "Forms of the Chronotope and of the Chronotope in the Novel," in *The Dialogic Imagination*,p. 84–258.

2. Moynahan, *Anglo-Irish*, p. 69. Apparently unacquainted with the eighteenth-century history of the Anglo-Irish novel, Moynahan also appears unfamiliar with the resurgence of critical work on the romantic novel over the last five to ten years.

INTRODUCTION

1. Evans, "Paraphrase of the 137th Psalm, alluding to the captivity and treatment of the Welsh Bards by King Edward I," in *Some Specimens of the Poetry of the Ancient Welsh Bards*, p. 143.

2. The 137th Psalm has had continuous resonance throughout British literature, from the poetry of Thomas Carew, Joel Barlow, and Byron to Samuel Richardson's *Pamela* (in which Pamela writes a topical version of the psalm during her captivity).

3. On the eighteenth-century development of antiquarian nationalism, see Hutchinson, *The Dynamics of Cultural Nationalism*, esp. chap. 2; Bell, ed., *The Scottish Antiquarian Tradition*; Brown, *The Hobby-Horsical Antiquary*; Morgan, *New History of Wales*, esp. chaps. 3 and 4; Jenkins, *The Foundations of Modern Wales*, esp. chaps. 6 and 10; Piggott, *Ruins in a Landscape* and *Ancient Britons*.

4. Innes, *A Critical Essay on the Ancient Inhabitants*, 2:471.

5. Ibid., 2:474, 2:423, and 1:iv.

6. Ibid., 2:476. But see also Giolla Bridhde Mac Con Midhe's mid-thirteenth-century "Defense of Poetry (addressed to a priest claiming to bring from Rome a condemnation of the Irish bards)," in Kinsella, ed., *The New Oxford Book of Irish Verse*, pp. 88–102; the end of bardic poetry would mean that "man's knowledge would reach back / no further than his father," that warriors "would have their stories hidden / for ages long . . . / nor know the roots that reared them," and that nobles "ignorant of their rights / and the complex kin of the Gael" (p. 100) would lose "access to their past" (p. 101), and thereby also lose their social position.

7. Innes' own account participates in the ongoing struggle between Irish and Scottish antiquarians over whether Ireland was initially settled by the Scots or Scotland by the Irish. Innes writes to defend the Scottish cause, yet sees his Irish counterparts moved by "private motives, and a national concern, to alter the records of settlements" (*A Critical Essay*, 2:484). The fact that "while all other nations have published their ancient antiquities" the Irish "had published none of their ancient histories" gives ground for suspicion that "they themselves distrust their authority" (2:502). Yet where there is a paucity of Scottish records, Innes laments the tragic "destruction of our historical monuments" by Edward I (as later by the Reformation), "that the Scots being quite destitute of all certainty of past transactions, and deprived of all proofs and evidences of their just rights and privileges, as

well as of the knowledge of all the braver actions of their ancestors, he might more easily enslave them, and impose what he pleased upon them without their being in a condition to produce either history or record, to defend themselves, or dispute his pretensions"(2:553).

8. During a twenty-year noviciate, the disciples of the Druidical Bards "learned an immense number of verses, in which they preserved the principles of that religious and civil polity by uninterrupted tradition for many centuries. Though the use of letters was familiar to them, they never committed their verses to writing, for the sake of strengthening their intellectual facilities, and of keeping their mysterious knowledge from the contemplation of the vulgar" (Jones, *Musical and Poetical Relicks*, p. 2).

9. Ibid., pp. 20–21. Ironically, Jones was known as the King's Bard (Bardd y Brenin), because he stood under the patronage of the crown prince. And Evans, ironically, was a correspondent and an associate of Thomas Percy and of Samuel Johnson; see Lewis, ed., *The Correspondence of Thomas Percy and Evan Evans*.

10. On the loss or perpetuation of tradition as the central preoccupation of *any* oral performance, see Gregory Nagy, "The Crisis of Performance," in John Bender and David Wellbery, eds., *The Ends of Rhetoric: History, Theory, Practice* (Stanford: Stanford University Press, 1990), pp. 43–59; on the changing self-understanding of bardic poetry in Ireland in the centuries after the conquest, see O'Riordan, *The Gaelic Mind*.

11. Jones, *Musical and Poetical Relicks*, p. 1.

12. O'Conor, *Dissertations*, p. 94.

13. Yet as we see already with Evans and Macpherson, the antiquarian desire for historical authenticity or plausibility is frequently overridden by other rhetorical and aesthetic considerations. The "Paraphrase" depends for its effect on an odd conflation of Hebrew God and pagan Druid. On the problem of anachronism in Macpherson, see Hume, "On the Authenticity of Ossian's Poems," esp. p. 417. Late-eighteenth-century and romantic illustrators of Macpherson dressed his characters alternately as Greeks, as Romans, and as medieval knights (see Hohl's *Ossian*); the illustrations to the 1805 Denham and Dick edition of *Poems of Ossian* combine details from all of these periods.

14. Nationalist discussions of the bard had strong aesthetic overtones as well. According to Macpherson and others, the bard was originally the poetic counterpart of the Druid; when the Druidic religion was suppressed, the bards took over some of their priestly functions and their religious aura. See Blackwell, *Inquiry*, p. 106; Hugh Blair, "Critical Dissertation on the Poems of Ossian," in *The Poems of Ossian*, ed. Gaskill, p. 350; Churchill's mockery of this tradition in "The Ghost," in *Poetical Works*, 2:58–59. Owenson's *Wild Irish Girl* describes a heroic age in which the bardic order was "sacred," "revered," and "inviolable" (p. 203) and portrays an elderly modern bard who, "with true druidical dignity, sat under the shade of a venerable oak" (p. 141). Even while the bard signifies collective and tribal memory, functioning as the repository and transmitter of tribal history, he becomes the representative of poetic art as a compensatory, secular religion. As Macpherson and Blair stress, Ossian lives in a world in which the Druidic religion has already died out, and in which Christianity has not yet been accepted by the Celtic tribes. In the interstices between religious world orders, only a fading heroic ethos and the

poetry that commemorates it give the Celtic warriors something to live and die for. The parallels with the late-eighteenth-century situation are unmistakable: the bard prefigures both its tendency toward the sacralization of culture and its sense of being caught between two ages.

15. According to Jones's *Musical and Poetical Relicks*, bardic duties became ever more specialized over the course of the centuries. Originally "a constitutional appendage of the druidical hierarchy, which was divided into three classes, priests, philosophers, and poets" (p. 1), the bards were redivided, at the end of the eleventh century, into new orders of poets, heralds, and musicians.

16. On these historical shifts, see Attali, *Noise*, esp. pp. 14–18, and Edmondstoune Duncan, *The Story of Minstrelsy*.

17. O'Halloran, *An Introduction*, p. ii. In eighteenth-century Ireland, argues Hutchinson, antiquarian nationalism is motivated not so much by outrage at English economic and political pressures as by the conviction that the English perceived "the Irish as *inherently* inferior and hence excluded from the full benefits of British civilization" (*Dynamics of Cultural Nationalism*, p. 63).

18. Roger Lonsdale, ed., *The Poems of Thomas Gray, William Collins, and Oliver Goldsmith* (London: Longman, 1969), p. 181.

19. Maturin, *The Milesian Chief*, 1:183–85. Aged bards make similar cameo appearances throughout early-nineteenth-century fiction, appearing at once as "a remnant of antiquity" and as the last of that "venerable race, whose profession had once been so respectable in Ireland" or Scotland or Wales (M'Henry, *O'Halloran*, 1:37).

20. Fox, *Annals of the Irish Harpers*, p. 97. See also Vance, "Celts, Carthaginians, and Constitutions," p. 228. The idea for the festival was derived from the Highland festivals already established in Scotland; in London, the month before the Belfast festival, Iolo Morganwg had staged an *eidisfodd* on Primrose Hill, reassembling a small group of London Welshmen as the druidical court of the "Bards of the Isle of Britain" (Humphreys, *The Taliesin Tradition*, p. 108; and Morgan, *New History of Wales*, p. 115).

21. See Bunting's *Ancient Music of Ireland* (1796), *A General Collection of Ancient Music of Ireland* (1809), and *Collection of the Ancient Music of Ireland* (1840), reprinted as *The Ancient Music of Ireland*. See also Andrew Carpenter, "Changing Views of Irish Musical and Literary Culture," in Kenneally, ed., *Irish Literature and Culture*, pp. 5–24, esp. 8, 24.

22. Fox, *Annals*, p. 5.

23. Tone, *Life*, 1:155–57.

24. McNeill, *Life and Times of Mary Ann McCracken*, esp. pp. 75–84.

25. Vance, "Celts, Carthaginians and Constitutions," pp. 228–31. On the aesthetic program of the United Irishmen, see Thuente, *The Harp Re-strung*.

26. Patricia Wilson, introduction to Galt, *Ringhan Gilhaize*, esp. p. vii.

27. The Friends of the People was founded in Scotland in 1792 and forcibly disbanded in 1793; twenty of its leaders were tried for sedition and transported, in 1794, to Botany Bay. In the meantime, however, Scottish radicals regrouped to form the United Scotsmen Societies, modeled (right down to its loyalty oath) on the United Irishmen. The organization remained in existence into the nineteenth century, although its 1797 uprising to establish a Scottish republic was abortive and

confined primarily to Perthshire. See here Ellis and Mac a'Ghobhainn, *The Scottish Insurrection*, esp. chaps. 3 and 4, but also John Brims, "Scottish Radicalism and the United Irishmen," in Dickson, Keogh, and Whelan, eds., *The United Irishmen*, pp. 151–66.

28. Lockhart, *Peter's Letters to His Kinsfolk*, 2:355.

29. In early-nineteenth-century Wales, in contrast, the novel did not become a major nationalist vehicle, or even (due to Methodist reservations about novel reading) a major literary form at all (Parry, *A History of Welsh Literature*, pp. 325–31). Despite the importance of Welsh scholarship and poetry to eighteenth-century bardic discussions, then, the Welsh novel will be discussed here only intermittently and unsystematically.

30. As Henry O'Halloran explains his political position on the eve of the revolution, "Irishmen have nothing to expect from English generosity. You are, I doubt not, well enough conversant in the history of our British connexion to know that it has been pregnant with nothing but oppressions and calamities to our ancestors and ourselves." The echo of Sylvester O'Halloran here is unmistakable; what is new is that such sentiments lead directly to political insurgency. See M'Henry, *O'Halloran*, 1:137.

31. See here Bowen's account of how a fear of democracy and an attendant "sense of dislocation" fostered a compensatory "cult of the glen and the tear" in early-nineteenth-century Anglo-Irish society (*Bowen's Court*, pp. 258–59).

32. Nairn, *The Enchanted Glass*, p. 174.

33. Ibid., pp. 258–59.

34. Nairn argues that the English compensate ideologically for the absence of a coherent national identity through their inordinate investment in the royal family: the royals offer a direct means of identification with the state, facilitated by the (re)invented rituals that accompany investitures.

35. See Durkacs, *The Decline of the Celtic Languages*, and Kilfeather, "'Strangers at home.'"

36. See Williams, *The Country and the City*.

37. Lockhart, *Peter's Letters*, 2:166–67.

38. Ibid., 2:354.

39. Throughout the eighteenth century, England formed the almost invariable setting of novelistic plots, even for novelists writing from Scotland or Ireland; if their novels were not actually English, they were written to pass as such. Englishness was, for the novel, the uninflected case, and therefore generally the ground for, as often as the explicit subject of, its stories. In English novels, at the same time, the treatment of Scottish or Irish culture remained superficial and stereotypical: Robert Bage's novels of the 1780s and 1790s, as Scott points out in his *Lives of the Novelists*, feature purely stage Irish and "Scotchmen" who are "still more awkward caricatures . . . the language which he puts in their mouths [is] not similar to any which has been spoken since the days of Babel" (p. 290). During the romantic period, the case is reversed: many novels—and several successive novelistic genres—derive their color, their interest, and their plots precisely from their un-Englishness. The purely English novel comes to appear quite pallid beside them (and indeed begins, in self-defense, to recast Englishness as a nationality or ethnicity whose complexity is comparable with that of the other cultures in Britain).

40. Jones's portrait of the English persecution of the Welsh bards, for instance, clearly derives from O'Conor's previous account of the English treatment of the Irish bards.

41. Over the first decades of the nineteenth century, old feelings of competitiveness begin to give way to a new mutual recognition. On a visit to Bangor in 1802, Edgeworth notes the failure of her party's attempts to communicate with the locals in English: "[T]he farmers entrenched themselves in their houses and shut their doors as fast as they could when we approached" (*A Memoir of Maria Edgeworth*, 1:109). When she visits the Highlands in 1823, however, she meets with a particularly warm reception *because* she comes from Ireland: the Highland guide "turned to me, and all reserve vanishing from his countenance, with brightening eyes he said, as he laid his hand on his breast, 'And you are Irish! Now I know that, I would do ten times as much for you if I could, than when I thought you were Southerns or English. We think the Irish have, like ourselves, more spirit.' He talked of Ossian, and said the English could not give the *force* of the original Gaelic" (2:227). It is in no small part the long-term influence of Edgeworth's Irish novels which has changed the tenor of intranational relations within Britain.

42. Green, *Scotch Novel Reading*, 1:47–51.

43. Ibid., 1:1, 1:8.

44. Austen, *Mansfield Park*, pp. 58–59. Austen's other novels are equally sardonic about fashionable harp playing. In *Persuasion* (written in 1815–16, published in 1818), Anne Eliot plays "a great deal better than either of the Miss Musgroves; but having no voice, no knowledge of the harp, and no fond parents to sit by and fancy themselves delighted, her performance was thought little of" (pp. 46–47). In *Emma* (1816), the foolish Mrs. Eliot sees harp-playing ability as a crucial selling point for a governess, the skill that will gain her entrée into any family circle (p. 301). And in *Sanditon* (written in 1817), when travelers arrive in a town attempting to transform itself into a tourist destination, they know they have reached "civilization" when they hear "the sound of a harp . . . through the upper casement" (p. 383). In turn, when the Misses Beaufort arrive in Sanditon, self-banished for their extravagances to this "small, retired place," they intend "to be very economical, very elegant and very secluded"; deciding on "the hire of a harp" for Miss Beaufort, they are determined to draw "praise and celebrity from all who walked within the sound of her instrument" (p. 421).

45. Demonstrating thorough familiarity with the tropes of romantic nationalism, Austen's juvenilia is strewn with journeys into Scotland and remote corners of Ireland, idyllic interludes in Welsh cottages and Scottish castles. In "Love and Freindship" (1792), Laura reveals her father to be "a native of Ireland and an inhabitant of Wales" and her mother "the natural Daughter of a Scotch peer by an Italian Operagirl" (p. 77). In "Lesley Castle" (1792), Lady Lesley's criticism of Scottish life ("These girls have no Music, but Scotch airs, no Drawings but Scotch Mountains, and no Books but Scotch Poems—and I hate everything Scotch" [p. 124]) echoes Johnson, recapitulates the satire of Smollett's *Humphry Clinker*, and anticipates the satire of Ferrier's *Marriage*.

46. For the large-scale social transformations of the period, see Foucault, *Histoire de la folie*, esp. chap. 2; and Thompson, *The Making of the English Working Class*; for the transformation of the British landscape, see Barrell, *The Idea of*

Landscape and *The Dark Side of the Landscape*; Bermingham, *Landscape and Ideology*; and Mitchell, ed., *Landscape and Power*.

47. McDowell, *Ireland in the Age of Imperialism*. Boland's historical novel *The Wild Geese* (1938) argues that the mid-eighteenth-century capitalization, improvement, drainage, and enclosure of the Irish countryside create a situation in which differential property laws intensify the enmity between Catholics and Protestants and in which familial—and even fostering—ties are sundered irrevocably by new economic expediencies.

48. On these social transformations, see Selkirk, *Observations on the Present State of the Highlands*; Youngson, *After the Forty-Five*; Phillipson and Mitchison, eds., *Scotland in the Age of Improvement*; Bumsted, *The People's Clearances*; as well as McGrath's play *The Cheviot, the Stag*. For poetry critical of the contemporary economic and political landscape, see, for instance, Charles Churchill's "Prophesy of Famine" (1763), Oliver Goldsmith's "The Deserted Village" (1770), and George Crabbe's "The Village" (1782). Within the late-eighteenth-century novel, both Smollett's socially critical picaresque novels (especially his 1771 *Expedition of Humphry Clinker*) and the sentimental novel launched by Henry Mackenzie's *Man of Feeling* (1771) contain more specific attacks on improvement, as on the new institutional texture of British life. See also the critique of urban slum life in the London poems of William Blake, as well as the critique of improvement at the beginning of William Holcroft's *Anna St. Ives* (1792), itself echoed by Austen in *Sense and Sensibility* (1811), *Mansfield Park* (1814), and especially *Sanditon*.

49. See Edgeworth, *Castle Rackrent* (1800), *Ennui* (written in 1804–5, published in 1809), and her treatise *The Absentee* (1812); Owenson, *The Wild Irish Girl* (1806), *Florence Macarthy* (1818), and *Absenteeism* (1825); Maturin, *The Wild Irish Boy* (1808) and *The Milesian Chief* (1812); Roche, *The Tradition of the Castle: Scenes in the Emerald Isles* (1824); John Banim, *The Anglo-Irish of the Nineteenth Century* (1828); and Owenson, *Absenteeism*. Owenson and the other novelists remain less optimistic than Edgeworth about the absentee's reclamation for the national community.

50. Benedict Anderson, "Numbers," Carpenter Lecture, University of Chicago, April 1993.

51. Hutchinson's *Dynamics of Cultural Nationalism* uses the case of Ireland to draw a fundamental distinction between cultural nationalism (which is typically shaped by antiquaries and other intellectuals, agitates primarily for cultural recognition and cultural autonomy, and develops a historicist account of its own traditions) and political nationalism (as a movement for political autonomy and an autonomous nation-state). Whereas political nationalists tend to be prostatist, cultural nationalists are suspicious of the state as "the product of conquest, and as imbued with an inherent bureaucratic drive that, exemplified in the cosmopolitan imperial state, seeks to impose a mechanical uniformity on living cultures. The glory of a country comes not from the political power but from the culture of its people" (p. 16).

52. "If nationalisms in the rest of the world have to choose their imagined community from certain 'modular' forms already made available to them by Europe and the Americas, what do they have left to imagine?" asks Chatterjee in *The Nation and Its Fragments*. "History, it would seem, has decreed that we in the postcolonial world shall only be perpetual consumers of modernity. Europe and the Americas,

the only true subjects of history, have thought out on our behalf not only the script of colonial enlightenment and exploitation, but also that of our anticolonial resistance and postcolonial misery. Even our imaginations must remain forever colonized" (pp. 5–6).

53. "Cultural nationalists," argues Hutchinson in *The Dynamics of Cultural Nationalism*, "should be seen . . . as moral innovators who seek by 'reviving' an ethnic historicist vision of the nation to redirect traditionalists and modernists away from conflict and instead to unite them in the task of constructing an integrated distinctive and autonomous community, capable of competing in the modern world" (p. 34). Yet see also Fanon's critique, in "On National Culture," of the idealizing rigidity of the nationalist vision (*Wretched of the Earth*, pp. 206–48).

54. For an introduction to this debate, see, for instance, the polemics in Nairn et al., *Nationalismus und Marxismus*.

55. As Thomas Davis will argue in 1843, quoting a traditional Welsh source, national identity is formed by a common language, by common laws, and by "cotillage land—for without these a country cannot support itself in peace and social union" ("Our National Language," *The Nation*, April 1, 1843, p. 394). Colonial identity, as Bowen argues, is deeply (if unstably) rooted in the confiscation and occupation of land. For the Anglo-Irish (including Bowen's own family), "the idea of power was mostly vested in property (property having been acquired by use or misuse of power in the first place). One may say that while property lasted the dangerous property-idea stayed, like a sword in its scabbard, fairly safely at rest. At least, property gave my people and people like them the means to exercise power in a direct, concrete, and therefore limited way. I have shown how their natures shifted direction—or the nature of the *débordement* that occurred—when property could no longer be guarenteed" (*Bowen's Court*, p. 455).

56. Since the early 1980s, the most influential accounts of nationalism have explained both its causality and the character of its identifications as constructed primarily or purely in the discursive realm; see, for instance, Hobsbawm and Ranger, eds., *The Invention of Tradition*; Anderson, *Imagined Communities*; and Handler, *Nationalism and the Politics of Culture in Quebec*, a radically dehistoricizing account that represents Quebecois nationalism as if it had no extradiscursive or even experiential basis. This tendency in the historiography of nationalism followed a more general constructivist and "discursive turn" in Anglo-American historiography, under the influence of Foucault, of Said's *Orientalism*, and more generally of structuralist and poststructuralist thought. Within literary studies, at the same time, the model proposed by Anderson and by Hobsbawm and Ranger continues to influence accounts that in other ways frame themselves as historicist. See, for instance, Bhabha, ed., *Nation and Narration*, and Armstrong and Tennenhouse, "A Novel Nation."

57. Chatterjee notes a similar pattern in the independence movements in the British Empire of the nineteenth and twentieth centuries, beginning as cultural movements (and a movement for cultural recognition) long before they become full-fledged political movements (*The Nation and Its Fragments*, pp. 5–6).

58. In Ireland, argues Carole Fabricant, Irish historians saw themselves as engaged in a long struggle to discredit centuries of Anglo-Irish propaganda. As Dennis Taafe protests in 1801, "We are beset with a chain of false witnesses,

descendants from Gyraldus Cambrensis" ("Swift as Irish Historian," in Fox and Tooley, eds., *Walking Naboth's Vineyard*, pp. 40–72, here 46). But see also Seamus Deane's more wary account of Irish antiquarian attempts to ratify "a specific Irish character and destiny." Deane recognizes the appeal and importance of antiquarian reconstruction for a colonized culture, yet he remains skeptical of the antiquarian wish for coherence and continuity ("Irish National Character," pp. 90–113, here 94–95).

59. Canny has argued that in Ireland all ethnic groups came to recognize conquest as the central determinant of Irish history, and they defined their own identities in relation to it ("Identity Formation in Ireland: The Emergence of the Anglo-Irish," in Canny and Pagden, eds., *Colonial Identity in the Atlantic World*, pp. 159–212).

60. In Ireland, argues Moore in *Memoirs of Captain Rock* (1824), the English conquerors have deliberately cultivated their own differences from the conquered, even though this has resulted in lasting unrest (pp. 12–13).

61. Teeling, *History of the Irish Rebellion of 1798*, p. 68.

62. O'Halloran goes so far as to argue that although Ireland is a legally and religiously segregated society, and although the division of rights and privileges rests primarily on ethnic identification, the actual course of the Irish occupation, which saw considerable intermarriage between occupying and occupied groups, makes apparently immutable ethnic divisions no more than a legal fiction (*An Introduction to the Study of the Histories*, p. i).

63. The very nomenclature "Britain" and "British," as a number of recent studies have argued, was put into circulation by Lowland Scots in the wake of the 1707 Act of Union. Determined to participate in the new multinational conglomeration, feeling themselves still very much Scots, yet tired of the continual English aspersions on Scottish "clannishness" and disloyalty, they proposed "British" as a term that neither mandated the assimilation of Scottishness to Englishness nor awakened accusations of undue national influence. See Crawford, *Devolving English Literature*; Colley, *Britons*; and Weinbrot, *Britannia's Issue*.

64. See Close, *The Early Years of the Ordnance Survey*, p. 100, and Andrews, *A Paper Landscape*, p. 9.

65. Friel's *Translations* (1981) uses the ordnance's anglicization of Irish place-names to raise the question of cultural imperialism. Yet J. H. Andrews argues that the survey's nomenclature became controversial only in the late eighteenth century, during the nationalist revival of interest in Gaelic. During the 1830s, the nationalist debate about the survey was focused rather on the decision not to compile "memoirs" (*A Paper Landscape*, chap. 4).

66. As a number of commentators complained, the survey made a categorical and polemical distinction between Protestant churches as institutions of established religion (marked on the ordnance maps in large Roman letters) and Presbyterian meetinghouses and Roman Catholic "chapels" (noted on the map in smaller italics) (J. H. Andrews, *A Paper Landscape*, p. 86).

67. In 1835 artist and antiquarian George Petrie set up the new Topographical Department of the Survey, which included Irish scholar Eugene O'Curry and poet James Clarence Mangan, and which worked to document place-names from histori-

cal documents and early literature. The department was broken up in 1842, presumably as a result of the memoir controversy (Seymour, ed., *A History of the Ordnance Survey*, p. 92).

68. The two commissioned pilot studies (of the local history and local geology of the county of Londonderry) that were to launch the project ended up sinking it instead, due in part to the dubious official choice of one of the country's largest population centers and most politically sensitive locales for the pilot (*A Paper Landscape*, esp. chap. 4).

69. Johnson, *Journey to the Western Islands of Scotland*, p. 158.

70. Yet see also Bowen's description of the mid-nineteenth-century construcion of a network of new, "official" roads in County Cork, Ireland, intended in part to give employment to the men who built them; precisely because they led nowhere, Bowen argues, they ended up becoming the "veins of local life . . . the people's roads" (*Bowen's Court*, pp. 288–89).

71. William Blake, "Proverbs of Hell," section of "The Marriage of Heaven and Hell," in *Complete Writings*, ed. Geoffrey Keynes (Oxford: Oxford University Press, 1971), p. 152.

72. See, for instance, O'Halloran, *Insula Sacra* (1770), and Jones (Myvyr) et al., eds., *The Myvyrian Archaiology of Wales* (1801), as well as Iain Gordon Brown, *The Hobby-Horsical Antiquary*, and Piggott, *Ruins in a Landscape* and *Ancient Britons*.

73. On the rather different political aesthetic of the English ruin, see, for instance, Goldstein, *Ruins and Empire*, and Janowitz, *England's Ruins*. Janowitz frames the eighteenth-century obsession with ruins as "a 'cultural affect' attending Britain as the nation moved into its imperial phase, while also indexing an imperial anxiety. . . . Though the spectacle of ruins in the landscape offers evidence of a nation possessed by a long history, the material that ruinists draw on to make figures may produce different meaning within some other group's imagination. The detritus of a Scottish castle may remind the Scottish viewer most powerfully of a defeat suffered, while Martello towers assert to the Irish the continuous and material presence of English domination. So, too, the evidence of ruined castles may remind those in opposition to central government that there has been a time when government was neither central nor uncontested" (pp. 2–3). The emphasis of Janowitz's own analysis, nonetheless, is on the English reception—and political neutralization—of the ruin rather than on the nationalist reconstruction of it. Seeing a shift from a historicist to an aestheticist reading of Chatterton and Macpherson in England, Janowitz identifies the same movement in the English reading of ruins, as the romantics free the ruin from antiquarian narratives of explanation to turn it into a freestanding aesthetic object in its own right. "Unmoored from an antiquarian grounding, the fragment opens itself up to a new poetic matter" (pp. 14–15). Janowitz describes the romantic and English reincarnation of the ruin; the effort of this account is rather to document what is lost or suppressed in the process of its "unmooring" and to account more fully for the power and coherence of the nationalist-antiquarian reading.

74. On the four-stage theory of the Scottish Enlightenment and its consequences for European ethnography, see Meek, *Social Science and the Ignoble Savage*.

75. For the Anglo-Irish, writes Bowen, the fact that Ireland is filled with ruins remains a source of ambivalent pride, for it provides evidence of their own (destructive) supremacy (*Bowen's Court*, p. 17).

76. In many ways their vision of—and this way of envisioning—national distresses remains deeply indebted to Enlightenment analysis. Under examination by an Ascendancy tribunal in 1798, radical Thomas Addis Emmet discusses the situation of Ireland's Catholics using an explicitly Enlightenment vocabulary of despotism, educability, and improvement: "[S]tronger measures are necessary for educating the Irish people than are necessary in England; in the latter country no steps were taken to counteract the progress of knowledge; it had fair play, and was gradually advancing; but in Ireland you have brutalized the vulgar mind, by long continued operation of the poper laws, which, though they are repealed, have left an effect that will not cease these fifty years" ("Examination of T. A. Emmet, 14 August 1798," in Gilbert, ed., *Documents Relating to Ireland*, p. 187). According to Emmet's diagnosis, the anti-Catholic laws have functioned, ironically, to entrench the Irish adherence to superstition. Yet he foresees the eventual end of Catholicism altogether under the advance of reason. "As the human mind grows *philosophic*, it will, I think, wish for the destruction of all religious establishments, and therefore, in proportion as the Catholic mind becomes *philosophic*, it will, of course, entertain the same wishes" (p. 186). Emmet's sense of national temporality thus stresses simultaneously the long-term effects of colonial oppression on the mentality of the Irish people and the ultimate sublation of their ensuing religious and political alliances into a new philosophical condition beyond history.

77. On the differences between Dublin and London, see Richard Lovell Edgeworth, *Memoirs*, 1:198.

78. "From my earliest youth," declares Wolfe Tone at his courtmartial, explaining why he attempted to direct the army of the French Republic in an invasion of Ireland, "I have regarded the connection between Ireland and Great Britain as the curse of the Irish nation, and felt convinced that, whilst it lasted, this country could never be free nor happy. My mind has been confirmed in this opinion by the experience of every succeeding year, and the conclusions which I have drawn from every fact before my eyes. In consequence, I determined to apply all the powers, which my individual efforts could move, in order to separate the two countries" ("Speech at Court-Martial," November 19, 1798, in *The Best of Tone*, ed. Mac Aonghusa and O'Réagáin, p. 183).

79. Koselleck, *Critique and Crisis*, p. 15.

80. Johnson, *Journey to the Western Islands*, p. 9.

CHAPTER 1

1. Young, *A Tour in Ireland*, 2:10.

2. See here Barrell, *The Idea of Landscape*, esp. chap. 2.

3. Young's *General Report on Enclosures* (1808; reprint, New York: Augustus Kelley, 1971) advocates enclosing the "wastes and commons" of England, Scotland, and Wales as well.

4. The 1892 edition appends John Wesley's even more cynical reading of the "Irish howl" in his *Journal* of 1750: "It was not a song, as I supposed, but a dismal,

inarticulate yell, set up at the grave by four shrill-voiced women, who (we understood) were hired for that purpose. But I saw not one that shed a tear; for that, it seems, was not in their bargain" (1:249).

5. Extolling liberty as a British birthright and as the foundation of colonial life, Young's *Political Essays Concerning the British Empire* appears unbothered by the slave labor deployed in many colonies. Young lauds Britain's "most beneficial commerce" with coastal Africa, the returns being "gold dust, ivory, guns and slaves" (p. 526), and he describes the purchase and maintenance of slaves in the American colonies under the heading "Sundry Articles" (p. 353).

6. Yet he argues against the practice of importing German workers, for "no country, whatever state it may be in, can be improved by colonies of foreigners" (*Tour*, 2:34).

7. Compare here Alexis de Tocqueville's *Journey in Ireland*. Observing Ireland in 1835 as a Catholic outsider, Tocqueville is interested not in the bog or land reclamation but in the distribution of property and wealth, as in the contrast offered by the pitiful Irish cabin and the splendid Protestant manor. Unlike Young, Tocqueville spends as much time talking to the local Catholic priests and intellectuals as to Protestant landlords, judges, and clergy. As a result, he learns a great deal about the long-standing religious and political tensions of the country. As the president of the Catholic college at Carlow tells him, "The people are treated as conquered by the landlords, and in fact the latter occupy the estates that have been confiscated from these same Catholics, who are dying of hunger" (p. 43). Tocqueville sympathizes with Catholic intellectuals who protest the Protestant church tithes, and even with Whiteboy activities, which he characterizes alternately as "acts of popular resistance" (p. 68) and as "popular justice" (p. 71).

8. As late as the 1920s, Corkery's influential book *The Hidden Ireland* continues to use Young and Edgeworth as primary guides to Irish conditions, defensively explaining Young's lack of insight into Gaelic culture as a significant historical indicator in its own right.

9. Edgeworth, *Castle Rackrent and Ennui*, pp. 121, 61.

10. As chapter 3 demonstrates, eighteenth-century picaresque and investigative travel writing is subsumed into early-nineteenth-century "traveling" plots; Irish and Scottish novels structured around a Youngian journey of discovery include Edgeworth's *Ennui* (1803–5, published in 1809), *The Absentee* (1812), and *Ormond* (1817); Owenson's *St. Clair* (1803), *The Wild Irish Girl* (1806), *O'Donnel* (1814), and *Florence McCarthy* (1818); Maturin's *The Wild Irish Boy* (1808) and *The Milesian Chief* (1812); Ferrier's *Marriage* (1818) and *Destiny* (1831); and M'Henry's *O'Halloran* (1825). A parallel group of stories, from Colpoys's *Irish Excursion* (1801), Christian Johnstone's *The Saxon and the Gaël* (1814), and Walter Scott's *The Heart of Midlothian* (1818) to Galt's *Gathering of the West* (1822), focus on journeys in the opposite direction, from the peripheries to local or imperial centers.

11. See Dunne's excellent " 'A Gentleman's Estate Should Be a Moral School,' " and Lloyd's *Anomalous States*, p. 148, as well as Gallagher's *Nobody's Story*, chap. 6. Philippe Hamon has brilliantly described the way in which Zola's fiction builds narrative action and even characterization around the need to provide description. See "What Is a Description?" in Tzvetan Todorov, ed., *French Theory Today* (Cambridge: Cambridge University Press, 1982), pp. 147–78. British nationalist fiction

could be read similarly, as didactic stories built around certain kinds of expository set pieces (whether political dialogues or landscape descriptions), which convey information about the state of the country *and* occasion meditations on ways of seeing.

12. See Owenson, *St. Clair*, *Wild Irish Girl*, *O'Donnel*, *Florence Macarthy*, and *The O'Briens and the O'Flahertys* (1827); Maturin, *Wild Irish Boy* and *Milesian Chief*; Walter Scott, *Rob Roy* (1817) and *Ivanhoe* (1819); Parnell, *Maurice and Berghetta* (1819); M'Henry, *O'Halloran*; Whitty, "The Last Chieftain," in *Tales of Irish Life* (1824); and arguably also Edgeworth, *Castle Rackrent* (1800), *Ennui*, and *Ormond*; Roche, *The Tradition of the Castle* (1824); and John Banim, *The Anglo-Irish of the Nineteenth Century* (1828); see also Trollope, *The Kellys and the O'Kellys* (1848), and Boland, *The Wild Geese* (1938). An influential group of early-nineteenth-century Scottish stories—Scott's *Waverley* (1814), *Guy Mannering* (1815), and *Bride of Lammermoor* (1819); E.H.H.'s *Highlander* (1819); Galt's *Entail* (1822); John Wilson's "Shieling," in *Lights and Shadows of Scottish Life* (1822); and Ferrier's *Destiny*—adapt the Irish chieftain plot to Scotland in various ways.

13. Melville, *The Irish Chieftain*, 2:4.

14. Owenson, *The Wild Irish Girl*, p. 79. Beginning her novelistic career under her maiden name, Sydney Owenson became Lady Morgan after her marriage in 1822, and thereafter she published under her married name. Although she is now known and reprinted as Lady Morgan, the focus here on her early works and the wish to avoid anachronism (and the misleading impression that she is innately an "aristocratic" author) have led to her identification in this book as Sydney Owenson as consistently as possible.

15. As James Chandler has suggested to me, the fen may have played a comparable role in seventeenth-century England: as long-time supports of peasant livelihood now under threat from the major landowners, both fen and bog become controversial and politicized terrain. In *Paradise Lost* (1667), they appear side by side as key features in the landscape of hell: "Rockes, caves, lakes, fens, bogs, dens, and shades of death— / A universe of death" (*The Poems of John Milton*, ed. John Carey and Alastair Fowler [London: Longmans, 1968], book 2, ll. 621–22). Cromwell's political career was launched when, as Lord of the Fens in the 1630s, he upheld the Huntingdon commoners' rights of common land, opposing the drainage of the fens by "court-supported great capitalist fen-drainers" (Christopher Hill, *God's Englishman: Oliver Cromwell and English History* [New York: Harper and Row, 1972], p. 261).

16. On the problem of an Anglo-Irish literary tradition, see McCormack, *Ascendancy and Tradition* and *Sheridan LeFanu*; Deane, *A Short History of Irish Literature*; Vance, *Irish Literature*; Lloyd, *Anomalous States*; and Eagleton, *Heathcliffe and the Great Hunger*, esp. chap. 5. All of these are critical accounts that position themselves against an earlier, affirmative historiography of Anglo-Irish literature. For a recent return to this mode, see Moynahan's breathtakingly pro-Ascendancy *Anglo-Irish*.

17. [Thomas Wharton?, later lord lieutenant of Ireland], "Lilli Burlero," in Deane et al., eds., *The Field Day Anthology*, 1:475–76; Sterne, *Tristram Shandy*, p. 56.

18. Julia Reinhard Lupton, "Mapping Mutability, or Spenser's Irish Plot," in Bradshaw et al., eds., *Representing Ireland*, pp. 93–115, here 98.

19. Moryson, *Shakespeare's Europe*, pp. 238, 247; see also Thomas Gainsford's description of bog warfare in *The Glory of England* (1618), in Hadfield and McVeagh, eds., *Strangers to That Land*, p. 70.

20. Gerard Boate, *Irelands Naturall History* (1652), reprinted in *A Collection of Tracts and Treatises*, 1:1–148; here 1:95–96.

21. King, "A Discourse Concerning the *Bogs* and *Loughs* of *Ireland*," p. 948.

22. Swift, "An Answer to Several Letters Sent Me from Unknown Hands" (1729), in *The Prose Works*, 7:130–34.

23. Joseph McMinn, indeed, reads Swift as an advocate of bog clearance: "Bogs were always a feature of the Irish landscape which frustrated Swift's ideal of a self-sufficient form of economy, a geological distortion which he hoped to reform out of existence" ("The Humors of Quilca: Swift, Sheridan, and County Cavan," in Fox and Tooley, eds., *Walking Naboth's Vineyard*, pp. 143–53, here 144).

24. Chaigneau, *The History of Jack Connor*, 1:66, 1:75.

25. See here Ian Campbell Ross, "An Irish Picaresque Novel."

26. Edgeworth found the prototype for this plot in family stories of Richard Lovell Edgeworth's own return to Ireland as a young man (*Memoirs of Richard Lovell Edgeworth*, 2:1–12).

27. Maria Edgeworth, *The Absentee*, pp. 94–95. On "Londonomania," see p. 199.

28. For Edgeworth's recasting of Davies, see chap. 5 here. Beaufort's 1792 *Memoir of a Map of Ireland* (which had Richard Lovell Edgeworth as one of its original subscribers) follows Young in its organization by locale and in its attempt to assemble a systematic statistical portrait of Ireland, county by county; unlike Young, Beaufort places considerable emphasis on local antiquities.

29. Owenson, *The O'Briens and the O'Flahertys*, p. 26.

30. Owenson, *Florence Macarthy*, 1:36–43. For recent debates over the political stance of Spenser's *View*, see Cairns and Richards, *Writing Ireland*; Coughlan, ed., *Spenser and Ireland*; Avery, "Mapping the Irish Other"; and Patterson, "The Egalitarian Giant," in *Reading between the Lines*, pp. 80–116.

31. Touring Ireland in 1842, on the eve of the Great Famine, Thackeray recounts a related cautionary tale. When the poor of Kilcullen clear a marshy common, to build cabins and feed their families upon the "rescued land," neighborhood land-owners resent the initiative of "these new colonists" and threaten them with prison (*The Irish Sketchbook*, in *Complete Works*, 20:22–23). To William Bennett, visiting Ireland at the height of the famine five years later, the horror of Irish living conditions begins with the fact that many cabins are simply "holes in the bog, covered with a layer of turfs, and not distinguishable as human habitations from the surrounding moor, until close down upon them" (*Narrative of a recent journey*, p. 25).

32. Haliburton, "Sam Slick's Opinion of the British," in *The Clockmaker*, pp. 69–73, here 71.

33. Sinclair, *The Code of Agriculture*, pp. 190–91.

34. Ibid., p. 191. *The Code of Agriculture* also establishes precise caste hierarchies within the mass of agricultural laborers, so the estate owner can give different terms of lease to each (p. 77).

35. Ibid., p. 189. When a bog in Haworth erupts in 1824, Patrick Brontë commemorates the event by writing not only a poem ("The Phenomenon, or an Account in Verse of the Extraordinary Disruption of a Bog . . .") but also a sermon on the subject. Reprinted in *Brontëana*. Even Harriet Martineau, touring Ireland in 1852 and convinced of the economic and public health benefits to be gained from the reclamation of Ireland's 3 million acres of bogs, sees the desolate Bog of Allen as an image of hell: "It makes the imagination ache, like the eye. . . . When Cromwell transplanted all disaffected families from other parts of Connaught, and when Connaught became the proverbial alternative of hell, the great bog was no doubt the uppermost image in men's minds. The disgraces of Connaught certainly recur with strong force to the traveller's mind when he traverses that bog for the first time" (*Letters from Ireland*, p. 76). See the similarly desolate portrait of the Bog of Allen in Roche, *The Munster Cottage Boy*, 2:167. The emotional armature and literary topoi developed during Britain's internal colonization are transported to the overseas empire: imperial representations of West Indian, African, and Indian tropical landscapes echo Anglo-Irish accounts of the Irish bog. As Struthers Burt argues in *Entertaining the Islanders* (New York: Charles Scribner's Sons, 1933), the swamp remains an important *paysage moralisé* for successive generations of British occupiers in the West Indies. The colonial administrator of the early nineteenth century feels an inchoate dislike of the local swamp: "[G]iven time, [he] would undoubtedly have diked it and drained it and planted it with something as formal as hibiscus. To this English mind, swamps were an insult to the British Empire." Brought over in midcentury to build a botanical garden, the Scottish gardener deliberately saves a small section of the original swamp, with a sign announcing "that here was a bit of the original West Indies"; its luxuriant plant growth and "venomous green struggle for survival" are a spectacle that "satisfied his sense of predestination." The twentieth-century English governor, in contrast, condemns the swamp as "immoral," with "the pragmatic excuses that swamps bred mosquitos, that they were inimical to white life, and that they occupied land that might be usefully employed, but pragmatism . . . did not account for the involuntary umbilical revulsion with which he viewed nature at its most fecund" (pp. 6–8). The swamp, then, gives concrete form to several distinct layers of imperial ideology and religious belief. It also appears as a long-standing locus of imperial struggle, a place that conjoins internal and external colonizations. The Celtic soul is compared to the dynamic, fecund terrain of the swamp, and the Scottish gardener's preservation of a piece of the swamp to commemorate indigenous life-forms alongside the cultivated imperial terrain functions as Celtic resistance to the British imperial project.

36. Sinclair's compendium is no longer the product of a single Enlightenment consciousness; instead, it collects local knowledge at long distance, through an open-ended questionnaire distributed to Church of Scotland ministers. Despite its localizing emphasis, the *Account* may well be influenced by Abbé Gregoire's famous inquiry into the regional traditions of postrevolutionary France, in order to provide the material foundation for linguistic and cultural standardization. See Balibar and Laporte, *Le français national*, and Certeau, Julia, and Revel, *Une politique de la langue*.

37. See, for instance, *Anthologia Hibernica, or Monthly Collections of Science, Belles Lettres and History* (published in Dublin, in 1793–94), a wide-ranging mis-

cellany grounded in the description of Irish antiquities. Most issues begin with an illustrated lead article on an ancient Irish monument. Although many of its articles are on nonantiquarian topics (from mathematics to geography and natural history), most discuss the historical aspects of Irish life (from its poetry to its superstitions) and enshrine them as national monuments in their own right. The two most influential early-nineteenth-century Scottish magazines, *The Edinburgh Review* and *Blackwood's Edinburgh Magazine*, follow this emphasis on antiquarian questions to an important extent. For the new, antiquarian travel writing, see Maria Graham Calcott's remarkable *Journal of a Residence in India* (1812) and *Letters on India* (1814), which read India through a survey of Hindu cultural practices, literary genres, and architectural monuments; seeking and finding important parallels between traditional culture in India and in the Scottish Highlands, Calcott develops a bardic model of Hindustani culture.

38. In the absence of such survey maps, Heaney's essay "The Sense of Place" (1977) evokes the traditional Irish poetic/exegetical genre of the *dinnseanchas*, which relates the original meanings and mythic associations of place-names (*Preoccupations*, pp. 131–49).

39. J. H. Andrews, *A Paper Landscape*, p. 148. Lancom's questions about cultural practices resemble the questions about bogs not only in form but in their presuppositions about the interrelationship of custom, habitat, and history. "Habits of the people. Note the general style of the cottages as stone, mud, slated, glass windows, one story or two, number of rooms, comfort and cleanliness. Food; fuel; dress; longevity; usual number in a family . . . early amusements and recreations? Patrons and patrons' days; and traditions respecting them? What local customs prevail . . . ? Peculiar games? Any legendary tales or poems recited around the fireside? Any ancient music, as clan marches or funeral cries? They differ in different districts, collect them if you can. Any peculiarity of costume? Nothing more indicates the state of civilization and intercourse" (p. 148).

40. In the long run, touristic writing becomes marked by both preoccupations, concerned with both evoking nostalgia and praising progress. Written during the 1830s, Howitt's *Visits to Remarkable Places* meditates on sites of Scottish history in tones of nationalist lament, expressing sorrow at postunion economic and cultural transformation. Yet when Howitt goes in search of Scott's Borders, his momentary chagrin at the transformation of the landscape that Scott describes ("What! is this that wild region of bogs and fastnesses into which the Liddisdale Borderers retreated when pursued by their enemies, and set all pursuit at defiance? Where are the bogs;- where are the dismal glens") is checked by his delight at the extent of its modernization, particularly its macadamized roads (2:548).

41. Carr, *The Stranger in Ireland*, p. 304.

42. The opening pages of Carey's *Lochiel, or The Field of Culloden* (1820) gather Highland characters around a cottage fire, stoked with peat and wood from the remains of the Caledonian forest (planted partly by the Romans). In a novel that goes on to trace the causes and course of the Jacobite Rebellion of 1745, this scene suggests the organic formation of the Highland landscape and way of life, shaped over millennia, in part by military history.

43. Some of Carr's examples clearly derive from King's 1685 "Discourse on the Bogs and Loughs of Ireland." As King observes, "[A] *Turf-Bog* preserves things

strangely, a Corps will ly intire in one, for severall years; I have seen a piece of leather pretty fresh dug out of a *Turf-Bog*, that had never in the memory of man been dug before; Butter has bin found, that had lain above 20 years. . . . Trees are found, and intire in them. . . . The Trees are supposed by the ignorant vulgar to have lyen there ever since the Flood, but the truth is, they fell on the surface of the Earth; and the *Bog* . . . swelling by degrees, at last covered them" (p. 954). Carr's reworking of these anecdotes is quite transformative: where King is interested simply in the way the bog's preservative powers raise questions of relative historical measurement, Carr raises larger questions of cultural transmission.

44. As late as the 1930s, O'Faolain's "Broken World" still invokes the bog in terms that echo Swift and Owenson, as a means of indicting the political economy and the corruptions of Anglo-Ireland (*The Finest Stories of Sean O'Faolain*, pp. 71–82). Overall, however, it is Carr's vision of the bog, as a site to contemplate the circular course of Irish history, that most influences Irish modernism. Joyce's *Ulysses* (1922) evokes a landscape of sand, silt, and sinking soil to meditate on the betrayals of Irish political history and the cultural sedimentation of language. In a Protestant school, Stephen is paid his salary for history lessons that constitute a cultural betrayal, within sight of a "tray of Stuart coins, base treasure of a bog" (p. 35), a reminder of the seventeenth-century English sellout of Ireland. Seamus Heaney's early poetry (reprinted in *Poems, 1965–1975*) explores the preservative powers of the bog, to consider the structure and circularity of Irish cultural memory. "Relic of Memory" (pp. 67–68) evokes the petrification of wood by the waters of the lough as a process that hardens their grain and "Incarcerate[s] ghosts / Of sap and season" (p. 67, ll. 6–7); "Bogland" (pp. 85–86) takes up Carr's examples of bog preservation to describe the organic quality and bottomlessness of Irish tradition; "The Tollund Man" (pp. 125–26), "Bog Queen" (pp. 187–89), and "The Grauballe Man" (pp. 190–91) describe the bog ground as the soil in which prehistoric corpses and ancient rivalries and punishments are preserved, to contemplate the fatal continuities of violence in Irish history, from the millennia before the conquest to the troubles of the present day.

45. Edgeworth, *Castle Rackrent and Ennui*, p. 329. For a similar critique of the enumerative fallacy in a contemporary travel account of Scotland, see the anonymous review of James Cririe's *Scottish Scenery* in *The Edinburgh Review* (January 1804): 328–34.

46. Dubois, *My Pocket-book*, p. 11. The Edgeworths' criticism seems to have informed Dubois in various ways. Carr sued Dubois for libel in 1808 but lost the case (*Castle Rackrent and Ennui*, p. 326).

47. "'A reclaimed bog' is a very uncertain gentleman, for if he is not 'kept drained,' he 'will *relapse*.' How kindly watchful our ministers are in this respect? If *draining the country* will do, we've nothing to fear" (Dubois, *My Pocket-book*, p. 98).

48. LeFanu, *Tales of a Tourist*, 1:27.

49. Even before Carr, many late-eighteenth-century travelogues were structured around extremely miscellaneous catalogs of antiquarian, geological, and cultural sights, from plant life to local superstitions and monuments; Pennant's *Tour in Scotland* (1771) moves in the course of a single page from "salmons" to "seals" to "servitude" (p. 157).

50. Richard and Maria Edgeworth, *Essay on Irish Bulls* (1802), reprinted in Edgeworth, *Tales and Novels*, 4:81–207; Kilfeather, "'Strangers in Ireland,'" chap. 1. In light of the Edgeworths' subsequent review of Carr in the *Edinburgh Review*, it is noteworthy that *Irish Bulls* received a condescending review in the same magazine (July 1803, pp. 398–402), which criticized it as a "rambling, scrambling book," mocked its Irish subjects, and belittled the claim of Maria Edgeworth's collaboration.

51. Edgeworth, *Castle Rackrent and Ennui*, p. 209.

52. Both Day's *Sandford and Merton* (1783–89) and *Ennui* present this fundamental insight into the primacy of circumstance and acculturation over individual character or inheritance, in ways that seems indebted to a striking scene in Chaigneau's *Jack Connor*. Abandoned by his mother, the young Connor is taken up by the family of Lord Truegood, to wait on Truegood's son Harry. When the boys fight, Jack accepts Harry's beatings without resistance, fearing the loss of Truegood's favor. Yet when Truegood learns of the fight, he punishes his son by ordering him to exchange clothes and position with Jack: by bullying his servant, the master loses any putative superiority of manner, and once he has lost his clothes as well, no stranger could recognize his superior status. Happily, the punishment is forestalled. Jack saves Harry from drowning and becomes a full member of the Truegoods, as Harry's adoptive brother.

53. *Memoirs of Richard Lovell Edgeworth*, esp. vol. 2. See here Eagleton's emphatically Lukácsian explication of Richard Edgeworth as a "world-historical" figure and his placement of Maria Edgeworth's fiction in relation to her father's historical exemplarity (*Heathcliff and the Great Hunger*, pp. 161–77, esp. 175); see also Dunne, "'A Gentleman's Estate,'" which reads Maria Edgeworth's Irish novels against her father's work as a reform landlord, intellectual, and agricultural improver.

54. One footnote glosses a phrase in the story with apparently useful background information. "*Her mark*. It *was* the custom in Ireland for those who could not write to make a cross to stand for their signature, as was formerly the practice of our English monarchs." Already the footnote threatens satire, invoking the illiteracy of the English monarchs; the cross is a substitute for a signature throughout Western Europe, not a peculiarity of Ireland. Yet the editor painstakingly "inserts the facsimile of an Irish *mark*, which may hereafter be valuable to a judicious antiquary." Even more than the "antique" night pot or kale pot proverbially "discovered" by the self-deluded antiquarian of satirical fame, the illiterate x of an obscure peasant woman has little value either as an "antique" aesthetic commodity or even as a historical trace (Edgeworth, *Castle Rackrent and Ennui*, p. 89).

55. Christensen's "Romantics at the End of History" interprets both "Essay on Irish Bulls" and the glossaries as attempts "to dissipate the English suspicion that there is some kind of essential character or form of thought that binds the Irish together, rejects English reason, and is unassimilable to polite society. . . . The 'depeculiarization' of Irish speech, which meant translating the demotic into the vernacular (both Maria Edgeworth's and Walter Scott's glossaries prosecute the same end), carried forward the Enlightenment's project of homogenizing mankind in the guise of the bourgeoisie and . . . of restricting character to what can be stamped on a commodity" (p. 473). More accurate about Scott's project than about

Edgeworth's, Christensen's comments take insufficient account of her efforts to reconstruct Ireland's complex cultural texture.

56. *Memoirs of Richard Lovell Edgeworth*, 2:62. He was also involved in the recovery of bog antiquities; he tried to obtain a fossilized animal skeleton from the bog to send to Edmund Burke, whom he admired (Butler, *Maria Edgeworth*, p. 129). A similar fossilized skeleton, "found in the lakes in the neighbourhood," appears in *The Absentee*, p. 113.

57. See also J. H. Andrews, *A Paper Landscape*, p. 6.

58. Butler, *Maria Edgeworth*, p. 211.

59. The model figures of synthesis are the cosmopolitan Annaly family, paradoxically the least rooted of the novel's several versions of Irish aristocracy. As their name suggests, they can unify Ireland by incorporating the different ages or orders that the novel represents. Ormond's own path of moral education (which leads him from one social chronotope to another, toward a final union with Miss Annaly) functions as an annal of the gradual civilizing of Ireland, as it moves past earlier stages of civil society (the virtues and excesses of traditional and hereditary government and the daring, unscrupulous reformism of the parliamentary era) to reach a synthesis of tradition and perfectibility in the Ascendancy.

60. Edgeworth, *Castle Rackrent and Ennui*, p. 191.

61. Edgeworth, *Ormond*, pp. 51–52.

62. *The Letters of David Hume*, ed. J.Y.T. Grieg. 2 vols. (Oxford: Clarendon Press, 1932), 1:330.

63. Adam Ferguson, *An Essay on the History of Civil Society*, p. 174.

64. Edgeworth, *A Memoir of Maria Edgeworth*, 2:8, 1:324, 2:7.

65. See also *The Absentee*, p. 143, where the bog is used to hide a still.

CHAPTER 2

1. The disparity between the two accounts is instructive. Whereas Johnson describes a sparse, barren, and underpopulated expanse, Boswell evokes a Scotland populated with an extended network of talkative intellectuals. On the generic differences between Johnson's account (ordered by locale) and Boswell's (organized as a diary), see Stuart Sherman's *Telling Time* (Chicago: University of Chicago Press, forthcoming). See also the parable Defoe uses to introduce the final, Scottish volume of his *Tour Thro' the Whole Isle of Britain* (1724–26): "I knew two Gentlemen who travelled over the greatest Part of *England* . . . together; the Result of their Observations were very different indeed; one of them took some Minutes of Things for his own Satisfaction, but not much, but the other . . . took an exact Journal," noting such things as the dates, the towns where they dined and lodged, and which inns had good claret (2:540).

2. Boswell, *Journal*, p. 391; subsequent references in the text are marked with *B*. As Rogers argues in *Johnson and Boswell* (chap. 7), Boswell is also reenacting the flight of the Pretender through the Highlands and Islands after Culloden.

3. Malcolm Andrews, *The Search for the Picturesque*, pp. 196–98.

4. M'Nicol, *Remarks on Dr. Johnson's Journey*, p. 7. See also Mackenzie, ed., *Report of the Highland Society*; Spittal, ed., *Contemporary Criticisms of Dr. Samuel Johnson*, esp. pp. 161–98; and J.C.D. Clark, *Samuel Johnson*, esp. pp.

238–39. Because of the lasting controversy around the *Journey*, Combe's *Tour of Doctor Prosody* (1821) can parody both Johnson's tone about Scotland and nationalist antiquarian claims, still assuming the reader's detailed familiarity with the *Journey*.

5. Boswell declares his "utter astonishment" that an "admirable work" like the *Journey* has been "misapprehended, even to rancour, by many of my countrymen" (B, p. 10). The defense of the *Journey* and his denunciation of the "shallow irritable North Britons" who criticize it appear again in his *Life of Johnson*, 2:300–308. As Crawford points out, however, Boswell also takes perverse delight in stimulating, embellishing, and arranging Johnson's anti-Scottish remarks (*Devolving English Literature*, pp. 75–88).

6. M'Nicol, *Remarks*, p. 7. For a contemporary reading of the *Journey* as an imperialist text, see Simon During, "Waiting for the Post: Some Relations between Modernity, Colonization, and Writing," in Adam and Tiffin, eds., *Past the Last Post*, pp. 23–45.

7. See Rogers, *Johnson and Boswell*, pp. 2–5, 217–24.

8. As Wechselblatt argues in "Finding Mr. Boswell," the *Journey* presents Scottish history as backward and random in its course, and Scots as a disconnected antilanguage.

9. "To see commerce flourish, industry rewarded and the poor have bread, are objects which would have given pleasure to a benevolent mind; and they would have been related with rapture. But England had not yet made any great progress in this branch; and the Doctor did not choose to acknowledge, that his own countrymen were in anything outdone by the Scots" (M'Nicol, *Remarks*, p. 42).

10. See *Journey*, pp. 9–10. Johnson's repeated criticisms of Scotland's treelessness arouse particular anger in his Scottish readers. As Womack argues in *Improvement and Romance*, pp. 65–68, this is a traditional complaint about Scotland which long precedes Johnson; see, for instance, *The North Briton* 13 (August 12, 1762).

11. Macpherson, "Carric-Thura," in *Poems of Ossian*, ed. Gaskill, p. 160.

12. Macpherson, "Calthon and Colmal," in *Poems of Ossian*, ed. Gaskill, p. 171. The wind replaces the song that carries the hero's fame and carries its echo even years later: as they perpetuate a collective tribal memory, oral traditions look back toward an original, natural language. From Herder onward, a whole strain of Ossian reception thus stresses the "naturalness" of the bard's epic song: it speaks from "natural" feelings, rather than being organized according to poetic "rules." Yet David Hume, skeptical of the poems' supposedly organic provenance, complains that in "Ossian, nature is violated, where alone she ought to have been preserved; is preserved where alone she ought to have been violated" ("On the Authenticity ," p. 418).

13. On Johnson's writing as "a fraying or dissolving into the texts of others," see Frederic Bogel, "Johnson and the Role of Authority," in Nussbaum and Brown, eds., *The New Eighteenth Century*, pp. 189–209; see also Thomas M. Curley, "Johnson's Last Word on Ossian: Ghostwriting for William Shaw," in Carter and Pittock, eds., *Aberdeen and the Enlightenment*, pp. 375–431.

14. See Youngson, *After the Forty-Five*; Womack, *Improvement and Romance*; and Peter Watkin's 1965 film *The Battle of Culloden*. On the long-term cultural and linguistic consequences of the military occupation, see Murphy, "Fool's Gold," esp.

pp. 568–69; Withers, *Gaelic in Scotland*, and Durkacz, *The Decline of the Celtic Languages*.

15. Bumsted, *The People's Clearance*.

16. Smollett, *The Expedition of Humphry Clinker*, p. 269; see also Hook's outstanding anthology *The History of Scottish Literature*, vol. 2, *1660–1800*; Youngson, *The Making of Classical Edinburgh*; and MacQueen, *The Enlightenment and Scottish Literature*, esp. vol. 1, *Progress and Poetry*. Tellingly, John Home's *Fatal Discovery, or Douglas* (1757) had huge success on the London stage until it was discovered to have been written by a Scot, whereupon "the success of the piece instantly ceased" (Henry Grey Graham, *The Social Life of Scotland*, p. 67).

17. *Letters of David Hume*, 1:255.

18. Calder's *Revolutionary Empire* views the Scottish Enlightenment as a "movement for self-colonisation" (p. 533), which consolidates Scotland's position as the "dreamland of eighteenth century 'political management'" (p. 682). On the role of the Scottish Enlightenment in consolidating or resisting British hegemony, and on its divided and contradictory attitude toward Scots speech and Scottish culture, see Daiches's *Literature and Gentility* and *The Paradox of Scottish Culture*, as well as Phillipson and Mitchison, eds., *Scotland in the Age of Improvement*, esp. Janet Adam Smith, "Some Eighteenth Century Ideas of Scotland," pp. 107–24, and John Clive, "The Social Background of the Scottish Renaissance," pp. 225–44; see also Simpson, *The Protean Scot*. Daiches sees linguistic dividedness as central to Scottish society: in the wake of the Union, Lowland literature either attempts a cosmopolitan, international style that can compete with English letters or patriotically resists a British standard, embracing the local and the antiquarian. The first position often implied either the wish to forget the existence of the Highlands, as embarrassingly backward, or the desire to improve it; the second, conversely, relied on the unassimilable "otherness" of clan life, to ground a nostalgic myth of inherent Scottishness.

19. See Simonsuuri, *Homer's Original Genius*; Rubel, *Savage and Barbarian*, esp. chap. 3; Weinbrot, *Britannia's Issue*, esp. chap. 6. Blackwell's argument partly overlaps with Vico's "Discovery of the True Homer" in *The New Science* (1725), which argues for Homer as the Greek people themselves, his two epic poems an expression of two different states of his society.

20. On Johnson's part in promoting Scottish self-consciousness about pronunciation, see Boswell, *Life of Johnson*, 2:158–61; Henry Grey Graham, *Social Life of Scotland*, p. 120; and Rogers, *Johnson and Boswell*, chap. 7.

21. Henry Grey Graham, *The Social Life of Scotland*, p. 114. See also Daiches, *Literature and Gentility*, *Paradox of Scottish Culture*, *Robert Fergusson*, and *Robert Burns*. On the Lowland vision of a British public and a British literature, see Crawford, *Devolving English Literature*, esp. chap. 2.

22. Mitchison, *A History of Scotland*, p. 311, and Daiches, *Scotland and the Union*. Watching the last session of the Irish House of Lords before the dissolution of the Irish Parliament and the Union with Britain, Thomas De Quincey notes the absence of a comparable epitaph: "[T]he Union was ratified; the bill received the royal assent without a muttering, or a whispering, or the protesting echo of a sigh. Perhaps there might be a little pause—a silence like that which follows an earth-

quake; but there was no plain-spoken Lord Belhaven as on the corresponding occasion in Edinburgh, to fill up the silence with, 'So, there's an end of an auld sang!' " (*Autobiographic Sketches from 1785 to 1803* [1852], reprinted in *Works*, 24 vols. [Edinburgh: Adam and Charles Black, 1863], 24:233–34).

23. Fergusson, "Elegy, on the Death of Scots Music," in *Works*, pp. 250–53.

24. On the linguistic patriotism of the eighteenth-century vernacular revival, see Pittock, *Poetry and Jacobite Politics*, esp. pp. 140–62.

25. Nineteenth-century Scottish fiction builds on the eighteenth-century revival of Scots vernacular poetry. See Letley, *From Galt to Douglas Brown*, and Donaldson, *Popular Literature*, chap. 2.

26. Hugh Blair, preface to *Fragments of Ancient Poetry*, in *Poems of Ossian*, by Macpherson, ed. Gaskill, p. 5.

27. Sher's *Church and University in the Scottish Enlightenment* argues for *Ossian* as the collective work of Macpherson and a "cabal" of Edinburgh literati who "provided the inspiration, incentive, financial support, letters of introduction, editorial assistance, publishing connections and emotional encouragement that brought Ossian into print" (p. 254) and links the poem's heroic code to the unsuccessful struggle for a Militia Bill to restore Scotland's right to military self-defense.

28. Grant, *Essays on the Superstitions of the Highlanders*, 2:45. In the wake of the Jacobite uprisings of 1715 and 1745, Graham argues, it was politically necessary to introduce "an uniformity of manners and of sentiments throughout the whole island" and to assimilate "the habits and manners of the Highlanders with those of the other subjects of the empire . . . yet it had almost proved fatal to the remains of our ancient national poetry" (*Essay on the Authenticity of the Poems of Ossian*, pp. 88–89). Macpherson's rescue of these remains, Graham argues, was timely; thirty years later, it would have been too late. According to several Highland informants, *Ossian* demonstrated how much the oral culture of the Highlands had been transformed under British occupation; in their own youth, the recitation of Ossianic poetry "was the favourite amusement of Highlanders, in the hours of leisure or of idleness; but . . . since the Rebellion 1745, the manners of the people had undergone a change so unfavourable to the recitation of these poems, that it was now an amusement scarcely known, and . . . very few persons remained alive who were able to recite them" (Mackenzie, ed., *Report of the Highland Society*, p. 78). *Ossian* also stirred English interest in Gaelic. See Withers, *Gaelic in Scotland*, esp. chap. 6, and Durkacz, *Decline of the Celtic Languages*, esp. chap. 5.

29. Macpherson, trans., *The Poems of Ossian*, p. 40.

30. Ibid., p. 41.

31. For the controversy surrounding the poems, see MacKenzie, ed., *Report of the Highland Society*; Lewis, ed., *The Correspondence of Thomas Percy and Evan Evans*, esp. pp. 19–20, 95–101, 117–18, 170–71; Graham, *Essay*; Sanders, *Life and Letters of James Macpherson*; Chapman, *The Gaelic Vision in Scottish Culture*, esp. chap. 2; MacKillop, *Fion mac Cumhaill*; and Gaskill, ed., *Ossian Revisited*. See also Pittock's defense of Macpherson's editorial practices in *Poetry and Jacobite Politics*, pp. 178–86.

32. It is this poem, with its repetitive and formulaic contents and its subsumption of narrative content to mournful invocation, that Werther translates into German

and reads aloud to Lotte at the end of Goethe's *Sorrows of Young Werther* (1774). Emotion invoked without any real plot to distract from it: this is the Ossianic/ oceanic feeling at its most intense, for what the voice carries is pure pastness, pure regret. See Simpson, *The Protean Scot*, chap. 2.

33. See Hauser, *The Social History of Art*, 3:4, 3:54, 3:85.

34. Churchill's "Prophecy of Famine: A Scots Pastoral" (1763) takes up the emblem of a ravenous Scotland (*The Poetical Works*, pp. 193–210).

35. Couper, *The Tourifications of Malachi Meldrum*, 2:57–58.

36. *The North Briton* 154 (March 10, 1770): 340–41. *The Briton* is reprinted in Smollett, *Poems, Plays, and the Briton*. For Wilkes's campaign against Smollett, see Nobbe, *The North Briton*, and Colley, *Britons*, esp. chap. 3. On Johnson's attitude toward anti-Scottish rhetoric, see Rogers, *Johnson and Boswell*, chap. 8. Temple's "Johnson and Macpherson" (pp. 363–64) has begun to trace a long line of anti-Macpherson parodies, in English newspapers, pamphlets, and pantomimes. In America, in contrast, *Ossian* becomes a key text for revolutionary intellectuals; see Jay Fliegelman, *Jefferson, Natural Language, and the Power of Performance* (Stanford: Stanford University Press, 1993), esp. chap. 4; Paul J. DeGategno, "'The Source of Daily and Exalted Pleasure': Jefferson Reads the Poems of Ossian," in Gaskill, ed., *Ossian Revisited*, pp. 94–108; and John Trumball's 1782 mock-heroic *M'Fingal. A Modern Epic Poem in Four Cantos* (New York: John Buel, 1795), which is dismissive of Macpherson as a "Scotch ministerial scribbler" (p. 1), yet derives a revolutionary lineage from *Ossian*: M'Fingal's "forefathers flourished in the Highlands / Of Scotia's fog-benighted islands; / Whence gained our 'Squire two gifts by right, / Rebellion and the Second-Sight" (p. 2). Macpherson himself opposed the American rebels in *The Rights of Great Britain Asserted against the Claims of America* (1776).

37. Boswell, *Life of Johnson*, 2:297; on the feud with Macpherson, see 2:292–89. Hume, in fact, chose not to print his skeptical essay "On the Authenticity of Ossian's Poems" during his lifetime, lest it embarrass friends who had championed Macpherson.

38. Stafford, *The Sublime Savage*, esp. chap. 2.

39. Wood, *An Essay on the Original Genius of Homer*, p. v. Couper satirizes this historicizing move by imagining Marlborough, Frederick of Prussia, Bonaparte, and Charles XII on pilgrimage "to the Troad, in order to adjust their plans and habiliments, according to what they could collect respecting the encampments and battles, the arms, accoutrements, and usual apparel, of Hector and Achilles . . . how the chiefs killed a sow, and how nicely they cut the spar-rib, for an entertainment— how they blew their noses in those days, before the amazing discovery of pocket handkerchiefs . . . that they might open, conduct, and conclude a campaign in the true Homeric stile and spirit" (*Tourifications of Malachi Meldrum*, 2:55–56).

40. As Temple points out, Johnson undertakes a similar journey to inspect Chatterton's manuscripts and the church where they were "discovered" in a less critical and vengeful spirit ("Johnson and Macpherson," p. 360). In 1764 Donald MacLeod of Glenelg invites "the gentlemen who deny Highlanders the honour of these monuments to the genius and prowess of his ancestors" to visit the Highlands, with interpreters, "that they may examine the matter themselves." They will be hospitably received, "and wherever they go to, the gentlemen and clergy will find out to them

the old men who still have in memory most of the works of Ossian, and the tradition-ary history of the Fingalians. I would engage that they should return home sufficiently satisfied that these poems being to the time and country to which they are ascribed" (Mackenzie, ed., *Report to the Highland Society*, appendix 131). On the influence of Johnson's journey and "the Ossianic sublime" on subsequent travel to Scotland, see Malcolm Andrews, *The Search for the Picturesque*, esp. chap. 8, and Cooper, *Road to the Isles*.

41. Sher, *Church and University*, pp. 10–11. See also John Clive, "The Social Background of the Scottish Renaissance," in Phillipson and Mitchison, eds., *Scotland in the Age of Improvement*, pp. 225–44; and Christensen, *Practicing Enlightenment*.

42. Kernan, *Printing Technology, Letters, and Samuel Johnson*.

43. Eagleton, *The Function of Criticism*, p. 35. See also Habermas, *The Structural Transformation of the Public Sphere*, and Sartre, *What Is Literature*.

44. See Blackwell's depiction of a golden age preceding the division of intellectual labor: "[T]here was as yet no *separation* of *Wisdom*: The Philosopher and the Divine, the Legislator and the Poet, were all united in the same Person" (*An Inquiry into the Life and Writings of Homer*, p. 84). See also Ferguson's defense of the "separation of arts and professions" as the precondition for civilizational progress (*An Essay on the History of Civil Society*, pp. 180–88).

45. Mackenzie, ed., *Report*, p. 54.

46. Ritson, *Pieces of Ancient Popular Poetry*, pp. vii–xi: "It is to an ENNIUS, perhaps, that we are indebted for a VIRGIL; to such writers as PEELE and GREENE, or others still more obscure, that we owe the admirable dramas of our divinest SHAKSPEARE; and if we are ignorant of the comparatively wretched attempts which called forth the deservedly immortal powers of HOMER or CHAUCER, it is by no means to be inferred that they were the earliest of poets, or sprung into the world . . . like Minerva out of the head of Jupiter, at full growth and mature." Maturin argues similarly that a realist tendency in modern English letters developed because prior bardic and ballad traditions had developed literary taste and had established the aesthetic power of ordinary language and occurrences (*Fatal Revenge*, 1:95–96).

47. Smollett, "The Tears of Scotland, Written in the Year MDCCXLVI," in *Poems, Plays, and the Briton*, pp. 23–26, here 23–24. On the romantic aesthetic of the ruin, see Janowitz, *England's Ruins*; Springer, *The Marble Wilderness*; and Bann, *The Clothing of Clio*.

48. M'Nicol counters that Scotland was never truly conquered, even in the post-Culloden occupation of the Highlands. The "whole glory of this conquest therefore, must belong to the *Doctor* alone. What could not be done in the field, he has accomplished in his closet" (*Remarks on Dr. Samuel Johnson's Journey*, p. 62).

49. Johnson, "Preface to *A Dictionary*," p. 235. Johnson's *Dictionary* worked both to naturalize social divisions and to displace contemporaneous progressive or radical linguistic theories; see Olivia Smith, *The Politics of Language*; Barrell, *English Literature in History, 1730–80* , esp. chap. 2; and De Maria, Jr., "The Politics of Johnson's *Dictionary*."

50. Johnson, "Preface," p. 235.

51. Ibid., pp. 241, 238.

52. Ibid., p. 255.

53. A satirical scene in Ferrier's *Marriage* (1818) lampoons Johnson's position: snobbish London bluestockings look down on a Scottish visitor because of her accent and speech, and they express their own patriotic wish that "every word we utter might be compelled to show its passport, attested by our great lawgiver, Dr. Samuel Johnson" (p. 204).

54. Johnson, "Preface," p. 258. On the relationship of *Dictionary* to *Journey*, see Lynch's suggestive " 'Beating the Track of the Alphabet.' "

55. Johnson, "Preface," pp. 257, 254.

56. Ibid., p. 256.

57. For the activities of the SPCK, see Withers, *Gaelic in Scotland*, and Durkacz, *Decline of the Celtic Languages*; for Evans's vehement polemics in the 1760s against the "popish" appointment of monolingual, English-speaking bishops to the Welsh church, see Lewis, ed., *The Correspondence of Thomas Percy and Evan Evans*, esp. pp. 144–45, 176–77.

58. *Johnson's Dictionary: A Modern Selection*, ed. E. L. McAdam, Jr., and George Milne (New York: Modern Library, 1965), p. 268; Henry Grey Graham, *Social Life of Scotland*, p. 179. See also John Wilkes's elaboration of Johnson's definition of *oats* in *North Briton* 40 (March 5, 1763), *The North Briton, No. 1 through LXVI Inclusive*, pp. 264–71.

59. See Combe's satirical portrait of Johnson as Paul Prosody, D.D., the antiquary baiter trapped within a book-dominated vision of the world; he reads books while walking and travels abroad "to find / What only centers in the mind" (*Tour of Doctor Prosody*, p. 2).

60. Fergusson, "To Dr. Samuel Johnson. Food for a New Edition of His Dictionary," in *Works*, pp. 203–6, here 203, ll. 1–11; p. 205, ll. 38–41.

61. Ibid., p. 206, ll. 62, 73–74.

62. Ibid., p. 205, ll. 54–55.

63. Fergusson, "Lines, to the Principal and Professors," in *Works*, p. 313. One model may be "The Description of an Irish Feast, translated almost literally out of the original Irish" (1720), Swift's translation of Aodh Mac Gabhráin's "Pléaráca na Ruarcach" (famous for its musical setting by Carolan). Swift's "Description" is one of the few efforts by early-eighteenth-century Anglo-Irish writers to take Gaelic poetry on its own terms and to challenge a long tradition of representing Gaelic in English as pure nonsense, as "Lilleburlero" (a tradition perpetuated in Johnson's reduction of the Erse oral tradition to "Radaratoo, radarate"). As a translation, however, the "Description" loses the pitch and timbre of the Gaelic original. Fergusson's Scots poems, in comparison, play the rhythm of the Lowland vernacular against the grain of English metrics. See also Andrew Carpenter, "Changing Views of Irish Musical and Literary Culture," in Kenneally, ed., *Irish Literature and Culture*, pp. 5–24, esp. p. 13.

64. Rousseau and Herder, *On the Origin of Language*. The stake of the shift that their work inaugurates is suggested forcefully in recent critiques of its liberatory rhetoric; see Derrida, *Of Grammatology*, and Kittler, *Discourse Networks, 1800/ 1900*. On English linguistic theory during the Enlightenment, see Aarsleff, *The Study of Language in England*, and Murray Cohen, *Sensible Words*.

65. For the history of this categorical divide between the literate and the illiterate mind, see Jack Goody, ed., *Literacy in Traditional Societies* (Cambridge: Cam-

bridge University Press, 1968) and *The Domestication of the Savage Mind* (Cambridge: Cambridge University Press, 1977); Walter Ong, *Orality and Literacy* (London: Methuen, 1982); Albert B. Lord, *The Singer of Tales* (Cambridge, Mass.: Harvard University Press, 1960); and Ruth Finnegan, *Oral Poetry* (Cambridge: Cambridge University Press, 1977).

66. Wood, *Essay*, pp. 259–60.

67. For a troubling continuation of Johnsonian debunking, see Hugh Trevor-Roper's "Invention of Tradition: The Highland Tradition of Scotland," in Hobsbawm and Ranger, eds., *The Invention of Tradition*, pp. 15–41, which insists on Scottish nationality and nationalism as a mere copy of an Irish original (while leaving intact Irish nationalism depicting popular culture as little more than an inheritance of romantic hoaxes).

68. Boswell, *Life of Johnson*, 1:310. In the wake of the *Ossian* controversies, Irish and Scottish nationalists repeatedly defend oral tradition as a valid historical source. Owenson follows Sylvester O'Halloran's line of defense, arguing in *The Wild Irish Girl* that contemporary historiographical practice already sanctions the use of oral sources. "Manuscripts, annals and records, are not the treasures of a colonized or conquered country. . . . [I]t is always the policy of the conqueror (or the invader) to destroy those mementos of ancient national splendour which keep alive the spirit of the conquered or the invaded" (p. 172); English attempts to discredit Irish claims of a long cultural history include deliberate efforts to keep even Irish *written* records from circulating. "Is it for those who have desolated the country, and razed every mark of power, or of resistance from the face of it," asks the chieftain in Maturin's *Wild Irish Boy*, "to demand where is the proof of power, or of resistance, and after beating down with the savageness of conquerors, the monuments of our strength and greatness, to ask with the insolence of conquerors, what monuments or strength and greatness are left to us?" (1:193).

69. Couper's *Tourifications* repeats McQueen's defense of Macpherson's "soldering hand" in assembling a "vast number of these scattered and detached pieces and poems" into an epic: "Did not Homer, or somebody, do all this for the Iliad?" (2:60)

70. Johnson would have learned more of living traditions, argues M'Nicol, "had he but known how to make his inquiries agreeable. But . . . his first question was generally rude and the second, a downright insult" (*Remarks*, p. 226).

71. Couper, *Tourifications*, 1:108.

72. See M'Nicol's critique of Johnson's interviewing strategy. "He might, for instance, question one of his *brogue-makers* concerning some nice point of antiquity, to which the poor fellow could make but a very imperfect answer. The next *taylor* he met might vary, in some circumstances, from the former; and a third person, not better informed than either of them, might differ a little from both. What then? Is there any thing surprising or uncommon in all this? or can such a variation in the accounts of illiterate mechanics justify the Doctor's general inference, 'that there can be no reliance upon Highland narration?' " (*Remarks*, p. 109).

73. William Wordsworth's "Solitary Reaper" (1805–7) might be read as an attempt to reconcile these two passages. Dorothy Wordsworth's *Recollections of a Tour Made in Scotland* identifies Thomas Wilkinson's *Tour in Scotland* as its primary inspiration, but these Johnsonian passages still seem its ultimate source.

74. See Withers, *Gaelic in Scotland*, chap. 7.

75. Yet as Thomas Davis protests in an 1843 article on the fate of Gaelic in Ireland, "To impose another language on such a people is to send their history adrift among the accidents of translation—'tis to tear their identity from all places—'tis to substitute arbitrary signs for picturesque and suggestive names—'tis to cut off the entail of feeling, and to separate the people from their forefathers by a deep gulf—'tis to corrupt their very organs, and abridge their power of expression. . . . A people without a language of its own is only half a nation. A nation should guard its language more than its territories—'tis a surer barrier, and more important frontier, than fortress or river" ("Our National Language," *The Nation*, April 1, 1842, p. 394).

76. On related orthographic reform efforts, see Olivia Smith, *Politics of Language*, and Donaldson, *Popular Literature in Victorian Scotland*, p. 54.

77. Johnson used mathematical games to overcome anxiety attacks (Bate, *Samuel Johnson*, pp. 73, 106, 415).

78. "These countries have never been measured, and the computation by miles is negligent and arbitrary. We observed in travelling, that the nominal and real distance of places had very little relation to each other" (Johnson, *Journey*, p. 75).

79. Denis Diderot, *Lettre sur les Aveugles*, in *Oeuvres philosophiques*, ed. Paul Vernière (Paris: Garnier, 1964), pp. 73–146.

80. Goldsmith, "The History of Carolan," p. 119.

81. Hume, *An Inquiry*, p. 28.

82. "Though speech and hearing were denied him, yet nature recompens'd him with a mind that glow'd with intelligence" (Thomas Holcroft, *Deaf and Dumb, or The Orphan Protected. A Historical Drama translated and adapted from the French of M. Bouilly* [Dublin: J. Stockdale, 1801], p. 35).

83. See also the comparison between agricultural cultivation and the teaching of sign language in ibid., p. 44.

84. Defoe, dedication and preface to his *Caledonia*, n.p.

85. Defoe, *The Second-Sighted Highlander*, p. 2; see Womack, *Improvement and Romance*, pp. 92–93.

86. George Chalmers made the attribution in 1790, but as Rodney Baine argued influentially in *Daniel Defoe and the Supernatural* (Athens: University of Georgia Press, 1968), no evidence supports Defoe's authorship of this or any of the works about Duncan Campbell traditionally attributed to him. Baine's own disattribution of *Duncan Campbell* (and reattribution to William Bond) is based mostly on dubious internal stylistic evidence (length of paragraphs as a hallmark of personal style). He does not address the text's possible relation to Defoe's other writings about Scotland.

87. Defoe, *Duncan Campbell*, p. 2. See also Defoe's *Memoirs of a Cavalier* (published only three months later), whose soldier narrator details the seventeenth-century English military campaigns in Scotland, railing against Scottish perfidy.

88. Swift's *Short View of the State of Ireland* (1727) makes an even more pointed comparison between Lapland and an underdeveloped Ireland: were a stranger to traverse Ireland, the "miserable Dress, and Dyet, and Dwelling of the People" and "the general Desolation in most Parts of the Kingdom" could make him believe

himself "travelling in *Lapland* . . . rather than in a Country so favoured by Nature as ours" (McMinn, ed., *Swift's Irish Pamphlets*, pp. 107–113, here 110).

89. Yet see also Defoe's "True Account of the Proceedings at Perth" (1716), in *The Versatile Defoe*, pp. 320–40, an unsympathetic portrait of Jacobite leadership during the '15.

90. Rebecca West, *The Judge* (1922; reprint, New York: Dial Press, 1980), pp. 144–45.

91. Smollett, *The Expedition of Humphry Clinker*, p. 277.

92. Andrew Gallie (Macpherson's friend and one of his hosts during his 1760s collecting trips) argues to the Highland Society that "[t]he names of Os, Fingal, Cumhal, Trenmor, their fathers and their heroes are still familiar, and held in the greatest respect. Straths [valleys], mountains, rocks and rivers, out of compliment to them, are named after them. . . . [A] high and craggy mountain in this same neighbourhood, perpetuates the fame of Fingal's favourite dog Bran. Every great and striking remain of antiquity, whose origin and use cannot be traced, is [even today] ascribed to Fingal and his followers" (Mackenzie, ed., *Report of the Highland Society*, pp. 41–42).

93. Blackwell, *Inquiry*, pp. 71, 114.

94. Yet as Ritson argues in the preface to *Pieces of Ancient Poetry*, the occasional character of such performances means that the poetry is transient and the scholarly reconstruction of "these fugitive productions" is difficult, if not impossible (pp. vii–xi).

95. Wood, *Essay*, p. 22.

96. Radcliffe probably draws on Hurd's "Dialogue III on the Golden Age of Queen Elizabeth between the Honourable Robert Digby, Dr. Arbuthnot and Mr. Addison" (1759), in which the ruins of Kenilworth Castle induce melancholy nostalgia and veneration in Dr. Arbuthnot, for whom they "revive the memory of some distinguishing character of the age," and righteous political anger in Addison, for whom they invoke "the memory of barbarous manners and a despotic government" (Hurd, *Letters on Chivalry and Romance*, p. 47).

97. Radcliffe, *Gaston de Blondeville*, 1:8–9.

98. Amory, *Memoirs*, p. xxi.

99. On the tension between the "oral" and the typographical in Amory, see Ian Campbell Ross, "Thomas Amory," pp. 71–85.

100. Maskell, *Old Tapestry*, 1:35.

101. Peacock, *Melincourt*, pp. 145–46. On a more Ossianic note, Derrydown argues that "Chevy Chase"—the ballad whose "rediscovery" and championing in *The Spectator* sparked the eighteenth-century ballad revival—is aesthetically superior to *Paradise Lost*.

102. Maturin, *The Albigenses*, 1:165–69.

103. See also, on the closing pages of Mary Hamilton's *Munster Village* (1778), the plein air masquerade to celebrate the establishment of an academic community for women. Arriving at the "temple of Minerva," guests are rowed over the "Styx" to "Elysium" and announced there by the boatman, "Charon" (p. 130). The masquerade becomes a virtual pageant of two thousand years of literary and cultural history: the first guests are dressed as Greeks (Demosthenes, Aristotle, Plato,

Pindar, and Praxiletes), followed by similar clusters of Romans (Cicero, Lucretius, Livy, Virgil, Horace, and Ovid), Italians (Lorenzo de Medici, Michelangelo, Raphael, Titian, Ariosto, and Tasso), and Englishmen of the Restoration, headed by the duke of Buckingham and including Dryden and Locke (pp. 131–33). To this point, the order of guests is strictly chronological, yet the final literary-historical guests to arrive—Homer and Ossian—are ancients rather than moderns, paired by affinity rather than by period. On Charon's ferry landing, they receive different receptions: accused of slighting women, Homer is not permitted to cross all the way to Elysium, whereas Ossian, "the first of men" (p. 144), is greeted rapturously and encouraged to perform a long rhapsodic poem. What his poetry cannot achieve, nonetheless, is the transmogrification of the fête champêtre, with its pantheon of Greco-Roman and Western European cultural heroes, back into the rugged sublimity of the Scottish Highlands.

104. Godwin, *Imogen*, p. 169.

105. Walpole, *Hieroglyphic Tales*, p. vi.

106. Kenneth Gross, introduction to Walpole, *Hieroglyphic Tales*, p. iv.

107. In Walpole's letters of 1760 and 1761, the years when Macpherson was publishing, first, selected Ossianic fragments and then the longer epic poem, "Fingal," Walpole expresses ever graver doubts about their authenticity.

108. Walpole, *Castle of Otranto*, p. 3.

109. See Richard Maxwell's forthcoming work on the motif of sanctuary in historical fiction.

110. Lee, "Advertisement," in *The Recess*, 1:n.p.

111. Marshall Brown, *Preromanticism*, pp. 165–70. Goldsmith's novel remains an important influence both on pastoral idyll and on early-nineteenth-century annalistic history.

112. Ryves, *The Hermit of Snowden*, p. viii.

113. Johnstone, *The History of John Juniper*, p. 86.

114. Macpherson, *The Poems of Ossian* (1805 edition). Mrs. Trimmer's *Series of Prints of ancient history* (1788) conflates Ossianically in the opposite direction: harps and harpists (drawn in very similar style) appear to illustrate the culture of the Celtic tribes, the education of King Alfred, and the rescue of Richard I by Blondel.

115. Maturin's *Melmoth the Wanderer*, pp. 495–96, offers a scene of literal "overcasting": a needlework rendition of a Christian scene is "repaired" by being embroidered over, so that its Christian content is suppressed and its latent classical or pagan resonances reemerge. Maturin links the process to textual revision and editing, and also to the social and historical milieu of Renaissance Spain in which imperial expansionism overlaps with a new secularism and a new interest in pagan culture (pp. 495–96).

116. "Magnus the Great: A Poem" and "The Chase: A Poem," in Charlotte Brooke, *Reliques of Irish Poetry*, pp. 33–65, 66–115.

117. Couper, *Tourifications*, 2:59.

118. Owenson, *St. Clair*, pp. 49–50. In LeFanu's *Tales of a Tourist*, "Mr. O'Carolan, a gentleman writing a book on the antiquities of Ireland," becomes involved in a debate with representatives of various sectors of Irish society about the origin of Ireland's round towers. The priest believes they were constructed by medi-

eval monks, the clergyman that they were built by the Medes, the landscape gardener ascribes them to the Druids, and so on. "Mr. O'Carolan floated in uncertainty between the different claims of the Scythians, Carthaginians, Phoenicians, Medes and Persians and could only come to the conclusion, that, whoever had the honour of constructing them, they were unquestionable proof of the high antiquity of the Irish nation" (2:212).

119. Owenson, *The Wild Irish Girl*, p. 97.

120. Scott, *The Antiquary*, 5:56.

121. For the possible sources of this episode, see Piggott, *Ruins in a Landscape*, esp. "The Roman Camp and Four Authors" and "The Ancestors of Jonathan Oldbuck"; and Robertson, *Legitimate Histories*, pp. 1–3. It has a long posterity in subsequent antiquarian satire: in "Strila's" "Anecdotes of Antiquaries," *Blackwood's Magazine* (May 1917): 135–38, a drunken Scottish peasant loses her kale pot in a peat bog; the antiquaries who find it one year later convince themselves that it is a Roman urn. See also LeFanu's *Tales of a Tourist*, 1:212; Dickens's *The Pickwick Papers* (original serial publication 1836–37), chap. 11; Prosper Merimée's *La Vénus d'Ille* (1837); and Gustave Flaubert's *Bouvard et Pécuchet* (written in 1872–80?). See also Richard Thomson's *Tales of an antiquary*, which provides a critical description of antiquarian activity (and credulity), even while reenacting antiquarian procedures to legitimate its own fictional reconstructions of London life over several centuries.

122. Richard Maxwell's "Searching for *Waverley*" (forthcoming) argues that *The Antiquary*'s pervasive Ossianisms link the themes of ancient and modern invasion to questions of authenticity, the relation between fact and fiction, and the Scottish militia controversy.

123. This barred window is also a "bard window." However facetiously, the passage links the interchange between aristocrat and beggar to the famous exchange of Richard I and his loyal servant Blondel through the barred prison window, their mutual recognition and communication made possible by a song. Chained and confined, an aristocratic spirit finds expression and recognition in the simple song of a wandering singer: the episode evokes the spirit of the ballad revival. Recounted in detail in the "Essay on Ancient Minstrels of England" in Percy's famous *Reliques of Ancient Poetry*, this story of Richard I and the "bard window" recurs in works concerned with cultural transmission (see Owenson, *Woman, or Ida of Athens*, 2:124–26) and becomes a perennial trope of the Gothic novel from Radcliffe's *Mysteries of Udolpho* to Sleath's 1810 *The Nocturnal Minstrel*.

124. See Michel Serres, *The Parasite* (Baltimore: Johns Hopkins University Press, 1982) and *Genèse* (Paris: Grasset et Fasquelle, 1982).

125. Griffin's *Tales of the Munster festivals* (1830) uses its frame narrative to restage *The Antiquary*'s opening meeting between Lovel and Monkbarn in far less cordial terms, to affirm both the political differences between cosmopolitan outsider and nationalist local historian and the generic separation between national tale and antiquarian history. Here, when the traveling narrator expresses his surprise that no one has yet written a national tale of Munster's picturesque beauties and customs, the elderly Irish antiquary gives him a stern lecture about the serious political and economic problems of "our forlorn and neglected country" (1:xix)—"a ruined

people stand in need of a more potent restorative than an old wife's story" (1:xviii)—then a detailed outline of the subjects from Irish history that most deserve fictional treatment.

126. Bage, *Hermsprong*, p. 44.

127. Peacock, *Crotchet Castle*, pp. 666–67. For the topicality of Peacock's satire, see Marilyn Butler, *Peacock Displayed*.

CHAPTER 3

1. Edwin Muir, *Scott and Scotland*, pp. 12–13, 161. Muir influences accounts of Scottish literature from Daiches' *Paradox of Scottish Culture* to Simpson's *Protean Scot*; but see also Nairn's critique in *The Break-up of Britain*, pp. 120–22. Muir's and Lukács's intellectual backgrounds offer interesting contrasts. Active in Glasgow socialism as in the Scottish avant-garde, Muir and his wife, Willa, lived during the 1920s in Czechoslovakia, Germany, Italy, and Austria, becoming the foremost translators of Central European modernism (Kafka, Hermann Broch, and Lion Feuchtwanger). Muir's *Scott* might fruitfully be read against Willa Muir's *Mrs. Grundy in Scotland*, a historical study of the Scottish ideology of respectability, written as an extended personification allegory and published in the same year and same series. It might also be read against contemporary Central European Marxist-modernist experiments in exemplary sociological biography—Siegfried Kracauer's 1937 *Orpheus in Paris: Offenbach and the Paris of His Time*, trans. Gwenda David and Eric Mosbacher (New York: Knopf, 1938), Benjamin's work on Baudelaire as a "lyric poet of High Capitalism," and Broch's *Hugo von Hoffmansthal and His Time* (written in 1947–50), trans. Michael Steinberg (Chicago: University of Chicago, 1984). Edwin Muir and Lukács part company, then, not only on modernism but in their approaches to historical exemplarity and totality.

2. "What is lacking in the so-called historical novel before Sir Walter Scott is precisely the specifically historical, that is, derivation of the individuality of characters from the historical peculiarity of their age. . . . Scott's extraordinarily realistic presentation of history [depends on] his ability to translate these new elements of economic and social change into human fates, into an altered psychology" (Lukács, *The Historical Novel*, pp. 19, 58).

3. Ibid., p. 30.

4. Postwar studies of Scott see him as a figure working in virtual isolation from the contemporary British novel. Davie's *Heyday of Walter Scott* reads Scott against the European classics; Arthur Melville Clark's *Sir Walter Scott: The Formative Years* and Millgate's *Walter Scott: The Making of a Novelist* depict Scott's formation as a self-fashioning. Fleischman's *English Historical Novel* criticizes a "Scott industry" that trumpets Scott's achievements (pp. 22–23) and briefly considers Scott's relationships to Edgeworth, Galt, and a few other contemporaries, yet feels they do not account for Scott's innovations. Although critical of Scott's influence on Scottish fiction, Craig's *Scottish Literature and the Scottish People* reads Galt as a distinctly minor author, in a chapter entitled "The Age of Scott."

The best recent work on Scott places his career in relation to contemporary politics or theory; see especially Sutherland, "Fictional Economies," and Ian Duncan, *Modern Romance*. Yet their emphasis is still on Scott's relation to classical, Renaissance, or eighteenth-century literature and to the Victorian novel, rather than to contemporary literature. Ferris's *Achievement of Literary Authority*, in contrast, reads Scott against novels by Edgeworth, Owenson, Hogg, and Galt, situating his authorship in relation to the realm of contemporary female writing as well as to the reviewing practices of the literary periodicals. See also W. B. Coley, "An Early 'Irish' Novelist" (1969), in Owens, ed., *Family Chronicles*, pp. 35–41; Garside, "Popular Fiction and National Tale"; Robertson, *Legitimate Histories*; Kerr, *Fiction against History*; MacQueen, *The Enlightenment and Scottish Literature*, vol. 2, *The Rise of the Historical Novel*; and Francis R. Hart's "Scott and the Novel in Scotland," in Alan Bell, ed., *Scott Bicentenary Essays*, pp. 61–79.

5. For Scott's "official" relationship to his contemporaries, see his *Letters*, including those to Edgeworth and Ferrier; Scott and Maturin, *The Correspondence of Sir Walter Scott and Charles Robert Maturin*; and Scott, *The Lives of the Novelists* and *On Novelists and Fiction*. See Frances Edgeworth, *A Memoir*, for Maria Edgeworth's impressions of Scott's poetry and fiction, her accounts of her visits to Scott in Edinburgh and Abbotsford, and her reaction to a wide range of contemporary novelists, including Radcliffe, Austen, Sophia Lee, Elizabeth Hamilton, Elizabeth Inchbald, Owenson, Barbara Hoole Hofland, John Gibson Lockhart, Peacock, the Banims, Gerald Griffin, Mrs. Monkland, Lady Caroline Lamb, and William Parnell. Austen's reading was just as catholic; see "Index to Literary Allusions," in Austen, *Works*, 5:295–306. For Austen's grudging admiration of Scott, see Austen-Leigh, "A Memoir of Jane Austen" (1870): "Sir Walter Scott has no business to write novels; especially good ones. It is not fair. He has fame and profit enough as a poet, and ought not to be taking the bread out of other people's mouths. I do not mean to like 'Waverley,' if I can help it, but I fear I must. . . . I have made up my mind to like no novels really, but Miss Edgeworth's, E's, and my own" (p. 332).

Scott, we should assume, read just as widely in the fiction of his own time; see Garside, "Popular Fiction." Robertson's *Legitimate Histories* discusses Scott's relationship to Maturin (pp. 214–25) and Lockhart's precedent-setting practice of regarding Scott as above, rather than within, the contemporary novelistic milieu (pp. 33–41). Scott's own pronouncements on the contemporary novel systematically mask his interest in the texts from which he borrows the most; he mentions and discusses at length Maturin's *Wild Irish Boy* rather than *The Milesian Chief*, Maria Edgeworth's *Castle Rackrent* rather than *Ennui* or *The Absentee* or *Ormond*, Charlotte Smith's *Old Manor House* rather than *Desmond*, Radcliffe's *Udolpho* rather than *Castles of Athlin and Dunbayne*, although it is clear he has read all of them. Commentators have not explored his indebtedness to these other novels in part because they have relied too exclusively on his own account of his influences, or they have underestimated its ironic play of revelation and concealment; an intertextuality readily apparent to Scott's contemporaries has been lost to later literary historians. The psychodynamics of Scott's relationship to his peers needs sustained rethinking. Scott acknowledged his debt to Owenson in particular, "with some hostility: invited to choose a name for one of his daughter Sophia's pet donkeys, Scott christened it 'Lady Morgan,'" presumably in mockery of Owenson's efforts at erudition (Nicola Watson, *Revolution and the Form of the British Novel*, p. 126).

Owenson was similarly abused by misogynist reviewers—see "Glorvina's Warning," *The Edinburgh Review* (March 1819): 720–22—and read with ambivalence even by dispassionate contemporaries. "[T]he condition one is [in] all the time one is reading Lady Morgan's book," writes Edgeworth in the early 1830s, is "alternately admiring and doubting and fearing to be taken in to believe what is all a sham" (Maria Edgeworth, *Letters from England, 1813–1844*, p. 453). For a modern dismissal of Owenson (and Maturin) as peripheral to the Irish novel, see McHugh and Harmon, *Short History of Anglo-Irish Literature*, pp. 110–12; for the first good overview of the national tale, see Gary Kelly, *English Fiction of the Romantic Period*, esp. pp. 86–98.

6. Literary-historical parameters for the romantic period include the increasing specialization of publishers and novelistic audiences; the shifting balance of power between trend-setting London publishers and alternative publishing centers in Edinburgh and Dublin; the generic expectations aroused or enforced by reviewers and by literary advertising; the effects of Scott's official and unofficial "patronage" on many literary careers; and the new "author functions" that Owenson and Scott inaugurate along with their new genres. Scott's prolonged masquerade as the anonymously antiquarian Author of *Waverley* is well known; Owenson's well-publicized glorification (and as Glorvina, personal embodiment) of a heroic, bardic female author was equally influential in its time; see Ferris, *Achievement*, and Mary Campbell, *Lady Morgan*. On post-Enlightenment authorship and audiences, see Klancher, *The Making of English Reading Audiences*; Butler, *Romantics, Rebels, and Reactionaries*; Mayo, *The English Novel*; Clive, *Scotch Reviewers*; Lockhart, *Peter's Letters to His Kinsfolk*, esp. letters 11, 12, and 35; Donaldson, *Popular Literature*; Shattock, *Politics and Reviewers*; and David Craig, *Scottish Literature*, pp. 297–300.

7. There are forerunners of the national tale already in the eighteenth century; see, for instance, Woodfin, *Northern Memoirs*. The early-nineteenth-century consolidation of the national tale as a genre is partly the result of Owenson's decision (or that of her publisher, Henry Colburn) to subtitle her novels with the generic designations "A National Tale" or "An Irish Tale." This label continued to be used by Colburn and other publishers for works ranging from Christian Johnstone's *Clan-Albin: A National Tale* (1815) and Mrs. Appleton's patriotic novel of medieval British life, *Edgar: A National Tale* (1816), to the 1834 series of Irish novels published by Colburn under the collective heading Irish National Tales. Eyre Evans Crowe's novels, for instance, appeared in this series under the two general subheadings "Today in Ireland" and "Yesterday in Ireland"; in its later usage, the designation "national tale" sometimes suggested a historical as well as a nationalist consciousness. Centered for part of its life in the publishing house of Henry Colburn, the genre might be understood partly as a marketing phenomenon; more work needs to be done on the role of specific publishers in shaping, commissioning, identifying, and classifying works in a particular genre.

8. As Ferris argues, this polarization was already accepted by Scott's public. Yet it has also been reinforced recently, as the first phases of the feminist reassessment of the novelistic canon gave particular attention to novels that could be read as explicitly feminist or protofeminist, in their foregrounding of female experience, education, and "the woman question"; see here Spencer, *The Rise of the Woman Novelist*; Spender, *Mothers of the Novel*; Schofield and Macheski, eds., *Fetter'd or Free?*; and Todd, *The Sign of Angellica*. The search for a separate, distinctively

female literary tradition (as emphasized in otherwise invaluable reprinting programs) runs the danger of ratifying the sexist ghettoization of "lady novelists" in earlier periods and literary histories. See the appreciative yet trivializing paean to contemporary female authorship in Walter Scott's *Lives of the Novelists*, p. 334; the chapters on female authors in Oliphant's *Literary History of England*, Anne Ritchie Thackeray's *Book of Sibyls*, and R. Brimley Johnson's *Women Novelists*; for a critique of this legacy, see Armstrong, *Desire and Domestic Fiction*, p. 48; see also Mellor, *Romanticism and Gender*.

9. Much of Owenson's work is marked by the confluence of feminist and nationalist concerns. See her discussion of the circumstances that produce national character and ideal womanhood in the preface to *Woman, or Ida of Athens* (1809), 1:ix–xxviii, and the extended discussion of female authorship (and the writing of the national tale in particular) as women's work at its most exalted and quotidian, most traditional and most radical, in *Florence Macarthy*, 4:35–38 and 4:142–51. See also her last work, *Woman and Her Master* (1840), with its synthesis of anthropological, sociological, and historical perspectives on female oppression since antiquity. Plots involving national identity and female socialization are also juxtaposed in Brunton's *Discipline* (1815), Ferrier's *Marriage* (1818), and, more implicitly, Maturin's *Women, or Pour et Contre* (1818), with its agonized wavering between two (secretly related) models of femininity embodied respectively by an English Methodist, locked into a repressive modesty, and a genial Italian actress (modeled on Corinne, Armida, and perhaps Owenson herself) who mounts public (and problematic) displays of her erudition and emotions.

10. If eighteenth-century Scottish history, writes Lecky in *A History of Ireland in the Eighteenth Century*, provides "one of the most remarkable instances on record of the efficacy of wise legislation in developing the prosperity and ameliorating the character of nations," the history of eighteenth-century Ireland shows "with singular clearness the perverting and degrading influence of great legislative injustices, and the manner in which they affect in turn every element of national well-being" (1:1).

11. Scott's *Waverley* is set "sixty years since," at a last battle for the Highlands, which by the time of writing belongs safely to the past. Edgeworth, *Ennui*; Maturin, *Milesian Chief*; Lamb, *Glenarvon* (1816); Parnell, *Maurice and Berghetta* (1819); M'Henry, *O'Halloran* (1824); Owenson, *The O'Briens and the O'Flahertys* (1827); John Banim, *The Anglo-Irish of the Nineteenth Century* (1828); and Michael Banim, *The Croppy: A Tale of the Irish Rebellion of 1798* (1828) all depict a far more recent failed rebellion, like Culloden in some ways, but utterly unlike it in others, including the fact that its suppression (and the official Act of Union in 1800) did not mark the end of guerrilla fighting.

12. On the line from *Tristram Shandy* to high modernism, see Eagleton's *Heathcliff*, esp. pp. 145–54.

13. Bowen, *Bowen's Court*, p. 5.

14. Swift, "The Story of the Injured Lady," in *The Prose Works*, 7:97–106, here 97–99.

15. Ibid., p. 97.

16. Ibid., p. 102. Stevie Smith's "Celts" (1957) updates Swift, envisioning the Celts as a whiny lady who hugs her grievances to herself.

17. Swift's allegorical story self-consciously recasts a long Anglo-Irish tradition that depicts Ireland salaciously. Luke Gernon's *Discourse of Ireland, Anno 1620*, for instance, depicts her as a lustful young nymph who "hath the greene sicknes for want of occupying . . . she wants a husband, she is not embraced, she is not hedged or ditched, there is no quicksett put into her" (Falkiner, ed., *Illustrations of Irish History*, pp. 344–62, here 349). Swift, in contrast, confronts the reader with the story of a rape and a forcible occupation, narrated by the resentful victim.

18. Swift, "Injured Lady," p. 97.

19. Ibid., pp. 97–98.

20. *The Anti-Union* 3 (January 1, 1799): 9–12, here 11.

21. Ibid., p. 11.

22. Ibid.

23. Ibid.

24. "A True Story," *The Anti-Union* 10 (January 17, 1799): 37–40, here 37.

25. Ibid., p. 37.

26. Ibid., p. 38.

27. Ibid., p. 40.

28. Ibid.

29. See Defoe's *Moll Flanders* (1722) and Swift's *Gulliver's Travels* (1726); Fielding's *Joseph Andrews* (1742) and *Tom Jones* (1749); Smollett, *Roderick Random* (1748) and *Humphry Clinker* (1771); Amory, *Memoirs* (1755) and *The Life of John Buncle* (1756–66); Goldsmith, *The Citizen of the World* (1760–61); Johnstone, *Chrysal* (1761) and *The History of John Juniper* (1781); and Hamilton, *Letters of a Hindoo Rajah* (1796).

30. Smith, *Desmond*, 1:197. See Cross, "An Earlier Waverley," pp. 87–88; Ty's *Unsex'd Revolutionaries* discusses Scott's declared dislike for *Desmond* and Leigh Hunt's hypothesis that it was an important source for *Waverley*.

31. Edgeworth structures "The Grateful Negro" (from her 1802 *Popular Tales*) around a parallel, didactic contrast in political economies, comparing the benevolent planter's pleasant, harmonious, and prosperous Jamaican plantation with his dissolute neighbor's ill-managed estate and rebellious slaves, in order to encourage agricultural reform and enlightened paternalism (*Tales and Novels*, 2:399–419).

32. This figure reworks a trope used in late-eighteenth-century fiction to discredit the rather different landscape transformations undertaken by modish "improvers": in Couper's *Tourifications* (2:118), Signor Pitoresco thus cuts down a stately avenue of trees at Meldrum Hall in order to improve the view; the trope appears again in Austen's *Mansfield Park*, when Fanny protests the chopping of trees at Sotherton.

33. National tales such as Edgeworth's *Ennui* and *The Absentee*, Owenson's *Florence Macarthy*, and Ferrier's *Destiny* have a powerful influence on the way early-nineteenth-century Irish and Scottish novel readers experience their native land. When Elizabeth Grant of Rothiemurchus describes her return to the Highlands in 1812, after a protracted stay in England, she writes like one of Edgeworth's, Owenson's, or Ferrier's returning absentees. "It has always seemed to me that this removal to Rothiemurchus was the first great era in my life. All our habits changed—all connexions, all surroundings. . . . The language, the ways, the style of the house, the visitors, the interests, were all so entirely different from what had

been latterly affecting us, we seemed to be starting as it were afresh. I look back on it now even as a point to date up to and a point to date on from; the beginning of a second stage in the journey" (*Memoirs*, p. 210).

34. See Nicola Watson, *Revolution*, esp. chaps. 1 and 3, for a contrasting account of *Desmond*, *The Wild Irish Girl*, and *Waverley*, as well as for the way the British novel rewrites Rousseau's *La nouvelle Helöise* and the French Revolution; see also Gary Kelly, *The English Jacobin Novel* and *Women, Writing, and Revolution*.

35. Scott, *Waverley*, in *The Waverley Novels*, 1:10.

36. West, *The Loyalists*, 2:220–21, 2:153.

37. Ibid., 2:6–7.

38. Ibid., 2:1–2.

39. Owenson's *Patriotic Sketches of Ireland* (1807) uses comparative political set pieces derived from Smith out of Radcliffe: of two Irish cabins visited on neighboring estates, one is poor under the abuses of the tenant system, the other prosperous under the influence of agricultural improvement. Yet Owenson's opening comparison of two cities, Sligo and Ballysidore, suggests a less pointed political program. By far the older town, Ballysidore was flourishing until "the vicissitudes of civil dissension" force its inhabitants to flee along the shore. Their temporary encampment grows into the city of Sligo, "now a large opulent and commercial town, while its parent city is one of the most ruinous and wretched villages in the province" (1:7). Despite the circumstances surrounding the respective fates of the two towns, however, Owenson draws a philosophical moral rather than a political one: their "vicissitudes" epitomize the inevitable "rise, climacteric, decline, and fall of every empire" (1:8–9). Owenson later condemns this impersonal, cyclical view of historical process, along with the exoticism and antiquarianism that characterize her first three novels. It is as if, in her early works, Owenson imitates Smith's use of a traveling plot to launch political observations, without understanding the full political implications of her literary and formal choices, nor how Smith's Jacobin and feminist politics fit together.

40. But see also M'Henry's *O'Halloran*. Although heavily indebted both to *The Wild Irish Girl* and to *Waverley*, *O'Halloran* is prefaced by a long polemic *against* Owenson's tendency to present Ireland as a society polarized between Anglo-Irish interests and Milesian claims. Owenson overlooks the importance of the Scotch-Irish as Ireland's major third cultural group, and of Presbyterian dissent as a political force, especially during the 1790s, when some Scotch-Irish agitated for Catholic emancipation, formed the nucleus of the United Irishmen, and eventually led the rebellion of 1798, and others, committed to more gradual reform, helped to uphold the government. The Scotch-Irish thus represent an independent (if unpredictable) third force in Irish politics. Scotch-Irish as Bradwardine Lowlanders: *O'Halloran* replaces the binarisms of *The Wild Irish Girl* with the equally schematic tripartite structure of *Waverley*, Owenson's partisanship with Scott's advocacy of a wavering, middle position.

41. Johnstone, *The Saxon and the Gaël*. On the history of national character as a conceptual category, see Deane, "Irish National Character."

42. Corkery, *Synge and Anglo-Irish Literature*, pp. 7–8.

43. *The Edinburgh Review* (April 1803) complains that Charles Vallancey's *Prospectus of a Dictionary of the Language of Air Coti, or Ancient Irish, compared*

with the Language of the Cuti, or Ancient Persians (pp. 116–23) invents completely spurious genealogies. "The Introduction," they scoff, "begins with several extracts relative to *Ireland*, translated from the Puranas! of the Indian Brahmins!" (p. 118). Instead of engaging in the "scientific labour" of real philological collation, "the Caledonian and Hibernian antiquaries waste long lives, and respectable learning, in establishing fictions which a child would ridicule, and in torturing the pliable orthography of a barbarous dialect, to give it a fanciful resemblance to Sanscrit or Phoenician" (p. 128).

44. See Appleton's *Edgar: A National Tale* (1816), whose didactic celebration of British nationality is buttressed with footnotes on "medieval" customs and justifications of its own anachronisms. Peck's *The Life and Acts of . . . Edmund of Erin . . . An Irish Historical Romance of the Seventh Century Founded on Facts: Blended with a Brief and Pithy Epitome of the Origin, Antiquity and History of Ireland with Copious Notes, Critical and Historical* presents the logical extension of this annotating impulse. Its exceptionally lengthy footnotes on the political history of Ireland, the inferiority of English to Irish intellectual traditions, or the parallels between Hibernian and Greek epic cultures turn into chapters in their own right, which block the plot for dozens of pages at a time.

45. *The Wild Irish Girl* synthesizes eighteenth-century nationalist, antiquarian, and local-color genres. Owenson sees herself as formulating "a national tale from those materials which the ancient and modern history, manners, and habits of my country supplied. . . . To blend the imaginary though probable incident with the interesting fact, to authenticate the questioned refinement of ancient habits, by the testimony of living modes . . . such was my prospectus" (*Patriotic Sketches of Ireland*, 1:vii–ix). She dabbles in antiquarian editing (see her 1805 *Twelve Original Hibernian Melodies*), and her footnotes to *The Wild Irish Girl* frame the novel as part of the antiquarian response to the Ossian controversy (her *Memoirs* stresses her indebtedness to Joseph Walker, author of the 1786 *Memoirs of the Irish Bards*). Yet see Dunne's "Fiction as 'the Best History of Nations' " on Owenson's continuing ambivalence toward antiquarianism.

The comparison of Owenson's national tale with a late-eighteenth-century forerunner, Brooke's 1769 *History of Emily Montague* (now known mainly as the first Canadian novel), makes clear both the national tale's origins in eighteenth-century travel fiction and its structural innovations. An epistolary novel like *The Wild Irish Girl*, *Emily Montague* is set in Quebec in the wake of the British conquest (seen as an exciting recent event rather than a political struggle), and it presents the final choice between places as purely economic, without political inflections. The English hero and heroines come out to Canada, fall in love, and write enthusiastic letters home about the Canadian landscape, French Canadian society, and the exotic customs of the Indians. Although they find Canada agreeable, they miss their families and their familiar surroundings; their final return to England is a happy one. Irish and Scottish national tales weigh their outcomes heavily in the opposite direction.

46. Owenson, *O'Donnel*, 1:20. The problem of tourist knowledge persists throughout Owenson's travelogues, from *Patriotic Sketches of Ireland* to *Italy* (1821), and as one of the motivating concerns of the national tale, as in Scottish and Irish literature more generally; see Goldsmith, *The Citizen of the World* (1760–61),

letter 23, pp. 90–93; Mrs. Wood's *Letters from the Irish Highlands*, letter 14, pp. 85–87; Combe, *Tour of Doctor Prosody*; and Lockhart's *Peter's Letters to His Kinsfolk*, which uses the traveler to Scotland as a vehicle for a highly sympathetic cultural exegesis. In his travels through northern Ireland, the Waverleyesque hero of M'Henry's *O'Halloran* discovers that he has misjudged his Scotch-Irish countrymen; taught to believe they are "a race of stiff, plodding, narrow-minded, avaricious people . . . so dry, so inhospitable, so selfish in their money, that they scarce deserved to be considered Irish . . . cunning Scotchmen . . . bigotted, ignorant Presbyterians," he is surprised to find that the Ulster peasantry "have all the good nature, simplicity and kindness of Arcadians . . . and their nobility and gentry, all the high-spiritedness, gallantry, and generosity of the days of romance. . . . Scottish in their industry and intelligence . . . they are altogether Irish in their manners and feelings" (1:138). So, too, when the hero of Elizabeth Hamilton's *Memoirs of the Modern Philosophers* (1800) reports of his "Tour Through Scotland," his newly enlightened view of Scotland was made possible by his decision to observe the country for himself, rather than to use his letters of introduction. From *O'Donnel* to John Banim's *Anglo-Irish of the Nineteenth Century*, the national tale discusses whether to tour with a guidebook or whether it will blind the traveler to all save the approved sights.

47. Owenson, *O'Donnel*, 1:87, 1:162, 1:163. A similarly satirical account of the self-absorbed tourist group and its misprisions appears again in Owenson's *Princess, or The Beguine* (1835), which retells the nationalist *O'Donnel/Florence Macarthy* plot in a Belgian rather than an Irish setting; British tourists visiting a Belgian gallery recognize only the already-known names of Italian artists and remain oblivious to the different aesthetic of Flemish art.

48. Although for the purposes of her plot, as she hastens to make clear in one footnote, her fictional travelers spend the night at "a new inn on the seacoast," "[i]t may be perhaps necessary to inform the English tourist, who may be induced to visit the Giant's Causeway by the coasting road from Belfast to Bush Mills, that no such inn at present exists, as is here mentioned" (Owenson, *O'Donnel*, 1:97).

49. Hamilton's *Memoirs of the Modern Philosophers*, 1:190–98, uses the discussion of Rousseau's *Nouvelle Heloïse* to establish a similar political bifurcation (with the opposite political sympathies); for Hamilton, Jacobin attitudes toward reading, quotation, and literary property metonymically point up the shortcomings of their political philosophy.

50. Owenson, *Florence Macarthy*, 1:14–17.

51. Like the travelers' arguments in Radcliffe's *Gaston de Blondeville*, Owenson's exegetical duel over the political meaning of the ruin probably derives from Hurd's "Dialogue III"; its staging, against the backdrop of the arrival and disembarkation in Dublin, is indebted to Edgeworth's *Absentee*—and recycled once again in Hall's *Whiteboy* (1845) (1:1–19), except that the Fitzadelm character is now an Englishman named Edward Spencer.

52. See also Roche's *Tradition of the Castle* (1824), which opens with a critical account of the 1802 Act of Union and the announcement of a parliamentarian who supports it that he will be moving his family to England, to live off their Irish rents. When he becomes dissolute and commits suicide, his son returns to Ireland, to fight for the restoration of his estates and for the novel's culminating romantic union with

the allegorically named Eveleen Erin. With its long delay between the declaration, by parliamentary fiat, of official political union and an actual, affective union, *Tradition* opens new political vistas for the national tale.

53. The trope of British intermarriage continues to be evoked in other forms of political discussion. Wood's *Letters from the Irish Highlands* presents it as a practical method of increasing international understanding by making "our English brethren acquainted with the true state of this portion of the empire. Any Englishman who has travelled in Ireland, every Irishman who has visited England, must have been struck by the mutual want of information prevailing among the inhabitants of the sister islands. . . . [A]n English lady, who, since her marriage with an Irish landed proprietor, contrives to reside part of every year in her own country . . . made it her business, in Ireland, to correct the erroneous opinions of her friends with regard to England, and in England, to set them right respecting Ireland" (pp. xv–xvi).

54. On the evolution of the marriage plot within Owenson's works, see Eagleton, *Heathcliff*, p. 180. Its dystopic rewriting may begin in Peregrine Puzzlebrain's *Tales of My Landlady* (11818); in "The Uses of Adversity" an Irish estate agent travels to London on business, wins the rich widow of an "eminent pork butcher," and brings her back to Ireland. "But almost immediately after their arrival in this country, mutual discontent took place of matrimonial harmony. Her Ladyship, proud of her wealth, her title, and her connections among, as she phrased it, the most *substantialist* and *toppingest* people in the city of *Lunnon*, found every thing in our poor little island insupportable. She declared, indeed, on her third day's residence in it, that it was the most barbarous, outlandish place on the face of the *yarsal* globe; and as to the people, she was sure that they had not half of the politeness of some *selvidges* which she had read about in history. As the *amor patriae* in M'Shaughlin's weak side, he defended his native land with more spirit than temper; and the consequence has been a succession of quarrels, which have nearly extinguished her love for her husband, as well as rendered their lives very uncomfortable" (1:252–53). Tellingly, it is Lady Muggins, not her Irish husband, who utters a series of "bulls" in the act of denouncing Irish savagery.

55. In Ferrier's *Marriage* (1818), an English heiress elopes to Scotland with a Highland nobleman, prepared for "romantic" Scotland but unprepared for Scottish weather, food, speech, and custom. After the marriage founders, her twin daughters are raised apart, one as English, the other as Scottish. When the Scottish daughter comes to London, she is rebuffed by her mother and twin, and she finally retreats with her husband to the Scotland they both love. The mother's comic inability to appreciate the values of Scottish life is offset by a loyal daughter who freely chooses her native Scotland over the blandishments of the metropole. Ferrier's *Destiny, or The Chieftain's Daughter* stages an even more elaborately failed intercultural marriage. The Chief of Glenroy marries an aristocratic English widow on a visit to London; back in the Highlands, the marriage founders on national differences and the couple's allergies to each other's worlds: the English wife suffers from rheumatism, "which she imputed entirely to the climate of Scotland," and her husband (who "despised every part of the globe save Scotland") suffers from gout, which he attributes to his one visit to London, so injurious that it must never be repeated (1:7). The rest of the novel centers on their two daughters, one sensible, loyal, and Scottish, the

other feckless and English. Like previous national tales, *Destiny* is concerned with local life, values, and loyalties. Yet its almost total avoidance of local color—Gaelic speakers are referred to only once, as "the aborigines of the country" (1:327) who are given church services in their own tongue—and its picture, closer to Austen than to Ossian, of the genteel pursuits of the Highland nobility mark one terminus of the national tale back into the novel of manners and female education from which it came.

56. Already in Owenson's *Woman, or Ida of Athens*, a transcultural love story is grafted onto an exotic locale, the Greek-Turkish war. Despite Owenson's own cultural and religious relativism, her novels help to establish the plot repertoire for the nineteenth-century biblical novel. See Lockhart's *Valerius: A Roman Story* (1821), a historical romance that rewrites *The Missionary* in reverse: a Briton arrives in imperial Rome, falls in love with a Christian maiden, converts to the new religion, and escapes Roman persecution by fleeing back to Britain with her. For an evangelical refusal both of *The Missionary*'s cosmopolitan implications and of the national marriage plot itself, see *The History of George Desmond* (1821, attributed to Mary Sherwood). Newly arrived in Bengal, Desmond is so disoriented by the unfamiliar Indian foods, perfumes, and ceremonies that he allows himself to be seduced by an evil "nautch girl" and goes native, setting up house with her. Eventually he deserts her and their child to marry a virtuous Englishwoman and return to white society. But his past continues to follow him, as the nautch girl confronts his wife with his impurities and finally poisons her. In the colonial context of India, it seems, the alliance with an allegorical national character is necessarily sinful, unhappy, and poisonous; a rapprochement with native culture can be achieved only at the price of betraying Christian values and the code of British civilization. But see also Mainwaring's *Suttee, or The Hindu Converts* (1800), in which—following Bernadin de Saint-Pierre's influential 1787 *Pierre et Virginie*—an English widow and a Hindu nurse raise their children together, against the background of British attempts at social reform in India (including the forcible suppression of suttee by British soldiers). The eventual marriage of their children, the English Mira and the Indian Mirza, reflects the productive "union" between Hindu culture and English government in British India; raised as Christians, the sons of Mira and Mirza become missionaries.

57. Owenson, *The Missionary*, 3:186–87. For its influence on Shelley's thinking about India, see Leask, *British Romantic Writers*, esp. pp. 115–18, 126–28. One source for Owenson's trope of bifurcated identity may be Wolfe Tone's recurring image of Ireland as a paralytic; in *An Argument on Behalf of the Catholics of Ireland* (1791), he urges the transcendence of traditional religious and ethnic divides by invoking an Ireland caught in historical and economic limbo: "Ireland is struck with a political paralysis, that has withered her strength, and crushed her spirits: she is not half alive; one side is scarce animated, the other is dead" (p. 11). A different precedent for Owenson's figuration of divided loyalties appears in *Ennui*, where the former Lord Glenthorn, renouncing an illegitimate birthright to become an ordinary citizen, finds himself still "apt to mistake between my old and my new habits," for which "people stared at me as if I was mad" (*Castle Rackrent and Ennui*, p. 293).

58. Maturin, *Melmoth the Wanderer*, p. 103. West's *Loyalists* describes the civil war in similarly bifurcated terms: "While the fanatics and levellers alternately

gained the ascendancy . . . [t]hat mighty Parliament . . . as different parties prevailed in it, countenanced the most rigorous coercion or permitted the wildest anarchy. . . . [It was a] strange combination of talent and extravagance, of praying demagogues and aspiring religionists" (2:220–21).

59. Other novels work with Owenson's and Maturin's notion of characterological schizophrenia, but often at the price of generic schizophrenia. John Banim's exploration of divided cultural identity in *The Anglo-Irish of the Nineteenth Century* begins as an national tale about the Protestant Ascendancy, using the education and return to Ireland of an Anglo-Irish absentee to analyze a neurotic micropolitics of cultural denial, self-loathing, and inferiority complexes. Then it uneasily shifts into a Waverleyesque historical novel plot whose macropolitical events—hostage takings and foiled uprisings—are meant to motivate its hero's change of political attitude, but which, in the wake of the detailed psychological analysis that has gone before, instead seem mechanical and anxious to lay to rest its own specters of permanent instability.

Such generic tensions between the national tale and the historical novel remain foundational to realism as late as Arnold Bennett's *Old Wives Tale* (1908), which marks the movements between its sections, allegorical protagonists, and places (Constance, the stasis of Bursley and the national tale, with its belief in an accreted knowledge of place, and Sophia, the cataclysms of late-nineteenth-century Paris and the historical novel, with its quest for wisdom through bitter experience) by moments of historical violence the characters witness, internalize, and repress. These traumas reappear belatedly but legibly as lingering medical symptoms, especially strokes, one even evident as partial facial paralysis, so that—as in Owenson's and Maturin's figures of uneven development and civil war—part of the personality continues to move forward in historical time, whereas the rest remains frozen in place.

60. As the name Armida indicates, Tasso's *Jerusalem Delivered* is a crucial intertext for *The Milesian Chief*, mirrored in many specifics of plot, in the epic emphasis on two polarized forces fighting over a Holy Land (in the love story between combatants trapped on opposite sides), and in its tragic sense of the cataclysmic, incomprehensible character of so-called holy wars. Tasso's love stories challenge the Manichaean religious and heroic economy of the epic form; the final reconciliation between Armida and Rinaldo, after the defeat of Armida's sorcery, amid the wreckage of a "delivered" Jerusalem, suggests a triumph of non-Christian alliances just as pagan forces are ostensibly defeated. At the same time, as a love triumphant, it provides one of the poem's scanty elements of positive closure, amid the apocalyptic destruction of the city. In *The Milesian Chief*, in contrast, a private happiness becomes impossible when nations break; public cataclysms destroy the heroic code of Tasso's world and the private sphere as a separable place. Here it is neither Armida's sorcery nor her relative's machinations that doom Connal's cause, but a new institutional reorganization of power, so impersonal it cannot be embodied allegorically, which renders obsolete the local loyalties of Connal's forces.

61. Maturin, *The Milesian Chief*, 1:181–85. Lamb's *Glenarvon* (1816) rewrites this as a scandalously autobiographical roman à clef: Lamb becomes the Armidian

Calantha, Lord Byron, the Connalesque Glenarvon. Foregrounding her own seduction and desertion (against a background of harp music and sublime Irish landscape), Lamb reduces the 1798 uprising to mere background action, come and gone in the space between chapters.

62. "The Outlaw," in LeFanu's *Tales of a Tourist*, makes Maturin's contrasts more explicit. Here an Irish aristocrat, raised primarily in England, compares her own decorous, long-distance patriotism to the headstrong rebelliousness of the United Irishmen, without knowing that her father and her lover have both been outlawed after the 1798 rebellion. Although deeply attached to "the mouldering records that tell of our ancient intellectual superiority," she is disturbed to think that Ireland's "'verdant paradise stocked with flocks of scholars' . . . has been defaced by strife . . . made the theatre of dissension, guilt, rebellion." Her lover's attempt to convince her of the "good intentions" of "those unhappy men who suffered death or exile" meets with complete incomprehension; she "'can never think with charity of those who, to . . . revenge imaginary grievances, plunged their country into all the miseries of civil war'" (1:116).

63. For a later, even more quietistic rewriting of *The Milesian Chief*, see Whitty's "Last Chieftain of Erin," in *Tales of Irish Life* (1824), 1:120–71. It deploys every plot device of the national tale from Edgeworth to Maturin, and every nationalist trope from the Ossianic reverie to the fostering nurse—only to turn against nationalist principles. The "last chieftain" loses his ruined castle and goes into exile with his bard and his priest. Rashly committing himself to the cause of national revolution, his son Cormac becomes an outlaw on his own ancestral lands but then rescues the Anglo-Irish landowner from danger and marries his daughter. This union seals the alliance between the old and new masters of Ireland, and Cormac recants all Jacobin and nationalist principles.

64. See here Kilfeather, "Strangers at Home"; W. J. McCormack, "Irish Gothic and After (1820–1945)," in Deane et al., eds., *Field Day Anthology*, 2:831–54.

65. "O Dove, Your Song Is Cause for Tears," in Kinsella, ed., *An Duanaire*, pp. 23, 21.

66. Owenson, *O'Donnel*, 1:vii.

67. Blackwell drew similar connections between historical crises and literary form. "It was when *Greece* was ill-settled, when Violence prevailed in many Places, amidst the Confusion of the wandering Tribes, that *Homer* produced his immortal Poem: And it was when *Italy* was torn in Pieces . . . in the Heat of the Struggle and Bloodshed of the *Guelfe* and *Ghibelline* Parties, that *Dante* . . . made the strongest Draught of Men and their Passions, that stands in the Records of modern Poetry. The Author of the *Eneid* lived in a Time of Disorder and publick Ruin. . . . And . . . it was when unhappy *Britain* was plunged in all the Calamities of *Civil Rage*, that our high-spirited Poem [*Paradise Lost*] took its Birth" (*Inquiry into the Life of Homer*, pp. 65–66). Owenson, in contrast, argues that new literary modes can be consolidated only in the wake of historical upheavals, hence the exhaustion of forms in her own epoch, "an era of transition [in which] changes moral and political are in progress" (Owenson, *Dramatic Scenes from Real Life* [1833], 1:v). Hamilton adapts this argument to justify the British conquest of India: "The thirst of conquest and the desire of gain, which first drew the attention of the most powerful and enlightened

nations of Europe towards the fruitful region of Hindostan, have been the means of opening sources of knowledge and information to the learned and the curious, and have added to the stock of the literary world" (*Letters of a Hindoo Rajah*, 1:vii–viii). The result of war is an enriched literary culture for the conquerors.

68. See Ferris's *Achievement* (esp. the introduction and chap. 3) for the initially critical reception of *Waverley*. Yet by 1825, Hazlitt's essay "Sir Walter Scott," in *Spirit of the Age*, flatly declares Scott the most popular writer of the age.

69. Well beyond its heyday, the national tale remains a repertoire of identifiable plot bits, linked to a recurring set of political concerns. Parnell's *Maurice and Berghetta* grafts the *Milesian Chief* plot line onto the idyll structure of *The Recess*; M'Henry's *O'Halloran* reassembles key elements of *The Wild Irish Girl*, *Waverley*, and *The Milesian Chief*; the anonymous *Ford Family in Ireland* (1845) is a tale of collective national comparison and discovery à la *O'Donnel* and *The Absentee*, crossed with the kidnapping/secret society/conversion plot of *Waverley* and *The Anglo-Irish* and ending in the hero's execution, as in *The Milesian Chief*.

70. From Radcliffe onward, the Gothic novel habitually performed acts of literary homage and self-legitimation in the form of its epigraphs, inserting itself into literary tradition at the beginning of every chapter. It is also, from its outset, linked not only to an Ossianic interest in the synchronization of voice and landscape but also to the specific topographies and traditionalisms of the peripheries; see, for instance, Lee's 1783–85 *Recess* (whose action moves both to Ireland with Essex's army and to a remote Scottish castle), Radcliffe's 1789 *Castles of Athlin*, and Roche's 1796 *Children of the Abbey* (whose characters circulate from northern Wales to northern Ireland to the west coast of Scotland).

71. On the differences between annal, chronicle, and nineteenth-century narrative history, see Momogliano, "Ancient History and the Antiquarian," and White, "The Value of Narrativity in the Representation of Reality," in White, *The Content of the Form*, pp. 1–25.

72. Owenson, *The O'Briens and the O'Flahertys*, p. 442. On the differences between Scott's and Owenson's modes of representing history, see Dunne's "Fiction," especially pp. 155–56.

73. Galt, *The Entail*, pp. 30, 61, 31.

74. Much of Galt's subsequent fiction uses first-person "autobiographical" narratives to explore the formation of political ideologies, life stories, and thus narrating voices. The panoramic scope of his novels as an ensemble and their nuanced attention to the circumstances that shape consciousness make Galt the most important and most innovative political novelist of his epoch. Galt's influence on subsequent Scottish fiction, however, is primarily as a sentimental annalist rather than a political satirist. See Moir's 1828 *Life of Mansie Wauch* (dedicated to Galt and a major influence on Victorian fiction), but also Alexander's *Johnny Gibb of Gushetneuk* (an ambitious 1871 attempt to revive a Galtian microanalysis of historical processes using the materials of local color and dialect fiction). The best work on Galt remains Costain, "Theoretical History and the Novel"; see also Waterston, ed., *John Galt*; MacQueen, *The Enlightenment and Scottish Literature*, vol. 2, *The Rise of the Historical Novel*; Hart, *The Scottish Novel*; Ian Campbell, ed., *Nineteenth-Century Scottish Fiction*; Letley, *From Galt to Douglas Brown*; and Gifford, ed., *The History of Scottish Literature,* vol. 3, *The Nineteenth Century.*

75. Galt, *The Provost*, p. 86.

76. Many postcolonial texts (from Alejo Carpentier's *The Lost Steps*, Salman Rushdie's *Midnight's Children*, and Gabriel Garcìa Márquez's *One Hundred Years of Solitude* to Alice Munro's *Lives of Girls and Women* and *Open Secrets*) unwittingly share political and formal concerns with romantic works such as *The Milesian Chief*, *Melmoth*, *The Entail*, and *The O'Briens*, themselves obsessed with questions of imperialism and colonial formation. It seems not at all fanciful, indeed, to speak of magical realism in connection with Gothic alternatives to emergent realism in the early nineteenth century, or of postcolonial historical novels in conjunction with the annalistic historical allegories of the romantic period (both reacting against the influence of the Waverley novels).

CHAPTER 4

1. Said, *Culture and Imperialism*, p. 96.

2. As Fraiman argues in "Jane Austen and Edward Said," Said fails to consider *Mansfield Park* in relation even to Austen's other works.

3. As Fleischman writes, in *A Reading of Mansfield Park*, of Sir Thomas Bertram's connection to Antigua, "The modern reader must be aware of public knowledge so widespread at the time that it need not be set out in the novel to have some effect in explaining the action" (p. 36).

4. On the rhetoric of radicalism, see Thompson, *The Making of the English Working Class*.

5. Ellis and Mac a'Ghobhainn, *The Scottish Insurrection*, p. 104.

6. Review of "Indian Recreations: Consisting chiefly of Strictures on the Domestic and Rural Economy of the Mahommadans and Hindoos. By the Rev. W. Tennant," *Edinburgh Review* (July 1804): 303–29, here 303–4.

7. [Mrs. Wood?], *Letters from the Irish Highlands*, p. 144; the book also draws extended parallels (198) between Irish middleman and West India proprietor.

8. See Perera's *Reaches of Empire*, chap. 1; Kilfeather, "'Strangers at Home,'" chap. 6; Kirkpatrick, "'Gentlemen Have Horrors upon the Subject'"; and Alan Richardson, "Romantic Voodoo."

9. Although *Translation of Letters from a Hindoo Rajah* presents Indian poetry as "the productions of the Hindoo bards" (p. xxxiii), Hamilton argues that India presents a remarkable degree of cultural preservation and continuity, so that its classical forms of culture are not in ruins (as they are in the Mediterranean) but rather remain alive and visible: "THERE the mouldering edifice, the fallen pillar, and the broken arch, bear, alone, their silent testimony to the genius and refinement of the states which produced them. But in Hindostan, the original features that marked the character of their nation, from time immemorial, are still too visible to be mistaken or overlooked" (p. xlv).

10. Kelly, *Women, Writing, and Revolution*, chaps. 4 and 8.

11. In its multiplication of parallel national plots, Owenson's oeuvre replicates the ambiguous organization of Abbé Raynal's five-volume compendium of the history of European imperialism, *Histoire ... des deux Indes* (1780, probably coauthored by Diderot). which was partly responsible for the rise of consciousness of the empire as a system. Each volume describes a separate continent, subdivided

into the separate histories of each European power's campaigns in the region. Raynal's organization makes the notion of a national empire newly coherent, at once implying and playing down the structural connections between disparate imperial ventures.

12. "There is a continual circulation," writes Smollett of trade and taxation, "like that of the blood in the human body, and England is the heart, to which all the streams which it distributes as refunded and returned" (*Expedition of Humphry Clinker*, p. 317). Circulation novels that meditate on the conjoined economic circuits of nation and empire include Charles Johnstone's *Chrysal, or The Adventures of a Guinea* (1760–65), which begins in a South American mine and ends by describing social and economic exchange within Europe, and Hubertus Scott's *Adventures of a Rupee* (1782), which moves from a survey of Indian society, and the Indian misadventures of two Scots (who follow the East India Company into captivity and death), to a traverse of Europe and meditations on commerce and circulation. See also Equiano's autobiographical description, in *Life of Olaudoh Equiano* (1789), of forced travels from Africa to Britain to the West Indies to America, as a slave and then a sailor in the British navy; the shorter narratives of slavery, transport, and cultural refashioning are collected in Edwards and Dabydeen, eds., *Black Writers in Britain*, and the novels of female travel to the colonies, from Brooke's *History of Emily Montague* (1769) to Goldsbourne's *Hartly House, Calcutta* (1789), are discussed in Nussbaum, *Torrid Zones*.

13. Lee's novel was popular for decades. Traveling to the West Indies in 1815, Matthew "Monk" Lewis notes that even the cabin boy is reading *The Recess* (along with *Werther*) (M. G. Lewis, *Journal of a West India Proprietor*, p. 33). Lewis, one of the few British romantic authors who owned slaves, deployed them (as his journal records) in private, and decadent, literary games: like other slaveholders, he gives his slaves names from classical mythology, then amuses himself with the intertextual incongruities that result when slaves named as gods engage in debased labor or court incongruous classical counterparts (without themselves grasping the joke).

14. Smith, *The Old Manor House*, p. 246.

15. Nugent's diary for February 12, 1803, describes Jamaican planters' children in similar terms. "Mrs. Skinner's little *Bonella* is a sweet child, but so spoiled that I am afraid she will be a little tyrant. Mrs. S., like all Creole ladies, has a number of servants with her, and all are obliged to attend to any caprice of the little girl, as well as her mother, and I grieve to see it.—It will, however, be a good lesson for me, and I am determined to make my dear little boy so amiable, that he shall be loved by all, and not feared. But, in this country, it will be difficult to prevent him from thinking himself a little king at least, and then will come arrogance, I fear, and all the petty vices of little tyrants" (*Lady Nugent's Journal*, p. 146).

16. This model of the colonial personality becomes a novelistic commonplace. Embittered by her slipping status in wartime England, the eponymous Anglo-Indian governess of Laura Talbot's *Gentlewoman* (1952, written at the height of decolonization) is still described in precisely such terms: "Miss Bowlby, with a part of her, seemed to want to be nice, and . . . India, somehow, came between the part of her that wanted to be" (p. 5). For the Rousseauian countertradition, see also Inchbald's

Nature and Art (1796): here young Henry, who was raised among African savages, has not absorbed their murderous violence; instead, he has remained a Rousseauian natural man, who shocks his cousin and uncle, on his return to England, by his inability to accept social convention at face value, as well as by his ceaseless concern for the sufferings of the poor.

17. Day, *The History of Sandford and Merton*, 1:1.

18. Austen, "Catharine," p. 203. The passage anticipates Jane Fairfax's protest in Austen's *Emma* (1816) that the "governess-trade" (p. 300) moves governesses from place to place, like chattels.

19. Bennett, *Anna*, 1:112. Mikhail Lermontov's *Hero of Our Time* (1840) suggests the applicability of this model for a different European empire as the (erotic) power relations generated during the Russian occupation of the Caucasus are transplanted back into Russia, with tragic results.

20. Hays, *Memoirs of Emma Courtney*, pp. 112–13.

21. Maaja A. Stewart, *Domestic Realities*, p. 111; Frank Gibbon, "The Antiguan Connection," p. 303.

22. Kirkham, "Feminist Irony and the Priceless Heroine" and *Jane Austen, Feminism, and Fiction*, esp. pp. 116–19. As she argues in "Feminist Irony," *Mansfield Park*'s Mrs. Norris may be named after John Norris, a former slave captain and proslavery advocate whom Clarkson debates at length.

23. Moira Ferguson, *Colonialism and Gender*, p. 82; Kirkham, "Feminist Irony," p. 244.

24. Reading *Mansfield Park* against *A Simple Story* (the 1792 novel by Elizabeth Inchbald, translator of Kotzebue's *Lover's Vows*), Stewart sees Austen's indirection as an affirmation of gender and geopolitical separation. "Austen's and Inchbald's novels each presents the patriarch's visit to the West Indies as an experience that the author, the other characters, and the reader cannot directly share, an experience known only through its momentous effects on the domestic space. . . . The separation between imperialism and domesticity reinforces the general ideological separation between imperial endeavor and metropolitan culture. That this separation allowed for forms of domination in the distant reaches of the empire not tolerable within the heart of the empire is often noted. That it also allowed for forms of extralegal sexual arrangements that explicitly departed from the increasingly idealized domestic family of the metropolis became a particular focus of anxiety and ambivalence among contemporary observers" (*Domestic Realities*, p. 106). Criticizing previous attempts to place Austen politically, Stewart argues that *Mansfield Park* is "not, of course . . . an abolitionist text. Rather . . . the West Indian discourses had penetrated the domestic realm, thereby changing the perceptions of power relations and affecting quotidian experiences" (p. 111).

25. Austen, *Mansfield Park*, p. 178.

26. See Austen's *Sense and Sensibility* (1811) for a related discussion of the long-term effects of travel on Colonel Brandon's personality. Whereas Marianne sees his journeys merely as the source of his boring touristic commonplaces—"he has told you that in the East Indies the climate is hot, and the mosquitoes are troublesome"—and Willoughby mockingly adds that "his observations may have extended to the existence of nabobs, gold mohrs, and palanquins," Elinor attributes

his sensibility to the fact that he "has seen a great deal of the world; has been abroad; has read, and has a thinking mind" (p. 51).

27. Moira Ferguson, *Colonialism and Gender*, pp. 68–69; see also Southam, "The Silence of the Bertrams."

28. Austen sets the Bertram plantation in Antigua, argues Maaja A. Stewart, because her brother singled out that island in his condemnation of West India slavery and because "[e]conomic forces further singled out Antigua when its local government declared bankrupcy in 1805" (*Domestic Realities*, p. 28). Sir Thomas's mission in Antigua, argues Fleischman, was probably to ensure that "his slaves did not die so readily of underfeeding, overwork, and the overseers' brutality"; although "the novel does not develop Sir Thomas's experience in Antigua," the novel suggests that it had profound personal consequences: on his return, Sir Thomas shows "a marked change of temperament," a "changed moral sensibility," which not only alters his relations with Fanny but "eventually issues in the discovery of his 'executive weakness' in the education of his children." The novel, for Fleischman, "may be accused of lacking an 'objective correlative' of the protagonist's emotion," so that "it is possible to reconstruct his experience only hypothetically. He goes to Antigua as a planter, presumably opposed to abolition; he occupies himself, for economic reasons, with improving the slaves' condition; he acquires some of the humanitarian or religious message of the Evangelical and other missionaries laboring in the same vineyard; and he returns critical of his own moral realm" (*A Reading of Mansfield Park*, pp. 38–39). Warren Roberts reaches similar conclusions in *Jane Austen and the French Revolution*: "While Austen touched only passingly on the slavery question . . . her way of doing so suggests that she considered it as an important issue. . . . Like other owners, Sir Thomas had to protect the lives of his slaves, which he could have done through the establishment of better working conditions, better nutrition and more decent housing. He probably went to Antigua for economic reasons . . . but upon arriving and becoming acquainted with conditions on the island and on his estate, he became interested in the slavery question on grounds that were not strictly economic. One can well imagine him going through stages leading from the strictly pragmatic to a mixture of practical and humanitarian and then centring on the ethical'" (p. 140).

29. Clarkson, *The History of the Abolition of the Slave Trade*, 2:583–85. The most influential nineteenth-century Anglo-American abolitionist literature, including Harriet Beecher Stowe's *Uncle Tom's Cabin*, advocates abolition to secure the moral redemption of white society as much as racial equality.

30. Stewart, *Domestic Realities*, p. 107. Instead "of the Slave-trade being a nursery for the British seamen, it was their grave" (Clarkson, *Abolition of the Slave Trade*, 2:60).

31. Hedge's *Samboe, or The African Boy* (1800?) offers related complaints about French revolutionary imperial policies. Like the abolitionist infant tales of the 1790s, Hedge's story links the imperial and the domestic in the journey—and the cultural shock—of its young African hero, as he leaves the Africa of his infancy and slavery for the chill of rural Wales. Hedge favors the repatriation of freed slaves to Sierra Leone; her comments on French Jacobin activity there—"advocates and patrons of the rights of man wantonly destroyed a settlement in which those rights

were peculiarly studied and held sacred" (p. 171)—reflect both conservative, anti-integrationist abolitionism and conservative outrage at the hypocrisies of French radicalism.

32. Even for Clarkson, emancipation is such a distant hope that it is mentioned only briefly, on the last page of his thousand-page *History of the Abolition of the Slave Trade*: "But here a new hope rises to our view. Who knows but that emancipation, like a beautiful plant, may, in its due season, rise out of the ashes of the abolition of the Slave-trade, and that, when its own intrinsic value shall be known, the seed of it may be planted in other lands?" (2:586).

33. As C.L.R. James argues in *The Black Jacobins*, the British government finally abolished the slave trade not for humanitarian reasons but to undermine French colonial power (pp. 51–54).

34. Maria Edgeworth, "The Grateful Negro," in *Tales and Novels*, 2:399–419, here 400.

35. Blackburn, *The Overthrow of Colonial Slavery*, p. 322. For less critical recent accounts of abolitionism, see Midgley, *Women against Slavery*, and Turley, *The Culture of English Antislavery*.

36. Early-nineteenth-century readers would have felt the continuity between didactic fiction and Austen's fiction with particular force; beginning their reading lives with moralizing infant literature, they then "would graduate to the stories and novels of Maria Edgeworth and Jane Austen" (Demers, *Heaven upon Earth*, p. 129).

37. Austen, *Sanditon*, pp. 421, 392.

38. Elizabeth Grant argues that *Guy Mannering* consolidated Scott's following. "*Waverley* came out, I think it must have been the autumn of 1814. . . . I did not like it. The opening English scenes were to me intolerably dull, so lengthy, and so prosy, and the persons introduced so uninteresting, the hero contemptible, the two heroines unnatural and disagreeable, and the whole idea given of the highlands so utterly at variance with truth. . . . Then burst out *Guy Mannering*, carrying all the world before it, in spite of the very pitiful setting, the gipsies, the smugglers, and Dandie Dinmont are surrounded by" (*Memoirs*, 2:72). Sydney Smith sees *Guy Mannering* as marking a high point of originality and freshness in Scott's novelistic career. By the time he publishes *The Abbot*, Scott "has exhausted the subject of Scotland, and worn out the few characters that the early periods of Scotch history could supply him with. Meg Merrilies appears afresh in every novel" (letter to J. A. Murray, September 3, 1820, in *Selected Letters of Sydney Smith*, ed. Nowell C. Smith [Oxford: Oxford University Press, 1981], p. 96).

39. Scott, *Guy Mannering*, 3:26. Dunbog evokes Irish Enlightenment bog-drainage discussions; the name of one man he displaces—John Young—reinforces the reference.

40. On *Guy Mannering* as a romance of modernization, see Ian Duncan, *Modern Romance*, pp. 111–35.

41. In chapter 4 the narrator situates the characters' beliefs within a temporal framework of which they are oblivious: "The belief in astrology was almost universal in the middle of the seventeenth century; it began to waver and become doubtful towards the close of that period, and in the beginning of the eighteenth century the art fell into general disrepute, and even under general ridicule" (3:34).

42. See my "Time of the Gypsies" for European theories about the origins of Gypsy culture and for the depiction of Gypsies in *Guy Mannering* and in Austen's *Emma*.

43. Leyden, *Scenes of Infancy*, pp. 123–25. For Leyden's travels throughout the British Empire and voluminous writings ("on the plan of Raynal") about Africa and India, see the "Biographical Memoir of John Leyden, M.D."

44. See Dallas, *The History of the Maroons*, for the so-called Maroon Wars, begun in 1790, with the uprising of the Trelawny Town Maroons. As Dallas makes clear, the Maroons occupy an anomalous position in the plantation hierarchy, comparable to the Gypsies' position on the feudal estate. In 1739, after a long war with the British colonial administration, the Maroons signed a treaty that granted them legal freedom and collective amnesty; in exchange, they pledged to help the government repel foreign invasions and, on the home front, to recapture escaped plantation slaves. Despite their continued hostility toward the British, the Maroons do not identify themselves with their slave compatriots, and in return they are thoroughly disliked by them. In Edgeworth's terms, they are at once insufficiently "grateful negroes" and overly loyal to colonial law.

45. Peter Garside, "Picturesque Figure and Landscape: Meg Merrilies and the Gypsies," in Copley and Garside, eds., *The Politics of the Picturesque*, pp. 145–74.

46. Leyden, *Scenes of Infancy*, p. 3.

Chapter 5

1. See Elizabeth Hamilton, *Letters on the Elementary Principles of Education*, 3d ed., 3 vols. (London: G. and J. Robinson, 1803); Leadbeater, *Cottage Dialogues*, esp. dialogue 16, "Nursing," pp. 86–90; and Sherwood, *Life of Mrs. Sherwood*, pp. 378–83.

2. See Fildes, *Breasts, Bottles, and Babies*, and *Wet Nursing*; for the continuation of such beliefs into the nineteenth century, see Gelpi, *Shelley's Goddess*, esp. part 1, "The Nurse's Soul." Whereas medieval medical treatises warn of the unsuitability of nursing across religious or ethnic lines, the Romans favor Greek nurses, who could accustom infants to the sounds of the Greek language. Rousseau, in contrast, wishes the nurse to sing only songs without words, lest she confound the natural unfolding of the child's linguistic abilities (Jean-Jacques Rousseau, *Emile*, trans. Barbara Foxley [London: Dent; New York: Dutton, 1974], p. 37).

3. The revolution in the nursery is a diffuse event, difficult to date. Fildes' *Wet Nursing* sees a new vogue for maternal breast-feeding after 1750, with wet-nursing dying out in England around 1800; yet Ann Roberts's "Mothers and Babies: The Wetnurse and Her Employer in Mid-nineteenth Century England" chronicles a renewed spate of polemics against wet-nursing almost thirty years later (*Women's Studies* 3 (1976): 279–93). On nineteenth-century nursery education, see Jonathan Gathorne-Hardy, *The Rise and Fall of the British Nanny* (London: Hodder and Toughton, 1972); Colin White, *The World of the Nursery* (London: Hervert Press, 1984); Kathryn Hughes, *The Victorian Governess* (London: Hambleton Press, 1993), and Alan Richardson, *Literature, Education, and Romanticism*.

4. Kittler, *Discourse Networks, 1800/1900*, pp. 25–69. See also Gelpi, *Shelley's Goddess*, esp. chap. 2, "Her Destined Sphere"; and Mellor, *Romanticism and Gender*, esp. pp. 80–84.

5. Shelley's poetry, argues Gelpi, is grounded in fantasies of the material realm, yet he suffers an almost pathological fear of the wet nurse as a bearer of cultural and physical contamination. See *Shelley's Goddess*, esp. chap. 1. See also Spivak's discussion of "the transition from the domestic to the 'domestic'" in her rich analysis of Mahasveta Devi's "Breast Giver," in "A Literary Representation of the Subaltern: A Woman's Text from the Third World," in *In Other Worlds*, pp. 241–68, here 256.

6. *Lady Nugent's Journal*, pp. 118–19, 122, 131, 154–55. Lady Nugent also describes "the agrémens of a Creole confinement" (pp. 124–25), including her shocked, fascinated exchanges with the slave midwife.

7. John Downman's 1806 portrait of Lady Nugent's family (reproduced in *Lady Nugent's Journal*, pp. 268–69) thus includes Nurse Hamilton, but on the very edge of the family group and the picture; only her head enters the painting.

8. For the cult of the dead nurse, see, for instance, Mrs. Sherwood's "Hours of Infancy" (1835), in *Social Tales for the Young*, pp. 87–104; W.M., "Nurse's Tale," *Chatterbox* 27 (June 1, 1867): 211; and Mrs. J. H. Ewing, *A Flat Iron for a Farthing, or Some passages in the life of an Only Son* (London: Bell and Daldy, 1873).

9. As Vladimir Propp puts it in "The Nature of Folklore," "Folklore is the womb of literature; literature is born of folklore. Folklore is the prehistory of literature. . . . Literature, which is born of folklore, soon abandons the mother that reared it. Literature is the product of another form of consciousness" (*Theory and History of Folklore* [Minneapolis: University of Minnesota Press, 1984], pp. 3–15, here 14). Folklore, in Propp's description, becomes the mother and prehistoric nurse, and literature the son who suckles himself in infancy on the folkloric but who eventually must leave his mother's arms to follow his destiny. Nineteenth-century progressives, indeed, come to see the folkloric not as the nourishing breast of national life but as the stuff of neurotic nightmares. Nineteenth-century nationalists narrate the course of cultural transformation rather differently. Writing in *The Nation* in 1843, critic D. F. MacCarthy thus hopes "that we can be thoroughly Irish in our feelings without ceasing to be English in our speech; that we can be faithful to the land of our birth, without being ungrateful to that literature which has been 'the nursing mother of our minds': that we can develop the intellectual resources of our country, and establish for ourselves a distinct and separate existence in the world of letters without depriving ourselves of the advantages of the widely-diffused and genius-consecrated language of England" (Lloyd, *Anomalous States*, p. 14).

10. When the grown nursling in Pushkin's *Eugene Onegin* (1823–31) tries to talk with her nurse about marriage and love, old Filatievna's memory fails, as though to emblematize the unbridgeable historical and social gap between the circumstances of her life and that of Tatyana: "Time was, I / stored in my memory no dearth / of ancient haps and never-haps . . . but everything to me is dark now, Tanya: / I have forgotten what I knew. . . . I'm all befuddled" (*Eugene Onegin*, trans. Vladimir Nabokov, 4 vols. [New York: Pantheon Books, 1964], 1:161, chap. 3, section 37, ll. 3–12.

11. Irving, *Abbotsford*, 4:14–15. See also Elizabeth Grant's description of her sister's 1825 wedding as the culmination and breakup of the old Highland clan system. Beginning with an Ormondesque collective leave-taking of the feudal aristocrat from the clan ("a mob of our people . . . raising such a shout as their pride—-ay, and their blessing, was driven away"), the passage shifts into the rhetoric of

wet-nursing and fostering: "She has been the nursing mother to all our people, in weal or woe their prop. Beloved every where, she was worshipped there. Doing her duty every where, she has taken the duties of others on herself there. . . . [Since her departure,] home, to me at least, never seemed like home since" (*Memoirs*, 2:192). Composed for her children and grandchildren as a familial legacy, Grant's compendious memoirs and diaries of the 1840s reflect her culture's new sense of urgency about conservation and cultural transmission.

12. Shelley, *Matilda*, in Wollstonecraft and Shelley, *Mary and Maria/Matilda*, p. 157. The passage echoes one from *Mary* (1788), by Shelley's own mother, Mary Wollstonecraft: "After the mother's throes she felt very few sentiments of maternal ternderness; the children were given to nurses, and she played with her dogs. . . . Her children all died in their infancy, except the two first. . . . Her children were left in the nursery; and when Mary, the little blushing girl, appeared, she would send the awkward thing away. . . . An old house-keeper told her stories, read to her, and, at last, taught her to read" (p. 7).

13. *Nicht Narren, Nicht Heiligen: Erinnerungen Russischer Volkstümler* (Leipzig: Reclam, 1984), p. 162, my translation.

14. Already in childhood, Figner dreamed of becoming a czaritsa, to raise her nurse along with her ("then my nurse will be dressed in silver, and I shall wear diamonds and rubies") (*Memoirs of a Revolutionist* [New York: International Publishers, 1927], p. 18). In adult life, Figner worked among the peasants as a doctor and a political agitator; she was eventually sentenced to twenty years in prison. In some ways, aristocratic anarchists inadvertently reproduced the system they condemned: as a relationship in which "we felt ourselves as human beings, children and masters," even Figner's utopian relationship between children and nurse leaves class hierarchies intact. On the servant as an embodiment of utopian promise, see Robbins, *The Servant's Hand*.

15. See Sigmund Freud, *The Psychopathology of Everyday Life*, trans. James Strachey, *Complete Psychological Works*, 20 vols. (1901; reprint, London: Hogarth Press, 1953–63), 2:49–51, and Jim Swan, "*Mater* and Nannie: Freud's Two Mothers and the Discovery of the Oedipus Complex," *American Imago* 31, no. 1 (1974): 1–64.

16. Freud, *Interpretation of Dreams*, in *Complete Psychological Works*, 4:247–48.

17. Ibid., 4:262.

18. See Carlo Ginzburg, "Freud, the Wolf-Man, and Werewolves," in *Clues, Myths, and the Historical Method*, trans. John and Anne Tedeschi (Baltimore: Johns Hopkins University Press, 1989), pp. 146–55.

19. Ferguson, *Essay on the Origins of Civil Society*, p. 81.

20. For an elaboration of Novalis's links between "a magician's den, a physicist's laboratory, a children's nursery," see Walter Benjamin, *The Origin of German Tragic Drama*, trans. John Osborne (London: New Left Books, 1977), p. 188.

21. My use of the word *uncanny* here is overdetermined, given not only Freud's literary-historical explication of the German *unheimlich* but the cultural and historical background of the "English" word itself. If the premises of this book are correct—if much of the tropic repertoire of English letters, particularly in describing the relationship of the collective and the individual psyche to a lost past, ultimately

originates in Scotland, Ireland, and Wales—then there is a clear need for a new psychohistorical philology, one that could explore the residues of cultural alterity and appropriation which reside in Scots words such as *uncanny* when used as parts of the English language.

22. In Chaigneau's *History of Jack Connor*, Lord Truegood forestalls such dangers by forbidding all nurses and domestics "to mention a single word, or idle story that could inspire fear into the minds of the children"; this "saved them many uneasy hours in their lives, which others feel for want of such management" (1:77).

23. An important 1776 Polish novel makes a similar critique: "The earliest years of my childhood were spent in the company of women. Nurses and nannies interpreted my as yet poorly articulated words to be extraordinarily sagacious responses. . . . Over the ensuing years I have concluded more than once . . . how evil and harmful it is to entrust even small children to unenlightened individuals. I heard far too many fables and dreadful romances. To this day my head is full of them. Although a thoroughly rational man, I must frequently struggle with myself not to lend credence to sorcery and superstition or to rid myself of some fear or other and not abhor the dark or solitude" (Ignacy Krasicki, *The Adventures of Mr. Nicholas Wisdom*, trans. Thomas H. Hoisington [Evanston, Ill.: Northwestern University Press, 1992], p. 11).

24. Blake experimented constantly with the ordering of the *Songs*; in some copies of the first edition, "The Ecchoing Green" does not stand next to "The Nurse's Song," and "The Voice of the Bard" appears toward the middle, not at the end, of the sequence. When he issued *Songs of Innocence and Songs of Experience* as a single volume, Blake moved "The Voice of the Bard" out of the *Songs of Innocence* section altogether, using it to end the *Songs of Experience* instead. Although we cannot give too much weight to any one ordering of the poems, the pairing of nurse and bard in some versions as anchoring presences is significant.

25. In the title image, a rapt audience reads at the nurse's knee, and above them, the tree's branches and leaves spell out the book's title. In the plate of the "Nurse's Song," similarly, the calligraphic text is ornamented with foliage and branches, and in the pictorial scene below the reading nurse extends the children's circle game (*Songs of Innocence and Experience*, figs. 5–9). See also the first engraving to "Spring," with its mother and child seated under the tree, and the first engraving of "The Ecchoing Green" (fig. 6), in which the children's play is framed by linked emblems of cyclical regeneration: several nurses, children at their knee, sit under the tree that occupies the center of the picture, framing the scene with arching branches.

26. Sherwood, "The Mail Coach," in *Social Tales for the Young*, pp. 1–28, here 18–19.

27. Owenson, *The Wild Irish Girl*, p. 53.

28. Johnstone, *Clan-Albin*, 1:60; I thank Ina Ferris for bringing this novel to my attention. As Scott tells Irving during his 1818 Abbotsford visit, "You will never weed these popular stories and songs and superstitions out of Scotland. . . It is not so much that the people believe in them, as that they delight in them. They belong to the native hills and streams of which they are fond, and to the history of their forefathers, of which they are proud." Poor country people pass winter nights "listening to some old wife, or strolling gaberlunzie, dealing out auld world stories

about bogles and warlocks, or about raids and forays, and border skirmishes; or reciting some ballad. . . . These traditional tales and ballads have lived for ages in mere oral circulation, being passed from father to son, or rather from grandam to grandchild, and are a kind of hereditary property of the poor peasantry, of which it would be hard to deprive them, as they have not circulating libraries to supply them with works of fiction in their place" (p. 46).

29. Owenson, *The O'Briens and the O'Flahertys*, p. 254.

30. Edgeworth, *Castle Rackrent and Ennui*, p. 160.

31. A related duality between the dissolute, tale-telling nurses and the virtuous future governess structures Elizabeth Hamilton's 1808 *Cottagers of Glenburnie*. As a young nurse, Mrs. Mason struggled with two evil fellow servants for control of the nursery; the frightening hobgoblin tales of the first leave a young listener emotionally scarred for life, and the second takes advantage of the nursery's physical isolation to stage midnight orgies there. Eventually (shades of *Jane Eyre*) she sets the house on fire and dies deservedly in the flames, while Mrs. Mason heroically rescues "her" infants from certain death and is burned and lamed in the fire. In reward, she is elevated to the status of governess. Eventually, Mrs. Mason becomes the governess and reformer of Glenburnie itself, transforming a slovenly, impoverished Scottish village into a model settlement.

32. Charles Dickens, "Nurse's Stories," reprinted in *The Uncommercial Traveller* (London: Dent; New York: Dutton, 1969), pp. 148–58, here 150, 157.

33. Charlotte Yonge's contemporaneous historical novel for children, *The Lances of Lynwood* (1855; London: J. M. Dent; New York: E. P. Dutton, n.d.), insists rather that in their original, archaic context, nurse's tales and bardic songs formed the basis for a literate culture at odds with the prevailing military ethos (p. 18).

34. See Nietzsche's "Uses and Disadvantages of History for Life" (1874), pp. 57–124.

35. Erich Auerbach places this scene of reunion at the beginning of the Western literary tradition. See "Odysseus' Scar," in *Mimesis: The Representation of Reality in Western Literature*, trans. Willard R. Trask (Princeton: Princeton University Press, 1968), pp. 3–23.

36. In Galt's *Entail* Claud Walkinshaw abandons Madge Dobble, the faithful nurse who has supported him for years.

37. Gaining new popularity with John Home's *Douglas* (1760), this plot becomes central to—and overused by—the Gothic novel; Sarah Green satirizes the Gothic novel reader who hopes "she yet might be able to find, in some hitherto concealed recess, the papers which contain the elucidation of her birth, when the confessions of her guilty nurse, and all the direful scenes of her iniquity would be proclaimed" (*Romance Readers and Romance Writers*, 1:141). See also Robert A. Erickson, *Mother Midnight: Birth, Sex, and Fate in Eighteenth Century Fiction* (New York: AMS Press, 1986), and Barbara Ehrenreich and Deirdre English, *Witches, Midwives, and Nurses* (Old Westbury: Feminist Press, 1973).

38. See Reeve, *The Old English Baron* (1777), esp. pp. 17, 37, 58, and Gunning, *Delves* (1796).

39. Canny, *Kingdom and Colony*, p. 41.

40. In Shakespeare's *Romeo and Juliet* (ca. 1595?), in contrast, the nurse's prolix narratives, particularly her long-winded speeches in act 1, are centered completely

around her foster child; she uses weaning, teething, and other nursing milestones as her principal temporal markers. Unlike Edgeworth, Shakespeare conceives the nurse's loyalties and mode of memory in emphatically nonbardic terms.

41. Edgeworth, *Castle Rackrent and Ennui*, p. 159. "They seldom nurse their own children, especially the wives of lords and gentlemen," writes Fynes Moryson in the *Itinerary* (1617). "For women of good wealth seek with great ambition to nurse them, not for any profit, rather spending much upon them while they live, and giving them when they die sometimes more than to their own children. But they do it only to have the protection and love of the parents whose children they nurse. And old custom is so turned into second nature with them as they esteem the children they nurse more than their own, holding it a reproach to nurse their own children. Yea, men will forbear their wives' bed for the good of the children they nurse or foster, but not nursing their own. Yea, the foster-brothers—I mean the children of the nurse and strangers that have sucked her milk—love one another better than natural brothers, and hate them in respect of the other. And by frequent examples we have seen many mourn for their foster-brothers much more than they would have done for their natural brothers; and some to oppose their own brothers to death that they might save their foster-brothers from danger thereof. The worst is that these nurses with their extreme indulgence corrupt the children they foster, nourishing and heartening the boys in all villainy, and the girls in obscenity" (Falkiner, ed., *Illustrations of Irish History*, p. 318). William Camden's *Britannia* (1695) argues that fostering prepares the ground for civil war: "All that have suckt the same breasts are very kind and loving, and confide more in each other than if they were natural brothers; so that they have even an aversion to their own brothers for the sake of these. If their parents reprehend them, they fly to their Foster-fathers for protection, by whom they are often excited to an open war and defiance against them; so that being seconded and brought up after this manner, they grow the vilest profligates in nature" (cited in Laurence, "The Cradle to the Grave," pp. 77).

42. *A Collection of Tracts and Treatises*, 1:671–72.

43. Writing a self-consciously Edgeworthian, annalistic family history of Anglo-Irish society, Bowen concurs with Edgeworth's assessment of the fostering system: "There exists between classes, at least in the country in Ireland, a good-mannered, faintly cynical tolerance, largely founded on classes letting each other alone. There does also, in many cases, exist a lively and simply spontaneous human affection between the landed families and the Irish people around them—this is said to have roots in the foster-system, which until quite lately prevailed. In a crisis, there may always be an alliance—against outsiders, in money troubles, against the law" (*Bowen's Court*, p. 126).

44. Johnstone, *Clan-Albin*, 1:18. But see Johnson's *Journey*, which discusses fostering in the Highlands as a financial arrangement and a mark of family favor (pp. 130–31).

45. For a contemporaneous anti-Papist and dystopic version of this story, see the anonymous *Irish Girl. A Religious Tale* (1814), in which a Catholic "tramper girl" is converted to Protestantism, only to be harassed and kidnapped by her Papist relatives, who wish to reclaim her. This is one of the rare instances (along with Patrick Brontë's 1818 *The Maid of Killarney*) in which the national tale is used to preach religious intolerance and paranoia.

46. Hogg, *The Brownie of Bodsbeck*, pp. 46, 99.

47. Scott, *Guy Mannering*, 4:318.

48. Homer, *The Odyssey*, trans. Robert Fitzgerald (Garden City, N.J.: Doubleday, 1963), p. 368.

49. Maturin's historical novel *The Albigenses* (1824) recasts *Guy Mannering*, using a minstrel (a composite of Blondel, Yorrick, and Meg Merrilies) to trigger and orchestrate the hero's reemergence from amnesia. "[E]very step of my earthly progress [is] marked by presages and voices that, though of the living, sound as if they issued from the grave! The voice, the song of that minstrel, recall to me images of years in which I seem to have lived;—I could methinks, repeat every word of his lay, echo every note of his harp;—but unless so touched, the chord of my early memory is broken, tuneless and irresponsive. . . . I could swear to that minstrel's voice—I could swear that in infancy I sat on his knees and listened to it. Hadst thou ever such thoughts of a life that began before thou hadst living consciousness. . . . Not the oaths of the holiest on earth . . . could make me believe I had not heard those words, those sounds, before,—though amid scenes I cannot, cannot recall. Oh those associations . . . that, far seen, and faintly remembered, we struggle after through mist and darkness, and grasp only their shadows—those spectres of departed memory that rise before us when the essence is gone forever" (1:174). Whereas in the early national tale and historical novel the nurse took on the characteristics of the bard, here the bard is described in terms associated with the nurse.

50. Hofland's *Stolen Child* (1828) rewrites *Guy Mannering* simultaneously as a children's story and a captivity narrative, so that this final movement becomes not only explicit but psychically essential. Manuel, a young Spanish immigrant to the American Southwest, initially fears the local Indians (who remind him of the Spanish Gypsies), yet soon makes friends among the Choctaws. When he is kidnapped by the Comanches and lives in captivity for several years, he helps to nurse Moscogi's baby and seems fully adopted by her family. But the male leaders of the tribe continue to make a categorical distinction between Manuel and their own sons—and after he witnesses the torture of Comanche prisoners (and the death of Diego, a faithful family servant who has come to rescue him), Manuel flees his captors and reenters the Christian world. Taken in by Mr. Osborne, he begins to piece together his fragmentary memories of his life before the kidnapping: he retains memories of household events, a birthday, his mother's dress, and his affection for his parents. "He was also fond of [his mother's] maid, who had accompanied him from Europe, but he could recollect the name of no other servant, nor had he any remembrance of his former friends, his usual playmates, occupations, or books. It appeared as if some things were completely eradicated from the tablets of memory, that others might be engraven there the deeper" (p. 151). On the basis of these slim clues, Mr. Osborne finds Manuel's parents, yet they initially hesitate to reclaim their son, afraid he has gone irredeemably native: "[I]f these wild people have rendered our child one of themselves, he is as much lost to us as if the grave had closed on him: so young,—so very young, he could be modelled to any thing" (p. 158). In the end they welcome him back into the family; the fact that he has safeguarded the memory of his parents proves to them that he has remained European at heart. In this children's version of *Guy Mannering*, the memory of the nursemaid is part of the armature that keeps Manuel culturally intact, throughout his captivity. Yet *The Stolen Boy* also evokes the primal fear of nineteenth-century parents that the fostering system will absorb and alienate their children.

51. Elizabeth Grant describes her own nurse in terms influenced by her subsequent reading of *Guy Mannering*: "It was when I was weaned there had come a tall randy kind of woman from Forres, a Meg Merrilies, to take care of me" (*Memoirs*, 1:8).

52. Maturin, "Leixlip Castle," p. 272.

53. As Clemit establishes in *The Godwinian Novel*, "Godwin read *Waverley* in Sept. 1815, *Guy Mannering* and *The Antiquary* (1816) in May 1816, started work on *Mandeville* in June 1816, and read *Old Mortality* while revising *Mandeville* for publication in Dec. 1817" (p. 97 n. 76).

54. Godwin, *Mandeville*, pp. 9–11. As Clemit's introduction makes clear, Godwin's account of the Ulster Plantation Uprising was influenced by *O'Donnel* and Maturin's Irish novels.

55. The English attempt to raise "an army of eight thousand Irish, principally Catholics," to fight the Covenanters backfires completely; many of these troops end up fighting with the Irish rebels against the English (*Mandeville*, p. 14).

56. "[W]e will have our rights. We will not be trampled upon as we have been by a handful of foreigners; we will not submit to have our estates torn from us, because we or our ancestors have meritoriously drawn our swords in the sacred cause of our country; we will not allow our inability to produce certain deeds and musty parchments, to be set up against immemorial possession to oust us of our lands; we are resolved that the holy Catholic faith, to which every man in Ireland is a sicere adherent, shall no longer go naked, like a dishonoured wanderer, but shall be clothed again in all her pristine magnificence and splendour" (*Mandeville*, p. 13).

57. In Traill's unpublished 1836 story, "My Irish Maid Isabella—A Night of Peril," however, the life story of Isabella Gordon, the Irish nurse of Traill's children, links the legacy of civil war in distant Ireland with the civil unrest surrounding the Upper Canada Rebellion. Born in Belfast, Isabella is the daughter of a kindly Protestant father and an "unloved" Roman Catholic mother, whose attempts to take her daughter "down among her own people in the wilds of Conemara" merely open "young Isabella's eyes to much she learned to abhor"; when her mother dies in Conemara "of famine fever," Isabella is happy to "escape back to her father" (Talbot, *Forest and Other Gleanings*, p. 103). Yet she is eventually forced to flee Ireland altogether, after she overhears "a wild set of disloyal men" plotting the murder of a clergyman's family and the burning of his church, informs on these "ribbon-men" to the magistrate, and remains "haunted" (101) by fears of reprisal. In Canada she can give free expression to her distrust of Irish Catholics and their spurious "love of liberty" (103), but now, with Ireland far away, she also indulges in a nostalgic reclamation of her Catholic legacy. She regularly taunts the Catholic shantymen by singing Orange songs—yet "after she had roused up '*a bit of the Devil in the boys*,' as she said, she would give them some specimens, on the contrary side" (101), "wild and pathetic" Irish songs (101), including a political lament composed about her own maternal uncle, hung "in the Rebellion of ninety-eight" (102). For all her Protestant loyalties, then, Isabella is "a strange mixture of races" (102): in some ways "as intolerant as the greatest of bigots," she also possessed "a power of strange eloquence when the subject touched her people and their wrongs. For though she railed at the Priests and attributed much of the misery of the Irish to the state of ignorance, superstition and subjection they were kept under, yet if I had

taken up the subject and even fully agreed with her she would have flamed out in vehement language defending them and asking me what I, an English woman, should know of the Irish and Ireland" (104). Like Nanny Elshinder, Isabella seems bifurcated by her own divided loyalties, but her allegiance to her mistress and nursling remains utterly undivided; when a drunken Irishman attacks Traill's child, her quick thinking and bravery save the hour. Isabella's loyalties, as Traill emphasizes, are *preexisting* ones, rooted in the history of Ireland rather than the history of Canada; so too, in Traill's presentation, the political upheavals of the Upper and Lower Canada Rebellions are imported from outside, echoes of the United Irishmen rebellion and of preexisting political problems there. Canada is, for Traill, emphatically not in the middle of its own civil war, so the bifurcation of the nurse's loyalties has no domestic consequences.

58. In Clark's *Esquimaux, or Fidelity* (1819), a Scottish family posted with the British Army in Labrador rescues and nurses an Inuit girl whose tribe has left her to die. Grateful to her rescuers, she follows them back to Britain, becoming a valued family retainer and nurse.

59. *Little Henry*'s influence on British children's literature is long and profound, beginning with Wilson's *History of Mr. Moland and Little Henry* (1815). On Sherwood's relationship to her own nurse and to her children's ayahs, see *The Life of Mrs. Sherwood*.

60. Sherwood's *Ayah and Lady* (1816) and *Ermina* (1831) feature native nurses who exchange sexually explicit stories over the heads of their charges, thereby corrupting them.

61. Sherwood, *The Babes in the Wood* , pp. 101–2.

62. According to C.L.R. James, some slave nurses and midwives in prerevolutionary San Domingo protested their enslavement by poisoning their young white charges (*The Black Jacobins*, p. 16).

63. For a contemporary treatment of these questions, see Gordimer, *July's People* (1981).

64. Moodie, *Roughing it in the Bush*, p. 149.

65. The story's allegory of Anglo-Irish relations is influenced by the national tale as well as by a contemporary habit (observable in the colonies and in Britain) of viewing Irish and Scottish servants and neighbors as the allegorical representatives of their nation's vices and virtues. As Edgeworth records in an 1818 letter, a dinner party she attended in England concluded with the hostess' expounding on the (ethnic?) character of the servants who have just served the meal: "Two old *family* servants waited—One Scotch, one Irish. Of both when they had left the room she told us characteristic anecdotes" (*Letters from England*, p. 133). A few years later, when Frances Stewart (a Belfast Scotch-Irish cousin of the Edgeworths) settles in the Upper Canada "bush" (in the neighborhood of Moodie's sister Catharine Parr Traill), she finds continuous pleasure, as her 1823 letters report, in the kindness of a neighbor, "our faithful Highlander Donald" McIntyre; when Stewart's daughter falls ill, he swims the river and walks many hours to summon the doctor; when the girl dies anyway, "the faithful Donald" is "one of the four who carried the tiny coffin." When Stewart goes into labor two months later, with no doctor or midwife within reach, "faithful Donald" again "came to our help," walking nine miles to press his mother into service as a childbed nurse (*Our Forest*

Home, pp. 43–47). On the relative virtues of Irish, Scottish, and English servants, see also Traill's "Female Servants in the Bush," in *Forest and Other Gleanings*, pp. 168–74, esp. 170–71.

66. See here Munro's short-story collection *Open Secrets*, which records Ontario's settlement history in overlapping, annalistic layers, from Moodie's era to the present. "A Wilderness Station" (pp. 190–224) recapitulates the volume's historical sweep, assembling a series of "documents" that narrate, with increasing obliqueness, the violent traumas that a female settler experienced in the 1850s and her apparent transformation, by the 1910s, into a harmless old sewing woman, a local character considered curious for her now-inexplicable beliefs and fears, a Jenny Buchanan concealing a Nanny Elshinder. See also Atwood's *Journals of Susanna Moodie* (1970), in which Moodie is seen as burying a disaffection bordering on insanity underneath her air of irreproachable gentility.

67. "My Australian girlhood," writes Praed in *My Australian Girlhood* (1904), "taught me to love Nature, and find in the old Nurse ever my best friend" (p. 1). Raised by Billabong Jenny, an Aboriginal nurse, Praed sees herself as an advocate for the Aborigines. Her persistent juxtaposition of her foster culture with the Australian bush shows both realms suffused with nursing stories, from the platypus's nursing habits, and the starvation of an Aboriginal baby because its mother's breasts have dried up, to the Aboriginal soldier whose service in the British Army so looses the ties of milk and blood that he willingly executes his own mother. Praed's comparisons between of the intact nursing practices of Australia's indigenous mammals and the breakdown of nursing and social bonds among Australia's indigenous people at once conflates the Aborigines with animals and protests the disruption of native life.

68. Moodie here announces a pervasive preoccupation of Canadian literature. As a literary tradition defined, from the eighteenth century onward, by female writers who compare colonial and female experience, Canadian literature might appear to be matriarchal. Yet it also demonstrates strong misogynist and matricidal tendencies. This is particularly evident in the literature of a French Canada whose English colonizers insistently described *Canadien* culture as effeminate and backward, whose Catholic leadership used the cult of the Virgin Mary to enforce social quietism, and whose rhetoric of Catholic nationalism emphasized not only "the revenge of the cradles" but the role of women as guarantors of cultural tradition. The postwar rebellion against the hegemony of church and colonial state adopted an inverse gender politics: Paul-Emile Borduas's 1948 "Refus Globale" called for the liberation of the colonial imagination through the recovery of Sade and French surrealism (both long censored in Quebec), and Pierre Vallières's 1968 account of Quebec's history of enslavement and colonization in *White Niggers of America* insists on the marital entrapment of the coureurs-de-bois, forced into involuntary marriages with the *filles du roi*, as crucial in the breaking of the *Canadien* spirit. Leonard Cohen's *Beautiful Losers* (1966), Michel Tremblay's *Les belles soeurs* (1968), and Denise Boucher's *Les fees ont soif* (1978) all attack the cult of female martyrdom. And although a series of radical texts from the 1960s insist on the necessary conjunction of sexual and national liberation, key texts of the 1970s, such as Victor-Levy Beaulieu's *Un rêve québécois* (1972), fantasize about violence toward women as political liberation and personal revenge.

In English Canada, as Mavis Gallant argues in "Varieties of Exile," remittance men embody the psychic dilemma of British emigrants: disinherited by their fathers and sent away to the colonies in disgrace, they spend their lives revering the memory of their mothers' goodness and of their father's petty tyrannies, raising their own children in an odd colonial imitation of their own families, and refusing to adjust to their place of exile, lest it unfit them for a return, someday, to their lost British homes. Forced to leave the land of their forefathers, terrified by the vastness and wildness of the colony in which they have landed, emigrants like Bogle Corbet and Moodie attempt psychic compensation by constructing a claustrophobic, authoritarian family sphere, in miniaturized replica of British society. A small population spread sparingly across one of the world's largest countries, English Canada defines itself, paradoxically, through its acute siege mentality (McGregor, *The Wacousta Syndrome*). And as virtually the whole sweep of English Canadian fiction suggests, the family assembled within the domestic blockade is necessarily severely dysfunctional. "Women are very dependent here," writes Anne Langton in a journal entry of 1838, "and give a great deal of trouble; we feel our weakness more than anywhere else. . . . The greatest danger, I think, we all run from our peculiar mode of life is that of becoming selfish and narrow-minded. We live so much to ourselves and mix so exclusively with one community" (*A Gentlewoman in Upper Canada*, p. 73).

69. Moodie, *Life in the Clearings*, p. 9.

70. Jameson, *Winter Studies*, p. 66. In compensation, as Moodie's sister Catharine Parr Traill argues in *The Backwoods of Canada* (1836), the isolation of the bush, the absence of nurses and social distractions, can also heighten the "maternal feelings" of individual mothers and strengthen family bonds. "[H]ere there is nothing to interfere with your little nursling. You are not tempted by the pleasures of a gay world to forget your duties as a mother; there is nothing to supplant him in your heart; his presence endears every place; and you learn to love the spot that gave him birth, and to think with complacency upon the country, because it is *his* country; and in looking forward to his future welfare you naturally become doubly interested in the place that is one day to be his" (p. 217).

71. For turn-of-the-century Irish-Canadian "dialect" poet William Drummond, the fostering system is merely an expedient support for the colonial state: the "habitants" of "The Habitant's Jubilee Ode" (*Poetical Works*, pp. 113–17) declare both filial love for the British Empire's distant matriarch and fraternal love for their English Canadian foster brothers, suckled at the same colonial breast.

> Long tam' for our moder so far away de poor Canayens is cry,
> But de new step-moder she's good an' kin', an' it's all right bimeby.
> If de moder is come dead w'en you're small garçon leavin' you dere alone,
> Wit' nobody watchin' for fear you fall, an hurt youse'f on de stone,
> An' 'noder good woman she tak' your han' de sam' your own moder do,
> Is it right you don't call her moder, is it right you don't love her too?
>
> (P. 115)

Grateful because the British conquest of Quebec spared them, in the nick of time, from the social upheavals of the French Revolution, Drummond's imaginary French Canadians conveniently conceive their political allegiances as family loyalties to a maternalistic imperial government who fostered, nourished, and educated the orphaned colony. For Drummond, intent on projecting ethnic stereotypes and An-glo-Canadian political agendas onto French Canada, the fostering system offers a conveniently binding model for imperial subjects. Under its cloaking rhetoric of mother love and parental guidance, the maternalist imperial state is just as authori-tarian as the paternalist one, only more successful in coaxing voluntary compliance with its law, coercing loyalty and obedience.

72. Moodie, letter of April 24, 1865, *Letters of a Lifetime*, p. 217.

73. Clarke, *His Natural Life*, p. 395.

74. Charles Dickens, *David Copperfield* (1850; Harmondsworth: Penguin, 1966), p. 765.

75. So brisk and sensible on the surface, David Copperfield's relationship to Peggotty has undercurrents of deflected sexual feeling and emotional transference. Sensing his mother will soon remarry, David asks Peggotty if she has ever married. She never has and never will, she reassuringly replies, squeezing her young charge in her arms until, as usual, she has popped several buttons off her dress. His mother, in contrast, chides him for his jealousy, and he is banished with Peggotty during the course of her wedding and honeymoon. Later, when his new stepfather banishes him to school, it is Peggotty, not his mother, who whispers through the locked nursery door to assure him of her continued love. In farewell, "[W]e both of us kissed the keyhole with the greatest affection—I patted it with my hand, I recollect, as if it had been her honest face—and parted. From that night there grew in my breast a feeling for Peggotty which I cannot very well define. She did not replace my mother; noone could do that; but she came into a vacancy in my heart, which closed upon her, and I felt towards her something I have never felt for any other human being" (p. 111). Peggotty takes up the vacancy in his heart left by his mother's desertion, and yet, because of that desertion, Copperfield guards himself against further emotional investment and loss. What marks this moment is both Copper-field's new ability to open himself to his nurse and his careful displacement, as he chastely plants the caresses intended for Peggotty's mouth onto the keyhole instead (although Freud would read the keyhole itself as erotically charged). In retrospect, even the earlier love scene between child and nurse was marked by a careful dis-placement, at once desexualizing and suggestive: if nurses were formerly identified, synecdochically, with their nipples, Peggotty is here identified by her buttons.

76. Laurence, *The Diviners*, pp. 228–29.

CHAPTER 6

1. G.P.V. and Helen B. Akrigg's *British Columbia Place Names* (Victoria: Sono Nis, 1986), p. 1; I thank W. H. New for this reference. Abbotsford's name is ambig-uous; although the town was long believed to be named for Scott's stately home, its founder claimed in 1924 to have named it after a general superintendent of the Canadian Pacific Railway (and the brother of Canadian prime minister Abbott).

2. For the unexpected, unwelcome gift of the emus, see *That Land of Exiles*, pp. 107–8. En route to conquer Java in 1811, Gilbert Lord Minto reads Scott's poetry (along with Ossian and Dugald Stewart) (Gibb, *Scottish Empire*, p. 211). Thomas Pringle dedicates *African Sketches* to Scott and sends the skin of the first lion shot by his party of Scottish settlers at the Cape, to be hung in the "Poet's antique armory

at Abbotsford" (p. 120). Scott had helped Pringle become the editor of *Edinburgh Monthly Magazine* (the precursor of *Blackwood's*, which satirized Pringle's short-lived editorship in the "Chaldee Manuscript," in its inaugural issue of October 1817), then secured permission for him to lead Scottish settlers to the Cape. Maria Edgeworth gave similar help to Belfast immigrants to Upper Canada (Stewart, *Our Forest Home*, p. 2).

3. Advertisement for "Beautiful Scottish Books," in Henry Grey Graham, *The Social Life of Scotland.*

4. Duncan, "The Hesitation of Miss Anderson," *The Pool in the Desert*, pp. 99–161, here 105.

5. Critical of the Scott family as social interlopers, Elizabeth Grant's *Memoirs* decries "the *Castle* at Abbotsford" as a "monument of human vanity, human absurdity and madness" (2:73).

6. See Irving, *Abbotsford*; Lockhart, *Peter's Letters*, 2:294–347; Henry F. Chroley, *Memorials of Mrs. Hemans*, 2 vols. (London: Saunders and Otley, 1837), 2:29–32; and Wainwright, *The Romantic Interior*, pp. 147–208.

7. Davey, "Abbotsford and India," in *The Abbotsford Guide to India*, p. 3. During the British occupation of India, Indians emigrated as indentured servants to colonial settlements in the West Indies, on the coast of Africa, and in British Columbia, doubling the routes of the slave trade.

8. Davey, "Abbotsford and India," pp. 3–5.

9. Davey, "Vijayangar," in *The Abbotsford Guide to India*, pp. 74–75, here 75.

10. But see the 1795 proposal that Anticosti Island be used to house "a settlement of convicts," who might settle freely after "their period of exile was elapsed"; the same author pleads against abolition in the Canadas (O'Leary, ed., *Canadian Letters*, p. 5).

11. On the effects of Canada's piecemeal construction on national identity, see Gilles Paquet and Jean-Pierre Wallot, "Nouvelle/France/Québec/Canada: A World of Limited Identities," in Canny and Pagden, eds., *Colonial Identity*, pp. 95–114.

12. See Elizabeth Waterston, "The Lowland Tradition in Canadian Literature," in Reid, ed., *The Scottish Tradition in Canada*, pp. 203–31; and MacLulich, *Between Europe and America*, pp. 61–86; what neither overview conveys is the investment in the Maritimes and Upper Canada as sites in which Scotland (and Ireland) could be reconstructed; John Young's pioneering treatise on Nova Scotian agriculture, for instance, takes as models the "improvements" of the Dublin Society and the Highland Society (*Letters of Agricola* [1818], esp. letter H, p. 23). Early Canadian children's literature is equally marked by Scottish influence; see Traill's *Young Emigrants* (1828), esp. pp. 72–75, and *Canadian Crusoes* (1852), in which the children of Highland soldiers, French Canadian habitants, and local Indians, stranded in the Canadian wilderness, form a new community, protected by dogs named Wallace, Bruce, and Wolfe.

13. Bowering, *A Short Sad Book*, p. 166.

14. Weinbrot argues a similar effect for *Ossian* (*Britannia's Issue*, p. 540).

15. Moodie, *Letters*, p. 22.

16. "[A]lmost all Canadian fiction written in the nineteenth century, in both English and French, falls into the category of historical novels modeled with greater or lesser understanding of the works produced by Scott" (Winnifred M. Bogaards, "Sir

Walter Scott's Influence on Nineteenth Century Canadian Historians and Historical Novelists," in J. H. Alexander and Hewitt, eds., *Scott and His Influence*, pp. 443–54, here 447); see Gerson, *A Purer Taste*, pp. 67–79; Kröller, "Walter Scott in America"; MacLulich, *Between Europe and America*, esp. pp. 37–60; and Gwendolyn Davies, *Studies in Maritime Literary History*, pp. 107–29.

17. For Scott's influence on Richardson, see Jay Macpherson, "Reading and Convention in Richardson: Some Notes," in Catherine Sheldon Ross, ed., *Recovering Canada's First Novelist*, pp. 63–86. For *Wacousta*'s centrality to subsequent Canadian fiction, see McGregor, *The Wacousta Syndrome*; yet see also New, *History of Canadian Literature*, pp. 78–80, and Davey's parodic "Wacouster," in *The Louis Riel Organ*, pp. 1–20.

18. Barr, "Literature in Canada," pp. 3–27, here 3, 7, 27. Barr echoes Wakefield's *Letter from Sydney* (1829), with its hypothetical insertion of Scott and other British intellectuals into colonial Australia: "Sir Walter Scott, Sir Humphrey Davy, and Mr. Malthus, would not earn as much in this colony as three brawny experienced ploughmen; and though the inordinate vanity of new people might be gratified by the possession of them, they would be considered as mere ornaments, and would often be wholly neglected, for things of greater utility" (p. 22).

19. Robert Owen, *A New View of Society and Other Writings*, ed. Gregory Clæys (Harmondsworth: Penguin, 1991), p. 172.

20. Hechter, *Internal Colonialism*; see also Angus Calder, *Revolutionary Empire*; Kearney, *The British Isles*, esp. chaps. 7 and 8; Francis Godwin James, *Ireland in the Empire*; and Connolly, *Religion, Law, and Power*, pp. 110–24.

21. See Bryant, "Scots in India"; Bumsted, *The People's Clearance*; Smailes, *Scottish Empire*; Fischer, *Albion's Seed*; and Hughes, *The Fatal Shore*, esp. pp. 181–95; see also Murray's *Peasant Mandarin* for a view of the British Isles as "England's oldest and longest lived empire," subjugating "her Scottish, Welsh and Irish neighbours" and initiating "the wholesale, if gradual and subtle, destruction of their native cultures" (pp. 236–37), and for Australia as a country settled by "an Anglo-Celtic rather than an Anglo-Saxon people" (p. 78).

On the presence of Scots and Irish in North America, see Brooke, *History of Emily Montague* (1769); Crévecoeur, "What Is an American?" in *Letters from an American Farmer* (1782), pp. 60–99; Breckenridge, *Modern Chivalry* (1792–1815); Simcoe, *Mrs. Simcoe's Diary*, esp. pp. 64–69; Knight, *A Year in Canada* (1816); Howison, *Sketches of Upper Canada* (1821); Jameson, *Winter Studies* (1838); Haliburton, *The Clockmaker* (1836), pp. 69–73; and Sellar, *A Scotsman in Upper Canada* (1915). Grant's *Memoirs* gives a vivid sense of Scottish society life against an imperial backdrop; her own Highland family moves to Bombay, and her brother becomes lieutenant governor of Bengal and governor of Jamaica. Oliphant's *Rector and the Doctor's Family* (1863) and the Linklaters' *Crossriggs* (1908) discuss the unanticipated repercussions of sending the young poor out to Canada or Australia to win their fortunes: if they fail, they will send *their* children back home to Britain to be raised.

22. Schaw, *Journal of a Lady of Quality*, pp. 81–82.

23. William Lyon Mackenzie, leader of the 1837 Upper Canada Rebellion, was raised in Dundee and fled to Canada, with hundreds of fellow Scottish radicals, after the Scottish insurrection of 1820. In York (Toronto), he published Radical

newspapers, which united reformers throughout Upper Canada. Ellis and Mac a'Gobhiainn, *The Scottish Insurrection*, p. 293.

24. Mitchel, *The Last Conquest of Ireland*, pp. 219–20. Mitchel's anti-imperialist rhetoric has precedents both in Swift and in the rhetoric surrounding the trial of Warren Hastings; see Burke, *Works*, vol. 9; Musselwhite, "The Trial of Warren Hastings"; and Suleri, *The Rhetoric of English India*, chap. 3, as well as Walpole, *Horace Walpole's Correspondence*. "The East India-Company," Walpole writes on July 19, 1769, "is all faction and gaming. . . . Such fortunes are made and lost every day as are past belief. Our history will appear a gigantic lie hereafter, when we are shrunk again to our own little island. People trudge to the other end of the town to vote who shall govern empires at the other end of the world. . . . Riches, abuse, cabals, are so enormously overgrown, that one wants conception and words to comprehend or describe them" (23:133). "[W]e have outdone the Spaniards in Peru!" he reiterated on March 5, 1772. "They were at least butchers on a religious principle, however diabolical their zeal. We have murdered, deposed, plundered, usurped— nay, what think you of the famine in Bengal, in which three millions perished, being caused by a monopoly of the provisions, by the servants of the East India Company?" (23:387).

25. Mitchel, *Jail Journal*, p. 194. On *Jail Journal* as a nationalist text, see Lloyd, *Nationalism and Minor Literature*, pp. 49–54, and Morash, *Writing the Irish Famine*, pp. 52–75.

26. Mitchel's personal failures of identification, in the meantime, are considerable. On the convict hull, he has only intermittent sympathy for ordinary felons; during the American Civil War, he will side with the Confederacy.

27. Thinking along parallel lines, Marx's "British Rule in India" (1853) links British internal colonialism and overseas expansion: Hindustan is "the Ireland of the East" (p. 301). Yet their differences of emphases are crucial: Marx denounces British military and social violence in India, but he condones the economic and political modernization inadvertently set into motion, "whatever bitterness the spectacle of the crumbling of an ancient world may have for our personal feeling." The English have "broken down the entire framework of Indian society, without any symptoms of reconstitution yet appearing. This loss of this old world, with no gain of a new one, imparts a particular kind of melancholy to the present misery of the Hindu, and separates Hindustan, ruled by Britain, from all its ancient traditions, and from the whole of its past history" (pp. 302–3). Yet by their forcible dissolution of India's traditional economies and communities, the English "produced the greatest, and to speak the truth, the only *social* revolution ever heard of in Asia. . . . [W]hatever were the crimes of England she was the tool of history in bringing about that revolution" (pp. 306–7).

28. Michael Normile, letter of November 11, 1855, in Fitzpatrick, ed., *Oceans of Consolation*, p. 74; see also John Mahony's letter of August 18, 1887, pp. 263–65.

29. "Jerilderie Letter" (1879), cited in Hughes, *Fatal Shore*, pp. 443–44.

30. "Children of the Gæl," reads the Gaelic inscription on the commemorative Celtic cross dedicated on Grosse Ile in 1909, "died in their thousands on this island having fled from the laws of foreign tyrants and an artificial famine in the years 1847–1848. . . . God bless Ireland!" (an echo of the Fenian slogan God Save [or Free] Ireland). The English and French inscriptions beside it declare the cross "sa-

cred to the memory of thousands of Irish emigrants who to preserve the faith suffered hunger and exile in 1847–8, and stricken with fever ended here their sorrowful pilgrimage." The French inscription also commemorates the French Canadian priests who entered the quarantine to "console and fortify" the sufferers. The cross addresses a highly differentiated audience: an official English Canada, a French Canada joined to Ireland in its Catholicism and experience of English occupation, and an angry Gaelic diaspora (Pádraic 'O Laighin, "Grosse Ile: The Holocaust Revisited," in O'Driscoll and Reynolds, eds., *The Untold Story*, pp. 75–101). On the continuing persecution of Irish immigrants during the Fenian scare, see See, *Riots in New Brunswick*.

31. O'Leary, ed., *Canadian Letters*, p. 80.

32. Canadian poetry marks the cultural transition from a stance critical of empire (and its displacements) to a celebratory one. In "The Deserted Village" (1770), Oliver Goldsmith mourned the wave of British emigration that followed enclosure; settled in Nova Scotia, his great-nephew and namesake Oliver Goldsmith writes his own counterpoem, "The Rising Village" (1824), as a paean to British conquest and settlement in North America. The critical attitude of the original poem is lost in its colonial reprise, which not only omits the dislocations suffered by the emigrant but explicitly forecloses any criticism of British conditions (David Sinclair, ed., *Nineteenth-Century Narrative Poems*, pp. 1–16).

There is a similar shift in perspective between Standish O'Grady's "Emigrant" (1831) and Alexander McLachlan's "Emigrant" (1861). O'Grady execrates the conditions that force the Irish into emigration: "[S]ad and lone and outcast," they await the "defeat" and "ruin" of the hated "Britannia" (*The Emigrant*, p. 10, ll. 53–56). In McLachlan's "Emigrant," in contrast, the primary emotion attributed to emigrants is elegiac nostalgia; their voyage to the colonies is accompanied by the homesick "lays" of "little Mac," who sings "of Scotia's bonnie woods and braes," landscapes he will never see again, and of his sorrow in parting with relatives and friends (Sinclair, ed., *Nineteenth-Century Narrative Poems*, pp. 115–56, here 124). McLachlan individualizes and stylizes emigration, occluding its socioeconomic causes, its mass character, and its link to forced clearances.

33. Clarke, *His Natural Life*, p. 614.

34. *Joseph Howe*, p. 76.

35. Gibson, *Perpetual Motion*, p. 113. "I wondered why I felt so bitter about Canada," writes Norman Levine at the end of *Canada Made Me* (1958). "After all, it was all part of a dream, an experiment that could not come off. It was foolish to believe that you could take the throwouts, the rejects, the human kickabouts from Europe and tell them: Here you have a second chance. Here you can start a new life. But no one ever mentioned the price one had to pay, how much of oneself you had to betray" (p. 277).

36. Praed's *Lady Bridget* (1915) demonstrates how an aggrieved Irish and Scottish nationalism is displaced, in the Australian outback, into genocidal racism against the Aborigines. Praed's novel works from, yet tilts and inverts, Owenson's radical national tales: the courtship and union of Lady Bridget O'Hara, radical Irish feminist intellectual (modeled both on Owenson and on Praed), and Colin McKeith, rugged Scottish rancher (engaged in a deadly vendetta against all Aborigines to avenge the murder of his own family), restage the union of British

national characters to imperial ends. Initially unable to accept her husband's murderous racism, the Irish heroine eventually sacrifices her principles and independence to be reunited with him: she will soften his racial hatred, but he will limit her anti-imperialist ideals. "And in that kiss," the novel concludes, "by the divine alchemy of true wedded love, all the past pride and bitterness were transmuted into a great abiding Peace" (p. 293).

37. Laurence, *The Diviners*, p. 85. Laurence's novel responds to a long and influential Scottish Canadian literary tradition in which Highland immigrant experience is elevated as a moral standard for the nation; see Connor's *Glengarry Schooldays* (1902), Macphail's *Master's Wife* (1939), and MacLennan's *Scotchman's Return* (1960). Following the sardonic account of Scotch-Canadian complacency in Sara Jeannette Duncan's *Imperialist* (1904), *The Diviners* depicts ethnic sentimentality as a dangerous moral and political trap.

38. Laurence, *The Diviners*, p. 86. For an explosive gloss on the contested ownership of historical suffering, see Leonard Cohen's *Beautiful Losers* (1965). Set simultaneously in the wake of the Holocaust, in the midst of Quebec's sexual revolution and radical separatist struggles, and within the hermetic colonial archive, the novel juxtaposes Indian, Jewish, and French Canadian martyrologies while travestying the impulse toward comparative victimology. Crosscutting between the historical evidence of the Jesuit *Relations*, a present-day story of national politics and a sexual triangle that crosses religious, racial, and heterosexual lines, the novel insists that Quebec, formed by the French conquest of the Indians and the English conquest of the French, takes its character from a sadomasochistic history of violence and repression, so that present-day attempts at sexual (and national) liberation necessarily move through erotic and political circuits still charged with this colonial logic.

39. Thomas Campbell's "Lines, Written at the Request of the Highland Society" (1809) envisions the rose, thistle, and shamrock entwining "in eternal union," as the independent Scot, the "generous" Englishman (l. 33), and the "fervid" Irishman unite to repel external invaders (*Complete Poetical Works*, pp. 200–202, here 201, ll. 35–36). The figure reappears in Canada in numerous contexts: on the arms of the Canada Company (W. H. Graham, *Tiger of Canada West*, p. 48); in a Standish O'Grady song celebrating the bravery of the "Glengarry Volunteers, composed of Scotch, Irish and English," in suppressing the Upper and Lower Canada Uprisings (*The Emigrant*, p. 83 n. 28); and, most ubiquitously, in the chorus of "The Maple Leaf Forever" (1867), a patriotic anthem written by Scottish Canadian Alexander Muir to celebrate Canadian Confederation. Laurence's *Diviners* offers a postcolonial gloss: the singing of "The Maple Leaf Forever" in Canadian schools' curriculum reinforces the long-standing social marginalization of French, Eastern European, and especially Native and Métis Canadians (pp. 69–70).

40. Moodie, *Life in the Clearings*, p. 26; the passage echoes and politicizes the observation, in Traill's *Backwoods of Canada*, that "[e]ven the Irish and Highlanders of the humblest class seem to lay aside their ancient superstitions on becoming denizens of the woods of Canada. . . . 'It is the most unpoetical of all lands; there is not scope for imagination; here all is new—the very soil seems newly formed; there is no hoary ancient grandeur in these woods; no recollections of former deeds connected with the country'" (p. 128). Moodie's *Life in the Clearings*, in contrast,

dwells on the contrast and potential conflict between different British national characters. The volume includes parallel stories about an Irish national character (Michael Macbride) and a Scottish one (Jeanie Burns), as well as a sketch that uses a fight between an English bulldog, a Scotch terrier, and an Irish greyhound to represent a debate over the Clergy Reserves.

Nineteenth-century Canadian fiction remains preoccupied with the similarities and differences between the Scottish and Irish communities. The narrator of the anonymous "Letters of Patty Pry" (published in *The Novascotian* in 1826) inveighs against Scottish literary tropes and cultural nostalgia but then hears the history of her own Irish family (and their emigration to Canada) from her father, who breaks into a brogue "as thick as *buttermilk*," the moment he starts talking of "his dear ould Ireland" (Arnason, ed., *Nineteenth Century Canadian Stories*, pp. 33–51, here 44). Opening with a feud, on the Ontario frontier, between Highland Presbyterians, Irish, and French Canadian "Papists," Connor's *Man from Glengarry* (1901) ends with the political confederation of Canada's disparate territories and the triumph of Christian forgiveness.

41. Howe, "Acadia," in *Poems and Essays*, pp. 5–40, here 31–32. Yet of the 1,200 Upper Canada settlers under his jurisdiction in 1826, Colonal Talbot reportedly finds the Highlanders and the Irish the most difficult "to manage, most difficult to satisfy, most craving" (Frances Stewart, *Our Forest Home*, p. 93).

42. On Pringle's colonizing work and literary influence, see Hay, ed., *Thomas Pringle*; Coetzee, *White Writing*, pp. 45–62; and David Bunn, " 'Our Wattled Cot': Mercantile and Domestic Space in Thomas Pringle's African Landscapes," in Mitchell, ed., *Landscape and Power*, pp. 127–73.

43. Pringle, *African Sketches*, p. 66. Scottish imperial literature resounds with scenes in which Scottish songs are sung in the isolation of the new outpost. Schaw travels from Edinburgh to the West Indies, in 1774, on a ship that disgorges a smuggled cargo of "wretched" and "disgusting" Highland emigrants and whose Scotch sailors speed the voyage with their melancholy singing of "Lochaber Nae maer" and "Heaven preserve my bonny Scotch laddie" (*Journal*, pp. 28, 59). In Sellar's *Scotsman in Upper Canada*, the Scots settlers (on a new estate called Bonnybraes precisely because "there's no Braes . . . that's what we left behind") sing Burns while they clear the woods, and "the age-old wilderness for the first time heard our Scottish melodies" (pp. 54–57). But see also the sardonic accounts of the singing of "Loch Lomond" in postcolonial Trinidad (Naipaul, *Middle Passage*, p. 65) and of "Highland" pipers (one of them black) playing "The Retreat from Gibraltar" on the streets of Montreal (Metcalf, *Kicking against the Pricks*, p. 4).

44. Pringle, *African Sketches*, p. 128.

45. The book adopts the sketch format of a British series in which the Hermit visits London, Edinburgh, and other European capitals.

46. Savery, *The Hermit of Van Diemen's Land*, p. 102. Other Australian literature, in contrast, evokes murderous ethnic rivalries. In "Moreton Bay," colonial Australia's most popular ballad, an Irish convict protests the sadism of a Scottish prison governor, rejoicing in his 1830 assassination (Manning Clark, ed., *Sources of Australian History*, pp. 186–87). Writing from the Australian bush of the 1840s, Annabella Boswell contrasts the pastoral calm of Glen-Alice (populated largely by Gaelic-speaking Highland settlers) with the drunken threats of its Irish laborers to

kill all the English (*Annabella Boswell's Journal*, pp. 36–41). In the remote bush station of Marcus Clarke's "Learning 'Colonial Experience'" (1873, *Stories*, pp. 5–10), English and Scottish friends quarrel about the Hanoverian cause and come to blows over Mary Queen of Scots; his 1871 "Horace in the Bush" (*Stories*, pp. 116–23) chronicles a similar quarrel between Scottish and Irish friends over their respective literary traditions.

47. Byrne, *Twelve Years' Wandering*, 2:124.

48. Some scholars question whether the same author could have written such different works; see Wilde et al., *The Oxford Companion to Australian Literature*, pp. 608–9.

49. See also Wakefield, *Letter from Sydney*, p. 24.

50. Quoted in Hughes, *The Fatal Shore*, p. 506. In an 1826 letter, Frances Stewart announces her intention to build a similar, personal collection in the Upper Canada bush. Maria Edgeworth, a friend and distant cousin, regularly sends Stewart her latest publications: "When I have completed my Edgeworth library I intend by degrees to get all Walter Scott's" (*Our Forest Home*, p. 95).

51. Crawford, *Devolving English Literature*, chap. 1; Viswanathan, *Masks of Conquest*.

52. In *The Convict Ships and England's Exiles*, hull chaplain Colin Arrott Browning describes his efforts to use the period of transport for an intensive course of spiritual reformation for the convicts, complete with a daily lesson plan (and literacy teaching). The goal is at once the convicts' inner transformation and their full socialization, beginning with deference to their guards and resulting in lasting respect for Australian law and order.

53. Frame's *Faces in the Water* describes the ritualized Sunday singing of "When Irish Eyes Are Smiling" and "The Road to the Isles" in a New Zealand mental hospital in strikingly similar terms: the nostalgic invocation of a long-lost national home both cheers and disciplines demoralized long-term inmates who fear they will never be allowed to go home again and that their electroshock or lobotomies will remove all memories of life before institutionalization (p. 48).

54. In 1837 she is delighted to find Scott (and Shakespeare) being read in a small village on Lake Simcoe (Jameson, *Winter Studies*, pp. 183, 542).

55. Mitchel, *Jail Journal*, p. 125.

56. Speech of Viscount Morpeth, in *The Abbotsford Subscription*, p. 16. For Scott's influence on nationalist writing in Europe, in the empire, and in America, see Lukács, *The Historical Novel*; Alexander and Hewitt, eds., *Scott and His Influence*; Green, *Dreams of Adventure, Deeds of Empire*; and Dekker, *The American Historical Romance*. Edgeworth remarks in 1818 on the enormous American popularity of the Waverley novels: "'Waverley,' 'Guy Mannering,' &tc., have excited as much enthusiasm in America as in Europe. . . . 'Boats are now actually upon the look-out for Rob Roy, all here are so impatient to get the first sight of it'" (*Memoir of Maria Edgeworth*, 2:9). As Twain argues in *Life on the Mississippi* (1883), the cult of the Waverley novels in the American South held back the region's development by a generation. "But for the Sir Walter disease, the character of the Southerner . . . would be wholly modern, in place of modern and medieval mixed. It was Sir Walter who . . . created rank and caste down there, and also reverence for rank and caste,

and pride and pleasure in them. . . . Sir Walter had so large a hand in making Southern character, as it existed before the war, that he is in great measure responsible for
the war" (p. 305).

57. Gooneratne, *English Literature in Ceylon*, p. 153.

58. Boswell, *Annabella Boswell's Journal*, p. 37.

59. Popular throughout Australia, the Waverley novels were the only novels included in the colony's first subscription library (established in 1826) (Temple, *That
Land of Exiles*, p. 106).

60. *Abbotsford Subscription*, p. 25.

61. Monkland, *Life in India*, 1:135–38.

62. Scottish ways of representing landscape and history, complains a proud New
Brunswicker in Haliburton's *Letter-Bag of the Great Western* (1840), threaten to
colonize North American prospects as well. "Byron has bedevilled the Rhine, as
Scott Loch Katrine. . . . May poetry and poets never damn our magnificent river
with their flattering strains. . . . Who ever sailed up the St. John without expressing
his delight at finding it so much more beautiful than he anticipated? and why? because he had heard no exaggerated account of it. . . . Whether we shall ever have a
poet, I know not. Shipbuilding, lumbering, stock-jobbing, and note-shaving, are not
apt to kindle inspiration; but if we shall ever be so fortunate, I most fervently hope
he will spare the river" (pp. 80–83).

63. Macpherson, *Poems of Ossian, in the Original Gaelic*, p. lxxxviii. To rescue
Ireland's "national instrument from ruin," Irish Anglo-Indians likewise donated
more than £1,100 to support a harping school (Bunting, *Ancient Music of Ireland*,
pp. 65–66).

64. Anderson, "Exodus." Lamming's *Pleasures of Exile* (1960) gives a more
positive account of the diasporic constitution of a unifying "West Indian" identity.

65. "Scott and Byron still dominated English literature in 1832, when the first
novel published in Australia appeared; and Australian literature grew out of English
literature. Scott provided the pattern for adventure—the result of two societies in
conflict—and the scenery. Byron provided the typical heroes, who admitted no social allegiance. . . . [T]he influence of Scott and Byron was to last longer in Australian fiction than in English. Colonization is the process by which a stronger society
overcomes a weaker" (Argyle, *Introduction to the Australian Novel*, p. 1). The radical potential of Byron and the critical potential of the Waverley novels disappear
over the course of this opening paragraph (as from nineteenth-century Australian
literature).

66. See Oliphant, *Annals of a Publishing House*; Klancher, *The Making of English Reading Audiences*; and Marilyn Butler, "Culture's Medium: The Role of the
Review," in Curran, ed., *The Cambridge Companion to British Romanticism*, pp.
120–47.

67. Azim, *The Colonial Rise of the Novel*, p. 115; Azim's book traces the formative influence of *Blackwood's* on the Brontës' juvenilia.

68. The phrase appears in the 1832 *Blackwood's* review (attributed to John Wilson) of Dunlop's "Statistical Sketches" (*Tiger Dunlop's Upper Canada*, p. 143).

69. *Blackwood's* influence on colonial literary life is so pervasive that when
Susanna Moodie visits the Toronto Lunatic Asylum in the early 1850s, she meets a

madman named David Moir, convinced he is the David Moir of *Blackwood's*, who signs his "strangely unconnected" poems as "Delta," the *Blackwood's* moniker of his famous namesake (*Life in the Clearings*, p. 270).

70. This diffusion was speeded by a transcolonial network of personal friendships. Pringle, protégé of Scott and early chronicler of the Cape, was in turn an early mentor of Susanna Moodie and a close associate, at the Cape, of Moodie's future husband, Orkneyman Dunbar Moodie (who published his own chronicle of Scottish settler life in Africa). Pringle's widow emigrated to Upper Canada, settling in the same area as Moodie's sister Catharine Parr Traill, and Frances Stewart, Maria Edgeworth's cousin and correspondent. See Dunbar Moodie, *Ten Years in South Africa*; Frances Stewart, *Our Forest Home*, p. 148; and Susanna Moodie's Pringle-inspired story of the Cape, "The Vanquished Lion" (1832), in *Voyages*, pp. 31–42.

71. Scott, *Waverley*, 1:xxxiv.

72. Especially for readers and critics committed to a "unified," English-dominated Canada, the novel's repeated homages to Scott provide gratifying evidence of the final ascendancy of British narrative forms and novelistic traditions over French Canadian material. The 1974 McClelland and Stewart reissue of the novel reiterates the conquest. As Lecker and Davey have recently argued, McClelland and Stewart's New Canadian Library series (begun in 1957) established a new canon for English Canadian readers and academics (Lecker, "The Canonization of Canadian Literature: An Inquiry into Value," in Lecker, ed., *Canadian Canons*; and Davey, "Critical Response," *Critical Inquiry* 16, no. 3 [spring 1990]: 656–89). The New Canadian Library conveyed only a highly foreshortened sense of French Canadian literature: Aubert de Gaspé's novel, the 106th in the series, was only the 9th—and the only pre-twentieth century—French Canadian work to be published. Even more startlingly, *Canadians of Old* was reissued without Aubert de Gaspé's name anywhere on the cover; instead it bears the name of the nineteenth-century English Canadian translator Sir Charles Roberts and announces *him* as the "Father of Canadian literature." Clara Thomas's nationalist introduction, finally, discusses the translation as much as the original, praises the novel's reconciliatory content, and gives little sense of its place within a Francophone tradition (*Canadians of Old*, pp. vii–xii, esp. xii).

73. Prebble's *Mutiny* presents Highland soldiers as "the first of Britain's colonial levies, called to arms to police their own hills and then to fight in the Crown's imperial wars" (p. 20). Several Highland Regiment mutinies, he argues, were catalyzed by the soldiers' sudden understanding of their role as imperial pawns. The first mutiny occurred during the initial mustering of the regiments in 1743; promised when recruited that they would not be posted outside Scotland, the soldiers mutinied when they learned they were ordered to the West Indies (feared for its extremely high mortality rate). "It naturally came into their heads," explained an anonymous *History of the Highland Regiments* (1743), "that they had been first used as rods to scourge their own countrymen and after having sufficiently tamed them were now to be thrown into the fire" (*Mutiny*, p. 48).

74. See here also Swift's "Memoirs of Captain John Creichton" (1731), in *The Works of Jonathan Swift*, pp. 521–43. The son of a Scotch-Irish family (with bitter memories of the Ulster Plantation Uprising), Creichton grows up in Ireland, serves the British Army in Scotland, and zealously persecutes suspected Covenanters.

When he is won over to the Jacobite cause, however, he learns what it is to be outlawed. John Mitchel read these memoirs with interest during his imprisonment.

75. Chaigneau, *Jack Connor*, 2:208.

76. Teeling, *History of the Irish Rebellion*, p. 118.

77. Jacobites could often gain pardon only by enlisting in the British Army; many remained openly cynical about the British cause (Pittock, *The Invention of Scotland*, p. 62).

78. According to Prebble, "[H]e believed that lingering resistance among the clans might finally be crushed by a contrived massacre, that the deliberate sacrifice of one of his patrols in the killing of the Macphersons' chief would justify the extirpation of the whole clan in reprisal. 'Wou'd you believe that I am so bloody?' he asked his friend William Rickson. The proposal remained a thought only, but he was ever amazed at his bloodthirsty dislike of the clans" (*Mutiny*, p. 94). In the 1750s "Britain was presented with the rather tasteless irony of General James Wolfe, once responsible for a sizable share of post-Culloden atrocities, leading the newly formed Fraser Highlanders in assaults on French holdings in North America" (Hill, *The Scots to Canada*, p. 13).

79. Hayter, "The Army and the First British Empire," p. 118.

80. See Benjamin West's painting *The Death of General Wolfe* (1770); Robert Fergusson's "Epitaph on General Wolfe," in Ramsay and Fergusson, *Poems*, p. 207; Galt's *Bogle Corbet*; and O'Leary's *Canadian Letters*, p. 4. In Green's *Romance Readers*, an elderly English veteran weeps as he studies "the last orders of General Wolfe" (1:2).

81. See here Colley, *Britons*, pp. 101–5, and Cullen, "The Art of Assimilation," p. 614.

82. *The Briton*, no. 4 (July 19, 1762), in Smollett, *Poems, Plays*, pp. 255–60, here 258–59.

83. See Crawford, *Devolving English Literature*, p. 17, on Scottish Enlightenment comparisons between the tribes, chieftains, and clans of the Highlanders and those of the Native Americans; see also Makdisi, "Colonial Space."

84. Johnstone, her husband, and William Blackwood had previously coedited the *Edinburgh Weekly Chronicle*, but the partnership dissolved, probably because Blackwood found the Johnstones too liberal. He went on to found *Blackwood's*, Scotland's first major Tory publication, and the Johnstones launched *Johnstone's Edinburgh Magazine* and other magazines of their own.

85. Johnstone, *Clan-Albin*, 1:112. For Johnstone, as for Edgeworth, such "universal talents" signal a world before the division of labor, now a dying way of life. Yet in Upper Canada, reports Jameson in *Winter Studies*, young Irish immigrants are forced to reinvent this mode, becoming "their own architects, masons, smiths, carpenters, farmers, gardeners" (p. 170).

86. For a postcolonial continuation of Johnstone's project, see Maillet's *Pélagie* (1982), which chronicles the epic nineteenth-century journey of the Acadians (cleared from Acadia to Louisiana by the British in 1755) back toward New Brunswick and the reconstruction—and ethnic broadening—of the Acadian nation in the process.

87. "The Shieling," in *Tales by Professor Wilson*, by John Wilson, pp. 166–75, here 170; Wilson dedicated this edition to Scott. On Wilson's influence on

Blackwood's, see Andrew Noble, "John Wilson (Christopher North) and the Tory Hegemony," in Gifford, ed., *The History of Scottish Literature*, vol. 3, *The Nineteenth Century*, pp. 125–52.

88. Yet see also Jameson's indictment of the "suffering, and injury, and injustice . . . inflicted, from the errors, ignorance, and remoteness of the home government" when it attempts to settle British Army veterans in Upper Canada in 1832. Of the 1,200 persuaded to exchange their pensions for Canadian land, only 800 ever reach Upper Canada, and only 450 survive the first five years of homesteading (with many requiring public assistance). "These were the men who fought our battles in Egypt, Spain, and France!" (*Winter Studies*, p. 538).

89. *Recollections of the American War*; rpt. in Dunlop, *Tiger Dunlop's Upper Canada*, pp. 1–62, here 19, 7.

90. Colley, *Britons*, esp. p. 14; Arnold, "On the Study of Celtic Literature," in *On the Study of Celtic Literature*, pp. 13–136; Meredith, *Celt and Saxon*; and Harvey, *Lectures*, pp. 136–95.

91. Dunlop, *Recollections*, in *Tiger Dunlop's Upper Canada*, p. 25. This is literally a scene from Christian Johnstone: the reconciliatory union at the end of her 1814 Scottish national tale *The Saxon and the Gaël* is allegorically recapitulated "at the SALUTATION, at Perth, where a Gael is shaking the hand of a Saxon, on the sign over the door" (4:45). The short novel of the Upper Canada Rebellion, *Two and Twenty Years Ago* (1859; sometimes attributed to Dunlop), carries this allegorical reconciliation even further, though its crucial categories are loyalty and family memory rather than ethnicity. During the Revolutionary War, an American family is politically divided: one brother sides with the Revolutionaries; the other, becoming a United Empire Loyalist, moves to Upper Canada. Sixty years later, on the eve of the Upper Canada Rebellion, the Loyalist's sons find themselves on opposite sides. One, proudly conscious of his Loyalist legacy, warns Sir Francis Bond that trouble is brewing; the other, seduced by "fanatical agitators" (p. 48), causes his own death and that of his mother.

92. Dunlop, *Statistical Sketches*, in *Tiger Dunlop's Upper Canada*, pp. 63–137, here 125.

93. Carl Klinck, introduction to *Tiger Dunlop's Upper Canada*, p. xi. See also W. H. Graham, *The Tiger of Canada West*, p. 22.

94. Dunlop, *Statistical Sketches*, p. 115. Frances Stewart similarly compares the Riceland of Upper Canada to Killarney, and the Otonabee River to the Liffey and the Boyne (*Our Forest Home*, pp. 20, 30).

95. Dunlop, *Statistical Sketches*, p. 68.

96. John Richardson, *Wacousta*, pp. 6–7.

97. See Ian A. Gordon's introduction to Galt's *Last of the Lairds*, pp. vii–xviii.

98. See Ferris, *Achievement of Literary Authority*, pp. 195–236; Gwendolyn Davies, *Studies in Maritime Literary History*, pp. 63–70; Bogaards, "Sir Walter Scott's Influence," esp. pp. 443–44; and Douglas S. Mack, "The Rage of Fanaticism in Former Days: James Hogg's *Confessions* and the Controversy over *Old Mortality*," in Ian Campbell, ed., *Nineteenth-Century Scottish Fiction*, pp. 37–50.

99. John Irving, "The Achievement of Thomas McCulloch," and Douglas G. Lockhead, "A Bibliographical Note," appendixes to McCulloch, *The Stepsure Letters*, pp. 150–59; and Klinck, ed., *Literary History of Canada*, p. 93.

100. Gwendolyn Davies, "The Club Papers: Haliburton's Literary Apprenticeship," in Tierney, ed., *The Achievement of Thomas Chandler Haliburton*, pp. 65–82; Ray Palmer Baker, *History of English Canadian Literature*, p. 60.

101. Haliburton, *A Historical and Statistical Account*; the line was also used as the motto for an 1826 series called Characteristics of Nova Scotia, in Halifax's *Acadian Magazine*. M. Brook Taylor, "Haliburton as a Historian," in Tierney, ed., *The Achievement of Thomas Chandler Haliburton*, pp. 103–22, 103 n. 1. See also MacMechan, *Headwaters of Canadian Literature*, pp. 41–42.

102. This position opposes a long tradition of promercantilist, proimperial literature; see Shields, *Oracles of Empire*.

103. McCulloch, *Stepsure Letters*, pp. 12–16.

104. Long before 1945, Caliban is invoked to stand for the moral problem of the West Indies: in *Peregrinations of Jeremiah Grant* (1763), Creole Jeremiah Grant frequents a "Wednesday Creole-club" in Bath which includes Phil Caliban, Will Hurricane, and Jack Muscavado (p. 89).

105. See also Egan's denunciation, in *Real Life in Ireland*, pp. 109–10, of the dehumanizing imperial view of convicts and Irishmen as the "living raw material" of empire.

106. Haliburton, *The Clockmaker* [1958 ed.], p. 17. Yet in an 1824 letter, Haliburton complains that "we are ourselves too poor to maintain or receive the paupers of other countries"; "low Irish—disbanded soldiers—hungry adventurers and Chesapeake blacks are not the class of emigrants we want." Instead, "a limited emigration of mechanicks and practical farmers possessing a property of from 500 to 1500 pounds each would be of infinite service to us" (*Letters*, p. 16).

107. A patronage-based civil service, complains Haliburton in the dedication to *The Letter-Bag*, denies even the most talented colonials their rightful place in imperial government (pp. v–xiv).

108. Haliburton, *Letter-Bag*, esp. letter 27, pp. 287–305.

109. Haliburton, *The Season-Ticket*, p. 1.

110. Timothy, *The Galts*; Waterston, ed., *John Galt*, esp. Gilbert A. Stelter, "John Galt as Town Booster and Builder," pp. 17–43. Galt's son settled in Canada, becoming one of the "Fathers of Confederation" in the 1860s; see Skelton, *Life and Times of Sir Alexander Tilloch Galt*.

111. "The literary world in Canada," writes Bharati Mukherjee in the same year, "is nascent, aggressively nationalist, and self-engrossed" (Blaise and Mukherjee, *Days and Nights in Calcutta*, p. 169). As Mukherjee elaborates in *Darkness* (1985), this nationalist climate reinforces Canada's cultural isolation and imperially derived racism—hence the lack of interest in the cross-cultural analysis that also became possible at this moment, whether in *Days and Nights* or in a full republication of *Bogle Corbet*. For other critiques of literary nationalism, see Lecker, ed., *Canadian Canons*, esp. Dermot McCarthy, "Early Canadian Literary Histories and the Function of a Canon," pp. 30–45; Metcalf, *Kicking against the Pricks*, *What Is a Canadian Literature*, and *Carry on Bumping*; Davey, *From Here to There* and *Postnational Arguments*.

112. Galt, *Bogle Corbet*. The partial nationalist reclamation of Sara Jeannette Duncan during the same period followed a similar pattern. Born in Ontario, Duncan spent most of her life outside Canada, traveling the empire, marrying an

Anglo-Calcuttan, and living in Bengal and Britain. Influenced by Austen, Meredith, and James, Duncan's novels dissect imperialist and colonial ideologies; *An American Girl in London* (1891), *The Imperialist* (1904), and *Cousin Cinderella* (or *A Canadian Girl in London*) (1908) place Canadian cultural identity in relation to American and British cultural imperialism, and her Anglo-Indian fiction—*The Simple Adventures of a Memsahib* (1893), *Vernon's Aunt* (1894), *His Honor and a Lady* (1896), *The Path of a Star* (1898), *The Pool in the Desert* (1903), and *The Burnt Offering* (1909)—explores Anglo-Indian attitudes toward native Indian society with increasing complexity; *Set in Authority* (1906), which uses a miscarriage of justice to illuminate the intellectual limits of Anglo-Indian society, anticipates (and probably influences) Forster's *Passage to India*. And her *Story of Sonny Sahib* (1894), inspired by the Mandevillian eyewitness narrative of an ayah who watched children being killed during the 1857 mutiny, reworks the ayah stories of Sherwood. In Canada, however, Duncan was long remembered solely for her one "Canadian" novel, despite the fact that *The Imperialist* also links small-town Ontario to the ideology and economics of empire. She is now finally receiving a fuller reprinting in Canada and fuller critical attention. See Fowler's Duncan biography, *Redney*; Tausky, *Sara Jeannette Duncan*; Misao Dean, *A Different Point of View*; and "You May Imagine My Feelings: Reading Sara Jeannette Duncan's Challenge to Narrative," in McMullen, ed., *Re(dis)covering Our Foremothers*, pp. 187–98.

113. Waterston's introduction to *Bogle Corbet* does not conceal the fact of abridgment, yet it goes on to discuss the radically truncated novel as if it formed an organic unity, a tendency taken up later by a number of Galt scholars; although half of the essays in Waterston's *John Galt: Reappraisals* (from the 1984 Galt conference she organized at Guelph) touch on *Bogle Corbet* (one of Galt's least-studied novels to that point), most seem to be using the Waterston abridgment as the basis for their remarks. This is particularly ironic given their simultaneous attention to the textual problems created by the intermittent censorship of Galt's publishers. (Dahlie's recent *Varieties of Exile* continues their trend; see p. 31.)

114. C. A. Oakley, *The Second City: The Story of Glasgow*, 4th ed. (Glasgow: Blackie, 1990), p. 10.

115. John Galt, *Bogle Corbet*. All citations are to the 1831 edition; where applicable, they are also keyed to the McClelland and Stewart abridgment (marked M&S).

116. Jameson's *Winter Studies* depicts Upper Canada as both spoiled Eden and "earthly elysium," noting at once "the mistakes of government, the corruption of its petty agents, the social backwardness and moral destitution of the people, as would shock you, and tempt you to regard Canada as a place of exile for convicts" and the country's "beauty" and "fertility . . . its glorious capabilities for agriculture and commerce . . . the goodness and kindliness and resources of poor-much-abused human nature, as developed amid all the crushing influences of oppression, ignorance and prejudice," which render the colony "the very paradise of hope" (p. 303).

117. See Christopher Columbus, *The Four Voyages*, ed. J. M Cohen (Harmondsworth: Penguin, 1969). On the Spanish obsession with cannibalism, see Hulme, *Colonial Encounters*, esp. pp. 13–44; Hulme and Whitehead, eds., *Wild Majesty*; Tzvetan Todorov, *The Conquest of America: The Question of the Other*, trans. Rich-

ard Howard (New York: Harper and Row, 1984), esp. pp. 1–50; on the Spanish cannibalization of the New World, see Eduardo Galeano, *Open Veins of Latin America*, esp. pp. 21–70.

118. See Dallas, *The History of the Maroons*, esp. 2:121–289. Imperial deportations could also move in the opposite direction. Participants in the Lower Canada Rebellion were forcibly expelled to the West Indies and Australia.

119. M'Culloch describes the Canadian landscape as causing a "shrinking" of the mind (*Colonial Gleanings*, p. 24).

120. "Bogle," in William Grant, ed., *The Scottish National Dictionary*, 10 vols. (Edinburgh: Scottish National Dictionary Association, 1936), 2:201.

121. See Nixon, "Caribbean and African Appropriations"; for alternative models of the Caribbean's developmental and psychic history, see also Naipaul's *Middle Passage*, which suggests how different patterns of European colonization shaped a highly variegated West Indian cultural landscape, and Lamming's *The Emigrants*, which thinks through the interrelationship of these cultures in Sartrean and Fanonian terms.

122. Anderson, *Imagined Communities*; Chatterjee, *Nationalist Thought*.

123. See Bruckner, "Whatever Happened to the British Empire?"

124. See Klinck, "The Transplanting of Traditions," in Klinck, ed., *Literary History of Canada*.

125. See Rushdie's "Commonwealth Literature Does Not Exist" (1993), in *Imaginary Homelands*, pp. 61–70.

126. See here Ashcroft et al., *The Empire Writes Back*, esp. the introduction and chap. 1.

127. Appadurai, "Disjuncture and Difference."

128. The 1960s and 1970s saw not only groundbreaking literary reexaminations of Canada's colonial history (Atwood's 1970 *Journals of Susanna Moodie*, Alice Munro's 1971 *Lives of Girls and Women*, Rudy Wiebe's 1973 *Temptations of Big Bear*, Timothy Findlay's 1977 *The Wars*, and George Bowering's 1980 *Burning Water*) but also the development of self-consciously cross-colonial models for understanding Canada's situation and imperial legacies of racism (Austin Clarke's 1967 *Meeting Point*, Leonard Cohen's 1965 *Beautiful Losers*, Ronald Lee's 1970 *Goddam Gypsy*, and Laurence's 1974 *Diviners*). In different ways, both bodies of work began to envision Canadian literature—like that of postindependence India, Jamaica, or Zimbabwe—as postcolonial. Yet as the thoroughly transcolonial background and subjects of many of Canada's most prominent current literary figures suggests, the "post" is not a going past or beyond, only a going through. Thus Daphne Marlatt (whose long poem *Steveston* (1974) explored West Coast Japanese Canadian settlement history, as shaped by official anti-Asian racism) is not Japanese; born in Malaya and a longtime resident of Australia before her immigration to Canada, she observes the situation of Asian Canadians from the background of the British colonies in Asia. Sam Selvon's writing is similarly informed by several layers of diasporic experience in the old British Empire: born into the long-standing ["East"] Indian community of Trinidad, he emigrated to London in the first postwar wave of West Indian immigration and became its premier chronicler (*The Lonely Londoners*, 1956) before moving on to Canada. Michael Ondaatje's *In the Skin of the Lion* (1988) depicts anarcho-syndicalist

agitation and multiethnic political union among Toronto's early-twentieth-century East European immigrant populations in terms that parallel his account, in *Running in the Family* (1982), of the life of his own casually multiethnic, multiracial family in early-twentieth-century colonial Ceylon; both versions of the multinational, in turn, feed *The English Patient* (1992) and its idyll of the calm before the end of the empire.

SELECT BIBLIOGRAPHY

PRIMARY SOURCES

Late-Eighteenth- and Early-Nineteenth-Century Novelists—Collected Works

Austen, Jane. *Works*. Edited by R. W. Chapman. 6 vols. London: Oxford University Press, 1954.

Edgeworth, Maria. *Tales and Novels*. 10 vols. 1874. Reprint, New York: AMS Press, 1967.

Godwin, William. *Complete Novels and Memoirs of William Godwin*. Edited by Pamela Clemit. 8 vols. London: Pickering, 1992.

Peacock, Thomas Love. *The Novels of Thomas Love Peacock*. Edited by David Garnett. London: Rupert Hart-Davis, 1948.

Scott, Walter. *The Waverley Novels*. 48 vols. Edinburgh: Cadell; London: Simkin and Marshall, 1829–33.

Shelley, Mary. *The Mary Shelley Reader*. Edited by Betty T. Bennett and Charles E. Robinson. New York: Oxford University Press, 1990.

Sherwood, Mary Martha. *The Works of Mrs. Sherwood*. 16 vols. New York: Harper and Brothers, 1834.

Wollstonecraft, Mary, and Mary Shelley. *Mary and Maria/Matilda*. Edited by Janet Todd. Harmondsworth: Penguin Books, 1991.

Novels (by date of original publication, unless otherwise noted)

1751

Chaigneau, William. *The History of Jack Connor*. 2 vols. 4th rev. ed. Dublin: Hulton Bradley, 1766.

1755

Amory, Thomas. *Memoirs: containing the Lives of Several Ladies of Great Britain. A History of Antiquities, Productions of Nature, and Monuments of Art*. London: John Noon.

1756

Woodfin, Mrs. A. *Northern Memoirs, or The History of a Scottish Family*. 2 vols. London: F. Noble and J. Nobel.

1756, 1766

Amory, Thomas. *The Life of John Buncle, Esq.* 3 vols. London: Septimus Prowett, 1825.

1760

Johnstone, Charles. *Chrysal, or The Adventures of a Guinea*. 2 vols. 2d rev. ed. London: T. Becket.

1760–67

Sterne, Laurence. *The Life and Opinions of Tristram Shandy*. Edited by Ian Campbell Ross. Oxford: Oxford University Press, 1983.

1761

Goldsmith, Oliver. *The Citizen of the World*. London: Everyman, 1934.

Sheridan, Frances. *Memoirs of Miss Sidney Bidulph*. London: Pandora, 1987.

1763

The Peregrinations of Jeremiah Grant, esq. Reprint, New York: Garland, 1975.

1765

Walpole, Horace. *The Castle of Otranto: A Gothic Story*. London: Oxford University Press, 1969.

1766

Goldsmith, Oliver. *The Vicar of Wakefield*. London: Collins, n.d.

1769

Brooke, Frances. *The History of Emily Montague*. Toronto: McClelland and Stewart, 1961.

1771

Mackenzie, Henry. *The Man of Feeling*. London: Oxford University Press, 1967.

Smollett, Tobias. *The Expedition of Humphry Clinker*. Edited by Angus Ross. Harmondsworth: Penguin Books, 1967.

1777

Reeve, Clara. *The Old English Baron: A Gothic Story*. Oxford: Oxford University Press, 1967.

1778

Hamilton, Mary. *Munster Village*. London: Pandora, 1987.

1781

Johnstone, Charles. *The History of John Juniper, Esq. Alias Juniper Jack*. 2 vols. Dublin: Printed for S. Price et al.

1782

Bage, Robert. *Mount Henneth: A Novel*. 2 vols. Reprint, New York: Garland, 1979.

Scott, Hubertus. *The Adventures of a Rupee, wherein are interspersed various anecdotes Asiatic and European*. London: J. Murray.

1783

Day, Thomas. *The History of Sandford and Merton*. 3 vols. 3d ed. London: John Stockdale.

1783–85

Lee, Sophia. *The Recess, or A Tale of Other Times*. 3 vols. Reprint, New York: Arno Press, 1972.

1784

Bage, Robert. *Barham Downs*. 2 vols. Reprint, New York: Garland, 1979.

Godwin, William. *Imogen: A Pastoral Romance from the Ancient British. Damon & Delia/Italian Letters/Imogen*. In *Collected Novels and Memoirs of William Godwin*. Edited by Pamela Clemit. Vol. 2. London: Pickering, 1992.

1785

Bennett, Mrs. [Agnes Maria]. *Anna, or Memoirs of a Welsh Heiress, Interspersed with Anecdotes of a Nabob*. 4 vols. London: William Land.

Walpole, Horace. *Hieroglyphic Tales*. Augustan Reprint Society. Los Angeles: University of California Press, 1982.

1787

Bage, Robert. *The Fair Syrian*. 2 vols. Reprint, New York: Garland, 1979.

1788

Wollstonecraft, Mary. *Mary*. In *Mary and Maria/Matilda*, by Wollstonecraft and Shelley. Edited by Janet Todd. Harmondsworth: Penguin Books, 1991.

1789

Goldsbourne, Sophia [Phebe Gibbes]. *Hartly House, Calcutta*. Calcutta: Stamp Digest, 1984.

Radcliffe, Ann. *The Castles of Athlin and Dunbayne: A Highland Story*. Reprint, New York: AMS Press, 1972.

Ryves, Elizabeth. *The Hermit of Snowden, or Memoirs of Albert and Lavinia. Taken from a faithful copy of the original manuscript, which was found in the hermitage, by the late Rev. Dr. L—, and Mr.—, in the year 17***. Dublin: H. Colbert.

1790

Austen, Jane. "Love and Freindship" (written). In *Works*. Edited by R. W. Chapman. Vol. 6. London: Oxford University Press, 1954.

1791

Inchbald, Elizabeth. *A Simple Story*. In *A Simple Story and Nature and Art*. London: Richard Bentley, 1849.

1792

Austen, Jane. "Catharine, or The Bower" (written). In *Works*. Vol. 6. London: Oxford University Press, 1954.

————. "Lesley Castle." In *Works*. Vol. 6. London: Oxford University Press, 1954.

Holcroft, Thomas. *Anna St. Ives*. London: Oxford University Press, 1970.

Radcliffe, Ann. *Mysteries of Udolpho*. Edited by Bonamy Dobrée. Oxford: Oxford University Press, 1980.

Smith, Charlotte. *Desmond. A Novel*. 3 vols. Reprint, New York: Garland, 1974.

1793

Smith, Charlotte. *The Old Manor House*. London: Oxford University Press, 1969.

1796

Bage, Robert. *Hermsprong, or Man as He Is Not*. Edited by Stuart Tave. University Park: Penn State University Press, 1982.

Gunning, Mrs. (Susannah Minifie). *Delves: A Welch Tale*. 3d ed. London: Lackington, Allen.

Inchbald, Elizabeth. *Nature and Art*. In *A Simple Story and Nature and Art*. London: Richard Bentley, 1849.

Roche, Regina Maria. *Children of the Abbey*. Philadelphia: J. B. Lippincott, 1879.

1797

Austen, Jane. *Northanger Abbey*. (Written in 1797–98; published in 1818.) In *Works*. Vol. 5. London: Oxford University Press, 1954.

Hamilton, Eliza[beth]. *Translation of Letters of a Hindoo Rajah; written Previous to, and During the Period of His Residence in England. To Which is prefixed a*

Preliminary Dissertation on the History, Religion and Manners, of the Hindoos.
2 vols. Boston: Wells and Lilly.

Hays, Mary. *Memoirs of Emma Courtney.* London: Pandora, 1987.

1799

Godwin, William. *St. Leon. A Tale of the Sixteenth Century.* In *Complete Novels.* Vol. 4.

Gunning, Susannah. *The Gipsy Countess: A Novel.* 4 vols. London: T. N. Longman and Orme Rees.

1800

Edgeworth, Maria. *Castle Rackrent, An Hibernian Tale taken from facts and from the manners of the Irish squires before the year 1782.* In *Castle Rackrent and Ennui.* Edited by Marilyn Butler. Harmondsworth: Penguin Books, 1992.

Hamilton, Elizabeth. *Memoirs of Modern Philosophers.* 3 vols. Reprint, New York: Garland, 1974.

[?]Hedge, Mary Ann. *Samboe, or The African Boy.* London: Harvey and Darton, 1823.

1801

Colpoys, Mrs. *The Irish Excursion, or I Fear to Tell You.* 4 vols. Dublin: H. Colbert.

Edgeworth, Maria. *Belinda.* London: Pandora, 1986.

1802

Edgeworth, Maria. "The Grateful Negro." In *Popular Tales.* Vol. 2 of *Tales and Novels.*

Owenson, Sydney. *St. Clair, or The Heiress of Desmond.* 3d rev. ed. London: J. J. Stockdale, 1812.

Radcliffe, Ann. *Gaston de Blondeville, or The Court of Henry III Keeping Festival in Ardenne.* (Written in 1802; published in 1826.) 2 vols. Reprint, New York: Arno Press, 1972.

1803

Couper, Robert. *The Tourifications of Malachi Meldrum, Esq., of Meldrum Hall.* 2 vols. Aberdeen: J. Chelmers.

1804

Opie, Amelia. *Adeline Mowbray, or The Mother and Daughter.* London: Pandora, 1986.

Sheridan, Anne Elizabeth (Mrs. Henry LeFanu). *The India Voyage.* 2 vols. London: G. and J. Robinson.

1806

Owenson, Sydney. *The Novice of St. Domnick.* London: Richard Phillips.

——— [Lady Morgan]. *The Wild Irish Girl.* London: Pandora, 1986.

1807

Maturin, Charles Robert. *Fatal Revenge, or The Family of Montorio.* 3 vols. Reprint, New York: Arno Press, 1974.

1808

Hamilton, Elizabeth. *The Cottagers of Glenburnie. A Tale for the Farmer's Ingle-nook*. Reprint, New York: Garland, 1974.

1809

Edgeworth, Maria. *Ennui*. (Written in 1803–5.) In *Castle Rackrent and Ennui*.

Maturin, Charles Robert. *The Wild Irish Boy*. 3 vols. Reprint, New York: Arno Press, 1977.

Melville, Theodore. *The Irish Chieftain and His Family: A Romance*. 4 vols. London: Lane, Newman.

Owenson, Sydney. *Woman, or Ida of Athens*. 4 vols. London: Longman, Hurst, Rees, and Orme.

1810

Green, Sarah. *Romance Readers and Romance Writers: A Satirical Novel*. 3 vols. London: T. and E. T. Hookam.

Sleath, Eleanor. *The Nocturnal Minstrel, or The Spirit of the Wood*. Reprint, New York: McGrath Publishing Company, 1972.

1811

Austen, Jane. *Sense and Sensibility*. In *Works*. Vol. 1. London: Oxford University Press, 1954.

Owenson, Sydney. *The Missionary. An Indian Tale*. Reprint, Delmar: Scholar's Facsimiles, 1981.

1812

Edgeworth, Maria. *The Absentee*. Edited by W. J. McCormack and Kim Walker. Oxford: Oxford University Press, 1988.

Maturin, Charles Robert. *The Milesian Chief*. 4 vols. Reprint, New York: Garland Press, 1979.

West, Jane. *The Loyalists. An Historical Novel*. 2 vols. Boston: Bradford and Read, 1813.

1814

Austen, Jane. *Mansfield Park*. In *Works*. Vol. 3. London: Oxford University Press, 1954.

Brunton, Mary. *Discipline*. 3 vols. 2d ed. Edinburgh: George Ramsey, 1915.

The Irish Girl. A Religious Tale. London: George Walker.

Johnstone, Christian, *The Saxon and the Gaël, or The Northern Metropolis, including a View of the Lowland and Highland Character*. 4 vols. London: Thomas Tegg; Edinburgh: T. Dick.

Owenson, Sydney. *O'Donnel: A national tale*. London: Henry Colburn, 1815.

Scott, Walter. *Waverley*. In *Waverley Novels*. Vols. 1–2.

Sherwood, Mary Martha. *The Story of Little Henry and his Bearer*. 3d. American ed. New Haven: John Babcock and Son, 1818.

1815

Johnstone, Christian Isobel M'Lersh. *Clan-Albin. A National Tale*. 3 vols. Philadelphia: Gale.

Scott, Walter. *Guy Mannering*. In *Waverley Novels*. Vols. 3–4.

Wilson, William. *The History of Mr. Moland and Little Henry*. Edited by Guy Fleet-way Wilson. London: Cassell, 1923.

1816

Appleton, Elizabeth. *Edgar: A National Tale*. 3 vols. London: Henry Colburn.

Austen, Jane. *Emma*. In *Works*. Vol. 4. London: Oxford University Press, 1954.

Hofland, Barbara Hoole. *Matilda, or The Barbadoes Girl*. London: A. K. Newman.

Lamb, Caroline. *Glenarvon*. Reprint, New York: Scholar's Facsimiles and Reprints, 1972.

Peacock, Thomas Love. *Headlong Hall*. In *Novels*.

Scott, Walter. *The Antiquary*. In *Waverley Novels*. Vols. 5–6.

———. *Old Mortality*. In *Waverley Novels*. Vols. 9–11.

Sherwood, Mary Martha. *The Ayah and Lady*. London: Christian Literary Society for India, 1902.

1817

Austen, Jane. *Sanditon*. (Unpublished fragment, written.) In *Works*. Vol. 6. London: Oxford University Press, 1954.

Edgeworth, Maria. *Ormond*. Dublin: Gill and Macmillan, 1990.

Godwin, William. *Mandeville: A Tale of the Seventeenth Century in England*. In *Collected Novels*. Vol. 6.

Peacock, Thomas Love. *Melincourt*. In *Novels*.

1818

Austen, Jane. *Persuasion*. (Written in 1815–16, published posthumously.) In *Works*. Vol. 5. London: Oxford University Press, 1954.

Brontë, Patrick. *The Maid of Killarney*. Reprinted in *Brontëana: His Collected Works and Life*. Bringley: J. Horsfall Turner, 1898.

Civilization, or The Indian Chief and the British Pastor. 3 vols. London: T. Egerton.

Ferrier, Susan. *Marriage*. Edited by Herbert Foltinek. Oxford: Oxford University Press, 1986.

Hogg, James. *The Brownie of Bodsbeck*. Edinburgh: Scottish Academic Press, 1976.

Maturin, Charles Robert. *Women, or Pour et contre*. Edinburgh: J. Ballantyne; London: Longman, Hurst, Rees, Orme, and Brown.

Owenson, Sydney. *Florence Macarthy: An Irish Tale*. London: Henry Colburn, 1834.

Peck, Frances. *The Life and Acts of the Renowned Chivalrous Edmund of Erin, commonly called Emun Ac Knuck, or Ned of the Hills. An Irish Historical Romance of the Seventh Century Founded on Facts: Blended with a Brief and Pithy Epitome of the Origin, Antiquity and History of Ireland with Copious Notes, Critical and Historical*. 3d ed. Dublin: Samuel J. Machen, 1842.

Puzzlebrain, Peregrine [pseud.], ed. *Tales of My Landlady*. 3 vols. London: M. Iley.

Scott, Walter. *The Heart of Midlothian*. In *Waverley Novels*. Vols. 11–13. Edinburgh: Cadell; London: Simkin and Marshall, 1829–33.

———. *Rob Roy*. In *Waverley Novels*. Vols. 7–8. Edinburgh: Cadell; London: Simkin and Marshall, 1829–33.

1819

Clark, Emily. *The Esquimaux, or Fidelity.* 3 vols. London: A. K. Newman.

E.H.H. *The Highlander, or Tales of My Landlady.* 2 vols. London: A. K. Newman.

Maskell, M. *Old Tapestry, A Tale of Real Life.* 2 vols. Edinburgh: W. and C. Tait and G. and W. B. Whittaker, 1819.

Parnell, William. *Maurice and Berghetta, or The Priest of Rahery: A Tale.* London: Rowland Hunter.

Shelley, Mary. *Matilda* (written). In *Mary and Maria/Matilda*, by Mary Wollstone-craft and Mary Shelley. Edited by Janet Todd. Harmondsworth: Penguin Books, 1991.

1820

Carey, Daniel. *Lochiel, or The Field of Culloden.* 3 vols. London: G. and W. B. Whittaker.

Galt, John. *Glenfell, or MacDonalds and Campbells. An Edinburgh Tale of the Nineteenth Century.* London: Sir Richard Phillips.

Maturin, Charles Robert. *Melmoth the Wanderer. A Tale.* Harmondsworth: Penguin Books, 1984.

Roche, Regina Maria. *The Munster Cottage Boy. A Tale.* 4 vols. London: A. K. Newman.

St. Clair, Rosalia. *The Highland Castle and the Lowland Cottage.* 4 vols. London: A. K. Newman.

Scott, Walter. *Ivanhoe.* In *Waverley Novels.* Vols. 16–17. Edinburgh: Cadell; London: Simkin and Marshall, 1829–33.

Sherwood, Mary Martha. *The Welsh Cottage.* Wellington, Salup: F. Houlston.

Sutherland, Alexander. *St. Kathleen, or The Rock of Dunmoyle.* 4 vols. London: A. K. Newman.

1821

Egan, Pierce. *Real Life in Ireland. By a Real Paddy, or The Day and Night Scenes, Rovings, Rambles and Sprees, Bulls, Blunders, Bodderation and Blarney of Brian Boru, Esq. and his Elegant Friend Sir Shaun O'Dogherty.* 4th ed. London: Methuen, 1904.

Galt, John. *Annals of the Parish and The Ayrshire Legatees.* Edinburgh: John Grant, 1936.

Lockhart, John Gibson. *Valerius: A Roman Story.* 3 vols. Edinburgh: Ballantyne.

McCulloch, Thomas. *The Stepsure Letters.* Toronto: McClelland and Stewart, 1960.

[Sherwood, Mary Martha?]. *The History of George Desmond; Founded on Facts which Occurred in the East Indies and Now Published as a Useful Caution to Young Men Going Out to that Country.* Wellington: F. Houlston and Sons.

1822

Galt, John. *The Entail, or The Lairds of Grippy.* Edited by Ian A. Gordon. London: Oxford University Press, 1970.

———. *The Gathering of the West.* Baltimore: Johns Hopkins University Press, 1939.

Galt, John. *The Provost*. Edited by Ian A. Gordon. London: Oxford University Press, 1973.

Wilson, John. *Lights and Shadows of Scottish Life*. Reprinted in *Tales by Professor Wilson*. Edinburgh: William Blackwood and Sons, 1870.

1823

Galt, John. *Ringhan Gilhaize, or The Covenanters*. Edited by Patricia J. Wilson. Edinburgh: Scottish Academic Press, 1984.

Sherwood, Mary Martha. *The History of Little Lucy and her Dhaye*. In *Works*. Vol. 3.

1824

Ferrier, Susan. *The Inheritance*. London: J. M. Dent, 1894.

Green, Sarah. *Scotch Novel Reading, or Modern Quackery, by a Cockney*. 3 vols. London: A. K. Newman.

Lockhart, John Gibson. *The History of Matthew Wald*. New York: E. Dukckinch et al.

Maturin, Charles Robert. *The Albigenses*. 4 vols. Reprint, New York: Arno Press, 1974.

M'Henry, James. *O'Halloran, or The Insurgent Chief. An Irish Historical Tale of 1798*. 2 vols. Philadelphia: H. C. Carey and I. Lea.

Morier, James. *Hajji Baba of Ispahan*. London: Oxford University Press, 1974.

Roche, Regina Maria. *The Tradition of the Castle, or Scenes in the Emerald Isles*. 4 vols. London: A. K. Newman.

Whitty, M. J. *Tales of Irish Life. Illustrations of the Manners, Customs, and Condition of the People*. 2 vols. London: J. Robins.

1825

Maturin, Charles Robert. "Leixlip Castle" (published posthumously). In *Gothic Tales of Terror*, edited by Peter Haining. Vol. 1, *Classic Horror Stories from Great Britain*. Baltimore: Penguin Books, 1973.

1826

Galt, John. *The Last of the Lairds, or The Life and Opinions of Malachi Mailings Esq. of Auldbiggings*. Edited by Ian A. Gordon. Edinburgh: Scottish Academic Press, 1976.

McCulloch, Thomas. *Colonial Gleanings. William and Melville*. Edinburgh: William Oliphant.

Shelley, Mary. *The Last Man*. Lincoln: University of Nebraska Press, 1965.

1827

Griffin, Gerald. *Tales of the Munster festivals*. 3 vols. London: Saunders and Otley, 1830.

Owenson, Sydney. *The O'Briens and the O'Flahertys. A national tale*. London: Pandora, 1988.

Shelley, Mary. "Roger Dodsworth, the Reanimated Englishman" (written). In *The Mary Shelley Reader*, edited by Bennett and Robinson.

Sherwood, Mary Martha. *Ermina*. London: Houlston and Son, 1831.

1828

Banim, John. *The Anglo-Irish of the Nineteenth Century*. 3 vols. London: Henry Colburn.

Banim, Michael. *The Croppy: A Tale of the Irish Rebellion of 1798*. 3 vols. Reprint, New York: Garland, 1978.

Hofland, Barbara Hoole. *The Stolen Child: A Story, Founded on Facts*. 2d ed. London: A. H. Newman, 1830.

Moir, David M[acbeth]. *The Life of Mansie Wauch, Tailor in Dalkeith, Written By Himself*. Edinburgh: William Blackwood and Sons, n.d.

Monkland, Anne Catherine. *Life in India, or The English at Calcutta*. 3 vols. London: Henry Colburn.

Morier, James. *Hajji Baba in England*. London: Oxford University Press, 1925.

Prichard, Thomas Jeffery Llewelyn. *The Adventures or Vagaries of Twn Shon Catti alias Thomas Jones, Esq. of Tragron, A Wild Wag of Wales*. 3d rev. ed. Llanidloes: John Pryse, 1873.

Thomson, Richard. *Tales of an antiquary: chiefly illustrative of the manners, traditions, and remarkable localities of ancient London*. 3 vols. London: Henry Colburn.

Traill, Catharine Parr. *The Young Emigrants, or Pictures of Canada*. London: Harvey and Barton, 1928.

1829

LeFanu, Alicia. *Tales of a Tourist*. 4 vols. London: A. K. Newman.

Peacock, Thomas Love. *The Misfortunes of Elphin*. In *Novels*.

Savery, Henry. *The Hermit of Van Diemen's Land*. Saint Lucia: University of Queensland Press, 1964.

1830

Carleton, William. *Traits and Stories of the Irish Peasantry*. 2 vols. Dublin: Mercier Press, 1973.

Galt, John. *Lawrie Todd, or The Settlers in the Woods*. 3 vols. London: Henry Colburn.

Mainwaring, M. *The Suttee, or The Hindu Converts*. 3 vols. London: A. K. Newman.

Savery, Henry. *Quintus Servinton. A Tale Founded upon Incidents of Real Occurrence*. Edited by Cecil H. Hadgraft. Brisbane: Jacaranda Press, 1962.

Sherwood, Mary Martha. *The Babes in the Wood of the New World*. Reprinted in *The Recaptured Negro and the Babes in the Wood of the New World*. London: Houlston and Wright, ca. 1860.

1831

Ferrier, Susan. *Destiny, or The Chieftain's Daughter*. London: J. M. Dent, 1894.

Galt, John. *Bogle Corbet, or The Emigrants*. 3 vols. London: Henry Colburn and Richard Bentley; abridged reprint, Toronto: McClelland and Stewart, 1977.

Peacock, Thomas Love. *Crotchet Castle*. In *Novels*.

1832

Galt, John. *The Member: An Autobiography*. Edited by Ian A. Gordon. Edinburgh: Scottish Academic Press, 1985.

Galt, John. *The Radical: An Autobiography*. London: James Fraser, 1877.

Richardson, John. *Wacousta, or The Prophecy: A Tale of the Canadas*. Edited by Douglas Clark. Ottawa: Carleton University Press, 1987.

1835

Owenson, Sydney. *The Princess, or The Beguine*. 3 vols. London: R. Bentley.

Sherwood, Mary Martha. *Social Tales for the Young*. London: William Darton, 1835.

1836

Haliburton, Thomas Chandler. *The Clockmaker, First through third series, 1836–40*. Ottawa: Tecumseh Press, 1995.

————. *The Clockmaker, or The Sayings and Doings of Samuel Slick of Slicksville*. Toronto: McClelland and Stewart, 1958.

Traill, Catharine Parr. *The Backwoods of Canada: Being Letters from the Wife of an Emigrant Officer, Illustrative of the Domestic Economy of British America*. 1836. Reprint, Toronto: McClelland and Stewart, 1989.

1836–37

Dickens, Charles. *The Pickwick Papers*. Edited by Robert L. Patten. Harmondsworth: Penguin Books, 1972.

1840

Haliburton, Thomas Chandler. *The Letter-Bag of the Great Western, or Life in a Steamer*. London: Richard Bentley.

Sherwood, Mary Martha. *The Last Days of Boosy, or Sequel to Little Henry and his Bearer* [ca. 1840?]. Philadelphia: American Sunday School Union, 1842.

————. *The Indian Chief*. London: Darton, n.d. [probably 1840–50].

1845

The Ford Family in Ireland. 3 vols. London: T. C. Newby.

Hall, S. C. *The Whiteboy. A Story of Ireland in 1822*. 2 vols. London: Chapman and Hall.

M'Combie, Thomas. *Arabin, or The Adventures of a Colonist in New South Wales*. London: Simmonds and Ward.

1848

Trollope, Anthony. *The Kellys and the O'Kellys, or Landlords and Tenants*. Edited by W. J. McCormack. Oxford: Oxford University Press, 1982.

1849

Haliburton, Thomas Chandler. *The Old Judge, or Life in a Colony*. Ottawa: Tecumseh Press, 1978.

1850

Dickens, Charles. *David Copperfield*. Harmondsworth: Penguin Books, 1966.

1852

Moodie, Susanna. *Roughing it in the Bush*. Toronto: McClelland and Stewart, 1986.

Traill, Catharine Parr. *Canadian Crusoes. A Tale of the Rice Lake Plains*. Edited by Rupert Schieder. Ottawa: Carleton University Press, 1978.

1853

Moodie, Susanna. *Flora Lyndsay, or Passages in an Eventful Life.* New York: De Witt and Davenport.

———. *Life in the Clearings versus the Bush.* Toronto: McClelland and Stewart, 1989.

1856

Traill, Catharine Parr. *Lady Mary and Her Nurse, or A peep into the Canadian Forest.* London: Arthur Hall.

1859

[Dunlop, William "Tiger"?]. *Two and Twenty Years Ago: A Tale of the Canadian Rebellion. By a Backwoodsman.* Toronto: Cleland's Book and Job Printing, 1859.

1860

Haliburton, Thomas Chandler. *The Season-Ticket.* London: Richard Bentley.

1861

Dickens, Charles. *Great Expectations.* Edited by Angus Calder. Harmondsworth: Penguin Books, 1965.

1863

Aubert de Gaspé, Philippe. *Les anciens Canadiens.* Translated by Charles G. D. Roberts as *Canadians of Old.* Toronto: McClelland and Stewart, 1974.

1870

Clarke, Marcus, *His Natural Life* [original title: *For the Course of His Natural Life*]. Edited by Stephen Murray-Smith. Harmondsworth: Penguin Books, 1980.

Antiquarianism: Literary History, Cultural History, and Bards

Arden, John, and Margaretta D'Arcy. *The Island of the Mighty.* London: Eyre Methuen, 1974.

Arnold, Matthew. *On the Study of Celtic Literature and Other Essays.* London: J. M. Dent; New York: E. P. Dutton, 1910.

Blackwell, Thomas. *An Inquiry into the Life and Writings of Homer.* 1735. Reprint, Menston: Scholar Press, 1972.

Blake, William, *Songs of Innocence and Experience.* 1789. Reprint, Paris: Trianon Press, 1967.

Brand, John. *Observations on Popular Antiquities, Chiefly Illustrating the Origin of our Vulgar Customs, Ceremonies and Superstitions.* Edited by Henry Ellis. 2 vols. London: F. C. and J. Rivington et al., 1813.

Brooke, Charlotte. *Reliques of Irish Poetry (1789) and a Memoir of Miss Brooke (1816) by Aaron Crossley Hobart Seymour.* Reprint, Gainesville, Fla.: Scholars Facsimiles and Reprints, 1970.

Bunting, Edward. *The Ancient Music of Ireland.* Dublin: Walton's Piano and Musical Instrument Galleries, 1969.

Clark, John, ed. *The Works of the Caledonian Bards. Translated from the Galic.* Edinburgh: T. Cadell, 1778.

Davies, Edward. *The Claims of Ossian.* Swansea and London: Longman, 1825.

Evans, Evan. *The Love of Our Country.* Carmarthen: J. Ross, 1772.

Evans, Evan [Ievan Prydydd Hir]. *Some Specimens of the Poetry of the Ancient Welsh Bards, Translated into English.* 1764. Reprint, Llandloes: John Pryse, n.d.

Graham, Patrick. *Essay on the Authenticity of the Poems of Ossian.* Edinburgh: James Ballantyne, 1807.

Grose, Daniel. *The Antiquities of Ireland: A Supplement to Francis Grose.* Dublin: Irish Architectural Archive, 1991.

Grose, Francis. *The Antiquarian repertory, a miscellaneous assemblage of topography, history, biography, customs and manners: intended to illustrate and preserve several valuable remains of old times.* 1807. Rev. ed. London: E. Jeffery, 1809.

————. *The antiquities of England and Wales.* London: S. Hopper, 1774.

————. *The antiquities of Ireland.* 2 vols. 1791. Reprint, Kilkenny: Wellbrook Press, 1982.

————. *A classical dictionary of the vulgar tongue.* 1785. Reprint, New York: Dorset Press, 1992.

Hume, David. "On the Authenticity of Ossian's Poems." In *Essays: moral, political, and literary.* Edited by T. H. Green and T. H. Grose. Vol. 2. London: Longmans, Green, 1898.

Hurd, Richard. *Letters on Chivalry and Romance with the Third Elizabethan Dialogue.* Edited by Edith J. Morley. London: Henry Frowde, 1911.

Innes, Thomas. *A Critical Essay on the Ancient Inhabitants of the Northern Parts of Britain, or Scotland.* 2 vols. London: William Innys, 1729.

Johnson, Samuel. "Preface to *A Dictionary of the English Language.*" In *Rasselas: Poems and Selected Prose,* edited by Bertrand Bronson. New York: Holt, Rinehart and Winston, 1958.

Jones, Edward. *The Bardic Museum of Primitive British Literature.* London: A. Stahan, 1802.

————. *Musical and Poetical Relicks of the Welsh Bards, Preserved by Tradition, and Authentic Manuscripts, From Remote Antiquity, with Native Pastoral Sonnets of Wales, likewise a History of the Bards.* London: Printed for the author, 1784.

Jones, Owen (Myvyr), William Owen Pughe, and Edward Williams (Iolo Morganwg), eds. *The Myvyrian Archaiology of Wales: Collected out of ancient manuscripts.* 1801–7. Reprint, Denbigh: T. Gee, 1870.

Lewis, Aneirin, ed. *The Correspondence of Thomas Percy and Evan Evans.* Baton Rouge: Louisiana State University Press, 1957.

Lhuyd, Edward. *Archaeologia Britannica.* 1707. Reprint, Menston, England: Scholar Press, 1969.

Mackenzie, Henry, ed. *Report of the Committee of the Highland Society of Scotland. Appointed to Inquire into the Nature and Authenticity of the Poems of Ossian.* Edinburgh: Edinburgh University Press, 1805.

Macpherson, James. *Fragments of Ancient Poetry, Collected in the Highlands of Scotland and Translated from the Galic or Erse Language.* 1760. Reprint, Heidelberg: Carl Winters Universitätsbuchhandlung, 1915.

————. *The Poems of Ossian and Related Works.* Edited by Howard Gaskill. Edinburgh: Edinburgh University Press, 1996.

————. *The Poems of Ossian, in the Original Gaelic, with a Literal Translation into Latin, by the late Robert MacFarlan, together with a Dissertation on the Authenticity of the Poems, by John Sinclair*. 3 vols. London: W. Bulmer, 1807.

————. *The Poems of Ossian, with Dissertations on the Aera and Poems of Ossian; and Dr. Blair's Critical Dissertation*. Leipzig: Bernhard Tauchnitz, 1847.

————, trans. *The Poems of Ossian, the Son of Fingal*. Edinburgh: Denham and Dick, 1805.

M'Nicol, Donald. *Remarks on Dr. Samuel Johnson's Journey to the Hebrides, in which are containd, Observations on the Antiquities, Language, Genius, and Manners of the Highlanders of Scotland*. London: T. Cadell, 1779.

Nietzsche, Friedrich. "On the uses and disadvantages of history for life" (1874). In *Untimely Meditations*, translated by R. J. Hollingdale. Cambridge: Cambridge University Press, 1983.

O'Conor, Charles. *Dissertations on the History of Ireland, and A Dissertation on the Historical Colonies, Established in Britain*. 1753. 2d rev. ed. Dublin: G. Faulkner, 1766.

O'Halloran, Sylvester. *A General History of Ireland, from the Earliest Accounts to the Close of the Twelfth Century, Collected from the most authentic records in which new and interesting lights are thrown on the remote Histories of other nations as well as both Britains*. 2 vols. London: A. Hamilton, 1778.

————. *Insula Sacra, or The General Utilites arising from some permanent Foundation, for the Preservation of our ANTIENT ANNALS*. Limerick: T. Welsh, 1770.

————. *An Introduction to the Study of the Histories and Antiquities of Ireland*. 1771. Reprint, London: J. Murray, 1772.

O'Keefe, Adelaide. *National Characters, Exhibited in Forty Geographical Poems*. Lymington: Darton, Harvey, and Darton, 1818.

Owenson, Sydney. *Twelve Original Hibernian Melodies, from the works of the ancient Irish bards*. London: Preston, 1805.

Percy, Thomas. *Reliques of Ancient English Poetry*. London: F. C. and J. Rivington, 1812.

Pownall, Thomas. *A Treatise on the Study of Antiquities*. London: J. Dodsley, 1782.

Prichard, Thomas Jeffery Llewelyn, ed. *The Cambrian Wreath. A Selection of English Poems on Welsh Subjects, Original and Translated from the Cambro-British, Historical and Legendary, including Welsh Melodies*. Aberystwyth: [John Cox], 1828.

————. *Welsh Minstrelsy*. London: John and H. L. Hunt, 1825.

Richards, George. *Songs of the Aboriginal Bards of Britain*. Oxford: Sold by J. Cooke et al., 1792.

Ritson, Joseph. *Ancient Songs and Ballads from the Reign of King Henry the Second to the Revolution*. 2 vols. London: Payne and Foss, 1829.

————. *Pieces of Ancient Popular Poetry: From Authentic Manuscripts and Old Printed Copies*. 1791. 2d ed. London: William Pickering, 1833.

————. *Scottish Songs*. 2 vols. Glasgow: Hugh Hopkins, 1869.

Roberts, Peter. *Cambrian Popular Antiquities, or An Account of some Traditions, Customs and Superstitions of Wales, with Observations as to their Origin*. London: E. Williams, 1815.

Smith, John. *Galic Antiquities*. Edinburgh: C. Elliot, 1780.

Stukeley, William. *Letter from Dr. Stukeley to Mr. Macpherson, on his publication of Fingal and Temora*. London: R. Hett, 1763.

Toland, John. *A Critical History of the Celtic Religion and Learning*. London: Lackington, 1740.

Trimmer, Mrs. Sarah. *A Description of a Set of Prints of Ancient History; contained in a set of Easy Lessons*. 2 vols. 3d ed. London: John Marshall, 1795.

———. *Scenes of Prints of Ancient History*. London: John Marshall, 1788.

Turner, Sharon, *A Vindication of the Genuineness of the Ancient British Poems*. London: E. Williams, sold by Longman and Rees, 1803.

Volney [Constantin-François Chassebeuf]. *A New Translation of Volney's Ruins*. 2 vols. 1802. Reprint, New York: Garland, 1979.

Walker, Joseph Cooper. *Historical Memoirs of the Irish Bards*. 1786. Reprint, New York: Garland Publishing, 1971.

Wolf, Friedrich August. *Prolegomena to Homer*. 1795. Reprint, Princeton: Princeton University Press, 1985.

Wood, Robert. *An Essay on the Original Genius and Writings of Homer*. 1775. Reprint, New York: Garland, 1971.

Ireland: Political, Cultural, and Literary History

Anthologia Hibernica, or Monthly Collections of Science, Belles Lettres and History. Dublin: Richard Edward Mercier, 1793–94.

The Anti-Union (1798–99).

Beaufort, Daniel Augustus. *Memoir of a Map of Ireland, Illustrating the Topography of That Kingdom, and Containing a Short Account of Its Present State, Civil and Ecclesiastical*. London: W. Faden, J. Debrett, and James Edwards, 1792.

Bennett, William. *Narrative of a recent journey of six weeks in Ireland*. London: C. Gilpin, 1847.

Boland, Bridget. *The Wild Geese*. 1938. Reprint, London: Virago, 1988.

Bowen, Elizabeth. *Bowen's Court*. 1942. Reprint, New York: Ecco Press, 1979.

Brooke, Henry. *An essay on the antient and modern state of Ireland*. Dublin: R. Griffiths, 1760.

Burke, Edmund. *The Works of the Right Honorable Edmund Burke*. 12 vols. 9th ed. Boston: Little, Brown, 1889.

Carr, John. *The Stranger in Ireland, or A Tour of the Southern and Western Parts of That Country, in the Year 1805*. 1806. Reprint, Shannon: Irish University Press, 1970.

A Collection of Tracts and Treatises, Illustrative of the Natural History, Antiquities, and the Political and Social State of Ireland. 2 vols. Dublin: Alex Thom and Sons, 1860.

Deane, Seamus, et al., eds. *The Field Day Anthology of Irish Literature*. 3 vols. Derry: Field Day; New York: Norton, 1991.

Dubois, Edward. *My Pocket-book, or Hints for "A Right Merrie and Conceitede" Tour, in Quarto; to be called, "The Stranger in Ireland," in 1805. By a Knight Errant*. New York: Ezra Sargeant, 1807.

Edgeworth, [Frances Anne]. *A Memoir of Maria Edgeworth, with A Selection from Her Letters.* 3 vols. London: Joseph Masters and Son, 1867.

Edgeworth, Maria. *Letters from England, 1813–1844.* Edited by Christina Colvin. Oxford: Clarendon Press, 1971.

Edgeworth, Richard Lovell. *Memoirs of Richard Lovell Edgeworth. Begun by himself and concluded by his Daughter.* 2 vols. London: R. Hunter, 1820.

Edgeworth, Richard Lovell, and Maria Edgeworth. *Essay on Irish Bulls.* In *Tales and Novels,* vol. 4, by Maria Edgeworth.

Falkiner, C. Litton, ed. *Illustrations of Irish History and Topography, Mainly of the Seventeenth Century.* London: Longmans, Green, 1904.

Friel, Brian. *Translations: A Play.* London: Samuel French, 1981.

Gilbert, John T., ed. *Documents Relating to Ireland, 1795–1804.* 1893. Reprint, Shannon: Irish University Press, 1970.

Goldsmith, Oliver. "The History of Carolan, the Last Irish Bard." In *Collected Works.* 5 vols. Oxford: Clarendon Press, 1966.

Grant of Rothiemurchus, Elizabeth. *The Highland Lady in Ireland: Journals, 1840–50.* Edited by Patricia Pelly and Andrew Tod. Edinburgh: Cannongate Classics, 1991.

Hadfield, Andrew, and John McVeagh, eds. *Strangers to That Land: British Perceptions of Ireland from the Reformation to the Famine.* Gerrards Cross: Colin Smythe, 1994.

Hall, Mrs. S. C. *Sketches of Irish Character.* London: Frederick Westley and A. H. Davis, 1831.

Heaney, Seamus. *Poems, 1965–1975.* New York: Farrar, Straus and Giroux, 1980.

_____. *Preoccupations: Selected Prose, 1968–1978.* New York: Farrar Straus and Giroux, 1980.

Joyce, James. *Ulysses.* 1922. Reprint, Harmondsworth: Penguin Books, 1971.

King, William. "A Discourse Concerning the *Bogs* and *Loughs* of *Ireland,* as it was presented to the *Dublin Society.*" *Philosophical Transactions* 15, no. 170 (April 20, 1685): 948–60.

Kinsella, Thomas, trans. and ed. *An Duanaire, 1600–1900: Poems of the Dispossessed.* Mountrath, Ireland: Dolman Press, 1981.

_____, ed. *The New Oxford Book of Irish Verse.* Oxford: Oxford University Press, 1986.

Leadbeater, Mary. *Cottage dialogues among the Irish peasantry.* Philadelphia: Johnson and Warner, 1811.

A Letter to the Publick Concerning Bogs. Dublin: G. and A. Wing, 1757.

MacOBonnichabbero of Drogheda. *Bogg-Witticisms, or Dear Joy's Common-Places, Being a Compleat Collection of the most Profound PUNNS, learned BULLS, Elaborate QUIBBLES AND WISE SAYINGS of some of the Natives of TEAGUE-LAND. Shet Fourd vor Generaul Nond disicaushion. And Coullected bee de grete Caare and Panish-Tauking of oour Laurned Countree-maun.* Printed for Evidansh Swear-all in Lack-Plaush Lane, [1700?].

Martineau, Harriet. *Letters from Ireland.* London: John Chapman, 1852.

Meredith, George. *Celt and Saxon.* London: Constable, 1910.

Mitchel, John. *Jail Journal.* 1854. Reprint, Dublin: M. H. Gill and Son, n.d.

Mitchel, John. *The Last Conquest of Ireland (Perhaps)*. 1860. Reprint, Glasgow: Cameron and Ferguson, n.d.

Moore, Thomas. *Memoirs of Captain Rock, The Celebrated Irish Chieftain, Written by Himself*. London: Longman, Hurst, Rees, Orme, Brown, and Green, 1824.

Moryson, Fynes. *Shakespeare's Europe: Unpublished Chapters of Fynes Moryson's Itinerary*. Edited by Charles Hughes. London: Sherratt and Hughes, 1903.

O'Faolain, Sean. *The Finest Stories of Sean O'Faolain*. New York: Bantam, 1959.

Owenson, Sydney. *Absenteeism*. London: Henry Colburn, 1825.

———. *The Book of the Boudoir*. 2 vols. 1829. Reprint, New York: J. and J. Harper, 1839.

———. *Dramatic Scenes from Real Life*. 2 vols. London: Saunders and Otley, 1833.

———. *Patriotic Sketches of Ireland. Written in Connaught*. 2 vols. London: Richard Philips, 1807.

——— *Woman and Her Master*. 1840. Reprint, Westport, Conn.: Hyperion Press, 1976.

Owenson, Sydney, and Sir Thomas Charles Morgan. *The Book Without a Name*. 2 vols. New York: Wiley and Putnam, 1841.

Smith, Stevie. "The Celts." In *Collected Poems*. New York: Oxford University Press, 1976.

Spenser, Edmund. *A View of the Present State of Ireland* and "A Brief Note of Ireland." Vol. 10 of *Works*, edited by Edwin Greenlaw et al. 10 vols. Baltimore: Johns Hopkins University Press, 1947–58..

Swift, Jonathan. *The Complete Poems*. Edited by Pat Rogers. Harmondsworth: Penguin Books, 1983.

———. *Irish Tracts, 1720–1723, and Sermons*. Edited by Louis Landa. Oxford: Basil Blackwell, 1948.

———. *The Prose Works*. Edited by Temple Scott. 12 vols. London: George Bell and Sons, 1905.

———. *Swift's Irish Pamphlets: An Introductory Selection*. Edited by Joseph McMinn. Savage, Md.: Barnes and Noble, 1991.

———. *The Works of Jonathan Swift*. Edited by D. Laing Purves. Edinburgh: William P. Nimmo, 1872.

Teeling, Charles Hamilton. *History of the Irish Rebellion of 1798: A Personal Narrative, and Sequel to the History of the Irish Rebellion of 1798*. 1876. Reprint, Shannon: Irish University Press, 1976.

Thackeray, William Makepeace. *The Irish Sketchbook*. Vol. 20 of *Complete Works*. 20 vols. New York: George Sproul, 1899.

Tocqueville, Alexis. *Alexis de Tocqueville's Journey in Ireland, July-August 1835*. Edited and translated by Emmet Larkin. Washington, D.C.: Catholic University of America Press, 1990.

Tone, Theobald Wolfe. *An Argument on Behalf of the Catholics in Ireland*. 1791. Reprint, n.p.: Connolly Books, 1969.

———. *The Best of Tone*. Edited by Proinsias Mac Aonghusa and Liam O'Réagáin. Cork: Mercier Press, 1972.

———. *Life of Theobald Wolfe Tone*. Edited by William Theobald Wolfe Tone. 2 vols. Washington: Gales and Seaton, 1826.

[Woods, Mrs.?, or Barbara Blake Attersall?]. *Letters from the Irish Highlands*. London: John Murray, 1825.

Young, Arthur. *A Tour in Ireland, with General Observations on the Present State of That Kingdom: Made in the Years 1776, 1777, and 1778*. 2 vols. 1780. Reprint, London: George Bell and Sons, 1892.

Scotland: Political, Cultural, and Literary History

The Abbotsford Subscription. Speeches Delivered at the Public Meeting Held at the Thatched House Tavern, on Sat. April 27, 1933 to Promote the Plan for Preserving Abbotsford Forever in the Line of Sir Walter Scott. London: James Moyes, 1933.

Alexander, William. *Johnny Gibb of Gushetneuk*. 1871. Reprint, Edinburgh: Douglas and Foulis, 1951.

"Biographical Memoir of John Leyden, M.D.," *Edinburgh Annual Register* 4 (for 1811, appears 1813): xli–lxviii.

Boswell, James. *Journal of a Tour to the Hebrides with Samuel Johnson, LL.D., 1773*. Edited by Frederick Pottle and Charles H. Bennett. New York: McGraw-Hill, 1961.

———. *Life of Johnson*. Edited by George Birkbeck Hill. 2 vols. Oxford: Oxford University Press, 1934.

Campbell, Thomas. *The Complete Poetical Works*. Edited by J. Logie Robertson. Oxford: Oxford University Press, 1907.

Chambers, Robert. *Popular Nursery Rhymes of Scotland*. 1841. Reprint, London: W. and R. Chambers, 1870.

Churchill, Charles. *Poetical Works*. Edited by Douglas Grant. Oxford: Oxford University Press, 1956.

Combe, William. *The Tour of Doctor Prosody in Search of the Antique and Picturesque, through Scotland, the Hebrides, the Orkney and the Shetland Isles*. London: Matthew Iley, 1821.

Defoe, Daniel. *Caledonia. A Poem in Honour of Scotland and the Scots Nation. In 3 Parts*. Edinburgh: Andrew Anderson, 1706.

———. *Discourse upon an union of the two kingdoms of England and Scotland*. London: A. Baldwin, 1707.

———. *An essay at removing national prejudices against a union with Scotland*. London, 1706.

———. *The Highland Visions, or The Scots New Prophecy*. London: J. Baker, 1712.

———?. *The History of the Life and Adventures of Duncan Campbell*. 1720. Reprint, London: J. M. Dent, 1902.

———. *The History of the Union*. Edinburgh: Heirs of Andrew Anderson, 1709.

———. *Memoirs of a Cavalier, or A Military journal of the wars in Germany and the wars in England*. 1720. Reprint, London: Dent; New York: E. P. Dutton, 1950.

———. *A Reply to the Scots Answer to the British Union*. Edinburgh, 1706.

———. *Scotland in danger, or A serious inquiry into the dangers which Scotland has been in, is now in, or may be in since the Union, with some humble proposals for the remedy*. Edinburgh: Heirs of Andrew Anderson, 1708.

Defoe, Daniel. *The Scot's narrative examin'd*. London, 1709.

———. *The Scots nation and union vindicated*. London: A. Bell, 1714.

———. *A Scots Poem, or a New-years gift*. Edinburgh, 1707.

———. *The Second-Sighted Highlander, Being Four Visions of the Ecylpse*. London: J. Baker, 1713.

———. *A Tour Thro' the Whole Isle of Britain*. 2 vols. 1724–26. Reprint, London: Frank Cass, 1968.

———. *Union and no Union. Being an enquiry into the grievances of the Scots. And how far they are right or wrong, who alledge that the Union is dissolved*. London: J. Baker, 1713.

———. *The Versatile Defoe: An Anthology of Uncollected Writings of Daniel Defoe*. Edited by Laura Ann Curtis. Totowa, N.J.: Rowman and Littlefield, 1979.

"Essay on the Present State of Education in Scotland." *Edinburgh Annual Register 1816* (1819): ccxv–cclviii.

Ferguson, Adam. *An Essay on the History of Civil Society*. 1767. Reprint, New Brunswick: Transaction Publishers, 1991.

Fergusson, Robert. *Works*. 1807. Reprint, Edinburgh: James Thin, 1970.

Grant, Anne. *Essays on the Superstitions of the Highlanders of Scotland*. 2 vols. London: Longman, Hurst et al., 1811.

Grant of Rothiemurchus, Elizabeth, *Memoirs of a Highland Lady*. Vols. 1 and 2. Edited by Andrew Tod. Edinburgh: Cannongate Classics, 1992.

Hogg, James. *Memoir of the Author's Life and Familiar Anecdotes of Sir Walter Scott*. Edited by Douglas Mack. Edinburgh: Scottish Academic Press, 1972.

Howitt, William. *Visits to Remarkable Places: Old Halls, Battle-Fields, and Scenes Illustrative of Striking Passages in History and Poetry*. 2 vols. London: Longman, Brown, Green, Longmans, and Roberts, 1856.

Hume, David. *An Inquiry Concerning Human Understanding*. 1748. Reprint, Indianapolis: Bobbs-Merrill, 1955.

Irving, Washington. *Abbotsford*. 1835. Reprint, vol. 4 of *Works*. New York: Nottingham Society, n.d.

Johnson, Samuel. *A Journey to the Western Islands of Scotland*. Edited by Mary Lascelles. 1775. Reprint, New Haven: Yale University Press, 1971.

Leyden, John. *Scenes of Infancy, Descriptive of Teviotdale*. Edinburgh: James Ballantyne; London: T. N. Longman and O. Rees, 1803.

Lindsay, Maurice. *The Discovery of Scotland: Based on Accounts of Foreign Travellers from the Thirteenth to the Eighteenth Centuries*. London: Hale, 1964.

Linklater, Jane and Mary. *Crossriggs*. 1908. Reprint, Harmondsworth: Penguin Books, 1986.

Lockhart, John Gibson. *Peter's Letters to his Kinsfolk*. 3 vols. Edinburgh: William Blackwood; London: T. Cadell and W. Davies; Glasgow: John Smith and Son, 1819.

McGrath, John. *The Cheviot, the Stag, and the Black, Black Oil*. 1974. Reprint, London: Eyre Methuen, 1981.

Millar, John. *The Origin of the Distinction of Ranks, or An Inquiry into the Circumstances which give rise to Influence and Authority in the Different Members of Society*. 4th ed. Edinburgh: William Blackwood; London: Longman, Hurst, Rees and Orme, 1806.

Muir, Willa. *Mrs. Grundy in Scotland*. London: George Routledge and Sons, 1936.

Oliphant, Margaret. *The Rector and The Doctor's Family*. 1863. Reprint, Harmondsworth: Penguin Books, 1986.

Pennant, Thomas. *A Tour in Scotland*. Chester: John Monk, 1771.

Ramsay, Allan, and Robert Fergusson. *Poems*. Edited by Alexander Manson Kinghorn and Alexander Law. Edinburgh: Scottish Academic Press, 1974.

Ruskin, John. *The Two Paths*. London: George Routledge and Sons, n.d.

Scott, Walter. *The Letters of Sir Walter Scott*. London: Constable, 1983.

Scott, Walter, and Charles Robert Maturin. *The Correspondence of Sir Walter Scott and Charles Robert Maturin*. Edited by Fannie E. Ratchford and William H. McCarthy, Jr. Austin: University of Texas Press, 1937.

Selkirk, Thomas Douglas Earl of. *Observations on the Present State of the Highlands of Scotland with a View of the Causes and Probable Consequences of Emigration*. 2d ed. Edinburgh: A. Constable, 1806.

Sinclair, John. *The Code of Agriculture, Including Observations of Gardens, Orchards, Woods, and Plantations*. London: Sherwood, Neeley, and Jones; Edinburgh: Archibald Constable; Dublin: M. Keene, 1817.

————, ed. *Statistical Account of Scotland, Drawn up from the Communications of the Ministers of the Different Parishes*. 21 vols. Edinburgh: William Creech, 1791–99.

Smollett, Tobias. *Poems, Plays, and the Briton*. Edited by O. M. Brack, Jr. Athens: University of Georgia Press, 1993.

Watkins, Peter. *The Battle of Culloden*. 1965. Motion picture.

Wilkes, John. *The North Briton, from No. 1 to No. XLVI inclusive, with several useful and explanatory notes . . . corrected and revised by A Friend to Civil and Religious Liberty*. 1763. Reprint, New York: AMS Press, 1976.

————. *The North Briton, from No. 1 to No. XLVII Inclusive*. London: W. Bingley, 1769.

Wordsworth, Dorothy. *Recollections of a Tour made in Scotland AD 1803*. 1874. Reprint, New York: AMS Press, 1973.

Empire

Arnason, David, ed. *Nineteenth Century Canadian Stories*. Toronto: Macmillan, 1976.

Atwood, Margaret. *The Journals of Susanna Moodie*. Oxford: Oxford University Press, 1970.

Ballstadt, Carl, ed. *The Search for English-Canadian Literature: An Anthology of Critical Articles from the Nineteenth and Early Twentieth Centuries*. Toronto: University of Toronto Press, 1975.

Barr, Robert. "Literature in Canada" (1899). In *The Measure of the Rule*. Toronto: University of Toronto Press, 1973.

Blaise, Clark, and Bharati Mukherjee. *Days and Nights in Calcutta*. Garden City, N.J.: Doubleday, 1977.

Borduas, Pierre. *Refus globale/Total Refusal: The Complete 1948 Manifesto of the Montreal Automatists*. Translated by Ray Ellenwood. Toronto: Exile Editions, 1985.

Boswell, Annabella. *Annabella Boswell's Journal*. Edited by Morton Herman. Sydney: Angus and Robertson, 1965.

Bowering, George. *A Short Sad Book*. Vancouver: Talonbooks, 1977.

Breckenridge, Hugh Henry. *Modern Chivalry*. Edited by Claude M. Newlin. 1792–1815. Reprint, New York: American Book, 1937.

Brown, Stewart, ed. *Caribbean New Wave: Contemporary Short Stories*. Oxford: Heinemann, 1990.

Browning, Colin Arrott. *The Convict Ship and England's Exiles*. London: Hamilton, Adams, 1847.

Byrne, J. C. *Twelve Years' Wandering in the British Colonies, from 1835 to 1847*. 2 vols. London: Richard Bentley, 1848.

Calcott, Maria Graham. *Journal of a Residence in India*. 2d ed. Edinburgh: Constable; London: Longman, Hurst, Rees, Orme, and Brown, 1813.

———. *Letters on India*. London: Longman, Hurst, Rees, Orme, and Brown; Edinburgh: A. Constable, 1814.

Clark, Manning, ed. *Sources of Australian History*. Melbourne: Oxford University Press, 1977.

Clarke, Marcus. *A Marcus Clarke Reader*. Edited by Bill Wannan. London: Angus and Robertson, 1964.

———. *Stories*. Sydney: Hale and Iremonger, 1983.

Clarkson, Thomas. *The History of the Rise, Progress, and Accomplishment of the Abolition of the African Slave Trade by the British Parliament*. 2 vols. London: Longman, Hurst, Rees, and Orme, 1808.

Cohen, Leonard. *Beautiful Losers*. 1966. Reprint, New York: Vintage, 1993.

Connor, Ralph. *Glengarry Schooldays: A Story of the Early Days in Glengarry*. Toronto: McClelland and Stewart, 1920.

———. *The Man from Glengarry*. 1901. Reprint, Toronto: McClelland and Stewart, 1965.

Crévecoeur, J. Hector St. John. *Letters from an American Farmer*. 1782. Reprint, New York: Signet, 1963.

Dallas, R. C. *The History of the Maroons, From their Origins to their Establishment in Sierra Leone*. 2 vols. 1803. Reprint, London: Frank Cass, 1968.

Davey, Frank. *The Abbotsford Guide to India*. Victoria: Press Porcépic, 1986.

———. *The Louis Riel Organ and Piano Company*. Winnipeg: Turnstone Press, 1985.

Duncan, Sara Jeannette [Mrs. Trevor Coates]. *An American Girl in London*. New York: D. Appleton, 1891.

———. *The Burnt Offering*. New York: Lane, 1910.

———. *Cousin Cinderella* [or *A Canadian Girl in London*]. 1908. Reprint, Toronto: University of Toronto Press, 1973.

———. *His Honor and a Lady*. New York: Appleton: 1896.

———. *The Imperialist*. 1904. Reprint, Toronto: McClelland and Stewart, 1990.

———. *The Path of a Star*. London: Methuen, 1899.

———. *The Pool in the Desert*. 1903. Reprint, Harmondsworth: Penguin Books, 1984.

———. *Set in Authority*. London: Archibald Constable, 1906.

————. *The Simple Adventures of a Memsahib*. New York: D. Appleton, 1893.

————. *The Story of Sonny Sahib*. New York: D. Appleton, 1901.

————. *Vernon's Aunt. Being the Oriental Experiences of Mrs. Lavinia Moffat*. New York: D. Appleton, 1895.

Drummond, William. *The Poetical Works*. New York: G. P. Putnam's Sons, 1912.

Dunlop, William "Tiger." *Tiger Dunlop's Upper Canada*. Toronto: McClelland and Stewart, 1967.

Edwards, Mary Jane, ed. *The Evolution of Canadian Literature in English: Beginnings to 1867*. Toronto: Holt, Rinehart, and Winston of Canada, 1973.

Edwards, Paul, and David Dabydeen, eds. *Black Writers in Britain, 1760–1890*. Edinburgh: Edinburgh University Press, 1991.

Equiano, Olaudoh. *Equiano's travels: his autobiography, the interesting narrative of the life of Olaudoh Equiano, or Gustavus Vassa the African*. 1791. Reprint, London: Heinemann, 1980.

Fay, Eliza. *Original Letters from India*. London: Hogarth Press, 1986.

Fitzpatrick, David, ed. *Oceans of Consolation: Personal Accounts of Irish Migration to Australia*. Ithaca: Cornell University Press, 1994.

Frame, Janet. *Faces in the Water*. New York: George Braziller, 1961.

Gibson, Graeme. *Perpetual Motion*. Toronto: McClelland and Stewart, 1982.

Gordimer, Nadine. *July's People*. New York: Viking, 1981.

Haliburton, Thomas Chandler. *A Historical and Statistical Account of Nova Scotia*. Halifax: J. Howe, 1929.

————. *Letters*. Edited by Richard A. Davies. Toronto: University of Toronto Press, 1988.

Harvey, M. *Lectures, Literary and Biographical*. Edinburgh: Andrew Elliot, 1864.

Hedges, William. *The Diary of William Hedges*. 3 vols. London: Hakluyt Society, 1950.

Howe, Joseph. *Acadia*. Edited by M. G. Parks. London, Ont.: Canadian Poetry Press, 1989.

————. *Joseph Howe: Voice of Nova Scotia*. Edited by J. Murray Beck. Toronto: McClelland and Stewart, 1964.

Howison, John. *Sketches of Upper Canada, Domestic, Local and Characteristic*. 1821. Reprint, New York: Johnson Reprint Corporation, 1965.

Hulme, Peter, and Neil L. Whitehead, eds. *Wild Majesty: Encounters with Caribs from Columbus to the Present Day*. Oxford: Clarendon Press; New York: Oxford University Press, 1992.

Jameson, Anna Brownell. *Winter Studies and Summer Rambles in Canada*. 1838. Reprint, Toronto: McClelland and Stewart, 1990.

Knight, Ann Cuthbert. *A Year in Canada and Other Poems*. Edinburgh: James Ballantyne, 1816.

Lamming, George. *The Emigrants*. London: M. Joseph, 1954.

Langton, Anne. *A Gentlewoman in Upper Canada: The Journals of Anne Langton*. Edited by H. H. Langton. Toronto: Clarke, Irwin, 1950.

Laurence, Margaret. *The Diviners*. Toronto: McClelland and Stewart, 1975.

Levine, Norman. *Canada Made Me*. 1958. Reprint, Ottawa: Deneau and Greenburg, 1971.

Lewis, M. G. *Journal of a West India Proprietor, 1815–17*. Edited by Mona Wilson. London: George Routledge and Sons, 1929.

MacLennan, Hugh. *Scotchman's Return and Other Essays*. New York: Charles Scribner's Sons, 1960.

Macphail, Sir Andrew. *The Master's Wife*. 1939. Reprint, Toronto: McClelland and Stewart, 1977.

Maillet, Antonine. *Pélagie*. Toronto: General Publishing Company, 1982.

Marryat, Frederick. *The settlers in Canada, written for young People*. 1844. Reprint, London: J. M. Dent and Sons, 1931.

Marx, Karl. "The British Rule in India." In *Political Writings*. Vol. 2, *Surveys from Exile*. New York: Random House, 1974.

M'neill, Hector. *Observations on the Treatment of the Negroes in the Island of Jamaica, including some account of their temper and character, with remarks on the importation of slaves from the Coast of Africa*. London: G.G.J. and J. Robinson, [1800?].

Moodie, Dunbar. *Ten Years in South Africa*. London: Richard Bentley, 1835.

Moodie, Susanna. *Letters of a Lifetime*. Edited by Carl Ballstadt, Elizabeth Hopkins, and Michael Peterman. Toronto: University of Toronto Press, 1985.

———. *Voyages: Short Narratives of Susanna Moodie*. Edited by John Thurston. Ottawa: University of Ottawa Press, 1991.

Mukherjee, Bharati. *Darkness*. Markham, Ont.: Penguin Books Canada, 1985.

———. *The Holder of the World*. Toronto: Harper Collins, 1993.

Munro, Alice. *The Lives of Girls and Women*. Scarborough: McGraw-Hill Ryerson, 1971.

———. *Open Secrets*. New York: Knopf, 1994.

Naipaul, V. S. *The Middle Passage*. 1962. Reprint, New York: Viking, 1981.

Nugent, Maria. *Lady Nugent's Journal of Her Residence in Jamaica from 1801 to 1805*. Edited by Philip Wright. Kingston, Jamaica: Institute of Jamaica, 1966.

O'Grady, Standish. *The Emigrant. A Poem*. Edited by Brian Trehearne. 1842. Reprint, London, Ont.: Canadian Poetry Press, 1989.

O'Leary, Thomas, ed. *Canadian Letters: Description of a Tour Thro' The Provinces of Lower and Upper Canada, in the Course of the Years 1792 and '93*. Montreal: C. A. Marchand, 1912.

Ondaatje, Michael. *The English Patient*. London: Bloomsbury, 1992.

———. *In the Skin of a Lion*. Harmondsworth: Penguin Books, 1988.

———. *Running in the Family*. New York: Norton, 1982.

Praed, Rosa. *Lady Bridget in the Never-Never Land*. 1915. Reprint, London: Pandora, 1987.

———. *My Australian Girlhood: Sketches and Impressions of Bush Life*. London: T. Fisher Unwin, 1904.

Pringle, Thomas. *African Sketches*. London: Edward Moxon, 1934.

Raynal, Guillaume-Thomas. *Histoire philosophique et politique des établissemens et du commerce des Européens dans les deux Indes*. 5 vols. Geneva: Jean-Leonard Pellet, 1780.

Schaw, Janet. *Journal of a Lady of Quality; Being the Narrative of a Journey from Scotland to the West Indies, North Carolina, and Portugal, in the years 1774 to 1776*. Edited by Evangeline Walker Andrews. New Haven: Yale University Press, 1923.

Sellar, Robert. *A Scotsman in Upper Canada: The Narrative of Gordon Sellar*. 1915. Reprint, Toronto: Clarke Irwin, 1969.

Simcoe, Elizabeth. *Mrs. Simcoe's Diary*. Edited by Mary Quayle Innis. Toronto: Macmillan of Canada, 1965.

Sinclair, David, ed. *Nineteenth-Century Narrative Poems*. Toronto: McClelland and Stewart, 1972.

Spender, Dale, ed. *The Penguin Anthology of Australian Women's Writing*. Ringwood, Australia: Penguin Books, 1988.

Stewart, Frances. *Our Forest Home. Being Extracts from the Correspondence of the Late Frances Stewart*. Edited by E. S. Dunlop. Montreal: Gazette Printing and Publishing, 1902.

Talbot, Laura. *The Gentlewoman*. 1952. Reprint, London: Virago, 1985.

Traill, Catharine Parr. *Forest and Other Gleanings: The Fugitive Writings of Catharine Parr Traill*. Edited by Michael A. Peterman and Carl Ballstadt. Ottawa: University of Ottawa Press, 1994.

Valliéres, Pierre. *White Niggers of America*. 1971. Reprint, Toronto: McClelland and Stewart, 1982.

Wakefield, Edward Gibbon. *A Letter from Sydney, and Other Writings on Colonization*. London: J. M. Dent; New York: E. P. Dutton, 1929.

Walpole, Horace. *Horace Walpole's Correspondence*. Edited by W. S. Lewis. 48 vols. New Haven: Yale University Press, 1937–83.

Wannan, Bill, ed. *The Heather in the South: A Scottish-Australian Entertainment*. Melbourne: Landsdowne Press, 1966.

Young, Arthur. *Political Essays Concerning the Present State of the British Empire*. London: W. Strahan and T. Cadell, 1772.

Young, John. *The Letters of Agricola. On Principles of Vegetation and Tillage. Written for Nova Scotia and Published first in the Acadian Recorder*. Halifax: Holland, 1822.

Yule, Henry, and A. C. Burnell. *Hobson-Jobson: A Glossary of Colloquial Anglo-Indian Words and Phrases, and of Kindred Terms, Etymological, Historical, Geographical and Discursive*. 1886. Reprint, New York: Humanities Press, 1968.

SECONDARY SOURCES

Aarsleff, Hans. *The Study of Language in England, 1780–1860*. Princeton: Princeton University Press, 1967.

Aberdeen, Jennie W. *John Galt*. London: Oxford University Press, 1936.

Adam, Ian, and Helen Tiffin, eds. *Past the Last Post: Theorizing Post-Colonialism and Post-Modernism*. Calgary: University of Calgary Press, 1990.

Adams, Percy G. *Travel Literature and the Evolution of the Novel*. Lexington: University Press of Kentucky, 1983.

Alexander, J. H., and David Hewitt, eds. *Scott and His Influence*. Aberdeen: Association for Scottish Literary Studies, 1983.

Allen, Michael, and Angela Wilcox, eds. *Critical Approaches to Ango-Irish Literature*. Gerrards Cross: Colin Smythe, 1989.

Alliston, April. "The Value of a Literary Legacy: Retracing the Transmission of Value through Female Lines." *Yale Journal of Criticism* 4, no. 1 (1990): 109–27.

Altick, Richard. *The English Common Reader*. Chicago: Chicago University Press, 1957.

Altman, Janet Gurkin. *Epistolarity: Approaches to a Form*. Columbus: Ohio State University Press, 1982.

Anderson, Benedict. "Exodus." *Critical Inquiry* 20, no. 2 (winter 1994): 314–27.

———. *Imagined Communities: Reflections on the Origin and Spread of Nationalism*. London: Verso Press, 1983.

Andrews, J. H. *A Paper Landscape: The Ordnance Survey in Nineteenth Century Ireland*. Oxford: Clarendon Press, 1975.

Andrews, Malcolm. *The Search for the Picturesque: Landscape Aesthetics and Tourism in Britain, 1760–1800*. Aldershot: Scolar Press, 1989.

Appadurai, Arjun. "Disjuncture and Difference in the Global Cultural Economy." In *Theory, Culture, and Society*. Vol. 7. London: Sage, 1990.

Appiah, Kwame Anthony. "Is the Post- in Postmodernism the Post- in Postcolonial?" *Critical Inquiry* 17, no. 2 (winter 1991): 336–57.

Arac, Jonathan, and Harriet Ritvo, eds. *Macropolitics of Nineteenth-Century Literature: Nationalism, Exoticism, Imperialism*. Philadelphia: University of Pennsylvania Press, 1991.

Argyle, Barry. *An Introduction to the Australian Novel, 1830–1930*. Oxford: Clarendon Press, 1972.

Armstrong, Nancy. *Desire and Domestic Fiction: A Political History of the Novel*. London: Oxford University Press, 1987.

Armstrong, Nancy, and Leonard Tennenhouse. "A Novel Nation, or How to Rethink Modern England as an Emergent Culture." *MLQ* 54, no. 3 (September 1993): 327–44.

Ashcroft, Bill, Gareth Griffiths, and Helen Tiffin. *The Empire Writes Back: Theory and Practise in Post-colonial Literature*. London: Routledge, 1989.

Attali, Jacques. *Noise: The Political Economy of Music*. Minneapolis: University of Minnesota Press, 1985.

Austen-Leigh, J. E. "A Memoir of Jane Austen" (1870). In *Persuasion*, by Jane Austen, edited by D. W. Harding. Harmondsworth: Penguin Books, 1965.

Avery, Bruce. "Mapping the Irish Other: Spenser's *A View of the Present State of Ireland*." *ELH* 57, no. 2 (summer 1990): 263–79.

Azim, Firdous. *The Colonial Rise of the Novel*. London: Routledge, 1993.

Bailyn, Bernard. *The Peopling of British North America: An Introduction*. New York: Knopf, 1986.

Bailyn, Bernard, and Philip D. Morgan, eds. *Strangers within the Realm: Cultural Margins of the First British Empire*. Chapel Hill: University of North Carolina Press, 1991.

Baker, Ernest A. *The History of the English Novel*. 10 vols. London: Witherby, 1934.

Baker, Ray Palmer. *History of English Canadian Literature to the Confederation*. Cambridge: Harvard University Press, 1920.

Bakhtin, Mikhail. *The Dialogic Imagination*. Translated by Caryl Emerson and Michael Holquist. Austin: University of Texas Press, 1981.

Balibar, Renée, and Dominique Laporte. *Le français national: Politique et pratiques de la langue nationale sous la Révolution française*. Paris: Librairie Hachette, 1974.

Balibar, Renée, G. Merlin, and G. Tret. *Les français fictifs: Le rapport des styles littéraires au français national*. Paris: Librairie Hachette, 1974.

Bann, Stephen. *The Clothing of Clio*. Cambridge: Cambridge University Press, 1984.

Barrell, John. *The Dark Side of the Landscape: The Rural Poor in English Painting, 1730–1848*. Cambridge: Cambridge University Press, 1980.

————. *English Literature in History, 1730–80: An Equal, Wide Survey*. London: Hutchison, 1983.

————. *The Idea of Landscape and the Sense of Place, 1730–1840*. Cambridge: Cambridge University Press, 1972.

Basker, James G. *Tobias Smollett: Critic and Journalist*. Newark: University of Delaware Press, 1988.

Bate, Walter Jackson. *The Burden of the Past and the English Poet*. New York: Norton, 1970.

————. *Samuel Johnson*. New York: Harcourt Brace Jovanovich, 1975.

Batten, Charles L., Jr. *Pleasurable Instruction: Form and Conventions in Eighteenth Century Travel Literature*. Berkeley: University of California, 1978.

Bell, Alan S., ed. *Scott Bicentenary Essays*. Edinburgh: Scottish Academic Press, 1971.

————. *The Scottish Antiquarian Tradition*. Edinburgh: John Donald Publishers, 1981.

Bender, John. *Imagining the Penitentiary: Fiction and the Architecture of Mind in Eighteenth-century England*. Chicago: University of Chicago, 1987.

Bermingham, Ann. *Landscape and Ideology: The English Rural Tradition, 1740–1860*. Berkeley: University of California Press, 1986.

Bhabha, Homi K., ed. *Nation and Narration*. London: Routledge, 1990.

Blackburn, Robin. *The Overthrow of Colonial Slavery, 1776–1848*. London: Verso Press, 1988.

Boerner, Peter. *Concepts of National Identity: An Interdisciplinary Dialogue*. Baden-Baden: Nomos Verlagsgesellschaft, 1986.

Bold, Alan, ed. *Sir Walter Scott: The Long Forgotten Melody*. London: Vision, 1983.

Bradshaw, Brendan, Andrew Hadfield, and Willy Maley, eds. *Representing Ireland: Literature and the Origins of Conflict, 1534–1660*. Cambridge: Cambridge University Press, 1993.

Bronson, Bertrand Harris. *Facets of the Enlightenment: Studies in English Literature and Its Contexts*. Berkeley: University of California Press, 1968.

————. *Joseph Ritson: Scholar-at-Arms*. Berkeley: University of California Press, 1938.

Browlie, William M. *John Galt, Social Historian*. Papers of the Greenock Philosophical Society. Greenock: "Telegraph" Printing Works, 1952.

Brown, David. *Walter Scott and the Historical Imagination*. London: Routledge and Kegan Paul, 1979.

Brown, Iain Gordon. *The Hobby-Horsical Antiquary: A Scottish Character, 1640–1830*. Edinburgh: National Library of Scotland, 1980.

Brown, Marshall. *Preromanticism*. Stanford: Stanford University Press, 1991.

Bruckner, Phillip, "Whatever Happened to the British Empire?" *Journal of the Canadian Historical Association*, n.s. 4 (1993): 3–32.

Bryant, G. J. "Scots in India in the Eighteenth Century." *Scottish Historical Review* 64, no. 1 (1985): 22–41.

Bumsted, J. M. *The People's Clearance: Highland Emigration to British North America, 1770–1815*. Edinburgh: Edinburgh University Press, 1982.

———. *The Scots in Canada*. Ottawa: Canadian Historical Association, 1982.

Butler, Marilyn. *Jane Austen and the War of Ideas*. Oxford: Oxford University Press, 1975.

———. *Maria Edgeworth: A Literary Biography*. Oxford: Clarendon Press, 1982.

———. *Peacock Displayed: A Satirist in His Context*. London: Routledge and Kegan Paul, 1979.

———. *Romantics, Rebels, and Reactionaries: English Literature and Its Background, 1760–1830*. Oxford: Oxford University Press, 1981.

Buzzard, James. "Translation and Tourism: Scott's *Waverley* and the Rendering of Culture." *Yale Journal of Criticism* 8, no. 2 (1995): 31–59.

Bysveen, Josef. "Epic Tradition and Innovation in James Macpherson's Fingal." Ph.D. diss.,, Uppsala University, 1982.

Cahalan, James M. *The Irish Novel: A Critical History*. Boston: Twayne, 1988.

Cairns, David, and Shaun Richards. *Writing Ireland: Colonialism, Nationalism, and Culture*. Manchester: Manchester University Press, 1988.

Calder, Angus. *Revolutionary Empire: The Rise of the English-Speaking Empires from the Fifteenth Century to the 1780s*. London: Jonathan Cape, 1981.

Calder, Jenni, ed. *The Enterprising Scot: Scottish Adventure and Achievement*. Edinburgh: Royal Museum of Scotland, 1986.

Camic, Charles. *Experience and Enlightenment: Socialization for Cultural Change in Eighteenth-Century Scotland*. Edinburgh: Edinburgh University Press, 1983.

Campbell, Ian, ed. *Nineteenth-Century Scottish Fiction: Critical Essays*. Manchester: Carcanet New Press, 1979.

Campbell, Mary. *Lady Morgan: The Life and Times of Sydney Owenson*. London: Pandora, 1988.

Campbell, Wilfred, and George Bryce. *The Scotsman in Canada*. 2 vols. Toronto: Musson Book, [ca. 1911?].

Canny, Nicholas. *Kingdom and Colony: Ireland in the Atlantic World, 1560–1800*. Baltimore: Johns Hopkins University Press, 1988.

Canny, Nicholas, and Anthony Pagden, eds. *Colonial Identity in the Atlantic World, 1500–1800*. Princeton: Princeton University Press, 1987.

Carter, Jennifer, and Joan Pittock, eds. *Aberdeen and the Enlightenment*. Aberdeen: Aberdeen University Press, 1987.

Castle, Terry. *Masquerade and Civilization: The Carnivalesque in Eighteenth-century English Culture and Fiction*. Stanford: Stanford University Press, 1986.

Chapman, Malcolm. *The Gaelic Vision in Scottish Culture*. London: Croom Helm, 1978.

Chatterjee, Partha. *The Nation and Its Fragments: Colonial and Postcolonial Histories*. Princeton: Princeton University Press, 1993.

———. *Nationalist Thought and the Colonial World: A Derivative Discourse?* London: Zed Books, 1986.

Chitnis, Anand. *The Scottish Enlightenment: A Social History*. London: Croom Helm, 1976.

———. *The Scottish Enlightenment and Early Victorian English Society*. London: Croom Helm, 1986.

Christensen, Jerome. *Practicing Enlightenment: Hume and the Formation of a Literary Career*. Madison: University of Wisconsin Press, 1987.

———. "Romantics at the End of History." *Critical Inquiry* 20, no. 3 (spring 1994): 452–76.

Clark, Arthur Melville. *Sir Walter Scott: The Formative Years*. Edinburgh: William Blackwood, 1964.

Clark, J.C.D. *Samuel Johnson: Literature, Religion, and English Cultural Politics from the Restoration to Romanticism*. Cambridge: Cambridge University Press, 1994.

Clarke, G. W., ed. *Rediscovering Hellenism: The Hellenistic Inheritance and the English Imagination*. Cambridge: Cambridge University Press, 1989.

Clemit, Pamela. *The Godwinian Novel: The Rational Fictions of Godwin, Brockden Brown, Mary Shelley*. Oxford: Clarendon Press, 1993.

Clive, John. *Scotch Reviewers: The Edinburgh Review, 1802–1815*. London: Faber and Faber, 1957.

Close, Charles. *The Early Years of the Ordnance Survey*. 1926. Reprint, Newton Abbott: David and Charles, 1969.

Coetzee, J. M. *White Writing: On the Culture of Letters in South Africa*. New Haven: Yale University Press, 1988.

Cohen, Murray. *Sensible Words: Linguistic Practice in England, 1640–1785*. Baltimore: Johns Hopkins University Press, 1977.

Colley, Linda. *Britons: Forging the Nation, 1707–1837*. New Haven: Yale University Press, 1992.

Collins, A. S. *The Profession of Letters: A Study of the Relation of Author to Patron, Publisher to Public, 1780–1832*. London: George Routledge and Sons, 1928.

Colls, Robert, and Philip Dodd, eds. *Englishness: Politics and Culture, 1880–1920*. London: Croom Helm, 1986.

Connolly, S. J. *Religion, Law, and Power: The Making of Protestant Ireland, 1660–1760*. Oxford: Clarendon Press, 1992.

Cooper, Derek. *The Road to the Isles: Travellers in the Hebrides, 1770–1914*. London: Routledge and Kegan Paul, 1979.

Copley, Stephen, and John Whale, eds. *Beyond Romanticism: New Approaches to Texts and Contexts, 1780–1832*. London: Routledge, 1992.

Copley, Stephen, and Peter Garside, eds. *The Politics of the Picturesque: Literature, Landscape, and Aesthetics Since 1770*. Cambridge: Cambridge University Press, 1994.

Corbett, Mary Jean. "Public Affections and Familial Politics: Burke, Edgeworth, and the 'Common Naturalization' of Great Britain." *ELH* 61 (1994): 887–97.

Corkery, Daniel. *The Hidden Ireland: A Study of Gaelic Munister in the Eighteenth Century*. 2d ed. Dublin: M. H. Gill, 1925.

———. *Synge and Anglo-Irish Literature*. 1931. Reprint, New York: Russell and Russell, 1965.

Costain, Keith M. "Theoretical History and the Novel: The Scottish Fiction of John Galt." *ELH* 43, no. 3 (fall 1976): 342–65.

Cottom, Daniel. *The Civilized Imagination: A Study of Ann Radcliffe, Jane Austen, and Sir Walter Scott*. Cambridge: Cambridge University Press, 1985.

Coughlan, Patricia, ed. *Spenser and Ireland: An Interdisciplinary Perspective*. Cork: Cork University Press, 1989.

Craig, David. *Scottish Literature and the Scottish People, 1680–1830*. London: Chatto and Windus, 1961.

Craig, Mary Elizabeth. *The Scottish Periodical Press, 1750–1789*. Edinburgh: Oliver and Boyd, 1931.

Crawford, Robert. *Devolving English Literature*. Oxford: Clarendon Press, 1992.

Cross, Wilbur L. "An Earlier Waverly." *Modern Language Notes* 17 (1902): 87–88.

Cullen, Fintan. "The Art of Assimilation: Scotland and Its Heroes." *Art History* 16, no. 4 (December 1993): 600–618.

Curley, Thomas M. *Samuel Johnson and the Age of Travel*. Athens: University of Georgia Press, 1976.

Curran, Stuart. *Poetic Form and British Romanticism*. New York: Oxford University Press, 1986.

———, ed. *The Cambridge Companion to British Romanticism*. Cambridge: Cambridge University Press, 1992.

Curtin, Nancy. *The United Irishmen: Popular Politics in Ulster and Dublin, 1791–1798*. Oxford: Clarendon Press, 1994.

Cutt, M. Nancy. *Mrs. Sherwood and Her Books for Children*. London: Oxford University Press, 1974.

Dahlie, Hallvard. *Varieties of Exile: The Canadian Experience*. Vancouver: University of British Columbia Press, 1986.

Daiches, David. *Literature and Gentility in Scotland*. Edinburgh: Edinburgh University Press, 1982.

———. *The Paradox of Scottish Culture: The Eighteenth-Century Experience*. London: Oxford University Press, 1964.

———. *Robert Burns*. London: G. Bell and Sons, 1952.

———. *Robert Fergusson*. Edinburgh: Scottish Academic Press, 1982.

———. *Scotland and the Union*. London: John Murray, 1977.

Dann, Otto, and John Dinwiddy, eds. *Nationalism in the Age of the French Revolution*. London: Hambleton Press, 1988.

Davey, Frank. *From Here to There: A Guide to English-Canadian Literature since 1960*. Erin: Press Porcepic, 1974.

———. *Post-nationalist Arguments: The Politics of the Anglophone-Canadian Novel since 1967*. Toronto: University of Toronto Press, 1993.

Davidson, Cathy. *Revolution and the Word: The Rise of the Novel in America*. New York: Oxford University Press, 1986.

Davie, Donald. *The Heyday of Walter Scott*. London: Routledge and Kegan Paul, 1961.

Davies, A. Richard, ed. *On Thomas Chandler Haliburton*. Ottawa: Tecumseh Press, 1979.

Davies, Gwendolyn. *Studies in Maritime Literary History, 1760–1930*. Fredericton, New Brunswick: Acadiensis Press, 1991.

Davis, Brion David. *The Problem of Slavery in the Age of Revolution, 1770–1823*. Ithaca: Cornell University Press, 1975.

Dean, Misao. *A Different Point of View: Sara Jeannette Duncan*. Montreal: McGill-Queen's University Press, 1991.

Deane, Seamus. "Irish National Character, 1790–1900." In *The Writer as Witness: Literature as Historical Evidence*, edited by Tom Dunne. Cork: Cork University Press, 1987.

———. *A Short History of Irish Literature*. London: Hutchinson, 1986.

de Certeau, Michel, Dominique Julia, and Jacques Revel. *Une politique de la langue. La Révolution française et les patois: L'enquête de Grégoire*. Paris: Gallimard, 1975.

Defoe, Daniel. *The Dumb Philosopher, or Great-Britain's Wonder*. London: Thomas. Bickerton, 1719.

Dekker, George. *The American Historical Romance*. Cambridge: Cambridge University Press, 1987.

De Maria, Robert, Jr. *Johnson's Dictionary and the Language of Learning*. Oxford: Clarendon Press, 1986.

———. "The Politics of Johnson's Dictionary." *PMLA* 104, no. 1 (January 1989): 64–74.

de Mause, Lloyd, ed. *The History of Childhood*. New York: Harper and Row, 1975.

Demers, Patricia. *Heaven upon Earth: The Form of Moral and Religious Children's Literature, to 1850*. Knoxville: University of Tennessee Press, 1993.

———, ed. *From Instruction to Delight: An Anthology of Children's Literature to 1850*. Toronto: Oxford University Press, 1982.

Derrida, Jacques. *Of Grammatology*. Translated by Gayatri Spivak. Baltimore: Johns Hopkins University Press, 1974.

Dickinson, W. Croft. *John Galt: "The Provost" and the Burgh*. Papers of the Greenock Philosophical Society. Greenock: "Telegraph" Printing Works, 1954.

Dickson, David, Dáire Keogh, and Kevin Whelan, eds. *The United Irishmen: Republicanism, Radicalism, and Rebellion*. Dublin: Lilliput Press, 1993.

Donaldson, William. *The Jacobite Song: Political Myth and National Identity*. Aberdeen: Aberdeen University Press, 1988.

———. *Popular Literature in Victorian Scotland: Language, Fiction, and the Press*. Aberdeen: Aberdeen University Press, 1986.

Dorson, Richard. *The British Folklorist: A History*. Chicago: University of Chicago Press, 1968.

Douglas, Bertram H. *Thomas Percy*. Boston: Wayne Publishers, 1981.

Duffy, Dennis. *Gardens, Covenants, Exiles: Loyalism in the Literature of Upper Canada/Ontario*. Toronto: University of Toronto Press, 1982.

Duncan, Edmondstoune. *The Story of Minstrelsy*. Detroit: Singing Tree Press, 1968.

Duncan, Ian. *Modern Romance and Transformations of the Novel: The Gothic, Scott, Dickens*. Cambridge: Cambridge University Press, 1992.

Dunne, Tom. "Fiction as 'the Best History of Nations': Lady Morgan's Irish novels." In *The Writer as Witness: Literature as Historical Evidence*, edited by Tom Dunne. Cork: Cork University Press, 1987.

———. "'A Gentleman's Estate Should Be a Moral School': Edgeworthstown in Fact and Fiction, 1760–1840." In *Longford: Essays in County History*, edited by Raymond Gillespie and Gerard Moran. Dublin: Lilliput Press, 1991.

———. *Theobald Wolfe Tone, Colonial Outsider: An Analysis of His Political Philosophy*. Cork: Tower Books, 1984.

Durkacz, Victor. *The Decline of the Celtic Languages: A Study of Linguistic and Cultural Conflict in Scotland, Wales, and Ireland from the Reformation to the Twentieth Century*. Edinburgh: John Donald Publishers, 1983.

Dwyer, John. *Virtuous Discourse: Sensibility and Community in Late Eighteenth Century Scotland*. Edinburgh: John Donald, 1987.

Eagleton, Terry. *The Function of Criticism: From the Spectator to Post-structuralism*. London: Verso Press, 1984.

———. *Heathcliff and the Great Hunger: Studies in Irish Culture*. London: Verso Press, 1995.

Ellis, P. Berresford, and Seumas Mac a'Ghobhainn. *The Scottish Insurrection of 1820*. London: Victor Gollancz, 1970.

Fabricant, Carole. *Swift's Landscape*. Baltimore: Johns Hopkins University Press, 1982.

Fanon, Frantz. *The Wretched of the Earth*. Translated by Constance Farrington. New York: Grove Press, 1968.

Favret, Mary. *Romantic Correspondence: Women, Politics, and the Fiction of Letters*. Cambridge: Cambridge University Press, 1993.

Ferguson, Moira. *Colonialism and Gender Relations from Mary Wollstonecraft to Jamaica Kincaid: East Caribbean Connections*. New York: Columbia University Press, 1993.

———. *Subject to Others: British Women Writers and Colonial Slavery, 1670–1834*. New York: Routledge, 1992.

Ferris, Ina. *The Achievement of Literary Authority: Gender, History, and the Waverley Novels*. Ithaca: Cornell University Press, 1991.

Fildes, Valerie. *Breasts, Bottles, and Babies: A History of Infant Feeding*. Edinburgh: Edinburgh University Press, 1986.

———. *Wet Nursing: A History from Antiquity to the Present*. London: Basil Blackwell, 1985.

Fischer, David Hackett. *Albion's Seed: Four British Folkways in America*. New York: Oxford University Press, 1989.

Flanagan, Thomas. *The Irish Novelists, 1800–1850*. New York: Columbia University Press, 1959.

Fleischman, Avrom. *The English Historical Novel: Walter Scott to Virginia Woolf*. Baltimore: Johns Hopkins University Press, 1971.

———. *A Reading of Mansfield Park: An Essay in Critical Synthesis*. Minneapolis: University of Minnesota Press, 1967.

Foster, R. F., ed. *The Oxford History of Ireland*. Oxford: Oxford University Press, 1992.

Foucault, Michel. *Histoire de la folie à l'age classique*. Paris: Gallimard, 1972.

Fowler, Marian. *The Embroidered Tent: Five Gentlewomen in Early Canada*. Concord: House of Anansi, 1982.

———. *Redney: A Life of Sara Jeannette Duncan*. Toronto: House of Anansi, 1983.

Fox, Charlotte Milligan. *Annals of the Irish Harpers*. London: Smith, Elder, 1911.

Fox, Christopher, and Brenda Tooley, eds. *Walking Naboth's Vineyard: New Studies of Swift*. Notre Dame: University of Notre Dame Press, 1995.

Fraiman, Susan. "Jane Austen and Edward Said: Gender, Culture, and Imperialism." *Critical Inquiry* 21 (summer 1995): 805–21.

Freeman, F. W. *Robert Fergusson and the Scots Humanist Compromise*. Edinburgh: Edinburgh University Press, 1984.

Freud, Sigmund. *Complete Psychological Works*. Translated by James Strachey. 24 vols. London: Hogarth Press, 1953–1963.

Frykman, Erik. *John Galt and Eighteenth Century Scottish Philosophy*. Papers of the Greenock Philosophical Society. Greenock: "Telegraph" Printing Works, 1953.

Galeano, Eduardo. *Open Veins of Latin America: Five Centuries of the Pillage of a Continent*. New York: Monthly Review Press, 1973.

Gallagher, Catherine. *Nobody's Story: The Vanishing Acts of Women Writers in the Marketplace, 1670–1820*. Berkeley: University of California Press, 1994.

Garlick, Raymond. *An Introduction to Anglo-Welsh Literature*. N.p.: University of Wales Press, 1970.

Garside, Peter. "Popular Fiction and National Tale: Hidden Origins of Scott's *Waverley*." *Nineteenth-Century Literature* 46, no. 1 (June 1991): 30–53.

Gaskill, Howard, ed. *Ossian Revisited*. Edinburgh: Edinburgh University Press, 1991.

Gelpi, Barbara Charlesworth. *Shelley's Goddess: Maternity, Language, Subjectivity*. New York: Oxford University Press, 1992.

Gerson, Carole. *A Purer Taste: The Writing and Reading of Fiction in English in Nineteenth-Century Canada*. Toronto: University of Toronto Press, 1989.

Gibault, Henri. *John Galt: Romancier Ecossais*. Grenoble: Publications de l'Université des langues et lettres de Grenoble, 1979.

Gibb, Andrew Dewar. *Scottish Empire*. London: Alexander Maclehose, 1937.

Gibbon, Frank. "The Antiguan Connection: Some New Light on *Mansfield Park*." *Cambridge Quarterly* 11, no. 2 (1982): 298–305.

Gifford, Douglas, ed. *The History of Scottish Literature*. Vol. 3, *The Nineteenth Century*. Aberdeen: Aberdeen University Press, 1988.

Gilbert, Sandra M., and Susan Gubar. *The Madwoman in the Attic: The Woman Writer and the Nineteenth Century Literary Imagination*. New Haven: Yale University Press, 1979.

Goldstein, Laurence. *Ruins and Empire: The Evolution of a Theme in Augustan and Romantic Literature*. Pittsburgh: University of Pittsburgh Press, 1972.

Gooneratne, Yasmine. *English Literature in Ceylon, 1815–1878*. Dehiwala: Tisara Prakasakayo, 1968.

Goslee, Nancy Moore. *Scott the Rhymer*. Lexington: University Press of Kentucky.

Gossmann, Lionel. *Between History and Literature*. Cambridge: Harvard University Press, 1990.

———. *Medievalism and the Ideologies of the Enlightenment: The World and Work of La Curne de Sainte-Palaye*. Baltimore: Johns Hopkins University Press, 1968.

Graham, Henry Grey. *The Social Life of Scotland in the Eighteenth Century*. 1899. Reprint, London: Adam and Charles Black, 1909.

Graham, W. H. *The Tiger of Canada West*. Toronto: Clarke, Irwin, 1962.

Green, Martin. *Dreams of Adventure, Deeds of Empire*. New York: Basic Books, 1979.

Habermas, Jürgen. *The Structural Transformation of the Public Sphere: An Inquiry into a Category of Bourgeois Society*. Cambridge: MIT Press, 1989.

Hamer, Mary. "Putting Ireland on the Map." *Textual Practice* 3, no. 1 (1989): 184–201.

Handler, Richard. *Nationalism and the Politics of Culture in Quebec*. Madison: University of Wisconsin Press, 1988.

Handler, Richard, and Daniel Segal. *Jane Austen and the Fiction of Culture: An Essay on the Narration of Social Realities*. Tucson: University of Arizona Press, 1990.

Harker, Dave. *Fakesong: The Manufacture of British "Folksong," 1700 to the Present Day*. Milton Keynes: Open University Press, 1985.

Hart, Francis Russell. *The Scottish Novel: From Smollett to Spark*. Cambridge: Harvard University Press, 1978.

Harvie, Christopher. *Scotland and Nationalism: Scottish Society and Politics, 1707–1977*. London: George Allen and Unwin, 1977.

Hauser, Arnold. *The Social History of Art*. 4 vols. New York: Vintage, n.d.

Hay, William, ed. *Thomas Pringle*. Capetown: J. C. Juta, 1912.

Hayter, Tony. "The Army and the First British Empire, 1714–1783." In *The Oxford Illustrated History of the British Army*, edited by David Chandler. Oxford: Oxford University Press, 1994.

Haywood, Ian. *The Making of History: A Study of the Literary Forgeries of James Macpherson and Thomas Chatterton in Relation to Eighteenth-Century Ideas of History and Fiction*. Cranbury, N.J.: Associated University Presses, 1986.

Hazlitt, William. "Sir Walter Scott." In *The Spirit of the Age, or Contemporary Portraits*. 4th ed. London: George Bell and Sons, 1894.

Hechter, Michael. *Internal Colonialism: The Celtic Fringe in British National Development, 1536–1966*. Berkeley: University of California Press, 1975.

Helgerson, Richard. *Forms of Nationhood: The Elizabethan Writing of England*. Chicago: University of Chicago Press, 1992.

Herzfeld, Michael. *Ours Once More: Folklore, Ideology, and the Making of Modern Greece.* Austin: University of Texas Press, 1982.

Hill, Douglas Arthur. *The Scots to Canada.* London: Gentry Books, 1972.

Hobsbawm, Eric. *Nations and Nationalism Since 1780: Programme, Myth, Reality.* Cambridge: Cambridge University Press, 1990.

Hobsbawm, Eric, and Terence Ranger, eds. *The Invention of Tradition.* Cambridge: Cambridge University Press, 1983.

Hohl, Hanna. *Ossian.* Paris: Ministere des musées nationaux, 1974.

Hook, Andrew, ed. *The History of Scottish Literature.* Vol. 2, *1660–1800.* Aberdeen: Aberdeen University Press, 1987.

Horn, Pamela. *The Rural World, 1780–1850: Social Change in the English Countryside.* London: Hutchison, 1980.

Hughes, Robert. *The Fatal Shore: The Epic of Australia's Founding.* New York: Vintage, 1986.

Hulme, Peter. *Colonial Encounters: Europe and the Native Carribean, 1492–1797.* London: Methuen, 1986.

Humphreys, Emry, *The Taliesin Tradition: A Quest for the Welsh Identity.* London: Black Raven Press, 1983.

Hunter, Paul. *Before Novels: The Cultural Contexts of Eighteenth-Century English Fiction.* New York: Norton, 1990.

Hurst, Michael. *Maria Edgeworth and the Public Scene: Intellect, Fine Feeling, and Landlordism in the Age of Reform.* London: Macmillan, 1969.

Hutchinson, John. *The Dynamics of Cultural Nationalism: The Gaelic Revival and the Creation of the Irish Nation State.* London: Allen and Unwin, 1987.

Jackson, Mary V. *Engines of Instruction, Mischief, and Magic: Children's Literature in England from Its Beginnings to 1839.* Lincoln: University of Nebraska Press, 1989.

Jacob, Margaret C. *The Radical Enlightenment: Pantheists, Freemasons, and Republicans.* London: George Allen and Unwin, 1981.

James, C.L.R. *The Black Jacobins.* 1936. 2d rev. ed. New York: Vintage, 1963.

James, Francis Godwin. *Ireland in the Empire, 1688–1770: A History of Ireland from the Williamite Wars to the Eve of the American Revolution.* Cambridge: Harvard University Press, 1973.

JanMohamed, Abdul R., and David Lloyd, eds. *The Nature and Context of Minority Discourse.* New York: Oxford University Press, 1990.

Janowitz, Anne. *England's Ruins: Poetic Purpose and National Landscape.* Cambridge: Basil Blackwell, 1990.

Jeffares, A. Norman. *Anglo-Irish Literature.* New York: Schocken Books, 1982.

Jenkins, Geraint H. *The Foundations of Modern Wales, 1642–1780.* Oxford: Clarendon Press and University of Wales Press, 1987.

Jestin, Loftus. *The Answer to the Lyre: Richard Bentley's Illustrations for Thomas Gray's Poems.* Philadelphia: University of Pennsylvania Press, 1992.

Johnson, Arthur. *Enchanted Ground: The Study of Medieval Romance in the Eighteenth Century.* London: Athlone Press, 1964.

Johnson, Claudia L. *Equivocal Beings: Politics, Gender, and Sentimentality in the 1790s. Wollstonecraft, Radcliffe, Burney, Austen.* Chicago: University of Chicago Press, 1995.

Johnson, Claudia L. *Jane Austen: Women, Politics, and the Novel*. Chicago: University of Chicago Press, 1988.

Johnson, R. Brimley. *The Women Novelists*. London: W. Collins, 1918.

Kay, Carol. *Political Constructions: Defoe, Richardson, and Sterne in Relation to Hobbes, Hume, and Burke*. Ithaca: Cornell University Press, 1988.

Kearney, Hugh. *The British Isles: A History of Four Nations*. Cambridge: Cambridge University Press, 1989.

Kee, Robert. *The Green Flag*. 3 vols. Harmondsworth: Penguin Books, 1989.

Kelly, Gary. *English Fiction of the Romantic Period, 1789–1830*. London: Longman, 1989.

———. *The English Jacobin Novel, 1780–1805*. Oxford: Clarendon Press, 1976.

———. *Women, Writing, and Revolution, 1790–1827*. Oxford: Clarendon Press, 1993.

Kelly, James. *Prelude to Union: Anglo-Irish Politics in the 1780s*. Cork: Cork University Press, 1992.

Kenneally, Michael, ed. *Irish Literature and Culture*. Savage, Md.: Barnes and Noble, 1992.

Kernan, Alvin. *Printing Technology, Letters, and Samuel Johnson*. Princeton: Princeton University Press, 1987.

Kerr, James. *Fiction against History: Sir Walter Scott as Story-Teller*. Cambridge: Cambridge University Press, 1989.

Kiely, Robert. *The Romantic Novel in English*. Cambridge: Harvard University Press, 1972.

Kilfeather, Siobhán Marie. "'Strangers at Home': Political Fictions by Women in Eighteenth Century Ireland." Ph.D. diss., Princeton University, 1989.

Kirkham, Margaret. "Feminist Irony and the Priceless Heroine of *Mansfield Park*." In *Jane Austen: New Perspectives*, edited by Janet Todd. New York: Holmes and Meier, 1983.

———. *Jane Austen, Feminism, and Fiction*. New York: Methuen, 1986.

Kirkpatrick, Kathryn J. "'Gentlemen Have Horrors upon the Subject': West Indian Suitors in Maria Edgeworth's *Belinda*." *Eighteenth-Century Fiction* 5, no. 4 (July 1993): 331–28.

Kittler, Friedrich. *Discourse Networks, 1800/1900*. Translated by Michael Meteer and Chris Cullens. Stanford: Stanford University Press, 1900.

Klancher, Jon P. "Godwin and the Republican Romance: Genre, Politics, and Contingency in Cultural History." *Modern Language Quarterly* 56, no. 2 (June 1995): 145–65.

———. *The Making of English Reading Audiences, 1790–1832*. Madison: University of Wisconsin Press, 1987.

Kliger, Samuel. *The Goths in England: A Study in Seventeenth and Eighteenth Century Thought*. Cambridge: Harvard University Press, 1952.

Klinck, Carl F., ed. *Literary History of Canada: Canadian Literature in English*. Toronto: University of Toronto Press, 1965.

———. *William "Tiger" Dunlop: Blackwoodian Backwoodsman*. Toronto: Ryerson Press, 1958.

Koehn, Nancy F. *The Power of Commerce: Economy and Governance in the First British Empire*. Ithaca: Cornell University Press, 1994.

Koselleck, Reinhart. *Critique and Crisis: Enlightenment and the Parthogenesis of Modern Society*. Cambridge: MIT Press, 1988.

Kramer, Dale. *Charles Robert Maturin*. Boston: Twayne, 1973.

Krishnaswamy, Revathi. "Evangels of Empire." *Race and Class* 34, no. 4 (April–June 1993): 47–62.

Kröller, Eva-Marie. "Walter Scott in America, English Canada, and Quebec: A Comparison." *Canadian Review of Comparative Literature* 7, no. 1 (winter 1980): 32–46.

Lascelles, Mary. *The Story-Teller Retrieves the Past: Historical Fiction and Fictitious History in the Art of Scott, Stevenson, Kipling, and Some Others*. Oxford: Clarendon Press, 1980.

Laurence, Anne. "The Cradle to the Grave: English Observation of Irish Social Customs in the Seventeenth Century." *The Seventeenth Century* 3 (1988): 63–84.

Leask, Nigel. *British Romantic Writers and the East: Anxieties of Empire*. Cambridge: Cambridge University Press, 1992.

Lecker, Robert, ed. *Canadian Canons: Essays in Literary Value*. Toronto: University of Toronto Press, 1991.

————. "The Canonization of Canadian Literature: An Inquiry into Value." *Critical Inquiry* 16 (spring 1990): 656–71.

————. *Making It Real: The Canonization of English-Canadian Literature*. Concord, Ont.: House of Anansi, 1995.

Lecky, William Edward Hartpole. *A History of Ireland in the Eighteenth Century*. 5 vols. London: Longmans, Green, 1923.

Leerssen, J. Th. "How *The Wild Irish Girl* Made Ireland Romantic" In *The Clash of Ireland: Literary Contrasts and Connections*, edited by C. C. Barfoot and Theo D'haen. Amsterdam: Rodopi, 1989.

Lenman, Bruce. *Integration, Enlightenment, and Industrialization: Scotland, 1746–1832*. London: Edward Arnold, 1981.

Letley, Emma. *From Galt to Douglas Brown: Nineteenth-Century Fiction and Scots Language*. Edinburgh: Scottish Academic Press, 1988.

Lindsay, Maurice. *The Discovery of Scotland: Based on Accounts of Foreign Travellers from the Thirteenth to the Eighteenth Centuries*. London: Robert Hale, 1964.

————. *The Eye Is Delighted: Some Romantic Travellers in Scotland*. London: Frederick Muller, 1971.

Lloyd, David. *Anomalous States: Irish Writing and the Post-Colonial Movement*. Durham: Duke University Press, 1993.

————. *Nationalism and Minor Literature: James Clarence Mangan and the Emergence of Irish Cultural Nationalism*. Berkeley: University of California, 1987.

Lovell, Terry. "Jane Austen and Gentry Society." In *Literature, Society, and the Sociology of Literature*, edited by Francis Barker et al. Chichester: University of Essex, 1977.

Lubbers, Klaus. *Geschichte der irischen Erzählprosa*. 2 vols. Munich: Wilhelm Fink Verlag, 1985.

Lukács, Georg. *The Historical Novel*. Cambridge: MIT Press, 1981.

Lukacs, John. *Historical Consciousness, or The Remembered Past*. New York: Harper and Row, 1969.

Lukacs, John. *The Literature of Change: Studies in the Nineteenth Century Provincial Novel.* Sussex: Harvester Press, 1977.

Lyell, Frank Hallam. *A Study of the Novels of John Galt.* Princeton: Princeton University, 1942.

Lynch, Deidre. "'Beating the Track of the Alphabet': Topography, Lexicography, and Johnson's Visions of the Ideal." *ELH* 57, no. 2 (summer 1990): 357–405.

———. "Nationalizing Women and Domesticating Fiction: Edmund Burke and the Genres of Englishness." *The Wordsworth Circle* 25, no. 1 (winter 1994): 45–49.

MacAndrew, Elizabeth. *The Gothic Tradition in Fiction.* New York: Columbia University Press, 1979.

McCormack, W. J. *Ascendancy and Tradition in Anglo-Irish Literary History from 1789 to 1939.* Oxford: Clarendon Press, 1985.

———. *Sheridan LeFanu and Victorian Ireland.* Oxford: Clarendon Press, 1980.

MacDonagh, Oliver. *The Nineteenth Century Novel and Irish Social History: Some Aspects.* Dublin: National Library of Ireland, 1970.

MacDonagh, Oliver, W. E. Mandle, and Pauric Travers, eds. *Irish Culture and Nationalism, 1750–1950.* London: Macmillan, 1983.

MacDonagh, Oliver, et al. *Irish and Irish-Australia: Studies in Cultural and Political History.* London: Croom Helm, 1986.

McDowell, R. B. *Ireland in the Age of Imperialism and Revolution, 1760–1801.* Oxford: Clarendon Press, 1979.

MacGillivray, Alan, "Exile and Empire." In *The History of Scottish Literature*, edited by Douglas Gifford. Vol. 3.

McGregor, Gaile. *The Wacousta Syndrome: Explorations in the Canadian Landscape.* Toronto: University of Toronto Press, 1985.

McHugh, Roger, and Maurice Harmon. *Short History of Anglo-Irish Literature, from Its Origins to the Present Day.* Totowa, N.J.: Barnes and Noble, 1982.

McKeon, Michael. *The Origins of the British Novel, 1600–1800.* Baltimore: Johns Hopkins University Press, 1987.

MacKillop, James. *Fionn mac Cumhaill: Celtic Myth in English Literature.* Syracuse: Syracuse University Press, 1986.

Maclean, Magnus. *The Literature of the Highlands.* Glasgow: Blackie and Son, 1904.

MacLulich, T. D. *Between Europe and America: The Canadian Tradition in Fiction.* Oakville: ECW Press, 1988.

MacMechan, Archibald. *Headwaters of Canadian Literature.* 1927. Reprint, Toronto: McClelland and Stewart, 1974.

McMullen, Lorrain, ed. *Re(dis)covering Our Foremothers: Nineteenth Century Canadian Women Writers.* Ottawa: University of Ottawa Press, 1990.

McNeill, Mary. *The Life and Times of Mary Ann McCracken, 1770–1866.* Dublin: Allen Figgis, 1960.

MacQueen, John. *The Enlightenment and Scottish Literature.* 2 vols. Vol. 1, *Progress and Poetry.* Vol. 2, *The Rise of the Historical Novel.* Edinburgh: Scottish Academic Press, 1982, 1989.

Makdisi, Saree. "Colonial Space and the Colonization of Time in Scott's *Waverley.*" *Studies in Romanticism* 34 (summer 1995): 115–87.

Manning, Susan. "Ossian, Scott, and Nineteenth Century Scottish Nationalism." *Studies in Scottish Literature* 17 (1982): 39–54.

Marshall, P. J., and Glendor Williams. *The Great Map of Mankind: British Perceptions of the World in the Age of Enlightenment*. London: Dent, 1982.

Mathias, Roland. *Anglo-Welsh Literature: An Illustrated History*. Bridgend: Poetry Wales Press, 1986.

Mayo, Robert Donald. *The English Novel in the Magazines, 1740–1815*. Evanston: Northwestern University Press, 1962.

Meek, Ronald L. *Social Science and the Ignoble Savage*. Cambridge: Cambridge University Press, 1986.

Meiz, Stephens, ed. *The Oxford Companion to the Literature of Wales*. Oxford: Oxford University Press, 1986.

Mellor, Anne. *Romanticism and Gender*. New York: Routledge, 1993.

Metcalf, John., ed. *Carry on Bumping*. Toronto: E. C. Press, 1988.

―――. *Kicking against the Pricks*. 1982. 2d ed. Guelph: Red Kite, 1986.

―――. *What Is a Canadian Literature*. Guelph: Red Kite Press, 1988.

Midgley, Clare, *Women against Slavery: The British Company, 1780–1870*. London: Routledge, 1992.

Miles, Robert. *Gothic Writing, 1750–1820*. London: Routledge, 1993.

Miller, D. A. *Narrative and Its Discontents: Problems of Closure in the Traditional Novel*. Princeton: Princeton University Press, 1981.

Miller, Nancy K. *The Heroine's Fiction*. New York: Columbia University Press, 1980.

Millgate, Jane. *Walter Scott: The Making of a Novelist*. Toronto: University of Toronto Press, 1984.

Minh-ha, Trinh T. *Woman, Native, Other: Writing Postcoloniality and Feminism*. Bloomington: Indiana University Press, 1989.

Mitchell, W.J.T., ed. *Landscape and Power*. Chicago: University of Chicago Press, 1994.

Mitchison, Rosalind. *A History of Scotland*. 2d ed. London: Methuen, 1982.

―――, ed. *The Roots of Nationalism: Studies in Northern Europe*. Edinburgh: John Donald Publishers, 1980.

Moir, Esther. *The Discovery of Britain: The English Tourists, 1540 to 1840*. London: Routledge and Kegan Paul, 1964.

Momigliano, Arnaldo. "Ancient History and the Antiquarian." In *Studies in Historiography*. London: Weidenfeld and Nicolson, 1966.

Morash, Christopher. *Writing the Irish Famine*. Oxford: Clarendon Press, 1995.

Morgan, Prys. *The New History of Wales: The Eighteenth Century Renaissance*. Llandybïe, Wales: Christopher Davies (Publishers), 1981.

―――, and David Thomas. *Wales: The Shaping of a Nation*. Newton Abbot: David and Charles, 1984.

Moss, John, ed. *The Canadian Novel II: Beginnings*. Toronto: NC Press, 1980.

Moynahan, Julian. *Anglo-Irish: The Literary Imagination in a Hyphenated Culture*. Princeton: Princeton University Press, 1995.

Muir, Edwin. *Scott and Scotland: The Predicament of the Scottish Writer*. London: George Routledge and Sons, 1936.

―――. *The Structure of the Novel*. New York: Hillary House, 1967.

Murphy, Peter T. "Fool's Gold: The Highland Treasures of MacPherson's Ossian." *ELH* 53, no. 3 (fall 1986): 567–91.

Murray, Les A. *The Peasant Mandarin: Prose Pieces*. St. Lucia: University of Queensland Press, 1976.

Musselwhite, David. "The Trial of Warren Hastings." In *Literature, Politics, and Theory*, edited by Francis Barker et al. London: Methuen, 1986.

Nabokov, Vladimir. *Lectures on Literature*. Edited by Fredson Bowers. New York: Harcourt Brace Jovanovich; London: Bruccoli Clark, 1980.

Nagy, Gregory. "The Crisis in Performance." In *The Ends of Rhetoric: History, Theory, Practise*, edited by David Wellbery and John Bender. Stanford: Stanford University Press, 1990.

Nairn, Tom. *The Break-up of Britain: Crisis and Neo-Nationalism*. London: New Left Books, 1977.

———. *The Enchanted Glass: Britain and Its Monarchy*. London: Radius, 1988.

Nairn, Tom, Eric Hobsbawm, Régis Debray, and Michael Löwy. *Nationalismus und Marxismus: Anstoß zu einer notwendigen Debatte*. Berlin: Rotbuch Verlag, 1978.

Napier, Elizabeth R. *The Failure of Gothic: Problems of Disjunction in an Eighteenth-century Literary Form*. Oxford: Clarendon Press, 1987.

New, W. H. *A History of Canadian Literature*. London: Macmillan, 1985.

Nixon, Rob. "Caribbean and African Appropriations of *The Tempest*." *Critical Inquiry* 15 (summer 1987): pp. 557–78.

Nobbe, George. *The North Briton: A Study of Political Propaganda*. New York: Columbia University Press, 1939.

Nussbaum, Felicity. *Torrid Zones: Maternity, Sexuality, and Empire in Eighteenth-Century English Narratives*. Baltimore: Johns Hopkins University Press, 1995.

Nussbaum, Felicity, and Laura Brown, eds. *The New Eighteenth Century: Theory, Politics, English Literature*. New York: Methuen, 1987.

O'Driscoll, Robert, and Lorna Reynolds, eds. *The Untold Story: The Irish in Canada*. Toronto: Celtic Arts of Canada, 1988.

Oliphant, Margaret. *Annals of a Publishing House. William Blackwood and His Sons. Their Magazine and Friends*. 1897. 2 vols. Reprint, New York: AMS, 1974.

———. *The Literary History of England, in the End of the Eighteenth and Beginning of the Nineteenth Century*. 3 vols. London: Macmillan, 1882.

O'Riordan, Michelle. *The Gaelic Mind and the Collapse of the Gaelic World Order*. Cork: Cork University Press, 1990.

Owens, Cóilín, ed. *Family Chronicles: Maria Edgeworth's "Castle Rackrent."* Dublin: Wolfhound Press; Totowa, N.J.: Barnes and Noble, 1987.

Parry, Thomas. *A History of Welsh Literature*. Translated by H. Idris Bell. Oxford: Clarendon Press, 1955.

Patterson, Annabel. *Reading between the Lines*. Madison: University of Wisconsin Press, 1993.

Perera, Suvendrini. *Reaches of Empire: The English Novel from Edgeworth to Dickens*. New York: Columbia University Press, 1991.

Phillipson, N. T., and Rosalind Mitchison, eds. *Scotland in the Age of Improvement*. Edinburgh: Edinburgh University Press, 1970.

Piggott, Stuart. *Ancient Britons and the Antiquarian Imagination: Ideas from the Renaissance to the Regency.* London: Thames and Hudson, 1989.

———. *Ruins in a Landscape: Essays in Antiquarianism.* Edinburgh: Edinburgh University Press, 1976.

Pittock, Murray G. H. *The Invention of Scotland: The Stuart Myth and the Scottish Identity, 1638 to the Present.* London: Routledge, 1991.

———. *Poetry and Jacobite Politics in Eighteenth Century Britain and Ireland.* Cambridge: Cambridge University Press, 1994.

Porter, Roy, and Mikulas Teich, eds. *The Enlightenment in National Context.* Cambridge: Cambridge University Press, 1981.

Potkay, Adam. "Virtue and Manners in Macpherson's Poems of Ossian." *PMLA* 107, no. 1 (January 1992): 120–30.

Power, Thomas P., ed. *The Irish in Atlantic Canada, 1780–1900.* Fredricton: New Ireland Press, 1991.

Pratt, Mary Louise. *Imperial Eyes: Travel Writing and Transculturation.* London: Routledge, 1992.

Prebble, John. *Mutiny: Highland Regiments in Revolt, 1743–1804.* Harmondsworth: Penguin Books, 1975.

Punter, David. *Literature of Terror: A History of Gothic Fictions from 1765 to the Present Day.* London: Longman, 1980.

Raleigh, Walter. *The English Novel: A Short Sketch of Its History from the Earliest Times to the Appearance of "Waverley."* London: John Murray, 1919.

Ranum, Orest, ed. *National Consciousness, History, and Political Culture in Early Modern Europe.* Baltimore: Johns Hopkins University Press, 1975.

Rattray, W. J. *The Scot in British North America.* 4 vols. Toronto: Maclear, n.d.

Reed, James. *Sir Walter Scott: Landscape and Locality.* London: Athlone Press, 1980.

Reid, W. Stanford, ed. *The Scottish Tradition in Canada.* Toronto: McClelland and Stewart, 1976.

Rendall, Jane. *The Origins of the Scottish Enlightenment.* New York: St. Martin's Press, 1978.

Rentis, Malsom D. *The Scots in Australia: A Study of New South Wales, Victoria, and Queensland, 1788–1900.* Sydney: Sydney University Press, 1983.

Retamar, Roberto Fernández. *Caliban and Other Essays.* Translated by Edward Baker. Minneapolis: University of Minnesota Press, 1989.

Richardson, Alan. *Literature, Education, and Romanticism: Reading as Social Practise, 1780–1832.* Cambridge: Cambridge University Press, 1994.

———. "Romantic Voodoo: Obeah and British Culture, 1979–1807." *Studies in Romanticism* 32 (spring 1993): 3–28.

Richetti, John J. *Popular Fiction before Richardson: Narrative Patterns, 1700–1739.* Oxford: Clarendon Press, 1969.

———, ed. *The Columbia History of the British Novel.* New York: Columbia University Press, 1994.

Robbins, Bruce. *The Servant's Hand: English Fiction from Below.* New York: Columbia University Press, 1986.

Roberts, Warren. *Jane Austen and the French Revolution.* New York: St. Martin's Press, 1979.

Robertson, Fiona. *Legitimate Histories: Scott, Gothic, and the Authorities of Fiction*. Oxford: Clarendon Press, 1994.

Rogers, Pat. *Johnson and Boswell: The Transit of Caledonia*. Oxford: Oxford University Press, 1995.

Rose, J. Holland, A. P. Newton, and G. A. Benians, eds. *The Cambridge History of the British Empire*. 8 vols. Cambridge: Cambridge University Press, 1940.

Ross, Catherine Sheldon, ed. *Recovering Canada's First Novelist: Proceedings from the John Richardson Conference*. Erin, Ont.: Porcupine's Quill, 1984.

Ross, Ian Campbell. "An Irish Picaresque Novel: William Chaigneau's *The History of Jack Connor*." *Studies* (summer 1982): 270–79.

———."Thomas Amory, *John Buncle*, and the Origins of Irish Fiction." *Eire-Ireland* 8, no. 3 (fall 1983): 71–85.

Rousseau, Jean-Jacques, and Johann Gottfried Herder. *On the Origin of Language*. New York: Frederick Ungar, 1966.

Rubel, Margaret Mary. *Savage and Barbarian: Historical Attitudes in the Criticism of Homer and Ossian in Britain, 1760–1800*. Amsterdam: North-Holland Publishing Company, 1978.

Ruoff, Gene W. "1800 and the Future of the Novel: William Wordsworth, Maria Edgeworth, and the Vagaries of Literary History." In *The Age of William Wordsworth: Critical Essays on the Romantic Tradition*, edited by Kenneth R. Johnston and Gene W. Ruoff. New Brunswick: Rutgers University Press, 1987.

Rushdie, Salman. *Imaginary Homelands: Essays and Criticism, 1981–1991*. London: Granta, 1991.

Said, Edward. *Culture and Imperialism*. New York: Alfred A. Knopf, 1993.

———. *Orientalism*. New York: Random House, 1979.

Sale, Roger. *Closer to Home: Writers and Places in England, 1780–1830*. Cambridge: Harvard University Press, 1986.

———. *English Literature in History, 1780–1830: Pastoral and Politics*. London: Hutchison, 1983.

Samuel, Raphael, ed. *Patriotism: The Making and Unmaking of British National Identity*. 3 vols. London: Routledge, 1989.

Sanders, Bailey. *The Life and Letters of James Macpherson Containing a Particular Account of his Famous Quarrel with Dr. Johnson, and a Sketch of the Origins and Influence of the Ossianic Poems*. 1894. Reprint, New York: Harkell House Publishers, 1968.

Sartre, Jean-Paul. *What Is Literature and Other Essays*. Cambridge: Harvard University Press, 1988.

Schivelbusch, Wolfgang. *The Railway Journey: The Industrialization of Time and Space in the Nineteenth Century*. Berkeley: University of California Press, 1986.

Schofield, Mary Anne, and Cecilia Macheski, eds. *Fetter'd or Free? British Women Novelists, 1670–1815*. Athens: Ohio University Press, 1986.

Scott, Walter. *The Lives of the Novelists*. London: J. M. Dent; New York: E. P. Dutton, n.d.

———. *On Novelists and Fiction*. Edited by Ioan Williams. London: Routledge, 1968.

Sedgwick, Eve Kosofsky. *The Coherence of Gothic Conventions*. New York: Methuen, 1986.

See, Scott W. *Riots in New Brunswick: Orange Nativism and Social Violence in the 1840s*. Toronto: University of Toronto Press, 1993.

Sencourt, Robert. *India in English Literature*. London: Simpkin, Marshall, Hamilton, Ken, n.d. [ca. 1923?]

Seymour, W. A., ed. *A History of the Ordnance Survey*. Folkstone: Dawson, 1980.

Shattock, Joanne. *Politics and Reviewers: The Edinburgh and the Quarterley*. London: Leicester University Press, 1989.

Sher, Richard. *Church and University in the Scottish Enlightenment: The Moderate Literati of Edinburgh*. Princeton: Princeton University Press, 1985.

Sher, Richard, and Jeffrey R. Smitten, eds. *Scotland and America in the Age of the Enlightenment*. Princeton: Princeton University Press, 1990.

Sherwood, Mary Martha. *The Life of Mrs. Sherwood, Chiefly Autobiographical*. Edited by Sophia Kelly. London: Darton, 1857.

Shiach, Morag. *Discourse on Popular Culture: Class, Gender, and History in Cultural Analysis, 1730 to the Present*. Cambridge: Polity Press, 1989.

Shields, David. *Oracles of Empire: Poetry, Politics, and Commerce in British America, 1690–1750*. Chicago: University of Chicago, 1990.

Simmons, Clare A. *Reversing the Conquest: History and Myth in Nineteenth-Century British Literature*. New Brunswick: Rutgers University Press, 1990.

Simonsuuri, Kirsti. *Homer's Original Genuis: Eighteenth-Century Notions of the Early Greek Epic (1688–1798)*. Cambridge: Cambridge University Press, 1979.

Simpson, Kenneth. *The Protean Scot: The Crisis of Identity in Eighteenth-Century Scottish Literature*. Aberdeen: Aberdeen University Press, 1988.

Skelton, Oscar Douglas. *Life and Times of Sir Alexander Tilloch Galt*. Edited by Guy MacLean. Toronto: McClelland and Stewart, 1966.

Sloan, Barry. *The Pioneers of Anglo-Irish Fiction, 1800–1850*. Gerrards Cross: Colin Smythe, 1986.

Smailes, Helen. *Scottish Empire: Scots in Pursuit of Hope and Glory*. Edinburgh: Scottish National Portrait Gallery, 1981.

Smith, Anthony D. *The Ethnic Origin of Nations*. Oxford: Basil Blackwell, 1986.

Smith, Naomi Royde. *The State of Mind of Mrs. Sherwood*. London: Macmillan, 1946.

Smith, Olivia. *The Politics of Language, 1791–1819*. Oxford: Clarendon Press, 1984.

Snyder, Edward D. *The Celtic Revival in English Literature, 1760–1800*. 1923. Reprint, Gloucester, Mass: Peter Smith, 1965.

Southam, Brian. "The Silence of the Bertrams: Slavery and the Chronology of *Mansfield Park*." *Times Literary Supplement*, February 17, 1995, pp. 13–14.

Spacks, Patricia Mayer. *Desire and Truth: Functions of Plot in Eighteenth Century Novels*. Chicago: University of Chicago Press, 1990.

Spencer, Jane. *The Rise of the Woman Novelist: From Aphra Behn to Jane Austen*. Oxford: Basil Blackwell, 1986.

Spender, Dale. *Mothers of the Novel: One Hundred Good Women Writers Before Jane Austen*. London: Pandora, 1986.

Spittal, John Ker, ed. *Contemporary Criticisms of Dr. Samuel Johnson: His Works and His Biographers.* London: John Murray, 1923.

Spivak, Gayatri Chakravorty. *In Other Worlds: Essays in Cultural Politics.* New York: Methuen, 1987.

Springer, Carolyn. *The Marble Wilderness: Ruins and Representation in Italian Romanticism, 1775–1850.* Cambridge: Cambridge University Press, 1987.

Stafford, Fiona J. *The Sublime Savage: A Study of James Macpherson and the Poems of Ossian.* Edinburgh: Edinburgh University Press, 1988.

Stafford, William. *Socialism, Radicalism, and Nostalgia: Social Criticism in Britain, 1775–1830.* Cambridge: Cambridge University Press, 1987.

Stallybrass, Peter, and Allon White. *The Politics and Poetics of Transgression.* London: Methuen, 1986.

Steeves, Harrison R. *Before Jane Austen: The Shaping of the English Novel in the Eighteenth Century.* New York: Holt, Rinehart and Winston, 1965.

Stewart, Maaja A. *Domestic Realities and Imperial Fictions: Jane Austen's Novels in Eighteenth Century Contexts.* Athens: University of Georgia Press, 1993.

Stewart, Susan. *Crimes of Writing: Problems in the Containment of Representation.* New York: Oxford, 1991.

———. *On Longing: Narratives of the Miniature, the Gigantic, the Souvenir, the Collection.* Baltimore: Johns Hopkins University Press, 1984.

Suleri, Sara. *The Rhetoric of English India.* Chicago: University of Chicago Press, 1992.

Summerfield, Geoffrey. *Fantasy and Reason: Children's Literature in the Eighteenth Century.* Athens: University of Georgia Press, 1985.

Summers, Montague. *The Gothic Quest: A History of the Gothic Novel.* London: Fortune Press, n.d.

Sutherland, Kathryn. "Fictional Economies: Adam Smith, Walter Scott, and the Nineteenth Century Novel." *ELH* 54, no. 1 (spring 1987): 97–127.

Swedenberg, Hugh Thomas, Jr. *The Theory of the Epic in England, 1650–1800.* Berkeley: University of California Press, 1944.

Sypher, Wylie. *Guinea's Captive Kings: British Anti-Slavery Literature of the Eighteenth Century.* Chapel Hill: University of North Carolina Press, 1942.

Tanner, Tony. *Jane Austen.* London: Macmillan, 1986.

Tausky, Thomas E. *Sara Jeannette Duncan: Novelist of Empire.* Port Credit: P. D. Meany Publishers, 1980.

Teich, Mikulás, and Roy Porter, eds. *The National Question in Europe in Historical Context.* Cambridge: Cambridge University Press, 1993.

Temple, Kathryn, "Johnson and Macpherson, Cultural Authority, and the Construction of Literary Property." *Yale Journal of Law and the Humanities* 5 (1993): 355–87.

Thackeray, Anne Ritchie. *A Book of Sibyls: Mrs. Barbauld, Miss Edgeworth, Mrs. Opie, Miss Austen.* London: Smith, Elder, 1883.

That Land of Exiles: Scots in Australia. Edinburgh: Her Majesty's Stationery Office, 1988.

Thompson, E. P. *The Making of the English Working Class.* New York: Vintage, 1966.

Thuente, Mary Helen. *The Harp Re-strung: The United Irishmen and Rise of Irish Literary Nationalism*. Syracuse: Syracuse University Press, 1994.

Tierney, Frank M., ed. *The Achievement of Thomas Chandler Haliburton*. Ottawa: University of Ottawa Press, 1985.

Timothy, H. B. *The Galts: A Canadian Odyssey*. 2 vols. Toronto: McClelland and Stewart, 1977, 1984.

Todd, Janet. *Sensibility: An Introduction*. London: Methuen, 1986.

———. *The Sign of Angellica: Women, Writing, and Fiction, 1660–1800*. London: Virago, 1989.

Tompkins, J.M.S. *The Popular Novel in England, 1770–1800*. London: Constable, 1932.

Tracey, Robert, "Maria Edgeworth and Lady Morgan: Legality vs. Legitimacy." *Nineteenth Century Fiction* 40 (1985): 1–22.

Trumpener, Katie. "The Time of the Gypsies: A 'People without History' in the Narratives of the West." In *Identities*, edited by Kwame Anthony Appiah and Henry Louis Gates, Jr. Chicago: University of Chicago Press, 1995.

Turley, David. *The Culture of English Antislavery, 1780–1860*. London: Routledge, 1991.

Twain, Mark. *Life on the Mississippi*. 1883. Reprint, New York: Dodd, Mead, 1968.

Ty, Eleanor, *Unsex'd Revolutionaries: Five Women Novelists of the 1790s*. Toronto: Unviersity of Toronto Press, 1993.

Vance, Norman. "Celts, Carthaginians, and Constitutions: Anglo-Irish Literary Relations, 1780–1820." *Irish Historical Studies* 22, no. 87 (March 1981): 216–38.

———. *Irish Literature: A Social History. Tradition, Identity, and Difference*. Oxford: Basil Blackwell, 1990.

Varma, Devendra P. *The Gothic Flame. Being a History of the Gothic Novel in England. Its Origins, Efflorescence, Disintegration, and Residuary Influences*. London: Arthur Baker, 1957.

Visram, Rozina. *Ayahs, Lascars, and Princes: Indians in Britain, 1700–1947*. London: Pluto, 1986.

Viswanathan, Gauri. *Masks of Conquest: Literary Study and British Rule in India*. New York: Columbia University Press, 1989.

Wainwright, Clive. *The Romantic Interior*. New Haven: Yale University Press, 1989.

Waterston, Elizabeth, ed. *John Galt: Reappraisals*. Guelph: University of Guelph Press, 1985.

Watson, Don. *Caledonis Australis: Scottish Highlanders on the Frontier of Australia*. Syndey: Collins, 1984.

Watson, Nicola. *Revolution and the Form of the British Novel, 1790–1825: Intercepted Letters, Interrupted Seductions*. Oxford: Clarendon Press, 1994.

Watson, Roderick. *The Literature of Scotland*. New York: Schocken Books, 1985.

Watt, Ian. *The Rise of the Novel: Studies in Defoe, Richardson, and Fielding*. Berkeley: University of California Press, 1957.

Webb, R. K. *The British Working Class Reader, 1790–1848*. New York: Augustus M. Kelley, 1971.

Wechselblatt, Martin. "Finding Mr. Boswell: Rhetorical Authority and National Identity in Johnson's *A Journey to the Western Islands of Scotland*." *ELH* 60 (1993): 117–48.

Weinbrot, Howard. *Britannia's Issue: The Rise of British Literature from Dryden to Ossian*. Cambridge: Cambridge University Press, 1993.

Wellek, Rene. *The Rise of English Literary History*. 1941. Reprint, New York: McGraw-Hill, 1966.

White, Hayden. *The Content of the Form: Narrative Discourses and Historical Representation*. Baltimore: Johns Hopkins University Press, 1987.

Wilde, William H., et al. *The Oxford Companion to Australian Literature*. Melbourne: Oxford University Press, 1985.

Williams, Glanmor. *Religion, Language, and Nationality in Wales*. Cardiff: University of Wales Press, 1979.

Williams, Patrick, and Laura Chrisman, eds. *Colonial Discourse and Post-colonial Theory: A Reader*. New York: Columbia University Press, 1994.

Williams, Raymond. *The Country and the City*. New York: Oxford University Press, 1973.

———. *Culture and Society, 1780–1950*. New York: Harper and Row, 1958.

———. *Keywords: A Vocabulary of Culture and Society*. London: Fontana, 1983.

Wilt, Judith. *Secret Leaves: The Novels of Walter Scott*. Chicago: University of Chicago Press, 1982.

Withers, Charles W. J. *Gaelic in Scotland, 1698–1981: The Geographical History of a Language*. Edinburgh: John Donald Publishers, 1984.

Witherspoon, Charles W. J. *Gaelic Scotland: The Transformation of a Cultural Region*. London: Routledge, 1988.

Wittig, Kurt. *The Scottish Tradition in Literature*. Edinburgh: Oliver and Boyd, 1958.

Womack, Peter. *Improvement and Romance: Constructing the Myth of the Highlands*. Houndsmills: Macmillan, 1989.

Young, James D. *The Rousing of the Scottish Working Class*. London: Croom Helm, 1979.

Youngson, A. J. *After the Forty-Five: The Economic Impact on the Scottish Highlands*. Edinburgh: Edinburgh University Press, 1973.

———. *The Making of Classical Edinburgh*. Edinburgh: Edinburgh University Press, 1966.

INDEX

About the Author

KATIE TRUMPENER is Associate Professor of English,
Germanic Studies, and Comparative Literature at the
University of Chicago.